The JFK Horsemen

Framing Lee, Altering the Altgens6 and Resolving Other Mysteries

The JFK Horsemen

Framing Lee, Altering the Altgens6 and Resolving Other Mysteries

Larry Rivera

MOON ROCK BOOKS

Save the World /Resist the Empire Series

And I suppose we didn't go to the Moon, either?
Nobody Died at Sandy Hook
And Nobody died in Boston, either
America Nuked on 9/11
From Orlando to Dallas and Beyond
White Rose Blooms in Wisconsin
Chronicles of False Flag Terror
Political Theater In Charlottesville
JFK: Who, How, and Why
The New Gutenberg Press

Jim Fetzer, Mike Palecek
Series Editors

The JFK Horsemen
Framing Lee, Altering the Altgens6 and Resolving Other Mysteries

Larry Rivera

ISBN 978-1-948323-04-8
Color edition

Copyright 2018 by Moon Rock Books

Moon Rock Books
6256 Bullet Drive • Crestview • FL • 32536
www.moonrockbooks.com

Printed in the U.S.A.

Also by Mike Palecek

Fiction:

SWEAT: Global Warming in a small town,
and other tales from the great American Westerly Midwest
Joe Coffee's Revolution
The Truth
The American Dream
Johnny Moon
KGB
Terror Nation
Speak English!
The Last Liberal Outlaw
The Progressive Avenger
Camp America
Twins
Iowa Terror
Guests of the Nation
Looking For Bigfoot
A Perfect Duluth Day
American History 101:
Conspiracy Nation Revolution
One Day In The Life of Herbert Wisniewski
Operation Northwoods: . . . the patsy
Red White & Blue
Welcome To Sugar Creek
CRUSHER vs. The Empire
Crusher in Wonderland
Geronimo's Revenge

Non-Fiction:

Cost of Freedom (with Whitney Trettien and Michael Annis)
Prophets Without Honor (with William Strabala)
The Dynamic Duo: White Rose Blooms in Wisconsin,
Kevin Barrett, Jim Fetzer & the American Resistance
And I suppose we didn't go to the Moon, either? (with Jim Fetzer)
Nobody Died At Sandy Hook (with Jim Fetzer)
And Nobody Died in Boston, either (with Jim Fetzer)
America Nuked on 9/11 (with Jim Fetzer)
From Orlando to Dallas and Beyond (with Jim Fetzer)
JFK Who, How, and Why (with Jim Fetzer)
Political Theater in Charlottesville (with Jim Fetzer)
White Rose Blooms in Wisconsin (with Chuck Gregory)

Dedication

To my father, Mercedes, the light of my life.

CONTENTS

Preface

I began this quest many years ago but did not really get serious about it until I realized in the year 2012 that computers could make a difference in finding out the truth about the JFK assassination.

The applications available to serious students of the case have now come of age. Word processors, imaging programs, search engines, mega document repositories—where scanned documents can now be searched and found—keywords which allow us to find these documents, give the new-age investigator tools that were never available to our predecessors and first-generation researchers. And now, a very special 3D open-source program by the name of Blender—which to those who have the patience to learn—can bear fruit as never before seen. The possibilities are endless. Technology is finally catching up with those who engineered the greatest tragedy of our nation's modern history.

Why is this important, one might ask? It is clear that our present is a direct result of what happened on 22 November 1963. The mainstream media insists on propagating—in the words of the great Jim Garrison—a "fairy tale" which the American public is not interested in overcoming. It has been up to brave Americans such as first-generation researchers Garrison, Harold Weisberg, my friend Vincent Salandria, Mark Lane, Shirley Martin, Sylvia Meagher, Ray Marcus, Roy Schaeffer, Penn Jones, Jr., J. Gary Shaw and Larry Ray Harris, Jack White, Robert Cutler, and many others who never accepted the official version of this heinous crime perpetrated against the American spirit.

The one motivating link that ties us together across generations is, of course, the full exoneration of Lee Oswald. I believe the inevitable will happen—history will eventually be revised, and Lee will take his place as a martyr who held this country together in times of extreme volatility—where provocation from either side could have doomed us all.

Martin Schotz, in his book *History Will Not Absolve Us*, maintained two key points in his thesis: JFK's American University peace speech of 10 June 1963, and the fact that the shirt worn by JFK that day showed a hole of entry well below the neck line, which in and of itself automatically proved the single-bullet theory was impossible—the speech, the motivating factor to take him out, the other a shirt hole, the evidence which has never been explained to this day by those who continue to propagate the lone nut theory.

In 2013, I began giving public presentations in earnest, and this exposure allowed me to meet and be in the company of living legends Jim Marrs, Cyril Wecht, Ed Tatro, Judyth Vary Baker, Jim Fetzer, and Phil Nelson, among others. Much time has been spent corresponding with others who share the same passion for truth, like Richard Hooke, Gary King, John Hankey, David Denton, Pat Shannan, Lola Quesada, and Ralph Cinque, have in one way or another assisted in my research, this book the culmination of it.

A very special thank you must be sent to Tyler Newcomb, whose father Fred wrote *Murder from Within* back in 1971, and who selected me to transcribe his father's raw recordings of the "JFK Horsemen," the four, key motorcycle escort who saw JFK gunned down right before their eyes. The information obtained from those recordings, I believe, has revolutionized and clarified what really happened on Elm Street that day.

Last but not least, I wish to thank David Gahary, with whom I spent endless, coffee-fueled nights, editing this book over Skype, and who surprised me by actually reading my work and fine-tuning its content. That is what editors are for.

—Larry Rivera

PART I
THE ALTGENS PHOTOGRAPHS

1

The Altgens' Photographic Timeline

Much has been written and speculated as to the authenticity and timing of the photographs taken by James "Ike" Altgens on 22 November 1963. This chapter brings forth some unknown facts and dispels some myths that prevail in the research community to this day.

The Movements of James Altgens

In May 1964, two key articles were published which brought national attention to 42-year-old James Altgens and his photograph. The first was Dom Bonafede's article, "The Picture With a Life of Its Own," published in the *New York Herald Tribune* on 24 May, which detailed Jones Harris's quest to find out who the man in the doorway really was. The second was published the following day by Maggie Daly in the *Chicago American*, where she publicized the fact that Altgens had been within 15 feet of the President, yet he had not been brought to testify before the Warren Commission—officially The President's Commission on the Assassination of President Kennedy.[1]

These two articles had the Federal Bureau of Investigation (FBI) up in arms about how to resolve Altgens6 and its "man in the doorway" dilemma. By the time Altgens was brought before the Commission on 22 July, he lamented how he wished it had been sooner, because he admitted that time had dulled his memory somewhat:

"Well I wish I would have been able to give you this information the next day when it was fresh on my mind because six months or so later, sometimes the facts might be just a little bit off and I hate to see it that way."[2] (It was actually eight months.)

Altgens stated in his FBI interview 2 June 1964 that after the final shots in Dealey Plaza, and after following Secret Service men and motorcycle cops up the embankment, then placing a phone call to his office, he headed straight to the Associated Press (AP) facilities located at the Dallas News Building five blocks away on Houston and Young, to deliver his film for processing. The FBI then established 12:57 PM CT as the time at which Altgens6 "moved" on the wire.[3]

3

Quite a feat when one considers the time it would have taken for Altgens to make sure no more bullets were flying in Dealey Plaza, the time he took to follow Secret Service men and policemen into the parking lot adjacent to the railroad yard, making sure there were no other victims to photograph, make a phone call, then "dash" back to AP to develop the film.[4]

Bear in mind that Altgens never provided a precise timeline of his activities after the shots. The severely cropped photograph, however, did not appear in newspaper print until the last evening editions in only a handful of newspapers, and was not shown on national TV until 6:35 PM by Walter Cronkite.[5]

The rest of the nation's newspapers did not publish Altgens6 until the following Saturday, 23 November.[6]

The following from Yahoo.com! is a generic timeline for developing film taken right out of a camera:

How long does it take to develop black and white film? Best Answer: To develop negatives, the film has to be in the developer for a period of between five and 10 minutes (usually). Subsequent steps are required to make your negatives permanent and then the negatives must dry before printing. Plan on two darkroom sessions, 30 min. minimum for negatives and a couple of hours for printing. You probably want to contact print first. It's fairly straightforward, and you should be able to make a good one in 10-30 minutes the first time.

What really happened to Altgens's film? Is this how it happened? Over the years, many researchers have accepted the official version and have never questioned the timing involved.

Richard Trask interviewed Altgens back in 1985 and maintained contact with him over the years for his 1994 volume *Pictures of the Pain: Photography and the Assassination of President Kennedy*.[7] His timeline for Altgens and his photographs has been accepted without questioning the logistics. For the sake of our discussion, and to put things into proper perspective, here is a possible timeline for James Altgens and his roll of film:

1. 12:30 PM shoots Altgens6 and Altgens7 (one-two minutes)

2. Snaps Altgens8 from his position on the south curb of Elm Street:

4

3. Runs up the embankment following Secret Service agents and motorcycle cops. Amid the confusion he must stay at least a few minutes to take in what is happening because he wants to make sure he captures the moment in which someone is arrested.[8]

4. Makes sure there are no other victims for him to photograph.[9]

5. Comes down from the grassy knoll and calmly stands at the north curb for a few minutes.[10] (see photographs below)

This four image sequence shows Altgens in the Mal Couch film. While everyone is running around, he calmly stays, "to take a long look around", (WC7H519) and does not look to be in any hurry.

Altgens seen in the Richard Bothun photograph calmly walking down to the sidewalk and curb of Elm Street.

Ike Altgens (back towards the camera) in one of the Cancellare photographs

Bill and Gayle Newman estimated they were on the ground for three minutes. Gayle, however, stated in an affidavit taken on 22 November that they got up and laid down a second time.[11]

This could have stretched this closer to five minutes.

Caught up in history

The Dallas Morning News   Saturday, November 22, 1986

Couple, sons stood watching only feet away as JFK was slain

By John Kirkpatrick
Staff Writer of The News

Building." No names of the mother
and father, no details. End of story

Newman says.
They watched and waited. Clay-

They stayed on the grass for
maybe three minutes. Tentatively,
they stood up. A Channel 8 reporter
spotted them. Billy recognized him
as the same man, Jerry Haynes, who
starred in a kiddie TV show. "That
man is Mr. Peppermint"

"After a TV interview, the Newmans spent hours at the sheriff's

6. Altgens crosses Elm Street to retrieve his gadget bag before moving on to find a "nearby phone."[12]

7. Locates a "nearby phone" and makes phone call to his office to inform that he has witnessed the assassination.[13] Bear in mind that every member of the media was scrambling to find a phone, which were at a premium in Dealey Plaza. Witness Robert McNeil went into the Texas School Book Depository (TSBD) looking for one to send NBC his first report.[14] (Anywhere from five-10 minutes.)

Altgens crosses Elm Street to retrieve gadget bag as the last press bus passes by (Slide No. 7 taken by Phillip Willis)

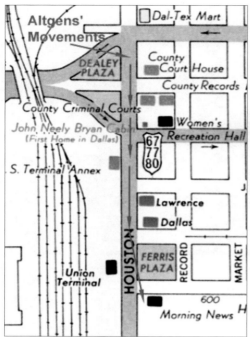

8. After talking to his office about witnessing the assassination, he "dashes" or "sprints" down Houston Street a quarter of a mile[15] carrying his camera and gadget bag, five blocks to Houston and Young, to the AP office located on the third floor of *The Dallas Morning News* building. Enters building, catches an elevator, runs down the hallways, etc. (Total time: six minutes)

9. Hands his camera to "someone" who rewinds unused film and removes his roll of film for processing.[16] (five minutes)

10. Depending on the efficiency of the personnel, the film must be removed from its metal cylinder in a dark room and placed in developer solution between five and 10 minutes.

11. Film is placed in fixer solution.

12. Film is placed in washing solution.

13. Negative film is dried for at least another 10 minutes.

14. First contact prints made of film roll Altgens2-8, Altgens1 is missing. (10 minutes)

15. Two positive 8.5" x 11" prints are printed, one for processing, one for the "morgue" for storage.[17]

16. Photographs are captioned and stamped for transmission.

17. AP supposedly sends Altgens4-7 out on the wire (five minutes) Altgens4,5,7 are the first to be published in newspapers. Altgens4 and Altgens6 are shown by Cronkite at 6:35 PM on CBS.[18] (Total minimum time: 60 minutes)

Altgens4 at 6:34:29PM   **Altgens6 at 6:34:46PM**

Wirephoto Transmissions of the 1960s

The reliable transmission of photographs via telephone lines came of age in 1935. In time, as technology advanced, the transmitting and receiving machines became more compact and portable.[19] This allowed more newspapers to come online and subscribe to wire services such as AP and United Press International (UPI). The speed of transmission was dictated by the quality of the telephone line and averaged eight-nine minutes time for a black and white photograph. Color photographs took three times as long. From then on, the received "thermofax" had to undergo further processing to get it ready for the newspaper press. In the 1960s, this was the norm.

The Trask Timeline

Pictures of the Pain devoted an entire chapter titled "The AP Man" to Altgens's photographs. Trask had Altgens arriving at his AP office by 12:39 PM, and then sticking around "for a few moments" to take phone calls to relay what he had witnessed. Afterwards, he was sent to Parkland Hospital along with AP photographer Henry "Hank" Burroughs, Jr. to continue covering the tragedy:

"Someone grabbed my camera, removed the film and took it to process it, because they wanted me on the telephone reporting what I saw. We did an extraordinary good job, because within 20 minutes of the assassination we had a picture rolling on the wire—and that's good. All over the world, at the same time that people got it in the US of A. It was fantastic. I saw some of the cable photos that came back in that night, and one or more of the pictures I had taken were on page one of many of the world newspapers." [20]

Trask never mentions the fact that Altgens called his office from "a nearby phone" as documented in his FBI interviews of 2 June

1964. The report states he sprinted back after talking on this phone.[21] Trask writes that Altgens informed AP Bureau Chief Bob Johnson about Kennedy being shot after he arrived at the AP offices following his mad dash down Houston Street. Trask concluded his timeline by asserting that Altgens6 was sent out at 1:03 PM, which is also in conflict with the time of 12:57 PM established by the FBI in the interview of 2 June 1964.[22] Trask conducted his interviews of Altgens on 21 November 1985, 22 years after the assassination.

Another issue that is not explained by Trask, is that if someone grabbed his camera as he entered the AP offices, it had to have been because they already knew about his pictures, of which he informed Johnson in his phone call beforehand while he was still in the field. That "someone" who grabbed his camera was never identified, despite Altgens having been on the job there for 26 years, and probably knew everyone who worked there. As a photographer who took pride in his craft and knowing the extreme importance of what was in his roll of undeveloped film, it would have behooved Altgens to have been completely aware of who took control of his camera, yet apparently this will never be known. Furthermore, it must be noted here that Altgens was primarily a wirephoto operator and photographer who did all the processing of the photographs that he took—from developing negatives, to printing and captioning, to actually working the transmitting equipment thermofax machines—during all of his career at AP in Dallas. Usually Altgens captioned the photographs that he sent on the wire.[23] According to Trask, the sign-off of the captioned wirephoto read: "AP Wirephoto cel61303 stf-jwa." This indicates that one Carl E. Linde operated the wire fax machine and sent out a photograph taken by James W. Altgens on a Friday at 1:03 PM. Trask writes that Altgens witnessed the transmission.

The rest of this chapter will discuss the improbability of this timeline and will offer other alternatives.

It would seem rather odd, that on this particular day, he would have been sent to continue covering the assassination at Parkland, especially when they already had "Hank" Burroughs carrying out that task.[24]

According to Trask, Altgens never obtained copies of the photographs extracted from his roll of film, and opens the door for scholars to question the number of photographs actually taken by Altgens in Dealey Plaza, and the control that AP had over these:

"In later years Altgens became unsure of the number of photographs he took that day of the assassination . . . it is evident that he is sure, or reasonably sure that he took five of the photos, but admits to leaving things to AP's judgement."[25]

This FBI report alone seems to derail the Trask timeline:

> ALTGENS advised that as the President's car disappeared he observed some Secret Service Agents and police officers with drawn guns on the north side of Elm Street running in the direction of the top of the triple overpass. He said he thought they were chasing someone who had fled from somewhere behind the President. ALTGENS related he also ran in this direction. After proceeding across Elm Street and up toward the triple overpass, ALTGENS stated he met the police officers returning. At this juncture, ALTGENS advised he then ran to a nearby telephone and informed his office that the President had been shot and that he had witnessed it. He then sprinted to his office in the Dallas News Building with the pictures he had taken. ALTGENS stated the pictures showing the President slumping in his seat with Mrs. KENNEDY bending over him moved on the Associated Press Wirephoto Network at 12:57 p.m. which was 17 minutes after the first news bulletin was sent out by Associated Press.

on __6/2/64__ at __Dallas, Texas__   File # __DL 100-10461__
            A. RAYMOND SWITZER and
by Special Agent __EUGENE F. PETRAKIS:vm__   Date dictated __6/3/64__

This document contains neither recommendations nor conclusions of the FBI. It is the property of the FBI and is loaned to your agency; it and its contents are not to be distributed outside your agency.

Clearly, the timeline mentioned in this FBI memorandum does not coincide with the time the cropped Altgens6 was sent out on the wire on 22 November 1963.

In his Warren Commission testimony, Altgens made it quite clear that Secret Service men and motorcycle policemen went up the embankment toward the picket fence area. Amazingly, Wesley Leibeler cut him off at that moment to ask him to elaborate as to the "little incline":

> There was utter confusion at the time I crossed the street. The Secret Service men, uniformed policemen with drawn guns that went racing up this little incline and I thought——   WC7H519

He then explained why he stuck around Dealey Plaza for quite some time:

Mr. ALTGENS. Yes, sir.

I started up the incline with—or, after the officers, because they were moving well ahead of me and I was moving behind them thinking perhaps if they had the assassin cornered I wanted a picture, but before I had gotten over one-quarter of the way up the incline, I met the officers coming back and I presumed that they were just chasing shadows, so to speak, because there was no assassin in the area apparently, but I didn't learn the location of the sniper's nest until I was en route out to Parkland Hospital to continue my assignment and I heard it on the radio, that the assassin's nest was in the sixth floor window of the Book Depository Building.

After that I made a good look through this area to see that no one else had been hit. I noticed the couple that were on the ground over here with their children, I saw them when they went down and they were in the area and laid there some time after the Presidential car had disappeared.

Mr. LIEBELER. They threw themselves on the ground in this grassy area that I have just described previously where you ran across after this last shot?

Mr. ALTGENS. Yes; but they were not hit. I looked at them and they weren't hit by a bullet, so I took another long look around before I started my dash back to the office, and as it turned out, my report was the first that our service had on the assassination and my pictures were the only pictures we had available for a period of about 24 hours. **WC7H519**

Interestingly enough, when one compares his Warren Commission testimony vis-à-vis his FBI interviews of 2 June 1964, it is noted that in his Warren Commission testimony he does not mention placing his phone call to his office, conversely, in his FBI interview he does not mention staying to make sure there were no other victims, and taking another "long look around" (The elapsed time could have clouded his recollection of events.) Perhaps that is the reason why the Warren Commission decided to drag their feet and were not overly excited about deposing James Altgens.

Needless to say, the timeline claimed by the FBI in their report of 2 June 1964 is physically impossible. Altgens would have taken at least 20-25 minutes just to get back to his office. It would have taken 30-35 minutes just to process his roll of film. The earliest Altgens's photographs could have been sent out via thermofax would have been closer to 1:30 PM. Another interesting tidbit about his Warren Commission testimony and the Trask timeline is the fact that he continued his assignment on to Parkland Hospital. This confirms that he was not around when his film was processed, therefore, Altgens did not really know the results of what he shot that day. Roy Schaeffer has been more specific about this, stating that "they sent him to Parkland to get him out of the way."[26]

1968: Richard Sprague Interviews Ike Altgens

In early 1968, Richard Sprague caught up with Altgens and interviewed him in a local Dallas restaurant. His 6 January 1969 letter to Harold Weisberg goes a long way in establishing the Altgens timeline from Ike Altgens himself:

Notes on Interview and Dinner with James (Ike) Altgens, Dallas Texas Friday, January 12, 1968. Also present, G. Nicholson

Main impression of him was a four-flusher who brags and exaggerates. He talked up the restaurant he took us to as though it were the Four Seasons. The place was empty, the food was awful, and it was worse than a roadhouse.

I showed him my display of the seven photos he had taken at the time of the assassination in Dealey Plaza. He vaguely remembered the four he had not been able to remember and said he had <u>told</u> the AP people in Dallas that there were more, but they kept insisting there were only three (1-4, 1-6 and 1-7).

He admitted that he just didn't kno w what to do with his camera, wandering across Elm and up and down the knoll and back across Elm. He said "I look pretty stupid, don't I," when we showed him the Rickerby photos of himself camera in hand, but not taking pictures.

He explained the collection of photos taken later in the day, about 5 p. m. , by saying his office sent him down to establish the place he was standing when he took 1-6. He took a series of photos (Altgens 2-4 through 4-18) from that spot facing the TSBD, the center of the Plaza, and the grassy knoll.

Rickerby photographs (above and below)

The images shown here precisely track the movements of Altgens and confirm that he was in no hurry whatsoever in the aftermath of the assassination: "wandering across Elm and up and down the knoll and back across Elm." This is exactly what we see in the photographic record and supports our contention that it would have been impossible for Altgens to return to the AP facilities in *The Dallas Morning News* building at 508 Young Street—five blocks South of Elm Street—in time to get his photos on the wire at 12:57 PM, according to the FBI and 1:03 PM, according to the AP timestamp.

This interview also reveals what we have suspected all along: that Altgens was sure he had taken more photographs, which he never saw because his camera was confiscated the second he entered the AP facilities. The Rickerby, Bothun, Willis, Cancellare, Couch, and other photos shown here tend to confirm this because as his colleagues, who arrived later, are seen frantically taking photographs of the scene, Altgens calmly stands around as if satisfied that he already has taken the photographs his competitors are belatedly trying to capture. This is the only explanation for the apparent aloofness he shows in all photographs and film. It also expands the timeline of what happened on Elm Street where he clearly has finished taking photos by the time his competitors have arrived. Sprague seems to have been on the right track when he puzzled over Altgens extended presence in Dealey Plaza, "not taking any pictures."

(Note: In a 2016 interview with *Dallas Morning News* employee Jerry Coley, which will be discussed at length in Chapter 19, he spoke of arriving back at *The Dallas Morning News* building between 12:45 PM and 12:50 PM.)

The Schaeffer Timeline

Recently, Mr. Roy Schaeffer and this author painstakingly reviewed and revisited the Trask timeline, and Altgens's FBI and Warren Commission interviews. Roy grew up in Dayton, Ohio and was reared in the newspaper business. In the 1950s, his father was president of the typographical union in Dayton, Ohio, where his responsibilities included negotiating labor contracts between the union and newspapers all over the U.S., including most major newspapers such as *The New York Times*, *Los Angeles Times*, and the *San Francisco Chronicle*, to name just a few.[27] Roy can be considered an expert of the highest order, with intricate knowledge of the newspaper business of the late '50s and early '60s and beyond. As fate would have it, Roy happened to be the person at the *Dayton Daily News* who received the Moorman and Altgens6 photographs and removed them from the thermofax machine at 7:15 AM, the morning of Saturday, 23 November 1963.[28] Schaeffer is extremely well-informed on alteration techniques and procedures and the equipment necessary to make these changes, and he immediately noticed opaquing techniques on the images that were received that morning.

Schaeffer is of the opinion that the image taken off of a wirephoto machine could not have been of sufficient quality where it might have been used to make alterations. Any alterations had to have been made locally in Dallas using the original negative or the original negative flown that afternoon to a place with the proper equipment to realize any alterations.[29] Two positives then had to be made off the original negative. One print would go into the AP morgue and the other to the wire operator who wrote the caption prior to it being sent over the wire. Either the negative had to be altered by a film stripper or a print of the original had to be made and then masking and opaquing of the positive had to occur prior to it being sent over the wire. Once a fax came off the wire, crude opaquing could be used. If it did occur, the opaque area would be darker or lighter than the rest of the altered photo. According to Schaeffer, the alterations to the Moorman and Altgens6 were done prior to them being sent over the wire, which would take about two hours. The altered original could have run five hours later in altered condition over the wire with its caption. After a newspaper received the AP wirephoto it would take another two hours to use a line camera and make two copies, one with a 55-line screen on it. Then a zinc engraving had to be made for a newspaper to run the AP altered wirephoto.[30] (For a complete breakdown of the history of wirephotos and their capabilities, see the appendix.)

Schaeffer tried for many years to get *The Dallas Morning News* to admit to the alterations of the Altgens and Moorman photographs, but to no avail. The fact that the original "morgue" copies of Altgens's photographs were never shown speaks volumes of the secrecy with which the photographs were treated. He believes the original, unaltered Altgens first generation positive prints still exist somewhere.[31]

The First Photos Shown By CBS, ABC And NBC Were Not Altgens's Photos

Despite the claims by Trask, that with unprecedented efficiency, AP had Altgens's images distributed on the wire, there is nothing further from the truth. At 1:08 PM CST, 38 minutes after the assassination, Cronkite showed this UPI photograph, and it was not one of Altgens's photographs[32] (lower left):

CBS (left) and NBC (right) showed the same UPI photograph, which was transmitted and received on the wirephoto thermofax machine, around the same time of 2:08PM Eastern.

And ABC showed it almost simultaneously:[33]

ABC News Ron Cochran shows the first UPI wirephoto on national television

Furthermore, this same UPI photograph was the very first one published in afternoon newspaper and extra editions that day. This one is from the *New York World-Telegram*:

President Kennedy in motorcade moving toward downtown Dallas just before he was shot.

And this is the original, non-cropped UPI photograph:

The Race Is On

It is quite obvious that the media were competing with each other to get the "scoop" in before the competition. AP and UPI were mortal enemies in this battle.[34] The *Dallas Times Herald* and *The Dallas Morning News* had couriers who were scooping up and catching rolls of film from photographers riding in the camera cars.[35] One particular instance which came to the attention of the Warren Commission was when *Dallas Times Herald* photographer Bob Jackson tossed a roll of film to courier Jim Featherstone as camera car No. 3 was on Main Street and close to making the turn onto Houston Street. He misjudged its flight in the wind and allowed it to fall and roll onto the pavement, much to the amusement of his colleagues in the camera car.[36] Featherstone then rushed this roll of film over to the *Dallas Times Herald* installations on Pacific Avenue for immediate distribution nationwide via wirephoto. This photo, taken as JFK's limousine made the turn onto Main Street, which was in that specific roll of film, was made available to the media roughly within an hour of the assassination.[37] The photo was severely cropped, as can be seen below.

Cronkite showed this cropped photo (left) at 2:32PM (1:32PM Dallas Time), wired by *The Dallas Times Herald.* ABC followed suit and showed the same photograph (right) at around the same time. NBC did not show this photograph.

Original, non-cropped version of the Dallas Times Herald *photograph*

John Caldbick was 17-years-old and had just started working the day before as a copyboy at the *Seattle Post-Intelligencer.*[38] This is how he described the scene that day:

Smaller groups gathered around the UPI wirephoto and AP telephoto machines, primitive faxes that took about five minutes to squeeze out a bad picture on wet, tissue-like paper that always made my fingers feel weird.

It was like watching a movie in extreme slow motion, the image burned into the chemicals of the paper one thin scanned line at a time, slowly building up to an entire picture and caption. Then there'd be a brief pause, and another one would start its slow vertical climb out of the machine. One of the staff artists' main and most hated jobs was retouching these things to make them passably usable. The first photo I remember seeing that day was of the Kennedys smiling and waving from the limousine, taken just a few minutes before the shots were fired.

(See *Dallas Times Herald* image above)

Here is a sample of a retouched wirephoto, as noted by Caldbick above:

President, center in car behind rear view mirror, grasps chest after being hit with fatal bullet

This scan by Richard Hooke of the *Oakland Tribune* of the late afternoon of 22 November 1963, shows an extremely cropped wirephoto with obvious retouching showing tracing around JFK's head, the rear-view mirror, Connally's head, Kellerman's shoulders and head, sun visors, to name just a few, exactly the procedure described by Caldbick above:

"One of the staff artists' main and most hated jobs was retouching these things to make them passably usable."[39]

Here are more front pages from 22-23 November, showing Altgens6 and Altgens7 wirephotos:

The Montana Standard, *23 November 1963*

The Philadelphia Bulletin, *late extra edition, 22 November 1963,*
Philadelphia, Pa.

The Evening Journal, *late extra edition, 22 November 1963,*
Wilmington, Delaware

AP was definitely in this horse race to get photographs out nationwide. The first AP wirephoto shown on 22 November by NBC was this one[40]:

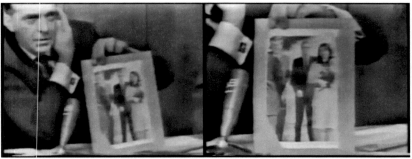

AP wirephoto showing JFK, Governor Connally, and Jackie
at Love Field shown by NBC at 2:07PM Eastern

This suggests that AP was actively transmitting photographs early that afternoon and raises the question as to why Altgens's photographs were delayed when compared to the rest of the photographs that they were distributing that day.

An interesting aside must be mentioned about this AP photograph taken between 11:00 AM and 11:15 AM at Love Field, while protocol greetings of dignitaries were being conducted. In his landmark study, *Inside the Assassination Records Review Board: The U.S. Government's Final Attempt to Reconcile the Conflicting Medical Evidence in the Assassination of JFK—Volume 5*, Douglas Horne had this to say about this photograph:

"Connally, captured between them, looks quite tense, is frowning, and appears to be staring off into the distance as if deep in thought. Sometimes a picture is worth a thousand words."[41]

The timing of this photograph should offer a pretty good benchmark with which to

Shortly after disembarking at Love Field, the President and First Lady are warmly received by local dignitaries.
Groden pg 3 credit AP/Worldwide

estimate the time it would take between taking a photograph, to sending it out on the wire. This process would involve sending the roll of film from the camera downtown via courier to the AP offices in *The Dallas Morning News* building for processing and transmission as described above. This would have taken approximately 20 minutes.[42] Applying these parameters, it is estimated that the approximate time elapsed before this particular photograph appeared on NBC was close to two hours.

Surprisingly, the next photograph to make its way on TV was the Cancellare photograph shown earlier in this study, which depicts the backside of Ike Altgens. It was broadcast by NBC around 2:40 PM ET that afternoon![43]

Altgens6 Makes Its Television Debut

At approximately 6:35 PM ET on 22 November 1963, Walter Cronkite presented for the first time on television, an extremely cropped version of the Altgens6 photograph to the American public. The glossy nature and the quality of the photograph shown by Cronkite suggests that it was re-photographed with a line camera after it was received as a wire fax at CBS that evening. This was a common technique at the time.

CRONKITE [narration]: "You see the secret service men, riding in back of the car, looking over their shoulder to the right rear where the shot came from."

These are snapshots taken from CBS footage of their JFK Assassination coverage the night of 22 November 1963. Unlike the low quality "wet paper" transmissions described by John Caldbick above, these images, particularly the third one below left, show the reflection from the glossy surface, which reinforces the inference that it was re shot as described above.

The Research of James Norwood

We would be remiss, of course, if we only presented one side of the Altgens photos timeline. Minnesota professor and JFK researcher James Norwood has taught JFK assassination courses at the University of Minnesota. Required reading used in these courses have been: James Douglass's *JFK and the Unspeakable* and Jim Fetzer's *Murder in Dealey Plaza.* Norwood is an extremely competent researcher who follows research protocol and relies mostly on primary source material.

In May 2015, Norwood tracked down three ex newspaper workers at the *Racine Journal-Times* who claim to have received, handled, processed and published Altgens6 the afternoon of 22 November 1963. With extraordinary and unprecedented efficiency, they managed to put the afternoon edition out by 2:00 PM CT, which included the extremely cropped Altgens6 photograph on the cover. This would have been a scant 90 minutes after the assassination. Norwood's meticulous work on the provenance and timing of the publication of Altgens6 by the *Racine Journal-Times* is impressive. He reports that his timeline coincides with the official version described by Trask, which we covered above. Recall that the "official" Altgens photograph caption fixed the time of transmission at 1:03 PM. The only problem with this, is the existence of the FBI memorandum of the interview of Altgens dated 2 June 1964, which is considered primary source material discussed above. Unless we accept the fact that the FBI was sloppy and incompetent in their work, then we must consider two key points reported by Special Agents A. Raymond Switzer and Eugene F. Petrakis:

1. After spending an extended amount of time at the scene of the crime—supported by the many photographs of Altgens taken by several photographers which track his movements—*Altgens searched for and found a telephone, spoke to his superiors* at the AP offices at *The Dallas Morning News* about what he had witnessed, then "raced" five city blocks, which span at least a quarter mile, entered the building, to finally hand his camera to an unknown person who removed the film and processed it. Also bear in mind, that the FBI reported that Altgens walked up to the triple overpass—also referred to as the triple underpass. From there on, Altgens was not even part of the chain of custody of his film. As we noted above, he told Richard Sprague he was positive he had taken more photographs than those released by AP.

2. The FBI report states time of transmission as 12:57 PM *not* 1:03 PM, as seen in the caption. Both cannot be right, and the time left available to process Altgens's film just does not fit this crucial piece of evidence left behind by FBI Special Agents Switzer and Petrakis.

The *Racine Journal-Times* had a 90-minute window to publish Altgens6. It took Altgens 15-20 minutes to reach the AP offices after the assassination at 12:30 PM CT. To this, we must add the approximate 30 minutes to expose, develop, prepare and print the photograph, as described above. From there, captioning and transmitting the photograph to the AP hub or distribution center in New York, nine minutes. The AP distribution center in N.Y. used a leased line network to distribute wirephotos.

This means that Altgens6 did not go out directly from Dallas to each individual newspaper across the country. Also, bear in mind that AP would have been in high demand to supply assassination wirephotos to hundreds of newspapers throughout the country and the world, and their ability to do so would have been limited by the available machines and phone lines. Even though they were capable of sending one transmission to multiple destinations, it still would have taken another nine minutes to reach small-market Racine, who was competing with large market subscribers, plus the television networks. It would be safe to say that large markets like New York, Chicago, Los Angeles, etc., would have had priority over small markets like Racine.

The TV networks had their own wirephoto equipment in house and were showing these as they were received in real-time. Second- and third-generation transmissions would have degraded the photograph where it would have required retouching as described by John Caldbick above. In this context, the *Racine Journal-Times* would have received Altgens6 approximately 68 minutes after the assassination, or 1:38 PM CT, leaving them with about 22 minutes to convert the transmitted wirephoto to hard copy, following the process described by Schaeffer above.

This simple chronological order of the wirephotos that were transmitted by different media that day suggests that the media were taking no prisoners when it came to getting the scoop over the competition. Conspicuous by its absence however, were Altgens's crucial photographs.

Simply put, they were not shown on TV that afternoon and only made their way onto a handful of newspapers on the West Coast and very late extra editions on the East Coast that day. Coupled with the analysis of the time it would have taken James Altgens to make his film available to the media, and the obvious delay his photos underwent, this now raises serious questions as to the real trajectory of his roll of film.

The Rigby Timeline for the Altgens6

Paul Rigby, a most respected JFK researcher from the UK, has provided the Oswald Innocence Campaign with a detailed time line of the Altgens6 photo and has proposed at least a two to three hour "window of opportunity" for alteration. Mr. Rigby's work deserves to be included here. He believes that there was a delay in the release of Altgens6 because it was initially wired to the AP headquarters in New York, but then appears to have been "cropped twice". On the basis of the available evidence, we can—provisionally at least—draw the following inferences:

(1) Altgens did not develop his own photos;
(2) Altgens6 went by fax, not to the world at large, but to the AP New York HQ, at just after 1:00 PM/CT;
(3) The negatives were sent by commercial airline, ostensibly to the same destination but did not arrive until hours after the initial fax;
(4) The dissemination of the image from NY did not occur until at least two hours after the fax arrived but before the arrival of the negatives;

(5) Both the AP and Altgens appear to have sought to conceal this hiatus;
(6) The AP acted against its own commercial interest in delaying release of Altgens6;
(7) The version which first appeared in the final editions of newspapers in Canada and the US on the evening of 22 November 1963 was heavily, and very obviously, retouched;
(8) Point (7) may not be the explanation, either full or partial, for the concealed delay; it is quite conceivable that obvious alterations were used to draw attention away from other more subtle stuff.

CONCLUSION

The surviving CBS, ABC, and NBC TV videos, which take us back to 22 November 1963, as riveting as they are, show a blow-by-blow account of the tragedy that was unraveling when this nation lost its innocence to an assassination that claimed its 35th president. Within these videos, we are able to discern the order in which the early images and photographs were propagated and disseminated to the world that day. In the case of Altgens's photographs, unfortunately it seems that these were set aside and were not sent out until later that afternoon. Despite concerted attempts to establish their dissemination early that afternoon, it appears that the two most important photographs—Altgens6 and Altgens7—were delayed long enough to cast serious doubt as to the integrity of their content.

ENDNOTES

1. CD1088, FBI Letterhead Memorandum of 05 June 1964 re: James W. Altgens, FBI 2 June 1964 DL100-10461, p. 1
2. WC7H525
3. CD1088, p. 6
4. WC7H519
5. YouTube CBS
6. DeLoach Memorandum
7. Trask, Richard, *Pictures of the Pain* (1994), p. 323, endnote 19
8. WC7H519
9. Ibid.
10. Ibid.
11. jfk.ci.dallas.tx.us/13/1312-001.gif
12. Willis slide No. 7.
13. CD1088, FBI Letterhead Memorandum of 05 June 1964 re: James W. Altgens, FBI 2 June 1964 DL100-10461, p. 6

14. nbcnews.com/id/3476061/ns/msnbc-jfk_the_day_that_changed_america/t/
covering-jfk-assassination
15. CD1088, p. 6, and WC7H519
16. Trask, Richard, *Pictures of the Pain* (1994), p. 318
17. According to Roy Schaeffer this is standard procedure for every photograph taken in the newspaper business.
18. CBS News Live Coverage of The Assassination of President Kennedy
Part 6 (6:30 PM - 7:30 PM)
19. time.com/3650882/associated-press-photowire-80th-anniversary
20. Trask, p. 318
21. CD1088, FBI 2 June 1964, DL100-10461
22. Trask, p. 318
23. Ibid. 308
24. Ibid. 318
25. Ibid. 318-19
26. Schaeffer email, 12 March 2015
27. "The Real Deal" interview, 17 February 2014
28. Schaeffer email, 12 March 2015
29. Schaeffer email, 19 March 2015
30. Schaeffer email, 21 March 2015 (email and/or interview on "The Real
Deal." See also taped telecon.)
31. Schaeffer email, 19 March 2015
32. CBS News Live Coverage of The Assassination of President Kennedy Part
6 (6:30 PM - 7:30 PM)
34. Trask, p. 391
35. Trask, top of p. 312; Featherstone, p. 439 top
36. WC2H158, Trask, p. 439
37. CBS and ABC. NBC did not show this photograph.
38. historylink.org/File/10670
39. Ibid.
40. Groden, Robert, *The Killing of a President: The Complete Photographic
Record of the JFK Assassination, the Conspiracy, and the Cover-up* (1993), p.
3 (credit AP/Worldwide)
41. Horne, Douglas, *Inside the Assassination Records Review Board*, p. 1431
42. dallas-lovefield.com/airport-directions.html
43. youtube.com/watch?v=SyAv1IlkiHQ

APPENDIX

Wirephotos

*The wirephoto process allowed photographic images to be
transferred through telephone lines. The process required a large,
expensive wirephoto machine both at the source and at the receiving
end. The original photograph was placed inside the wirephoto
machine. Much like with today's computer scanner, an electronic eye
scanned the photograph and translated it into electrical impulses.*

These impulses were sent through the telephone wire to the identical wirephoto machine at the receiving end. At the receiving machine the impulses were translated to light that was used to develop the image onto photographic paper.

The development would take minutes to over an hour, as the photographic paper was slowly exposed line by line. In fact, the ultimate way to identify the wirephoto (the received image) is to look for the tiny horizontal or vertical lines in the image.

sportscollectorsdaily.com/photos-telephone-history-guide-wirephotos

Qualities that identify wirephotos

Tiny horizontal or vertical lines in the image. The wirephotos were developed in lines, much like a computer print or television image. In fact, the wirephoto machine was the father of the television. In the receiving wirephoto machine, the emitted light was slowly passed over the photographic paper line by line. Under close inspection the wirephoto will often have a line pattern.

Sometimes it can be seen up close with the naked eye. Sometimes a magnifying glass is needed. It often appears as jaggedness to a person or car's edge in the image. If there was an interruption in the telephone line during transmission, there sometimes is an obvious "break" line, squiggles or similar marks in the image. The line pattern is the ultimate way to identify wirephotos.

A wirephoto could be sent simultaneously to many receivers. For example, AP could put the original photograph into the wirephoto machine and send copies to *The Seattle Times*, *The New York Times*, *San Francisco Chronicle* and *Green Bay Press-Gazette* all at once. The AP's main office in New York City could send wirephotos to its regional office in Atlanta, and the Atlanta office could send wirephotos to the New York City office. As you can imagine, this made photograph distribution quicker and more efficient than transporting a box of photos by train.

"While the wirephoto process was invented in 1921, and AT&T had its first commercial wirephoto service in 1925, it took at least a decade for the process to be used widely.

The early machines were large, overly expensive and the process was unreliable. The early wirephotos were usually of poor quality and hostage to the fickleness and 'breaks' of the telephone lines. When someone sent a wirephoto across the telephone lines, it often took more than an hour and the sender had no idea if a recognizable image would be received at the other end. Before 1935, wirephotos were only used for especially important, breaking news."

In 1934 AP, the world's largest news service, installed an advanced and effective wirephoto system. Starting the following year, the wirephoto system became practical. Soon after, other major news services installed their own wirephoto systems.

This included AP's rivals International News Photos, United Press Association and ACME. Though press photos were still distributed the old-fashioned way, and a local newspaper would still hire its own photographers for local stories, the wirephoto system was the dominant form of photo distribution from 1935 until the mid-1970s.

cycleback.com/pressphotos/three.htm

Roy Schaeffer email, 19 March 2015

Probably when the Altgens film strip was drying the alteration to DN5 were being considered. In checking over five newspapers that ran the AP Altgens DN5 were all altered. December 14, 1963 Saturday Evening Post showed most of a total print and was severely edited throughout the photo that appeared in that edition.

As I said, the Moorman UPI and Altgens DN5 were each altered when I took them off the AP and UPI lines and they both ran on page 5 in section D of the Sunday edition of the Dayton Daily News. *This proves that the both were altered prior to 23 November 1963 &:15 pm. EST.*

This was my timeline.

Only the negative from Altgens film was ready to be altered in about 2.5 hours after it being delivered to The Dallas Morning News. Two positives then had to be made off the original negative.

One print went into the AP morgue and the other to the wire operator who wrote the caption prior to it being sent over the wire. So either the negative had to be altered by a film stripper or a print of the original was made and then masking and opaquing of the positive had to occur prior to it being sent over the wire. This would take about two hours. My best guess that the altered original ran five hours later in altered condition over the wire with its caption. Then after a newspaper receives the AP wire it takes another two hours to use a line camera and make two copies, one with a 55-line screen on it. Then a zinc engraving has to be made for a newspaper to run the AP altered wire. I think the main reason Altgens made his statement as such was he knew the negative film was replaced with an altered negative.

I pointed this out to Burl Osborn, president of The Dallas Morning News in 1994. He then referred it over to his lawyer who declined to expose this fact. In about 2004, I contacted the president of World Wide who then owned Altgens which was altered. I proved this in 1989 when I was sent Altgens5 and Altgens6 for book publication.

Roy Schaeffer

2

The Jaggars-Chiles-Stovall Connection

"I have long suspected that all is not right with that firm."

—Beverly Brunson

JFK researchers are quite familiar with the firm Jaggars-Chiles-Stovall (JCS). It was Lee Oswald's second place of employment after returning from the USSR, and he worked there for six months between October 1962 to April 1963.[1] As we shall now see, many loose ends and unanswered questions remained in the investigation of this company, some of which we will attempt to bring into focus.

We decided to take another look at the physical layout of downtown Dallas and noted that the address of JCS, at 522 Browder Street, was in proximity to Dallas City Hall, which in 1963 was on Harwood Street, and to *The Dallas Morning News* building at Houston and Young:

JAGGARS-CHILES-STOVALL INC
522 Browder-RI 1-5501
Jaggars Prntg Co—See
[1965 Phone Book listing] Jaggars-Chiles-Stovall Inc

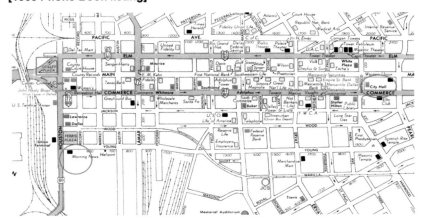

As noted in the previous chapter, British researcher Paul Rigby's timeline established at least a three-hour window before Altgens6 was published in some late editions of newspapers in Canada and the U.S. The major East Coast papers did not publish the photograph until the following Saturday, and Walter Cronkite did not show the photograph until 6:35 PM ET.

JFK researcher Beverly Brunson's suspicion of JCS's involvement was well-founded. On 26 October 1991, author Harry Livingstone interviewed the Reverend Jack Shaw in relation to his research on Roscoe White. In passing, Reverend Shaw stated that JCS was used as a base of operations for the assassination.[2] In her research, Brunson noted that Seth Kantor had written an account of his experiences that day, which was published as an exhibit in Volume 20:

> The interesting thing about this rumor is that Kantor gives someone from Jaggars Chiles Stovall part of the credit for spreading the rumor. I have long thought, because of the "Walker" letter, which denotes a time when Oswald had to be working for Jaggars-Chiles Stovall. and was yet engaging in some mysterious activity,(which Jaggars must have covered at least when they tuned over work reports that indicated Oswald was regularly employed from Oct. 13 to April 6th) -I have long suspected that all is not right with that firm. Ofstein their employee thought so too. If Jaggars-Chiles-Stovall was interested in spreading a rumor that a secret service man was wounded (Kantor also says that the rumor incorporated that the secret service man was in on the plot to kill Kennedy), then it could only have been to explain that spot of blood which so many saw that day, and to scotch the rumor that it was not the motorcycle officer who was wounded.

The fact that Seth Kantor reported that a JCS employee was responsible for spreading a "rumor" about another wounded victim makes this information extremely significant.

It indicates that at least one JCS employee, who appears to have wanted to make sure Kantor knew of his employment, was actively involved in the propagation of information (or disinformation) during the assassination.[3]

> 1 p.m.) I went ot an office down the hall and placed a call to Washington. It was difficult getting a line out of the hospital. The nurses in this office-- there were a handful-- seemed to be stunned-- and they looked at each other dreadfully as they listened to my conversation to Washington. A western union man who had been with us since we came down from from Andrews Force Base came into the office. A nurse asked him about a report that a Secret Service agent had been killed out on the street. He said the, it was true. This was one of the immediate rumors which sprung up . It took several days for this particular rumor not to be believed in Dallas itself (fellow in Jaggars-Chiles-Stovall) who got it from a friend who got it from a postman supposed to have been at the death scene that the shot and bleeding SS man was picked up and whisked away and it was all hushed up. Why? I asked. Because they even have to die in secret, he said.) He and others hinted that maybe the SS man was in on the plot to kill the President.)
>
> **Kantor Exhibit 4, WC20H410**

In a rare 1978 letter from the great Sylvia Meagher to Harold Weisberg, after reviewing Edward Eptseins's book *Legend: The*

Secret World of Lee Harvey Oswald, Sylvia had this to say about her suspicions of JCS, and their possible role in setting up Lee Oswald as the patsy:

> *The second item is Epsteins's claim in the body of the book that John Bowen (at JCS) and Gary Taylor both saw the rifle in Oswald's possession (in the footnote, this is changed to Gary Taylor and Alexandra De M. Taylor, with Bowen dropped). But Gary Taylor said no such thing in his Warren Commission testimony—why should one believe him now? As for Bowen, he is an ex-convict, using an alias, and I would like to know if he was paid for giving Epstein an interview.*[4]

But exactly what was JCS capable of doing besides advertising artwork and other commercial ventures?

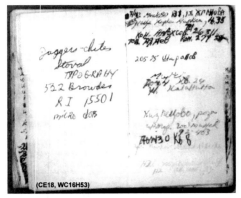

(CE18, WC16H53)

In his book *Spy Saga: Lee Harvey Oswald and U.S. Intelligence*, Philip H. Melanson noted that this company had been practically ignored by previous researchers.[5] When he dug a little deeper, he noted that Lee Oswald had annotated two intriguing terms in his address book below the reference to the company: "Typography" and "micro dots." This led Melanson to try to contact ex-employees of the company and on 14 May 1981 he spoke to Mr. Steven Baker. Baker confirmed for Melanson what John Graef had already told the Commission in 1964 in this excerpt from *Spy Saga*:

> *These references have been only partially deciphered by previous research. 522 Browder Street was of; RI1 1150, its telephone number. Typography can refer to almost any aspect of the advertising or printing trade, from typesetting to photographic composition. In May 1981 the author talked with Mr. Steven Baker, who then worked in Jaggars' advertising department. He indicated that at Jaggars, typography had a more specialized meaning: it described the sophisticated techniques of photographic reduction and modification performed by the firm in its advertising work. In 1962-63, Baker asserted, Jaggars*

used "modification cameras" and other complex equipment which were more sophisticated than the photographic equipment available in most photo labs.[6] Microdot is a system employed in espionage to store and transmit intelligence data. Using sophisticated techniques of photographic reduction, the system affords the storage of large volumes of strategic information within a tiny spot the size of a semicolon or an exclamation point. Such a spot is then concealed within the text of a letter or document for storage or transmittal. It might be fruitful to examine all of Oswald's correspondence, notes and documents to see if any contain microdot. Neither the Warren Commission nor the House Committee did that. If microdot data could be found, it might reveal much about Oswald's spy missions and about the identity of those who controlled him. If the Commission or the Committee had become curious about microdots, however, they most likely would have asked the nation's premier espionage agency to analyze Oswald's papers.

Melanson also acknowledged that JCS employees and management claimed ignorance about microdots, but in the final analysis, it is obvious that this type of classified work would have been denied in any investigative setting.

Surely, any outfit equipped to manufacture microdots would have had unlimited capabilities of photographic manipulation. A microdot is in effect a reduced negative, (see appendix) and as we shall see, the re-generation of Altgens's negatives after alteration of the photographs is fundamental to the production of positive prints for later dissemination.

This is how John Graef, who was director of the photographic department at JCS, described their capabilities:[7]

> Mr. GRAEF. That's correct. All our cameras are different from the ordinary cameras you find in commercial printing shops or printing establishments.
> Mr. JENNER. Are these portable cameras or fixed cameras?
> Mr. GRAEF. No, fixed cameras—dark room cameras.
> Mr. JENNER. When I used the expression "fixed," I had in my own mind that they would be these large-size cameras, fixed in the sense that they would be adjacent to a wall or a bench or a table.
> Mr. GRAEF. Or the floor?
> Mr. JENNER. Or the floor.
> Mr. GRAEF. Yes.
> Mr. JENNER. And be so heavy as not to be portable or so firmly secured as not to be removable?
> Mr. GRAEF. Yes; that's right.
> Mr. JENNER. Would you indicate their size?
> Mr. GRAEF. I would say approximately 8 feet long total length, with 6 or 7 feet of the front of the camera projecting through a wall, which on the outside of

184

that wall have the exposure lights to light whatever you are going to shoot. Then, the back of the camera sticks through the wall in the darkroom and on the back of the camera, of course, you place your light-sensitive film and make your exposure this way.

Mr. JENNER. And do you use light-sensitive film plates?

Mr. GRAEF. No; ordinary commercial Litho film or Ortho film that are generally available from large companies.

Mr. JENNER. Indicate the size of the frames?

Mr. GRAEF. Approximately 20 by 24 inches. The difference in these cameras—they are commonly known as modification cameras. As I said previously, you could take a line of type and twist it or curve it or stretch it out of proportion. As they are different compared with ordinary cameras that are used in most places throughout the country in that they do not have any scales on them. Ordinarily you measure a piece of copy and you set the cameras on a certain number, and for example, the same size—if you wanted to make the same size shot, you would set your copy board on No. 1, and you would set your film carrier on No. 1, put your film in and make your exposure, and you get a same size shot, but our cameras have no scales and you have to find visually and manually your sizes, everything is flexible on the camera. The boards move——

Mr. JENNER. What boards?

Mr. GRAEF. The copy boards can twist. The film carrier can twist.

Mr. JENNER. When you say "twist" do you mean twist the image?

Mr. GRAEF. On its axis—actually twist on its axis.

Mr. JENNER. You mean "twist" as distinguished from "turn"?

Mr. GRAEF. Well, let me say "turn"—then. Can turn on its axis. The lens camera can be shifted up or down or to the right or left. There are various devices that are supplied with the camera, consisting of prisms through which you can make distortions, various other forms which can be used to make various complicated bends and waves in type or illustrations, or what have you.

Mr. JENNER. Now, the bends or waves—when you say bends or waves in type, you mean you do not bend or twist the copy itself—that is, the thing to be photographed, but by use of prisms and other distortion devices, the image implanted on the film is a twist or distortion of the copy or photograph?

Mr. GRAEF. Yes; except we do both.

Mr. JENNER. You do straight photographing as well as distortion photography?

Mr. GRAEF. Well, many times, we will take the actual copy and twist it. Anything goes to get the final results, whatever has to be done, for example if we want to make a curved shot of a label, a flat two-dimensional label, a printed label, and we wanted to curve that label, we might take an empty tin can and paste that on the tin can and tip the tin can so that the lens looking at it would pickup the curve. We would tilt the can to such a degree that the lens in its position would pickup this curve of the label, and, of course, we would make an exposure, so anything goes in camera modification.

You start with the fundamentals of learning film and paper; the characteristics of them—we have many grades of paper, many contrasts of paper; we have several different varieties of film; the time developing these various papers—all of these have to be learned by an applicant before he can go on to beginning the camera, so it is a progression of a trade that takes time.

Mr. JENNER. Does this include color work?

Mr. GRAEF. No; all black and white.

Mr. JENNER. Oh, all black and white?

Mr. GRAEF. All black and white. We shoot color copy occasionally, but we don't do color work.

Mr. JENNER. That is, when I say color work, I intended two things—first, color film and secondly, colored ultimate product.

Mr. GRAEF. Colored film, no; we do not develop colored film and we don't shoot colored film. We might, in black and white, make a two-color a set of two-color negatives or something, for example, we might shoot part of a label and furnish a negative that would print the black on something and we might furnish an additional negative that would register with the first, that would print a color. For example, a colored border around the black copy and we

Clearly, these passages describe very specialized work in the field of photographic optics, enhancement and manipulation, using equipment not normally found in commercial facilities. In his effort to please the Commission, perhaps Graef was just a bit too revealing about the capabilities of JCS.

Which again brings us back to Altgens6 and Altgens7. It has been pointed out by researchers how fast key TSBD witnesses Billy Lovelady, Bill Shelley, Danny Arce, Bonnie Ray Williams, Charles Givens, and others were taken to City Hall for affidavits that day, literally before there had been a chance for the smoke to clear in Dealey Plaza. Other witnesses like Bill and Gayle Newman were taken to the Sheriff's office on Main Street. Jean Hill and Mary Moorman were taken to an interview office on the third floor of the Dallas County Criminal Courts building on Houston Street overlooking Dealey Plaza.[8] These are classic examples of divide and conquer tactics. Furthermore, Buell Wesley Frazier, another TSBD employee and possible patsy, who was on the steps of the entrance, was missing in action, and was not heard from until 6 PM later that day. Frazier's saga will be discussed in a later chapter. The logistics would have dictated the need to divide and control these key witnesses.

In Lovelady's case, we know that Detective James Leavelle took his affidavit at City Hall that afternoon:

After the arrest of Oswald at the Texas Theatre I was told over the police radio that Squad 91 had the witness to the shooting and was enroute to the city hall. I then returned to the city hall and my office. I assisted other officers in taking affidavits an answering the telephone. I took affidavits from Charles Douglas Givens and Billy Nolan Lovelady.   **James Leavelle #36 Report**

Because of the obvious reactions of Secret Service Agents John Ready, Paul Landis and Glen Bennet, who are seen looking in the direction of the TSBD, Altgens6 offered the conspirators a perfect opportunity to show the world from where the shots should be perceived. If you were trying to frame the patsy, this photograph was perfect "evidence" showing that the shots were fired from behind Kennedy, the building where Lee Oswald and the other potential patsies worked. The only problem they confronted was a plethora of unwanted evidence captured in the photograph, specifically the people in the doorway, and the reactions of Roy Kellerman, Bill Greer and Emory Roberts. Other people standing at the curb had to be air-brushed out as well, apparently people who were not supposed to be in Dealey Plaza that day. As mentioned earlier, the very first versions of the photograph were severely cropped. The first attempt to show the non-cropped photograph was this one by *The Saturday Evening Post* of 14 December 1963:

One hundred yards more and they would have reached the   safety of an overpass. Then three shots rang out.

Even this version of Altgens6 was not intact, where the top portion had been cropped to remove the upper parts of the fire escape of the Dal-Tex Building in the background. To this day it is unknown how far up the original photograph reached.[9]

By far, the largest obstacle preventing the immediate dissemination of Altgens6 had to be the presence of Lee Oswald, Buell Wesley Frazier, Billy Lovelady and Joe Molina in the doorway. All of them were potential patsies and this concept will also be covered in a later chapter of this book. Their presence in the doorway would have been the primary reason to send the negatives on to JCS for alteration. All four of these men were altered in one way or another. Then, the government tried desperately to convince the critics that the man in the doorway was really Billy Lovelady, by co-opting and intimidating a couple of witnesses into identifying Doorway Man as Lovelady. The prize for identifying Lovelady as Doorway Man—that they themselves would not be accused of pulling the trigger.

As mentioned earlier in the article by Bonafede, Jones Harris actually commissioned a thorough study by an expert by the name of Bernard Hoffman, who enhanced the extant photograph, and only served to raise even more questions which prevail to this day. To his credit, Harris tried everything in his power to obtain a photograph of Billy Lovelady for comparison and was met with hostile resistance in Dallas every time. A fellow by the name of William Francis Beckman, who had been sent by Harris, was run out of town after incidents outside the TSBD, including one with Patricia Lovelady.[10] Shirley Martin sent her young son Steve along with his sister Teresa

to try to snap a picture of Lovelady while he was lounging around the rear entrance of the TSBD after lunch one day.[11] Only Mark Lane was eventually successful in taking this picture of Lovelady, which revealed that he was practically bald.

Following the assassination, Altgens himself tried unsuccessfully to interview and photograph Lovelady. In an extremely rare letter dated 8 April 1976 to an unspecified recipient, Altgens gave hints that he might have been much more interested in the issue of the man in the doorway than has ever been published or discussed on Internet forums. One day, out of the blue, Lovelady called him to obtain a copy of his iconic photograph. Altgens tried to trade a private interview and "photo session" opportunity for a print of his photograph, but he was flat-out refused by Lovelady. He expressed his dismay that he had tried to obtain access to Lovelady and had been unsuccessful in doing so. The letter also reveals that Altgens was in contact with both Billy and Patricia Lovelady and was privy to the problems that he went through as a result of his notoriety as the supposed man in the doorway.[12]

Detailing the Alterations

Altgens6 immediately induced early researchers Harold Weisberg, Shirley Martin, Beverly Brunson and many others to break out their magnifying glasses and study every last pixel of the image.

The alterations are numerous and need to be broken down in left and right halves as shown in these two brightness-adjusted images:

No matter which side of the Altgens6 argument a person is on, one of the most egregious instances of obfuscation of the photograph—discovered by Dennis Cimino—has to be the area of the mouth of Secret Service agent in charge of the detail that day, Emory Roberts:

Emory Roberts at the Main and Market Street intersection, seconds before the assassination   **Emory Roberts in Altgens6**
LR

Any layman would suggest that Roberts was probably speaking into the microphone of a radio, and those who manipulated the photograph on 22 November 1963 did not want this to be so obvious.

Whatever Roberts was doing, or whomever he was speaking to on radio, will never be known.

Again, Dennis Cimino has done a commendable job in identifying areas of alteration using modern computer software gamma techniques. Cimino's techniques reveal simple instances of obfuscation where blobs of ink via airbrushing seem to cover several key areas of the image.

Other traces of manipulation such as edit lines also are revealed by Cimino. For example, someone has been erased next to the man with the sunglasses, above.

An African-American man was calmly sitting on the fire escape of the Dal-Tex Building—as seen here in Altgens5—where the motorcade is traveling on Houston Street as it approaches the intersection with Elm Street:

Altgens5 black
man on Dal Tex
fire escape

In his book *Photographic Whitewash: Suppressed Kennedy Assassination Pictures*, Harold Weisberg discussed the man on the fire escape of the Dal-Tex Building (p. 48):

> Part of the story of the man on the fire escape in the Altgens picture (WHITEWASH II, inside front cover). Scissoring of this picture eliminated this part and the man from the evidence and the *Report*. The truth is that this unidentified man, elevated on the fire escape as he was, had by far the best and least obstructed view of the crime and the scene in every direction except in back of him. For this reason alone, he should have been called as a witness. He was not. More intriguing, however, is the fact that, half-way through the assassination, he seems suddenly to have been distressed. He seems to have lost his balance and awkwardly trying to regain it. The most obvious explanation is that he was shocked by what he was seeing. Pictures taken of this man as the motorcade approached the corner of Houston and Elm Streets, on the northeast corner of which the Dal-Tex Building stands, show him to be sitting normally and watching. It is only after the shooting began that he started to fall.
> *Photograhic Whitewash*, pg 48

this almost looks like a human being coming down this fire escape and someone obscured the area in front of him for some reason and that is not normal

looks like left elbow face looking down maybe but they purposely obscured what is in front of him

The Dal Tex Fire escape and the figure running or falling down the stairs of fire escape. (Cimino)

Cimino has zeroed in and identified a black ink splotch, via air brushing, that has been placed at waist level and below, in front of the figure, and in the process, obscuring the vertical frame post of the fire escape. When compared to the same man, enlarged in Altgens5 above, it is obvious that this anomaly is only present in Altgens6. Weisberg's observation above, of the supreme importance and obliteration of this man from history, certainly, has its repercussions. This African-American witness was never identified, sought, or brought forth to describe what he witnessed, and if he volunteered to come in, he was certainly suppressed by those investigating the case. In 1963 Dallas, Texas, it is up to the reader to draw their own conclusions as to why this African-American would not want to get involved.

Occupants of Lyndon B. Johnson's (LBJ) Secret Service follow-up car erased. (analysis credit: Dennis Cimino)

Nice and clear top of the windshield earlier in the motorcade.

Windshield now shows dark amorphous blob on the upper edge.

This color-coded collage vividly illustrates the alterations to the windshield. The aqua outline represents the normal area of the tint of the windshield. The dark areas marked by purple and green outlines appear to be masking added after the fact.

The Dallas Morning News Reporters

Dallas Morning News junior reporter Mary Woodward, society editor Ann Donaldson, employee Miss Aurelia Alonzo and copy editor Margaret "Maggie" Brown were standing right between the R.L. Thornton and Stemmons Freeway signs on the north curb of Elm Street.[13]

It appears from witness maps that all four were captured in Altgens6. All versions of Altgens6, with the lone exception of *The Saturday Evening Post* printed 14 December 1963 shown earlier, have been cropped to partially remove these women. When we zoom into that area, we realize why:

One of the women for sure, and possibly two or more, were filming and/or taking photographs of the motorcade. Witness maps suggest the woman in the dark dress was actually Maggie Brown (It is also possible that it was Donaldson).

In Altgens6, the hand strap of the camera is clearly seen. Bear in mind that this woman is cropped out of most of the versions of the photograph.

Many frames from the Zapruder film confirm she was holding a camera at face level. Some frames even show what appears to be a dark square camera case at the feet of one of them (shown below).

Here is frame Z150 which shows her holding a camera at face level:

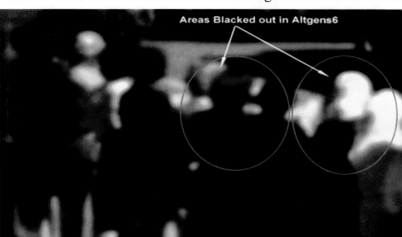

Frame 116 of the Zapruder film shows another unidentified woman, the sixth person to the right of Brown, also taking photographs of the motorcade. These have never surfaced either.

When we plot the line-of-sight of the woman filming the motorcade, we come up with this:

One hundred yards more and they would have reached the safety of an overpass. Then three shots rang out.

It appears that she had her camera trained right at LBJ's car, which brings us to another crucial and unexplained alteration of the photograph. Author Phil Nelson has pointed out that Johnson was ducking at the instant that Altgens snapped his photograph,[14] which would suggest that LBJ had foreknowledge of what was going to happen in Dealey Plaza. The following closeup shows a little more detail:

Retouching of the areas of LBJ's car is quite evident. Agent Rufus Youngblood received a commendation for supposedly jumping over the seat and covering Johnson with his body so that no harm could come to him.[15] There is not a single witness who ever mentioned seeing this action by Youngblood, and Senator Ralph Yarborough emphatically denied it ever happened.[16]

But what about the women from *The Dallas Morning News*? As trained reporters and newspaper women, surely they would have been of interest to any investigative body, especially if one or more were taking pictures or filming that day. Only the youngest, Mary Woodward, was interviewed by the FBI on 6 December 1963, probably because she had written an article (below) that same afternoon about what she and her companions had witnessed. The other three women were summarily dismissed in the following manner:

1
DL   · 89-43
        BJO:mja

        ,ANN DONALDSON, 4812 Alcott, Society Editor;
MARGARET BROWN, 9334 Peninsula Drive, Copy Editor; and
Miss AURELIA ALONZO, 4011 Travis, Reporter, all employees
of Women's News Department, Dallas Morning News, Dallas,
Texas, were interviewed December 6, 1963, by SAS HENRY J.
OLIVER and LOUIS M. KELLEY. All furnished the same information
as that previously furnished by MARY ELIZABETH WOODWARD.

No one from the Dallas Police Department (DPD), the FBI or Secret Service ever spoke to them about what they witnessed that day. Whichever films or photographs they took, have never been seen. Even more intriguing is the fact that none of them came forward, except for Mary Woodward, who many years later, in 1988, had this to say in Nigel Turner's documentary, *The Men Who Killed Kennedy*, episode No. 3:

Civic leaders and responsible people whether it be the mayor, the managing editor of the paper, almost felt a responsibility to kind of not rock the boat, perhaps, and the answer was the version that came to be the most widely accepted that there were three shots and they had all come from the Texas School Book Depository building and they were all fired by Lee Harvey Oswald.

—Mary Woodward

45

AFTER ACKNOWLEDGING our cheers, he faced forward again and suddenly there was a horrible, ear-shattering noise coming from behind us and a little to the right. My first reaction, and also my friends', was that as a joke, someone had backfired their car. Apparently the driver and occupants of the President's car had the the President start slumping in the car.

THIS WAS followed rapidly by another shot. Mrs. Kennedy stood up in the car, turned half-way around, then fell on top of her husband's body. Not until this minute did it sink in what actually was happening. We had wit-

Introducing Blender

Many years ago, Richard Sprague predicted that computers would eventually become essential in solving the JFK assassination.[17] That time has arrived with the advent of modern 3D computer graphics and digital imaging applications. By using assassination photographs as reference images, it is possible to replicate these in 3D space, thereby allowing researchers to study these like never before. This book will offer numerous examples of how these applications can be applied to the study of the JFK assassination. Open source program Blender (blender.org) is an extremely robust computer graphics and modeling application that is used worldwide to create just about anything that can be copied in life, including full length animations, movies, modeling, and game rendering. Most universities now include Blender in their curricula.

Altgens6 offers a perfect opportunity to create a 3D model of Dealey Plaza and everything seen in the photograph as the assassination occurred. For example, shadows can be exactly replicated by positioning the sun and establishing its position in the sky at 12:30 PM that day. This allows us to correctly position the models in the scene by "working backwards" and using Altgens6 as our reference image. Before we continue, it is imperative that we establish Ike Altgens's exact position when he took Altgens6. Most people think he took it from the infield as he is seen in the Zapruder film. Not surprisingly, Blender correctly places Altgens in the middle of the left lane of Elm Street at the time he took his photograph. In a later chapter we will discuss new revelations about the speed of the motorcade but suffice it to say that Altgens began his sequence of photographs at the intersection of Main and Houston, then had enough time to cross the north infield of Dealey Plaza, down the south curb of Elm Street, to position himself for his iconic photograph. Furthermore, Jim Fetzer has also offered compelling evidence that Mary Moorman was standing on the pavement at the time she took her Polaroid.[18]

The inference points in the direction that the motorcade was traveling so slow that these people felt they were not in danger by stepping onto the street to take their coveted pictures. It appears to be the case with Ike Altgens:

In order to obtain a compatible rendering of Altgens6 which replicates the angles and perspectives of the many components of the photograph, it is necessary to place Ike Altgens in the middle the left lane of Elm Street, as seen in the above illustration. If we move Altgens onto the infield as seen in the Zapruder film, this is the result:

Clearly, these are not the angles, shadows, and perspectives seen in the extant Altgens6, and the only way to replicate these, is by placing Altgens in the street.

Returning to our discussion of *The Dallas Morning News* women, Blender allows us to study their position in relation to the motorcade and the vehicles as they approached that position on the north curb of Elm Street. We can therefore hypothesize as to the direction in which the camera is pointing, as seen in the two-dimension Altgens6. Above, we saw the red arrow tracing the possible line-of-sight onto LBJ's car. With Blender, we can represent these lines of sight into 3D renderings using generic models, where these seem to confirm that they indeed filmed the LBJ vehicle at the time that Altgens took his photograph, which also corresponds in time to Zapruder film frame 255.

As we have seen here, by placing multiple cameras in our Blender scene, we can accurately represent the line-of-sight of each individual or model. Here is how the scene looks like from above in our Blender "viewport."

This exercise certainly suggests that this woman had LBJ's car in her viewfinder and filmed what was going on in that car as the assassination was taking place. Catching Johnson as he ducked would have been more than enough reason to deep six her film.

Altgens7

The alterations were not limited to Altgens6. Photographic expert Jack White was convinced that Altgens4-7 had been altered in one way or another.[19] A few researchers have discovered that Altgens7 is also rich in alterations. Among these:

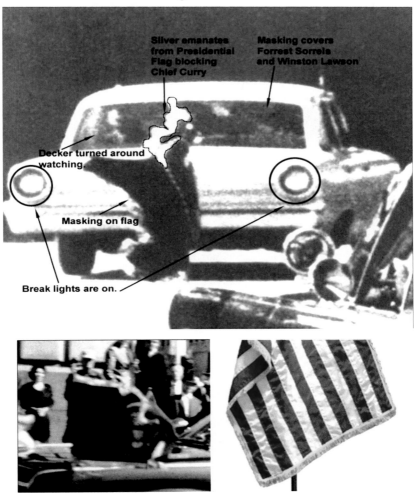

The key to understanding the alterations to Altgens7 can be found in the presidential flag. As seen above in Willis slide No. 2, the border of the flag contained a golden fringe, which was uniform on three sides—top, bottom and outer. (Fringes on flags are used in formal settings such as parades, inaugurations, dedication ceremonies, etc., see appendix) Furthermore, this particular flag had no loose tassels or

49

any other loose ornaments. Altgens7 contains a prominent sliver of sorts, which conveniently splits the rear windshield, covering Chief Curry and facilitating the right side of the glass to be masked and opaqued. Schaeffer describes this alteration:

"They added a slight white opaque to the top of the flag to conceal the slight masking on the rear of Curry's back car windshield to help hide their view in the plaza."[20]

Altgens 5

Altgens 6

Altgens 7

Presidential Flag comparison in Altgens photos

WHEN THE BULLETS STRUCK: Mrs. Kennedy moving to the aid of the President after he was hit by a sniper yesterday in Dallas. A guard mounts rear bumper. Gov. John B. Connally Jr. of Texas, also in the car, was wounded.

Above (previous page) is Altgens7 which was sent on the wire, scanned from the original copy of *The New York Times* of 23 November 1963. Sheriff Bill Decker and the left tail light have been cropped out, as well as the upper portion of the photograph which showed the top portion of the overpass.

After showing that alterations were indeed performed on these photographs, the obvious question remains: where could these alterations have taken place?

Roy Schaeffer breaks this down:

In truth, I think three places could have altered Altgens6. Assuming that JCS could have done it, The Dallas Morning News had the equipment to do so. The key thing is where the negative was developed and looked at.[21]

The Altgens photo could have been altered at JCS or The Dallas Morning News. For example, the Dayton Daily News would use what is called a Job Shop, Craftsman photo craft. The newspaper would use this if they didn't have the necessary equipment to change a photo or mask out or opaque certain things in the photo or negative that the newspaper didn't want published. I am on the fence about as whether The Dallas Morning News or JCS altered the Altgens film. One thing's for sure, a copy of the original film strip was remade or re-shot after it was altered. This could have been done at JCS. No newspaper has this equipment. Period.[22]

Once again, the revelations of the Reverend Shaw, who told Harry Livingstone that JCS was used as a base of operations for the assassination, makes this outfit the primary suspected culprit for the activities whereupon the Altgens photographs would have been altered. We have shown here that they certainly had the capability and equipment to do so. *The Dallas Morning News* building, which housed AP's office, was a hub of frenzied activity that afternoon and weekend. Any activity by strangers involving photos of the assassination would have attracted an inordinate amount of attention. The physical proximity of JCS—only eight short blocks east—in a very quiet and unassuming setting, and in relative proximity of City Hall on Harwood Street, would have made JCS the ideal venue for this type of operation. Once the altered negative was produced, it would quietly make its way back to *The Dallas Morning News* building at Houston and Young for nationwide distribution. One final argument in favor of JCS has to be the simple fact that Lee Oswald had worked there for six months—from 13 October 1962 to 6 April 1963—and his appearance and physical characteristics were very well known to the company.

Based on the arguments presented so far, which cast plenty of suspicion on JCS, here is one possible scenario:

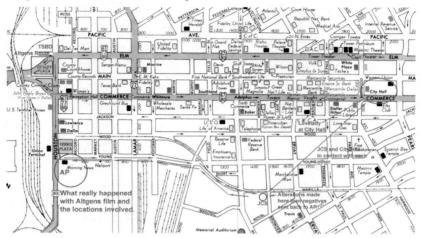

Altgens arrives at 12:50-12:55 PM at AP's facilities on the third floor of *The Dallas Morning News* building at Houston and Young and "someone" grabs his camera because they already know he has witnessed the assassination and has potentially explosive photographs, having discussed this by telephone with his boss Bob Johnson prior to arriving, while he is still in Dealey Plaza. This "someone" has never been identified.

In trying to beat out the competition to put photographs on the wire as soon as possible, the negative is developed and examined on a light table. The first 8.5" x 11" prints are made, one of which goes to the "morgue." Judging by the swiftness with which competitors the *Dallas Times Herald* and UPI have put some of their photos on the wire that day, with couriers intercepting photographers riding in camera cars, it can be safely assumed that Altgens's negatives are available within an hour of his arrival at AP, at 1:50 PM CT. AP, via live TV, is aware that CBS News with Walter Cronkite, NBC with Bill Ryan and Frank McGee, and ABC with Ron Cochran, are already showing photos shot by the competition. They are now frantic and trying to catch up. It is this author's opinion that a major mistake was made when they sent out the photograph which was shown by NBC around 2:07 PM ET depicting the President with John Connally and Jackie at Love Field immediately after deplaning. This shows they were actively in competition to wire photographs to the rest of the country. It also shows the efficiency which they were capable of. By estimating this photo to have been taken around 11:00 AM, and assuming that it is immediately rushed to AP offices in downtown Dallas via courier, (which was pointed out, takes about 20 minutes), it can be estimated that the photo takes at least an hour to be processed and shown by NBC on TV around 1:00 PM CT. Altgens4 and Altgens6, however, do not make it onto TV until 6:35 PM. This is key to understanding the timeline of the Altgens photographs.

At least four images are identified, which show the president immediately before and after the shots, Altgens4-7. Schaeffer believes that at least one other photograph is possible to have been shot by Altgens between Nos. 6 and 7. (This one was scratched entirely. Could it have shown what several motorcycle escort and at least 60 different witnesses said about the complete stoppage of the motorcade that day, and Secret Service Agents dismounting and running past the JFK limo and others going up the embankment, as reported by Altgens himself?) At this moment, the images must be thoroughly inspected by "someone" who knows what needs to be taken out. In following the timeline of UPI and the *Dallas Times Herald* photographs, which were the first images put on the wire, by 1:50 PM CT, the Altgens photos should have been captioned and sent out via thermofax, yet they were not. As mentioned earlier, Cronkite shows the *Dallas Times Herald* photograph within an hour of the assassination, but does not show Altgens's photographs No. 4 and No. 6 until 5:35 PM CT. This leaves a time void of three hours and 45 minutes where his photos are unaccounted for. (It's important to realize that in the case of Altgens photographs, it had to be all or none because the suppression would have been obvious.)

Altgens6 and 7 are deemed unsuitable for public consumption and the negative strip is sent down the street to JCS. The positive prints are enlarged so they can be worked on. Airbrushing, masking and opaquing are the only techniques available at the time. As noted above, Altgens6 undergoes at least a dozen alterations. Altgens7 is altered in the area of the rear window of Chief Jesse Curry's lead car to hide the actions of the Secret Service Special Agent in Charge (SAIC) of the Dallas district, Forrest V. Sorrels, Secret Service Agent Winston Lawson and Curry, who appear to be turned around like Sheriff Bill Decker, watching the events behind them unfold while the motorcade is at a standstill. The upper portion is chopped off to remove the cement railing at right of the triple underpass. Once the alterations are in place and new negatives are produced, the images are re-shot, and a new negative produced on Tri X Pan film. The original negatives are destroyed. The resultant negatives are sent back to AP at *The Dallas Morning News* building and these are then processed in the normal manner and distributed nationwide.

Here is what happens next, as described by Roy Schaeffer:

Working backwards, the original negative had a print made to go over the wire service from Dallas to the Dayton Daily News on the AP wire Saturday morning 23 November 1963 at 7:15 P.M. After I watched it print out on the wire machine, on the way to engraving to have a zinc plate made from it, I noticed the editing in the area of the front windshield, mainly the area on the passenger side of the Presidential limousine. I also notice that the motorcyclist was much more clear or darker than the front windshield of the limousine. I also noticed that the flag was darker than the persons in the front of the Presidential limousine. While in the engraving department, Sony Delator shot the AP fax using a line camera to crop the photo so it would fit in a three column space. So, working backwards the AP fax when received by me was 18 hours later. When Altgens called AP in Dallas, he gave the info the caption writer would write when he received the photo after it was developed. After checking the Cincinnati Enquirer, Indianapolis Star later that week all had the same ALTERED (photo), what is now referred to as the AP6, or DN5. The process is the negative has to be developed and dried. Someone then examined the emulsion side of the developed Altgens film strip and then altered it for some reason that I didn't know at that time. [23] If the Cronkite #6 positive photo was shown as it appears in an altered state at 6:30 PM that Friday, 22 November 1963, so now we have a timeline of five hours. My photograph training tells me that Altgens6 was altered by someone who knew what he was doing. [24] On 14 December 1963, The Saturday Evening Post ran an almost full photo of it. I found at least eight places where the photo has been retouched. I think in this case the AP photo editor had already typed out the caption with a time/date but the photo wasn't attached to the photo to be sent out. ONE MUST REMEMBER ONE THING: THE FAX SENT OVER THE WIRE WAS SEVERELY ALTERED. This suggests that one can't trust the time/stamp as to when AP went over the wire in an unaltered state. [25] My work started on the altered

Altgens photo from the beginning. My problem in telling workers at the newspaper of the altered Altgens I had no reason for this to occur in December 1963. The fly in the ointment is the entire negative had to be reshot using Pan X film on a duplicating film stock. The proof of the correct timeline is when the AP photo arrived at the newspaper it was sent over the AP wire. In my opinion the timeline was at about 5:30 PM Dallas time. The time to alter Altgens6 would be about 4:30 PM for the altered AP photo to be sent out to various newspapers who bought the AP wire service.

Roy Schaeffer[26]

We cannot conclude this chapter without pointing out the death of Ike Altgens—and his wife Clara—in what appear to have been suspicious circumstances in 1995 at the age of 78. The obituary, dated 19 December 1995, informs that both Ike and his wife Clara had been suffering from the flu, however, the police "were looking into the possibility that they had died of carbon monoxide poisoning from a defective furnace." This coincides with the peak of activities of the Assassination Records Review Board (ARRB), where witnesses were being called upon to clarify their experiences the weekend of 22 November 1963.

> Mr. Altgens, who was retired, and his wife, Clara, 73, were both found dead at the home, The Associated Press reported. The Dallas Morning News reported on Friday that relatives said the couple had been suffering from the flu but that the police were looking into the possibility that they had died of carbon monoxide poisoning from a defective furnace.

ENDNOTES

1. Warren Commission Vol. 23: JCS Time Sheets pp. 529-625 (CE1850)
2. Livingstone, Harrison, *High Treason 2—The Great Cover-Up: The Assassination of President John F. Kennedy* (1992), p. 466
3. Warren Commission Vol. 20 (See Kantor Exhibit No. 44)
4. jfk.hood.edu/Collection/Weisberg%20Subject%20Index%20Files/M%20

Disk/Meagher%20Sylvia%201969%20to/Item%20126.pdf
5. Melanson, Phil, *Spy Saga*, p. 149
6. Ibid. 151
7. Warren Commission Vol. 10, pp. 184-185
8. Sloan and Hill, *JFK: The Last Dissenting Witness* (1992), pp. 27-34.
9. Weisberg, Harold, *Whitewash II* (1966)
10. Bonafede, Dom, *New York Herald Tribune*, "The Picture With a Life of Its Own," 24 May 1964, pp. 4-5
11. Interview with Steve Martin, "The Real Deal," January 2015
12. jfk.hood.edu/Collection/White%20%20Files/JFK%20Assassination%20Photos%20Book/Pages%20651-687.pdf, p. 3
13. Don Roberdeau witness map at imgur.com/QcAKTOp

14. Nelson, Phil, *LBJ: The Mastermind of the JFK Assassination* (2011), p. 477
15. Ibid. 482
16. Ibid. 473, also see Marrs, Jim, *Crossfire: The Plot That Killed Kennedy*, (1989) pp. 249-250, (see also, senatoryarborough.tripod.com/index.htm, "The Senator who suspected a JFK conspiracy")
17. Sprague, Richard F., "The Assassination of President John F. Kennedy: The Application of Computers to the Photographic Evidence," *Computers and Automation*, May 1970 (jfk.hood.edu/Collection/Weisberg%20Subject%20Index%20Files/S%20Disk/Sprague%20Richard%20E%20Computers%20and%20Automation/Item%2006.pdf)
18. Fetzer, Jim, *Murder in Dealey Plaza: What We Know Now that We Didn't Know Then* (2000), pp. 346-347
19. deeppoliticsforum.com/forums/archive/index.php/t-2191.html
20. Roy Schaeffer email, 29 March 2015
21. Schaeffer email, 20 March 2015
22. Schaeffer email, 25 March 2015
23. Schaeffer email, 26 March 2015
24. Ibid.
25. Ibid.
26. Ibid.

APPENDIX

Microdots

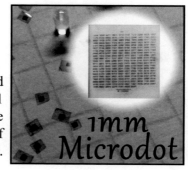

The microdot is a page-sized photograph that has been reduced to 1 mm in diameter. The microdot became a popular and commonly used form of steganography during World War II.

The process of creating a microdot is straightforward but requires a few specialized pieces of equipment. First, a photograph of the message is taken which reduces it to roughly the size of a postage stamp. Next, the image is shrunk further with a reverse microscope, bringing it down to 1 millimeter. The negative is then developed and the image is punched out of the film. A common way to do this was with a syringe needle in which the point had been filed down. Once the needle separated the dot from the rest of the film, it was placed on the cover text, over a period or under a stamp, and cemented in place. Professor Walter Zapp is credited with creating a device that could perform most of these processes mechanically.

flylib.com/books/en/1.496.1.12/1

Hollow British one pound coin has a specially designed "cavity" for storage of a bullet lens reader and a "well" to store microdots and films. Opening of the coin exposes both the microdot(s) and the 160x microdot reader lens. The lens has been specially designed to read microdots and is made to fit in the coin. It can be used to view dots as large as 2 millimeters. Included is an ultra-high-resolution microdot of a KGB cipher. The cipher contains over 1,100 digits in less than 1 square millimeter.

stanhopemicroworks.com/spy-coins-microdots.html

An intriguing entry in Oswald's address book is the word "microdots" appearing on the page on which he has notated the address and phone number of Jaggers-Chiles-Stovall (CE 18, p. 45). Microdots are a clandestine means of communication developed by German intelligence during World War II and still in general use among espionage agencies. The technique is to photograph the document to be transmitted and vastly reduce the negative to a size that will fit inside a period. The microdot can be inserted in an innocuous letter or magazine and mailed, or left in a "dead drop"—a prearranged location for the deposit and pickup of messages.

Ramparts January 1968 page 50

PART II
THE MAN IN THE DOORWAY

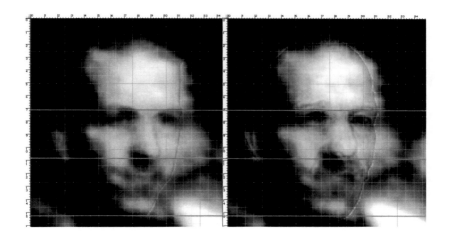

3

Lady by the Doorway

There is much controversy raging these days regarding who exactly were the figures present at the TSBD doorway/entrance during the assassination of JFK. As we saw in the first two chapters, the cropped version of this image was supposedly circulated immediately after the assassination, therefore it was thought to be in pristine state. According to Altgens, he used a 35mm Nikkorex camera with a 105mm telephoto lens loaded with Eastman Kodak Tri-X film set at 15 feet focal length.[1] His picture supposedly was "on the wire" within minutes (12:57 PM) of the assassination, and forwarded to AP in N.Y., and the negative remained at the Dallas AP.[2]

Because this negative was subsequently lost, controversy has surrounded this picture from day one.[3]

In the mid-1960s, Weisberg wrote entire chapters about these problems, and over the years many researchers have documented several anomalies in the non-cropped version of the image:

1. LBJ's Secret Service protection already jumping out of their car to protect him[4]

2. Some type of commotion going on in the closet window behind the fire escape of the second floor of the Dal-Tex Building[5]

3. Jackie already holding JFK's left wrist in response to the president choking on a bullet

4. A bullet hole in the windshield right of the rear-view mirror (as viewed from the front)[6]

5. White traffic road lines disappearing[7]

6. Several figures which have been "blacked out" or altered[8]

7. Image blurred on purpose and not printed as clearly as it could have been[9]

8. What seems like strange projection of figures

Later on, in the 1990s, two very complete articles were written which dealt with the issues of Altgens6: Roy L. Schaeffer's "Was Lee Harvey Oswald the Person in the James Altgens Photograph?"[10] and Dr. John J. Johnson's excellent "Man-in-the-Doorway: An unbelievable coincidence."[11]

Robert Groden also tried to address this controversy in his 1993 work *The Killing of a President: The Complete Photographic Record of the JFK Assassination, the Conspiracy, and the Cover-up.*[12] Altgens6 still has a few more secrets to reveal.

Dave Weigman filmed the motorcade from the seventh car in the motorcade.[13] His film has been broken down into individual slides or images and at least seven of his images show the entrance of the TSBD and the adjacent area up to the white monument.[14]

The Towner and Hughes color movies also show crucial images of the entrance but fail to reveal any detail.[15]

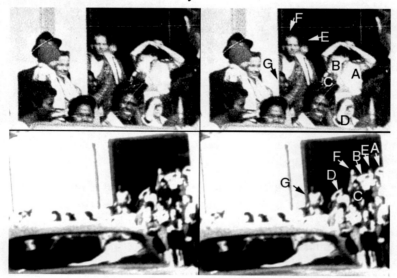

The images above pertain to research that has already been done comparing Weigman and Altgens, and which tries to reconcile some figures in question, but has never attempted to reconcile the left part of the image containing "Fedora Man" and the "Woman and Child" figures because at first glance they do not seem visible in any other pictures taken that day.

Since there is already a study in the public domain with letters assigned to these figures, we will continue to use them for reference. For this study we will assign Fedora Man and Woman and Child the letters (H) and (I) respectively. The rest of this chapter will focus on these two figures (H) and (I).

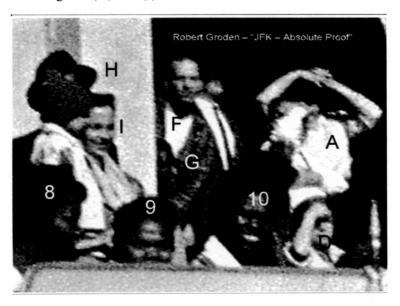

To appreciate the effect of Altgens's telephoto lens, focal length, and his location in relation to the entrance[16] of the TSBD, we must first consider how it affects the three African-American women, marked 8, 9 and 10.

These three women in the foreground have all been located in the Croft picture.

Again, the perspective of the Altgens photo seems to place them in front of the TSBD, when in reality they are much further down Elm Street, beyond the white monument.

This is known as foreshortening.

63

Martin Hinrich[17] has compiled this excellent comparison which verifies the position of the three women further down Elm Street than they appear in Altgens.

Croft/Altgens6 composite color image (credit Bill Miller)
jfkassassinationgallery.com

As we move up, we encounter figures (H) and (I) established earlier. The woman (I) is holding an infant who is wearing a wool cap. The other figure is Fedora Man wearing a suit (H).

Both appear to be standing on the sidewalk near the curb.

The Woman and Child figure (I) is blocking Fedora Man (H) in the Altgens image, therefore we cannot see his face.

He seems to be looking in the direction of the cars as they make the turn onto Elm Street, same as the African-American man (G) in the doorway.

Here is another 3D perspective in Blender:

This image using generic models shows the relationship in 3D space between four of the people seen in Altgens6, where foreshortening has brought these together to create the illusion that they are very close to one another.

Some have questioned whether Fedora Man and Woman and Child are actually in the photograph, alluding an obscure agenda of alteration via superimposition.

Blender 3D renderings however, place the trio on the sidewalk, near the monument, as seen in the Towner film.

There has also been doubt regarding the size of the child and the mother's ability to hold him in the position shown for a prolonged amount of time.

Consider this image captured from our Blender view port. The proportions are correct for a four-year-old and his mother:

This pose shows how easy it would have been to hold the child with only one arm, as the child would have naturally braced himself in the manner shown above, a possible reason why we do not see his little arm in the photograph.

In Altgens6, we note how the infant's head still partially blocks the profile of the woman. Who was this woman? Now there is a good probability that it is Mrs. Peggy Hawkins and her four-year-old son John, Jr. [18] Peggy's husband John, Sr. worked on the third floor of the TSBD as an agent for textbook publisher Allyn & Bacon.

Peggy arrived around noon on 22 November 1963 with her son John and immediately went up to the third floor to check in with her husband. She went out to the curb in front of the TSBD with some of John's co-workers to wait for the presidential motorcade. As the president's limousine turned the corner of Elm Street she immediately recognized the loud report as gunfire. Being only 50 feet away, she saw JFK hit and witnessed the limousine pulling up to a complete stop further down the street. Fearing for the safety of her son, she took refuge at the retaining wall that runs parallel to the service drive in front of the TSBD. Mrs. Hawkins, nor her husband John, were ever called to testify before the Warren Commission. Her FBI statement was "mailed in" and buried in Commission Document 897 under the heading "FBI Gemberling Report of 04 Apr 1964 re: Oswald-Russia/Cuba." Why she never came forward or identified herself as the woman with the child in the Altgens photograph remains a mystery.

Amazingly enough, John Hawkins was *never* accounted for or interviewed by anyone after the assassination. We know that he was present that day in his office because Peggy stated in her FBI interview dated 26 March 1964, and contained in p. 36 of CD897, that when she arrived downtown at noontime, she went up to see him before meeting up with some of his coworkers to watch the parade down at the curb. In fact, Hawkins is not mentioned in any witness list or even in the employee roster of Allyn & Bacon published by the Warren Commission in Commission Document 87, pp. 787-788:

ALLYN & BACON COMPANY - Room 301

Steven F. Wilson, Manager
903 Carney Drive
Garland, Texas   BR 8-2753

CO-2-34030
12-7-63
Page 13

Miss Ruth Hendrix
2011 North Prairie
Dallas, Texas   TA 3-2615

Mrs. Mary Lea Williams
3718 Inwood Road
Dallas, Texas   LA 7-1775

Mrs. Billie P. Clay
6934 Casa Loma
Dallas, Texas   DA 1-2761

Mrs. Rudell Parsons
3437 Amherst
Dallas, Texas   EM 8-4953

Mrs. Sue Dickerson
7310 Brierfield Drive
Dallas, Texas   CA 4-4792

With the thousands upon thousands of pages of documentation, derived from two investigations of the JFK assassination, FBI and Secret Service reports and interviews, literally thousands of books, articles and essays on the subject, digital web repositories, it seems that no one has ever wondered about the missing Mr. and Mrs. Hawkins. Peggy's stunning FBI interview dated 1 April 1964, buried in CD897, tells of how when she realized more shots could be forthcoming, she ran for cover with her young son seeking protection "behind the retaining wall in front of the TSBD for shelter." Peggy should have been all over the newspapers and newscasts that weekend, especially after seeing herself and her son prominently shown in Altgens6 the following day! Could there have been a better story to tell by the mass media? Bill and Gayle Newman became world famous for doing exactly the same thing for their two young sons. Yet, she and her husband elected to avoid the limelight! Inquisitive minds would immediately infer that there might have been a reason for this.

It is important to point out that we only know of John Hawkins's existence because Peggy mentions him in CD897, a portion of which is shown below: (see complete document in appendix)

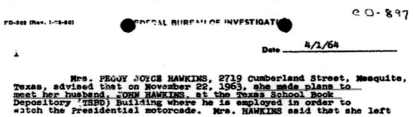

FD-302 (Rev. 1-25-60) FEDERAL BUREAU OF INVESTIGATION

CD-897

Date ____4/1/64____

Mrs. PEGGY JOYCE HAWKINS, 2719 Cumberland Street, Mesquite, Texas, advised that on November 22, 1963, she made plans to meet her husband, JOHN HAWKINS, at the Texas School Book Depository (TSBD) Building where he is employed in order to watch the Presidential motorcade. Mrs. HAWKINS said that she left

Further confirmation of their identities comes from the Warren Commission statements of Allyn & Bacon employees Mary Lea Williams and Georgia Ruth Hendrix contained in CE1381.[19] The background, identity and role, if any, of John Hawkins is a dark and unexplored area which has *never* been properly explained or investigated by JFK researchers. (Note: why would Ms. Williams volunteer the exact address of the Hawkins family in this interview? Was this some kind of hint?)

(CE1381) "On November 22, 1963, I left the Depository building at approximately 12:20 PM to view the arrival of the Presidential Motorcade. I was accompanied by Mrs. Sue Dickerson, Billie Clay, Ruth Hendrix, all employees of Allyn and Bacon, Inc., and Mrs. John Hawkins and her four year old son, John. Mrs. Hawkins is wife of John Hawkins, an agent for Allyn and Bacon, Inc., and resides at 2719 Cumberland Drive, Mesquite, Texas. Our group took up a position along the motorcade route about halfway between the first and second light poles on the curbside slightly west of the Depository building. We were on the north side of Elm Street as it leads into the underpass.

Mary Lea Williams CE1381

Fedora Man Also Pinpoints Hawkin's Location

Fedora Man (H) is a tall individual, at least six feet. He towers above everyone in the Towner slides. There is no doubt the area of Fedora Man and Woman and Child in Altgens6 has been misinterpreted over the years because of the optical phenomena displayed therein. Warren commissioners Rankin and Dulles assumed the figures were much closer to the entrance than they were, while Marguerite Oswald was convinced that Woman and Child were actually Marina Oswald and her daughter June.[20]

Even though we believe we can now put all of these suppositions to rest, we are still left with the mystery of who Peggy and John Hawkins really were, and why they were ignored by JFK investigations.

ENDNOTES

1. Weisberg, Harold, *Whitewash II* (1966), p. 251
2. Ibid. 245-46, 248
3. Ibid. 248-249
4. Fetzer, Jim, *Murder in Dealey Plaza* (2000), p. 149
5. Ibid.
6. Ibid. 139, Douglas Weldon chapter on windshield of limousine. Bullet hole slightly visible in Altgens6.

7. Weisberg, *Whitewash II*, p. 256
8. Refer to the end of Chapter 2 for detailed alterations
9. Weisberg, *Whitewash II*, p. 300
10. The Weisberg Collection. Hood College, Frederick, MD, USA
11. *The Fourth Decade*, May 1998, Vol. 5, No. 4
12. Groden, Robert, *The Killing of a President: The Complete Photographic Record of the JFK Assassination, the Conspiracy, and the Cover-up* (1993), pp. 186-187
13. Marrs, Jim, *Crossfire: The Plot That Killed Kennedy* (1989), p. 58
14. Weigman collection at jfkassassinationgallery.com/thumbnails. php?album=13
15. Towner gallery at jfkassassinationgallery.com/thumbnails.php?album=40; Hughes gallery at jfkassassinationgallery.com/thumbnails.php?album=8
16. Don Roberdeau's map of witnesses, places Altgens almost opposite Zapruder on the south side of Elm, visible at Z348; droberdeau.blogspot. com/2011/01/discovery-close-jfk-assassination.html
17. Croft collection at jfkassassinationgallery.com/thumbnails.php?album=27
18. CD897, pp. 35-36, FBI Gemberling Report of 04 Apr 1964 re: Oswald— Russia/Cuba. Buried within this 600-page document we inexplicably find Peggy Hawkins's FBI report, classified under "Other witnesses and Related data" (Cannot think of a more irrelevant place to put this document. Some of the content of CD897 is nothing but empty pages.)
19. CE1381 Why would Mary Lee Williams go out of her way to mention Peggy Hawkins's exact and complete address in her statement?)
20. WC Vol. I, pp. 215-16

APPENDIX

FD-302 (Rev. 1-25-60)

FEDERAL BUREAU OF INVESTIGATION

C O - 8 97

Date 4/1/64

Mrs. PEGGY JOYCE HAWKINS, 2719 Cumberland Street, Mesquite, Texas, advised that on November 22, 1963, she made plans to meet her husband, JOHN HAWKINS, at the Texas School Book Depository (TSBD) Building where he is employed in order to watch the Presidential motorcade. Mrs. HAWKINS said that she left home at approximately 11:15 AM and arrived at the TSBD Building at around 12:00 Noon. She said that she went to the offices of the Allyn and Bacon Company on the third floor of the building where she met other employees of this company and then proceeded to the sidewalk in front of the building on Elm Street in order to watch the parade. Mrs. HAWKINS said that the car containing the Presidential party had just passed in front of the building shortly after noon when she heard two or three shots fired in the near vicinity. She said she immediately recognized them as firearm shots and not as fireworks and had the impression that they came from the direction of the railroad yards adjacent to the TSBD Building. Mrs. HAWKINS stated that she did not see where the shots came from nor did she see any individual firing a rifle or any other weapon at this time. She said that she was looking at the President's car at the time and saw the President straighten up in the back seat and then slump over on his side.

She stated she was aware that the President had been shot and was concerned for her own safety and that of her small child who was with her. She estimated that the President's car was less than fifty feet away from her when he was shot, that the car slowed down almost coming to a full stop and then started off again. Mrs. HAWKINS said that she automatically took several steps toward the President's car, then realized that there might be further shots and took her small child behind the retaining wall in front of the TSBD Building for shelter. She said she did not realize at any time that the shots had come from the TSBD and saw no one at the windows of the building.

She stated she stayed behind the retaining wall until she realized there would be no more shots and then walked back to the front of the TSBD Building. She said that a motorcycle police officer was in front of the building at this time and that she heard over his radio some remarks about the railroad yards near the building.

On	3/26/64	at	MESQUITE, TEXAS	File #	DL 100-10461

by SA J. HALE MC MENAMIN & SA RAYMOND J. FOX/lea   39   Date dictated 3/31/64

This document contains neither recommendations nor conclusions of the FBI. It is the property of the FBI and is loaned to your agency; it and its contents are not to be distributed outside your agency.

CD 897

DL 100-10461
2

Mrs. HAWKINS said that she then re-entered the TSBD Building by the front door and went upstairs to the third floor by elevator. She said that during this time she was excited and quite shaken by the events and cannot recall who she saw on her way back into the building and up to the third floor. She said that she believed that sufficient time had elapsed after the shots and her re-entry into the building for many persons to have left the building. Mrs. HAWKINS stated that she did not know LEE HARVEY OSWALD and cannot recall having seen him in the vicinity of the TSBD Building at the time of the shooting. Mrs. HAWKINS advised that she was born September 6, 1934, at Scottsville, Arkansas, and that she resides at Mesquite, Texas with her husband, JOHN HAWKINS, and one small child.

4

The Untold Story of Joe Molina

Seldom do we see in JFK Assassination history a case quite like the one we have with Joe R. Molina. Molina was ostracized after 22 November and was almost run out of town in the wake of the JFK assassination. That he was later able to recover from the aftermath of what was done to him and his family in Dallas is a testament to his resiliency and drive.

Joe Rodriguez Molina was born in Dallas, Texas, on 18 June 1924. He was one of five brothers and sisters born to Pedro Rodriguez and Luisa Molina, both Mexican immigrants who settled in Dallas in the 1920s.[1]

Hispanic names go by first name, father's surname, mother's surname, therefore somewhere along the line, as new U.S. citizens, the family adopted his mother's surname of Molina. Molina graduated from Crozier Tech High School in Dallas and fresh out of high school served in the U.S. Navy from 26 February 1943 to 5 January 1946.[2] In the Navy he was trained as a machinist and he attended machinist courses at the University of Missouri in Columbia.[3] He was honorably discharged on 5 January 1946.[4]

The Texas School Book Depository

In February 1947, Joe began working at the TSBD while the company was still located at 2210 N. Pacific Ave.[5] Five years later, the company moved to the first floor of the Dal-Tex Building, where most of the textbook companies operated out of.

In the summer of 1962, president James "Jack" Charles Cason moved the company's operations to 411 Elm Street just across Houston Street, west of the Dal-Tex Building, and overlooking Dealey Plaza on the North side.[6] The building on 411 Elm Street had been in use as a grocery warehouse for the past 20 years.

Extensive renovations were undertaken to bring the building up to the minimum requirements of the company. Even the elevators had to be refurbished.[7] The timing of this move has always been questioned.[8]

Joe Molina held several positions at TSBD. Initially, he worked as an accountant or bookkeeper in the credit department. At the time of the assassination he had been credit manager for three or four years.[9] "He handled over 10,000 accounts using an adding machine, making bank deposits, supervising the credit department, operating a Sensimatic posting machine, writing letters of credit and other miscellaneous duties."

He could also type 50 words per minute.[10] These skills provided Joe with a desk job very few Mexicans in Dallas could attain at the time. It also helped that he is a light-complected Mexican-American.

His immediate supervisor was 63-year-old Otis Williams. Williams was supervisor of the bookkeeping and credit department and was with Molina at the time of the shooting. According to secretary Virgie Mae Rackley, Williams and Molina were very close friends. She also described Molina as "a very religious man and a very fine man."[11]

The GI Forum, Dallas, and McCarthyism of the 1950s

William Lowery was famous for infiltrating "Communist Organizations" since the late '40s and had the GI Forum in his sights in the '50s when McCarthyism was at its peak.[12] (His 33-page House Select Committee on Assassinations (HSCA) testimony is still classified.[13]) He appears to have befriended Molina and campaigned to have him elected chairman of the GI Forum in 1955.[14] Joe tried to talk about him during his Warren Commission testimony but was cut short by Joseph Ball.[15]

Mr. MOLINA: I just wanted to state in the record that I want to deny any accusations if there is any doubt in anybody's mind.

Mr. BALL: No, there is nobody I ever heard has accused you of anything.

Mr. MOLINA: I know there's a fella that I talk with that belongs to the or had worked with the FBI *that knows my position in this thing.* [Emphasis added]

Mr. BALL: I never heard anybody accuse you of any wrongdoing in connection with this matter.

Mr. MOLINA: In fact, Bill Lowery worked with the FBI.

Mr. BALL: You don't have to worry about that. No one is accusing you of anything.

Some say there is a possibility Joe was also infiltrating Communist Party elements in the GI Forum and working with Lowery. There is much information on Lowery at the Education Forum. The consensus there is that Joe must have been involved in some capacity as an informant for Lowery.[16] JFK researcher William Weston believes his association with Lowery raises a red flag. A Navy veteran Mexican-American with four kids informing on his fellow countrymen under the guise of helping them with their discrimination and employment problems? Highly unlikely.

From 1954 to 1959, Lowery kept close tabs on Molina, then did not report anything on him again until 29 August 1962. Shortly after, Molina left the GI Forum for good, reasons unknown. Besides Lowery, the following persons informed on Joe Molina while he was with the Forum:[17]

Felix Botello (Informant Code No. DL T-1): Posted reports on Molina for many years. There is an elementary school in Dallas which bears his name. Botello worked closely with the FBI and was charged with infiltrating Communist Party organizations in Dallas.

Margarita Landin (Informant Code No. DL T-2): Reported on Joe's activities as chairman of the GI Forum on 22 July 1957. Wife of Joe Landin who on 20 August 1964 was a current, active informant of the Dallas FBI office.

Ruth Lowery (Informant Code No. DL T-4): Concealed apparently because she was the younger sister of William Lowery.

During his tenure as chairman of the GI Forum in Dallas, Joe Molina engaged various Dallas institutions about discrimination towards Mexican-Americans.

Two examples of Joe's activism can be seen in the fact that he organized a committee in July 1957 to ". . . protest the refusal of Vickery Park swimming (pool) to accept Mexican-Americans as patrons."[18]

On 12 February 1958, Joe went to see the mayor of Dallas, R.L Thornton ". . . to see what could be done to prevent discrimination against Latin-Americans in Dallas."

Mayor Thornton received Joe's committee and agreed to contact some people about discrimination issues if they would submit an initial letter of protest.[19]

22 November 1963

The day of 22 November 1963 started out like any other day for Joe Molina. His wife dropped him off at work that morning and he arrived at 7:00 AM. Since he had his own key, he settled in for the day's work which hardly ever drew him away from his office on the second floor.[20] At noon, he broke away from his routine and went to the cafeteria on the 2nd floor and had lunch with "the girls" who included Ms. Virgie Mae Rackley.[21] At 12:15 PM, he went outside to find a spot in the doorway to watch the motorcade with his friend and supervisor Otis Williams.[22]

So, who was at the doorway steps with Joe? The following statements have been compiled according to witness testimonies, most of them obtained from CE1381 and other sources.

1. Otis N. Williams: Molina's boss and best friend ". . . was standing on the top step against the railing on the east side of the steps in front of the building." (CE1381) This is confirmed by Joe's own testimony in 6H370:

Mr. MOLINA: Yes, I was standing on the front steps.

Mr. BALL: With whom?

Mr. MOLINA: Right next left of me was Mr. Williams and close to there was Mrs. Sanders [Pauline]

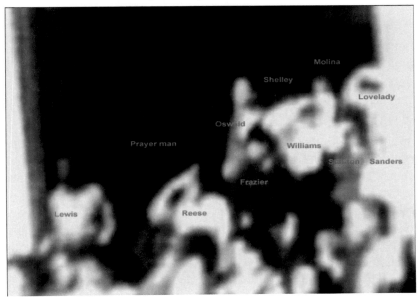

This was also confirmed by Virgie Mae Rackley's 23 November 1963 statement to the DPD: "Molina went outside with a Mr. Williams, of the department." Otis Williams however, did not reciprocate, and by the time his statement was taken on 19 March 1964, Molina had been long gone from his TSBD employment. Mr. Williams then contracted a mysterious case of amnesia regarding who was around him: "I do not recall who was standing at either side of me . . ." (CE 1381) (So much for being best friends!) Regarding his position, in those days the railing was in the center of the stairs, therefore, he was roughly at the center of the entrance at the top step.

2. Pauline Sanders: "I took up a position at the top of the front steps of the [TSBD] building facing Elm Street. To the best of my recollection I was standing on the top step at the east end of the entrance . . . I noticed Mrs. Sarah Stanton standing next to me, but I am unsure as to the others." (CE 1381)

3. Sarah Stanton: "I was standing on the front steps of the TSBD with Mr. William Shelley, Mr. Otis Williams, Mrs. R.E. Sanders and Billy Lovelady." She did not even mention Molina who was standing right next to her! (CE 1381)

4. Madie Belle Reese: ". . . took up a position on the second step from the bottom to the right or west side of the main entrance of the [TSBD] building. Mrs. Dean was standing directly to my left at the time of the assassination . . ." (CE 1381)

5. Buell Wesley Frazier: "I was standing on the front steps of the building when the parade came by." [Handwritten statement taken the night of 22 November 1963 at the DPD. Affidavit was also prepared based on this one document.] When Frazier's CE 1381 statement was taken on 18 March 1964, he was now suddenly accompanied by Shelley and Lovelady.

After the shooting ended, Molina went to the embankment by the railroad tracks like so many other TSBD employees who thought the shots came from that direction.[23] His impression was that the shots had come from the west side.[24] After hanging around in the lobby of the TSBD, he left around 2:00 PM. He walked over to Sanders restaurant on Main to wait for his wife to pick him up because the area of the building had been cordoned off. At Sanders, he ran into Eddie Piper, who for some unknown reason told him that Oswald had "not been accounted for at the depository."[25]

The Night of 22 November 1963

The night of 22 November, early morning of 23 November 1963, would be one Joe Molina and his family would never forget. There are two conflicting versions of these events. According to the DPD, Joe and his family had not yet gone to bed at 1:30 AM,[26] presumably still watching the TV reports and talking about the assassination that had taken place earlier that day. However, Joe's WC6H368 testimony states quite the opposite: "That's right, woke up my wife and children; scared my wife half to death."

His testimony reveals that his family was awoken up by a large group of policemen at 1:30 AM, an act that terrified his wife, Soledad. It turned out Joe received a visit from the cream of the DPD, among them Captain William Gannaway, Lieutenant Jack Revill, and if that were not enough, the notorious Assistant D.A. Bill Alexander.[27] Alexander was a "self-avowed right wing extremist,"[28] and was infamous (and proud of it) for sending many convicted murderers to the gallows. Once, he threatened a witness at gunpoint in the courtroom.[29] On 22 November 1963, Alexander was around Dealey Plaza and the TSBD right after the assassination.[30] Around 1:00 PM he drove out to Oak Cliff with Detective Gerald Hill in time to see a dead Officer Tippit, then swung over to the Texas Theater and was seen in the alley with his gun drawn, waiting to shoot down the "communist-assassin."[31] When they confronted Joe that morning, they had a search warrant issued by Judge David Johnson,[32] but when Joe politely asked them in and gave them permission to search the house, it was not executed. "Sure, I don't have anything to hide, look around," was Joe's response to their arrival.[33]

Captain Gannaway later reported to the FBI: "Molina made a remark stating that he had been expecting us."[34]

The obvious question here is, did Bill Lowery tip Molina off that he would be visited that night by the DPD? Or was this just another lie by the DPD? Unknown to Joe at the time,[35]—and probably still is, if he has not had access to the FBI reports—they were looking for *"anything that might connect Mr. Molina with Lee Harvey Oswald."*[36] [Emphasis added]

Captain Gannaway was a little more specific: "He said that the officers searched Molina's premises for weapons, ammunition, explosives, or anything else to connect Molina with Lee Harvey Oswald."[37]

Bill Alexander: Right-wing Assistant D. A. and, on November 22, part-time cop.

J. Gary Shaw has pointed out how odd it seemed that the assistant district attorney "would be playing cop at such a time."[38] Apparently Alexander was putting in a lot of overtime and his day had not yet ended when he went to see Molina. At one point during the search, they met in the kitchen and spoke in lowered voices so Molina could not hear.[39] Speculation: were they debating whether to plant evidence at Joe's house? Did the fact it was a small two-bedroom house with six occupants and three very inquisitive teenagers (Joe Jr., 16; Linda Molina, 14; and adopted daughter Sylvia, 14) dissuade them from doing this? Why was the top brass of the DPD summoned to serve a search warrant at 1:30AM? Why was "taking care" of Joe Molina of such importance? Why were the top cops of the DPD and the assistant district attorney trying to *find and link confederates* [Emphasis added] to Lee Oswald in the early hours of 23 November? This would suggest the conspirators had not made up their minds yet to pin this entirely on the one patsy.

23 November 1963

On 23 November 1963, Molina spent seven hours at the DPD, from 10:00 AM to 5:00 PM.[40] Little did he know that while he was being seen by the top cops of the DPD, his secretary Virgie Mae Rackley, 18, was being questioned by two DPD patrolmen about "strange conversations" she overheard Joe having on the telephone. She also mentioned how unusual it was for Joe to have had lunch that day with the girls in the cafeteria when he was known to always eat lunch by himself in his office.[41] During this time at the station, he was interviewed again by Captain Gannaway about the GI Forum, then he was interviewed again by Lieutenant Revill, only now they wanted him to: "...write a statement as to the political sympathies of the various members of the American GI Forum, *which he declined to do*, [Emphasis added] stating he had no first-hand knowledge as to which of them, if any, were Communist Party members or had communist sympathies."[42]

They also asked him if he was acquainted with John Stanford— "A state official of the Communist Party from San Antonio against whom Lowery had testified in Subversive Activities Control

Board (SACB) hearings in Washington on 23 September 1963"— to which he answered "No."[43] The evidence that Joe Molina was neither communist, nor had communist friends was overwhelming. William Lowery had reported on Molina more than eight years earlier as follows: ". . . Molina appeared to be strongly opposed to the Communist Party [CP] . . . Joe Molina is not sympathetic to the CP and it is doubted that Molina could ever be recruited into the CP. Molina opposed the CP faction within the GI Forum." Informant William Lowery, Jr., 25 July 1955.[44]

Finally, they made him sign an affidavit about the GI Forum, when it was organized, who attended the charter meeting back in 1955, naming the charter members and how and when he failed to "renew my membership after July 1962."[45] This appears to have been harassment on the part of the DPD, especially now that we have seen Molina's Dallas FBI file in its entirety and its assorted cast of characters who spied on Molina. Furthermore, the correct date of incorporation of the Dallas GI Forum was 29 September 1954.[46]

Later that day, *The Dallas Morning News* published a story in their afternoon edition which read in part:

Dallas Police Saturday questioned a man said by Police Chief Jesse Curry to have been listed on the department's subversive files as they continued a massive investigation of the slaying of the president here Friday. The man being questioned was said to have been acquainted with Lee Harvey Oswald, the 24-year-old self-styled Marxist charged with murdering President Kennedy with a sniper's bullet. Chief Curry told reporters he did not know whether the man being questioned Saturday was listed on FBI subversive lists, but said he has been on lists maintained by the DPD for some time. The man was not described as a suspect. Police said he came to Police Headquarters voluntarily at their request.[47]

Even though Molina was not mentioned by name in the article, it was quite clear that Curry was referring to him. Curry already had involvement with Joe Molina in the past which could have tainted his judgment in handling Joe's particular predicament.

The Shenanigans of Chief Jesse Curry

On 23 November 1963, obviously with an ax to grind, Chief Curry stated: " ...Molina had caused the [DPD] considerable trouble in the past by demanding such things as listing Mexicans as white persons rather than as Mexicans, and generally protesting alleged discrimination against Mexicans."[48] After spending most of the day of 23 November at the DPD, Joe was taken home by the police because he did not have any transportation. When he got home, his wife Soledad was waiting for him with the news that he was on TV from coast-to-coast and they had labeled him a subversive and communist.[49] Later that night, Molina again called the DPD and tried to talk to Curry about a retraction, but Curry gave him the runaround and would not speak to him.[50] Despite all of this he was still told only Curry could give the retraction. Who leaked Joe's name to the media about being a "subversive"? Curry was under a lot of pressure from the national media for having mentioned Molina as a subversive and possible accomplice of Lee Oswald. Even though he was caught on video and audio speaking to the media, he denied or did not recall talking about Molina to the press, therefore, did not think a retraction was necessary.[51] Eight months later, despite denying throwing Molina under the bus, Curry knew the docket number of Molina's civil lawsuit against local radio station WRR, the date it was filed, *and* the name of the judge presiding the case in Dallas District Court, 86946-B filed 30 April 1964 Judge Julian Hyer.[52] Molina's attorney was Otto E. Mullinax, a longtime friend and fellow member of the GI Forum.

Molina Loses His Job at the TSBD

On 13 December 1964, Molina was called in by his supervisors and advised he was being let go due to automation. The funny thing about this is that he never saw any new machines being delivered to the accounting offices, which further aroused his suspicions about the real reason he was being fired. Joe told [his supervisors] in no uncertain terms: "I don't really think that's the reason why you're letting me go, it's probably because of this other thing."[53]

Besides the obvious "other thing" being the JFK "thing," was Joe trying to say something here about other activities he may have seen or heard at the TSBD? Joe remained as a lame duck at the TSBD until the end of December. His responsibilities were shifted to another person in the company.[54]

Why did the TSBD deny Molina was fired due to the publicity and subversive reports that came out about him? Why did they lie about automating his position? Roy Truly, superintendent of the TSBD,[55] and O.V. Campbell, TSBD's vice president,[56] tried to justify and explain his termination in a manner that comes across sort of condescending. O.V. Campbell described how Joe had to be brought in at least once a year to be reprimanded for his independence and unwillingness to take orders and suggestions.[57] They tried to make up for their actions by revealing the "generous" severance package that was given to Molina as well as glowing references for his next job at the Neuhoff Employees Credit Union.[58] What they did not mention was that Molina had to take a pay cut at his new job from $6,000 to $4,500 per year.[59] Also, that his new employment happened to be the result of his affiliation to his Church at Holy Trinity where people cared and were worried about what was happening to him.[60]

In contrast, as will be seen in the following pages, Billy Lovelady— who was arrested at the TSBD company 11 months earlier as a running felon and thrown in jail—had been recently court-martialed for gun running at one of the most important U.S. Air Force (USAF) bases in America—Andrews Air Force Base, where Air Force One is kept, and where the president plays golf—but was protected and allowed to work there throughout the assassination and beyond.[61] Laura Kittrell, a 30-year Texas Employment Commission (TEC) counselor and case manager, revealed in her 1966, 80-page manuscript, how strict the TSBD company had historically been about hiring questionably discharged individuals there.[62]

Meanwhile, in the wake of the assassination, the halls of the TSBD had to have been buzzing about what was happening to Joe, a trusted employee for more than 16 years. Joe was brought in five times for questioning, 23 November 1963, 30 November 1963, 25 March 1964, 15 July 1964, 14 August 1964, plus his Warren Commission testimony of 7 April 1964, which was at his own request. The FBI even took to calling him at his new place of employment to interview him right there on the premises of Neuhoff Employees Credit Union![63]

They (the Warren Commission, FBI, DPD, Secret Service, etc.) did not want to bring Joe Molina into this. It was he who initiated contact with the Warren Commission, not the other way around. Molina wanted the committee to ". . . record my story concerning the aftermath of the tragic events of 22 November 1963 . . . so that I may be cleared and exonerated from the false rumors that were heard from coast to coast."[64] As stated earlier, a very astute Joseph Ball did not allow him to shift his testimony towards William Lowery, and quickly terminated it. Joe's confirmed presence at the front steps of the TSBD is the holy grail of the assassination. He was intimidated and pressured into going along with the Warren Commission testimonies of Frazier, Shelley, Lovelady and Sarah Stanton.

Shirley Martin Comes Calling

In 1967, Joe agreed to an interview with Mrs. Shirley Martin. Mrs. Martin, from Hominy, Oklahoma, was a JFK supporter, was a self-motivated housewife-turned-researcher who started working on the JFK case on 24 November 1963.[65] Immediately after the assassination, she began to visit Dallas with her entire family to track down and interview witnesses, survey Dealey Plaza, do re-enactments, take pictures, she even got her kids Steven and Teresa involved one time by going to the rear of the TSBD to see if they could snap a photograph of Billy Lovelady for comparison with Altgens6.[66] On other occasions, she used hidden tape recorders to document conversations. She quickly established close ties with researchers Mark Lane, Sylvia Meagher, and particularly Harold Weisberg. She was not interested in writing books or articles, only in providing researchers with leads for further investigation.[67] In September 1964, she sent a telegram to Warren Commissioner Rankin, informing him of some of her findings. On 17 September 1964, two unidentified FBI agents were sent to visit her in Oklahoma regarding her telegram. After toying with them for a while, she advised them if the Commission wanted her information, they were going to have to subpoena her to Washington and take her testimony under oath.[68]

During her many trips to Dallas, with her southern charm and beautiful daughter Vickie at her side, she was able to interview people like Ruth and Michael Paine, Jean Hill and Mary Moorman, and Father Oscar Huber, the priest who gave JFK his last rites.[69] On the first observance of JFK's death, she again went to Dallas with her family in tow. They attended mass at Father Huber's Holy Trinity Church and afterward, requested a few minutes with the good Father. In one of the most incredible acts of homegrown intelligence ever

 seen, she secretly recorded her conversation with Huber, where he described a bullet hole right above JFK's left eyebrow. Father Huber, of course, denied ever talking to Shirley.[70] That's when Shirley went ballistic and

went public with her tape. Then, she had Penn Jones publish an open letter editorial in the *Midlothian Mirror* in her name calling out the priest as the liar that he was.[71] At the end of her 24 February 1967 letter to Weisberg, she wrote in longhand this most poignant note: "This hardly seems important anymore—however, it is for the record. God alone (and Huber) knows what Father Huber really saw—but I know what he told me!"[72]

Shirley and her children also became quite close with Marguerite Oswald who they affectionately called Mama O.[73]

When Shirley Martin came knocking on Joe Molina's door, she described him as a "frightened man." In a letter to Harold Weisberg in July 1967 she wrote that: "Joe Molina claims to be the man in suit ["Black Tie Man"] standing next to Lovelady-Oswald figure in Altgens photo. My inclination is that Molina was lying about this."[74]

Moreover, she felt Molina had notified someone before her visit and that person was in the house the day she interviewed him.[75] Could this have been William Lowery?

Later that year, her daughter Vickie, 22, was involved in a tragic car accident which took her life. After Vickie's death, Shirley's involvement diminished considerably, but she never stopped investigating the case. She died in 2006.[76]

Time and The Federal Government Heals All Wounds

In 1988, Molina gave an interview for the 25th observance of the assassination to *The Dallas Morning News*. The article included this photo of Joe.[77]

After the assassination, Joe landed a job with the United States Postal Service (USPS) in 1966 as a postal clerk.

JOE MOLINA:
25 years after being questioned in
Kennedy assassination.

He went back to school and graduated in 1969 from El Centro Community College and was soon promoted in 1969 to the position of Postal Contract Compliance Examiner. From there he went on to the General Services Administration, and in 1978 he started work with the U.S. Department of Labor as an equal opportunity specialist.

No doubt his unrelenting activism and battles to improve living conditions for Mexican-Americans in Dallas during the '50s and '60s prepared him for this line of work. He retired in March 1988.[78] In his own words, he lives comfortably and has money in the bank.[79]

These images show Black Tie Man in the doorway in Weigman 658 and the corresponding Altgens6, where Molina himself identified his position in the doorway.

Robert Groden – "JFK – Absolute Proof"

Joe Molina admitted to being "black tie man" to Shirley Martin in July 1967

Joe Molina claims to be the man in suit standing next to Lovelady-Oswald figure in Altgens photo. My inclination is that Molina was lying about this. He was a frightendd man when I spoke to him; I have always felt he had someone in the house the night I interviewed him, and that he had notofied someone ahead of time that I was coming. He was in the process of buying a new home when I last talked to him. However, this could have been only an inference. I have no way to be positive. At any rate, he was leaving Brown Street. I do not know where he is now.

Your book is excellent. I am still reading. More later.
Appreciated your appreciation of your wife's hard work. This has been hard on he
Love,
S.

ENDNOTES

1. FBI DL100-9847, p. 2, 15 July 1964
2. Ibid
3. FBI DL100-9847, p. 39b, 14 August 1964
4. National Personnel Records Center (NPRC) report
5. Warren Commission, 6H370
6. Weston, William, "The Spiders Web," *Dealey Plaza Echo*, Vol. 10, No.1, March 2006, pp. 1, 9. This has been corrected by interview with Roy Lewis, who on 30 December 2015 stated the move was in the summer of 1962.
7. Ibid.
8. Ibid.
9. DPD, 23 November 1963 interview with Molina by R.L. Senkel
10. FBI DL100-9847, p. 39c, 14 August 1964
11. City of Dallas Office Memorandum, 23 November 1963, by Patrolmen Trotman and Shelton
12. *Dallas Morning News* 26 September 1963, Lewis Harris, "Dallas Salesman Describes Role as Counter Spy"
13. contentdm.baylor.edu
14. FBI DL100-9847, p. 30, 16 July 1964
15. WC6H373
16. Weston, William, "The Spiders Web," *Dealey Plaza Echo*, Vol. 10, No.1, March 2006, p. 9
17. FBI DL100-9847, pp. 4-7, 20 August 1964
18. FBI DL100-9847, p. 6, 20 August 1964, Informant DL T-2, 22 July 1957
19. Ibid. Informant DL T-3, 13 February 1958 (Note: There is also the 10 November 1954 committee led by Molina to see Dallas County Clerk Bill Shaw, regarding alleged discrimination against Mexican-Americans on Dallas County grand juries.)
20. WC6H372
21. City of Dallas Office Memorandum, 23 November 1963 interview with Ms. Rackley by Patrolmen Trotman and Shelton
22. Ibid.
23. WC6H372
24. WC6H371
25. DPD interview with Detective R.L. Senkel, 23 November 1963, p. 2
26. FBI DL100-9847, p. 1, 16 July 1964
27. FBI DL100-9847, p. 22, 15 July 1964

28. Shaw, J. Gary, *Cover-Up: The Governmental Conspiracy to Conceal the Facts About the Public Execution of John Kennedy* (1976), pp. 100-101
29. Ibid.
30. Ibid. 100
31. Ibid. 101
32. FBI DL100-9847, p. 28a, 15 July 1964
33. WC6H369
34. FBI DL100-9847, p. 28b, 19 August 1964
35. FBI DL100-9847, p. 12, 16 July 1964
36. FBI DL100-9847, p. 22, 15 July 1964
37. FBI DL100-9847, p. 2, 16 July 1964, by FBI Special Agent Joseph E. Jones
38. Shaw, J. Gary, *Cover-Up: The Governmental Conspiracy to Conceal the Facts About the Public Execution of John Kennedy* (1976), p. 101
39. FBI DL100-9847, p. 12, 16 July 1964
40. FBI DL100-9847, p. 14, 16 July 1964
41. DPD City of Dallas Memorandum, 23 November 1963, Patrolmen Trotman and Shelton, undated DPD doc signed by Detective R.L. Senkel
42. FBI DL100-9847, p. 14, 16 July 1964
43. Ibid.
44. FBI DL100-9847, p. 4, 20 August 1964
45. DPD, 23 November 1963, affidavit taken by William Biggio
46. FBI DL100-9847, p. 3, 20 August 1964
47. DL-100-9847, p. 39, 15 July 1964
48. DL100-9847, p. 8a, 23 November 1963
49. WC6H370
50. DL100-9847, p. 8a, 23 November 1963
51. FBI DL100-9847, p. 31, 16 July 1964
52. Ibid.
53. WC6H370
54. Ibid.
55. FBI DL100-9847, p. 33, 14 July 1964
56. FBI DL100-9847, p. 35, 14 July 1964
57. FBI DL100-9847, p. 36, 15 July 1964
58. FBI DL100-9847, p. 35, 14 July 1964
59. DL100-9847, p. 16, 20 July 1964
60. WC6H371
61. Rivera, Larry, "Lovelady Revisited"
62. Laura Kittrell unpublished manuscript, p. 68 (Kittrell worked at the TEC for more than 30 years)
63. FBI DL100-9847, p. 12, 15 July 1964 at 2821 Alamo Street, Dallas, TX
64. Molina letter to Warren Commission 31 March 1964
65. efmpress.com/fecteau/ColdCaseKS_JFK_ShirleyMartin.pdf
66. Ibid.
67. Ibid. 2
68. FBI 89-43-4997, 21 September 1964, unidentified FBI agents out of Oklahoma City, OK

69. efmpress.com/fecteau/ColdCaseKS_JFK_ShirleyMartin.pdf

70. Lewis, Richard W., "The Scavengers," *New York World Journal Tribune*, 22 January 1967

71 *Midlothian Mirror*, 2 March 1967, open letter editorial by Shirley Martin

72. Weisberg letter, 24 February 1967, The Weisberg Collection. Hood College, Frederick, MD, USA

73. efmpress.com/fecteau/ColdCaseKS_JFK_ShirleyMartin.pdf

74. Shirley Martin, July 1967 letter to Weisberg, The Weisberg Collection. Hood College, Frederick, MD, USA

75. Ibid.

76. efmpress.com/fecteau/ColdCaseKS_JFK_ShirleyMartin.pdf

77. *The Dallas Morning News*, Ken Stephens, 20 November 1988, "Where Are They Now? Joe Molina: the 'second man'"

78. Ibid.

79. Ibid.

5

Roy Edward Lewis and Altgens6

Fifty-three years after he took his photograph of JFK during the assassination on 22 November 1963, little could Ike Altgens imagine the controversy it would create, as it has now become the most scrutinized photograph of all time. The photograph corresponds to Zapruder frame 255, which shows JFK reacting to shots fired from in front and behind him. Within Altgens6—in an area that encompasses no more than 1/8"—there is a reunion of sorts at the entrance of the TSBD, which depicts a cross-section of the people who worked there. In particular, the image of an African-American man's profile can be seen in front of Doorway Man, which is already looking to his left and in the general direction of the Dal-Tex Building, a known source of gunfire that day.

It is painfully obvious that the JFK investigation relegated African-American people as the least important witnesses and were treated as such. Well before the civil rights era, it is not hard to imagine the degree of intimidation they must have been subjected to, as were most of the African-American community in the South and particularly Dallas in the 1960s. Under these adverse conditions, they were by far the easiest group to sway. A prime example can be seen when one examines Don Roberdeau's witness map of Dealey Plaza. The positions taken up by almost all the African-American witnesses on the north curb of Elm Street, citizens who are clearly visible in the Croft image as well as Altgens6 and some early frames of the Zapruder film, are people who remain unidentified to this day.

By process of elimination, we have tentatively identified 18-year-old Roy Edward Lewis (figure G below) as the African-American man in the stairway of the entrance of the TSBD. There is very little information on Lewis in early assassination documentation. He was born in Carthage, Texas in September 1946,[1] and at the time of the assassination he had been working there approximately four months. The DPD interviewed him on 18 February 1964, and the report only states general information such as his address and the fact that he had only been working there for seven months at the time, but also states *he saw Oswald at 10:00 AM that morning.*[2] His official "testimony" was taken one month later in Dallas by FBI agent J. Hale McMenamin on 18 March 1964, and was included in CE1381, the Commission document that briefly reported what TSBD employees did that day. His statement of 18 March 1964 does not mention he had seen Lee Oswald at 10:00 AM.[3] Neither document was signed by Lewis. At the time of the assassination, Lewis was firmly ensconced on the west side of the entrance, in contact with the wall, while the rest of his white coworkers stayed on the other side of the hand railing.

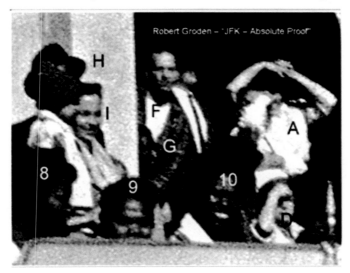

Doorway of Altgens6

From CE1381:

"On 22 November 1963, *I stood by myself on the inside of the front entrance of the Texas School Book Depository* [Emphasis added] to watch President John F. Kennedy come by the building in a motorcade. I heard three shots fired from somewhere above me but was unable to see the person who fired them."

His statement also contains a very cryptic but revealing passage: "I was acquainted with Lee Oswald but he was not with me at the time I heard the shots."

The rest of his testimony parroted what the others said—they did not see Lee Oswald that morning, did not see anyone who was not supposed to be in the building, and briefly described what each of them did after everyone was dismissed for the day. What is very strange about Roy's testimony is that he was never shown a copy of

Altgens6, was never asked who was with him, behind him or around him at the stairway, was never asked about Billy Lovelady's shirt (plaid, striped or solid color), and was never asked to confirm the presence of Shelley, Lovelady, Arce, Frazier, and Molina. Conversely, these five individuals were never asked about the presence of Lewis in the doorway![4] This selective treatment confirms what is suspected regarding the African-American witnesses. Certainly, the most logical person to ask regarding who was at the entrance of the TSBD would have been the one visible in the most pictures and movies taken that day. Lewis appears in Altgens6, at least three Weigman slides, the Skaggs slide, and Willis slide No. 8.

From Weigman movie clip

In a very rare interview, perhaps the only one he had ever given until we caught up with him, Larry A. Sneed interviewed Lewis for his 1998 book, *No More Silence: An Oral History of the Assassination of President Kennedy*, where he made some very interesting observations. First, on the direction of the shots:

"Unlike some witnesses, I didn't see any smoke or smell any gun powder, nor could I tell the direction of the shots because it was like an echo there. But no way did I suspect anything coming from the [TSBD]." Contrary to what the Warren Commission and FBI reported, which we have cited above, Lewis began working for the TSBD in

August or September 1962, which was right after the company moved into the building at 411 Elm Street.

In the Sneed volume, Lewis offers some very specific details about the daily life at the TSBD, and his own and other coworkers responsibilities there. A very interesting observation of Lee Oswald that perhaps had never been pointed out before, was the fact that he was teased about wearing his hair longer than normal, and that "hair would be growing down his neck."

Lewis's account gives Lee Oswald a human quality, which is in sharp contrast to the mean, disgruntled loner that the Warren Commission characterized him in their report.

One of the most striking revelations was Sneed's description of the difference in physical characteristics between Oswald and Lovelady, where he stated:

I've been told that some people confused Billy Lovelady with Oswald, but Lovelady was much heavier, and even though Oswald's hair was thinning, Billy's was about all gone up there.

Describing his exact location during the assassination, he stated: "Due to my lack of excitement, I was one of the last ones out of the building before the motorcade arrived. That's why I wasn't outside near the street like most everybody else. Instead, when I came out, I was standing with some ladies from up in the offices right in the middle of the steps in front of the building that led to the sidewalk beyond the glass door."

Lewis stated how he had been neglected as a witness but did not find that odd because he figured the investigators had plenty of witnesses:

"I'm not sorry about not getting involved. *If they had contacted me* [Emphasis added], there probably wouldn't have been much that I could have told them, more than I'm saying now, so my life never changed much as a result of the assassination. *Now if I'd have been interviewed by the FBI or Secret Service* [Emphasis added] at my home, I'd have been in the limelight and received a lot of publicity." This indicates that his supposed statement to the FBI in CE1381 might have even been fabricated.

Regarding his opinion on Lee Oswald's guilt, here is what he had to say: "But I'm still not convinced that he did it, and because of his murder, it's for certain we're never going to get to the bottom of it. I'll never be convinced that Oswald did it or that he acted alone."

In Willis slide No. 8, Lewis remained at the entrance, only now he had moved to the other side of the center hand railing. It is possible he saw or heard something going on east of him, in the general direction of the Dal-Tex Building. More than likely, he was staring at the two vans that were parked on Elm, east of Houston Street which can be seen in the Towner film. But what exactly was it that attracted Roy's attention for so long?

The last official reference to Roy Lewis occurred when he and his coworkers were finger-and-palm-printed by the FBI on 15 June 1964.[5] The belatedness of this action cannot be understated and reconciled unless it was to make sure Lewis understood they were keeping tabs

on him and the others, and he was keeping his mouth shut about what
he had witnessed. Could this have included his personal knowledge
of who was standing behind him in the doorway?

The Roy Lewis Interview

On 30 December 2015, this author was finally able to track down
Roy Lewis and interview him for close to 90 minutes. A listing of 27
questions had been formulated for him based on the information that
we had been able to gather, which we surmised he might have had
personal knowledge of. Some highlights of the interview are detailed
herein:

1. Buell Wesley Frazier

He advised that Frazier is key to finding out the truth of the
assassination. The following are new revelations:

• *"The main guy you want to talk about is Wesley Frazier, he
would pick him up every day and bring him to work."* [Emphasis
added] Frazier used to give Lee Oswald rides to work *every day*, not
just on weekends.

• Edward Shields—an African-American TSBD employee—
said Frazier would drop Lee off on Houston adjacent to the northeast
entrance of the TSBD and park his car on the bend of Houston to Ross
Ave. He was good friends with Shields, and says that all African-
American witnesses knew of this. Lewis confirmed what Shields said.
Despite not knowing for sure where Frazier parked on 22 November
1963, he found it to be extremely unlikely, because the area in front
of the state building had all kinds of obstacles like railroad tracks,
ditches, etc.

• Lewis advised that he and the African-American workers
spoke among themselves about the supposed package Lee was
supposed to have brought in, and confirms that none of them saw
this, and it was common knowledge that it had been made up. They
wondered why he would bring curtain rods to work to begin with.

2. Refurbishing of the sixth floor

• Roy Lewis categorically stated this was *false*. There was no
type of refurbishing going on up there that week. As the youngest
employee involved in moving boxes and material around, he would
have been carrying material and tools had this been the case. He
never saw any plywood, electric saws, or any specific carpenter's

wares at all. He was never asked or involved in the movement of this material or tools. Furthermore, he stated the freight elevators were the main tool used by him and the other warehouse workers, as well as dollies or hand trucks. Had there been any work of this type on the sixth floor, he would have been involved in it. Furthermore, he stated that the lighting up there was extremely poor, and this would have entailed the use of special lighting for this purpose, and this was not the case. This is confirmed by the Alyea film, which shows DPD detectives using flashlights to search the sixth floor of the TSBD.

• Lewis revealed that the sniper's nest, where boxes had been moved over to form the barricade at the southeast windows of the sixth floor, had been arranged and been in place since between 10:30 AM and 11:00 AM.

• Lewis said that warehouse workers *never* went to the second-floor lunchroom except to use the vending machines, because there were no vending machines in the "domino room" on the first floor of the northeast corner of the building where they would change into their work clothes and leave their coats and jackets.

3. Lewis knew the differences between Lovelady and Oswald

• Lewis confirmed that Lovelady was almost totally bald and was shorter and heavier, and when shown the Mark Lane photograph, he pointed out that this is what Lovelady really looked like.

• Lewis purchased a 1957 or 1958 Pontiac from Lovelady, which suggests that he knew Lovelady pretty well. Lewis was unaware of Lovelady's troubles at Andrews AFB, but he was aware that Lovelady had been arrested at the TSBD but did not remember when.

• Lewis said he cannot understand how one could have been mistaken for the other. He said Lee Oswald was much thinner and used to wear his hair long and his coworkers used to kid him that they were going to gang up on him and cut it for him. He said Oswald would keep to himself, and on his free time at lunch, most of the time he had his nose in the newspaper.

• Lewis advised that Lee did have access to the fourth, fifth and sixth floors. He did not remain confined to the first floor. He also said that order packers never went up there; they normally stayed on the first floor. Junior Jarman would take care of going up to correct packing mistakes.

Employment Records, Time Sheets, and Method of Payment to Warehouse Employees

Mr. Lewis was not paid in cash. This is very important because it indicates that the Warren Commission was not entirely truthful about these workers being paid in cash, whereby supposedly detailed payroll records did not exist.

According to Lewis, employees were required to sign in and out on a daily basis. This suggests that time sheets and logs should exist showing the exact time and attendance records of each employee. According to O.V. Campbell and Bill Shelley, the person in charge of keeping payroll records was H.S. Aiken.

Aiken had 20 employees to keep track of, and it would be crucial to keep an orderly record of attendance which could later be used in case an employee was laid off and they filed for unemployment benefits with the TEC.

These benefits are always calculated according to hours worked, and any employer would require accurate records to make sure that laid off employees would not file for more benefits than they would have been entitled to. The only way to make sure of this would have been either time clocks or signed time sheets, which Lewis has now confirmed indeed existed. Here are the time sheets of October and November 1963, as published in the Warren Commission as Commission Exhibit 1949:

The next three documents try to explain away the lax and sloppy record keeping or lack thereof. This information completely contradicts what Lewis has revealed:

FD-302 (Rev. 1-25-60)

FEDERAL BUREAU OF INVESTIGATION

Date _3/24/64_

1

Mr. O. V. CAMPBELL, Vice President, Texas School Book
Depository (TSBD), 411 Elm (RI 7-3521), stated that all records
pertaining to LEE HARVEY OSWALD's employment at TSBD have previously
been furnished to Agents of the FBI. He stated the only employee
records maintained by TSBD that would contain OSWALD's handwriting
and/or signature are OSWALD's application for employment and
Employee's Withholding Exemption Certificate which have previously
been furnished.

Mr. CAMPBELL stated the only records maintained by Texas
School Book Depository that would show the hours worked by OSWALD
are the payroll records reflecting the employment of OSWALD from
October 16 through November 22, 1963. Mr. CAMPBELL pointed out
that these records are prepared in their entirety by Mr. H. S. AIKEN,
employee of TSBD, and OSWALD did not participate in any manner in
preparation of same. He stated TSBD does not utilize a time clock
or other device to record an individual's times of arrival and
departure as such information is maintained by Mr. AIKEN and
employees in the warehouse are paid in cash; are not required to
sign any type of receipt for their pay; therefore, there is no
additional record pertaining to OSWALD's employment at TSBD.
Regarding the payroll records maintained by TSBD, Mr. CAMPBELL
pointed out that copies of same had previously been furnished to
an Agent of the FBI.

CE 1887

On _3/18/64_ at _Dallas, Texas_   File # _DL 100-10461_

by _SA EMORY E. HORTON:vm_   Date dictated _3/21/64_

This document contains neither recommendations nor conclusions of the FBI. It is the property of the FBI and is loaned to
your agency; it and its contents are not to be distributed outside your agency.

Date   December 9, 1963

1

On December 9, 1963, Mr. WILLIAM H. SHELLEY,
Warehouse Foreman, Texas School Book Depository (TSBD), Dallas, Texas
advised that no time clock or register of any kind is
maintained for the warehouse employees of TSBD. The only
record maintained is the payroll record that shows whether
or not the employee was present on a specific date. Each
morning after working hours begin, he checks to see that
each employee is present and on the job, and if any employee
is missing, he notes this fact and advises Mr. TRULY, who
in turn notifies Mr. AIKEN, who keeps the payroll records.
The only permanent record maintained is that record maintained by Mr. AIKEN for the payroll.

Mr. SHELLEY stated specifically that on the
morning of November 22, 1963, he did not see OSWALD with
any package and, in fact, did not actually see OSWALD
arrive at work but did see him at about the time the work
day commenced, and at that time OSWALD had no package.

Mr. SHELLEY stated there is no way to determine
what other employee, or employees, arrived for work at
about the same time as OSWALD on that or any other date.

On 3/18/64 Mr. O. V. CAMPBELL, Vice-President, TSBD, texas advised that all records pertaining to OSWALD's employment at TSBD had previously been furnished to Agents of the FBI. He stated the only employee records that would contain OSWALD's handwriting and/or signature are his application for employment and employee's withholding exemption certificate (identified as Laboratory Nos. K23 and Q483 respectively).

He stated the only records that would show the hours worked by OSWALD are the payroll records reflecting employment of OSWALD at TSBD from 10/16 through 11/22/63 (Item 3 above). Mr. CAMPBELL pointed out that these records are prepared in their entirety by Mr. H. S. AIKEN, employee of TSBD, and OSWALD did not participate in any manner in the preparation of same. He stated TSBD does not utilize a time clock or other device to record an individual's times of arrival and departure as such information is maintained by Mr. AIKEN and employees in warehouse are paid in cash, are not required to sign any type of receipt for their pay, therefore, there is no additional record pertaining to OSWALD's employment at TSBD.

4. Altgens6

- Roy Lewis identified himself as" Black Profile Man," which is also the African-American man in the Weigman slide and in Willis slide No. 8 and the Skaggs. *He identified himself in these as well.*

- Lewis identified Lee Oswald as Doorway Man. The first time Roy saw the Groden enlargement of the doorway, his immediate and first reaction was "That's Lee Harvey Oswald!" and "It looks like him."

- Lewis identified Billy Lovelady as "Black Hole Man" based on the rolled-up shirt sleeve seen on the left arm. He said that Lovelady had the habit of wearing his shirts in this manner. (much more on this in Chapter 8)

- Lewis did not see or hear firecrackers or see any streamers.

Altgens6 closeup

Weigman slide

Regarding Willis slide No. 8, Lewis remarked: "Why do they have me looking that way?" We pointed out the "Towner vans" at Elm and Houston, and he stated that could have been what drew his attention. When asked if he was aware about the possibility that Lee Oswald might have been standing right above him and towards the center railing, he stated that he was not aware of who was behind him because he was focused on Kennedy and the limousine. This is important because it would indicate that Lee Oswald could have been a late arrival at the TSBD entrance, possibly when the motorcade was just making the turn from Main onto Houston.

Willis slide No. 8

Above left: Roy Lewis has identified himself as this individual in Willis slide No. 8. Above right: Lewis and Doorway Man in Hughes slide.

5. Shots

• Roy Lewis was standing at the bottom steps of the entrance of the TSBD doorway. He heard three shots, first one, then two in succession, almost one on top of the other. "I heard boom, then boom-boom."

• From his vantage point he could not tell if the motorcade stopped or the actions of the motorcycle patrolmen. He only saw JFK brush his hair to the side with his hand.

• He rushed to the grassy knoll after a few minutes, most probably after he was captured in Willis slide No. 8.

6. African-American witnesses

Roy Lewis advised that the African-American witnesses were not intimidated, however they *were* ignored. For example, when the FBI went looking for him at his apartment building, they did not knock on his door. They asked a couple of his neighbors, who protected him and told the FBI that he did not live there. The agents were satisfied with this and did not go knocking door-to-door in an attempt to verify this. They never came back. He says this indicated their lack of interest in pursuing new leads. He says nobody had ever taken the interest to thoroughly ask him about 22 November 1963 until now.

7. Transplantation of the TSBD company

• Is 100% positive that the TSBD company which employed him was already at 411 Elm Street when he started working there in August 1962.

> ROY S. TRULY, Warehouse Manager, Texas School
> Book Depository, advised that the Texas School Book Deposi-
> tory has occupied the building at 411 Elm Street for only
> a few months. Prior to this time, the building was oc-
> cupied by a wholesale grocery company engaged in supplying
> restaurants and institutions and during the course of their
> occupancy, the floors of the building became oil soaked and
> this oil was found to be damaging the stock of the School
> Book Depository stack thereon. In view of this, they had
> instituted a process of covering the floors with sheets of
> plywood. This process was being performed by the regular
> warehouse employees whenever they had slack periods of
> work.
>
> The southwest corner of the 6th floor had been
> cleared of stock in order that plywood could be laid over this
> floor and the southwest corner was consequently empty of stock
> on November 22, 1963, making the windows to the southwest
> corner of the building readily accessible.

- This must mean that the Truly interview above, where he states the TSBD company had only occupied the building at 411 Elm Street for a few months is mistaken and *he was probably referring to close to a year and a few months.*

- The text book company agents, on the other hand, could have moved in after the TSBD company. Example: Scott Foresman, McMillan, Allyn & Bacon.

Analysis

Roy Lewis is what we would call a pristine, uncontaminated witness. There are very few of these left.

When interviewed he was 69-years-old, and a happily married religious man, who cherished the time he spent with his 24 grandchildren. From what could be perceived, he had great relationships with his neighbors, warmly greeting them outside of his middle class, well-kept home.

After the assassination, and the perfunctory attempts to contact him by the FBI, he slipped into oblivion and nobody had ever taken the time or made the effort to investigate what he saw and heard. In 1998, Larry Sneed interviewed Roy for his book, and wrote one of the chapters on him. However, Sneed did not go into the detail that we went into with him. Roy has never read the Warren Report or any of the information contained in the 26 volumes of Exhibits and Hearings. He has never read any books or been interested in the aftermath of the assassination of JFK. It is obvious that he had never seen the images which depict him at the entrance of the TSBD, such as Altgens6, Weigman slide 658 and others, the Skaggs, Willis slide No. 8, and especially the enlargement of the doorway in Altgens6. He has readily identified himself in all of these images. At the church where he is a member, the congregation there considers him a celebrity because they know that he knew Lee Oswald. However, that is where it ends.

At the beginning of the interview, Roy was asked to try to recall the events to the best of his ability, and this author found him to be extremely lucid and sober. The revelations Roy offered will indeed make investigators, researchers, and historians re-write the accepted conclusions put forth by the Warren Commission and those who insist on supporting its fairy tales.

To summarize, these are:

1. Wesley Frazier arrived every day with Lee Oswald, not just on weekends. This would indicate one of two things:

•   Frazier would pick him up in Oak Cliff on his way in from Irving

•   Lee Oswald never really stayed at Earlene Roberts's rooming house, and always stayed with Ruth and Michael Paine.

It has never really been revealed how Lee Oswald arrived at the TSBD every day while living in Oak Cliff. If we consider Roy's story as valid, the most probable option has to be that Frazier picked him up there every day. Roy also confirmed the ongoing thesis that Frazier would park on Houston/Ross and drop Lee off at the northeast corner of the building, *never* down by the railroad tracks south of the state building, and especially on 22 November, as it had been raining in the morning. Most importantly, without ever seeing Edward Shields's HSCA interview, Lewis confirmed exactly what Shields testified to. (see appendix for transcript)

2. There was no floor work being done on the sixth floor. Lewis categorically denied this to be the case, supported by the lack of photographs depicting any tools or material essential for this endeavor. The poor lighting up there would have prevented this type of work, and he never saw any supplemental lighting being used.

3. The sniper's nest had already been constructed between 10:30-11:00 AM because he saw it and was a witness to it.

4. The TSBD company never paid the warehouse employees in cash as stated many times in the Warren Commission by Bill Shelley and O.V. Campbell. This is false. Moreover, the TSBD company kept track of employee attendance by keeping signed time sheets where each employee would sign in and out at specific times. The time sheets supplied by the Warren Commission show nothing of the sort. The actual time sheets have never surfaced.

5. When he started working at the TSBD in August 1962, they were already operating at 411 Elm Street. It is entirely possible the move happened in the summer of 1962, with the text book agents following in the spring and summer of 1963.

6. The African-American witnesses were totally ignored and were not pursued to give their impressions of what happened on 22 November 1963. Case in point, they were never asked about the

supposed package Lee brought into the building. He was emphatic that this had been discussed among the African-American workers and they had determined this not to be the case.

7. Roy Lewis was shown the overlays, discussed in Chapter 8. After seeing the Oswald and Lovelady overlays and animations on a laptop computer, he agreed that Doorway Man is indeed Lee Oswald, and that if this is the case, then Oswald could not have been on the sixth floor shooting at JFK.

ENDNOTES

1. CE1381, p. 61 (image below)
2. DPD, 18 February 1964, Lewis interview by Detectives Brumley and Parks (image below)
3. *Op. cit.*
4. WH6H363-367 Arce, WH6H336-341 Lovelady, WH6H368-373 Molina, WH2H210-245 Frazier, WH6H327-334 Shelley
5. CE3131 p. 5 (image below)

18 February 1964

Captain W. P. Gannaway
Special Service Bureau
Dallas Police Department

Thru:
Lieutenant Jack Revill
Criminal Intelligence Section
Special Service Bureau
Dallas Police Department

SUBJECT: CRIMINAL INTELLIGENCE (6)
ROY EDWARD LEWIS C/M/21

Sir:

Pursuant to the instructions of Captain W. P. Gannaway SUBJECT investigation was conducted with the following results.

SUBJECT, who resides at 5906 WOODVILLE, has been an employ of the TEXAS SCHOOL BOOK DEPOSITORY, HOUSTON & ELM, for seven months. SUBJECT stated that he knew LEE HARVEY OSWALD when he saw him but that he did not associate with him. He stated that OSWALD stayed by himself most of the time. SUBJECT stated that he was in the entrance of the building when the President was assassinated. SUBJECT stated that he did not see anyone leave the building after the shots were fired. SUBJECT stated that on the day of the assassination he saw OSWALD only one time and that was at 10:00 A. M. SUBJECT said he had never seen JACK RUBY until he saw him on television.

Respectfully submitted,

R. H. Brumley, Detective
Criminal Intelligence Section

From CE1381

1

DL 100-10461
JHM/cms

"Dallas, Texas
March 18, 1964

"I, Roy Edward Lewis, make the following voluntary
statement to J. Hale McMenamin who has identified himself to
me as a Special Agent, Federal Bureau of Investigation.

"I am a male Negro, and was born September 18, 1946
at Carthage, Texas. I presently reside at 5906 Woodville,
Dallas, Texas, and am employed in the warehouse of the Texas
School Book Depository, 411 Elm Street.

"On November 22, 1963 at approximately 12:25 PM
I stood by myself on the inside of the front entrance of the
Texas School Book Depository Building to watch President
John F. Kennedy come by the building in a motorcade. I heard
three shots fired from somewhere above me, but was unable to see
the person who fired them.

"I was acquainted with Lee Harvey Oswald, but he was
not with me at the time I heard the shots.

"During the morning of the assassination of
President Kennedy, I saw no individuals in the Texas School
Book Depository who were not known to me to be employees.

"Following the assassination, all employees were
dismissed from work, and I left the building about 1:15 P.M.

"I have read this statement, and it is true and
correct to the best of my knowledge.

"/s/Roy Edward Lewis

"Witnesses:
"/s/J. Hale McMenamin, SA, FBI, Dallas, Texas 3/18/64.
"/s/Raymond J. Fox, SA, FBI, Dallas, Texas, 3/18/64."

61

LEE HARVEY OSWALD

On September 2, 1964, fingerprints and palm prints
of the following individuals who were employees of the TSBD
on November 22, 1963, were submitted to the Latent Fingerprint
Section of the Identification Division of the FBI for comparison
with the identifiable latent fingerprints and palm prints on
the four cardboard cartons.

Roy S. Truly
Carl Edward Jones
Harold Dean Norman
Edward Shields

It should be noted that on June 15, 1964, fingerprints
and palm prints were obtained from the following employees of
TSBD and submitted to the Latent Fingerprint Section of the
Identification Division of the FBI for comparison with the
identifiable latent fingerprints and palm prints on the four
cardboard cartons:

Daniel Garcia Arce
Jack Edwin Dougherty
Buell Wesley Frazier
Charles Douglas Givens
James Earl Jarman, Jr.
Frankie Kaiser
Roy Edward Lewis
Billy Nolan Lovelady
Eddie Piper
William Hoyt Shelley
Troy Eugene West
Bonnie Roy Williams

- 5 -

COMMISSION EXHIBIT No. 3131—Continued

APPENDIX

Lewis: My concept is that he let him off in the back, that is my concept.

Rivera: Then he went and parked.

Lewis: *Then he went and parked—right. That is my concept. Now I didn't see him, I can't say because I wasn't an eyewitness—he put him out in the back—now you say he drove with him on weekends, now he drove with him every day—Monday through Friday.* [Emphasis added]

Rivera: He did? We didn't know that.

Lewis: He would bring him—he would let him out in the back—and come in the back [entrance].

Rivera: And another thing, he usually never parked all the way back there, he used to park right there on Houston . . .

Lewis: Uh Huh.

Rivera: . . . on the bend of Houston. This is what I'm interpreting, only on that day, supposedly he parked behind the railroad tracks in front of the state building, when he usually always parked right there on the bend of Houston . . .

Lewis: Uh huh.

Rivera: . . . where it turns into Ross Ave.

Lewis: Right.

Rivera: That's something that we have always been questioning, wondering . . . so if you say that he never parked all the way down there, they are making it up, or only on that day he parked all the way up there; that seems kind of strange.

Lewis: Yeah, it does, but now . . .

38. VIEW FROM ROOF OF TEXAS SCHOOL BOOK DEPOSITORY
LOOKING NORTH TOWARD PARKING LOT NO. 1. (ARROW)

Mr. D: Now, let me back up a little bit. Are you telling me that this fella said that somebody who worked in the book depository, the building down on Elm and Houston, hollered out the window and asked Frazier where was his rider?

Mr. S: Mm-hmm.

Mr. D: Are you talking about the morning of the assassination?

Mr. S: I think it was, Mr. Davis, if I'm not mistaken. I think it was.

Mr. D: And how did you come about this information?

Mr. S: Well, I was down on the floor when they hollered out and said and the answer he gave them, I don't know, I think he said:"I dropped him off at the building." Now, whoever it was hollering asked him, I don't know.

Mr. D: This is the morning of the assassination?

Mr. S: Mm-hmm

Mr. D: Somebody hollered out the window at Frazier and say: "Where is your rider?" And to your recollection, Frazier says: "I dropped him off at the building."

Edward Shields Interview 1978 HSCA (Mr. S below)

Mr. S: Wesley Frazier - right. You're correct.

Mr. D: Alright. He rode to work with him.

Mr. S: Wesley Frazier - yes. And they would park their car right on Houston Street and get out and walk to the building on Elm Street.

Mr. D: Alright. The day of the assassination, did you see Oswald come to work with Frazier?

Mr. S: No, I didn't. They told me that he let him out at the building. He did not come on the parking lot.

Mr. M: You say they told you?

Mr. S: Yeah.

Mr. D: Who told you they...

Mr. S: Jerman, them, and all of --
the fellows that work there at the building.

Mr. D: Alright. This is just...Can you tell me a
specific person that told you that?

Mr. S: Yeah. I think Charles Gibbons hollered out
there and asked Frazier where was his rider and he told him:
"I dropped him off at the building." Yeah, that was it.

6

Lovelady Revisited: Andrews Air Force Base—The Fugitive

The release of FBI documents pertaining to Billy Nolan Lovelady makes this individual a person of extreme interest in ways that had never been considered before.[1] The controversy surrounding his presence in Altgens6 must now be viewed in an entirely different light. The dean of early researchers, Harold Weisberg, wrote entire chapters devoted to this, where he protested the manner in which the Lovelady affair had been conducted from day one by the FBI and later the Warren Commission.[2] If only Weisberg had known then what we know now!

Story of an Ever-Changing Shirt

Lovelady was photographed in his red-and-white vertical striped shirt on 29 February 1964 by the FBI in Dallas.[3] He stated that during the assassination "he was wearing a red-and-white vertical striped shirt and blue jeans." At that time the FBI was only concerned with making his shirt look more like Doorway Man's by leaving the top three buttons unbuttoned. A little more than a month later on 7 April 1964, his sworn, *unsigned* testimony was taken by Joseph Ball in Dallas, a vague exchange, where he was shown a cropped version of

108

Altgens with an arrow already pointing at Doorway Man, and where Ball changed the subject at will, and did not seem interested in pursuing any new information.[4] For example, for the record and supposedly under oath, he was never asked the simple question of what shirt he wore that day.[5] Later, and as mentioned in the first chapter of this book, in May of that year, Dom Bonafede of the *New York Herald Tribune* wrote a most comprehensive article on this issue. Bonafede wrote about Jones Harris, who was the first investigator to actually commission enhancements of Altgens6 and later tried to photograph Lovelady in Dallas. He reported Lovelady was an inch shorter than

Lee Oswald, and he "was wearing a red-and-white striped sport shirt buttoned near the neck."[6] Two years later, when Weisberg wrote *Whitewash II: The FBI-Secret Service Cover-Up* (1966), questions kept arising regarding Lovelady's shirt versus that worn by Doorway Man. Josiah Thompson's *Six Seconds in Dallas: A Micro-Study of the Kennedy Assassination* (1967), tried to reconcile this as well.[7] By 1971, the issue would not go away and Lovelady was finally photographed in the doorway of the TSBD by Bob Jackson in a plaid checkered red and dark shirt with the top buttons unbuttoned. Amazingly, Jackson placed Lovelady on the third step of the doorway when his Warren Commission deposition clearly stated he was on the top step (WC6H339). The story of the plaid shirt did not come full circle until the HSCA published its report in the late '70s.[8] There are problems with that conclusion as we shall see.

Lovelady Gets in Trouble

The mystery of Lovelady's apparent change of direction regarding the shirt he wore on 22 November 1963 is compounded by the fact that he had been in serious trouble when he was an Airman Second Class at Andrews AFB in 1960-61, because of the illegal sale of stolen guns.[9] This case was investigated by the Office of Special Investigations (OSI),[10] and culminated in penalties ranging from a suspended sentence and two-year probation for Charles Williams, to

$200 fines for Lovelady and Paul Crouse.[11] Once the civil portion of this case was resolved on 11 April 1961, Lovelady and his partners were quickly court-martialed and separated from the USAF on 14 June 1961 with a duty status of "discharge."[12] This is why he never finished his tour of duty. As a civilian, it appears that Lovelady had actually been on the lam for more than a year after skipping town on his $200 fine—he had only paid $125 of the $200. He was finally tracked down in Dallas as a fugitive in early January 1963 and immediately arrested and incarcerated by the FBI. The balance of $75 fine was paid by O.V. Campbell who "advanced" him the money.[13] On 29 January 1963, the FBI closed the case.[14] As the father of young children, how pliable would Lovelady have been with this sword of Damocles hanging over his head? When Harold Weisberg appeared before a grand jury during the Garrison investigation before the Clay Shaw trial in New Orleans in 1967, he was asked point blank if he thought Lovelady had been lying about his identification as Doorway Man in Altgens6, and he answered with an emphatic "Yes."[15] (Roy Schaeffer even suggests he might have been one of the shooters![16]) Lovelady, who refused to be photographed by anyone after the assassination,[17] who was caught in a vortex of unknown proportions, was hounded throughout his life and moved to Colorado to avoid investigators and others who wanted to talk to him.[18] He died of an apparent heart attack on 14 January 1979, there was no autopsy performed,[19] and was never officially interviewed by the HSCA. (see next chapter). His wife Patricia passed away on 10 March 1996 at the age of 57.[20]

There are published articles that make reference to HSCA Vol. VI, p. 287, which in effect changed Lovelady's initial FBI report of 2 March 1964.[21] Within this document, footnoted reference No. 252 points to *Six Seconds in Dallas*, p. 227, and "outside contact report" with Lovelady *5 July 1978 Document 009727*. Unless it is classified, this document is *nowhere to be found on this good Earth*. Outside contact reports were used by the HSCA to document supplemental information which was not taken under oath, perhaps in a telephone conversation. Is there any tangible and attributable evidence to support this conclusion? The HSCA reference traces back to Josiah Thompson's 1966 volume where the author cites Lovelady's Warren Commission *unsigned* deposition of 7 April 1964 (6H338-339), Wesley Frazier's 22H647 (CE1381), Sara Stanton in CE1381, and Bill Shelley's 6H328. Danny Arce's obviously coached *and unsigned* (6H365-67) Warren Commission testimony has also been used in other articles to corroborate Lovelady's presence in the doorway,[22] but for some unknown reason, Thompson refrained from using his testimony as a reference. Thompson finishes the Lovelady issue by quoting what he "told" CBS News regarding the shirt, and does not give a date, nor does he offer any tangible evidence of this "interview," which must be regarded as hearsay.[23] Surely CBS would have videotaped such an important statement! This was the first time Lovelady "changed" his mind about the shirt, which was now "long-sleeved and patterned in large squares."[24] Given what we now know about CBS, Time Life, and other media giants during the Cold War, and their intelligence connections,[25] these alleged statements by Lovelady are highly suspect and unlikely.

Similarly, most Warren Commission testimony, statements and depositions regarding the movements and exact positions of Lovelady and Oswald in the doorway have the earmarks of having been cooked. Carolyn Arnold's— O.V. Campbell's secretary— testimony was tweaked to say she saw Oswald on the first floor at 12:15 PM instead of the true time of 12:25 PM.[26] Victoria Adams's— an employee of Scott Foresman and Company, housed in the TSBD building—testimony was changed to discredit her statement of having reached the first floor via the back stairway in the time frame she had established of 90 to 120 seconds where she, according to the Commission, met Shelley and Lovelady on the first floor.[27] Never mind that Lovelady and Shelley testified they immediately raced to the railroad tracks, and after watching the police search cars in the parking lot "for a little while," re-entered the building via the rear entrance where the loading docks were located.[28]

Her coworker Sandra Styles, who was with Ms. Adams during and after the assassination, was very superficially interviewed by the Warren Commission.[29] Young and impressionable kids like Danny Arce and Buell Wesley Frazier—both only 19-years-old—were totally intimidated to say whatever was needed to conform to the government's version.[30] For example, Sarah Stanton's "affidavit" is part of a 73-witness "bundle" (CE1381) taken by the FBI which seems to have been put out with a cookie cutter. Joe Molina, as we saw in the previous chapter, was paid a visit by the top brass of the DPD and the assistant district attorney at 1:30 AM the night after the assassination.[31] The Commission did not ask any witnesses to look at an enlargement of Altgens6, and they were only interested in asking them their race, where they were, their duties and when they left the TSBD at the time of the assassination.[32] Of the few who were known to have contact with Lee Oswald, they were only asked when was the *last* time they had seen him, and never were they asked specifically if he was in the doorway.[33] The Commission did not "bring Lovelady with his shirt and photograph him in the doorway" to try to duplicate Altgens6 and dispel the rumors that were going on from coast-to-coast.[34]

Lingering Questions About Lovelady

There remains much to be investigated about Lovelady—what exactly were his activities and assignments at Andrews AFB as a member of the base supply squadron; was he proficient in the handling of guns and rifles?

According to TEC counselor/interviewer Laura Kittrell, who spent 30 years working for the TEC, the TSBD company was famous for employing only "clean" candidates, and frowned upon workers who had been dishonorably discharged from the service, not to mention someone with a criminal record such as Lovelady's.[35] So how did he end up working with the TSBD company as a running felon?

How did he manage to convince O.V. Campbell to advance him $75 so he could pay his fine off? If he couldn't pay the $75, how did he secure the $1,000 personal recognizance bond in Dallas?

Why was he not fired for being arrested at his place of employment, thereby embarrassing the company? Did Campbell ever find out about the details of his felony and subsequent court-martial and discharge? Was there a prior relationship there, and how was he able to start his trucking business in Denver given the background and notoriety he now possessed?

Could Oswald, Lovelady, Larry Crafard, Richard Case Nagell, and perhaps even Thomas Arthur Valle[36] been steered and influenced because of the threats of dishonorable discharge? Was this some patsy's club from which the conspirators could draw from at will? Finally, why did Patricia Lovelady attempt to sell the checkered shirt to Harold Weisberg for $5,000?[37]

Why did Kenneth Brooten, counsel for the HSCA, later become Lovelady's personal attorney? (see appendix) These questions obviously need to be scrutinized by researchers.

In a strange twist of fate, Special Agent Francis X. O'Neill, Jr. of Sibert and O'Neill fame,[38] was one of the FBI agents who investigated the Andrews AFB gun running case and took at least one statement on 15 September 1960.[39]

ENDNOTES

1. maryferrell.org/mffweb/archive/docset/getList.do?docSetId=1828
2. Weisberg, Harold, *Whitewash II* (1966), "The Lovelady Diversion," p. 241, and, "The Lovelady Caper," p. 295
3. Shaw, J. Gary, *Cover-Up: The Governmental Conspiracy to Conceal the Facts About the Public Execution of John Kennedy* (1976), p. 41. Original reference to *Whitewash II* by Harold Weisberg, "The Lovelady Caper," p. 295. An FBI report dated 2 March 1964, documented the session where Lovelady was photographed in the vertically striped shirt at the FBI in Dallas on 29 February 1964.
4. CE369 (see appendix v) (Author's comment: Talk about leading a witness!)
5. WC6H338-339
6. Bonafede, Dom, "The Picture With a Life of Its Own," *New York Herald Tribune*, 24 May 1964, pp. 5- 6
7. *Six Seconds in Dallas: A Micro-Study of the Kennedy Assassination* (1967), p. 227
8. HSCA Vol VI 287 (see appendix iv)
9. *The Washington Post*, 28 September 1960, "8 Andrews Airmen Arrested by FBI," also see aarc-fbi587-04_0016_0006, FBI report dated 6 October 1960
10. Ibid.
11. aarc-fbi587-04_0002_0006 and aarc-fbi587-04_0002_0007, 11 January 1963
12. NPRC letter, 17 October 2012, in response to Standard Form 180, Request Pertaining to Military Records
13. aarc-fbi587-04_0002_0008
14. aarc-fbi587-04_0002_0003 and aarc-fbi587-04_0002_0004
15. Harold Weisberg: Grand Jury Proceedings New Orleans 28 April 1967, p. 24. "BY A JUROR: Q. You think Lovelady was lying? A. Yes. I think there was no question about it. I think everybody who was handling this knew he was lying. May I suggest this also to you, on February 29 they had this after Lovelady was on the stand, there were those pictures in their file and there were no questions asked as to whether Lovelady told the truth." The Weisberg Collection. Hood College, Frederick, MD, USA
16. Schaeffer, Roy, "Was Lee Harvey Oswald the Person in the James Altgens Photograph?"
17. Weisberg, *Whitewash II* (1966), pp. 299, 303
18. *Dallas Times Herald*, 18 January 1979 article, says he died "Sunday" which would establish the date of 14 January 1979
19. Ibid.

20. mrholga.com/2012/05/texas-school-book-depository-worker-billy-n-lovelady

21. FBI report dated 2 March 1964, taken by Robert P. Gemberling and Emory E. Horton on 29 February 1964, file DL 100-10461 (see appendix ii) (Could these two FBI agents have been trying to "blow the whistle" on this thing by documenting and locking in Loverlady's shirt?)

22. Knuth, Magen, "Was Oswald in the Doorway of the Depository at the time of the JFK Assassination?"

23. Thompson, Josiah, *Six Seconds in Dallas*, p. 227

24. Ibid.

25. Fetzer, Jim, "JFK, the CIA and *The New York Times*," jamesfetzer. blogspot.com/2015/09/by-jim-fetzer-central-intelligence.html

26. Fetzer, Jim, *Murder in Dealy Plaza* (2000), pp. 29, 366

27. Earnest, Barry, *The Girl on the Stairs,* 2010 Kindle Version, p. 348 (The object of this, of course, to manipulate her and Sandra Styles's timeline of not seeing Oswald come down the same stairs from the sixth floor seconds after the assassination.)

28. WC6H330 Shelley and WC6H340 Lovelady

29. Ibid pp. 350-353 (She was never formally interviewed, only a short statement which is included in CE1381.)

30. O'Toole, George, *The Assassination Tapes* (1975), pp. 201-203 (Frazier lied on many key points about 22 November 1963.)

31. WC6H368

32. Weisberg, Harold, *Whitewash II* (1966), pp. 296-97

33. Ibid.

34. Ibid.

35. Laura Kittrell unpublished manuscript, p. 68 (Kittrell worked at the TEC for more than 30 years.)

36. Douglass, James, *JFK and the Unspeakable* (2007), p. 202. NPRC Crafard discharged from U.S. Army due to unsuitability, character and behavioral disorders. The story of Richard Case Nagell, who shot up a bank in El Paso two months before the assassination to make sure he was in custody when it took place, is described in Dick Russell's *The Man Who Knew Too Much*.

37. Harold Weisberg to Roger Feinman letter dated 18 September 1988, The Weisberg Collection. Hood College, Frederick, MD, USA

38. Lifton, David, *Best Evidence* (1988), pp. 101-108

39. Statement of John Reid Barnes, 15 September 1960, aarc-fbi587-04_0016_0049

APPENDIX i: Lovelady timeline according to FBI documents (September 1960- January 1963) at maryferrell.org and FOIA requests to the NPRC

1. Billy Nolan Lovelady enlisted in the USAF 3 December 1957 (NPRC)

2. In 1960, Lovelady was a member of military personnel attached to the 1001th Base Supply Squadron, Andrews AFB (aarc-fbi587-04_0002_0006) Lovelady's rank was Airman Second Class. (aarc-fbi587-04_0016_0007)

3. On 3 or 4 September 1960, Andrews AFB reported three Smith & Wesson stolen revolvers. On 9 September 1960, all suspects were identified by witnesses in a lineup conducted by the OSI (aarc-fbi587-04_0016-006).

4. 26 September 1960 complaint against Lovelady, and his two friends, Airmen Williams and Crouse that on or about early September 1960 they were accused of stealing revolvers. Williams admitted theft of guns, Crouse admitted manipulating records pertaining to the guns, and Lovelady admitted sale of the guns. These were very serious charges. (aarc-fbi587-04_0002_0007)

5. 10 January 1961, Lovelady charged with two counts of violating Title 18 U.S. Code Section 641, which pertains to the theft of public money, property or records. (aarc-fbi587-04_0013_0003)

6. 10 February 1961, Lovelady appeared in U.S. District Court in Baltimore, MD for arraignment (aarc-fbi587-04_0008_0007)

7. 17 March 1961, Lovelady arraigned and entered plea of not guilty (Ibid).

8. 11 April 1961, Lovelady entered plea of guilty and fined $200 payable in installments of $25; indictments dismissed. (aarc-fbi587-04_0008_0003)

9. 14 June 1961, Lovelady quickly court-martialed by his superiors and separated from the USAF with a duty status of "discharge." (NPRC letter dated 17 October 2012 in response to Standard Form 180, Request Pertaining to Military Records FOIA) After 3.5 years in the service, Lovelady was not allowed to complete his six-year tour of duty and was again a civilian.

10. October 1961, Lovelady stopped paying $25 monthly installments of his fine.

11. 16 December 1961, Lovelady started working at the TSBD while they were still located in the Dal-Tex Building. (CE1381) The company moved to 411 Elm St. during the summer of 1963.

12. 7 December 1962, U.S. Attorney Robert J. Carson reported Lovelady only paid $125 of his fine. His last payment had been made over a year ago and his office started looking for him. Lovelady was nowhere to be found and all letters were returned undeliverable. Judge Tomsen issued a bench warrant for his arrest and $1,000 bail. (aarc-fbi587-04_0002_0007)

13. 26 December 1962, Lovelady considered a fugitive by the FBI (aarc-fbi587-04_0002_0005)

14. 7 January 1963, Lovelady arrested at the TSBD by FBI agents and incarcerated in the Dallas County Jail. O.V. Campbell offered to pay remaining balance of MD fine if charges were to be dropped, and Lovelady released on $1,000 personal recognizance bond and ordered to appear 9 January 1963. (aarc-fbi587-04_0002_0008)

15. 9 January 1963, Lovelady appeared before U.S. Commissioner Hill and after several communications between MD and Dallas, and U.S. District Court of MD agreed to dismiss the warrant once the $75 was received. He was released on own recognizance. (Ibid)

APPENDIX ii: FBI Lovelady Statement of 2 March 1964

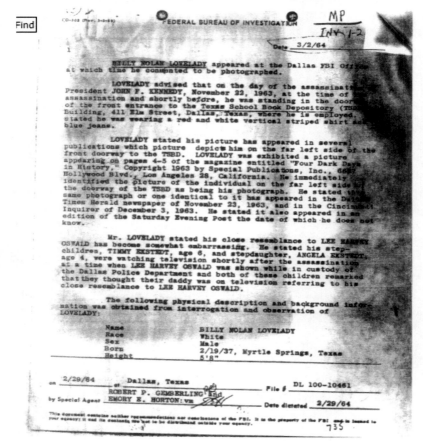

APPENDIX iii: HSCA Vol. VI, p. 287 with reference 252

287

to the Warren Commission after Lovelady had been interviewed and photographed in 1964 by FBI agents, (*251*) Lovelady was reported to have been wearing a short-sleeved red and white, vertically striped shirt. (See fig. IV–67.) Lovelady later explained that when he was interviewed and photographed by the FBI, he had not been told to wear the same shirt he had worn on the day of the assassination and that, in fact, he had been wearing a long-sleeved, plaid shirt when he was standing in the Texas School Book Depository doorway. (*252*) (See fig. IV–67.)

318

(*238*) Repeatability of Height Measurements from Photos and Other Sources, a report by the House Select Committee on Assassinations. By W. K. Hartmann, April 1978 (JFK Document 007221).

(*239*) Testimony of Cecil Kirk, Sept. 25, 1978, IV House Select Committee on Assassinations-JFK Hearings, 362–365.

(*240*) Ibid.

(*241*) Ibid.

(*242*) Clyde Snow and Joan Williams, "Variation in Premortem Statural Measurements Compared to Statural Estimates of Skeletal Remains," Journal of Forensic Sciences, October 1971, vol. 16, No. 4, p. 456.

(*243*) Testimony of James W. Altgens, July 22, 1964, 7 Warren Commission Hearings, 517; the photographic evidence panel correlated the Altgens photograph in time to Zapruder frame 255.

(*244*) Warren report, p. 644.

(*245*) Testimony of Billy Nolan Lovelady, Apr. 7, 1964, 6 Warren Commission Hearings, 338–39.

(*246*) Testimony of William H. Shelley, Apr. 7, 1964, 6 Warren Commission Hearings, 328; statement of Buell W. Frazier, Mar. 18, 1964 (CE 1381), 22 Warren Commission Hearings, 647; statement of Sarah D. Stanton, Mar. 18, 1968 (CE 1381), 22 Warren Commission Hearings, 675.

(*247*) See ref. 2, Lane, pp. 354–356; Shaw, pp. 39–42.

(*248*) See ref. 2, Meagher, p. 362.

(*249*) CE 1408, May 24, 1964, New York Herald-Tribune story, 22 Warren Commission Hearings, 793–94; see ref. 2, Model and Groden, pp. 147–49; Meagher, p. 363; and Thompson, pp. 225–27.

(*250*) Ibid.

(*251*) Letter from FBI Director J. Edgar Hoover to J. Lee Rankin, Mar. 9, 1964, Commission document 457.

(*252*) See ref. 2, Thompson, p. 227; outside contact report with Billy Nolan Lovelady, July 5, 1978 House Select Committee on Assassinations (JFK Document 009727).

(*253*) Memorandum from Robert Groden to the House Select Committee on Assassinations, July 21, 1978 (JFK Document 010209).

(*254*) See ref. 210, RIT report, p. 36.

APPENDIX iv: Commission Exhibit 369

COMMISSION EXHIBIT 369

* *

Billy Nolan Lovelady, 41, the Oswald look-alike who also worked with Oswald at the Texas School Book Depository, died at his home in Denver, Colorado, of an "apparent heart attack". No autopsy was performed.

At the very instant the President was shot, a photograph of the Presidential limousine was snapped by James Altgens. It showed a man who strongly resembled Oswald standing in the front doorway of the Book Depository, dressed just as

= 4 =

Oswald was dressed when he was arrested for the murder of Officer Tippit. But the Warren Commission accepted Lovelady's testimony that it was he, Lovelady, and not Lee Harvey Oswald, in the doorway, thus disposing of a sticky problem for the Commission.

Lovelady's family attorney, Kenneth Brooten, said that Lovelady "was under a lot of stress. He paid for it dearly." Brooten and Lovelady's wife, Patricia, indicated that alleged "harassment" of Lovelady by assassination researchers had somehow precipitated or aggravated Lovelady's condition. Interestingly enough, Brooten said that he became acquainted with Lovelady while he, Brooten, was working as a counsel for the Assassinations Committee, and went on to become his lawyer.

HSCA photographic consultant Robert Groden, a long time Warren Commission critic and author, said of the man in the doorway (in the Altgens photograph) recently, "I could prove to anybody that it was Lovelady."

Maybe so, but Groden did not probe the more perturbing question: what was Lovelady doing in Oswald's clothes, and how and when did they switch back?

* *

Grassy Knoll Gazette (725.pdf, 6 March 1979)

7

The HSCA Activities of Kenneth Brooten and Robert Groden

"The Select Committee on Assassinations was born in the septic tank of House politics."

—Gaeton Fonzi, *The Last Investigation* (1993), p. 175

The House Select Committee on Assassinations (HSCA) bill, which reopened the JFK assassination and probed the Martin Luther King assassination, was introduced in 1976 by Congressmen Henry Gonzalez (D-TX) and Thomas Downing (D-VA). Gonzalez had been in the motorcade of 22 November 1963, where JFK's limousine was ambushed by gunfire.

After the bill was approved, and it was time to convene the Committee, Gonzalez was passed over as chairman in favor of Downing, even though the latter was not running for reelection in 1976. Gonzalez was none too happy with this and made sure people knew about his feelings.[1] Philadelphia attorney Richard A. Sprague was brought on by Gonzalez and Downing as director and chief counsel of the Committee. Sprague was director and chief counsel for only six months[2] and submitted his resignation on—of all dates—the night of the death of George De Mohrenschildt in Florida.[3]

The controversy surrounding his resignation was due to the fact that he and his staff intended to investigate all intelligence ties to Oswald, and he refused to be bound and limited by any disclosure agreements which would preclude any access to sensitive data or witnesses within any U.S. government agency.

One of the legal counsels Gonzalez hired was a young 32-year-old Florida attorney by the name of Kenneth E. Brooten, from Gainesville, Florida, who had been an assistant on Capitol Hill to Gonzalez.[4]

The activities of HSCA legal counsel Brooten provide for interesting reading. This chapter explores and contrasts two of Brooten's known assignments: the Mexico City trip and the Aurora, Colorado trip.

In attempting to write a timeline of Brooten's short-lived tenure on Richard Sprague's staff, one is limited by the fact that records are missing which correspond to the early months of the committee.[5] As far as we can tell from surviving documents, Brooten began actively working for the committee around 20 October 1976, where he is mentioned in a CIA communication as the originator of a telephone call to the CIA's Office of Legislative Counsel asking for unspecified information.[6]

Eight days later, Brooten is mentioned in a letter by Jacqueline Hess to the FBI Office of Legislative Liaison informing the FBI that he was a recent addition to the staff of the HSCA.[7] (see appendix)

Because of the charged political atmosphere, the expectation to provide immediate, dramatic results, and under the constant threat of losing funding for the committee, Sprague decided to toss his Hail Mary pass and tackle one of the most controversial aspects of the case against Oswald: the supposed Mexico City visit of 27-28 September 1963. Brooten was involved in three extremely crucial facets of the game plan:

1. The deposition of David Atlee Phillips (pp. 119-131), which was taken under closed executive session on Saturday, 27 November 1976.

The document pertaining to this deposition was withheld a total of 86 times before it was finally made public on 22 September 1998, because of the President John F. Kennedy Assassination Records Collection Act of 1992 (the JFK Records Act) and the mandate of the AARB.[8]

2. The investigation and interviews of Boris and Anne Tarasoff, who at the time of Oswald's supposed visit to Mexico City were employed by the CIA as Russian language translators and transcribers. The interviews were recorded by Brooten in Guadalajara, Mexico, on 29-30 November 1976.[9]

This trip yielded a 109-page report which was not fully released until 26 March 1997 and had previously been postponed for declassification a total of 45 times.[10]

3. The interview of U.S. Ambassador Joseph John Jova on 2 December 1976 in Mexico City, regarding possible contact with the Cuban Embassy regarding information on Lee Oswald. Since there weren't any diplomatic relations with Cuba, this would have to be handled indirectly through the Swiss government.

The Phillips Deposition

On Saturday, 27 November 1976, the closed executive testimony[11] of the CIA's former chief of operations for the Western hemisphere David Atlee Phillips, was taken for the HSCA by Richard Sprague and Kenneth Brooten, in the presence of Congressmen Richardson Preyer and Charles Thone, both of whom contributed some very minor questions.

The enigmatic Phillips had directed CIA operations in Cuba, Mexico and the Dominican Republic[12] and was in Cuba in the late 1950s when the cauldron of the Cuban revolution was boiling over, and was a veteran of the Bay of Pigs operation.[13]

On the recommendation of Desmond Fitzgerald in July or August 1963, he was named head of Cuban Operations of the Mexico City station, and was there at the time of Oswald's supposed visit to the Russian Embassy and Cuban Consulate.[14]

Phillips's HSCA testimony was preceded by a late-night session the night before, where Sprague's staff laid out the outline of what would be covered in his deposition.[15]

Even today there are many areas of redaction still masked in its 135 pages of testimony. A careful analysis of this document typifies Sprague's thoroughness, inquisitive disposition, and his ability to uncover the multiple layers of complexity of the intelligence trade, and more importantly, his ability to follow the chain-of-command, which ultimately seemed to lead to the upper echelons of Langley. It is entirely possible that Sprague's fate could have been sealed by the way he performed during this deposition.

Interestingly, *the very next day*, Sunday, 28 November, Brooten and Jonathan Blackmer flew to Mexico City,[16] apparently under the guise of finding out about any Oswald contact with the Cuban Embassy there. It is quite obvious that Sprague wished to follow up portions of Phillips's testimony with actual field work and interviews before some unforeseen event.

In fact, Brooten's and Blackmer's very first order of business was to locate former Russian language translators Boris and Anne Tarasoff. According to a CIA cable, Brooten was not supposed to speak to former CIA personnel, and it was so stated in this copy of the cablegram dated 3 December 1976:

1. IN SECOND CONVERSATION WITH[   ] WHILE WAITING FOR
APPOINTMENT WITH AMBASSADOR JOVA ON 3 DECEMBER, MR. KENNETH
E. BROOTEN, JR,, HOUSE SELECT COMMITTEE COUNSEL, SAID THAT
THE PURPOSE OF THEIR TRIP TO MEXICO WAS SOLELY IN CONNECTION
WITH POSSIBLE CONTACT WITH CUBAN EMBASSY (SEE REF B) AND THA
HE AND MR. BLACKMER DID NOT INTERVIEW NOR HAD ANY PLANS TO
INTERVIEW FORMER AGENCY EMPLOYEES IN MEXICO.

A close examination of two memoranda found in the Tarasoff document shows how meticulous Brooten was in reporting his day-to-day work and itinerary to Richard Sprague. Brooten and Blackmer immediately made plans to fly to Guadalajara to meet the Tarasoffs. This, of course, ran counter to what the CIA had surmised the purpose of their trip had been:

"He [Brooten] and Mr. Blackmer did not interview nor had any plans to interview former agency employees in Mexico," reads the cable shown above.

Anyone could interpret the above as a conscious effort by Sprague and his legions to mislead the CIA about the true nature of Brooten's trip to Mexico City. But why? The truth of the matter is that by the time this cable was sent, Brooten and Blackmer had already interviewed "former agency employees" in Mexico. As noted below, both Boris and Anne Tarasoff had indeed worked for "The Company":

Mr. Brooten: And, at which, how long did you work for the Company?

Mr. Tarasoff: About 15 years.

Mr. Brooten: All right sir. And in 1963 what was your duty station?

Mr. Tarasoff: Well, I came here from Washington, D.C. It must have been the 6th of June, if I'm not mistaken.

Mrs. Tarasoff: The 5th of June.

Mr. Tarasoff: The 5th of June 1963.

Mr. Brooten: All right sir. And, were you on temporary assignment then or what?

Mr. Tarasoff: No, that was to be my permanent assignment. By permanent, you put in two years. And if you are not satisfactory, they ship you back.

Mr. Brooten: All right.

Mr. Tarasoff: But I managed to survive for [redacted] years in the same capacity.

Mr. Brooten: All right sir, who did you relieve in your job when you came?

Mr. Tarasoff: George Miscow was my predecessor.

Mr. Brooten: And where did you work specifically when you came from Washington to Mexico City.

Mr. Tarasoff: Do you mean on permanent assignment?

Mr. Brooten: Yes sir, I mean when you were changed, where did you work, for what department or . . .

Mr. Tarasoff: I don't know which department.

Mr. Brooten: Was it with, were you a translator sir?

Mr. Tarasoff: I was translator and transcriber at the same time. There is a difference, sometimes they use two people for those two jobs.

The transcript bears out that Tarasoff eventually acknowledged that as far as he was concerned, *it would have been impossible to confirm and prove that Oswald had visited the Soviet Embassy*:

Mr. Blackmer: This officer determined that Oswald had been at the Soviet Embassy on 26 or 28 September 1963, and had talked with Kostikov, a member of the counselor section. Now do you know for a fact whether he was at the Soviet Embassy?

Mr. Tarasoff: We could never know that.

Mrs. Tarasoff: No.

Mr. Blackmer: You never knew that. And do you know for a fact whether or not he talked to Kostikov on the telephone?

Mr. Tarasoff: Well, as I said before, it's a very doubtful proposition and we could jump at conclusions all weekend.

Mr. Blackmer: But, you don't know for a fact that he did?

Mr. Tarasoff: Not as a fact.

This information alone refutes any of the lone nut, communist-driven scenarios with which Warren Commission apologists have characterized Oswald.

Moreover, it suggests a reason why the Tarasoff document was repressed for over 20 years.

These two memoranda, published here in their entirety, show how detailed and meticulous Brooten normally was in submitting reports to Richard Sprague.

Furthermore, Gaeton Fonzi wrote how most staff had to practically work for nothing due to funding problems and how they had to wait after submitting expense reports for reimbursement.[17]

It would be very safe to infer that to get paid, anyone working for the committee would have made sure to document every last second working on behalf of the committee.

MEMORANDUM

TO: Richard A. Sprague

FROM: Kenneth E. Brooten, Jr.

IN RE: Mexico City Trip -- Brooten & Blackmer   11-28-76 to 12-4-76

1.   We initially had reservations to depart on an American Airlines Flight at 7:15 a.m. on Sunday, November 28, 1976. Jonathan had called American to confirm the fact that we only had to show our official passports to get a tourist visa for Mexico. We arrived at the airport at 6:30 a.m. and were advised that they could not issue Mexican Tourist Cards on Official Passports. I called the operations desk at the Department of State who said the Official Passport was proof of American Citizenship and that should be sufficient. American Airlines employees would not accept that so rather than create a confrontation as to who we were we took a later flight and traveled on our personal passports.

2.   Upon our arrival in Mexico City we were met by William J. Roche, the Chief of Security for the Embassy. The Embassy had reserved rooms for us.

3.   On Monday, November 29, 1976, Mr. Roche made airline reservations for us to Guadajalara -- it is a 1 hour flight and approximately 355 miles from Mexico City. He arranged to have us met by Mathias Ortwein the Consul General. Mr. Ortwein made arrangements for our hotel and offered us the use of his personal vehicle.

4.   We made initial contact with Boris Tarasoff at approximately 3:30 p.m. His wife was not at home and had been in Guadajalara for 5 or 6 days at their daughters taking care of her sick children. Our interview with Mr. Tarasoff lasted until approximately 9:00 p.m. when we went to Guadajalara to meet with his wife. We interviewed her until approximately 11:00 p.m.

5.   Following our telephone conversation on Tuesday, November 30, we taped the formal interview which is transcribed. Jonathan is preparing a separate Memorandum on the specific areas of inquiry which I asked him to make.

6.   We returned to Mexico City on Thursday, December 2, 1976, and took up the matters at the Embassy which are the subject of my separate Memoranda. We returned to Washington on Saturday, December 4, 1976.

MEMORANDUM   12-5-76

TO: Richard A. Sprague

FROM: Kenneth E. Brooten, Jr.

IN RE: Contacts with Ambassador John Joseph Jova, U. S. Embassy Mexico
         City and [   ]

1.   I initially met with William Calderhead, Deputy Chief of Mission
         U. S. Embassy, Mexico City and advised him of the following:

         a)   I had received information from the Committee Staff indicating
              that someone had contacted them advising that the Cuban Embassy
              personnel in Mexico City would be willing to meet with us and
              provide us with the information which they had on Lee Harvey
              Oswald.

         b)   I had not been advised of the source of the information by
              the Committee Staff and I did not know the reliability of
              the source.

         c)   I had discussed the matter with you for "instructions" and
              had been advised by you that I should take the matter up with
              the Ambassador.

         Mr. Calderhead suggested that we make a formal contact through the
         Department of State and have them go through the Swiss, since the
         Swiss represent the interest of the U. S. Government in Havana.

2.   I met with Ambassador Jova at his residence on December 2, 1976, and
         advised him of the foregoing. I also advised that while the Committee
         would be most interested in obtaining any information we could from
         the Cubans we were very much aware of the complications which could
         arise should the information prove to be erroneous.

         I further advised the Ambassador that we did not want to do anything
         which could cause embarrassment to the U. S. Government or the
         Congress and that we wanted to proceed with his consent and advice.
         The Ambassador advised:

         a)   The official U. S. position is that there are to be no official
              contacts with the Government of Cuba.

         b)   He knows the Ambassador from Cuba on a social basis and could
              make a discrete approach and inquiry.

         c)   He would have to get "instructions" from Washington to make an
              approach and inquiry from the Cuban Ambassador.

         d)   He very much appreciated our consulting with him since it was a
              very delicate matter.

(Author's note: The thoroughness of these reports is absolutely
impressive and mind-boggling.)

         I suggested that possibly the C.I.A. could have some source either
         direct or indirect which could verify whether or not the Cubans wanted
         to meet with us.

He stated that he had not discussed our visit with [ ] out with my consent would do so. He offered to have the [ ] come to his residence or have us meet him at his residence.

3. I met with [ ] and advised him of the situation and requested his assistance and judgement. He advised:

   a) That some of his people had informal contacts with the Cubans and could make an inquiry to see if a "responsible official" of the Cuban Embassy would meet with us. To do so he would have to get "instructions" from C.I.A. Headquarters - but at my request he would proceed to do so.

   b) He said that the Cubans would probably have to go to Havana for "instructions" before they would reply. He further stated that most of the information would probably be in Havana.

   c) I asked if he had any other method of determining the validity of the information and he said that he was not prepared to confirm whether there were wiretaps at this time. Later in the conversation he said as a result of the story - a copy of which is attached that the Cubans had been saying less on the phone.

   d) We agreed to meet with the Ambassador the next day to discuss how to proceed.

4. On Friday, December 3, 1976, I again met with the Ambassador and [ ] had not yet received a reply to his request for instructions," from C.I.A. Headquarters and again advised that the Cubans would most likely go to Havana for "instructions" before replying.

   Ambassador Jova said he would seek instructions from State on making an informal social contact with the Cuban Ambassador but suggested that that would take time. He said the most proper method would be to go through the Swiss and State here in Washington.

   I advised that while we certainly wanted to obtain the information that we wanted to use the most conservative approach so as not to create an incident. The Ambassador again expressed his appreciation for our sensitivity to a "delicate situation."

5. ACTION TO BE TAKEN:

   a) Contact C.I.A. Headquarters to follow up on [ ] request for "instructions."

   b) Contact the Department of State and request that they go through the Swiss with a formal contact to the Cubans in Havana and follow up on Ambassador Jova's request for instructions.

MEMORANDUM 12-5-76
Page 3

   c) Both of these follow up actions should, in my judgement, be initiated immediately.

   d) If we can confirm the contact with the Cubans it will be necessary for me to return to Mexico City, and I would purpose to do so as soon as we receive a confirmation.

6. Jonothan Blackmer accompanied me to each of the meetings.

Almost a year and a half later, Tarasoff was still adamant about not positively identifying Oswald as the man speaking in the Mexico City surveillance tapes. Here is a passage from his actual HSCA testimony:

> Mr. Genzman. I am referring to this document and this
> document alone at the moment. From this particular document
> which relates to a conversation, were you able to determine
> that the speaker was Lee Harvey Oswald?
>
> Mr. Tarasoff. I would have no idea who was talking at
> that time.   Boris Tarasoff 4/12/78 HSCA testimony page 1-25

The Aurora, Colorado Trip

In mid-November 1976, a scant two weeks after Kenneth Brooten began working for the Committee, and two weeks b*efore his trip to Mexico City,* Brooten and HSCA photographic consultant Robert Groden traveled to Aurora, Colorado, to see Billy Lovelady and photograph him in his checkered colored shirt. The controversy generated by the man in the doorway in Altgens6 by early critics of the Warren Commission, particularly Harold Weisberg, prompted the Committee to try to dispel the continued rumors that the man in the doorway had been Oswald. One of only two documents that exist today that corroborate this visit happens to bethis HSCA "Audio Accession Preservation List," which inventories four—or two—(see below image under "Remarks") original microcassettes containing approximately five hours of interview material with Billy and Patricia Lovelady. These tapes, were recently retrieved and digitized by researcher Karl Golovin.[18]

AUDIO ACCESSION PRESERVATION LIST

RG _233 JFK_   RESTRICTED   3

Subject No. #	TITLE – DATE – DESCRIPTION	Running Time	Disc 16"	12"	Reel 10"	7"	Orig. Cass.	Orig. Other	New Mag.	Ref. Cass.	Remarks
.001914	Lila Hurtado (Libra) speaking on the "Judas Movement" also Dr. John Happas at Hypnosis Motivation Institute, Van Nuys, Ca Dec. 9, 1976	50:00					1		1	1	5" 3-3/4 ips
.002224	R. C. Nagell and C. W. Lynn Interview	120:00					1		1	1	
.002225	Billy Nolan Lovelady and Patricia Lovelady Interview (Brooten)	5 hrs?					4		4	4	2-orig micro-cassettes

This discussion will review the first tape, where Brooten and Groden showed the Loveladys an underexposed copy of a frame from the John Martin film and where Lovelady described his movements immediately after the assassination, and are pertinent to the timing of the Martin film that requires our scrutiny.

The John Martin Film

The DCA motion picture compendium collated the individual films of 18 amateur photographers who made their film available to try to make a profit for their owners.[19] The original commercialized product came out in 1964.[20] Wolper Productions purchased the rights of the film shortly thereafter.[21] What is known as the John Martin film is included in the DCA film, and shows, among other things, part of what was going on in front of the TSBD a few minutes after the assassination.[22] In the first incarnation of the DCA film, the Martin film was mostly underexposed,[23] which rendered the images much darker than normal and made their study that much more difficult. Harold Weisberg noticed the underexposure and surmised that this happened right at the time when Martin was filming the entrance of the doorway, as Martin inadvertently changed the exposure setting of his 8mm camera.[24] For all the pages that Richard Trask dedicates to the Martin film in his 1994 book *Pictures of the Pain,* he never once mentions anything about its under exposure.

Initially, the FBI did not even know about the existence of the Martin film. The undeveloped film was immediately secured by *Life* magazine the day of the assassination and sent to N.Y. for "development and review."[25] The film remained there until 9 December 1963, when at the behest of Postal Inspector Harry Holmes, the FBI decided it might be time to develop the film and study its pertinence to the events of 22 November.[26] By 11 December 1963, the FBI was finally documenting the existence of the Martin film:

```
DL 89-43
NY 89-75
JPO

RE:  MOVIES TAKEN BY JOHN MARTIN,
     DALLAS, TEXAS
     NOVEMBER 22, 1963

          On December 11, 1963, the Dallas Division advised
that JOHN MARTIN, Superintendent of Safety, United States
Post Office, Dallas, Texas, took a roll of 8 mm color
movies of the Presidential motorcade in Dallas on
November 22, 1963.  According to MARTIN, the movies were
taken of the motorcade as it neared the spot where President
KENNEDY was assassinated and he thought possibly he had a
shot of the window in the Texas School Book Depository
```

Building from which the fatal shots were fired. According
to information available to the Dallas Division, the film
was in the possession of Life Magazine, New York City.

On December 17, 1963, the film taken by MARTIN
was obtained by SA ROBERT J. LAWSON from DICK POLLARD, Time
and Life, Inc., 50th Street and 6th Avenue, New York City.
On the same date the film was forwarded to the Federal Bureau
of Investigation, Washington, D. C. for review.

In 1993, John R. Woods II wrote the most important and complete study of the JFK photographic record ever published, titled, *JFK Assassination Photographs—Comprehensive listing of the Photographic Evidence Relating to the Assassination of President John F. Kennedy.* Wood wrote about the Martin film:

"Footage shot by John Martin prior, during and after the assassination. Sadly, the majority of this important footage was underexposed. Because of this, *additional footage may have been edited out from the original film.*" [Emphasis added][27]

What could have been so mysterious about this film? Why did Life magazine keep the undeveloped film for almost three weeks before handing it over to the FBI? Could part of it have been edited out, as Wood suggests above? Did *Life* magazine have the general task of snapping up as much film as possible, which is exactly what they did with the crown jewel of assassination films, the Zapruder film?

In mid-1967, Richard Sprague (no relation to HSCA Chief Counsel Sprague) viewed the Martin film and reported to Weisberg that it showed men running away from the grassy knoll behind the picket fence.[28] This gives us a pretty good indication of the timing of this film.

Richard Trask wrote that Martin ". . . remained near the Book Depository for some 10 minutes taking film of the activities in front of the building, including witness Charles Brehm being interviewed, cops holding shotguns, views of Houston and Elm Streets including the entrance of the Book Depository. . ."[29] This information fixes the estimated timestamp of the sequence of the doorway to be approximately 10 minutes after the assassination.

During the life of the HSCA, and in his attempt to disprove Oswald as Doorway Man, Groden had access to, and worked with, among other negatives and films, the Martin film:

(763) This contradiction [about Doorway Man] was partially resolved by photo-optical work performed by Robert Groden, a Warren

Commission critic and photographic consultant to the committee. During his work with the committee, Groden made photographically enhanced enlargements of the original 35 mm black and white Altgens negative and frames of the Bell,Martin, and Hughes color motion picture films, which also showed the spectator in the doorway, and detected a pattern of lines that correspond in pattern and color more closely to Lovelady's plaid shirt than to Oswald's tweed-patterned shirt. (See Figure IV-67 in appendix.)[30]

The question that begs to be answered is, why did Groden, as the HSCA photographic expert, elect to show Lovelady such a low quality, underexposed print of the Martin film? For his book, *The Killing of a President: The Complete Photographic Record of the JFK Assassination, the Conspiracy, and the Cover-up* (1993), Groden published a very clear, black and white image of the man in question, which Harold Weisberg harshly criticized.[31] Later, in 2003, it was Robert Groden himself who distributed the brightness-adjusted Martin film sequence in his DVD video *The Assassination Films: JFK, The Case For Conspiracy.*[32] As noted above, it was the darker, underexposed photograph the one which was shown Lovelady on 13 November 1976.

Returning to our discussion of Brooten's interview of Lovelady, where Lovelady admits he did not see Lee Oswald on the sixth floor:

KB: Now when you were on the sixth floor, did you see Lee Harvey Oswald?

LOVELADY: No, not on the sixth floor.

KB: Did you see Oswald at all that morning?

LOVELADY: Yes, sure did, he was working filling orders just as usual, working on the fifth and sixth floor, you know, came up later, filling orders.

KB: Do you recall how often you saw him that day?

LOVELADY: Not very many times.

Lovelady admits that Oswald **could have** been standing in the doorway with him! The stunned silence of the participants leaves us wondering why Brooten did not follow up on this explosive admission:

KB: Was Lee Oswald on those steps?

LOVELADY: No, Frazier.

KB: Would it have been possible, from where you were, sitting—from where you was, that hec ould have been there? (25:50)

LOVELADY: Could have . . . he was [unintelligible] (25:51-25:55)

During this interview, Brooten appears to cleverly skirt the issue and seems merely preoccupied with establishing the checkered colored plaid shirt that Lovelady supposedly was wearing on 22 November, as seen in the John Martin film. Brooten also goes through machinations trying to establish that Lovelady was wearing a crew cut, and more importantly, that he had a two-day growth of beard, which is what Gorilla Man appears to have in the film. He therefore repeatedly makes a point of establishing Lovelady's shaving habits, especially on 22 November 1963, and is quite insistent about it. The images shown below are from the original DCA film.[33]

But other clearer, non-cropped, versions of frames from the Martin film do not show the individual with a "growth of beard," as described by Brooten in the interview, merely the slightly unshaven face of a man.[34]

Not only did underexposure make the individual appear to have an exaggerated growth of beard, it also obfuscated the presence of a left breast pocket which included a well-defined and buttoned flap. Here is a side-by-side closeup for comparison. Below left is the HSCA image, below right is from Robert Groden's DVD, *The Assassination Films,* posted on YouTube.[35]

Upon close examination in digitized form, the red color appears to bleed downward, obliterating the white outline of the flap. This leaves us with the possibility that the photo shown Lovelady that day might have been manipulated to conceal the obvious presence of that pocket, in an effort to match his own checkered plaid shirt in which Groden photographed him that day. It also tended to blend the different colors and square patterns, apparently in an attempt to make it look more like the shirt worn by the man in the doorway.

The timing of the doorway Martin film clip is vitally important. This event was also captured in the Hughes film, which further confirms the timing established by Trask of approximately 10 minutes after the assassination, and it depicts employees being screened as they re-enter the TSBD. Both films show normal levels of exposure.

Martin film   Hughes film

But in this first tape, Lovelady informed Brooten that he did not go back into the TSBD via the front entrance, in fact, he never mentioned hanging around the TSBD front entrance steps at any time after he went with Shelley to the railroad yard after the assassination:

LOVELADY: Bill Shelley . . . he and myself, actually the girl told us about the event, we start running towards those railroad track we took off and . . . towards those railroad tracks. And then . . . Bill Shelley and myself . . . we got to about the railroad tracks, wondering what we were doing out there (30:50) *and came in the back entrance of the building. Went back in the building.* [Emphasis added]

And this is backed up by Bill Shelley's own Warren Commission testimony, where he states that he and Lovelady stood there and watched them search cars in the parking lots for a little while before re-entering the building:

> Mr. BALL. What did you and Billy Lovelady do?
> Mr. SHELLEY. We walked on down to the first railroad track there on the dead-end street and stood there and watched them searching cars down there in the parking lots for a little while and then we came in through our parking lot at the west end.
> Mr. BALL. At the west end?
> Mr. SHELLEY. Yes; and then in the side door into the shipping room.   **WC6H330**

Is it Really Lovelady in the Martin Film?

Modern computer digital imaging overlay techniques now allow us to examine and scrutinize photographs like never before. Complete details and methodology are covered in the next chapter. The results of overlays using the Martin film and a known profile of Billy Lovelady yield interesting results. This eight-panel collage, which increases in opacity from top to bottom, illustrates major differences between the two individuals.

Martin Film-Billy
Lovelady overlay

LR

The next collage (left) is a vertical photogrammetric comparison which shows how Lovelady's chin drops straight down and protrudes much more than Gorilla Man, who seems to lack a chin altogether, and appears to have a much larger head as well. Even though the man in the Martin film is shown blowing a puff of smoke from a cigarette he is smoking, the features still do not appear to line up when digital forensic overlays are performed.

Amy Joyce Finds Gorilla Man in Zapruder and Skaggs Films

In a stunning new development, JFK researcher and image specialist Amy Joyce appears to have finally solved the mystery of Gorilla Man, seen in the John Martin film. We have just offered compelling evidence showing that the man seen in the Martin film *is not* Billy Lovelady.

Now Amy seems to have found an individual wearing the exact same clothing as Gorilla Man, locating him in a Jay Skaggs slide. As the JFK limo makes the turn from Main on to Houston, his position is on the west curb of Houston Street. Here is a closeup of that slide:

Photographer Jay Skaggs's position was right at the corner of Elm and Houston Streets, on the east curb of Houston. Here he is seen in Bothun photo No. 3:

Amy has also located what appears to be the same individual in the Zapruder film, seen in frames Z193 though Z218. Here is a very clear isolation of frame Z205. The checkered shirt is an exact match! This individual also shows a prominent bald spot, exactly as exhibited by Gorilla Man:

He is moving south-to-north with a purpose and at a brisk pace, parallel with Houston, right along the reflecting pools which are located there. Watch closely as Z200 shows him lifting his left arm and hand as he takes a drag from his cigarette. Below is Z200 showing this action.

Here are frames Z216 and Z217, both of which also show the same bald spot. He is again raising his left arm and hand to take another drag from is cigarette:

Closeup of Zapruder frames 216 and 217

This guy is doing exactly what Gorilla Man is seen doing in the Martin film: smoking a cigarette! The image below shows him in the process of exhaling:

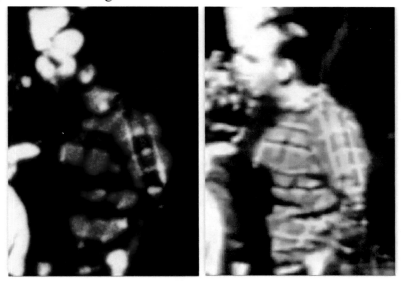

The similarities are so striking, that even the forward tilt or slouch of his neck is seen in both Zapruder frames! Here is a closeup of frame Z217:

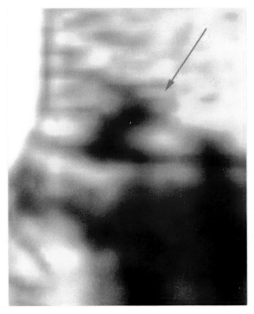

But there is more. Here is Australian JFK researcher John Costella's—who is an optics expert—Z217, which shows the entire frame:

Besides what appears to be the identification of Gorilla Man in the Zapruder frames and the Skaggs slide, a second, even more disturbing problem exists: Why is he not turned around facing and following the JFK limousine as it is already traveling down Elm Street, well to his left? The view from that position was unobstructed.

In fact, other people around him are not looking at the JFK limousine either! Jim Fetzer has maintained that the composition known as the extant Zapruder film was created by splicing footage used *before the JFK limousine arrived in Dealey Plaza*, with the motorcade subsequently added using film editing techniques available at the time. This may very well be the smoking gun that proves that his hypothesis is correct.

So, what does this all mean? First, those who claim Gorilla Man is Billy Lovelady, shown 10 minutes after the assassination hanging out in front of the TSBD entrance, have a major problem.

If Lovelady is Doorway Man, then how could he also be roaming around Houston Street as the assassination is unfolding? If the identification of Gorilla Man in the Skaggs and Zapruder film is correct, Kenneth Brooten and Robert Groden appear to have a lot of explaining to do, since they went to Aurora, Colorado in November 1976—in representation of the HSCA—to show Lovelady the Martin frame and obtain his alleged positive identification of himself. In the final analysis, we are left with the mystery of who exactly was this guy and what, if any, was his role in all of this.

The Vicky Adams/Sandra Styles "Encounter" with Billy Lovelady and Bill Shelley

"All I can say," she finally answered, "is that Shelley and Lovelady were definitely not on the first floor when we got there."

—Sandra Styles to Barry Earnest, p. 190

A very interesting and new revelation that comes out of this tape has to do with Victoria Adams and Sandra Styles, briefly discussed in the previous chapter, were two young women who worked at Scott Foresman, and had been on the fourth floor along with Dorothy Mae Garner and Elsie Dorman, who had been filming the motorcade from above.[36]

Motivated by youthful curiosity, Adams and Styles immediately went down the northwest stairway towards the back of the building, the same stairway the Warren Commission alleged that Oswald had used to get down to the second floor lunchroom within two minutes, buy his cola and encounter Officer Marrion Baker and Roy Truly.

Adams clearly stated that nobody came down the stairs, nor did she or Sandra hear anybody coming down that way in the immediate aftermath.[37] Her Warren Commission testimony contains an event that she would refute much later on—whether she encountered Lovelady and Shelley on the first floor.[38]

While researching his book *The Girl on the Stairs: My Search For A Missing Witness To The Assassination Of John F. Kennedy* (2010), Barry Earnest conducted a decades-long investigation where he finally caught up with both Victoria Adams and Sandra Styles in 2002. Troubled by the possibility that Vicky's Warren Commission testimony might have been altered, he sought her to corroborate what she had seen and heard that day. He noted how the "divide and conquer" technique had been applied to these young women, where only Adams had been called to testify, leaving her corroborating witness, Sandra, completely out of the picture, discarded and forgotten to history.

He wrote how Adams had repeatedly told those who interviewed her to please talk to Sandra about what they had both witnessed that day.[39]

Earnest's research points at possible malfeasance by David Belin and Joseph Ball, as they tried to establish a timeline of a supposed encounter Adams and Styles had with Bill Shelley and Billy Lovelady on the first floor of the TSBD, when these two came back into the building, after running towards the railroad tracks where a multitude of people and policemen had congregated.

Earnest explains that the reason this scheme was concocted had been to establish that Adams and Styles had actually come down much later than they thought they had, with that being the reason they saw nor heard anyone in the stairway at the time, because Oswald had already allegedly used the stairs.

In the Brooten recording, however, Billy never mentions anything about encountering Adams and Styles after he and Shelley re-entered the building via the back entrance:

KB: Right. Now, we move on to immediately after you heard the shots and went back in the building. What did you, what did you see inside the building?

LOVELADY: All the other employees [Emphasis added] had gotten back into the building by that time we stood around and wondered whether we should go back to work or find out what happened, whether they thought we would have to go back to work . . .

KB: Did they have any kind of roll call to find out who was there, or anything like that? . . . anything like that? (31:40)

This statement by Lovelady also demolishes the timeline the Warren Commission had established for his re-entering the TSBD along with Bill Shelley. If all the other employees had already returned and were inside the building, this had to have been at least 10-15 minutes after the assassination.

There is more. Billy's original handwritten statement is a very strange one, indeed. The upper portion is in his handwriting:

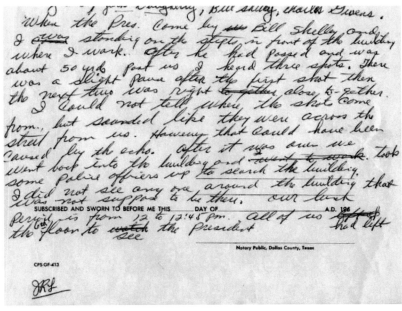

AFFIDAVIT IN ANY FACT

THE STATE OF TEXAS
COUNTY OF DALLAS

BEFORE ME,_____

a Notary Public in and for said County, State of Texas, on this day personally appeared *Billy*

Nolan Loveladg W-M-36 7722 Hume Dr. Dallas, Tex

Who, after being by me duly sworn, on oath deposes and says:

I live at 7722 Hume Dr. Dallas, Tex. I work at Texas School book depository 411 Elm. On Friday Nov. 22, 1963, I worked on the 6th floor along with Danny Arce, Jack Dougherty, Bill Shelley, Charles Givens.

But the lower portion appears to be written by someone else, and has key phrases crossed out and replaced:

...Dougherty, Bill Shelley, Charles Givens. When the Pres. Come by Bill Shelley and I was standing on the steps, in front of the building where I work. After he had passed and was about 50 yds. past us I heard three shots. There was a slight pause after the first shot then the next two was right close, to-gether. I could not tell where the shots come from, but sounded like they were across the street from us. However that could have been caused by the echo. After it was over we went back into the building and took some police officers up to search the building. I did not see any one around the building that was not suppose to be there. our lunch period is from 12 to 12:45 pm. all of us had left the 6th floor to see the president

CPS-GF-413

A prime example is the way Bill Shelley's name is written in the top portion versus the lower portion:

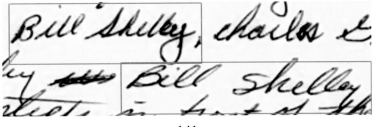

The JFK Horsemen

It is obvious that these are not written by the same person. The letter "B" in "Bill" is entirely consistent with Billy's signature, and the second one is not. The letters "S" and "y" in the word "Shelley" are not even close.

So, why would this be important in this discussion? Because his statement has the following phrase crossed out: ". . . we went back into the building and went to work," which has been replaced with "took some police officers up to search the building," by someone other than Lovelady.

Certainly, the detail of taking police officers upstairs to search the building would have been something Lovelady would have never forgotten, yet he completely fails to tell Brooten about it not once, but twice.

In fact, Lovelady is quite clear when he tells Brooten that "All the other employees had gotten back into the building by that time we stood around and wondered whether we should go back to work or find out what happened, whether they thought we would have to go back to work . . ."

And right at the very end of the interview:

KB: OK. Did the police come inside?

LOVELADY: They sure did.

KB: Alright. Do you recall who it was who came inside.

LOVELADY: No.

KB: Do you recall what they did when they came inside?

LOVELADY: *Well they . . . went up there . . .* [Emphasis added]

These two passages appear to confirm that in those crucial 10-15 minutes after the assassination, Billy Lovelady did not "take any police officers up to search the building," as documented in his affidavits, where his first one seems to have been obviously altered to include the event that he had supposedly taken police officers to the upper floors of the TSBD.

Bill Shelley, on the other hand, who was foreman and supervisor at the TSBD company, would have been the logical person tasked with this action since he was part of management, and that is exactly what is stated in both his handwritten and typed affidavits.

AFFIDAVIT IN ANY FACT

THE STATE OF TEXAS
COUNTY OF DALLAS

BEFORE ME, _____ Mary Rattan _____

a Notary Public in and for said County, State of Texas, on this day personally appeared
William H. Shelley w/m/37 of 126 S. Tatum, FE7 1969. Bus: 411 Elm, RI7 3521

Who, after being by me duly sworn, on oath deposes and says: Today approximately 12:30 pm November 22, 1963 I was standing on the front steps at 411 Elm watching the President in the parade. The President's car was about half way from Houston Street to the Triple Underpass when I heard what sounded like three shots. I couldn't tell where they were coming from. I ran across the street to the corner of the park and ran into a girl crying and she said the President had been shot. This girl's name is Gloria Calvery who is an employee of this same building. I went back to the building and went inside and called my wife and told her what happened. I was on the first floor then and I stayed at the elevator and was told not to let anyone out of the elevator. I left the elevator and went with the police on up to the other floors. I left Jack Dougherty in charge of the elevator.

William H. Shelley

Final Thoughts on the Brooten-Groden Aurora Trip

One begins to wonder why meticulous records regarding this trip are not in existence today, like those filed by Brooten for his Mexico City and Guadalajara trips just two weeks later, which have been discussed above. Full day-to-day reports, transcripts of taped conversations, affidavits, if any, should have been filed and made part of the official HSCA record. Billy Lovelady had very interesting things to say when Brooten and Groden called on him on 13 November 1976. By far, the most important revelation by Lovelady is the fact that he admitted that Oswald could have been standing on the steps with him. This he never followed up on, and we are left with the impression that Brooten might have ignored the information Lovelady was providing that tended to exonerate Oswald. Conversely, Brooten seemed intent on justifying the man seen in the John Martin film with the plaid checkered shirt buttoned up to the neck, sporting a "two-day growth of beard," and making his best effort to turn this man into Billy Lovelady.

A good example of what appears to be manipulation of Lovelady's story can be seen in his Warren Commission testimony where Weisberg observed:

*That Lovelady "verified" that Oswald was not there is a plain lie. He did testify that he was there but not that Oswald wasn't. **Lovelady did not testify he was standing where that man is standing in the Altgens picture.** [Emphasis added] He did testify to those with him, by name, and they are not in that part of the Altgens picture.*[40]

Here is the actual testimony that Weisberg was referring to in the above citation:

Mr. Ball: I have got a picture here, Commission Exhibit 369. Are you on that picture?

Mr. Lovelady: Yes, sir.

Mr. Ball: Take a pen or pencil and mark an arrow where you are.

Mr. Lovelady: Where I thought the shots are?

Mr. Ball: No, you in the picture.

Mr. Lovelady: **Oh, here.** [indicating] [Emphasis added]

Mr. Ball: Draw an arrow down to that; do it in the dark. You got an arrow in the dark and one in the white pointing toward you. Where were you when the picture was taken?

Mr. Lovelady: **Right there at the entrance of the building standing on the top of the step, would be here.** [indicating] [Emphasis added]

Mr. Ball: You were standing on which step?

Mr. Lovelady: **It would be your top level.** [Emphasis added]

Mr. Ball: **The top step, you were standing there?** [Emphasis added]

Mr. Lovelady: Right.(WC6H338-339)

Since this was official sworn testimony being recorded by a stenographer, Joseph Ball clearly should have followed up with something like, "Let it be established for the record that Mr. Lovelady has identified himself, by indicating that he is the *leftmost individual in Commission Exhibit 369.*" This obviously was not the case.

It appears that the photograph extracted from a frame of the John Martin film created more problems than it solved for the HSCA, via its emissaries Kenneth Brooten and Robert Groden.

The time estimate of this image—eight-12 minutes after the assassination—does not reconcile with the recollections of Billy Lovelady, which are backed by the documented experiences of Bill Shelley that day.

The extremely poor quality and apparent alteration of the image suggests an ulterior motive, and the missing pocket and flap on Billy's shirt is obviously a major problem for those who insist it is Billy Lovelady in the Martin film.

The Aurora Documents

The official documents which deal with the result of the Colorado visit are covered in two very brief HSCA addenda presented here, which are not part of the 12 volumes published by the HSCA, not released until 1993. (see Appendix ARRB: JFK Assassination Form System ID 19 August 1993) They are the only documents in existence that indirectly "document" Brooten and Groden's visit, and will be discussed shortly:

1. RIF#: 180-10114-10405, which contains these three photographs that were taken by Groden during the Aurora trip of Lovelady wearing a checkered colored plaid shirt.

Title: NO TITLE, SUBJECTS: LOVELADY, WILLIAM; PHOTOGAPHS AND FILMS
Author: n/a
Pages: 2
Agency: HSCA
RIF#: 180-10114-10405
Subjects: LOVELADY, WILLIAM; PHOTOGAPHS AND FILMS
Source: n/a

ANGUISH... Lovelady with photographic analyst Groden shortly before his death.

2. RIF#: 180-10114-10406, which contains the underexposed image of very poor quality mentioned earlier, of what is commonly known as Gorilla Man, reproduced from the Martin film. On the back of this photograph, a crude handwritten statement supposedly witnessed and signed by Brooten and Groden.

Title: NO TITLE, SUBJECTS: PHOTOGRAPHS AND FILMS; LOVELADY, WILLIAM
Author: n/a
Pages: 3
Agency: HSCA
RIF#: 180-10114-10406
Subjects: PHOTOGRAPHS AND FILMS; LOVELADY, WILLIAM
Source: n/a

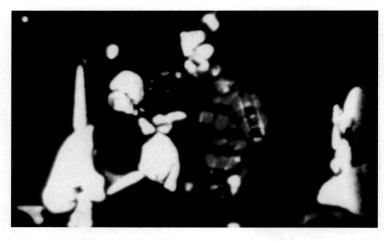

In 1998, researcher John Johnson published two very good articles in *The Fourth Decade* which dealt with the man in the doorway issue, the second, which noted the difference in the plaid shirts, present the two HSCA exhibits shown above. Johnson concluded his study:

"The pattern of Lovelady's shirt is close to that of the shirt in the Martin film-very, very close. But how does the old expression go? Close, but no cigar. If Lovelady's shirt does not exactly match the one in the Martin (or Bell) film, it would be evidence of an elaborate hoax. It is simply inconceivable that a simple man like Billy Lovelady would concoct such a hoax all by himself."[41]

Johnson's analysis centered on the pocket flap, which was noted by Australian researcher Jim Baker. He also briefly dealt with the "statement" which was on the back of the Martin photograph in 180-10114-100406. It is now time to take a much closer look at this document.

146

The HSCA Statement by "Billy N. Lovelady"

The following handwritten statement, on the back of the photo which is part of RIF#: 180-10114-10406, stands out because it bears the signature of witnesses Kenneth E. Brooten and Robert Groden. This mysterious and informal document speaks for itself inasmuch as it tries, in a very awkward way, to settle once and for all the identity of the *"man standing in the entrance of the doorway, with the "plaided" (sic) shirt on,"* [Emphasis added] seen in Altgens6. Assuming he was in charge, it is incomprehensible why an experienced attorney of the stature of Brooten, who was representing and acting on behalf of a bona fide congressional committee, would resort to this improvisation, instead of preparing an official and formal affidavit, signed and witnessed by an independent, local, notary public. Also, do bear in mind, that all of his work with the Tarasoffs in Mexico was painstakingly documented, and contrasts sharply with what will now be presented for consideration.

From DPD Affidavit 11/22/63

From HSCA handwritten statement dated 11/13/76 "witnessed" by Kenneth Brooten, Patricia Lovelady, and Robert Groden

This statement is supposedly signed by both Billy Lovelady and his wife Patricia. Below is a comprehensive analysis of "Lovelady's" signature, including overlays of each exemplar. Lovelady signed one original and one carbon copy of his affidavit of 22 November 1963, which offer a perfect opportunity to examine his signature across different documents. These can be found at the City of Dallas JFK document repository, Nos. 0470-001 and 0471-001.[42] These are facsimiles of the original color documents, written with a blue colored ball point pen, which reveals Lovelady's signature in intricate detail.

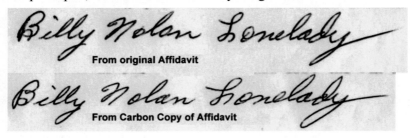

From original Affidavit

From Carbon Copy of Affidavit

After closely examining these with computer imaging and enhancement techniques, the following anomalies were noted:

1. Letters "B" and "y" are not even close. Notice the pronounced loops in the letters "B."

2. The real Lovelady did not loop his letter "i" in "Billy."

3. There is a pause between the second "L" and "y" in "Billy" in the HSCA signature, as if this had been traced over his real signature.

Exemplar #1

Dallas City Document 0470-001

Dallas City Document 0471-001

4. There is a pronounced separation in the HSCA, "Lovel ady", not seen in the Dallas document.

5. If you extend a line across the top of each signature from the top of the "B" on, you will notice that in the real Lovelady signatures the last two letters, "L" and "d" all reached that height or extended above, where the Brooten-Groden statement stay well below that line.

The images below are overlays where we matched the size of the "B"s and let the rest of the images fall as they would:

Exemplar #2

The Opinion of a Professional

Recently, a thorough handwriting analysis of this document was performed by certified handwriting expert Kim Johnsen, CMHA. This is the result of her study:

"Clearly, the two signature exemplars look little alike. One is bigger than the other. One uses a middle name; the other does not. In addition, there are numerous variances in letter formations, accompanied by major differences in at least seven separate graphology areas. Furthermore, other than diacritical heights, upper zone widths and capitals widths, there are no modes (measurements) alike (however, I did not anticipate that the diacriticals, upper zone and capitals would fall within the same mode; this gives me a bit of pause).

Kindly remember that such measurements are mostly subconsciously driven and automatic."[43]

"Some flagrant stroke or letter formation differences are briefly listed here:

Exemplar #1: Angular upper zone formations. Exemplar #2: Upper zone formations are rounded.

Exemplar #1: The Capital B in "Billy" is embellished; Exemplar #2 is not.

Exemplar #1: Final signature stroke varies completely from Exemplar #2.

Exemplar #2: Middle initial "n" much smaller than rest of signature; Exemplar #1 is not.

Exemplar #2 has a broader "d" loop in Lovelady than #1.

Exemplar #2 has decided directional pressure, "y" in Lovelady. #1 does not.

Exemplar #2 has decided varying heights of the two "l"s in "Billy," while #1 does not; this is however not conclusive. More handwriting samples desired.

Exemplar #2 has broader "e" loop than Exemplar #1. However, this particular trait is not fixed.

Exemplar #1 has a left-leaning final stroke, "L" in Lovelady; #2 does not. (Evidence of slow writing.) *

Exemplar #1 "stabs" his ovals; #2 uses garlands.

Exemplar #2 has a "fish hook" on his Capital "L," Lovelady. It is absent in #1. [Emphasis added]

Exemplar #1 uses retracing strokes on "Billy" (indicating much tension); #2 does not.

Exemplar #2 has eliminated the final "y" in Lovelady; in #1 it is evident."

Important Postscript: The handwritten note dated 13 November 1976, which begins, "The man standing in the entrance . . . " contains a lie. In other words, the writer is lying when he identifies the man as "Billy N. Lovelady." (Author's note: This is a portion of the 13-page report by CMHA Kim Johnsen)

And finally, by comparing the signature of HSCA counsel Kenneth Brooten in a 7 April 1977 letter to Weisberg, it is noted that this document also casts serious doubts as to Brooten signing it at the time of its creation.

The handwritten statement purportedly signed by Billy Nolan Lovelady in Aurora, Colorado, on 13 November 1976, on the back of a photograph, in the presence of HSCA counsel Kenneth E. Brooten and Robert J. Groden, raises serious questions as to its authenticity, and even more questions about the ethical behavior of those involved in its apparent forgery. The most astonishing aspect of this document is that it was filed away among HSCA addenda and would probably have never seen the light of day had it not been for the President John F. Kennedy Assassination Records Collection Act of 1992.

> **YESTERDAY in its first meeting under chairman Stokes, the committee voted to fire the only two members of the staff known to be loyal to Gonzalez. ... Letters of dismissal were mailed to Edyth Baish and Kenneth Brooten. ... See PROBE, A-11**

Brooten later claimed to have resigned shortly thereafter, on 8 March 1977. This excerpt of an article written by Jeremiah O'Leary and published on 10 March 1977, by *The Washington Star*, however, states that he had been fired by the Committee's new chairman, Louis Stokes. The reason for Brooten's "resignation" is mentioned in a letter he wrote to Harold Weisberg on 7 April 1977, where he expressed the following:

"My personal feelings were that the committee had compromised itself to such an extent that their final product has already been discredited."

This is a stunning admission from someone who had worked closely with Richard A. Sprague, and who at one point was interim director and chief counsel of the Committee at the tender age of 32.[44] Inexplicably, Brooten soon became Lovelady's personal attorney and remained as such until the day he died in 1979. (see appendix) This has never been properly explained and has puzzled researchers over the years.

```
Dear Harold:

Thank you very much for sending me the copy of your letter to
Jack Kershaw. As you know I resigned from the committee
effective March 8, 1977 upon the acceptance by the House
of Representatives of the resignation of Chairman Gonzalez.
My personal feelings were that the committee had compromised
itself to such an extent that their final product has already
been discredited.  I simply refused to compromise my personal
or professional integrity for a group of politicians and
accordingly have returned to the practice of law here in
Florida.
```

As far as Groden is concerned, as HSCA photographic consultant who accompanied Brooten to Aurora and was present at the time the Martin slide was shown to Lovelady, it would seem strange that he would stand idly by and allow what was obviously an underexposed photograph to have been used on such a sensitive mission. Absent any documentation similar to that filed for Brooten's Mexico trip, one gets the feeling that everything that went on in Aurora has never been fully revealed.

As shown here, the activities of Kenneth Brooten with the HSCA, particularly when contrasting the two trips he undertook for the Committee, are beginning to answer many of the questions raised in the previous chapter pertaining to Billy Lovelady.

Brooten was not just any assistant counsel entrusted with very sensitive aspects of the investigation, perhaps two of its very most crucial, which had to do with the perceived guilt or innocence of Oswald: his alleged trip to Mexico City, and the extremely controversial man in the doorway issue of Altgens6. According to handwriting expert Kim Johnsen, the informal "statement" written on the back of a photograph, converted from a frame of the John Martin film, which accompanies the HSCA document shown here, is not Lovelady's signature and suggests an obscure agenda. Brooten failed to follow up on the most important revelation by Lovelady, where he stated *that Lee Oswald could have been on the steps of the TSBD entrance at the time of the assassination.* Lovelady cracked the door open and Brooten failed to kick it in, by expanding on that line of questioning! His reaction to this incredible statement by Billy was, *"Right. Now we move on to the next page of questions . . ."* Any competent attorney interested in finding out the truth about who was in the doorway would have feasted on this low hanging fruit! This is reminiscent of the way Warren Commission counsels Joseph Ball, David Belin, Arlen Specter, Wesley Liebeler, and others took pains to avoid and suppress any testimony that could have exculpated Oswald.

Hopefully, after digesting and evaluating this information, the reader will be able to make an informed decision if Brooten was able to, in his own words, *"preserve his personal or professional integrity for the sake of a group of politicians."*

ENDNOTES

1. Fonzi, Gaeton, *The Last Investigation* (1993), p. 181
2. Russell, Dick, *On the Trail of the JFK Assassins: A Groundbreaking Look at America's Most Infamous Conspiracy* (2008), Chapter 6, Kindle position 794

3. Ibid. Chapter 6 "The Take down of the House Investigation"
4. Weisberg, Harold, *Mailer's Tales of the JFK Assassination*, (unpublished manuscript) Chapter 3, p. 23, The Weisberg Collection. Hood College, Frederick, MD, USA
5. jfkcountercoup.blogspot.com/2012/08/nana-seeks-hsca-records-of-richard.html (Bill Kelly blog)
6. mffpdf_106120, maryferrell.org, CIA's Office of Legislative Counsel, 20 October 1976
7. mffpdf_10069, maryferrell.org, Hess letter to Paul Daley, FBI, 28 October 1976, p. 308
8. ARRB David Atlee Phillips deposition cover page (see appendix below)
9. HSCA 180-10110-10030 Tarasoff, p. 37
10. Ibid. cover page (see appendix below)
11. mffpdf_41076, HSCA Executive Session, 27 November 1976, David Atlee Phillips deposition, p. 2
12. Ibid. 119
13. Fonzi, Gaeton, *The Last Investigation* (1993), p. 41
14. *Op. cit.* pp. 6, 7
15. mffpdf_41076, HSCA Executive Session, 27 November 1976, David Atlee Phillips deposition, p. 12
16. HSCA 180-10110-10030, Tarasoff, p. 25
17. Fonzi, Gaeton, *The Last Investigation* (1993), pp. 180, 181
18: Email 2/12/18 Karl Golovin, HSCA Recording at the National Archives.
19. Trask, Richard, *Pictures of the Pain* (1994), pp. 568-69
20. Ibid. (Also see jfkassassinationfiles.wordpress.com/2016/03/28/dca-film) DCA combined sequences taken by 18 photographers, including John Martin and Charles Mentesana; for others, see H. Weisberg, *Photographic Whitewash: Suppressed Kennedy Assassination Pictures* (published by author, 1967), pp. 254, 251-300. John R. Woods II, 1993 *JFK Assassination Photographs—Comprehensive listing of the Photographic Evidence Relating to the Assassination of President John F. Kennedy*
21. Ibid. 570
22. Trask, p. 574
23. "An underexposed image is the sort of photograph that one might consider to be too dark." photographylife.com/underexposure-and-overexposure-in-photography
24. Weisberg, Harold, *Inside the Assassination Industry*, p. 1036 (Note: Weisberg erroneously called it "overexposure," which is the opposite effect, where too much light is allowed through the camera. David Wrone, in obtaining his information from Weisberg, replicated the same mistake.) See, Wrone, David: *The Zapruder Film: Reframing JFK's Assassination* (2003), p. 178
25. Trask, p. 574
26. Ibid.
27. Woods II, John R. *JFK Assassination Photographs—Comprehensive listing of the Photographic Evidence Relating to the Assassination of President John F. Kennedy* (1993), p. 77

28. Weisberg, Harold, *Whitewash III: The Photographic Whitewash of the JFK Assassination* (1967), p. 106
29. Trask, p. 571
30. HSCA Vol. 6, p. 289
31. Groden, Robert, *The Killing of a President* (1993), p. 187; Weisberg, Harold, unpublished manuscript, *Picturing the Corruption* (1996), Chapter 4, p. 10. "Where the greatest dishonesty comes in is on that pair of pictures, the one taken from the overexposed Martin film and one not in color similar to and next to it."
32. jfkassassinationfiles.wordpress.com/2016/03/28/dca-film
33. youtube.com/watch?time_continue=2&v=n1gLqYN0pHo (underexposed video at 7:51 mark)
34. youtube.com/watch?v=KqMtbnBxIYU (5:42 mark) from: DVD The Assassination Films
35. Ibid
36. Earnest, Barry, *The Girl on the Stairs,* 2010 Kindle Version, pp. 13, 23
37. Ibid. 187, 189, 190
38. WC6H388
39. Earnest, Barry, *The Girl on the Stairs,* 2010 Kindle Version, p. 187. "However, once I realized it, I kept asking why the Warren Commission wasn't calling for Sandra Styles." Victoria Adams
40. Weisberg, Harold, unpublished manuscript, *Picturing the Corruption* (1996), Chapter 4, p. 8
41. Johnson, John Dr., *The Fourth Decade*, July 1998, "The man in the doorway—the plot thickens," pp. 36-37
42. jfk.ci.dallas.tx.us
43. Johnsen, Kim, CMHA, "Handwriting Analysis: Billy Nolan Lovelady," 8 October 2014 (13-page report)
44. Harold Weisberg letter to Dr. Cyril Wecht, 1 February 1992, p. 2

APPENDIX

David Atlee Phillips 27 November 1976 HSCA testimony cover documents:

Assassination Records Review Board
Final Determination Notification

```
           AGENCY : HSCA
    RECORD NUMBER : 180-10131-10328
    RECORD SERIES : SECURITY CLASSIFIED TESTIMONY
AGENCY FILE NUMBER : 014726
```

September 22, 1998
Status of Document: Postponed in Part
Number of Postponements: 86

The redactions in this document have been postponed under the provisions set forth in The John F. Kennedy Assassination Records Collection Act of 1992.

The number within the brackets is provided to represent the appropriate substitute language from the list below.

Board Review Completed: 09/14/98

```
                                              v09-16-96ccr
                          JFK RECORDS

                                      Cross Reference: None

Status in System:

----------------------------------------------------------------
- - - - - -
              AGENCY : HSCA                                        \
       RECORD NUMBER : 180-10131-10328
       RECORD SERIES : SECURITY CLASSIFIED TESTIMONY
 AGENCY FILE NUMBER : 014726
 Other Agency Equity:
----------------------------------------------------------------
- - - - - -
                      DOCUMENT INFORMATION

           ORIGINATOR : HSCA
                 FROM : PHILLIPS, DAVID ATLEE
                   TO :
                TITLE :
                 DATE : 11/27/76
                PAGES : 135
        DOCUMENT TYPE : TRANSCRIPT
          SUBJECT(S) : OSWALD, LEE, POST RUSSIAN PERIOD, TRAVEL, TRIP TO
                       MEXICO; CIA, METHODOLOGY; PHILLIPS, DAVID A., TESTIMONY
                       BEFORE THE COMMITTEE;
       CLASSIFICATION : UNCLASSIFIED
         RESTRICTIONS : 256
       CURRENT STATUS : REFERRED
 DATE OF LAST REVIEW : 08/21/93
             COMMENTS : Box 5

 Date in: 01/26/96

 F F F F F F F
 T F F F F F F
```

The Tarasoff HSCA document:

Assassination Records Review Board
Final Determination Notification

```
----------------------------------------------------------------
              AGENCY : HSCA
       RECORD NUMBER : 180-10110-10030
       RECORD SERIES : SECURITY CLASSIFIED TESTIMONY
 AGENCY FILE NUMBER : 014849
```

March 26, 1997

Status of Document: Postponed in Part

Number of releases of previously postponed information: 0

Number of Postponements: 45

```
                                                    Date : 07/27/95
                                                    Page : 1

                        JFK ASSASSINATION SYSTEM
                         IDENTIFICATION FORM
----------------------------------------------------------------
                         AGENCY INFORMATION

                AGENCY : HSCA
         RECORD NUMBER : 180-10110-10030
         RECORDS SERIES : SECURITY CLASSIFIED TESTIMONY
     AGENCY FILE NUMBER : 014849
----------------------------------------------------------------
                        DOCUMENT INFORMATION

            ORIGINATOR : HSCA
                  FROM : TARASOFF, BORIS; TARASOFF, ANNE [ R ]
                    TO :
                 TITLE :
                  DATE : 11/28/76
                 PAGES : 109
              SUBJECTS : TARASOFF, BORIS, TESTIMONY BEFORE THE COMMITTEE [ R ]

                         TARASOFF, ANNE, TESTIMONY BEFORE THE COMMITTEE [ R ]

                         OSWALD, LEE, POST-RUSSIAN PERIOD, TRAVEL, TRIP TO
                         MEXICO

                         CIA, METHODOLOGY

         DOCUMENT TYPE : TRANSCRIPT
        CLASSIFICATION : UNCLASSIFIED
          RESTRICTIONS : 3
        CURRENT STATUS : RELEASED WITH DELETIONS
   DATE OF LAST REVIEW : 11/14/96
       OPENING CRITERIA :
              COMMENTS : Includes attachments and summaries.
Box 10.
```

**APPROVED FOR RELEASE 1993
CIA HISTORICAL REVIEW PROGRAM**

OLC 76-3632
10 December 1976

MEMORANDUM FOR THE RECORD

SUBJECT: Meeting with Staff Members from the House Select
Committee on Assassinations - 10 December 1976

   1. Another meeting with the staff of the House Select
Committee on Assassinations was held at 1400 hours on
10 December in the office of the Chief Counsel, Mr. Richard
Sprague. The meeting, which lasted for about an hour and a
half, was attended by Mr. Sprague, Mr. Stephen Fallis, and
Mr. Kenneth Brooten, of the Committee staff. Mr. Sidney
Stembridge, Deputy Director of Security, and Mr. Douglas T.
Cummins, of my office, were with me to represent the Agency.

11 May 1977 phone call to Brooten by CIA Douglas T. Cummins

OLC 77-1971
16 May 1977
CHRONO

**HSCA
77-0041**

MEMORANDUM FOR THE RECORD

SUBJECT: Telephone Conversation with Mr. Kenneth Brooten, Former
Assistant Counsel, House Select Committee on Assassinations
(HSCA)

1. On 11 May 1977, the Office of Legislative Counsel received a telephone call from the office of Representative Henry Gonzalez (D., Texas) asking that this office contact Mr. Brooten, who is now practicing law in Florida. It was stated that he had information of interest about the House Select Committee on Assassinations. The undersigned responded to this request but was unable to reach Mr. Brooten until this date, since he was out of town.

2. I reached Mr. Brooten in his office in Florida and identified myself to him as representing the Office of Legislative Counsel of the CIA. I reminded him of the last time we had met in December 1976 when he was still a member of the HSCA staff. He said that he recalled that meeting. Mr. Brooten stated that he had been receiving "dribbles of information", which he termed as third hand and hearsay, indicating to him that someone who purported to represent CIA was making general inquiries about the modus operandi of Mr. Richard A. Sprague, the former Chief Counsel of the HSCA. When I learned the intent of his call, I asked Mr. Brooten for his permission to have my secretary monitor the conversation so that we could have an accurate transcript. He agreed to this. The purpose of his contacting us was to offer his views on how Sprague and his people had operated in the past and would operate in the future.

I declined his offer. When I mentioned that Mr. Sprague was no longer with the Committee, Brooten answered most emphatically by saying Sprague "hired most of the people on that staff except me." I responded that the HSCA was George Cary's and my account and that I knew nothing about any such inquiries nor would I even know why such questions would be asked.

Journal - Office of Legislative Counsel   Page 4
Monday - 16 May 1977

14. (Unclassified - DTC) LIAISON Called Kenneth Brooten, former Assistant Counsel, House Select Committee on Assassinations (HSCA), regarding a call received from the office of Representative Henry Gonzalez (D., Texas) asking that this office contact Mr. Brooten. It was stated that he had information of interest about the HSCA. (See Memorandum for the Record).

5. I mentioned to Mr. Preyer that Ken Brooten, formerly of the House Assassinations Committee, had been in touch with us and offered to provide us with information about the methods of operation of former Chief Counsel, Richard Sprague, and others whom he hired on the Assassinations Committee staff but that we had declined to receive this information. I said that Brooten may well have had the best of motives but we did not feel that we should be the recipients of this kind of information. Mr. Preyer said he agreed with the way we handled the call.

GEORGE L. CARY
Legislative Counsel

CIA INTERNAL USE ONLY SECRET

Journal - Office of Legislative Counsel   Page 4
Wednesday - 20 October 1976

77-0010 J-13

13. (Unclassified - LLM) LIAISON Ken Brooten, on the
staff of the House Select Committee on Assassination, called requesting
any summary information the Agency might have on the Kennedy
assassination. I told Brooten that I had met with Richard Sprague,
also on the Committee staff, yesterday and Sprague had asked for
the same information and that I was in the process of determining
if it exists. Brooten was unaware that Sprague had requested this
information.

October 28, 1976

Mr. Paul Daley
Office of Legislative Liason
Federal Bureau of Investigation
J. Edgar Hoover Building
Room 3658
Washington, D.C. 20535

Dear Mr. Daley:

Per your telephonic request, please be advised that the following
persons have been employed by the House Select Committee on Assassinations:

  Richard A. Sprague
  Kenneth E. Brooten, Jr.
  Jeremy Ray Akers
  Robert C. Ozer
  Joseph Kiel
  Donovan L. Gay
  Richard Joseph Feeney
  Vivian Leigh McPherson
  Billie Gay Larson
  Carole Hanson Amato
  Jacqueline Hess
  Patricia M. Orr

ENCLOSURE

Richard Augustus Edwards, III has been detailed from Congressman
Downing's staff to work as Press Assistant. Patricia Wendling
Costello is a staff volunteer until November 17, 1976.

If I may be of additional service, please do not hesitate to call.

                    Sincerely, 62.117290-4
                    Jacqueline Hess
                    Jacqueline Hess   5 NOV 4 1976

JH/bgl

and was about to get himself fired. I remember clearly what I told him, if not the exact words. It was not
very long this was recalled by one of Sprague's assistant counsel, Ken Brooten. Brooten was a Gainesville,
Florida lawyer with much experience on Capitol Hill. He then was an assistant to Texas Congressman Henry
Gonzalez. Gonzalez, who was a member of that committee had a leading role in getting it established.

"The Congress is a different world," I told Sprague. "In it you do not have the liberty and authority you enjoyed as the district attorney of a great city. I know the Congress. I worked for it for four years. The way you are going it will not be long before you are cut off at the knees."

That is what happened just as I told Sprague it would. That was the easiest of predictions. It was inevitable. Sprague had left the Congress no real choice by his conduct and by his steady flow of unjustified statements to the press that embarrassed, really demeaned the House.

Then, briefly, Gonzalez was acting committee chairman and Brooten was its temporary general counsel and staff director.

The evening of the day it happened, before I had become aware of it, Brooten phoned me to tell me:

"If ever a man was Merlin, remembering the future, you were the day you told
Sprague what was going to happen to him. It did this afternoon. He was fired."

28 November 1976—4 December 1976: Mexico City Trip—MEXICO CITY FILE INDEX FOLDER:

Tarasoff interviews transcript—Interviews of Boris and Ann Tarasoff, former contract employees of the CIA at Mexico City Station. Taken by Jonathan Blackmer and Ken Brooten on 29-30 November 1976, regarding intercepts of Oswald's phone calls to the Soviet Embassy from the Cuban Embassy. (two copies) Interview with Boris Dimitry Tarasoff and Ann Tarasoff at Ranch Contento, Guadalajara, Mexico on Tuesday, 30 November 1976, 1:15 PM (local time).

Mr. Blackmer: This officer determined that Oswald had been at the Soviet Embassy on 26 or 28 (unclear) September, 1963 and had talked with Kostikov, a member of the Counselor section. Now do you know for a fact whether he was at the Soviet Embassy?

Mr. Tarasoff: We could never know that.

Mrs. Tarasoff: No.

Mr. Blackmer: You never knew that. And do you know for a fact whether or not he talked to Kostikov on the telephone?

Mr. Tarasoff: Well, as I said before, it's a very doubtful proposition and we could jump at conclusions all weekend.

United Press International

GAINESVILLE — The attorney for Lee Harvey Oswald look-alike Billy Nolan Lovelady said Thursday the strain of being hounded by conspiracy theorists during 15 years may have contributed to his client's early death.

Lovelady, 41, reportedly died in his sleep Sunday at an undisclosed location in Colorado, where he had gone into self-imposed seclusion. A post-mortem examination will be performed.

Lovelady was an employee of the Texas School Book Depository in Dallas, Texas and was photographed standing in the building's doorway on Nov. 22, 1963, the day former President John F. Kennedy was assassinated.

HIS UNCANNY resemblance to Oswald, who the Warren Commission named as the lone assassin, led some conspiracy theorists to contend that the photo showed Oswald, not Lovelady, and therefore Oswald could not have shot Kennedy.

The Warren Commission later concluded that the man in the doorway was Lovelady, not Oswald, but offered little supporting evidence.

Gainesville attorney Kenneth Brooten, who served as chief counsel for the House Assassinations Committee in 1977 and later represented Lovelady before the committee, Thursday said conspiracy theorists pestered Lovelady.

Brooten, who reported Lovelady's death Wednesday, said his client was "hounded out of Dallas" and took his family into hiding to Colorado.

"A NUMBER of people went out to exploit it (his resemblance) by writing books, doing investigations. Some were well-intentioned and some intentioned to personally gain by it. For whatever reasons and for whatever motivations, they all seemed to contact Billy Nolan Lovelady," he said.

Brooten noted that the House subcommittee probing the Kennedy assassination recently agreed with the Warren Commission that Lovelady definitely was the man photographed in the depository doorway.

Asked whether the subcommittee's finding and Lovelady's death had brought to an end another chapter in the Kennedy assassination saga, Brooten said:

"Whether or not it was Billy Nolan Lovelady in the doorway or Lee Harvey Oswald, I think, has probably been resolved. It's been resolved by the House Assassinations Committee by photo analysis, and I think, in the minds of a great number of people. That has closed the last chapter on it."

* * * * * * * * * * * * * * * * * * *

Billy Nolan Lovelady, 41, the Oswald look-alike who also worked with Oswald at the Texas School Book Depository, died at his home in Denver, Colorado, of an "apparent heart attack". No autopsy was performed.

At the very instant the President was shot, a photograph of the Presidential limousine was snapped by James Altgens. It showed a man who strongly resembled Oswald standing in the front doorway of the Book Depository, dressed just as

Oswald was dressed when he was arrested for the murder of Officer Tippit. But the Warren Commission accepted Lovelady's testimony that it was he, Lovelady, and not Lee Harvey Oswald, in the doorway, thus disposing of a sticky problem for the Commission.

Lovelady's family attorney, Kenneth Brooten, said that Lovelady "was under a lot of stress. He paid for it dearly." Brooten and Lovelady's wife, Patricia, indicated that alleged "harassment" of Lovelady by assassination researchers had somehow precipitated or aggravated Lovelady's condition. Interestingly enough, Brooten said that he became acquainted with Lovelady while he, Brooten, was working as a counsel for the Assassinations Committee, and went on to become his lawyer.

HSCA photographic consultant Robert Groden, a long time Warren Commission critic and author, said of the man in the doorway (in the Altgens photograph) recently, "I could prove to anybody that it was Lovelady."

Maybe so, but Groden did not probe the more perturbing question: what was Lovelady doing in Oswald's clothes, and how and when did they switch back?
* * * * * * * * * * * * * * * * * * *

HSCA Identification forms for 180-10114-10405/06

```
                                                    Date:08/19/93
                                                    Page:1
                          JFK ASSASSINATION SYSTEM

                             IDENTIFICATION FORM
--------------------------------------------------------------------
                             AGENCY INFORMATION

              AGENCY : HSCA
       RECORD NUMBER : 180-10114-10405

       RECORDS SERIES :
   NUMBERED PHOTOGAPHIC MATERIALS

   AGENCY FILE NUMBER :
--------------------------------------------------------------------
                            DOCUMENT INFORMATION

         ORIGINATOR : HSCA
               FROM :
                 TO :

              TITLE :

               DATE : 00/00/00
              PAGES : 3

           SUBJECTS :
   LOVELADY, WILLIAM
   PHOTOGAPHS AND FILMS
```

```
         DOCUMENT TYPE : PHOTOGRAPH
        CLASSIFICATION : U
          RESTRICTIONS : OPEN IN FULL
        CURRENT STATUS : O
   DATE OF LAST REVIEW : 07/08/93

      OPENING CRITERIA :


              COMMENTS :
   Folder list in Box 1. Some material subject to copyright provisions. Box 1.
```

```
                                                        Date:08/19/93
                                                        Page:1
                        JFK ASSASSINATION SYSTEM

                          IDENTIFICATION FORM
   ------------------------------------------------------------------------
                          AGENCY INFORMATION

                AGENCY : HSCA
         RECORD NUMBER : 180-10114-10406

        RECORDS SERIES :
   NUMBERED PHOTOGRAPHIC FILES

   AGENCY FILE NUMBER : 000265
   ------------------------------------------------------------------------
                          DOCUMENT INFORMATION

            ORIGINATOR : HSCA
                  FROM :
                    TO :

                 TITLE :


                  DATE : 11/13/76
                 PAGES : 1

              SUBJECTS :
   PHOTOGRAPHS AND FILMS
   LOVELADY, WILLIAM

         DOCUMENT TYPE : PHOTOGRAPH
        CLASSIFICATION : U
          RESTRICTIONS : OPEN IN FULL
        CURRENT STATUS : O
   DATE OF LAST REVIEW : 07/08/93

      OPENING CRITERIA :


              COMMENTS :
   Folder list in Box 1. Some material subject to copyright provisions. Box 1.
```

On February 2nd, the House voted to reconstitute the Assassinations Committee—temporarily. Still under sharp attack by certain conservative lawmakers suddenly deeply concerned with civil liberties. the Committee was, as the *Washington Star* put it, "given less than two months to justify its existence under conditions that . . . make it almost impossible to develop new evidence." The House had kept the Committee alive, but gave it just barely enough to cover the already reduced salaries of its staff. (Everyone had taken a 40 percent pay cut while waiting reconstitution.)   **Fonzi pg 180**

Gonzalez had been furious at not being named chairman of the Committee when it was originally formed. He automatically stepped into the post, however, when Downing retired and the new Congress convened in January. (It was, of course, something of a Catch-22 position since the Committee, not yet reconstituted, was officially nonexistent.) Gonzalez, however, wanted more than just the title. He wanted control and the power to stack the staff with his own people. Sprague wasn't about to give him that.

In December, Gonzalez had told Sprague that, under the formula in the Congressional Rules, the Committee could operate with a budget of $150,000 a month until it was officially reconstituted. On that basis, Sprague began beefing up his original start-up staff with new additions, all of whom were put on the payroll January 1st. I was in that group. Gonzalez, however, had been mistaken about the Committee's budget. The rules actually permitted it only $84,337 a month in expenses while awaiting reconstitution. When Gonzalez was called on the carpet by the Rules Committee for the budget over-run, he said that Sprague had hired the new staffers without his knowledge or permission.   **Fonzi pg 181**

With no recourse but to view it in the larger terms of human folly, Tanenbaum roared with laughter. "What an asshole!" he shouted. But it really wasn't funny. Since all Congressional committees use the postal franking privileges of its chairman, and every expense voucher, travel order and most directives and requests to other Government agencies are made under the chairman's signature. Gonzalez, in effect, was stopping the operation of the Committee.   **Fonzi pg 181**

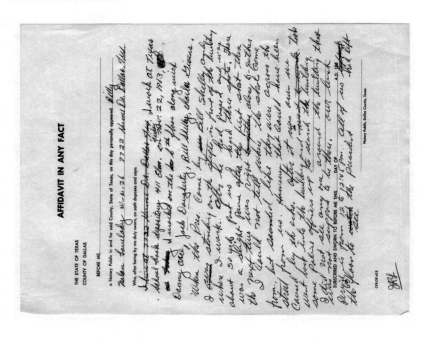

SPECTATOR IN TSBD DOORWAY:

(Hughes Film)

(Altgens Photo)

(Bell Film)

Oswald Arrest Shirt

Lovelady in Dealey Plaza Nov. 22, 1963 (Martin Film)

Lovelady photographed by FBI in 1964

Lovelady in 1963 shirt (1976)

FIGURE IV-67.—Photographic evidence evaluated in Robert Groden's shirt analysis.

162

8

The Man in the Doorway Identified

*A*uthors note: This chapter follows scientific protocol as it establishes a hypothesis, previous research and published material, followed by materials and methods and finally results and discussion.

James Altgens photo No. 5, aka Altgens6

Abstract/Hypothesis

The man in the doorway in Altgens6 can now be positively identified using modern computer graphics techniques. The techniques used here can be completely and reliably reproduced using the materials and methods described herein.

Introduction

At 12:30 PM on 22 November 1963, John F. Kennedy was assassinated in broad daylight on the streets of Dallas in the presence of a multitude of people who were hoping to get a glimpse of the President of the United States as he drove through that city in a motorcade. As soon as AP photographer Ike Altgens fifth photograph, now known as Altgens6, was published nationwide and around the world, many people noticed a figure in the background standing in the entrance of the TSBD, who resembled the accused assassin, Lee Oswald, the obvious implication being that the image offered the perfect alibi for Mr. Oswald.

On the weekend of the assassination, the FBI immediately went out of its way to proclaim the man in the doorway as another employee of the TSBD company by the name of Billy Nolan Lovelady.

The issue was further compounded when the FBI photographed Lovelady on 29 February 1964 in the shirt he claimed to have worn, which was a short-sleeved vertical striped, red and white shirt, a shirt which in no way resembled the one worn by the man in the doorway.

Commission No. 457b found in Commission Document 457

Within months, Jones Harris would become the first person to commission special enhancement studies of the photograph, by having Bernard Hoffman scan the image and construct a mosaic which detailed every last pixel, which at the time technologically offered the most sophisticated enlargement for study.[1]

According to Dom Bonafede, this exercise proved inconclusive because Harris could not obtain contemporary photographs of Lovelady for comparison basis.[2]

Lovelady and his employer fiercely resisted every attempt by photographers to obtain images of the famous "man in the doorway."[3] Lovelady claimed that he did not want some "crazy S.O.B. take a shot" at him.[4] Despite all of this, Mark Lane was successful in taking this photograph of Lovelady, sometime after the assassination, which was shown in a previous chapter.

Even though the area in question is extremely small, one of the arguments among early critics was the fact that the shirt worn by Doorway Man very closely resembled and seemed to match the shirt worn by the accused assassin Oswald. Harold Weisberg was the first author to publish a nine-point study which documented these similarities.[5]

The FBI, Warren Commission, and the HSCA never conducted reenactments of the figures in the doorway using the same equipment and film Altgens had used that day. Weisberg complained repeatedly that they should have brought Lovelady with the shirt he claimed to have worn and simply stood him in the doorway and taken pictures to settle the matter once and for all.[6]

It was not until November 2012, 49 years later, that a Texas researcher by the name of Ralph Cinque decided to commission a thorough reenactment of the figures in the doorway of Altgens's photograph by utilizing the exact same equipment, position, camera, film and focal length settings that Altgens had used.[7]

Cinque conducted his experiment at the exact same time of day—12:30 PM—that the photograph had been taken in order to ascertain the effect of the shadows cast by the figures seen in the doorway. Moreover, despite the passage of time, Cinque was able to prove the exact position of Doorway Man in the center of the stairway, standing on the landing that led to the glass door of the front entrance. Because of the foreshortening optical effect seen in the photograph, many had assumed that Doorway Man was standing against the west wall of the entrance. The first clear enlargement of the photograph was later conducted by Robert Groden, where he also proclaimed the figure as Lovelady.

This chapter will explain the procedures of image processing and overlay in facial recognition as it is applied to biometrics and offer new empirical data that should enable us to draw comparisons and make an informed decision as to the identity of the man in the doorway.

Image Overlaying in Facial Recognition

Facial recognition using image overlaying software is widely used and accepted in the field of forensic science. (see "Face Recognition in Forensic Science—Part 1," pp. 4-5, what-when-how.com/face-recognition/face-recognition-in-forensic-science-face-recognition-applications-part-1).

The following is quoted verbatim from this source:

The procedure of the comparison can be qualitative or quantitative, using relative or absolute dimensions. In a morphological comparison, the location and size of facial features is measured relatively, not absolutely. If the perspectives of the questioned and known images are similar and the position of the head is similar, the image depicting the known individual can be scaled to that of the questioned individual by using the interpupillary distance or other consistent features within the image. An overlay of the scaled known image and the questioned image can then be made in order to determine if the relative alignment of other facial features is consistent. This overlay of images is also referred to as the superimposition method and can be performed with video editing or image processing equipment. A variation of the overlay approach is a photogrammetric one: a side-by-side of the images is prepared and two sets of three or more parallel lines are drawn through facial features, such as the jawline, pupils, nasal bridge, on both images and compared by position.

*For both a photogrammetric and overlay approach, the images must be of the same perspective, but the key difference is that an overlay allows one to view the length and width simultaneously although viewing the lines in the photogrammetric approach leaves more to human perception as one looks across both images. Superimposition can appear to be doctoring the evidence if not properly explained because scaling implies changing the images to effect alignment, **but the method is sound.**"* [Emphasis added]

Consider that if you scale an image of Abraham Lincoln to the same eye corner-to-corner distance as that of George Washington, that scaling will not force the length of the face or shape of the jaw to match up, and rightly so because they are different individuals. Just as scaling two images of Abraham Lincoln to the same interpupillary distance will demonstrate the similar locations of facial marks and the consistent sizes of facial features because the images do depict the same individual. Therefore, a superimposition can provide extremely beneficial information to determine if features appear to be the same and if the relative locations and dimensions relate. With an overlay, the examiner can "blink" back and forth between questioned and known imagery to assist in the comparison by identifying similarities and dissimilarities. In this type of comparison, facial landmarks, standard reference marks generally defined by the underlying structure of the skull, are used in the main as guides and are not typically measured.

Biometric Parameters and Identifiers

The digital era of computers has opened a vast field in the science of biometrics which goes hand-in-hand with forensic science and photogrammetry.

Biometric recognition, or simply biometrics, is a rapidly evolving field with applications ranging from accessing one's computer, to gaining entry into a country. Biometric systems rely on the use of physical or behavioral traits, such as fingerprints, face, voice and hand geometry, to establish the identity of an individual. The deployment of large-scale biometric systems in both commercial (e.g., grocery stores, amusement parks, airports) and government (e.g., US-VISIT [United States Visitor and Immigrant Status Indicator Technology]*) applications, increases the public's awareness of this technology. This rapid growth also highlights the challenges associated with designing and deploying biometric systems. Indeed, the problem of biometric recognition is a* grand challenge *in its own right. The past five years have seen a significant growth in biometric research resulting in the development of innovative sensors, robust and efficient algorithms for feature extraction and matching, enhanced test methodologies and novel applications. These advances have resulted in robust, accurate, secure and cost effective biometric systems.*

springer.com/us/book/9780387710402

Biometric parameters are now being used from individual applications in medicine to assess fetal development, to the deployment of security systems of mass recognition as cited above. Identification systems ranging from finger, hand and palm recognition to retina scans, all fall under the umbrella of biometrics. Photogrammetric, side-by side comparison can be used as a key component of biometrics, which can subsequently be used to verify and quantify the results of facial image overlaying.

Examples of Facial Overlaying and Calibration of the System

A simple example of overlay techniques used in facial recognition can be seen when we compare these two images, who are obviously not the same person:

The very first task is to match interpupillary distance between the two individuals, followed by scaling, in this manner:

When we try to line up the rest of the features such as nose, lips, chin, ears, etc., the rest of the features fail to line up, obviously because they are not the same person:

Our next example compares two females who at first glance look very much alike:

Marilyn Monroe-Jane Mansfield comparison

When we apply the same overlay techniques, it is quite evident that eyebrows, nose, and mouth do not line up, and overall facial structures differ in shape and general contour.

Now we try two different photos of the same person—in this case Marilyn Monroe:

Which yields the following:

Both components of this overlay fall into perfect alignment and are a match in all biometric and photogrammetric parameters.

Yet Another Example

In 1971 Ramón Flores was accused of murder in Ohio and fled that state to hide out in Puerto Rico, in the southern town of Juana Diaz. Recently, after 40 years on the lam and in hiding, authorities caught up with Flores, and the following photographs were released.

The difference between the two photographs is approximately 40 years:

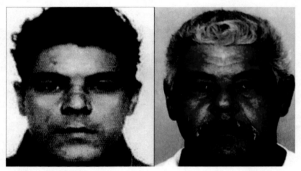

When we applied the same overlay techniques to these two photographs, the results were the following:

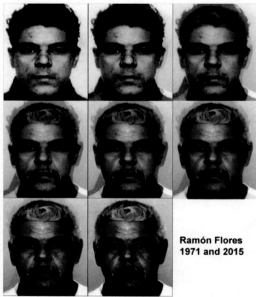

**Ramón Flores
1971 and 2015**

Despite there being 40 years difference between the photographs, once the interpupillary distance was set and images scaled accordingly, the rest of the features lined up perfectly. A small difference in ear size can be attributed to normal cartilage enlargement as the human body ages.

The preceding exercises have allowed us to calibrate and establish the reliability and accuracy of the system which will now be used to identify the man in the doorway.

Lee Oswald Images and Overlays

The same procedures and techniques can be applied to known photographs of Oswald and Lovelady.

The following is a four-image collage showing Oswald at different times in his life. A grid and ruler has been overlaid to facilitate comparison. The top two images are from the late '50s, first a photograph when he was in the U.S. Marines, and the second his passport photograph. The bottom two are the mug shots in New Orleans and Dallas, respectively left and right:

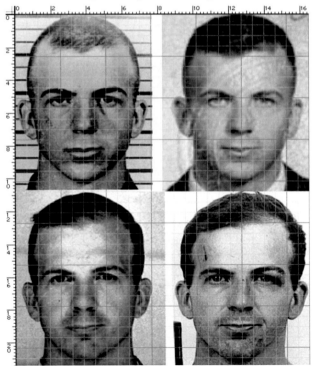

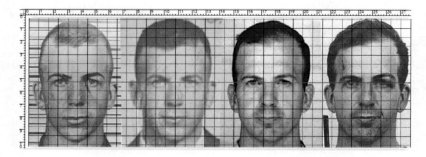

When we color code each individual photograph, we come up with this photogrammetric study. This exercise shows a relatively consistent pattern in features and cranial size. Here is the color-coded overlay onto the first image at top left, with the next three images at 50% opacity:

This overlay contains all four photographs of Oswald shown in the two collages above.

Next, we compare the New Orleans and Dallas mug shots. These offer a unique opportunity to appreciate the shape and dimensions of Oswald's face and head:

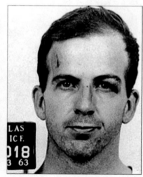

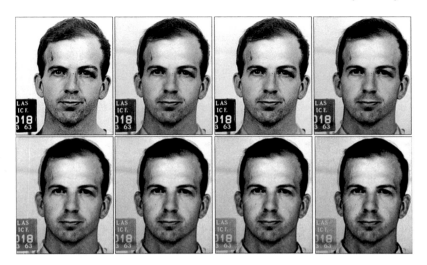

This overlay sequence shows a remarkable degree of similarity between the Oswald arrested in the summer of 1963 and the Oswald arrested in Dallas on 22 November 1963. As shown in our earlier Marilyn Monroe example, the difference between these two images is almost negligible. The inescapable conclusion here must be that they are the same person. (Note: there are two small dark spots on the right side of his face—left as seen in photo—of the NOPD photo, which are anomalies placed after it was taken.)

Lovelady Images and Overlays

There are very few images of Lovelady, however, the two that have been picked confirm the identity as the same person who was photographed by the FBI on 29 February 1964:

CBS photo (1967)   *Groden photo (1976)*

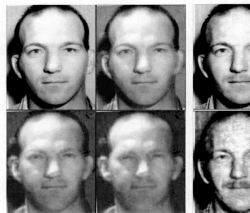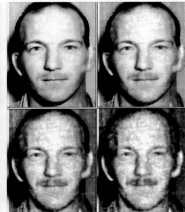

The Task at Hand

First-generation researcher Ray Marcus was the first person to attempt to do overlays of Altgens6 using a clear sheet of plastic in the mid-1960s.

Marcus, however, in a reversal of the methodology that will be presented here, attempted to overlay an enlarged image of the man in the doorway over facial enlargements of Oswald and Lovelady. Another limitation of his methodology was the use of frontal shots of the subjects as opposed to Doorway Man who is at a slight angle, showing 3/4 of his face.[8]

According to interviews of Marcus conducted by John Kelin for his book *Praise from a Future Generation: The Assassination of John F. Kennedy and the First Generation Critics of the Warren Report* in 2000, Marcus reported that, "They (Oswald) seemed to roughly match," and he admitted the limitations of his methods.[9]

Obviously, the technology of the time did not allow for detailed analysis. Besides Marcus, as far as we know, no other researcher has ever undertaken the task of performing overlay experiments using the image of Doorway Man as a control image and superimposing confirmed photographs of the two possible candidates cited by those on either side of the issue, Lee Oswald and Lovelady.

The Symmetry of the Faces of the Gallery (Test) Images

To validate the procedures in this study, and even though human faces are not perfectly symmetrical, it is important to first establish

174

the symmetrical properties of the faces of the individuals being tested. The following images show a high degree of symmetry for both individuals. Indications of this near-perfect symmetry are revealed in this photogrammetric comparison, when we overlay a grid and ruler which allows for easy measurable parameters. By applying the proper biometrics, it is possible to demonstrate this degree of symmetry. This exercise will be extremely important when we move on to the methodology portion of this paper. At first glance, this side-by-side, photogrammetric comparison suggests that Lovelady's head was larger, longer, and wider than Lee Oswald's head.

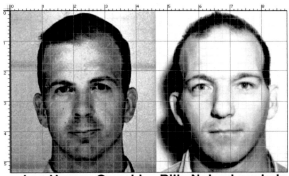

Lee Harvey Oswald   Billy Nolan Lovelady

However, by taking our methodology one step further, we can provide even better indications of the symmetrical properties of both subjects by superimposing flipped images of these frontal photographs:

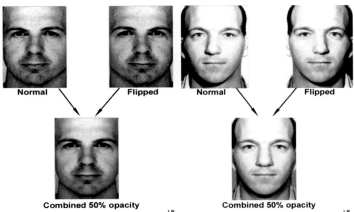

The next two images are enlargements of the Lovelady's 29 February 1964 FBI photograph and the Oswald NOPD mug shot. Both have been slightly tilted to adjust the horizontal plane of the eyes. Again, a grid and ruler have been superimposed, where this time the grid contains intersecting points or crosshairs that line up with the pupils of the eyes. This procedure shows measurable interpupillary distance between the two subjects.

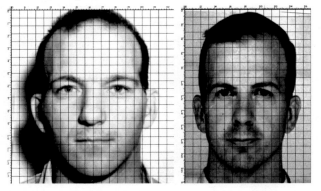

When we look at both subject's profiles, we note the following important difference in the location of the ears:

About the Control Image or "Probe"

The image or photograph to be tested is known as the "probe." The provenance of our probe or control image is an enlargement (or scaling up) of the Groden scan shown earlier above.

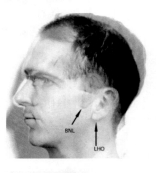

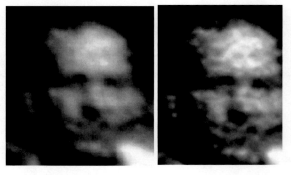

Control or "Probe" Image (Doorway Man)

The image first appeared in Robert Groden's book, *The Search for Lee Harvey Oswald: A Comprehensive Photographic Record* (1995). Many in the JFK research community have used the image to either confirm or refute the identity of Lovelady as Doorway Man. It is not known how Groden enhanced the photograph to obtain the enlargement. Above, Dennis Cimino has removed the haze and "mottled" condition of Groden's image to facilitate its study. No other adjustment has been made.

Bear in mind that Groden has already used this scan to identify Lovelady as the man in the doorway and has continued to proclaim Lovelady as Doorway Man as recently as the weekend of 17-18 October 2015, where he addressed a gathering of researchers in New Orleans observing the 76th birthday of Lee Oswald. It appears, Groden has never submitted the image to any bona fide, peer-reviewed scientific analysis, and published the results in the manner as is being done here. Most of the JFK research community has merely accepted his proclamation of Lovelady as Doorway Man.

But in the mid-1970s, Groden was of the persuasion that it was Lee Oswald in the doorway! In 1976, Groden and Pete Model published the paperback book, *JFK: The Case for Conspiracy*, where he wrote, "It is precisely at this point that one of the single most important still photos was taken—not only of the president but of his "assassin.""[10] On the very next page he wrote: "He bears an uncanny likeness to Lee Harvey Oswald. *Indeed, he could have been and probably was Oswald!*"[11]

In the fall, Groden began working for the HSCA, and in late October traveled to Denver, along with Kenneth Brooten, as detailed in the previous chapter, to interview and photograph Lovelady in his checkered colored shirt,[12] as can be seen below.

Groden's argument now resided in his contention that Lovelady's shirt was actually a black and red checkered patterned plaid shirt, and cited the "presence" of Lovelady outside the TSBD entrance in the John Martin film.[13] Groden overlooked the fact that the shirt worn by the man in the Martin film contains a breast pocket on the left side which has a distinctive flap, whereas the shirt he himself photographed Lovelady in 1976 does not exhibit this feature, as can be seen below. Moreover, Harold Weisberg noted that the individual in the Martin film, shown here, has his shirt buttoned all the way to the neck, whereas the man in the doorway has his shirt splayed open almost to his navel.[14]

As noted in the previous chapter, in 1998, researcher Dr. John Johnson published two exquisite articles in *The Fourth Decade*, which dealt with the man in the doorway issue. Recall that Johnson's analysis centered on the pocket flap, which was pointed out by Australian researcher Jim Baker. The following enhanced collage revisits the breast pocket with a flap and button of some type:

Above left, frame from the Martin film. The photographs above right, all taken by Groden in 1976.[15]

Furthermore, in 2014, Judyth Vary Baker conducted a computerized study of the pixel pattern exhibited by Doorway Man's shirt and concluded that it most closely resembled the rust-colored, richly textured shirt worn by Oswald the day and night of 22 November 1963.[16] These issues can certainly be clarified, and all doubts put to rest, if the probe (or control) image can be successfully submitted to the same forensic facial recognition overlay tests which have been described here.

Materials and Methods

1. There are three images in the public domain that offer the unique opportunity to perform overlay experiments on Doorway Man,

because of the angle in which he is presented in Altgens6, where he is showing the right side of this face and ear, which is an approximate 3/4 profile.

There are two photos of our subjects that offer the opposite orientation, which would be the left side of the face and ear. (see appendix) The introduction has shown the uncanny symmetrical properties of the faces of these two individuals, so when these images are flipped, we are able to produce these two workable facsimiles, which in forensic face recognition jargon are known as the "gallery":

The third image to be tested is a non-flipped photograph (right) of Lovelady published on 18 January 1979 by the *Dallas Times Herald* at the time of Lovelady's death. The photograph was taken by Bob Jackson in 1971. (See appendix.)

2. The computer program which allows us to conduct these experiments is one which is extremely popular, powerful and sophisticated—Adobe Photoshop. Another very good and open source program by the name of GIMP—GNU Image Manipulation Program—can also be used, however Photoshop has been chosen for this study because of program familiarity.

3. A screen-capture program which shows precise coordinates on a computer monitor is necessary to copy each individual rendition as the overlay is increased in opacity. In the case that an animation constructed from each progressive image is required, it is of utmost importance to avoid shifting of the resultant images to provide a much smoother transition. Gadwin PrintScreen has been chosen for this task.

4. Optional. In case animation is required, as mentioned in No. 3 above, a very good open source graphics editing program to use is PhotoScape.

Procedure

1. The control or probe (background) image is opened in Photoshop, followed by the two gallery or overlay images that will be used for testing. The gallery photos have been tinted magenta for Lovelady and blue for Oswald. This will allow differentiation of the exemplars.

2. In separate procedures, the image which will be superimposed, is selected with the select tool:

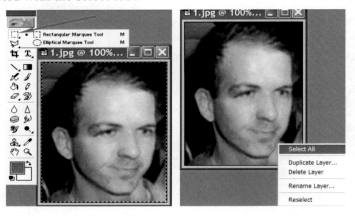

Alternatively, (above right) the user can right click on the image and select the entire image. The next step is to copy it into the clipboard, via Edit > Copy

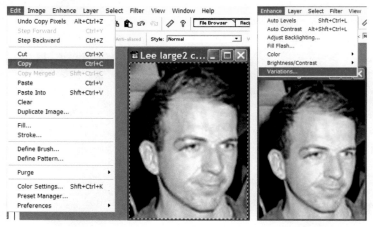

In order to color code the test images we must first modify them by using the color VARIATIONS tool, which is under the ENHANCE tab. This will take us to the variations page, where the image can be tinted to any color necessary:

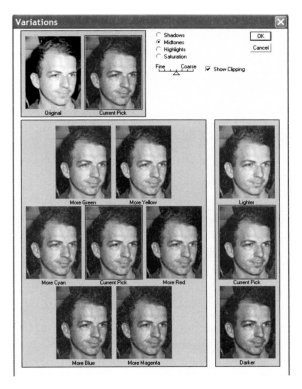

Next, cut out and isolate the heads of the individuals using the "polygonal lasso tool." This tool will neatly separate the heads from the gallery photos:

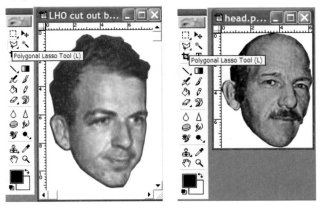

And finally, before trying to do any overlays, we must render the white areas transparent—this is also known as the "alpha channel"— so that only the heads are overlaid onto our probe image, excluding all other elements of the gallery photograph. This is done in different manners, depending on the version of Photoshop.[17] (See ENDNOTES section for details.)

Once the heads have been isolated, right click on the control image to activate, and paste the contents of the clipboard over the control image:

3. We have thus defined our first layer. The LAYER function at the top of the screen, allows manipulation of opacity values of the test image which can be overlaid onto the control image. There are two ways to control this function: 1. By directly entering the percentage value in the dialog box, or 2. By sliding the control triangle right or left:

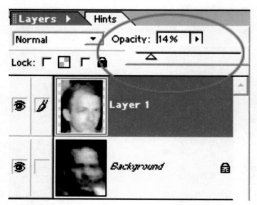

By slightly changing the opacity it is now possible to line up features. In this experiment, the eyes and ears have been scaled to match the control image, Doorway Man. At this juncture, the move tool is indispensable to tilt, size and move the overlay image to align and match the control image as much as possible:

4. Once satisfied with the position of the overlay, we are ready to start capturing the results. Unfortunately, this is not a function of Photoshop. To capture different degrees of opacity, it is necessary to use Gadwin PrintScreen. The process must be repeated after every adjustment of the opacity levels mentioned above. In this experiment we went from zero, to 5%, 10%, 15%, 20%, 25% and 30% opacity. After each capture, the opacity value is raised to the next level. Gadwin will place the captured image into the clipboard. Returning to Photoshop, we go to File > New > OK to create the new image with the correct dimensions:

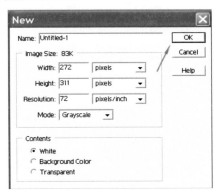

Paste the contents of the clipboard into Photoshop with Edit > Paste. Each resultant file is saved in JPEG format (Joint Photographic Experts Group), with a distinctive name which allows and defines an ascending order, i.e., LHO5%.jpg, LHO10%.jpg, etc.

By experimenting with the opacity levels, it is possible to obtain as many different versions of the overlay onto the control image as necessary, with varying intensities and opacity. The next illustration shows one of the gallery images in the process of being scaled, positioned and overlaid onto the probe image with a 25% degree of opacity:

Results and Measurements

After superimposing and overlaying all three exemplars onto our control image of Doorway Man, it is clear there is quite a bit of difference between them. The following collages and images show the empirical results of our tests and procedures.

Lovelady

Billy Lovelady-Doorman Overlay Collage

This first collage of results shows our flipped image of Lovelady.

Observations

Once interpupillary distance had been set, we attempted to scale the head of Lovelady as much as possible to match that of Doorway Man.

Here are some of the anomalies:

1. Nose is rounder, larger and more bulbous. The bridge is different. *Nose shifts to the right, displacing it from the shadow cast by the nose of Doorway Man.*

2. There is slightly more space between the lower lip and the tip of the chin which brings the mouth slightly higher.

3. Eyebrows are more arched and there is more space between eyes and brow ridge.

4. Shape of the chin is different, and the face is wider.

5. The forehead is swept back at a different, lower angle.

Our second set of results show how the *Dallas Times Herald* photograph of Lovelady of the article dated 18 January 1979 lines up in our overlay procedures:

Billy Lovelady-Doorman Overlay Collage using non-flipped Dallas Times Herald photograph

Observations

Once interpupillary distance had been set, once again, we attempted to scale the head of Lovelady as much as possible, to match that of Doorway Man. Here are some of the anomalies:

1. Nose is rounder, larger and more bulbous. The bridge is different. *Nose shifts to the right, displacing it from the shadow cast by the nose of Doorway Man.*

2. There is slightly more space between the lower lip and the tip of the chin which brings the mouth slightly higher.

3. Eyebrows are more arched and there is more space between eyes and brow ridge.

4. Shape of the chin is different, and the face is wider.

5. The forehead is swept back at a different, lower angle.

A key aspect of this overlay reveals and confirms that because Lovelady's face was wider than Doorway Man's, the horizontal adjustment required to match interpupillary distance drew the face inward, making it narrower, to the point of throwing the ear completely out of alignment. Here the right ear (left on photograph) fails to line up with Doorway Man's and does not even reach the required position.

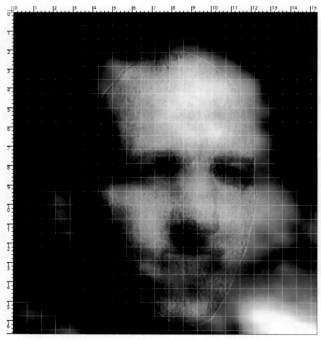

And the reason for this is probably because physiologically and anatomically speaking, the ear location on both subjects is different, as shown earlier in this study.

Oswald

Lee Oswald-Doorman Overlay Collage

Observations—Key Identifiers

1. Interpupillary distance between Oswald and Doorway Man is the same. This makes the eyes line up perfectly.

2. Nose matches, including bridge and general conformation. *More importantly, the nose is in perfect position to cast the shadow seen below Doorway Man's nose, (which was caused by the noon sun).*

3. Lips, which are pursed in a particular and specific manner, are a match.

4. Eyebrows and brow ridge are more horizontal and are a match. High forehead is a match.

5. Chin matches in size and shape. The face matches in both width and height.

6. The ear is a perfect match in location and size. (Note: Oswald had suffered a bruise over his left eye, which had caused swelling—when the image is flipped this area stands out somewhat.)

Photogrammetric Comparisons

Working backwards, we can now apply photogrammetric techniques using the results obtained above. First by using the flipped image of Lovelady:

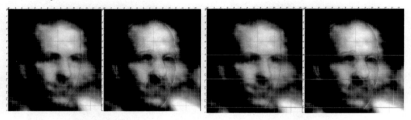

And finally, the photogrammetric comparisons using the *Dallas Times Herald* non-flipped photograph of Lovelady:

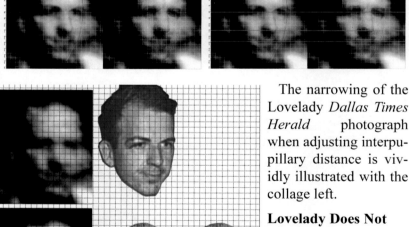

The narrowing of the Lovelady *Dallas Times Herald* photograph when adjusting interpupillary distance is vividly illustrated with the collage left.

Lovelady Does Not Fit Doorway Man

The empirical data obtained in this final exercise suggests that even if we were to exclude Lee Oswald as one of the subjects being tested using accepted facial forensic recognition and comparison protocol, both images of Lovelady, flipped and non-flipped, fail to line up with the features of Doorway Man. The evidence also clearly suggests that Bob Jackson's covert intention in 1971 was to pose Lovelady to make his features look like Doorway Man by pursing his lips and squinting his eyes. In doing so, the results presented here render him as an absurd carica-ture, not unlike "The Coneheads" of *Saturday Night Live* fame.

Lovelady Identified

But if Lovelady was not Doorway Man, then where was he located in Altgens6? Let's begin by reviewing Lovelady's Warren Commission testimony:

Mr. Ball: Where were you when the picture was taken?

Lovelady: Right there at the entrance of the building standing on the top of the step, would be here (indicating).

Mr. Ball: You were standing on which step?

Lovelady: It would be your top level.

Mr. Ball: The top step you were standing there?

Lovelady: Right.

Since we have proven that Doorway Man is not Lovelady, the figure known as Black Hole Man would be the most logical place to start, because he is one of only three people visible on the top step.

Here is our control or probe image:

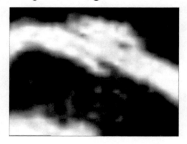

This image does not show the eyes of the individual in question; however, it does show the nose and mouth, including the lips, the upper lip area, and the philtrum. As established earlier, *interpupillary distance or other consistent features within the image* can be used.

These are the anatomical features that we will compare:

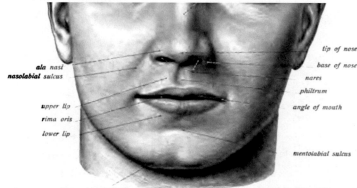

By Dr. Johannes Sobotta - Sobotta's Atlas and Text-book of Human Anatomy 1906, Public Domain, https://commons.wikimedia.org/w/index.php?curid=29847473

This is the first of our two gallery images. It is the same non-flipped photograph used earlier in this study, a contemporary photograph of Lovelady in his photo shoot with the FBI on 29 February 1964:

By applying exactly the same techniques detailed in this chapter, we should be able to draw empirical data that should allow us to narrow the possible identity of this man. Indeed, that is the case:

Billy Lovelady - "Black hole man"
comparison overlay

LR

1. The area and size of mouth and lips are a perfect match.

2. The distance covered between the nose and the upper lip, including the philtrum, is a perfect match.

3. The tip of the nose, which contains a slight skin tone, is a perfect match to Lovelady's nose in both size and width. More importantly, and as shown above, its placement is consistent with the shadow cast by the nose of our probe image.

4. The perioral creases of the probe image are somewhat more pronounced because it appears the individual is squinting his eyes in the noon sun, which tends to involuntarily draw these features slightly upward.

And here is the photogrammetric study of this overlay:

Photogrammetric comparison

191

Even though the probe image does not allow us to set interpupillary distance as in earlier examples, the features below the eyes are visible enough to allow the use of digital overlay technology, which aids in the identification of this individual.

Our second gallery image is the same one used in the calibration section above. As noted, it was taken by CBS in 1967 as part of an investigative program which was never broadcast. When squinting his eyes, Lovelady, like many people, had the involuntary habit of creasing the perioral areas around his mouth, as seen in the above photograph. This made the area more prominent, with light reflecting off of it. This anatomical detail yields results that are even more compelling than those shown in our previous test:

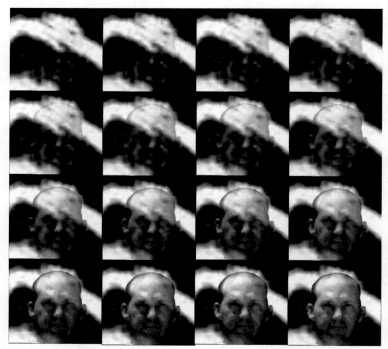

16 image collage with increasing opacity values.

LR

When we overlaid the 1967 CBS photograph onto our probe image, even Lovelady's perioral creases lined up perfectly with those of Black Hole Man.

Again, working backwards, when we ran our photogrammetric comparison, this was the result obtained:

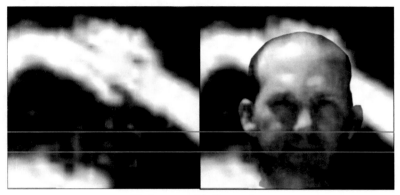

Photogrammetric Comparison

The Shirts Also Tell A Story

As mentioned earlier in this chapter, Judyth Baker has been working on pixel degradation and blurring of the shirts of our test subjects. The following collage replicates her work.

The image at left is from Lovelady's plaid shirt from the same Bob Jackson 1971 photo shoot.

The shirt at right is Lee Oswald's shirt, rendered in black and white. Both have been subjected to the same increases in blur values and changes in brightness and contrast, to try to replicate the pattern of the shirt seen on Doorway Man.

Hopefully, the reader will be able to make a comparison, using not only the pattern of the fabric, but the way shadows are cast on both samples.

And this is what the Altgens6 doorway probably looked like on 22 November 1963, before it was altered:

A Blender Closeup

This Blender representation of the doorway figures show how the shadows have been very closely replicated in our scene. A chin comparison with our probe image reveals the possibility that the notch projected as a shadow below Doorway Man's chin actually belongs to Lee Oswald. But then again, we already knew that it certainly was Lee Oswald in the TSBD doorway.

Conclusion

This chapter has confirmed the reliability of photographic overlays in the comparison, assessment and measurement of biometric and photogrammetric parameters, which when properly applied, can aid in the identification and/or refutation of the individuals in question. The methodology used in this study, and the empirical data obtained, unequivocally prove that the key identifiers stated above match up perfectly with Lee Oswald, who truly was "the man in the doorway." Conversely, these same identifiers exclude Lovelady to a high degree of certainty as Doorway Man. Additional image overlay testing of the second figure in the doorway reveal that "Black Hole Man" was indeed Lovelady. And finally, our Blender closeup of the doorway replicates the shadow of Lee Oswald's chin.

ENDNOTES

1. Bonafede, Dom, *New York Herald Tribune*, 24 May 1964, "The Picture With a Life of Its Own," p. 2
2. Ibid. 4
3. Ibid. (Francis Beckman, who had been sent by Harris to take a picture, was almost thrown in jail for "harassing" Lovelady)
4. Ibid. 5
5. Weisberg, Harold, *Whitewash II* (1966), image section
6. Ibid.
7. Cinque used the same 35mm Nikkorex camera with 105mm telephoto lens loaded with Eastman Kodak Tri-X film set at 30 feet focal length.
8. John Kelin provided copies of the actual sheets of the Ray Marcus overlays.

9. Kelin, John, *Praise from a Future Generation: The Assassination of John F. Kennedy and the First Generation Critics of the Warren Report* (2007), p. 227
10. Groden and Model, *JFK: The Case for Conspiracy,* p. 147
11. Ibid. 148
12, Rivera, Larry, "HSCA Activities of Kenneth Brooten, Legal Counsel," 25 January 2015 (see HSCA RIF#: 180-10114-10406)
13. Groden, Robert, *The Killing of a President* (1993), p. 187
14. Weisberg, Harold, *Picturing the Corruption of the JFK Assassination* (1996), p. 35
15. HSCA RIF#: 180-10114-10405, *The Killing of a President* (1993), p. 187
16. jamesfetzer.blogspot.ca/2015/07/jfk-judyth-vary-baker-cements-oswald-in.html
17. Photoshop: Mode > Indexed color > Mode > Color Table > Select Eyedropper tool > "touch" white area with eyedropper to render transparency. Note: To overlay the colorized gallery image, it is necessary to convert the probe to "RGB color" via Mode > RGB Color. If this is not done, the gallery image will revert to black and white.

Original non-flipped images of subjects

9

The Travails of the Rust-Colored Shirt

From day one, the shirt that Oswald wore on 22 November 1963, became a lightning rod for controversy and speculation. To paraphrase early researcher and author Sylvia Meagher, "nothing less than the total exoneration" of the accused assassin hung in the balance.[1]

Inasmuch as James Altgens's fifth photograph taken that day showed what seemed to be a person in the doorway at the top of the entrance steps of the TSBD wearing the same shirt, and who looked remarkably like Oswald. As mentioned several times in this book, Harold Weisberg wrote entire chapters on this issue, and did a nine-point study comparing the shirt of Doorway Man and the one worn by Lee the night of 22 November.[2]

Later that weekend, after parading Oswald around City Hall in his distinctive richly textured shirt, and submitting him to a couple of identification lineups, he was suddenly stripped of it and laid bare in the T-shirt he had been wearing underneath.

Oswald vehemently protested the fact that he had been stripped of this shirt and was being shown in the final lineup in a plain white T-shirt, while others were being shown in normal shirts and jackets.[3]

OSWALD complained of a lineup wherein he had not been granted a request to put on a jacket similar to those worn by some of the other individuals in the lineup.

on __11/23/63__ at __Dallas, Texas__	File #	__DL .89-43__
by Special Agent __JAMES W. BOOKHOUT__ /wvm	Date dictated	__11/24/63__

103

This document contains neither recommendations nor conclusions of the FBI. It is the property of the FBI and is loaned to your agency; it and its contents are not to be distributed outside your agency.

But what seemed to attract so much attention to Oswald's shirt? On the night of the 23rd, the FBI had already visited Lovelady and obtained his assurance that he was the man in the doorway,[4] so why the insistence in documenting what he had been wearing?

On 30 November and 4-5 December 1963, the FBI interviewed a cross-section of witnesses, including DPD officers who had seen and interacted with Oswald on 22 November, to obtain their impressions on what he had been wearing, and if possible, to identify what color shirt he had on.

They were shown the actual "rust brown colored" shirt.[5] This chapter analyzes the travails of that "rust brown colored shirt" and how the opinions of the witnesses served to cement the shirt that Oswald was wearing, hence, his presence in the doorway.

FBI agents Vernon Mitchem and John T. Kessler did most of the legwork, interviewing employees of the TSBD and witnesses in Irving.[6]

Starting with the very controversial Mary Bledsoe, who many researchers have noted "turned her head away from him not wishing to converse with him" because he looked so "dirty and disheveled," we note that her very first impression when shown the shirt was, "No, no that is not the shirt."

Then, she flipped when she supposedly noted the "ragged elbow" on the *right sleeve* which had a hole in that area. Later in the same interview, we are told that "her first impression was that the left sleeve on Oswald's shirt was the sleeve that had the ragged elbow; however, she was not positive."[7]

The following excerpts are from the Oswald 201 File, Vol. 8 (mffpdf_95643 pp. 301-318, in PDF file 129-146, under heading *C. Shirt of Lee Harvey Oswald*), which as mentioned above, instead of shedding light on the shirt Oswald was wearing that day, only serve to raise more incertitude about the entire affair. One possible reason for this might have been because those in control of the investigation knew the shirt worn by Doorway Man would be a problem in maintaining Oswald as the "patsy."

Our next witness, Buell Wesley Frazier, who allegedly saw Oswald carry a small package cupped under his arm pit, was completely unable to identify the "rust-colored" shirt that was shown to him on 5 December 1963, perhaps because he wore a blue jacket into work that day that was later found in the basement employee dressing room of the TSBD company:[8]

FRAZIER was shown a rust brown sport shirt with a hole in the right sleeve at the elbow, which, according to the arresting officers, was being worn by OSWALD at the time of his arrest on November 22, 1963. FRAZIER was unable to identify this shirt as having been worn by OSWALD on November 22, 1963.

on ___12/5/63___ at ___Dallas, Texas___   File # ___DL 89-43___

by Special Agent ___VERNON MITCHEM AND JOHN T. KESLER: mam___   304 Date dictated ___12/5/63___

CS COPY   201-28924

This document contains neither recommendations nor conclusions of the FBI. It is the property of the FBI and is loaned to your agency; it and its contents are not to be distributed outside your agency.

Roy Truly stated that the shirt looked familiar, but as previously stated, he believed Oswald was wearing light clothing and had on a white T-shirt or light-colored sport shirt.

Mr. TRULY was shown a rust brown sport shirt with a hole in the right sleeve at the elbow, which, according to the arresting officers, was being worn by OSWALD at the time he was arrested on November 22, 1963. TRULY stated that the shirt looked familiar to him but as previously stated he believes that OSWALD was wearing light clothing and had on a white tee-shirt or a light colored sport shirt.

on _____12/5/63_____ at _____Dallas, Texas_____ File # _____DL 89-43_____

by Special Agents_____VERNON MITCHEM AND JOHN T. KESLER: mam_____ 305 _____ Date dictated _____12/5/63_____

This document contains neither recommendations nor conclusions of the FBI. It is the property of the FBI and is loaned to your agency; it and its contents are not to be distributed outside your agency.

Charles Givens stated the above described sport shirt appeared to be like the one Oswald was wearing on 22 November 1963, but that he could not definitely identify this as the shirt.

GIVENS was shown a rust brown sport shirt with a hole in the right sleeve at the elbow, which, according to the arresting officers, was being worn by OSWALD at the time of his arrest on November 22, 1963. GIVENS stated the above-described sport shirt appeared to be similar to the one OSWALD was wearing on November 22, 1963, but that he could not state definitely that this was the shirt.

on _____12/5/63_____ at _____Dallas, Texas_____ File # _____DL 89-43_____

by Special Agents_____VERNON MITCHEM AND JOHN T. KESLER: mam_____ 306 _____ Date dictated _____12/5/63_____

This document contains neither recommendations nor conclusions of the FBI. It is the property of the FBI and is loaned to your agency; it and its contents are not to be distributed outside your agency.

Linnie Mae Randle, Wesley Frazier's sister, was completely out of the ballpark on the issue of the rust-colored shirt, failing to identify the shirt, and thinking it had been "solid color and light," which was not even close to reality. This is the same "witness" who reported Oswald had placed a package in her brother's car the morning of 22 November 1963.

Mrs. RANDLE was shown a rust brown sport shirt with a hole in the right sleeve at the elbow, which, according to the arresting officers, was being worn by OSWALD at the time of his arrest on November 22, 1963. Mrs. RANDLE stated that the above-described shirt does not look familiar to her, that OSWALD could have been wearing this shirt, but she believes that the shirt OSWALD was wearing on the morning of November 22, 1963, was a solid color and light.

on _____12/5/63_____ at _____Irving, Texas_____ File # _____DL 89-43_____

by Special Agents_____VERNON MITCHEM AND JOHN T. KESLER: mam_____ 308 _____ Date dictated _____12/5/63_____

This document contains neither recommendations nor conclusions of the FBI. It is the property of the FBI and is loaned to your agency; it and its contents are not to be distributed outside your agency.

Junior Jarman said it looked "vaguely familiar" to him, but could not recall with certainty what type of shirt Oswald had worn that day:

> JARMAN was shown a rust brown sport shirt with a hole in the right sleeve at the elbow, which, according to the arresting officers, was being worn by OSWALD at the time of his arrest on November 22, 1963. JARMAN stated that the above-described shirt was vaguely familiar, but he could not recall if this shirt was worn by OSWALD on November 22, 1963.

on __12/5/63__ at __Dallas, Texas__   File # __DL 89-43__

by Special Agent __VERNON MITCHEM AND JOHN T. KESLER: mam__   Date dictated __12/5/63__

307

This document contains neither recommendations nor conclusions of the FBI. It is the property of the FBI and is loaned to your agency; it and its contents are not to be distributed outside your agency.

This next witness, Mrs. Robert Reid, tells a truly amazing tale. Mrs. Reid had been down at the curb in front of the TSBD building at the time of the shots.

She supposedly made it back up to her office on the second floor in time to see Oswald cross all the way in front of her from the rear lunch room, supposedly mumbling to himself.

Bear in mind that Oswald allegedly had just come down from the sixth floor, purchased his soft drink from the vending machine, and had just had an "encounter" with police officer Marrion Baker and Roy Truly in the second-floor lunchroom.

Her description of what she saw Oswald wearing completely contradicts Baker.

> Mrs. REID stated that to the best of her recollection, OSWALD was wearing a white tee-shirt and a pair of pants, color unknown. She stated that she had never seen OSWALD wear a regular shirt.
>
> Mrs. REID was shown a rust brown sport shirt with a hole in the right sleeve at the elbow, which, according to arresting officers, was being worn by OSWALD at the time of his arrest on November 22, 1963. She said that she could not recall ever seeing this shirt before and was certain that OSWALD did not have this shirt on at the time she saw him on November 22, 1963.

on __12/5/63__ at __Dallas, Texas__   File # __DL 89-43__

by Special Agent __VERNON MITCHEM AND JOHN T. KESLER: mam__   Date dictated __12/5/63__

309

CS COPY

201-28924

This document contains neither recommendations nor conclusions of the FBI. It is the property of the FBI and is loaned to your agency; it and its contents are not to be distributed outside your agency.

Below is Mrs. Reid's actual handwritten account of the above:

He had a cope in his hand

I did not under stand what he said.
When I saw him he was dressed in a
white T-shirt and I don't recall what his trousers
was like. I did not see him any more
after that.

Marrion Baker stated in his Warren Commission testimony that even though he was in a hurry and did not see Oswald for an extended period, he was positive he had been wearing a light brown jacket of some kind, which he later realized had been a shirt which hung out over his pants, with a white undershirt, which is exactly the attire seen on Doorway Man. Despite Baker being unsure about it being a "shirt" or a "jacket," he was sure that is what Oswald had been wearing, and not a bare T-shirt as described by Mrs. Reid.

Mr. BELIN. Did you notice what clothes the man was wearing as he came up to you?
Mr. BAKER. At that particular time I was looking at his face, and it seemed to me like he had a light brown jacket on and maybe some kind of white-looking shirt.
Anyway, as I noticed him walking away from me, it was kind of dim in there that particular day, and it was hanging out to his side.
Mr. BELIN. Handing you what has been marked as Commission Exhibit 150, would this appear to be anything that you have ever seen before?
Mr. BAKER. Yes, sir; I believe that is the shirt that he had on when he came— I wouldn't be sure of that. It seemed to me like that other shirt was a little bit darker than that whenever I saw him in the homicide office there.
Mr. BELIN. What about when you saw him in the School Book Depository Building, does this look familiar as anything he was wearing, if you know?
Mr. BAKER. I couldn't say whether that was—it seemed to me it was a light-colored brown but I couldn't say it was that or not.
Mr. DULLES. Lighter brown did you say, I am just asking what you said. I couldn't quite hear.
Mr. BAKER. Yes, sir; all I can remember it was in my recollection of it it was a light brown jacket. WC3H257

Bonnie Ray Williams wanted nothing at all to do with the "rust-colored shirt" and failed to identify it in any way, shape or form:

WILLIAMS was shown a rust brown sport shirt with a hole in the right sleeve at the elbow, which, according to the arresting officers, was being worn by OSWALD at the time of his arrest on November 22, 1963. WILLIAMS was unable to identify this shirt and could not recall ever seeing OSWALD either wearing this shirt or a shirt similar in appearance.

on 12/5/63 at Dallas, Texas File # DL 89-43
by Special Agent S VERNON MITCHEM AND JOHN T. KESLER: mam 310 Date dictated 12/5/63
This document contains neither recommendations nor conclusions of the FBI. It is the property of the FBI and is loaned to your agency; it and its contents are not to be distributed outside your agency.

This next mysterious passage of an interview conducted on 22 November the day of the assassination, was not dictated until a week later, and was finally written up on the 30th, where FBI agent Gary S. Wilson interviewed an *unnamed person* who distinctly remembered Oswald wearing only a *"white or extremely light-colored shirt"* while being brought outside the Texas Theater on 22 November:

Date __November 30, 1963__

1

On the afternoon of November 22, 1963, as LEE HARVEY OSWALD was being removed from the Texas Theater by police officers, I had occasion to view him. I distinctly remember that he was wearing either a white or extremely light colored shirt and dark trousers. This observation was made outside the theater while officers escorted him from the theater entrance to a waiting police car. There were several officers around OSWALD, and my only definite recollection is of the color of his clothing. Subject was not wearing a hat at this time.

on __11/22/63__ at __Dallas, Texas__ File # __DL 89-43__

by Special Agent __GARY S. WILSON/gm__ Date dictated __11/29/63__

This document contains neither recommendations nor conclusions of the FBI. It is the property of the FBI and is loaned to your agency; it and its contents are not to be distributed outside your agency.

The Strange Case of Paul Bentley

It is necessary to pause now and consider Paul Bentley, who was senior polygraph examiner at the DPD.[9] Bentley was involved in the arrest of Lee Oswald at the Texas Theater that afternoon, along with Officers Montgomery and Carroll.

According to a 23 November 1963 article by *The Dallas Morning News*, *"Detective Paul Bentley sprained an ankle during the fracas."*[10] Years later, when George O'Toole interviewed Bentley for his 1974 book, *The Assassination Tapes,* Bentley advised O'Toole that he had this ankle in a cast[11] that same day, with the inference being that he had been unable to administer Buell Wesley Frazier's polygraph because of this incident.

He was also in the squad car with Oswald as he was being driven to City Hall and removed his billfold from his rear left pocket while in the car.[12] If anyone had a good look at what Oswald was wearing that day, it was Paul Bentley. Bentley positively identified the rust-colored shirt as that worn by Lee Oswald at the time of his arrest at the Texas Theater:

BENTLEY stated that as he recalled, LEE HARVEY
OSWALD was wearing a brown long sleeved sport shirt, a pair
of dark trousers and no jacket.

This color photograph by Jim McCammon unequivocally confirms
what Lee Oswald was wearing when arrested at the Texas Theater.

As an aside, the McCammon photograph, which for many years
had been published cropped and in black and white, shows Bentley
in full splendor, cigar in mouth, hair neatly combed, enjoying his
moment of glory, showing no ill-effects of a severely sprained ankle,
which later supposedly required it to be immobilized in a cast.[13]

Lieutenant PAUL BENTLEY of the Dallas Police
Department stated that he was at the scene of the arrest
of LEE HARVEY OSWALD by the Dallas Police Department
on November 22, 1963, following the shooting of Officer
J. D. TIPPIT of the Dallas Police Department. BENTLEY
stated that he observed OSWALD wearing this shirt and
that this shirt was worn by OSWALD all during the time
of his arrest, subsequent to his arrest, and transportation to the Homicide Bureau of the Dallas Police Department and turned over to Captain WILL FRITZ of the Dallas
Police Department.

BENTLEY stated that he accompanied OSWALD to
the Dallas Police Department after his arrest where he
was released to Captain WILL FRITZ, Homicide Bureau,
Dallas Police Department, Dallas, Texas.

on 12/4/63 at Dallas, Texas File # DL 89-43

by Special Agent VINCENT E. DRAIN/gmt Date dictated 12/4/63

CS COPY 201-28924

This document contains neither recommendations nor conclusions of the FBI. It is the property of the FBI and is loaned to
your agency; it and its contents are not to be distributed outside your agency.

Officer Ray Hawkins certified that "at no time did Oswald remove" his rust brown colored shirt until he had been turned over to Captain Will Fritz.

> RAY HAWKINS stated, after viewing this shirt on December 4, 1963, that this was positively the shirt that LEE HARVEY OSWALD was wearing at the time he was arrested on November 22, 1963, following the shooting of Officer J. D. TIPPIT of the Dallas Police Department.
>
> HAWKINS stated that he was a patrolman with the Dallas Police Department and participated in the arrest of OSWALD on November 22, 1963. HAWKINS related that he accompanied OSWALD to the office of Captain WILL FRITZ of the Dallas Police Department and that at no time was this shirt removed from OSWALD until he was turned over to Captain WILL FRITZ in the Homicide Bureau at the headquarters of the Dallas Police Department, Dallas, Texas.

on __12/4/63__ at __Dallas, Texas__ File # __DL 89-43__

by Special Agent __VINCENT E. DRAIN/gmf__ Date dictated __12/4/63__

This document contains neither recommendations nor conclusions of the FBI. It is the property of the FBI and is loaned to your agency; it and its contents are not to be distributed outside your agency.

Similarly, Captain W.R. Westbrook was "fairly certain" about the shirt being the same one in which Oswald had been arrested.

> On December 4, 1963, one brown shirt in color, which shirt had been previously obtained from Captain GEORGE M. DOUGHTY and Lieutenant CARL DAY of the Crime Laboratory of the Dallas Police Department on November 22, 1963, and which shirt had been examined by the FBI Laboratory on November 23, 1963, was exhibited on this day to the following individual:
>
> Captain W. R. WESTBROOK of the Dallas Police Department after viewing this shirt on December 4, 1963, stated he "is fairly certain" that this is the same shirt that he saw LEE HARVEY OSWALD wearing at the time of his arrest on November 22, 1963.

on __12/4/63__ at __Dallas, Texas__ File # __DL 89-43__

by Special Agent __VINCENT E. DRAIN/gmf__ Date dictated __12/4/63__

This document contains neither recommendations nor conclusions of the FBI. It is the property of the FBI and is loaned to your agency; it and its contents are not to be distributed outside your agency.

Bob Carroll, helped arrest Oswald in the Texas Theater, and supposedly helped disarm him, along with Officer MacDonald. When shown the rust-colored shirt, he was positive it was the same one that Oswald had on at the time of arrest.

---

5 1   Date __December 4, 1963__

On December 4, 1963, one brown shirt in color, which shirt had been previously obtained from Captain GEORGE M. DOUGHTY and Lieutenant CARL DAY of the Crime Laboratory of the Dallas Police Department on November 22, 1963, and which shirt had been examined by the FBI Laboratory on November 23, 1963, was exhibited on this day to the following individual:

BOB K. CARROLL, an officer of the Dallas Police Department, stated that upon seeing this shirt on December 4, 1963, that this was the shirt that LEE HARVEY OSWALD was wearing at the time he arrested him on November 22, 1963, following the shooting of Dallas police officer J. D. TIPPIT. CARROLL states that he accompanied OSWALD, after the arrest, to the Homicide Bureau of the Dallas Police Department, namely, to the office of Captain WILL FRITZ. At no time was this shirt removed from OSWALD and he was wearing this shirt at the time OSWALD was turned over to Captain WILL FRITZ on November 22, 1963.

on __12/4/63__ at __Dallas, Texas__ File # DL 89-43

by Special Agent __VINCENT E. DRAIN/gmf__ Date dictated __12/4/63__

315

This document contains neither recommendations nor conclusions of the FBI. It is the property of the FBI and is loaned to your agency; it and its contents are not to be distributed outside your agency.

The omnipotent Captain Will Fritz was shown the same shirt on 4 December 1963 and also confirmed for the FBI that the rust-brown colored shirt was the same one Oswald was wearing when he was brought into his office.

Fritz did, however, inform the FBI exactly what shirt he was wearing, which was confirmed years later when a copy of his handwritten notes surfaced in the late 1990s, namely that Oswald admitted only to have changed his pants or "britches." (see Fritz's notes in appendix at the end of Chapter 13)

---

1   Date __December 4, 1963__

On December 4, 1963, one brown shirt in color, which shirt had been previously obtained from Captain GEORGE M. DOUGHTY and Lieutenant CARL DAY of the Crime Laboratory of the Dallas Police Department on November 22, 1963, and which shirt had been examined by the FBI Laboratory on November 23, 1963, was exhibited on this day to the following individual:

Captain WILL FRITZ, Homicide Bureau of the Dallas Police Department, Dallas, Texas, was exhibited this shirt on December 4, 1963. Captain FRITZ stated

that he could positively state that this was the same
shirt that OSWALD was wearing at the time he was brought
to his office by the arresting officers of the Dallas
Police Department following LEE HARVEY OSWALD's arrest
on November 22, 1963.

FRITZ stated that OSWALD in an interview told
him on November 22, 1963, that he had changed his
trousers that day but had not changed his shirt that
day prior to his arrest by the Dallas Police Department
on the afternoon of November 22, 1963. FRITZ related,
however, that on the following day, November 23, 1963,
OSWALD claimed that he had changed his entire clothing.

on __12/4/63__ at __Dallas, Texas__ — File # __DL 89-43__

by Special Agent __VINCENT E. DRAIN/gmf__ — 316 — Date dictated __12/4/63__

This document contains neither recommendations nor conclusions of the FBI. It is the property of the FBI and is loaned to
your agency; it and its contents are not to be distributed outside your agency.

It is only at the end of this document that we find the addition of
Oswald supposedly claiming that he changed his "entire clothing."

Detective Jim Leavelle is the man seen in the light-colored suit
reacting to Jack Ruby's shooting of Oswald in the basement of City
Hall on 24 November 1963. Leavelle confirmed exactly the same
information as stated by Captain Fritz above and could "positively"
identify the shirt worn by Oswald.

On December 4, 1963, one brown shirt in color,
which shirt had been previously obtained from Captain
GEORGE M. DOUGHTY and Lieutenant CARL DAY of the Crime
Laboratory of the Dallas Police Department on November
22, 1963, and which shirt had been examined by the FBI
Laboratory on November 23, 1963, was exhibited on this
day to the following individual:

Detective JAMES R. LEAVELLE, Homicide Bureau,
Dallas Police Department, Dallas, Texas, was exhibited
this shirt on December 4, 1963. Detective LEAVELLE
stated that he could positively state that this shirt
is the same shirt that he observed on LEE HARVEY OSWALD
at the time he was brought by the arresting officer to
the office of Captain WILL FRITZ of the Dallas Police
Department on November 22, 1963.

on __12/4/63__ at __Dallas, Texas__ — File # __DL 89-43__

by Special Agent __VINCENT E. DRAIN/gmf__ — 317 — Date dictated __12/4/63__

This document contains neither recommendations nor conclusions of the FBI. It is the property of the FBI and is loaned to
your agency; it and its contents are not to be distributed outside your agency.

The final entry in Volume 8 of the Oswald 201 file is an interview
conducted by New Orleans FBI SAIC Warren De Brueys of Detective

Fay Turner, DPD. "Turner identified this shirt as being the shirt *that he personally seized* [Emphasis added] by search warrant from Lee Harvey Oswald's room, 1026 North Beckley Street (sic), Dallas, on November 22, 1963, *in the presence of Detective Walter E. Potts and District Attorney BILL ALEXANDER*." [Emphasis added]

This inexplicable entry runs completely counter to what all other DPD officers, detectives, and captains told the FBI on 4-5 December, about their identification of the rust-brown colored shirt.

---

1   Date ___12/4/63___

                 Detective FAY M. TURNER, Dallas Police Department, was shown a faded brown long-sleeve shirt which was included among material received from the Dallas Police Department, November 26, 1963, as having been seized by search warrant from the room of LEE HARVEY OSWALD, 1026 North Beckley Street, Dallas, on November 22, 1963.

                 Detective TURNER identified this shirt as being the shirt that he personally seized by search warrant from LEE HARVEY OSWALD's room, 1026 North Beckley Street, Dallas, on November 22, 1963, in the presence of Detective WALTER E. POTTS and District Attorney BILL ALEXANDER.

---

on __12/4/63__ at Dallas, Texas   DL 89-43
                                       File # __100-10461__
by Special Agent __WARREN C. DE BRUEYS: mam__   Date dictated __12/4/63__

This document contains neither recommendations nor conclusions of the FBI. It is the property of the FBI and is loaned to your agency; it and its contents are not to be distributed outside your agency.

Conclusions

The documentation presented above leaves no doubt, that the "rust-brown" colored shirt in which Oswald was photographed the night of the assassination, is the same one he wore during the entire day, while being arrested at the Texas Theater, and especially while standing in the doorway of the TSBD. The few instances which disagreed with DPD personnel, namely Mary Bledsoe, Mrs. Robert Reid, the unknown FBI witness, and Detective Fay Turner, were so wild and out-of-touch with reality, that any statistical analysis would have discarded their statements because of lack of credibility. And finally, in a taped interview of Lovelady by Kenneth Brooten of the HSCA on 13 November 1976, Lovelady had this to say about the clothes he saw Oswald wearing that day:

KB: Do you recall how he [Oswald] was dressed that day?

LOVELADY: [unintelligible] . . . ordinary top work shirt and a T-shirt.

KB: Did you see pictures of him after his arrest?

LOVELADY: Sure did.

KB: Did he have the same . . . after his arrest?

LOVELADY: Yes, he was, when he was at work.

ENDNOTES

1. Meagher, Sylvia, *Accessories After the Fact: The Warren Commission, the Authorities & the Report on the JFK Assassination* (1966), p. 84
2. Weisberg, Harold, *Whitewash II* (1966), pp. 241, 251
3. FBI 105-82555 Oswald HQ File, Section 21, p. 103. Also see *Dealey Plaza Echo*, Vol. 3, No. 2, July 1999, maryferrell.org/showDoc.html?docId=16241&search=Howard_Brennan#relPageId=1&tab=page
4. Bonafede, Dom, *New York Herald Tribune*, 24 May 1964, "The Picture With a Life of Its Own," p. 2
5. Oswald 201 File, Vol. 8, pp. 301-318 (in PDF file 129-146 under heading *C. Shirt of Lee Harvey Oswald*)
6. Ibid.
7. Ibid. 302
8. jfk.hood.edu/Collection/Weisberg%20Subject%20Index%20Files/K%20Disk/Kaiser%20Frankie/Item%2001.pdf (CE163 is the photo of the blue jacket)
9. O'Toole, George, *The Assassination Tapes* (1974), p. 173
10. *The Dallas Morning News*, 23 November 1963
11. O'Toole, George, *The Assassination Tapes* (1974), p. 181
12. Ibid.162
13. time.com/3804560/an-end-to-conspiracy-rare-photo-of-lee-harvey-oswalds-arrest-suggests-why-hes-guilty

10

Why Was Buell Wesley Frazier Erased from Altgens 6?

"The world is a dangerous place, not because of the people who are evil; but because of the people who don't do anything about it."

—Albert Einstein

We are not going to talk about curtain rods in this chapter. The curtain rod story is a red herring; therefore, we will do away with it right from the top. This chapter will not argue if it was Lovelady or Oswald in the doorway, or the difference between their shirts. That has already been answered and proven in Chapter 8. The next order of business is to find out why was Buell Wesley Frazier appears to have been erased from Altgens's famous photograph.

Buell Wesley Frazier was born 4 June 1944.[1] At 19, he arrived in Irving in early September 1963 from the town of Huntsville, 200 miles away, to find work and live with his sister Linnie Mae Randle, her husband Bill, and their three children.[2] With his mother also visiting with Linnie in November 1963,[3] he was left with no choice but to sleep on the couch of the Randle's living room.[4] There are two versions of how he obtained his employment at the TSBD. His Warren Commission testimony states he went through the Massey Employment Agency.[5] They referred him there, and the same day he interviewed with Roy Truly, he was hired.[6] However, his sister stated she was the one who enabled him to land the job at the TSBD,[7] where he was making the minimum wage of $1.25 per hour.[8] At any rate, he did end up working there on 13 September 1963, and the rest is history.

22 November 1963

Frazier got up at 6:30 AM, had breakfast with his mother and family at 7:15,[9] picked up Oswald, who had been waiting for him outside, after walking half a block from the Paine residence. He took Stemmons Freeway downtown and arrived at the TSBD parking lot in time for work. The following image shows this was not just any parking lot. It was well removed from the work place. From there they walked the three blocks to work.[10] It was cold and foggy and had been raining that morning.[11] At this point he supposedly got separated from Oswald, who advanced ahead of him and went into the building. Frazier's excuse for staying behind was that he wanted to "charge" the car's battery.[12] After at least a half-hour ride, it would be unnecessary to do this because the alternator/generator would have charged the battery by virtue of the time it would have taken to drive from Irving. Frazier worked alongside Lee Oswald on the first-floor filling orders until 11:00 AM.[13]

39. FRAZIER'S CAR PARKED IN APPROXIMATELY SAME LOCATION USED ON NOVEMBER 22, 1963. TEXAS SCHOOL BOOK DEPOS-ITORY IN BACKGROUND. (ARROW)

Frazier was standing on the TSBD front stairs[14] when the motorcade drove by, heard the shots, stayed for a few minutes at that position, then went back inside to eat his lunch in the basement. If true, Frazier was the only TSBD employee who did not leave the building to find out what everyone else was reacting to, and it would appear that the assassination of the President of the United States would not spoil his appetite.[15] He left the TSBD between 1:00 PM and 2:00 PM and went straight home.[16] The evidence shows, however, that Frazier did not go home, but supposedly went back to Irving to see his stepfather David Williams at the Irving Professional Center, who had been convalescing there for a month.[17] The only problem with this is that Frazier left Huntsville to "stay away from an abusive, alcoholic stepfather,"[18] so why would he be looking for solace from him of all people on this most tragic day? Between 4:00-5:00 PM, Linnie Mae approached the officers who were at the Paine's and advised Detective Adamcik that "her brother was visiting her father at Parkland Hospital, and *we* [Emphasis added] could reach him there."[19] According to the documents, Linnie Mae sent the officers to Parkland Hospital, which would appear she was buying time for Frazier, who could have been unaccounted for up to six hours. Since his car was not enclosed in any way, he could have left anytime, and apparently, he did.

He was arrested around 6:45 PM and taken to the Irving Police Department to wait for DPD agents Stovall, Rose and Adamcik. The policemen searched his car on the spot with "negative results."[20] Next, they went to the Randle residence and conducted a thorough search there where they found a .303 caliber British rifle with ammunition which was confiscated.[21]

His sister arrived at the house and the urban legend of Lee Oswald carrying a long package was born when Linnie Mae supposedly told the police about the long "suspicious" package she "saw" Lee with that morning. She was here to defend her brother at all cost. She then arranged for a Baptist priest to accompany all of them to City Hall in Dallas.[22]

These photographs taken the night of 22 November 1963, show what he was wearing at 12:30 PM that day; Frazier never had a chance to change his clothes.

The official story is that at 9:00 PM the DPD finished taking affidavits from both Buell and his sister Linnie Mae. They started back to Irving when a radio call came in asking them to turn around and go back to Dallas.[23] Captain Fritz ordered Frazier to take a polygraph test, which he allegedly passed "conclusively."[24] The test lasted until

12:10 AM, 23 November 1963. Many researchers believe this test was rigged. Much more on this will follow.

Frazier Gets Drafted

What better way to keep tabs on Buell Wesley Frazier? He was drafted into the Army and inducted on 2 August 1965 at the age of 21.[25] He was shipped to Europe as soon as he finished his basic training in October 1965, 23 months after the assassination.[26] Seven months later, he returned to the continental U.S. and was assigned to Fort Lewis, Washington.[27] This happened to be close to Seattle, a major embarkation point for Vietnam.[28] He was undoubtedly exposed to other young men who were on their way to 'Nam, some never to return alive. Frazier spent more than a year in suspense and limbo at Fort Lewis from June 1966 to August 1967.[29] **After two years of service as a cook, in August 1967, Frazier was "released from active duty" and transferred to *U.S. Army Reserve*.**[30] [Emphasis added.] According to Frazier in his HSCA interview, since he was not going to make a career out of the Army, he was given the choice of deferring his active duty service for later on. While the Vietnam War was raging and some of our major cities burning, he quietly went back to civilian life in Irving.[31]

At the age of 23, Buell Wesley Frazier completely missed the Vietnam War as if it had never happened. Most of his contemporaries were humping in the rice paddies of Vietnam, many returning in body bags. The implication is pretty obvious. From where he was in Fort Lewis, Washington he could have been in Saigon within 18 hours.[32]

In between Army stints, Frazier testified at the Shaw trial on 13 February 1969, but not without providing stiff resistance via his attorney Hollebeck. One of his conditions for testifying was that he would not be available to the press in New Orleans.[33] In his testimony under oath, he misstated his, Lovelady's and Shelley's positions, stating he was "at the top of the stairs," and Lovelady and Shelley were "right down in front of me at the bottom of the steps."[34]

At 28, Frazier returned to active duty and re-enlisted towards the end of the Vietnam war on 26 March 1973 at Ft. Polk, Louisiana. He went through Advanced Individual Training at Ft. Sill, Oklahoma on 16 July 1973. He returned to Texas 9 August 1973 at Ft. Bliss and went through artillery training in September 1973. From there he was transferred to Ft. Hood, Texas on 20 September 1973.[35] Frazier was promoted to Administrative Specialist on 1 October

1976 with the Headquarters Company 2nd Armed Division in Ft. Hood.[36] He finished his call of duty doing security for officers at base headquarters,[37] and was discharged on 25 March 1977 at the age of 32, at Ft. Hood, with the rank of sergeant.[38] He earned the following distinctions: National Defense Service Medal, Marksman Badge w/ Rifle Bar, Good Conduct Medal, Army Commendation Medal, and Expert Badge w/Rifle Bar.[39]

The Assassination Tapes

In 1975, Penthouse Press published George O'Toole's *The Assassination Tapes*. Douglas Horne praised this volume as "a delightful gem of a book" and "the evidence he presented is just as relevant—and just as valid—today, as it was in 1975."[40] Harold Weisberg criticized the book for two reasons: (a) he felt O'Toole had borrowed way too much from *Whitewash IV: The Top Secret Warren Commission Transcript of the JFK Assassination* (bordering on plagiarism) without giving him credit, and (b) he thought some of his wild speculation was too much for him to handle. Weisberg did not impugn however, the actual technology and methodology used by O'Toole.[41] Mark Lane totally embraced the technology and wished he had it when he was seeing and recording witnesses in Dallas; it would have sent him in other directions of investigation.[42]

Despite the controversy, O'Toole's investigation, which is based on voice stress analysis, is full of intrigue. The Psychological Stress Evaluator was invented in 1971[43] and patented in 1976 by Bell, McQuiston and Ford.[44] Their model PSE 1000 was marketed by the Dektor Counterintelligence and Security Co.[45] According to O'Toole, this device opened up a whole new playing field for investigators. He was now able to use recorded exchanges to chart the degree of stress in voice recordings no matter how old or far away.[46] O'Toole went back and retroactively analyzed voice recordings of Oswald and determined he was telling the truth about "not shooting anyone."[47]

Next, O'Toole analyzed Frazier's CBS interview shortly after the assassination,[48] and determined his degree of deception to have gone through the roof during the entire 42-second exchange:

"Judging from the PSE charts, when Buell Wesley Frazier made that statement, he was in a condition of sheer terror."[49]

Now O'Toole was ready to deal with Frazier. His first order of business was, of course, to find him. After failing to find him in Dallas, he visited Linnie Mae who quickly brushed him off. The only thing he could get out of her was the fact that Frazier was in the Army and could not be contacted.[50]

While in Dallas he called Paul Bentley, senior polygraph examiner at the time of the assassination. Bentley claimed not to have been on duty that night because of a sprained ankle that was in a cast. (He detected hard stress in his voice.)[51] Next, he decided to talk to R.D. Lewis, who, according to DPD documents, was the technician who administered the polygraph. Lewis denied administering any polygraph "connected to Oswald" that night (hard stress).[52] Furthermore, O'Toole established that Lewis never signed the DPD report that had Rose and Stovall's name on it, and "Lewis had not gone on record anywhere to the effect that Frazier had passed the test."[53] Lewis never testified before the Warren Commission.

For his next interview, he spoke to Detective Gerald Hill at his home. Hill advised O'Toole that Fritz could not have ordered the polygraph: "'cause Fritz didn't believe in polygraphs. He wouldn't use 'em." (near maximum stress).[54] He returned and spoke to Bentley again, who told him that was not true, he had run "many, many" examinations for Captain Fritz.[55]

He decided to see Detective Richard Stovall, who was with Frazier most of the early evening and night of 22 November until he dropped him off after midnight.[56] The first thing he found out from Stovall was that he was not present for Frazier's polygraph. (Hard stress appeared)[57] This directly contradicted his WCVIIH192 testimony.[58] He spoke to Gus F. Rose, the detective who was with Stovall and

Adamcik that day. Rose now contradicted Hill regarding Fritz's confidence in the polygraph test.[59]

O'Toole then contacted Lewis again, armed with information contained in Jim Bishop's 1967 book *The Day Kennedy Was Shot* and Warren Commission references that mentioned the polygraph. Bishop's book is highly prejudiced about the supposed guilt of Lee Oswald, however, and some of the information gleaned from his book deserves comment at this time.

Bishop wrote that Detective "Guy" (sic) [Gus] Rose was anxiously trying to locate Wesley Frazier, having contacted every "hospital, sanitarium, and clinic in and around Dallas,"[60] following information provided by Linnie Mae, who in a very general manner had informed Rose that Frazier was at "some hospital if the police wanted him."[61] That's a lot of man-hours to spend on vague and general information when time is of the essence. How could Linnie Mae have not known that Frazier's stepfather, David Williams, had been at the Irving Professional Center for more than a month?

Bear in mind that Linnie Mae had to have known exactly where Williams was being "dried out" for his alcoholism. Frazier and her own mother, who was married to Williams, had been staying at her house! Then Bishop gave us an indication of how superficial, skewed and ill-informed his book really is: "He [Rose] dialed the Irving Professional Center and identified himself. A nurse supervisor said yes, *they had a Mr. Frazier senior as a patient.* "[62]

This is just an example of how Bishop's book, one which lacks any citations, footnotes or sources, is plagued by misinformation and reads like a novel of sorts, which can be classified as fiction.

Bishop, however, seems to have had "inside information" as to the actual procedure of Frazier's polygraph test and specifically those who were involved in its administration. In his narrative, he points out how Frazier "bordered on controlled hysteria" when asked the simple question if he had recently fired a gun.

Here are some actual questions that Bishop detailed, questions that could only have been obtained by reading the actual polygraph report, or interviewing someone who had been intimately involved in the test, yet had not forgotten its details.[63]

This "anonymous man" was probably R.D. Lewis, according to O'Toole [64]:

- Do you live with your sister?

- Ever fire a gun?

- Control question: Ever did anything you were ashamed of?

- Control question: When you were little, did you ever lie to your mother?

This polygraph report has mysteriously disappeared from DPD files, and it happens to be the basis of O'Toole's investigation. Here is a sample DPD polygraph report taken by Paul Bentley of Policeman Roy Vaughn, regarding the access that Jack Ruby might have had coming down the ramp at City Hall before he shot Lee Oswald:

City of Dallas
OFFICE MEMORANDUM

To Mr. J. E. Curry   December 6, 1963
    Chief of Police

Subject: Polygraph Examination
          Roy E. Vaughn

A polygraph examination was given Roy E. Vaughn (W/M/28) at the request of Deputy Chief N. T. Fisher. This examination was given on November 28, 1963. Below is a list of pertinent questions that were asked during this examination.

1. Did you see Jack Ruby near the Main Street entrance of the City Hall between 9:30 a.m. and 11:30 a.m. last Sunday morning? Answer—No

2. Did you allow Jack Ruby to enter the basement of the City Hall last Sunday morning? Answer —No

3. Did you talk with Jack Ruby last Sunday morning? Answer —No

4. Did you allow anybody to enter the basement of the City Hall last Sunday morning that did not show you proper identification other than the two men you told Chief Fisher about? Answer —No

No Number: Did you lie to Chief Fisher regarding this incident?
           Answer——No

           Have you told Chief Fisher the complete truth regarding this
           incident?   Answer —Yes
It is the opinion of this Examiner this person answered each of the questions
with the truth.

                                        P. L. Bentley
                                        P. L. Bentley
                                        Detective of Police
                                        Identification Bureau
nw   *The only reason you and I are here is to assist the people of Dallas*   102

Returning to O'Toole's investigation, Rose now started to vaguely remember maybe giving Frazier a polygraph test that night. Finally, O'Toole concluded that there was no credibility to Frazier having passed the polygraph test.[65]

It was now time to get serious about finding Frazier. He checked with an Army contact and was told there had never been anyone by that name in the Army.[66] From there he heard from another contact with "very good FBI connections" that Frazier was working at the Boeing Corporation, in Renton. (not the only source of this) Then he went chasing him through most of the bases he had been in the South, sometimes just missing him.[67]

On a visit to Dektor, he happened to meet Tony Pellicano, an expert at finding people.[68] With the help of Pellicano, he finally located Frazier in December 1973 in Texas, stationed at Fort Hood, only 100 miles south of Dallas. Frazier was living on base and commuting to Irving on weekends.[69] When he finally recorded his interview with Frazier, it was no less than stunning. O'Toole and Pellicano detected Frazier repeatedly lying when asked the following questions, which produced maximum hard stress or good-to-hard stress.[70]

1. Did he (Oswald) take that package up with him into the building?

2. Did he tell you he was going to go home with you that night?

3. There was nobody else in the (polygraph) room with you?

4. Did he (the examiner) tell you that you passed the test?

5. Do you know Paul Bentley?

6. You never knew he (Oswald) had this gun then?

In closing this chapter, O'Toole wrote:

"The midnight polygraph examination of Buell Wesley Frazier lies at the very heart of the mystery of November 22, 1963. Why does it provoke hard stress, false statements, and curious lapses of memory among the Dallas police officers who should be the most familiar with it? The answer to these questions can only be the darkest speculation."[71]

Frazier and the HSCA

While he was being discharged from the Army in 1977, the HSCA was forming to investigate the JFK and MLK assassinations. Again, Frazier offered stiff opposition to testifying. "Frazier continues to procrastinate. Definite resistance."[72]

Frazier was finally interviewed by Investigators Jack Moriarity and Clarence Day of the HSCA, but never testified under oath. The reason is pretty obvious when one reads the transcripts.

Four audio tapes were made of these interviews which lingered in oblivion at the National Archives until Greg Parker decided to transcribe them. Tapes Nos. 1 and 2 were useless because of time deterioration.[73] Tape No. 3 described how he stayed put on the steps:

"I continued to stay right on the steps where I was. I didn't move from there, I didn't talk with someone who was sitting there that, uh, was—was on the stairs, as I said earlier. With the same two people. And the shots came from—apparently now—they came from around in a group of people scrambling." Later on the same topic, "And I moved to the right. *'Cause I was very interested in staying—there is no way to get caught. Standing there in the middle.*"[74]

Then Day asked him a very simple, important and relevant question:

Day: Are you in any pictures?

Frazier: No—I don't remember. What . . . I was gonna say is that it sounded—sounded like they were taken in the fall. It was then that was, you know, perfect. But being there at that time I didn't know.[75]

This tape also contains what seem to be other incoherent statements from Frazier. However, they seem incoherent if you do not know about his induction into the Army.

His references to "military" and "Seattle" are not a coincidence. Had this man been mentally tormented, with the specter of being sent to Vietnam at the whim of the people who were running this operation? It was crucial that they keep a lid on Frazier. This was the star witness that helped "convict" Lee Oswald in the public eye.

Consider the following exchange from p. 6 of the HSCA tapes:

"And anyways they terminated asking questions and when I answered back I tried to—*I tried to tell them the truth. And that made them very angry.*"[76] [Emphasis added]

The only thing that comes to mind that could elicit this type of reaction would have been that he told them that perhaps his friend Lee Oswald was right next to him standing at the stairs of front entrance.

On tape No. 4 he talked about the advantage the TSBD employees had being on the steps at a higher level and in the sunlight to avoid the crowded curbs, and how he kept going from the doorway to the sunshine and again, confirming his position when the motorcade drove by, next to the "big heavy-set lady"[77] These details are very important because they refute the argument that *he was in the shadows of the doorway* [Emphasis added] when the motorcade drove by:[78]

"So, we stepped back out then down on—out on to the steps. . . . *so we stepped back into the sunlight* [Emphasis added] then where actually we could see better. Because that's, you know, it's not every day that you can see the President of the United States come by in a motorcade a few feet away."

FRAZIER: OK, I know some of the girls that worked in the . . . offices above and ***they stepped out into the sunlight with me*** [Emphasis added] there and I know the big heavy-set woman she was right there.[79]

Above, one of the least-cropped versions of Altgens6. Notice the red highlights where alteration have been performed. According to Roy Schaeffer, an expert in this field, who is mentioned previously, this is the result of masking and opaquing.

To the right we have zoomed in and isolated the area of the entrance of the TSBD. Notice how the suit coat of Secret Service Agent Jack Ready (red circle) has been extended from the chest area forward.

The light streak or artifact running vertically, parallel to his jacket, which is not part of the limo, is the tip of the stick that holds the flag of the presidential flag, which shows evidence of airbrushing. For the sake of simplicity, we will only assign Nos. 1-3

from bottom to top, only to the figures that have their hands up at their foreheads trying to visor their eyes from the sun.

Take a look at the same area, but from the angle of Dave Weigman, who was traveling in one of the press cars, seventh car in the motorcade, a few seconds after the last shots. The three people shielding their eyes are still there, right? Now focus on the man sandwiched in between these three.

These images confirm this is a young, tall, slim, long limbed man with long neck, black hair, triangular shaped combination of head and hair. He is wearing a long-sleeved dark colored shirt or light jacket, rolled up right below the elbow.

Why is this man not seen in Altgens6? The three people in photograph who are shielding their eyes with their hands are accounted for. Doorway Man is also accounted for as well as the African-American man who is at his lower right.

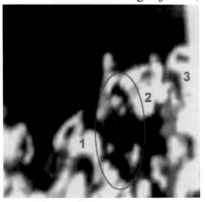

When the 22 November 1963 photograph taken of Frazier is flipped and compared to the figure in Weigman, a perfect match is obtained. He happens to be standing exactly on the stairs in the sunlight where he said he was, in his own handwritten statement the night of 22 November 1963.[80]

Frazier standing "in the sunlight" on the steps of the entrance by the center hand rail

Despite the blurriness of the Weigman frame, distinctive features of Frazier can be matched, such as the long neck, the shadow that his face casts on his neck, his upper hairline, and the triangular shaped face, in the collage at left. His Warren Commission testimony was taken 11 March 1964 by Mr. Joseph Ball. In his testimony, Frazier confirmed his

Overlay of City Hall photo (right) onto figure in sunlight on stairs standing by the hand rail.

position, stating he was "one step down from the top there," and "Yes sir, standing by the rail."

He was shown CE 362, which is only a schematic drawing of the first floor as seen from above to establish his position at the time.[81]

Down the Road of Deception, Lies and Duress

Here is where things get dicey. It has just been proven that Frazier was standing in the sunlight in the middle of the steps, and it was documented as early as the night of the assassination.[82]

In his Warren Commission testimony, he was asked if he would take a look at CE369, a version of Altgens6 which is severely cropped—quoting p. 242 of his testimony:

Mr. BALL: We have got a picture taken the day of the parade and it shows the President's car going by. Now, take a look at that picture. Can you see your picture any place there?

Mr. FRAZIER: No, sir; I don't, because *I was back up in this more or less black area here*. [Emphasis added]

Mr. BALL: I see.

Mr. FRAZIER: *Because Billy, like I say, is two or three steps **down in front of me**.* [Emphasis added]

Mr. BALL: Do you recognize this fellow?

Mr. FRAZIER: That is Billy, that is Billy Lovelady.

Mr. BALL: Billy?

Mr. FRAZIER: Right.

Mr. BALL: Let's take a marker and make an arrow down that way. That mark is Billy Lovelady?

Mr. FRAZIER: Right.

Mr. BALL: That is where you told us you were standing a moment ago.

Mr. FRAZIER: Right.

Mr. BALL: In front of you to the right over to the wall?

Mr. FRAZIER: Yes.

Now, let's take a look at Billy Lovelady's Warren Commission testimony regarding his position in the doorway:

Mr. BALL: Draw an arrow down to that; do it in the dark. You got an arrow in the dark and one in the white pointing toward you. Where were you when this picture was taken?

Mr. LOVELADY: Right there at the entrance of the building standing on the step, would be here (indicating).

Mr. BALL: You were standing on which step?

Mr. LOVELADY: *It would be your top level.* [Emphasis added]

Mr. BALL: *The top step you were standing there?* [Emphasis added]

Mr. LOVELADY: Right.[83]

The deception orchestrated by Joseph Ball in Frazier's and Lovelady's Warren Commission testimonies requires scrutiny.

As seen in a forthcoming chapter, Joseph Ball appears to have been a major player in deceiving the American public about what went on in the doorway of the TSBD during the assassination, and documenting for the Commission the apparent deceit. As seen in the above-noted exchanges, there are contradictions which cannot be reconciled with the photographic record such as Weigman 658 shown above.

Which brings us to the added deception and ridiculous manipulation by Bob Jackson in 1971.

This photograph speaks volumes. It shows Lovelady standing *on the third step* which contradicts what he told the Commission about *standing on the top level as quoted above.*

It is obvious Jackson did not care to understand the visual dynamics of Altgens6 and the unique optical effects Altgens's telephoto lens, film and upwards angle created. One has to wonder if he even had a copy of Altgens6 while he was snapping this shot.

In 1971 photographer Bob Jackson posed Lovelady in front of the School Book Depository wearing the same shirt as on November 22, 1963. At a distance of 8 years and with Lovelady having lost hair, grown sideburns, and gained weight, it was still evident he was one and the same as the 1963 figure.

The image above is from Ralph Cinque's Altgens6 re-enactment conducted on 7 November 2012 and 13 November 2012, the first time this was ever done using the exact same equipment and film Altgens used in 1963.

It is presented here to confirm the position of Doorway Man *at the top step of the stairway right of center, next to the rail.* It took Cinque a couple of weeks of trial and error to finally pinpoint Doorway Man's exact position in Altgens6.[84] Again, this is also confirmed by Altgens6 and Weigman 658. This image only shows the top three of seven steps that make up the stairway itself.

Using Blender, we can strip away the extraneous figures and zero into the doorway in 3D. The model used in place of Frazier is plainly visible:

This next image corresponds to Dave Weigman's perspective, but at the time Altgens6 was taken, which matches Zapruder frame 255.

Note that by the time Weigman drove by, the people standing there had moved slightly.

Changes at the Entrance

These images are from the Warren Commission. At left is a schematic drawing of the first floor of the building, the area where Lee Oswald and Wesley Frazier worked side-by-side filling orders. According to Frazier's testimony, the only reason for order-fillers to have gone up to the sixth floor would have been to process book returns. This was a very simple procedure which required very little time. That morning it was

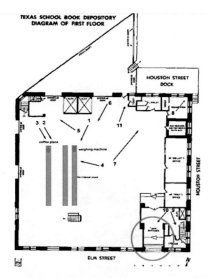

Frazier who had been to the sixth floor at least once. When asked if he had seen Oswald on the sixth floor of the building at any time that morning, he answered "No."[85]

The second image below is the Elm Street main entrance of the building as seen from inside. Notice how restricted the top landing of the entrance was in those days—it could not have been more than three feet of horizontal space towards Elm Street, which probably could only accommodate one row of people.

Moreover, the radiator against the wall allows us to estimate the space on the other side of the door. The schematic drawing above also confirms the door opened both ways and was right in the middle of the landing. This is where Frazier supposedly was, "more or less this dark area here." Here is another image taken from the end of the Alyea film depicting two DPD policemen guarding the entrance. Not much space there at all!

10 ENTRANCE LOBBY.

-särskilt runt skolbokslagret
kort efter skottlossningen-

Years later, the entire doorway was replaced with thick, ornate wooden frames, and the door itself pushed further inside the entrance by a whopping nine feet, one inch, which greatly increased the area of the landing, as we see today. (photo credit Rosey Cinque)

In 1986, Oswald posthumously received his long-awaited trial, with the star witness, of course, Buell Wesley Frazier.[86] Oswald was defended by Gerry Spence, who many feel was not very well prepared for this one.[87]

The prosecutor was Vince Bugliosi of *Helter Skelter* fame. For the purpose of this study, the single most important part was Frazier's 10:52 minute testimony. At 9:57 into his testimony:

SPENCE: You recall these 23 years later that Mr. Lovelady was standing in front of you at that precise moment, *about four steps in front of you*, is that correct? [Emphasis added]

FRAZIER: Yes sir, that is.

SPENCE: Have you ever said that to anybody in the world prior to today?

FRAZIER: I don't know whether anyone asked me that or not.

SPENCE: But my question is, did you ever tell that to anyone in the world prior to today?

FRAZIER: Not that I know of, sir.

SPENCE: But you did tell that to Mr. Bugliosi, with the 'g' silent, didn't you?

FRAZIER: Well, I asked this question a while ago sir.

There are major problems with this. Again, Frazier was right in the middle of the group that was on the stairs, in the sunlight, one or two steps from the top. Every time Frazier testified about his and Lovelady's position at the stairs of the entrance of the TSBD, no matter in which forum, he gave a different story. In his Warren Commission testimony, he gave two different positions (as seen above) within the same session! Doorway Man is obviously above him, *not two, three or four steps in front of him!* Thanks to Gerry Spence, we have videotaped testimony which shows Frazier misleading the court with impunity under oath.

Frazier wearing his "Texas Future Farmers of America" jacket and light-colored denim pants.

Above, we see the last image of Weigman's last pan, before he got out of the car and headed to the grassy knoll. The actions of the individual circled in red are completely consistent with Frazier's HSCA interview quoted above in detail *and* his original statement and affidavit of the night of 22 November *and* an FBI report written on 23 November 1963. Frazier is still in the middle of the stairway, below Doorway Man, in the sunlight, wearing the same attire he was photographed in the night of 22 November, looking around to see what happened. He stated in his official Warren Commission testimony he thought shots came from the railroad tracks.[88]

Frazier points out to Gerry Spence where he thought the shots came from in 1986 mock trial

Alterations of Our Own

Using 21st century technology, when the alterations of the doorway of Altgens6 are reverse engineered, this composite is revealed.

Once Frazier's head is scaled, rotated, blurred, and transferred back to where he used to be, it is a perfect fit.

Even Secret Service Agent Jack Ready, seen below, returns to his original, correct size, as seen when compared to his partner, Paul Landis, right next to him.

Both were looking right in the direction of the stairway entrance. This also supports the Blender image shown above.

After careful analysis of all of the evidence presented here, there is an extremely high probability that Buell Wesley Frazier and possibly Sarah Stanton were removed from Altgens6.

Once we come to terms with this concept, we begin to understand the terrible life of duress Buell Wesley Frazier has lived. He may live well and comfortable today, but he will always know in the back of his mind what really happened, and how his testimony helped frame an innocent man.

After carefully compiling and noting all of his different statements and positions over the years, the following table can be constructed:

Date	Venue	Frazier's and/or Lovelady's Location
11/22/63	Dallas Police Department	"Standing on the front steps" (Hand written statement and affidavit)
03/11/64	Warren Commission ("two for the price of one") by Mr. Joseph Ball	1. "One step down from the top there," and "Yes sir, **standing by the rail**." [Emphasis added] (WC2H233) 2. "I was back up in this **more or less black area here**. [Emphasis added] Because Billy, like I say, is two or three steps in front of me." (WC2H242)

02/13/69	Clay Shaw Trial, New Orleans	"At the top of the stairs", and Lovelady and Shelley were "Right down in front of me at the bottom of the steps." (Shaw Trial Transcript p. 26)
1978	HSCA Interview by Moriarity and Day, audio tape transcription.	"Continued to stay right on the steps where I was. So we stepped back out then down on - out on to the steps. . . . so we stepped back into the sunlight then where actually we could see better. Cause I was very interested in staying—there is no way to get caught. Standing there in the middle" (III-2) "So we stepped back out then down on—out on to the steps. . . . so we stepped back into the sunlight then where actually we could see better. Because that's you know it's not every day that you can see the President of the United States come by in a motorcade a few feet away." (IV-14)
1986	Lee Oswald Mock Trial, London England	SPENCE: You recall these 23 years later that Mr. Lovelady was standing in front of you at that precise moment—about 4 steps in front of you, is that correct? FRAZIER: Yes sir, that is.
04/07/64	Warren Commission: Billy Lovelady testimony taken by Joseph Ball and Samuel Stern.	Mr. BALL: You were standing on which step? Mr. LOVELADY: *It would be your top level.* [Emphasis added] Mr. BALL: The top step you were standing there? Mr. LOVELADY: Right. (WC6H339)

Discussion: Was Frazier a Possible Patsy?

Why was Frazier removed from Altgens6? When Altgens6 was first viewed on 22 November around 1:30 PM, there was a group of TSBD employees spilling out from the very restricted top landing area down onto the seven doorway steps as seen in Weigman 658, including Frazier, Lovelady, Joe Molina, Roy Lewis, Pauline Sanders, Otis Williams, Bill Shelley and Sarah Stanton. Frazier and Stanton were in Altgens's line of sight. Thanks to the Warren Commission entrance photo exhibit No. 10, and the Alyea film, we know the landing area of the stairway was smaller than it is today.

Despite the difference in distance, and much like we see in this Skaggs image at right, Hughes right below, and very faintly in Weigman 658, part of the glass divider and silver metal frame should have been visible in the background of Altgens6.

Today, this area is mostly obscured. Years later the entrance was retrofitted and remodeled to match Frazier's "more or less black area" story.

Besides Frazier having disappeared for at least five hours that day, DPD detectives found a British Enfield .3030 rifle with ammunition among his belongings at his sister, Linnie Mae Randall's house.

The rifle was confiscated according to this evidence receipt by Detectives Stovall and Rose. This would suggest that Frazier was one of a small group of possible patsies, depending on how the evening played out.

Form CPS—PC—447	**POLICE DEPARTMENT** CITY OF DALLAS		

PROPERTY CLERK'S INVOICE OR RECEIPT

Nov 23 1963 _____ 19____

Received of **R S Stovall & G R Rose** _____ the following described articles,

§ recovered stolen property:

Evidence in Offense No._____ Arrest No._____ Charge **Confiscated, Evidence**

QUANTITY	ARTICLE	BIN NO.	DISPOSITION
1	Rifle, British Infield, Pk Mk 1, peep sight, ser #U21616, 21 3/4" bl, blue steel, wooden stock with brass butt, bolt action, with 1 magazine clip and rings for fastening shoulder straps	AK-1	
10	Rounds British R P 303 ammo	F-33	

Recently, Frazier revealed an interesting episode the night of the 22nd, when Captain Will Fritz entered the interrogation room where he was being held. Coincidentally, this information never made it into Jim Bishop's book. This is how Frazier described the incident on 13 July 2013, during a question and answer session with the Sixth Floor Museum:

"We went another round of questioning for quite some time. They had talked to Captain Will Fritz, he was head of, ah, he was head of homicide, and ah, they had explained to me after that, this kid is telling us everything he knows. So, ah, but Captain Will Fritz would not buy that, he would not accept that. So they go out of the room, and in comes Captain Will Fritz, never seen him in my life, never talked to him, he brought in a typed statement he had a pen, he says, 'here, sign this.' He gave me a pen and I started reading it. Well, they wanted me to confess to be a part of, or having knowledge of, the assassination of John F Kennedy. I read about two sentences of that and I looked at him and I says, that's ludicrous, I said, 'I'm not signing that!' So he drew his hand back to hit me and I did my arm up like this. He's about where you are sitting, and I told him, I said,—he got very red-faced, he wasn't a real big man, of course physical, I hear he got a temper, anyway—I told him, I says, you know, 'I know there's a policeman outside the door,' but I said, 'before they get in, you and I are going to have a hell of a fight,' and I said, 'I'll get a good lick or two and you'll remember me.' Well, he snatched up the paper and the pen and walked out the room—never did see him again ever . . . The way he treated me, the way he tried to make me sign that statement—we could never be friends."

This is a stunning admission by Frazier! Its significance cannot be understated. Frazier was one of a short list of possible patsies, there is no other explanation. In the early 1990s JFK researcher Sheldon Inkol wrote two articles which dealt with alternate patsies in which he named Frazier, Joe Molina, and a fellow by the name of Donald Wayne House as possible patsies.[89] In another article, published in the same journal, he offered his theory that Frazier could have been impersonated by Jack Lawrence, just like Lee Oswald had been impersonated in the weeks leading up to the assassination.[90] Inkol cites a very strange incident which occurred at the Sports Drome Rifle Range on Sunday, 17 November 1963, in which Mr. and Mrs. (Lucille) Garland Slack stated they had seen Lee Oswald in the company of a man whom they referred to as "Frazier from Irving."

> In an effort to resolve discrepancies in information furnished by Mr. SLACK concerning this incident, Mrs. SLACK contacted Mr. SLACK during the interview. According to Mrs. SLACK, Mr. SLACK maintained that OSWALD was at the rifle range on November 17, 1963, and that he had been brought there by a man named "FRAZIER" from Irving, Texas. Mrs. SLACK stated she felt her husband was confused as to the date when he observed the individual he believed to be OSWALD at the range, but he was sincere in the statement he had previously made to Agents of the FBI and during his testimony before the President's Commission.

The reason Inkol believed Frazier had been impersonated is that because Frazier later denied the supposed incident in an FBI interview on 11 September 1964. (CD1546 pp. 138-140)

> In an effort to resolve discrepancies in information furnished by Mr. SLACK concerning this incident, Mrs. SLACK contacted Mr. SLACK during the interview. According to Mrs. SLACK, Mr. SLACK maintained that OSWALD was at the rifle range on November 17, 1963, and that he had been brought there by a man named "FRAZIER" from Irving, Texas. Mrs. SLACK stated she felt her husband was confused as to the date when he observed the individual he believed to be OSWALD at the range, but he was sincere in the statement he had previously made to Agents of the FBI and during his testimony before the President's Commission.

FD-302 (Rev. 3-3-59)   **FEDERAL BUREAU OF INVESTIGATION**

1   Date _____ 9/14/64 _____

> Mr. BUELL WESLEY FRAZIER, 1413 Shady Grove, Apartment 27, Irving, Texas, employed at Texas School Book Depository, advised that on no occasion did he ever take LEE HARVEY OSWALD to a rifle range. He advised that he did not take OSWALD to the Sports Drome Rifle Range, Dallas, Texas, on either November 10, or 17, 1963, or on any other date.

If the conspirators were trying to make Frazier a patsy for the assassination, then it would have been necessary to erase any evidence of him being in any pictures that day. The only other record of Frazier being in the doorway is the Weigman film, as mentioned earlier in this chapter. Since the Weigman film was not released until the late '60s by NBC, the only proof that Frazier was in the doorway would have been Altgens6.

Those who tampered with the photograph made sure Frazier was not seen on the steps of the doorway, leaving the door open to accuse him of the assassination, in case other candidates had to be discarded. A second reason to erase him from Altgens6 has to be the fact that Lee Oswald and Frazier knew each other (albeit for less than a couple of months), worked side-by-side filling orders, and supposedly car pooled on weekends. This was too clear and solid a connection. Once the legend of Oswald as a loner, communist and malcontent was established immediately after the assassination, Oswald being with Frazier in the doorway could not be permitted.

Over the years between 1963 and 1986, Frazier has misstated his position on five different occasions, sometimes under oath. According to O'Toole, he was caught lying six different times, and as stated earlier, the results of his supposed midnight polygraph test have never surfaced.

Based on the premise that Oswald owned a rifle, if Frazier was complicit in setting up Oswald, even in a passive way, his role could have been delivering the rifle from the Paine's garage. This could easily have been accomplished by putting the Carcano in the trunk of his car in the early hours of 22 November or the night before. Being only half-a-block away, either of the Paines could have facilitated this exchange, and with a spare copy of Frazier's car key, he would not even have had to get off of the couch he slept in. Perhaps the true reason for Frazier lagging behind was to make sure Oswald did not see *him* bringing a rifle into the TSBD. If he was passively involved, he may have left the rifle in the trunk of his car and allowed others to retrieve it. They would have had all morning to plant it.

Notice on the first page of this chapter how far and isolated from the TSBD his car was parked. Those three blocks seem to be close to a quarter-mile distance to the building as shown in CE361 below. The distance from his car to the TSBD according to the scale shown was approximately 2,250 feet. Another unmentioned possibility, if he was actively involved, could have been as a chauffeur or getaway driver for any one of the real participants. His five-to-six-hour absence now starts to look pretty suspicious. By taking McKinney Avenue or Munger Street, he could have left the scene of the crime without being noticed.

Furthermore, the map shown as CE361 was falsified by the Warren Commission. This image is supposed to depict CE361, which shows Houston Street going on right through the railroad yard, however the following image proves that Houston turned east right after the TSBD.

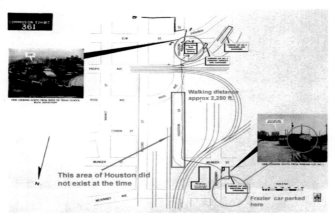

COMMISSION EXHIBIT 361

Frazier tried to point out the discrepancy in his Warren Commission testimony, when in response to Joseph Ball showing him CE361, he answered:

Mr. Frazier: I see *that is right there where you say* [Emphasis added]that is the street going up to the parking lot there.

The HSCA Testimony of Edward Shields

But is that the way it really happened? As seen in Chapter 5, according to African-American employee Edward Shields, that is not where Frazier normally parked his car, and on 22 November, several of his coworkers witnessed Frazier drop Lee Oswald off at the bend of Houston Street near the east rear entrance of the TSBD. Here is the actual HSCA interview:

```
    Mr. S:  Wesley Frazier - right. You're correct.
    Mr. D:  Alright. He rode to work with him.
    Mr. S:  Wesley Frazier - yes. And they would park
their car right on Houston Street and get out and walk to the
building on Elm Street.
    Mr. D:  Alright. The day of the assassination, did you
see Oswald come to work with Frazier?
    Mr. S:  No, I didn't. They told me that he let him out
at the building. He did not come on the parking lot.
    Mr. M:  You say they told you?
    Mr. S:  Yeah.
    Mr. D:  Who told you they...
    Mr. S:  Jerman, them, and all of
the fellows that work there at the building.
    Mr. D:  Alright. This is just...Can you tell me a
specific person that told you that?
    Mr. S:  Yeah. I think Charles Gibbons hollered out
there and asked Frazier where was his rider and he told him:
"I dropped him off at the building." Yeah, that was it.
```

```
    Mr. D:  Now, let me back up a little bit. Are you telling
me that this fella said that somebody who worked in the book
depository, the building down on Elm and Houston, hollered out
the window and asked Frazier where was his rider?
    Mr. S:  Mm-hmm.
    Mr. D:  Are you talking about the morning of the
assassination?
    Mr. S:  I think it was, Mr. Davis, if I'm not mistaken.
I think it was.
    Mr. D:  And how did you come about this information?
    Mr. S:  Well, I was down on the floor when they
```

> hollered out and said and the answer he gave them, I don't know,
> I think he said:"I dropped him off at the building." Now,
> whoever it was hollering asked him, I don't know.
>
>   Mr. D: This is the morning of the assassination?
>   Mr. S: Mm-hmm
>   Mr. D: Somebody hollered out the window at Frazier and
> say: "Where is your rider?" And to your recollection, Frazier
> says: "I dropped him off at the building."

Perhaps Frazier doesn't know how close he came to becoming the fall guy for the assassination of John F. Kennedy. When we consider Frazier's comment about remaining at the steps, *"'Cause I was very interested in staying—there is no way to get caught. Standing there in the middle,"* [Emphasis added] this scenario takes on a whole new meaning. That is why it was imperative that Frazier be erased from Altgens6.

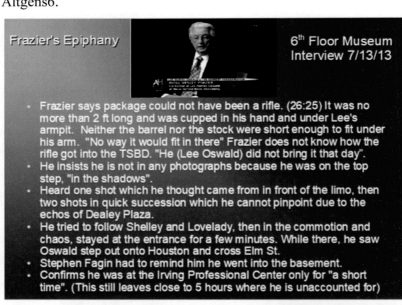

Frazier's Epiphany

6th Floor Museum Interview 7/13/13

- Frazier says package could not have been a rifle. (26:25) It was no more than 2 ft long and was cupped in his hand and under Lee's armpit. Neither the barrel nor the stock were short enough to fit under his arm. "No way it would fit in there" Frazier does not know how the rifle got into the TSBD. "He (Lee Oswald) did not bring it that day".
- He insists he is not in any photographs because he was on the top step, "in the shadows".
- Heard one shot which he thought came from in front of the limo, then two shots in quick succession which he cannot pinpoint due to the echos of Dealey Plaza.
- He tried to follow Shelley and Lovelady, then in the commotion and chaos, stayed at the entrance for a few minutes. While there, he saw Oswald step out onto Houston and cross Elm St.
- Stephen Fagin had to remind him he went into the basement.
- Confirms he was at the Irving Professional Center only for "a short time". (This still leaves close to 5 hours where he is unaccounted for)

- Regarding the interrogations at the Dallas Police Department that night: "Why can't they accept what I'm telling them?" (44:22)
- Captain Fritz walked in with a typed statement for him to confess that he had knowledge of the JFK assassination. He read the first two sentences and protested he was not going to sign that (46:41). A red-faced Fritz raised his hand as if to hit him, to which Frazier reacted and told Fritz that even with cops standing outside, he would be sure to get a couple of good "licks" in and "you will remember me". Fritz snatched the unsigned statement and stormed out of the room.
- Regarding Lee's guilt; "I don't know anybody who can prove that, it's a theory." (55:23)

> • On the Warren Commission. "They already had their answers and weren't interested in anything I had to say and they tried to make me change my testimony" (55:38)
> • On Joseph Ball: "I ran into one of the sharpest attorneys I have ever seen in my life, Mr. Ball. He was good, but I could not accept what he was trying to feed me."
> • We should walk a couple of miles in his "moccasins".

ENDNOTES

1. CE 1381, NPRC report
2. WC2H211
3. Ibid.
4. *The Dallas Morning News*, 16 November 2008, Aynesworth, "Oswald co-worker no longer silent about JFK assassination role"
5. WC2H212
6. Ibid.
7. WC2H246 "When you live in a place you know some places that someone with, you know, not much of an education can find work"
8. *The Dallas Morning News*, 16 November 2008 Aynesworth, "Oswald co-worker no longer silent about JFK assassination role"
9. DPD handwritten statement, p. 1 and affidavit 22 November 1963
10. WC2H214
11. WC2H227
12. WC2H228
13. DPD Affidavit 22 November 1963, p. 2 by Mary Rattan
14. DPD handwritten statement and affidavit, 22 November 1963
15. WC2H235
16. CE 1381, 1:00-2:00 PM was quite a generous time frame
17. Greg Parker article, 22 September 2009, "Whose line is it anyhow?"
18. *The Dallas Morning News*, 16 November 2008, Aynesworth, "Oswald co-worker no longer silent about JFK assassination role"
19. DPD Rose/Stovall/Adamcik, four-page Report on Investigation of the President's Murder
20. Ibid.
21. DPD 148-001
22. DPD Rose/Stovall/Adamcik
23. DPD Rose/Stovall/Adamcik report, and Shaw, Gary J., *Cover-Up: The Governmental Conspiracy to Conceal the Facts About the Public Execution of John Kennedy* (1976), pp. 90-91
24. DPD Rose/Stovall/Adamcik p. 4
25. HSCA Tape 4, p. 2 NPRC report
26. NPRC FOIA report p. 2
27. Ibid.
28. GI's Diary 174ahc.org/diary01.htm by SP4 Horace Cassels
29. NPRC report, p. 2
30. NPRC, HSCA tape 4, p. 2
31. HSCA tape 4, p. 2

32. GI's Diary 174ahc.org/diary01.htm by SP4 Horace Cassels
33. Armstrong, Box 16, Notebook No. 3, Tab 28, p. 7
34. Clay Shaw trial (1969) BWF, p. 26
35. NPRC p. 3
36. NPRC p. 4
37. Ibid.
38. Ibid. 1
39. Ibid.
40. Horne, Douglas, *Inside the ARRB Vol V*, (2009), p. 1654
41. Weisberg letter 28 July 1975 (Oswald to buy car and meet FBI in Texas Theater to collect the $200)
42. Mark Lane's foreword of *The Assassination Tapes* (softcover edition)
43. Horne, Douglas, *Inside the ARRB Vol V*, (2009), p. 1655
44. Copy of patent available.
45. vsa-avsa.blogspot.com The first supplier of VSA technology was Dektor, who manufactured the PSE 1000, an analog machine, that was later replaced by the PSE 2000.
46. O'Toole, George, *The Assassination Tapes* (1975), pp. 83-84
47. Ibid. 125
48. Ibid. 171
49. Ibid. 172
50. Ibid.
51. Ibid. 181
52. Ibid. 174
53. Ibid. 181
54. Ibid. 175
55. Ibid. 177
56. Ibid. 177-179, DPD Report, and WCVIIH192
57. Ibid. 178
58. WCVIIH192
59. O'Toole, George, *The Assassination Tapes* (1975), pp. 183-184
60. Jim Bishop, *The Day Kennedy was shot* (1968), p. 335
61. Ibid.
62. Ibid.
63. Ibid. 472
64. O'Toole, George, *The Assassination Tapes* (1975), p. 181
65. O'Toole, George, *The Assassination Tapes* (1975), p. 187
66. Ibid. 190
67. Ibid. 196
68. Ibid.
69. Ibid. 197
70. Ibid. 201-203
71. Ibid. 206
72. Armstrong HSCA RG233 handwritten notes
73. ReopenKennedyCase.org (Greg Parker's website)
74. Tape III-2
75. Ibid.

76. Tape III-6
77. Ibid.
78. Ibid.
79. Tape IV-14
80. DPD handwritten statement and affidavit, 22 November 1963
81. WC2H233
82. DPD handwritten statement and affidavit, 22 November 1963
83. WH6H339
84. Ralph Cinque
85. WC2H232
86. *The Dallas Morning* News, 16 November 2008, Aynesworth, "Oswald co-worker no longer silent about JFK assassination role," p. 4
87. Mark Lane would have been a better choice. Spence allowed Bugliosi to lead witnesses at will.
88. WC2H242, despite Ball trying his best to confuse him
89. Inkol, Sheldon, *The Third Decade*, Vol. 6, No. 4, May 1990, "Other Patsies"
90. Inkol, Sheldon, *The Third Decade,* Vol. 7, No. 5, July 1991, "Jack Lawrence: Assassin or Fall Guy"

11

Who Was in the TSBD Doorway? The Patsies

Chapter 8 of this book has gone a long way to identify Lee Oswald as the man in the doorway in the famous and iconic Altgens6 photograph. As logic dictates, if Oswald was in the doorway at the time that President John F. Kennedy is seen reacting to bullets that have already struck him, then he could not have been shooting from the southeast window of the sixth floor of the TSBD. Early research legends Mark Lane, Vincent Salandria, as well as noted authors and scholars Gerald McKnight, David Wrone, Phil Nelson and a host of distinguished men and women, are all in agreement. This is not a new concept, inasmuch as Harold Weisberg was the very first researcher and author to publish two very important chapters devoted to this issue in his second book, *Whitewash II: The FBI-Secret Service Cover-Up*, which still prevails to this day, and where he came up with a study that showed nine points of similarity between the shirt worn by the figure known as Doorway Man and the shirt worn by Oswald the day and night of 22 November 1963. Moreover, Sylvia Meagher had this to say about the Doorway Man dilemma:

> Neither the Report nor the Hearings and Exhibits provides any visual means of judgment since no photograph of Lovelady is found in any of the volumes. Merely asserting that it is Lovelady and not Oswald in the doorway, the Commission presents no supporting visual evidence by which one can appraise the resemblance between Lovelady and the man in the doorway, or Lovelady and Oswald, although nothing less hangs on the accurate identification of the doorway man than Oswald's possible total innocence of the assassination. **Meagher P362**

More recently, Richard Hooke, using computer techniques and his training in anthropology, has expanded Weisberg's study to more than 50 points of similarity, all of which would prevail in any judicial setting.

But what about the other figures in the doorway? What can be reconstructed from the few strands of information left over by the flawed and biased pseudo investigations done by the Warren Commission, the HSCA, the FBI and the DPD, which appear to have been fashioned to railroad an innocent man? Were there other

242

possible candidates to take the blame for the assassination of John F. Kennedy?

The Dave Weigman Film

There happens to be a film taken by Dave Weigman, which can be considered almost a mirror image of Altgens6, taken from a different angle of perhaps 90° as Weigman was passing in front of the TSBD in the seventh car, camera car, No. 1, which was a 1964 yellow Chevy Impala convertible. This film was quietly suppressed by NBC, just like *Life* magazine did with the Zapruder film, and did not surface until the late 1960s.

NBC is also the owner of several important pieces of photographic evidence. A TV film taken by NBC photographer David Weigman was suppressed by NBC and not made available to researchers. It shows the grassy knoll in the background just a fraction of a minute after the shots. Some of the assassination participants can be seen on the knoll.　　　*Taking of America 1,2,3* Richard Sprague 1976 pg 53

10. CAMERA CAR #1 National Motion Picture Cameras

1. Driver
2. John Hofan-NBC sound
3. David Wiegman, Jr.*-NBC B&W movie
4. Thomas J. Craven, Jr.*-CBS B&W movie
5. Cleveland "Cleve Ryan"-Lighting
   Technician
6. Thomas "Ollie" Atkins*-United States Navy,
   White House color movie

vehicle: yellow 1964 Chevrolet Impala
　　　2-door convertible Super Sport (SS)
　　　provided by Earl Hayes Chevrolet Dallas
　　　through Sam Bloom
aka: Press Photo Car (CE 767)
　　　Press Pool Convertible (CE 768)
　　　Cam 1 (Cutler)
　　　Movie Cam 1 (Trask)
　　　National Press Car (N&A)
relevant photos/film: Stoughton 1, Towner 2,
　　　Wiegman film, Couch film, DCA film, Zapruder film,
　　　Hughes film, Nix film, Martin film, Bell film, Atkins film.
occupant sources: CE 768, C&A Article, Trask.
notes: Wiegman, Atkins, and Craven jump out of car at head of Elm
　　　Street and run up the knoll to film the Newmans. Camera Car
　　　#1 pulls out of line at the base of the knoll and Wiegman,
　　　Atkins, and Craven re-enter the car. SA Lem Johns also
　　　enters this car at this point. Camera Car #1 then rejoins
　　　the motorcade between cars #15 and #16. At the Trade Mart it
　　　gets out of line and then rejoins the motorcade again,
　　　between cars #16 and #17. It arrives at Parkland at 12:45-
　　　12:50 PM (18H774).

When it did, the film seemed to have lost some of its sharpness, and what we see today is a fuzzy sequence which looks suspiciously as if it has been altered. Just one case in point, Roy Schaeffer has noted the edit lines that appear in various frames, notice the difference between one frame and the other:

Is this proof of Weigman alteration?

This technique is called "overlay mask" and was detected by Roy Schaeffer. He has seen evidence that Weigman has been extensively edited. "Using this technique you can see some removal or edited parts of the Weigman film" Roy Schaeffer

Even though the film appears to have been worked on, there is still enough information to help identify the rest of the people who were in the doorway that day. These are the people we believe were in the doorway that day:

Who's Who in the Doorway

1. Buell Wesley Frazier

In the previous chapter we meticulously established the presence of Frazier on the steps of the doorway to the front entrance of the TSBD based on the Weigman film. Photographs and film taken that same night at City Hall, when he was summoned to take a polygraph test by Captain Will Fritz, shows a tall, long-limbed young man, with the same hair style, wearing the same clothing that Frazier was wearing that day and night.

Buell Wesley Frazier at DPD and in the TSBD Doorway LR

However, and as noted in the previous chapter, when we isolate and extrapolate that particular area from the Weigman to Altgens6, we note that Frazier is missing from the photograph and there is an unusual darkening in front of Agent John Ready's suit coat. He should be right off the left shoulder of figure No. 1 seen above. All of which leads us to believe that Frazier has been removed from Altgens6, as shown in the following collage:

This is where they erased Frazier by airbrushing.

Airbrush bleeds into the foyer roof.

Salandria reenactment of Altgens6 7/64

Part of Landis's forehead lopped off.

Overlay at left shows trunk of Live Oak tree would not have blocked Frazier. Above extrapolation of tree trunk.

JFK research legend Vincent Salandria's Altgens6 reenactment in the summer of 1964 is probably one of the most important photographs ever taken. It reveals areas of Altgens6 that were blocked by both limousines, and spectators that were lining the curb of Elm Street in front. It also shows the area of the TSBD doorway and the live oak tree in pristine condition, which proves that Frazier could not have been blocked by this tree.

247

The situation with Frazier is compounded by the different versions over the years of his location (see Chapter 10).

When we see this in Weigman 658, we should see this in Altgens6

Yet we do not. The reason: Buell Wesley Frazier was removed from Altgens6.

Note: This is what the Altgens6 probably looked like before alteration.

Buell Wesley Frazier has yet to come clean as to his true location in the doorway and continues to cling to the story that he was standing in the nonexistent "dark area" of the TSBD entrance.

Area where Frazier says he was in WC2H242...."more or less this black area here"

Area Frazier says he was in WC2H233 "One step down from the top"

Bugliosi points to "dark area" Frazier insists he is in Altgens6 (1986 *"Trial of Lee Harvey Oswald"*)

On 3 August 2013, as mentioned in the previous chapter, Rosie Cinque measured the depth of the entrance of the top landing of the doorway and discovered that the entrance had been pushed in from approximately three feet to slightly over nine feet. When we spoke to architect, JFK author and researcher J. Gary Shaw in October 2013, he stated that the remodeling of the entrance probably occurred in the 1980s when the county took over the building.

2. Joe Molina

Joe Molina held several positions with the TSBD company. When first hired, he worked as an accountant or bookkeeper in the credit department. His work attire as credit manager consisted of a dress shirt, coat, and tie. Molina "took up a position on the top step of the entrance of the TSBD for the purpose of watching the Presidential Motorcade." (CE1381, p. 66).

He also testified before the Warren Commission on 7 April 1964, and 25 years later was interviewed by *The Dallas Morning News* on 20 November 1988, on the 25th observance of the assassination. He has never been interviewed or spoken in public since. As noted in chapter 4, in July 1967, Shirley Martin visited Molina and showed him a copy of Altgens6. Joe advised Shirley that he was the man next to the "Oswald-Lovelady" figure, known as Black Tie Man. Shirley's immediate reaction was to disbelieve Molina, however, under the circumstances he was living in, and by process of elimination, Molina's claim seems believable.

This man appears to be wearing a suit, however, this also looks suspiciously like what are known as "daggar strokes," a common technique used in airbrushing. See howtoairbrush.com

The reason to do this, of course, to make Doorway man's shirt appear to have vertical stripes, which is what Lovelady was wearing for his photo shoot with the FBI on 2/29/64. As noted in chapter 6, the checkered shirt did not make its debut until at least 1967.

So, who else was in the doorway with Joe Molina and Buell Wesley Frazier? The following statements have been compiled according to witness testimonies, obtained from CE1381 and DPD affidavits.

Right: This collage shows what is commonly known as Black Tie Man in the Altgens6 photograph. In the Altgens6 this figure appears to have been retouched.

Joe Molina admitted to being "black tie man" to Shirley Martin in July 1967

3. Otis N. Williams

Joe Molina's boss and best friend "...was standing on the

top step against the railing in the east side of the steps in front of the building." (CE1381) This is confirmed by Joe's own testimony in 6H370:

Mr. Molina: Yes, I was standing on the front steps.

Mr. Ball: With whom?

Mr. Molina: Right next left of me was Mr. Williams and close to there was Mrs. Sanders [Pauline]

Otis Williams

This was also confirmed by Virgie Mae Rackley's 23 November 1963 statement to the DPD: "Molina went outside with a Mr. Williams, of the department." Otis Williams however, did not reciprocate, and by the time his statement was taken on 19 March 1964, Molina had been long gone from his TSBD employment. Mr. Williams then contracted a mysterious case of amnesia regarding who was around him: "I do not recall who was standing at either side of me . . ." (CE1381)

Otis Williams as "Obfuscated man" in the Altgens6. Same physical characteristics.

From Larry Snead's "No more Silence" 1998

So much for being best friends!

Regarding his position, in those days the railing was located in the center of the stairs, therefore he was roughly at the center of the entrance at the top step.

4. Pauline Sanders

"I took up a position at the top of the front steps of the Depository building facing Elm Street. To the best of my recollection *I was standing on the top step at the east end* [Emphasis added] of the entrance. I noticed Mrs. Sarah Stanton standing next to me, but I am unsure as to the others." (CE1381)

5. Sarah Stanton

"I was standing on the front steps of the TSBD with Mr. William Shelley, Mr. Otis Williams, Mrs. R.E. Sanders and Billy Lovelady." (CE1381)

She did not even mention Molina who was standing right next to her!

6. Madie Belle Reese

". . . took up a position *on the second step from the bottom to the right or west side* [Emphasis added] of the main entrance of the Depository building. Mrs. Dean was standing directly to my left at the time of the assassination . . ." (CE1381)

Robert Groden – "JFK – Absolute Proof"

Height analysis and comparison of figures on the top step or landing of the entrance of the TSBD This collage shows what is commonly known as Black Tie Man in Altgens6.

7. Billy Lovelady

Mr. Ball: You were standing on which step?

Mr. Lovelady: *It would be your top step.* [Emphasis added]

Mr. Ball: The top step you were standing there?

Mr. Lovelady: Right. (WC6H336)

In April 1961, while in the process of being court-martialed out of the USAF, Lovelady was known to have the following physical characteristics:

Name	BILLY NOLAN LOVELADY
Birth data	February 19, 1937
	Myrtle Springs, Texas
Height	5'8"
Weight	160
Eyes	Green
Hair	Brown
Complexion	Ruddy
Scars	Appendectomy scar

Two years later, and as a civilian, it can be safely assumed that he would have probably gained at least 10 pounds, weighing in at 170 to 175 pounds, possibly even more.

This is confirmed by the statements of Roy Lewis below, and it contrasts sharply with Lee Oswald's weight of 145 pounds. In Chapter 8 we conclusively pinpointed his position in Altgens6.

The shirt appears to have been whited out, possibly in an attempt to hide the vertical striped red and white short-sleeved shirt he was wearing that day:

 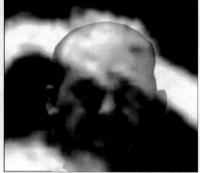

8. Bill Shelley

"I recall that as the presidential motorcade passed by I was standing just outside of the glass doors of the entrance. At the time President John F. Kennedy was shot I was standing at this same place." (CE1381)

Mr. BALL: You were standing where?

Mr. SHELLEY: Just outside the glass doors there.

Mr. BALL: That would be on the top landing of the entrance?

Mr. SHELLEY: Yes.

WC6H328

9. Roy Lewis

As we saw in chapter 5, 17-year-old Roy Lewis had obtained employment at the TSBD the year before, as he married very young, and at the time of the assassination his wife was expecting a baby due the following February. Roy later named this baby daughter Jacqueline in honor of the First Lady.

"Due to my lack of excitement, I was one of the last ones out of the building before the motorcade arrived. That's why I wasn't outside near the street like most everybody else. Instead, when I came out, I was standing with some ladies from up in the offices right in the middle of the steps in front of the building that led to the sidewalk beyond the glass door."

"I've been told that some people confused Billy Lovelady with Oswald, *but Lovelady was much heavier,* **and even though Oswald's hair was thinning, Billy's was about all gone up there."** [Emphasis added]

—Roy Lewis (*No More Silence: An Oral History of the Assassination of President Kennedy*, pp. 84-88)

Besides Oswald, Roy Lewis is the only figure in Altgens6 who is recognizable beyond any shadow of doubt. Many researchers have puzzled over Roy's profile being in the position that it is. The answer to that question is that Roy's attention appears to have been drawn in the direction of what is known as the "Towner vans." These are two vans that were parked on the north curb of Elm Street, east of Houston," and can be seen briefly in Tina Towner's film:

Altgens6 corresponds to Zapruder frame 255, and by then at least four to five shots have already been fired at JFK. Whatever it is that attracted Roy's attention that day seems to have impacted him in a special way, because as everyone else is running and storming the grassy knoll, Roy is still looking in that direction, even several minutes later, as seen in Willis slide No. 8. Another strange thing about this Willis slide is that Roy has wrapped his arm around the center rail of the stairway.

Roy's personal thoughts about Lee Oswald were recorded by Larry Sneed in this manner:

"Two days after the assassination when Oswald was shot, though I know they didn't let it happen intentionally, I still wondered how that could happen in the police department. I was mad at Oswald at the time, but I'm a sympathetic person, and I hate to see anything bad happen to anybody. *But I'm still not convinced that he did it, and because of his murder, it's for certain we're never going to get to the bottom of it. I'll never be convinced that Oswald did it or that he acted alone."* [Emphasis added]

—Roy Lewis (*No More Silence: An Oral History of the Assassination of President Kennedy*, pp. 84-88)

If Roy was *"never convinced that Oswald did it or that he acted alone,"* perhaps it is because he knows that Oswald was standing right above him in the doorway that day, which is exactly what he said in Chapter 5. Furthermore, Roy appears to know by personal experience that Lovelady could never pass as Doorway Man.

After careful analysis, the identification of the people in the doorway shapes up like this:

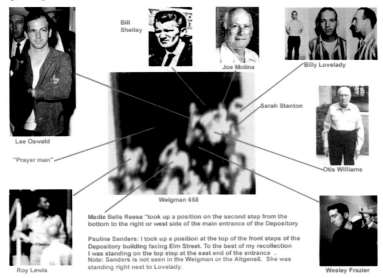

Madie Belle Reese "took up a position on the second step from the bottom to the right or west side of the main entrance of the Depository

Pauline Sanders: I took up a position at the top of the front steps of the Depository building facing Elm Street. To the best of my recollection I was standing on the top step at the east end of the entrance . Note: Sanders is not seen in the Weigman or the Altgens6. She was standing right next to Lovelady.

The Alternate Patsies Are All in the Doorway

The uncertainty and difficulty involved in setting up a person to take the blame for any crime is an extremely complex undertaking. Even more so for an event that is filmed and photographed, such as a presidential motorcade. A whole set of circumstances and requirements need to be just right. If any of these cannot be fulfilled, redundancy must be built into the operation because of contingencies that may arise that cannot be controlled. The "patsification" of Oswald was no exception. The conspirators could not have possibly known if he would remain in the doorway during the assassination. Had he been caught in more photographs that could not be controlled and intercepted by the FBI, secondary scenarios would have been necessary. Let's review some of these:

1. Billy Lovelady

As we saw in Chapter 6, Lovelady was kicked out of the USAF for the illegal theft and trafficking of guns at Andrews AFB in 1960-61. Recall that he and two others were prosecuted by the OSI and later removed from the USAF via court-martial. When Lovelady failed to pay his $200 fine, he fled Maryland's jurisdiction and ended up working for the TSBD company in December 1961.

In January 1963, the FBI finally caught up with him and he was arrested and incarcerated as a fugitive in Dallas. O.V. Campbell, VP of the TSBD company, paid the remaining $75 of his fine and was released on a $1,000 personal recognizance bond. This would have been the perfect background to set him up as a patsy and as a member of the work crew that was supposedly laying down plywood on the sixth floor; he could have been easily placed in the sniper's nest.

2. Buell Wesley Frazier

Frazier's case is even more intriguing because the DPD confiscated an Enfield .303 rifle with ammunition at his sister Linnie Mae Randall's house. Frazier was unaccounted for five hours after the assassination and was finally arrested at 6:30 PM in Irving. His possible removal from Altgens6 would of course, be very suspicious, especially when viewed in the context of what happened to him the night of the 22nd.

Frazier is probably aware how close he came to being in Oswald's shoes. As we saw in the previous chapter, in a short interview in the days following the assassination with CBS, which was analyzed for voice stress analysis, George O'Toole determined that Frazier was scared out of his wits:

"Judging from the PSE charts, when Buell Wesley Frazier made that statement, he was in a condition of sheer terror." (*The Assassination Tapes*, O'Toole, p. 172)

And with good reason. The first reports coming out of WBAP-TV in Dallas that day identified a British Enfield rifle as the weapon used to assassinate the president. The empty shells that were planted in the sniper's lair could have easily turned into .303 ammunition. Frazier was soon drafted into the Army as a cook and remained unavailable for years. When he refused to sign his confession around midnight, the conspirators shifted into high gear and paid Joe Molina a visit.

3. Joe Molina

In Chapter 4 we thoroughly discussed how 22 November 1963 changed Joe Molina's life. This portion of a document seemed to, or attempted to, involve Molina somehow in the periphery of the assassination:

> On 11/27/63, OSVALDO IGLESIAS, 1851 East 26th Avenue, Tampa, advised that he had made a statement, while watching television about the assassination of President KENNEDY, to the effect that the man shown passing out propaganda with LEE HARVEY OSWALD in New Orleans appeared to him to be identical to RODRIGUEZ MOLINA, the man arrested for questioning with OSWALD in Dallas.

This document is full of innuendo and third hand, uncorroborated hearsay information. (John Armstrong Collection Box 16, Notebook 3, Box 27, file No. 33158, p. 7) Despite later being exonerated from any connection to Oswald, news about Molina was released from coast-to-coast and he was never able to get a retraction from Chief Jesse Curry. As we saw in Chapter 4, by Christmas he had been "let go" from his employment at the TSBD.

And where were these four patsies located that day? The probability of these four men being together in the same restricted space of the doorway, practically touching each other, is astronomical. Moreover, all four figures seem to have been subjected to some form of alteration in Altgens6! The four patsies in the entrance stairway identified as Doorway Man, "Obfuscated Man," Black Hole Man, and the removal of Frazier from the photograph, are strong indications that a very sophisticated operation was indeed executed in Dallas on 22 November 1963.

PART III
FRAMING LEE HARVEY OSWALD

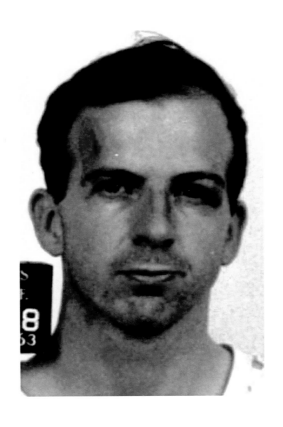

12

The Sinister Role of Bill Decker

In 1979, towards the end of the HSCA, Bolt, Beranek and Newman[1] analyzed the surviving Dictabelt recording where a total of four shots were detected. This recording was presumably the result of Officer J.B. McClain's radio mic being stuck in the "on" position, thereby adding gunshots to what was being recorded at DPD headquarters.[2] Over the years, many researchers, among them Todd Vaughan, Steve Barber, Chris Scally and Gary Mack (aka Larry Dunkel) have thoroughly dissected and debated the content and significance of these Dallas Police radio transmission tapes.[3]

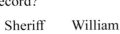

Within these recordings it has been well established that Sheriff Bill Decker participated in only a couple transmissions where he gave orders to his men to mobilize to the area of the railroad tracks and the TSBD that fateful day.[4] Was Sheriff Decker involved in more than what is stated in the official record?

Sheriff William Decker's ties to the underground, narcotics, the Dallas mafia, bootlegging, gambling and other improper activities have been well documented by many researchers and even the HSCA. Anthony Summers wrote how Joseph Civello was the "Dallas Mafia figure widely acknowledged to have been Texas representative for Carlos Marcello."[5] Furthermore, Summers wrote how Civello was one of the men arrested in the famous organized crime Apalachin meeting of 1957.[6]

When Joseph Civello was asked about Bill Decker in his deposition before the HSCA, this is how he answered: [7]

Q. We had discussed just very briefly Sheriff Decker. What was your relationship with Mr. Decker?

A. Like a son.

Q. I wonder if you could just tell us how that relationship developed and just characterize it for us.

A. Well you know ever since I was a little boy, why he knew of our family and he knew the Italian families, and everybody loved Decker. Decker made a lot of friends with a lot of people. Decker never had any problems with the Italian families here.

As I grew up and knew of Decker and just like grew up with him you know and I guess the man loved me and I loved him. I love Mrs. Decker. I would go down to the courthouse and I would always make it a point to go by and holler at him, sit down, and talk to him.

Paul Roland Jones, a career criminal who operated in the Dallas area for many years and in many areas of criminal activity, was even more specific about Decker's criminal pedigree. [8]

—Jones states that Bill Decker was an "old-time bootlegger here and he's rather a popular sort of fellow and he's been the under sheriff all of the time." Jones claims Decker and Dean Gauldlin (the district attorney) asked Jones if he wanted Dallas, and Jones declined the offer.

And Steve Guthrie, ex-Sheriff of Dallas County in the 1940s had this to say about Decker: [9]

—Guthrie stated that "We all know Bill Decker is a payoff man with Bennie Binion" and Butler agreed with Guthrie.

Decker in Action on 22 November 1963

Todd Vaughan's excellent study, *Presidential Motorcade Schematic Listing* (1993), detailed Chief Jesse Curry's lead car and its occupants: [10]

3. LEAD CAR

1. DPD Chief Jesse E.(J.E.) Curry
   (DPD Call #1)
2. SA Winston George "Win" Lawson (SSR)
3. DC Sheriff James Eric (J.E.) "Bill" Decker
   (DPD Call Dallas #1)
4. SAIC Forrest V. Sorrels

vehicle: white Ford Mercury 4-door sedan
    Lisc. TX #N or M U 8631 - provided by DPD
aka:
relevant photos/film: DCA film, Croft 1, Altgens 1-3,
    Martin film sequence, Hughes film sequence, Weaver 1, Altgens
1-7.
occupant sources: CE 768, CE 771, 4H170 Curry, 17H628 Lawson.
notes: SA Lawson has portable DCN SS radio tuned to "Charlie"
    frequency, however, according to Curry it "wasn't working
    too well" at the time of the assassination, and thus there
    was "no radio contact" between the Lead Car and the
    Presidential Limousine (Curry 2).

Early in the motorcade, images from the DCA film show the rear passenger-side window where Secret Service Agent Forrest Sorrels is clearly visible sitting in the back seat with his right forearm and elbow over the top of the back door and holding the window frame. The rear windshield is clearly visible and transparent as well.

Later in the film compilation, Chief Curry's lead car is shown at the 4:05 minute mark.[11] Seated in the back seat on the driver's side is Sheriff Bill Decker. His left arm, shown by the shirt cuff inside the suit jacket, is not visible in these frames as the car approaches the person filming the motorcade:

youtube.com/watch?v=KqMtbnBxIYU (DCA film: 6:48 running time)

Sheriff Bill Decker.

Left arm resting over the door is Chief Jesse Curry's.

"Twin-V" Radio, 15″ housing

Suddenly, we see the movement of the left hand as it raises up to Decker's face. The shirt cuff is now at an approximate 45° angle and continues to move to Decker's mouth.

Meanwhile, the car's headlights are not on, only the red police blinkers. Decker's hand continues to move toward his mouth, holding what appears to be a hand-held radio microphone. The following images require no description as to what is going on in the back seat.

The Official Version of Decker's Transmissions

The Warren Commission published the transcripts of the radio transmissions of channel Nos. 1 and 2 that day between the hours of 10:00 AM and 3:00 PM.[12] The only official record of DPD radio transmissions, as noted above, are contained in Commission Exhibit 1974 (Vol. 23). The implications are interesting. These transcripts *never* mention Decker communicating to *anybody* before 12:30 PM, and then only briefly to state the following:

First transmission by Decker at 12:30 PM: "I am sure it is going to take some time to get your men in there. Pull every one of my men in there."[13]

Second transmission by Decker at 12:30 PM: "Have my office *move all available men out of my office* [Emphasis added] into the railroad yard to try to determine what happened in there and hold everything secure until *Homicide* [Emphasis added] and other investigators should get there."[14]

Furthermore, Roger Craig later questioned Decker's specific orders to the "street" policemen and plainclothesmen that they were not to get involved in the security of the motorcade, and Craig and others were ordered to remain in front of police headquarters at 505 Main Street:[15]

> About 10:30 a.m. November 22, 1963, Bill Decker called into his office what I will refer to as his street people—plain-clothes men, detectives and warrant men, myself included—and told us that President Kennedy was coming to Dallas and that the motorcade would come down Main Street. He then advised us that we were to stand out in front of the building, 505 Main Street and represent the Sheriff's Office. We were to take no part whatsoever in the security of that motorcade. (Why, James Eric?) So . . . the stage had been set, all the pawns were in place, the security had been withdrawn from that one vulnerable location. Come John F. Kennedy, come to Elm and Houston Streets in Dallas, Texas and take your place in history!

A more sinister interpretation may be the possibility that perhaps Decker was speaking to Harry Weatherford, whom he had ordered atop the County Records building during the assassination.[16]

If that was the case, then the other occupants of the car should have heard what Decker was saying. A few weeks earlier, Weatherford had a silencer built by Deputy Sheriff Pat Boyd for his .30 carbine.[17]

In 1964, just months after the assassination and right before the publication of Warren Commission report, German author and researcher Joaquim Joesten published his wonderful treatise, *Oswald: Assassin or Fall Guy?*

Well ahead of his contemporaries, Joesten had to publish his work overseas. His only sources were published materials such as newspapers and magazines, and a short trip to Dallas right after the assassination. He was so well-informed that the FBI sent agents in March 1964 on behalf of the Warren Commission to try to find out if he had secret connections and whether he was obtaining documents from the FBI and the CIA.[18]

According to Joesten, the *Dallas Times Herald* published the following in its afternoon editions:

"Sheriff Decker came on the air at 12:25 PM."

"I don't know what's happened. Take every available man from the jail and the office and go to the railroad yards off Elm near the triple underpass . . ."

George Carter, an ace reporter for the *Times Herald* was glued to the radio at police headquarters, which is the reason the *Times Herald* beat out its competitors for this scoop.

Joesten observed how both afternoon editions of 2:30 PM and 4:30 PM continued to carry the report of Decker's transmissions that day.

Strange Happenings at the Dispatchers?

According to an officer at the Dallas Police Department, her job was of vital importance in "coordinating the dispatch of communications for officers in the field." She received emergency calls and issued information directly to the dispatch officer in the downtown division headquarters, located approximately one mile from Dealey Plaza. In her key position she was privy to all transmissions, and would also have heard all communications regarding the murder of Officer J. D. Tippit.

Very few researchers know about how Margie Barnes, a secretary in the communications division, with a designation of "Police Clerk 4" of the DPD Radio Patrol Division, was relieved of her duties at The Eleventh Hour, when she received an "unsolicited and unexpected engraved invitation" to attend the President's Luncheon at the Trade Mart on 22 November.

"She was moved out of her crucial position in a manner which she described as "astonishing." Barnes was never called by the Warren Commission or interviewed by anyone about the activities at the Radio Patrol Division of the DPD.[19]

For decades, British JFK researcher Chris Scally has studied the dispatcher's transcripts and has published several articles about his findings. Scally has determined that what survives today are second and third generation copies of the dictabelts, and that it is impossible to conclusively state if the extant recordings are a genuine representation of the corresponding transcripts.[20] The absence of Bill

Decker speaking in any of these transcripts before the time of 12:30 PM is an obvious cause for concern. Furthermore, he sees nothing nefarious about the removal of Barnes from her position that day.[21]

The Evolution of Altgens7

Although it may seem peripheral to the Decker story, we must now once again turn our attention to Altgens7. As noted in Chapter 2, this version of Altgens7, supposedly printed from the original negative, should be pristine and unaltered. Right away one notices where the cement railing of the overpass has been chopped off at right, along with spectators who were in that area.

Surviving "non-cropped" version of Altgens7.

Cropped version of Altgens7.

The cropped version of Altgens7 shows the brake lights on, indicating the driver, Chief Curry, has stopped the car.

Finally, we zoom in to show the lead car driven by Chief Jesse Curry. What was Decker doing while the motorcade was grinding to a halt? In Altgens7, he is seen rotated 180°, watching the successful execution of the ambush on the JFK limousine. That same afternoon, he told reporters for the *Dallas Times Herald* that "he may have seen one of the bullets hit the concrete and bounce."[22] This further supports the hypothesis that *he was turned* toward the JFK limousine, as seen in Altgens7. The only way he could have seen these two events would have been while facing the trailing motorcade.

As noted, his second statement transmitted over the radio now takes on more ominous implications:

"Have my office *move all available men out of my office* [Emphasis added] into the railroad yard to try to determine what happened in there and hold everything secure until *Homicide* [Emphasis added] and other investigators should get there."

1. Why did he order some of his men to remain in his office during the motorcade?

2. More importantly, how did he know as early as 12:30 PM, that "Homicide" personnel were going to be needed in Dealey Plaza, unless he knew right there and then that someone was mortally wounded?

It also raises serious doubts about the truthfulness of Chief Jesse Curry regarding how the occupants of the lead car found out about the mortal wounds of the president, since Curry maintained all along it was motorcycle patrolman James Chaney who drove up to inform them. This concept will be discussed at length in Chapter 20.

Summarizing, Altgens7 reveals several anomalies in the rear area of Chief Jesse Curry's automobile:

• Decker was turned completely around, facing JFK's limousine.

• The lead car's brake lights were on, indicating Curry had stopped or was in the process of stopping the car. This gives more credence that the entire motorcade came to a stop.

• What appears to be obfuscation in the area where we should see Sorrels and possibly Lawson, where the only reason to erase them would have been because they too were turned around viewing the assassination.

• A "sliver" of some type, emanating from the presidential flag which covers an area of the middle of the rear windshield, which is not visible in the other Altgens photographs. The area that it covers matches the area where Chief Jesse Curry should have been visible. Was Curry also turned around watching the assassination?

• Darkened inner portion of the presidential flag where other Altgens images show the presidential logo was printed on both sides of the flag itself.

WHEN THE BULLETS STRUCK: Mrs. Kennedy moving to the aid of the President after he was hit by a sniper yesterday in Dallas. A guard mounts rear bumper. Gov. John B. Connally Jr. of Texas, also in the car, was wounded.

Finally, this is the Altgens7 sent out by AP and printed Friday, 22 November in many afternoon editions in the Midwest United States and the West Coast.

The scan above is from the front page of *The New York Times* of Saturday, 23 November. Sheriff Bill Decker and the left tail light, have been cropped out of the photograph.

Over the years, many researchers have discounted the notion of alteration of Altgens7 because of its early publication in evening editions of newspapers in the time zones noted.

It is quite evident Altgens7 was also subject to alteration in the same manner that Altgens6 was altered to hide a slew of evidence the conspirators did not want to come out.

James Douglass provided us with a glimpse of Bill Decker's very sinister role. Citing the work of Penn Jones, Jr. in *Forgive My Grief III,* Douglass related how Decker interrupted the preliminary interrogations in the afternoon of 22 November of Oswald by Homicide Captain Will Fritz, to request an immediate meeting in person. This request required Fritz to stop what he was doing and travel 15 blocks to 505 Main Street to hold a private conversation with Sheriff Decker that could not be carried out by telephone, and thus became the object of much speculation.[23] What was spoken between those two will never be known, but given the bevy of the evidence presented here, it is not hard to imagine what that could have been.

For more than 50 years, Sheriff Bill Decker enjoyed a long and duplicitous career in law enforcement in the state of Texas. Among the criminals he pursued were Bonnie Parker and Clyde Barrow and Raymond Hamilton.[24]

He died in 1970 with Harry Weatherford at his bedside.[25] It now seems evident that 22 November 1963 immortalized Decker, but for all the wrong reasons.

ENDNOTES

1. HSCA Vol. V, pp. 644-652
2. Ibid. (Chris Scally later determined that the open microphone could have been from Bobby Hargis's motor, see p. 35, "Acoustics Discussion Paper," March 1983)
3. *The Continuing Inquiry,* Penn Jones, editor, Vol. VI, Nos. 2 (22 September 1981), 4 (22 November 1981), and 5 (22 December 1981)
4. CE1974
5. Summers, Anthony, *Conspiracy* (1989, update 1991), p. 467
6. Ibid. 468
7. HSCA Vol. 9, p. 412
8. Ibid. 513
9. Ibid. 516
10. Vaughn, Todd Wayne, *Presidential Motorcade Schematic Listing* (1993)
11. DCA film, 4:05
12. CE1974 p. 2
13. Ibid. 163
14. Ibid.
15. Craig, Roger, *When They Kill a President* (unpublished manuscript 1971), p. 1
16. Shaw and Harris, *Cover-Up: The Governmental Conspiracy to Conceal the Facts About the Public Execution of John Kennedy* (1975), p. 144

17. Ibid.

18. Joestem, Joachim, *Oswald: Assassin or Fall Guy?* (1964, Kindle location 81)

19. Flynt, Larry, *The Los Angeles Free Press*, *"JFK Murder Solved"* (1978), p. 35

20. Scally, Chris, "The Dallas Police Department's Channel 1 Dictabelts: The Chain of Possession"

21. Chris Scally email 18 February 2015

22. Shaw and Harris, *Cover-Up: The Governmental Conspiracy to Conceal the Facts About the Public Execution of John Kennedy* (1975), p.125, (see pictures of bullet marks on p. 124), also Eugene Aldredge letter to Weisberg, 16 September 1968

23. Douglass, James, *JFK and the Unspeakable* (2008), pp. 275-276

24. tshaonline.org/handbook/online/articles/fde69

25. Fetzer, Jim, *Murder in Dealey Plaza* (2000), p. 94

APPENDIX

Re: ASSASSINATION OF PRESIDENT
JOHN FITZGERALD KENNEDY,
NOVEMBER 22, 1963, DALLAS, TEXAS

Caller	Conversation
Dispatcher (HENSLEE)	12:30 p.m. KKB 364.
1 (Chief of Police JESSE E. CURRY)	Go to the hospital - Parkland Hospital. Have them stand by.
1 (Chief of Police JESSE E. CURRY)	Get a man on top of that triple underpass and see what happened up there.
1 (Chief of Police JESSE E. CURRY)	Have Parkland stand by.
Dallas 1 (Sheriff J. E. "BILL" DECKER)	I am sure it's going to take some time to get your man in there. Pull every one of my men in there.
Dispatcher (HENSLEE)	Dallas 1 (Sheriff J. E. "BILL" DECKER), repeat, I didn't get all of it. I didn't quite understand all of it.
Dallas 1 (Sheriff J. E. "BILL" DECKER)	Have my office move all available men out of my office into the railroad yard to try to determine what happened in there and hold everything secure until Homicide and other investigators should get there.
Dispatcher (HENSLEE)	10-4. Dallas 1 (Sheriff J. E. "BILL" DECKER) - Station 5 (Dallas County Sheriff Dispatcher) will be notified.

Dispatcher (HENSLEE)   1 (Chief of Police JESSE E. CURRY), any
information whatsoever?

– 163 –

COMMISSION EXHIBIT No. 1974—Continued

Fritz met Craig outside his office in the City Jail Building. He looked through the glass and told Fritz that was the man he had seen escape the area of the killing. The two men entered the room where Oswald was and Fritz said, "This man saw you leave."

Oswald replied with agitation, "I told you people I did."

Fritz said, "Calm down, son, we are just trying to find out what happened. What about that CAR?" (1)

Oswald answered, "That STATION WAGON (2) be-
1 and 2: Emphasis ours.

FORGIVE MY GRIEF III   31

longs to Mrs. Paine, don't try to get her involved in this."

Craig distinctly remembers that Fritz said "car" and Oswald replied "station wagon."

Just about this time Captain Fritz got a telephone call from Sheriff Decker requesting Fritz to come to talk with him. Fritz left the questioning of Oswald and retraced the 15 blocks from city hall to Decker's office which is less than a block from the School Book Depository. Apparently this was not only a personal conversation, it was something which could not be said over the telephone or police radio. The need for a personal conversation must have developed after the ride from Parkland Hospital to the School Book Depository, as Decker caught a ride with Fritz from Parkland.

13

The Cab Ride That Never Happened

It is generally accepted that taxicab driver William Whaley drove Lee Oswald to his rooming house on North Beckley in Oak Cliff, a suburb of Dallas, after Oswald allegedly assassinated President John F. Kennedy on 22 November 1963. Even many researchers who do not believe Oswald shot anyone that day have never disputed the alleged bus and cab ride. The evidence offered by the Warren Commission has essentially been acknowledged and unchallenged by scholars, historians and students of the case.

The importance of this cannot be overstated because it reinforces the lone nut notion that Lee acted alone and was not involved in any type of conspiracy. Once we start scrutinizing and peeling away the layers of this convoluted onion, we begin to realize that what other witnesses and investigators have reported regarding his actions immediately after the assassination might not be so farfetched after all.

Harold Weisberg was one of the few who thoroughly dissected both of Whaley's depositions, and concluded that it had all been fabricated. By applying simple computer handwriting and graphics analysis, this chapter will re-examine the long-standing and possibly flawed evidence that has led to the conclusion that Oswald made his great escape in William Whaley's taxi cab.

Connecting the Dots with the Evidence

The Warren Commission, taking its cue from the FBI,[1] claimed that Whaley volunteered to come in when he supposedly saw Oswald's picture in the newspaper the following day, and recognized him as the man who had hired him to drive him to Oak Cliff the day before around noon time. Whaley, supposedly wrote two very intriguing statements on 23 November, which in turn were the foundation of his official DPD affidavit that was later presented during his Warren Commission testimony.[2] They appear to have been written by a stenographer, and if that is the case, we do not have a copy of Whaley's actual signature. The first statement, written in the first person, bears his name at the top and ends about 2/3 down the page where he describes the age of his passenger as "25 or 26 years old." At top right, the document bears the name of one "E.C. Hardin," who turns out to be FBI Special Agent Edmond C. Hardin. Hardin was present for Whaley's interrogations that Saturday and wrote the very first FBI report dated 23 November, cited above, which documented Whaley's supposed, and now well-known movements, the day of the assassination.

The mere fact that both statements are undated and unsigned should raise suspicions in any unbiased investigator. Moreover, the belated disclosure the next day, 23 November, that Oswald hired a cab to reach his rooming house at 1026 N. Beckley Avenue should also be a focus of interest to researchers. Here is a copy of the first handwritten statement by "William Whaley":

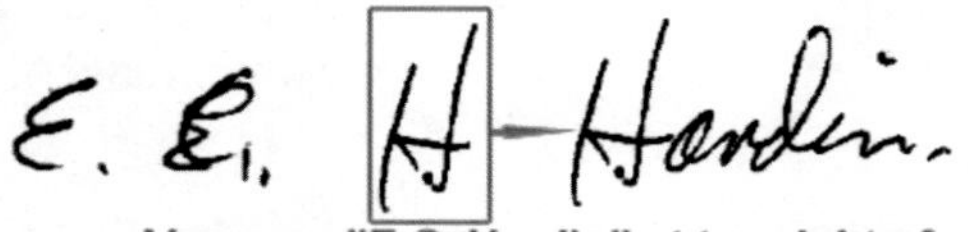

E. E,   *Hardin.*

E. E, [H] *Hardin.*

Above an "E.C. Hardin" at top right of
Whaley's 1st handwritten statement with
letter "H" isolation. E.C. Hardin is FBI
Special Agent Edmond C. Hardin.

Comparison of the words "He" and
"Houston" in Whaley's 1st handwritten
statement.

It's possible Whaley's handwritten statements could have been written by FBI Special Agent Edmond C. Hardin himself, so above is a comparison, so the reader can analyze and decide if Hardin may have written Whaley's handwritten statements.

Below, we note the letter "E" in the same style of the E.C. at the top, along with what appear to be the initials "LDM." These initials should correspond to Detective L.D. Montgomery, who by his own admission, testified before the Warren Commission that he brought in Whaley for questioning:

Mr. BALL. Did you talk to witnesses that had anything to do with the shooting of Tippit?

Mr. MONTGOMERY. Well, we went out and got two of them and brought them down.

Mr. BALL. Who were they?

Mr. MONTGOMERY. Let's see, there was a taxicab driver—Whaley—one of them was Mr. Whaley and there was another one.

Here is a sample of L.D. Montgomery's signature and handwriting:

There certainly are various elements of Montgomery's handwriting which match Whaley's statements:

As stated earlier, another possibility would be that a stenographer or clerk could have written Whaley's statements, and annotated Hardin's name at the top of the first statement, Document 0138-001, to acknowledge the presence of the FBI. This could also be a possibility, because of the error we find in his initials, which were corrected to "E.C." from the original "E.E." It would have been unlikely for Hardin to misspell his own name. The FBI brought in a virtual army of clerks and stenographers from neighboring cities such as Houston, San Antonio, Little Rock, New Orleans, and Oklahoma City.[3]

In the absence of a confirmed sample of Whaley's true handwriting, any analysis is a daunting task. It does not preclude the fact, nonetheless, that many suspicious anomalies exist in the handling of Whaley's statements and taxicab call log the weekend of the assassination, yet the evidence available still allows us to reasonably reconstruct a more coherent interpretation of what might have happened.

Later that day, a second version of this same statement was apparently re-written where both Whaley and Hardin's names were omitted at the top, and an addendum marked with a star was added at the bottom, detailing his interaction with an elderly lady who wanted the cab for which he had already activated the meter.[4] This second version of Whaley's statement contained a second page which will be closely examined.[5]

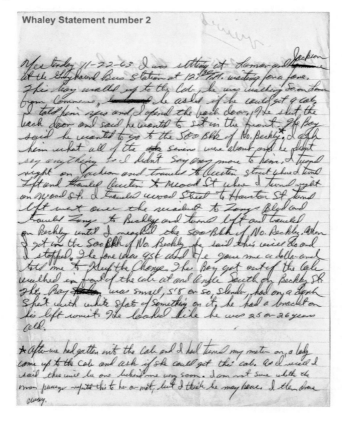

Whaley Statement number 2

The two pages shown above are the first and second statements by William Whaley; is this his true handwriting? Is this his true signature?

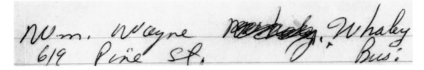

Why were there two different versions of Whaley's handwritten statements and why did they contain so many corrections and modifications?

For example, the first line states "Lamar and Commerce," which was corrected to "Lamar and Jackson."

Then, the statement went from "this boy was walking south on Lamar from Commerce" to "this boy walked up and asked if he could get a cab." Any layperson could easily interpret that they were avoiding any mention of Commerce Street as the route used by the cab rider who arrived at Whaley's post.

Why is William Whaley's signature lacking at the bottom of both of these first-generation versions of his handwritten statement, which was later transcribed into the typewritten affidavit of 23 November 1963?

> Mr. BELIN. When you saw the statement the first time, did you see the statement before you went down to see the lineup?
>
> Mr. WHALEY. No; I didn't see the statement. I don't think I did. I am not for sure.
>
> I think I signed it after I came back. It was on paper. They were writing it up on paper.
>
> Mr. BELIN. They were writing?
>
> Mr. WHALEY. Before I left there, I signed this typewritten, because they had to get, a stenographer typed it up. I had to wait.
>
> Mr. BELIN. But was this before or after you saw the lineup?
>
> Mr. WHALEY. After she typed it up. It was after.
>
> Mr. BELIN. It was after?
>
> Mr. WHALEY. That is when I signed it, after.
>
> Mr. BELIN. Now, when you signed it—what I want to know is, before you went down, had they already put on there a statement that the man you saw was the No. 3 man in the lineup?
>
> Mr. WHALEY. I don't remember that. I don't remember whether it said three or two, or what.

In his second appearance before the Warren Commission Whaley described some problems he confronted that day while the authorities were processing his statements and affidavit.[6]

"I signed my name because they said that is what I said."
[Emphasis added]

This last remark is an extremely strong indicator of how detached Whaley was from any voluntary actions of his own, and as remarkable as it may seem, it is very possible he did not even sign any statement and/or affidavit attributed to him. Here we note Belin's immediate reaction to Whaley's off-the-wall remark, which also gives a good indication of the extreme pressure Whaley was under.

> Mr. BELIN. Well, Mr. Whaley——
> Mr. WHALEY. I know, sir, but I don't think you can understand what I had to put up with that afternoon.
> Mr. BELIN. You mean with the press?
> Mr. WHALEY. Yes, sir; with everything.

In this example, Belin tried to deflect responsibility to the "press," but Whaley answered, "with everything."

The second page of his handwritten statement supposedly written by Whaley, is even more intriguing and deserves even more scrutiny because outside of his apparently contrived Warren Commission testimony above, it is the only document in existence where Whaley supposedly "identifies" Oswald as "the number 3 man" out of the police lineup he attended at 2:15 PM Saturday the 23rd, as his fare the day before between the times of 12:15 and 12:45 PM.

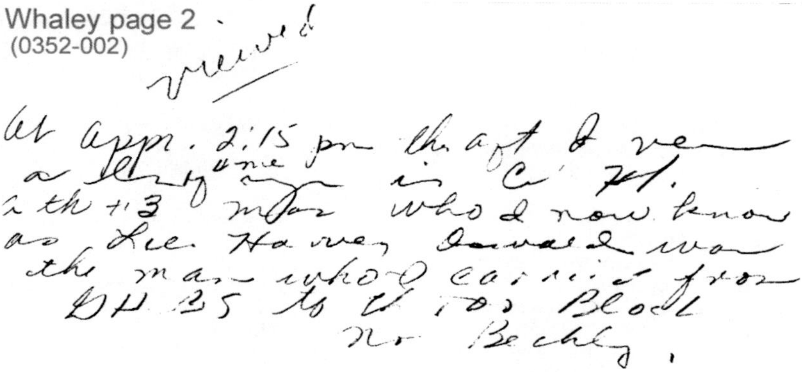

Whaley page 2
(0352-002)

Thus, the notations (see appendix for isolation) seen above translate into the following:

> At approximately 2:15 pm this afternoon I viewed a line up of 4 men in this City Hall. The number 3 man who I now know as Lee Harvey Oswald was the man who I carried from the Greyhound Bus Station to the 500 block of North Beckley.XXXXXXXXXX XXX

Several issues here are inescapable. As noted above, William Whaley never signed any of his handwritten statements. Secondly, the handwriting does not match "Whaley's" handwriting on the first page of the second "statement." In fact, the abbreviations contained in the so very important second page bear the characteristics of shorthand used by stenographers. This shorthand contains a combination of half-words and symbols. When we isolate and analyze the handwriting of the first and second pages, we find many discrepancies between the two pages of his supposed second statement:

The phrase "500 Block of No Beckley" on the second page do not match.

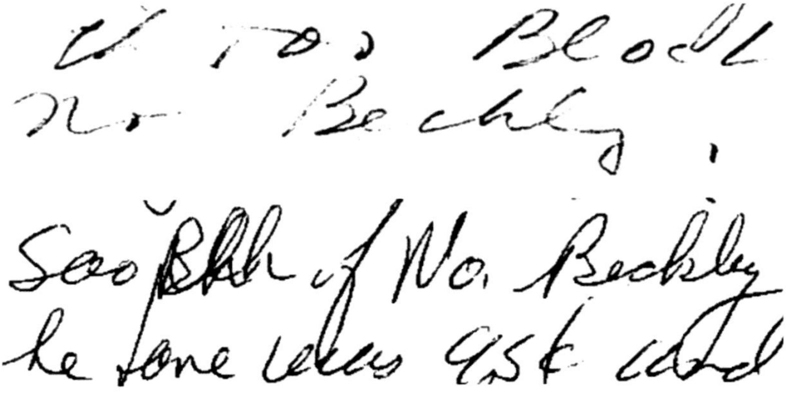

More importantly, the word "Beckley" has been misspelled to read "Beckly," perhaps indicative of an out-of-town stenographer, as mentioned earlier. (see footnote 3) There is not a single instance in Whaley's handwritten statements where Beckley is misspelled except for in the second page of his second statement.

But there are even more problems with this short paragraph. The very first line reads:

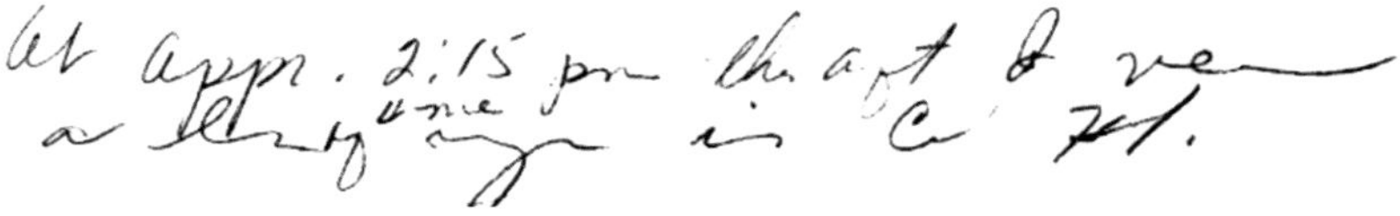

"At appr. 2:15 pm this aft I ve a line of 4 me up in Cit Hl"

Not only is this a very cryptic rendition which contains shorthand symbols unlikely to have been known by Whaley, but they also show the signs of a person with dyslexia!

The statement continues:

"A th #3 man who I now know as Lee Harvey Oswald was the man who I carreid (sic) from GH BS to th 500 Block No Beckly (sic)."

281

More shorthand notations not used in the first page:

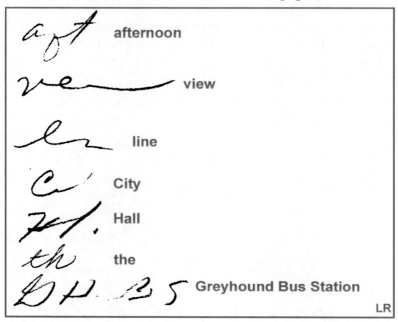

This collage shows and isolates the many instances of shorthand notation used in the very brief second page of Whaley's second handwritten statement, Document 0352-002, which are only found in this document and not in the other two pages of handwritten pages.

Note comparisons of the word "Beckley":

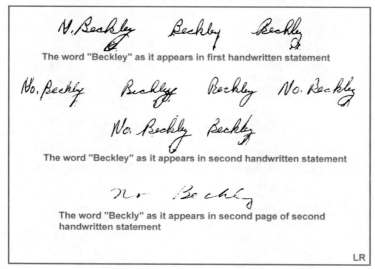

Right, we examine the word "the" as written by "Whaley" in the first page, versus the second page. Note that "Whaley" never abbreviated the word "the." Furthermore, when crossing the letter "t," he always ran it across the letter "h" as well, and he never looped his letter "t" when spelling the word "the."

The word "the" contained in the first page.

The word "the" contained in the second page.

Right "Oswald" and "carried" (not in script) from the second page of Whaley's second "statement." If you really want to get technical, notice that the word "carried" is misspelled as "carried."

Moreover, this letter "d" comparison proves beyond any reasonable doubt that these were not written by the same person. Numerous applications of the letter "d" by the "real William Whaley" are not even close to matching those contained in the second page of his statement, right.

As noted above, the handwritten statement by Whaley was transcribed into an official affidavit, ostensibly signed by William Whaley in the presence of Notary Patsy Collins.

> Mr. BELIN. Did you sign an affidavit for the Dallas Police Department?
> Mr. WHALEY. Yes, sir.
> Mr. BELIN. I will hand you a document which I am calling Whaley Deposition Exhibit A, and ask you to say if your signature appears on there?
> Mr. WHALEY. Yes, sir; that is my signature.

However, when we analyze the signatures contained in "Whaley Deposition Exhibit A" (DPD affidavit), we come up with this:

Affidavit signature comparison for cab driver William Whaley taken by notary Patsy Collins.(Vol 21 page 727)

William Wayne Whaley.

SUBSCRIBED AND SWORN TO BEFORE ME THIS 23 DAY OF November A.D. 1963

Patsy Collins Patsy Collins

CPS-OF-413

Not only are various elements of both signatures virtually identical, but the slant of both samples of writing are identical as well.

Below is the only actual spelling of Whaley's name contained in any of the handwritten statements. If this is the real William Whaley signature, you do not need to be a professional forensic calligrapher or handwriting expert to note that it's not even close to what is shown in his affidavit.

Furthermore, this color version clearly shows that his last name, which had been scratched out, was originally misspelled as *"Whaly"* *instead of "Whaley."* Once the offending script is removed, this becomes quite evident, as shown in this overlay collage:

Another interesting aspect noted here is that the letter "y" in "Whaley" had to be cut short because the word "Bus:" had already been written on the next line. This clearly suggests that the correction occurred after the statement had been written up.

This collage shows the DPD's practice of duplicating affidavits, and in the process duplicates the apparent falsification of Whaley's signatures.

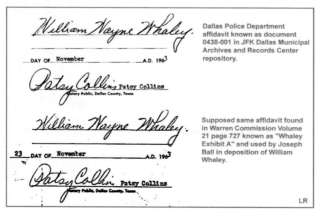

Dallas Police Department affidavit known as document 0438-001 in JFK Dallas Municipal Archives and Records Center repository.

Supposed same affidavit found in Warren Commission Volume 21 page 727 known as "Whaley Exhibit A" and used by Joseph Ball in deposition of William Whaley.

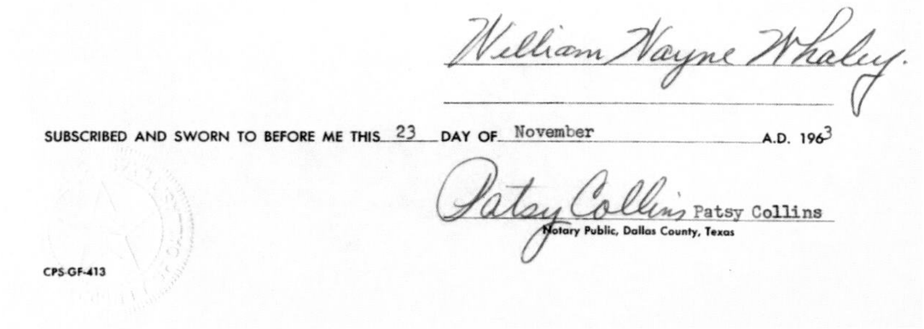

William Wayne Whaley.

SUBSCRIBED AND SWORN TO BEFORE ME THIS 23 DAY OF November A.D. 196³

Patsy Collins Patsy Collins
Notary Public, Dallas County, Texas

CPS-GF-413

Call Log Comparison

But let's dig a little deeper and examine Commission Exhibits 370 and 382, which are William Whaley's actual taxi cab logs which supposedly document his fares and activities on the day of 22 November 1963. These exhibits were presented by Joseph Ball in his examination of Whaley on 12 March 1964,[7] but mysteriously were not used by Belin in his second round of testimony 8 April 1964.[8]

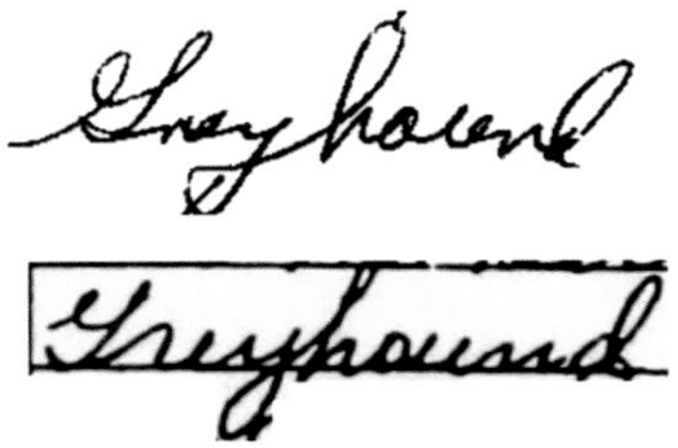

Right: The word "Greyhound" by Whaley above versus "Greyhound" by unknown below.

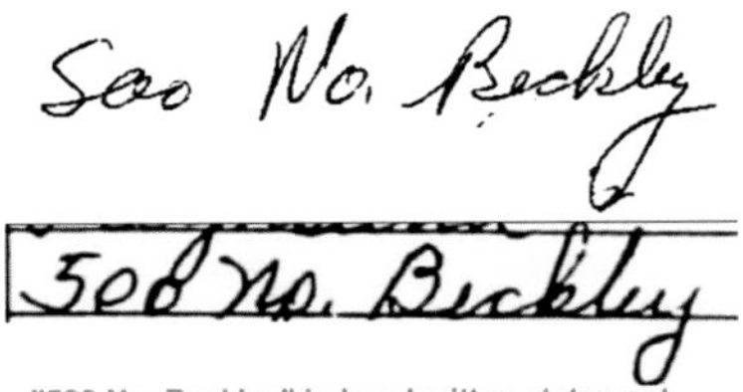

The word "Greyhound" comparison, above from handwritten statement, below from CE370/CE382 call log.

Right: "500 No Beckley" comparison, and, below, this simple rendition of "95 cents" stands out because "Whaley" consistently wrote it in his statements with the "cent symbol," ¢, whereas in his call log it is written with a decimal point and the cent symbol is omitted.

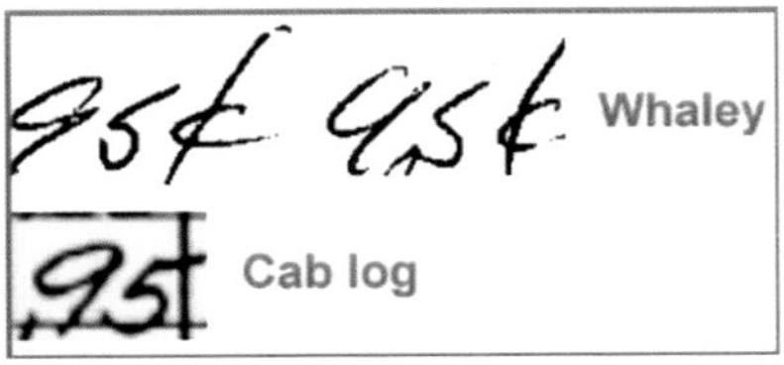

"500 No. Beckley" in handwritten statement above, versus CE370/CE382 below.

Finally, when we examine Whaley's supposed signature at top left of his log, we find the basic components of the signature are a perfect match to Notary Patsy Collins's forged signature contained in his affidavit of 23 November 1963:

Whaley

Cab log

285

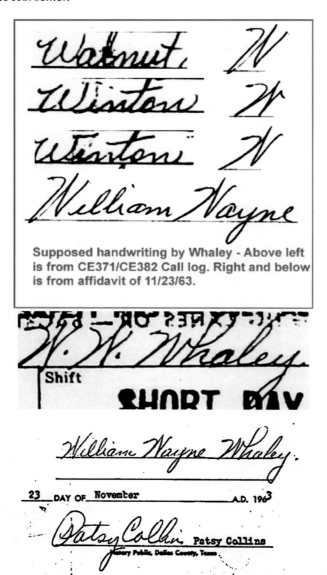

Supposed handwriting by Whaley - Above left is from CE371/CE382 Call log. Right and below is from affidavit of 11/23/63.

Shift

SHORT DAY

William Wayne Whaley.

23 DAY OF November A.D. 1963

Patsy Collin Patsy Collins
Notary Public, Dallas County, Texas.

Commission Exhibits 370 and 382 are clearly documents which do not contain any actual entries by the real William Whaley. They were probably written in one sitting. Moreover, they are much too neat and organized to have been written in the uncomfortable environment of a taxi cab, by a driver who was in constant stop-and-go traffic. It contains no folds, crumpling or creases of any kind, typical of the movement that would have been caused by a taxi cab thrashing about in an eight-hour shift. Granted, Whaley probably would have used a pad or clipboard of some kind to write on, however, the report is much too pristine to have been in the environment of a taxi cab. We have exactly the same situation as Oswald's supposed bus transfer ticket—Commission Exhibit 381A—which lacks any evidence of having been in anybody's pants pocket, and which was not produced until the next day.[9]

Consider Whaley's actual statements in this video, concerning the entries of his daily log:

youtube.com/watch?v=o3G8FZ92vjs

Whaley: "Yes sir, in the time element and what I put down on my sheet, they wanted to know why I approximated my time and I explained to 'em I put the trips down as every 15 minutes, as for an hour which is usually the run of it, you can't put 'em down exactly to the minute 'cause you'd have to stop on them traffic or re-writing while you're moving and that's dangerous, so I'd approximate mine it runs on to 15 minutes."[10]

Regarding the log entries themselves, historian Michael L. Kurtz rightfully noted that the entries were not even organized in 15-minute increments.[11] (see actual cab log above as filed under CE382) Furthermore, the key entry which corresponds to the ride from the Greyhound terminal to 500 North Beckley Avenue is logged at 12:30 PM, the exact time of the assassination.

In synthesis, after a careful and methodical analysis of the available evidence, the inevitable conclusion one must draw is that the surviving documents pertaining to William Whaley are extremely flawed, and to borrow one of Jim Fetzer's favorite phrases, are not even internally consistent between one another. Remarkably, the three pages of handwritten documents that are in the first person were the basis for his official affidavit dated 23 November and notarized by Patsy Collins, which in turn was used by the Warren Commission to substantiate Whaley's transportation of Oswald to his boarding room at 1026 North Beckley Avenue.

It is most likely that both William Whaley's signature on his affidavit, and the taxicab log attributed to him for 22 November 1963, and published by the Warren Commission as CE370 and CE382, have been forged. Notary Patsy Collins emerges as a major player in the so very important staged cab ride by Oswald to North Beckley Avenue in Oak Cliff to supposedly pick up the revolver with which he allegedly murdered Officer J.D. Tippit.

Yet, these falsified exhibits were unashamedly used by Warren Commission Counsel Joseph Ball to support Whaley's purported pickup of Oswald at the Greyhound station on 22 November 1963. The question that remains to be answered is why William Whaley went along with the charade and supported the Warren Commission's railroading of Oswald.

While questioning Whaley's DPD affidavit as valid, Dorothy Kilgallen wrote the following, only weeks before the publication of the Warren Report:

Dorothy Kilgallen, *New York Journal-American* 9/26-64

● On Nov. 23, a cab driver named William Wayne Whaley signed an affidavit saying he had picked up a fare "who I now know to be Lee Harvey Oswald" a few minutes after the assassination, and drove him a short distance—95 cents on the meter.

Yet on Nov. 24, District Attorney Henry Wade of Dallas county held a press conference in which he told reporters:

". . . He asked the bus driver to stop, got off at a stop, caught a taxicab driver, Darryl Click—I don't have the exact place—and went to his home in Oak Cliff, changed clothes hurriedly, and left."

William Wayne Whaley became Darryl Click, almost as casually and rapidly as the Mauser became a Carcano.

Kilgallen, however, was pursuing other information and rumors that were running rampant in Dallas, namely, that Henry Wade had mentioned Darryl Click, not William Whaley, as the cabbie who drove Oswald to Oak Cliff that day. This might have been one of the angles of investigation which she alluded to when she said she was going to break the case "wide open." It is well-known that Kilgallen herself became one of the mysterious deaths shortly thereafter.

U.S. Postal Inspector Harry Holmes could not recall Oswald even talking about how he left the TSBD after the assassination:

Following this, he simply walked out the front door of the building. I don't recall that anyone asked why he left or where or how he went. I just presumed that this had been covered in an earlier questioning. Postal Instpector Harry Holmes Interview of Lee Oswald CE2064

Discussion

William Whaley was a decorated World War II veteran who won the Navy Cross for his service to our country in Iwo Jima. Moreover, he was a Navy reservist attached to the air wing staff at the Naval Air Station in Dallas.[12] This background would suggest that

Whaley would not have been a person susceptible to willingly lie or participate in any false pretenses. The evidence strongly suggests that Whaley refused to sign his name on any document that contained false statements about his activities on 22 November 1963. Indeed, Whaley never directly referred to his passenger as "Oswald," rather as his "fare," or "passenger."

At the other end of the spectrum we have Whaley's perplexing, bizarre, and disorganized Warren Commission testimony where he knowingly accepted a forged taxi cab log as his own and allowed Joseph Ball to lead him as he pleased, leaving Belin to later try to control the damage for the Commission.

For example, consider the following exchange by Whaley and Ball regarding Oswald's clothing:

> Mr. BALL. I have some clothing here. Commission Exhibit No. 150, does that look like the shirt?
> Mr. WHALEY. That is the shirt, sir, it has my initials on it.
> Mr. BALL. In other words, this is the shirt the man had on?
> Mr. WHALEY. Yes, sir; that is the same one the FBI man had me identify.
> Mr. BALL. This is the shirt the man had on who took your car at Lamar and Jackson?
> Mr. WHALEY. As near as I can recollect as I told him. I said that is the shirt he had on because it had a kind of little stripe in it, light-colored stripe. I noticed that.

The clothing described by Whaley in his deposition does not match what Oswald wore that day at all. Whaley stated the man he drove to Oak Cliff wore two jackets and a shirt with a little light-colored stripe. Oswald wore neither of these, and as much as Ball tried, he could not steer Whaley in this direction. However, the FBI had already questioned Whaley in December about the clothing that Oswald wore that day:

The FBI knew since mid-December 1963 that Whaley could not identify the clothing worn by Oswald on 22 November 1963!

FD-302 (Rev. 3-3-59)

FEDERAL BUREAU OF INVESTIGATION

1

Date 12/18/63

WILLIAM WAYNE WHALEY, residence, 619 Pine Street, Lewisville, Texas, employed as a cab driver for Yellow Cab Company, Oak Cliff Cab Division, examined a brown long-sleeved man's sport shirt and stated that he cannot definitely say whether this is or is not the shirt worn by LEE HARVEY OSWALD on November 22, 1963, when he took OSWALD from the Greyhound Bus Station to the 500 block of Beckley, Dallas, Texas.

He stated that this may well be the shirt since, as he recalls, OSWALD was wearing grey work pants and a grey work jacket and had on a darker shirt which had a gold streak in it. He also recalled that this shirt was opened down the front to about the fourth button, and he does not recall OSWALD's wearing an undershirt. He also recalled that the shirt, as well as the rest of OSWALD's attire, was unpressed and wrinkled, as though it had not been ironed after washing or as though he had slept in the clothes.

on 12/18/63 at Dallas, Texas   File # DL 100-10461

by Special Agent BARDWELL D. ODUM: mam   Date dictated 12/18/63

This document contains neither recommendations nor conclusions of the FBI. It is the property of the FBI and is loaned to your agency; it and its contents are not to be distributed outside your agency.

And here is JFK research great Beverly Brunson's opinion of the entire William Whaley affair:

I may be wrong; but I never did think Oswald was in Whaley's cab. Remember that Whaley came up with his story (essentially preposterous) only after Oswald had accused Capt. Fritz of not protecting his identity. There was no point in Oswald's not mentioning this taxi ride since it was not incriminating. I think the production of Whaley the next day was part of an effort by Fritz to reassure Oswald. Oswald must have had some idea that he might pass himself off as Hidell up until the time he confronted Craig about 5:00 and he must have been counting on Fritz to help him. It was then only the next day that Oswald happened to mention that he had been in that taxi and Fritz produced Whaley who made an ass of himself all through his testimony, as you demonstrated.

Beverly Brunson
Box 296
Baxter Springs, Kansas 66713

(Item 13 pg 5)

Harold Weisberg wrote about the problem the Commission had with Whaley's identification of Oswald's clothing: [13]

Everybody else said Oswald was not wearing a jacket, the Commission says it found the jacket he wore to work (even if it didn't meet the description given by Frazier). Whaley is shown the gray zipper jacket, and Oswald had that one on. Shown the next jacket, which the table of contents describes as a blue zipper jacket, Whaley said that

291

Oswald was wearing one or the other. But by definition, "like
set" with the pants already described as blue, then Oswald had o the
blue jacket on. Finally he decided that Oswald was wearing both.

If not prior to this point, at this very moment the Commission
should have dispensed with Whaley as a witness. This makes everything
else he has said completely incredible.

It also points more and more in the direction that Whaley might
have been a reluctant participant in the cover-up that ensued after the
assassination:

Then Whaley pulls his most monstrous boner: "I signed that statement
before they carried me down to see the lineup. I signed this statement,
and then they carried me down to the lineup at 2:30 in the afternoon."
He undoubtedly correctly got the tone of voice, besides the meaning of
the words, in Belin's rejoinder, "You signed this affidavit before you
saw the lineup?" Whaley says he is confused and that Belin is doing
it to him.

As noted by Weisberg, these excerpts from Whaley's second Warren
Commission testimony speak for themselves:

Mr. BELIN. All right. Now in here it says, "The No. 3 man who I now know
is Lee Harvey Oswald was the man who I carried from the Greyhound Bus
Station * * *"
Was this the No. 3 or the No. 2 man?
Mr. WHALEY. I signed that statement before they carried me down to see
the lineup. I signed this statement, and then they carried me down to the line-
up at 2:30 in the afternoon.
Mr. BELIN. You signed this affidavit before you saw the lineup?
Mr. WHALEY. Well, now, let's get this straight. You are getting me con-
fused.
Mr. BELIN. Now, I will put it this way. There was an FBI reporter. FBI
interviewer with you?
Mr. WHALEY. Yes, sir; there was.
Mr. BELIN. And there was an interview with the Dallas Police Department?
Mr. WHALEY. Yes. And Bill Alexander from the district attorney's office
was there, also.
Mr. BELIN. All right, now, the last sentence.
Mr. WHALEY. Let me tell you how they fixed this up. They had me in the
office saying that. They were writing it out on paper, and they wrote it out
on paper, and this officer, Leavelle, I think that is his name, before he finished
and before I signed he wanted me to go with him to the lineup, so I went to
the lineup, and I come back and he asked me which one it was, which number
it was, and I identified the man, and we went back up in the office again, and
then they had me sign this. That is as near as I can remember. (WC6H430)

Is Jim Leavelle the DPD Detective who might have written
Whaley's statements?

Mr. WHALEY. That is the way it is right now. I don't think it will change again.

But on that afternoon, all I saw was the man that I hauled up there, and they asked me which number he was, and I said No. 2. I am almost sure I did, but I couldn't get up to swear to it that I did, sir.

Chief Justice Earl Warren was present during Whaley's first deposition in Washington and was obviously not impressed, because Whaley was called a second time on 8 April for Ball's tag team partner, David Belin, to have a crack at him. But before bringing him in a second time, the Commission flew two of its staff members, Burt Griffin and Leon Hubert, to Dallas to try to figure out how they were going to train Whaley for his second round of testimony.

Weisberg totally demolished the Commission's depositions of William Whaley, while casting serious doubts as to both Joseph Ball and David Belin's integrity:[14]

In using Whaley, they not only utilized a man who should have known in advance to be thoroughly and completely undependable, a man who was wrong on almost everything. In addition to destroying his own credibility as a witness, which in itself weakens the Commission's case, he casts doubt upon the important clothing identifications of other witnesses, and if anybody ever had any question about the complete dishonesty of the police lineup and the complete falsity of the police

statements that Oswald didn't want any lawyer, Whaley certainly shattered it. He came as close as any one man can come to proving that the whole case against Oswald was a frame-up. He destroyed the lineup, which could have been destroyed without him, and he also said that the police prepared statements for people to sign, including identifications before the identifications were made, and then ordered the witnesses to sign the statements.

And finally, Weisberg had this to say about the quality of witness Whaley made:

Whaley is only one in an apparently unending series of people who can not be dignified by description with the word "witness". In Whaley's case, he was totally unnecessary unless the Commission felt that his supervisor having notified the police they could not ignore him. However, this has not been compelling in the Commission's reconstructions pr hearings.

And Whaley had this to say about his own performance before the Warren Commission:

> **Mr. WHALEY.** I don't want to get you mixed up and get your whole investigation mixed up through my ignorance, but a good defense attorney could take me apart. I get confused. I try to tell you exactly what happened, to the best of my ability, when they brought Oswald out in the lineup of four. He was the third man out. I don't know which way they count them.

An Alternate Route for Lee Oswald: The Murray Photograph

After establishing the improbability of Oswald making his getaway via William Whaley's taxicab, one must now seriously consider Roger Craig, who adamantly insisted he saw and heard Oswald whistle as he raced down the grassy knoll to board a Rambler station wagon driven by a dark-complected Hispanic-looking man.

The only Jim Murray image that is not available on websites on the Internet is below, (provided by J. Gary Shaw, who in turn obtained it from Richard Sprague), in the self-published 1976 book *Cover-Up: The Governmental Conspiracy to Conceal the Facts About the Public Execution of John Kennedy*, coauthored by Larry Ray Harris. Shaw and Harris were the first researchers to advance the idea that confirmed what Roger Craig witnessed that day.[15] Witnesses who independently corroborated Roger Craig, but who never testified before the Warren Commission, include Helen Forrest, James Pennington,[16] Marvin C. Robinson[17] and his employee Roy Cooper.[18]

Photo credit J. Gary Shaw

Irish researcher Harry Irwin published a portion of some of Roger Craig's letters to Ed Tatro and one "M.G." of Bellport, N.Y. (written in 1970), in *The Continuing Inquiry* on 22 May 1977. In one of these letters, Craig wrote about the Murray photograph shown alongside. Craig first saw this photograph in New York, and he expressed surprise that it even existed, and even more surprise that Richard Sprague had not disseminated it:

As for the man running down the grassy knoll and the station wagon, Dick Sprague has pictures of this as well as the clock showing what time 12:44pm. I saw them in New York, why he doesn't show them I will never understand.   **TCI Vol 1 No. 10 5/22/77 pg 4**

Returning to William Whaley, bear in mind that well before Whaley was brought in on Saturday the 23rd, *The Dallas Morning News* printed a story that same morning which documented what Craig saw (see insert below).[19]

And Sheriff's Deputy Roger D. Craig, 27, identified Oswald as the man he saw running from the Texas School Book Depository building at Elm and Houston, from where President Kennedy's assassin fired a high powered rifle.   Dallas Morning News 11/23/63

Even though this image is blurry and grainy, it shows an individual closely resembling Oswald, not wearing a jacket, where his shirt looks puffed, his hair disheveled, as he seems to be in full stride on his way to board the Rambler station wagon described by Craig. Later that afternoon when Craig was summoned to Captain Will Fritz's office, Oswald was confronted by Craig's observations, which are best summed up in these collages offered by Richard Hooke:

Deputy Sheriff Roger Craig

Deputy Sheriff Roger Craig (arrow) in the office of Captain Will Fritz the evening of November 22, 1963. Fritz denied that Craig had been there that night until this photo showed up years later.

Captain Fritz denied Roger Craig was ever in his office, lied about it for 6 years, until retired Dallas Police Chief Jesse Curry screwed up and published this photo in his book, JFK - Assassination File. They were trying to hide the fact that Lee Oswald got picked up at 12:40 in front of the TSBD, in Mrs. Paines station wagon, and thus LEE OSWALD was meerly a pawn in A MASSIVE CIA ORCHESTRATED HIT on JFK.

Deputy Sheriff Roger Craig was not mistaken; and James Pennington and Helen Forest said it was Oswald getting into the wagon also. Additionally, Lee , agreed it was he and said it was Ruth Paine's car he was getting into. Also, at a subsequent visit with attorney Joseph Ball, Craig identified the shirt (that Ball produced out of evidence) as having been the overshirt Oswald was wearing. NO, THERE IS NO MISTAKE HERE, THERE WAS NO BUS / CAB RIDE AND THE AMERICAN PEOPLE HAVE BEEN COMPLETELY TAKEN TO THE CLEANERS!!!

November 22, 1963, 5 pm, Deputy Sheriff Roger Craig went to Captain Fritz's office, in Homicide Bureau of the Dallas PD. Oswald was sitting behind the desk. Fritz said,

"Is this the man?" pointing to Oswald.
Craig replied that it was. Fritz said to Oswald,
"This man saw you leave the building."
"I told you people I did" Oswald answered excitedly.
"Now take it easy, son," said Fritz, "we're just trying to find out what happened. What about the car?"
"That station wagon belongs to Mrs. Paine-don't try to drag her into this." Answered Oswald, and then he sat back, disgustedly, in his chair, and added,
"Everybody will know who I am now."

TRAIL OF BLOOD

Additionally, the people all along the bogus bus /cab ride died suspiciously, shortly thereafter: Cecil McWatters (bus driver), Mary Bledsoe (passenger), William Whaley (cab driver), Earline Roberts (landlady) and her sister Bertha Cheek, and Lee Oswald.

WILLIAM WHALEY

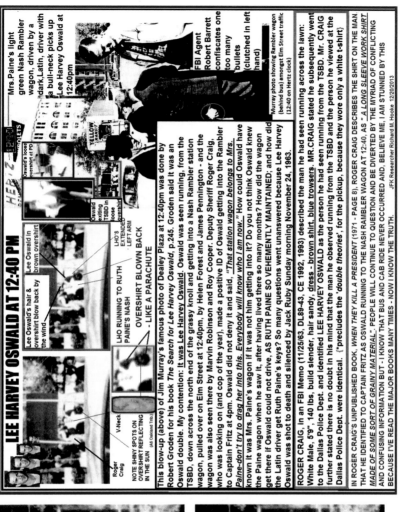

LEE HARVEY OSWALD AT 12:40 PM

(At Oakland Trib.)

Roger Craig

NOTE SHINY SPOTS ON OVERSHIRT REFLECTING IN THE SUN

V-Neck

Lee Oswald's hair & overshirt blow back by the wind

Lee Oswald in brown overshirt

LHO RUNNING TO RUTH PAINE'S NASH

LHO'S EXTENDED LEFT ARM

OVERSHIRT BLOWN BACK - LIKE A PARACHUTE

Oswald's loose overshirt at PD

Oswald exiting TSBD in loose overshirt

Mrs.Paine's light green Nash Rambler wagon, driven by a dark,Latin, driver with a bull-neck picks up Lee Harvey Oswald at 12:40pm

FBI Agent Robert Barrett confiscates one too many bullets (clutched in left hand)

Murray photo showing Rambler wagon (behind bus) amongst Elm Street traffic (12:40 on Hertz clock)

This blow-up (above) of Jim Murray's famous photo of Dealey Plaza at 12:40pm was done by Robert Groden for his book *The Search for Lee Harvey Oswald*, p.245. Groden said it was an Oswald double. My contention: It was Lee Harvey Oswald. Oswald was seen running, from the TSBD, down across the north end of the grassy knoll and getting into a Nash Rambler station wagon, pulled over on Elm Street at 12:40pm, by Helen Forest and James Pennington - and the wagon was also seen there by Marvin Robinson and Roy Cooper. Deputy Sheriff Roger Craig, who was looking on (and cop of the year), made a positive ID of Oswald getting into the Rambler to Captain Fritz at 4pm. Oswald did not deny it and said, *"That station wagon belongs to Mrs. Paine–don't try to drag her into this. Everybody will know who I am now."* How could Oswald have known it was Mrs. Paine's wagon if it was not him getting into it? Do you not think Oswald knew the Paine wagon when he saw it, after having lived there so many months? How did the wagon get there if Oswald could not drive, AS RUTH PAINE SO VEHEMENTLY MAINTAINED; and how did the Latin driver get Ruth Paine's keys? So many questions went unanswered because Lee Harvey Oswald was shot to death and silenced by Jack Ruby Sunday morning November 24, 1963.

ROGER CRAIG, in an FBI Memo (11/25/63, DL89-43, CE 1992, 1993) described the man he had seen running across the lawn: White Male, 5'9", 140 lbs, build slender, hair sandy, dress - brown shirt, blue trowsers. MR.CRAIG stated he subsequently went to the Dallas Police Dept. and identified LEE HARVEY OSWALD as the person he had seen running from the TSBD. Mr. CRAIG further stated there is no doubt in his mind that the man he observed running from the TSBD and the person he viewed at the Dallas Police Dept. were identical. (*precludes the 'double theories', for the pickup, because they wore only a white t-shirt*)

IN ROGER CRAIG'S UNPUBLISHED BOOK, *WHEN THEY KILL A PRESIDENT* (1971 - PAGE 8), ROGER CRAIG DESCRIBES THE SHIRT ON THE MAN THAT HE IDENTIFIED TO CAPTAIN FRITZ AS OSWALD RUNNING TO THE NASH RAMBLER WAGON AT 12:40, AS " A LONG SLEEVE WORK SHIRT MADE OF SOME SORT OF GRAINY MATERIAL". PEOPLE WILL CONTINUE TO QUESTION AND BE DIVERTED BY THE MYRIAD OF CONFLICTING AND CONFUSING INFORMATION BUT - I KNOW THAT BUS AND CAB RIDE NEVER OCCURRED AND, BELIEVE ME, I AM STUNNED BY THIS BECAUSE I'VE READ THE MAJOR BOOKS MANY TIMES - NOW I KNOW THE TRUTH.

JFK Researcher Richard M. Hooke 12/20/2013

NOTE SHINY SPOTS ON OVERSHIRT REFLECTING IN THE SUN

LHO RUNNING TO RUTH PAINES RAMBLER

LHO'S EXTENDED LEFT ARM

OVERSHIRT BLOWN BACK - LIKE A PARACHUTE

Mr. Craig. And the station wagon stopped almost directly across from me. And—uh—the man continued down the hill and got in the station wagon. And I attempted to cross the street. I wanted to talk to both of them. But the—uh—traffic was so heavy I couldn't get across the street. And—uh—they were gone before I could——

Mr. Belin. Where did the station wagon head?

Mr. Craig. West on Elm Street.

Mr. Belin. Under the triple underpass?

Mr. Craig. Yes.

Mr. Belin. Could you describe the man that you saw running down toward the station wagon?

Mr. Craig. Oh, he was a white male in his twenties, five nine, five eight, something like that; about 140 to 150; had kind of medium brown sandy hair—you know, it was like it'd been blown—you know, he'd been in the wind or something—it was all wild-looking; had on—uh—blue trousers——

Mr. Belin. What shade of blue? Dark blue, medium or light?

Mr. Craig. No; medium, probably; I'd say medium.

And, a—uh—light tan shirt, as I remember it.   WC6H266

Mr. Belin. Anything else about him?

Mr. Craig. No; nothing except that he looked like he was in an awful hurry.

A More Plausible and Likely Scenario

Whaley could have been selected because of his background as a decorated Navy veteran who had seen action in Iwo Jima.

Somewhere along the way he seems to have been recruited by being sold on the premise that Oswald was a Communist ex-defector who shot the president and Governor Connally, and they needed Whaley to fulfill his patriotic duty and help put him away permanently.

The evidence suggests, however, that Whaley refused to sign any documents which might compromise his integrity. It is therefore possible that his signature in his so very crucial affidavit and in his cab activity log for Friday, 22 November 1963, might have been forged.

As we have seen here, Notary Patsy Collins figured prominently in both of these. The second page of his second statement was an outright fabrication, where the architects of the scheme did not even hide the stenographic shorthand notations that remained in his "statement."

Subsequently, Whaley was interviewed by the FBI on 18 December by Bardwell Odum regarding a description of Oswald's clothing, and on 19 December by Edmond Hardin again, on the possibility of his knowledge of a relationship between Jack Ruby and Oswald. Then, the Warren Commission brought him to D.C. to face the godfathers of the Commission, with Earl Warren himself present at his first deposition of 12 March 1964.

With Warren obviously unconvinced by the Whaley charade, they had to regroup and send Burt Griffin, Leon Hubert and FBI Agent

John Howlett to Dallas on Sunday, 22 March 1964, to fix the situation and try to bring Whaley back into the fold for his second round on 8 April 1964.

This time, Warren was nowhere near the proceedings, and with Belin desperately trying to plug his finger into the dike, it all came crashing down on them, drowning any possibility that Whaley could remain a credible witness.

Sylvia Meagher questioned the timing of the actual cab ride and pointed out the obvious problems the Commission had with this aspect of Oswald's alleged getaway.[20]

Why would Whaley allegedly drop off Oswald at the 500 block of North Beckley Avenue, when his rooming house was in the 1000 block, namely 1026? As noted by Meagher, this would have obviously thrown the "official" timeline completely off, subtracting crucial minutes to Oswald's trip to his rooming house and placing him there well before the time that was required by the Commission. On 22 November 2014, this author walked the distance from the 500 block of North Beckley Avenue to the house located at the 1026 address, and the actual time it took to cover the distance at a brisk walk was eight minutes and 37 seconds. The distance covered was approximately 7/8 of a mile.

> **(4) OSWALD got out of the taxicab on North Beckley and walked north toward his rooming house at 1026 North Beckley, Oak Cliff section of Dallas, at about 12:55 p.m.**
>
> **(5) OSWALD entered the rooming house about 1:00 p.m. and left shortly thereafter.**
>
> Warren Commission has Oswald covering the distance from the 500 block of North Beckley in 5 minutes. Actual walking time at a brisk pace is 8 minutes and 37 seconds verified by author on 11/22/14.   LR

Yet, this is how the out-of-town Warren Commission counsels explained away how Whaley, a cab driver for 37 years in Dallas, could have confused the 500 block for the 1000 block.

As ridiculous as it may seem, this internal memorandum, which is now in the public record, reveals the reactionary ways of the Commission, and given Whaley's first unsuccessful deposition, offers a great example of how they went about fixing the official record to frame Oswald.[21]

OPTIONAL FORM NO. 10
1010-104

UNITED STATES GOVERNMENT

Memorandum　　　ROUGH DRAFT

TO : Mr. Rankin　　　　　　　　　DATE: March 23, 1964

FROM : Mr. Griffin and Mr. Hubert

SUBJECT: Activities of Dallas on Sunday, March 22, 1964.

Beginning at about 10 a.m., Mr. Griffin, Mr. Hubert, and SA John Joe Howlett visited the area between 1026 N. Beckley and 223 South Ewing Street. It was noted that the 1000 block on North Beckley begins at 5th Street. This may explain the taxi driver's notation that he let Oswald out of his cab in the 500 block. The cab driver may have been confusing 5th Street with the 500 block. We noted in the 1026 North Beckley area that there is an Enco Service Station directly across the street from that address and that diagonally across Zangs Boulevard is a Sleight Spped Wash-Dry establishment. We further noted that the distance from 1026 North Beckley Street to the nearest bus stop on Marsalis via 5th Street was one-half mile. We observed also that although the spot at which Tippett was shot is closer to Ruby's residence via Patton Street than 10th Street, the 10th Street route would probably

When interviewing Oswald during the weekend of the assassination, Postal Inspector Holmes quoted him as having complained about how little money he made at $1.25 an hour, and that he could hardly feed himself on this income:

He stated that 'How could I afford to order a rifle on my salary of $1.25 an hour when I can't hardly feed myself on what I make.'
Postal Inspector Harry Holmes Interview of Lee Oswald CE2064

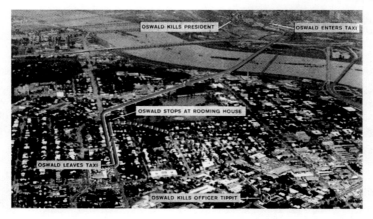

Later, *Life* magazine joined in the deception by publishing this aerial photograph where Oswald is supposed to have ridden Whaley's cab

past his rooming house on 1026 N. Beckley Avenue to the 500 block, only to double-back on foot and spend more money on cab fare, on his meager minimum wage salary, no less. But in doing so, *Life* inadvertently documented—for all posterity—how deceitful Griffin, Hubert and Howlett had been by justifying Whaley's mistake, in this manner:

"It was noted that the 1000 block on North Beckley begins at 5th Street. This may explain the taxi driver's notation that he let Oswald out of his cab in the 500 block. The cab driver may have been confusing 5th Street with the 500 block."

According to John Armstrong in his landmark study *Harvey and Lee*, a "Lee Oswald" drove up alone in a light-colored Rambler station wagon and walked into the Tidy Lady Laundromat (or Launderette) to use a payphone around 12:50 PM that day. Armstrong drew this information from Commission Document 1518, which contains the belated FBI interviews of Oda and Wesley Pennington, conducted by Richard J. Burnett on 1 September 1964, (see appendix) just as the Commission's proceedings were coming to an end. At this stage of the game, General Counsel F. Lee Rankin, by his own admission, was closing doors rather than opening them,[22] so it is highly unlikely that the FBI alerted the Commission as to the existence of these two witnesses.

In advancing the two Oswald scenario, Armstrong has unfortunately accepted the cab ride as valid. Furthermore, Armstrong cited Captain Will Fritz without providing a source, as confirming that Oswald made his getaway via a bus and cab ride:

> *NOTE: When interviewed on November 22nd* **Harvey** *Oswald told Captain Fritz that he rode the bus home. The following day Captain Fritz again interviewed Oswald and asked him if he had taken a cab ride after he left the TSBD. Oswald replied, "Yes, I did ride the cab....."* — John Armstrong, *"Harvey and Lee"* pg 826

If anything, this uncorroborated statement by Fritz provides even more evidence of an Oswald frameup. As an aside, it is interesting to note that when Captain Fritz's notes surfaced in 2007, for the entry dated Friday, 22 November 1963, they briefly mentioned a bus ride, but contained no mention of a cab ride.[23] The cab ride story did not surface until the next day. (see appendix)

As shown here, it is clear that U.S. Navy veteran William Whaley was thrown into a cauldron of deceit, and unfortunately for him, destiny dictated that he would become a linchpin in the framing of

Oswald for a murder he did not commit. The documents that prevail to this day are extremely flawed and do not pass the test of proper scrutiny.

Notary Patsy Collins clearly compromised her integrity by participating in the falsification of affidavits and taxi cab call logs. As noted by first-generation researchers Weisberg and Meagher, Whaley's Warren Commission testimony borders on laughable and reveals the incredible scheming that corrupt counsels Ball, Belin, Hubert and Griffin had to go through in order to frame his testimony as believable, a task in which they failed miserably.

Death of William Whaley

Whaley's extensive record as a taxicab driver in the city of Dallas was impeccable, having not once been involved in any accidents for over 19 years. Whaley, however, was killed the evening of Saturday, 18 December 1965, when he crashed head-on with an 83-year-old driver by the name of John Henry Wells on the Trinity viaduct in Dallas.

Wells hit Whaley's cab head-on when he inadvertently drove on the wrong lane of the divided highway of the Trinity River Bridge. Even though many have classified Whaley's unfortunate accident as one of the mysterious deaths surrounding the assassination of JFK, it is highly unlikely there was anything nefarious about his death.

ENDNOTES

1. mffpdf_95616, p. 101 FBI Hardin document, 23 November 1963
2. City of Dallas JFK document repository 0138-001, 0352-001, and 0352-002
3. See FBI 105-82555 Oswald HQ File, Section 209, pp. 53-55
4. City of Dallas JFK document repository 0352-001
5. Ibid. (0352-002)
6. WC6H431
7. WC2H254-255
8. WC6H428-434
9. jfkthelonegunmanmyth.blogspot.com/2012/10/oswalds-escape-from-...2
10. youtube.com/watch?v=o3G8FZ92vjs
11. Kurtz, Michael, *Crime of the century: The Kennedy assassination from a historian's perspective* (1982), p. 133
12. *The Dallas Morning News*, 19 December 1965
13. The Weisberg Collection. Hood College, Frederick, MD, USA
14. Ibid.
15. Shaw, J. Gary, "Fritz is the Liar—Not Roger Craig,"pp. 8-9, *The Continuing Inquiry* (TCI 571.pdf)
16. Kurtz, Michael, *Crime of the century: The Kennedy assassination from a historian's perspective* (1982), p. 133
17. CD5, p. 74
18. FBI memorandum from S.A. Earle Haley to SAC Dallas (89-43), 23 November 1963. The Weisberg Collection. Hood College, Frederick, MD, USA
19. Jones, Penn, *Forgive My Grief Vol IV* (1974), p. 33
20. Meagher, Sylvia, *Accessories After the Fact: The Warren Commission, the Authorities & the Report on the JFK Assassination* (1966), p. 84
21. 23 March 1964, internal Warren Commission memorandum by Griffin and Hubert "Activities of Dallas on Sunday 22 March 1964"
22. Epstein, Edward, *The New Yorker*, "A Reporter at Large," 13 July 1968, pertaining to the discovery of Sylvia Odio
23. See copies of Fritz's notes in appendix. The cab ride suddenly surfaced in his notes on the 23rd, the same day they produced Whaley as the alleged driver.

APPENDIX

William Whaley, the cab driver who took Oswald to his roominghouse is dead of a two car crash on the Trinity River bridge in Dallas. Whaley is the first Dallas cab driver to be killed while on duty since 1937, but details on Whaley's accident are not available. Whaley had a chance to talk to Oswald alone after the assassination of President Kennedy.

174
FORGIVE MY GRIEF-VOLUME I   by Penn Jones

303

Whaley, who had more seniority than any man in the taxi system, was a Navy gunner during World War II, winning the Navy Cross for action off Iwo Jima.

Dallas Morning News 12/19/65

WHALEY WAS ALSO a Navy reservist, attached to the air wing staff at the Naval Air Station.

④

AFFIDAVIT IN ANY FACT

THE STATE OF TEXAS
COUNTY OF DALLAS

BEFORE ME, _____Patsy Collins_____

a Notary Public in and for said County, State of Texas, on this day personally appeared _____

William Wayne Whaley, 619 Pine Street, Lewisville 2, Texas, Bus 610 S. Akard
Bus phone RI-2-9191

Who, after being me duly sworn, on oath deposes and says: Yesterday 11-22-63 I was sitting at Lamar and Jackson at the Greyhound Bus Station at 12:30 pm waiting for a fare. This boy walked up to the cab, he was walking South on Lamar from Commerce, he asked if he could get a cab, I told him, yes, and I opened the back door. He shut the back door and said he wanted to sit in the front. The boy said he wanted to go to the 500 Block of North Beckley. After we had gotten into the cab and I had turned my meter on, a lady came up to the cab and ask if she could get this cab. As i recall I said there will be one behind me very soon. I am not sure whether the man passenger repeated this to her or not, but I think he may have. I then drove away. I ask him what all of the sirens were about and he didn't say anything so I didn't say any-more to him. I turned right on Jackson and traveled to Austin Street where I turned left and traveled Austin to Wood Street where I turned right on Wood Street. I traveled Wood Street to Houston Stre t turned left went over the viaduct to Zangs Blvd. and traveled Zangs to Beckley and turned lef t and traveled on Beckley until I reached the 500 Block of North Beckley. When I got in the 500 Block of North Beckley he said this will do and I stopped The fare was 95 cents and he gave me a dollar and told me to keep the change. The boy got out of the cab and walked in front of the cab at an angle south on Beckley Street. This boy was small, five feet eight inches, slender had on a dark shirt with white spots of something on it. He had a braclet on his left wrist. He looked like he was 25 or 26 years old. At approximately 2:15 pm this afternoon I viewed a line up of 4 men in this City Hall. The number 3 man who I now know as Lee Harvey Oswald was the man who I carried from the Greyhound Bus Station to the 500 block of North Beckley.XXXXXXXXXX XXX

William Wayne Whaley.

SUBSCRIBED AND SWORN TO BEFORE ME THIS __23__ DAY OF __November__ _____ A.D. 196_3_

Patsy Collins Patsy Collins
Notary Public, Dallas County, Texas

CPS-GF-413

304

Regardless of the identity of the man who allegedly boarded Whaley's cab, there are several points that stand out in Hardin's FBI report, because of their contradictory nature. The phrase "from the direction of Commerce Street" suggests that Whaley's rider did not walk from Elm Street which was to the north of Whaley's position (see map below) The phrase "did not appear to be in a hurry" is not the profile of someone who had just murdered the President of the United States. Moreover, the fact that Whaley's cab was the only cab standing at that location is quite unusual, especially during lunch hour *and* the fact that the motorcade had passed within feet of that location, right down Main Street, and there were literally thousands of people in the downtown area. In the world of taxi cab life and the competition for fares, how convenient was it that there would not be any other cabbies available to corroborate Whaley's pickup?

At about 12:30 p.m., on this date, he noticed in his rear vision mirror a young man come up to his cab from the rear, from the direction of Commerce Street, that is, from the north, and "mosied up there" and did not appear to be in a hurry. Mr. WHALEY's cab was the only cab standing at that location at that time. The location was about seven blocks from the spot where President KENNEDY was assassinated. This man could have gotten off a bus nearby without his having seen him do so and he does not recall seeing him approaching at a great distance from the cab. The young man approached him and asked "Can I get the taxicab?". to which he answered in the affirmative.

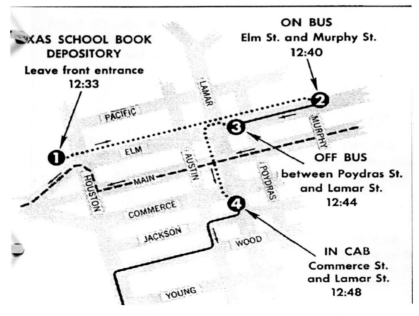

From the John Armstrong site at Baylor University, Box 16, Notebook 4, Tab 34 (33650.pdf)

The Edmond C. Hardin FBI report dated 23 November 1963

FD-302 (Rev. 3-3-59) FEDERAL BUREAU OF INVESTIGATION

Date ___11/23/63___

WILLIAM WAYNE WHALEY, 619 Pine Street, Lewisville, Texas, Route 2, was interviewed in the office of the Homicide Bureau, Dallas Police Department, by SA HARDIN and Detective L. Lee MONTGOMERY, Homicide Bureau, Dallas Police Department, and Mr. W. F. ALEXANDER, Assistant District Attorney, Dallas County. Mr. WHALEY furnished the following information:

He has been a capable driver for the city transportation company for the past 37 years, presently driving Cab #36. He is so employed at Dallas, Texas.

During the morning of November 23, 1963, he noticed a photograph of an individual named OSWALD in a Dallas newspaper and learned that this was the photograph of a suspect in the assassination of President JOHN F. KENNEDY on November 22, 1963, a few minutes following the assassination of Mr. KENNEDY. He explained this incident as follows:

At about 12:30 p.m., November 22, 1963, he was sitting in his cab at the cab stand located at the Greyhound Bus Terminal at Lamar and Jackson Streets, Dallas. A few minutes earlier he had begun to hear sirens and noticed a few blocks away that people were running about excitedly. He thought perhaps it was due to a robbery of some sort and did not connect this unusual activity with the shooting of President KENNEDY and Governor CONNALLY. At about 12:30 p.m., on this date, he noticed in his rear vision mirror a young man come up to his cab from the rear, from the direction of Commerce Street, that is, from the north, and "mosied up there" and did not appear to be in a hurry. Mr. WHALEY's cab was the only cab standing at that location at that time. The location was about seven blocks from the spot where President KENNEDY was assassinated. This man could have gotten off a bus nearby without his having seen him do so and he does not recall seeing him approaching at a great distance from the cab. The young man approached him and asked "Can I get the taxicab?", to which he answered in the affirmative. The man got inside the cab and stated "I want to get to the 500 block of North Beckley". Just before pulling away with the young man a woman came up to the cab and asked him if she could have the cab, whereupon he told her the cab was taken. She then asked him if he would call her another cab, whereupon he explained

on __11/23/63__ at ___Dallas, Texas___ File # __DL 89-43__

by Special Agent ___EDMOND C. HARDIN / mac___ Date dictated __11/23/63__

348

This document contains neither recommendations nor conclusions of the FBI. It is the property of the FBI and is loaned to your agency; it and its contents are not to be distributed outside your agency.

2

DL 89-43

to her that he could but added it would do no good, inasmuch as another cab would be along before he could get one to come by calling. He recalls that just as the woman asked for the cab, the young man opened a door and then closed it again immediately. He may have said something to the woman which may have been a repetition of what he had told the woman about the cab being taken or about another cab coming along very soon.

He does not recall definitely just what conversation, if any, took place between the young man and the woman. He then pulled away with the young man and immediately after, starting up, he told the young man "I wonder what's going on", referring to the unusual activity in connection with the sirens and apparently excited people a few blocks away. The young man did not say a word but remained silent throughout the entire trip and did not appear to be excited or to notice the unusual activity to which Mr. WHALEY referred above.

Mr. WHALEY took the young man to the 500 block of Beckley Street, where the man stated "This will do right here". He then got out, gave Mr. WHALEY a dollar bill to pay the fare of $.95, and stated "Keep the change". The man then angled across the street and started walking down Beckley Street in a southward direction. At that point, Mr. WHALEY left him and did not see him any more.

Mr. WHALEY estimated that he drove this man a distance of about 2-3/4 miles and dropped him off about seven blocks from the spot where OSWALD allegedly shot a police officer a few minutes later. The spot where he dropped this man off was located about one mile from the theater where OSWALD was arrested a few minutes following this.

He recalled that the young man he drove in his cab that day was wearing a heavy identification bracelet on his left wrist, he appeared to need a haircut and was dressed in gray khaki pants which looked as if they had been slept in. He had on a dark colored shirt with some light color in it. The shirt had long sleeves and the top two or three buttons were un-buttoned. The color of the shirt nearly matched the pants, but was somewhat darker. The man wore no hat. He appeared to be

349

3

DL 89-43

about 25 years of age, 5' 7" to 8", tall, about 135 pounds, with brown hair thick on top. He had a long thin face and a high forehead. He did not appear to have a noticeable accent but rather talked as people in this area normally do.

A photograph of LEE HARVEY OSWALD, New Orleans Police Department #112723, was shown Mr. WHALEY, who stated that this is definitely the photograph of the man referred to above whom he drove in his cab November 22, 1963.

On November 23, 1963, immediately following inter-view with Mr. WHALEY, Mr. WHALEY was present at a lineup at the Dallas Police Department Lineup Room, where LEE HARVEY OSWALD appeared with three other white males of similar ages and descriptions. Mr. WHALEY without hesitation stated that OSWALD is definitely the man whom he drove in his cab on November 22, 1963, as related above.

FRITZ IS THE LIAR - NOT ROGER CRAIG   by J. Gary Shaw

Marvin C. Robinson is a name long familiar to researchers as the man who gave the FBI corroborative testimony relating to Roger Craig's Oswald-Rambler Station Wagon story. What is not common knowledge is that Robinson was actually requested to appear and give deposition before Warren Commission Staff. This writer recently obtained a copy of the Commission's letter of request to Mr. Robinson dated March 26, 1964. The initials KP appear in the upper right hand corner of the letter indicating that up until that date the potential witness was considered a "Key Person" in the investigation.

Robinson however, never appeared before Commission attorneys. A previously scheduled Navy Reserve cruise caused the witness to phone the U.S. Attorney's office in Dallas and request that he be called at a later date. He was never contacted again. On April 1, 1964, Craig gave his testimony as scheduled and the Commission's "lone and unaided assassin" story received one of its most severe jolts. There must not be corroborating evidence to this story. Robinson was forgotten and his statement to the FBI buried among the voluminous unpublished records of the commission investigation.

Recently this writer interviewed Robinson and was given the story the Warren "Rubber Stamp" Committee chose not to hear. The following is what the committee would have heard had they desired to give the nation an honest report on the death of its president.

Robinson, proceeding west on Elm Street, had stopped his car just short of the Houston Street intersection. There was one other car between his and the intersection. He sat with motor running, windows up, and air conditioner on. A friend was in a car just behind him. Robinson heard no shots. As soon as the motorcade passed, a Dallas policeman quickly stepped out and began to direct the Elm Street traffic into Dealy Plaza. (Later, upon learning of the shooting, this action puzzled Robinson. He was amazed that the area was not immediately sealed off.*)

As Robinson crossed Houston he noted the panicky situation of the crowd and had turned his attention from driving to trying to ascertain what was happening.

Upon returning his attention to driving he discovered that a light-colored Rambler Station Wagon had pulled quickly in front of him and he had to hit his brakes in order to prevent hitting the auto from the rear. It was during this moment that he observed a man wearing a light-colored coat run down the incline to his right and hurriedly jump into the station wagon. The station wagon then pulled out of Robinson's traffic lane and sped toward the tripple-underpass and out of Dealy Plaza.

Later, after relating this event to his friend and at this friend's insistence, Robinson decided to report what he had seen. He did so by contacting Dallas Police Inspector J. Herbert Sawyer, who lived directly across the street from Robinson's home. Sawyer in turn called in the FBI.**

Dallas Police Captain Will Fritz appeared before Commission attorneys on April 22, 1964, and called Craig's story untrue. Craig, Fritz said, was telling a story that "didn't fit with what we knew to be true." The Police captain, it seems, knew what was true and what wasn't within two hours of the murder. Not bad. In a May 26, 1964 letter from Commission General Counsel J. Lee Rankin, Fritz was given detailed instructions as to his writing of a deposition in which he again calls Craig's story a lie.*** The Dallas Sheriffs Deputy's testimony must be discredited at all cost.

To have heard Marvin Robinson's testimony would have cast further doubt on

the "Lone Assassin" case. Therefore, it's alright for a Dallas police captain to lie. It's alright to hide and ignore corroborating testimony which pointed to a conspiracy. After all, the lives of other men could be at stake...the men who killed John Kennedy.

---

*   The actions of this Dallas officer raises additional questions concerning one of the lead motorcycle patrolmen who can be seen in the Zapruder film as he leaves the motorcade at the Houston-Elm intersection. Some have speculated that this was perhaps the motorcycle patrolman who opened the mike on his radio just minutes prior to the shooting of President Kennedy, thus blocking radio communication from the Dealey Plaza area during and right after this critical time. Now the question must be asked, was this also the officer who quickly directed the backed-up traffic into the killing area? Patrolman J. M. Smith, an officer assigned this intersection, testified that he quickly vacated his post to look for a potential assassin behind the grassy-knoll area. Further investigation is needed regarding this unidentified Dallas Policeman.

**   It was convenient for Sawyer to contact the FBI. His wife was employed by the Dallas Bureau and Sawyer himself was a graduate of the FBI Academy.

*** See T.C.I. Mar. 22, 1977. "Instructing a Witness". See also Forgive My Grief Vol. III Revised: Page 101, "LBJ Ordered Fritz to Stop Investigating Oswald".

FD-302 (Rev. 3-3-59)

FEDERAL BUREAU OF INVESTIGATION

Date ___September 2, 1964___

1

    JOHN WESLEY PENNINGTON, 405 North Clinton Street, Dallas, Texas, advised that he is retired.

    Mr. PENNINGTON advised that sometime between 12:00 noon and 1:00 p.m., Friday, November 22, 1963, his wife, ODA, and he had taken some wash to the Tidy Lady Launderette, 1227 Davis Street, which is located at the northeast corner of Davis and North Clinton in the Oak Cliff section of Dallas, Texas, approximately two blocks from their place of residence.

    His wife and he were the only individuals in the laundromat, which is a self-service, coin-operated establishment.

    After they were inside the laundromat waiting on their wash, an unknown individual drove up alone in a light-colored station wagon, year and make unknown, and parked on the east side of North Clinton Street, just north of the Davis - Clinton intersection, and by the side door of the laundromat.

    This unknown person hurried around the corner onto the north side of Davis, walked several feet, turned around, entered the laundromat, and went directly to the pay phone located inside this laundromat. He did not appear to notice the PENNINGTONS sitting in the laundromat.

    This individual made a local telephone call, spoke briefly to some unknown person, and left the laundromat walking at a quick pace, crossed Davis Street, and headed south on North Clinton Street. He did not re-enter his automobile.

    Mr. PENNINGTON stated he did not overhear any of this person's telephone conversation. Mr. PENNINGTON stated that he mentioned to his wife that the man acted as if he were in some kind of trouble.

93

on _9/1/64_ at _Dallas, Texas_   File # _DL 100-10461_

by Special Agent _RICHARD J. BURNETT /jtf_   Date dictated _9/2/64_

This document contains neither recommendations nor conclusions of the FBI. It is the property of the FBI and is loaned to your agency; it and its contents are not to be distributed outside your agency.

DL 100-10461

2

    He advised that he paid no particular attention to this incident until shortly after he arrived home when he received a long distance telephone call from his daughter in Phoenix, Arizona, asking him if they heard about the

assassination of President KENNEDY. Up until this telephone
call, Mr. PENNINGTON stated that neither his wife nor he
had heard the news of the assassination.

Later when his wife and he had viewed the photograph
of LEE HARVEY OSWALD on television, they commented that OSWALD
appeared to be the same person they had seen at the laundromat
on Friday, November 22, 1968.

Mr. PENNINGTON stated the person they saw at the
laundromat, who they believe was possibly identical to LEE
HARVEY OSWALD, was wearing a medium brown jacket with dark
brown vertical stripes, closed to the collar, and dark pants.
He does not recall whether the jacket was a zipper or button-
up style. The individual wore no hat.

FD-302 (Rev. 3-3-59)

FEDERAL BUREAU OF INVESTIGATION

Date ___September 2, 1964___

1

Mrs. ODA PENNINGTON, 405 North Clinton Street,
Dallas, Texas, advised she is the wife of JOHN WESLEY
PENNINGTON. Mrs. PENNINGTON furnished substantially the
same information as her husband regarding the individual
she believes was identical with LEE HARVEY OSWALD, who
stopped at the Tidy Lady Launderette, on the northeast
corner of Davis and North Clinton Streets, Dallas, sometime
shortly after noon on Friday, November 22, 1963.

Mrs. PENNINGTON noted that she is hard of hearing
and could not hear any of this person's telephone
conversation inside the laundromat. She was unable to
describe this person's automobile other than it was a light-
colored station wagon.

95

on __9/1/64__ at __Dallas, Texas__ File # __DL 100-10461__

by Special Agent __RICHARD J. BURNETT /ltf__ Date dictated __9/2/64__

DL 100-10461
RJB:jtf
1

        In regard to the foregoing information furnished
by Mr. and Mrs. JOHN WESLEY PENNINGTON, the following is
noted:

        Previous investigation has determined that LEE
HARVEY OSWALD was reportedly wearing a light gray cotton
jacket with a full-length zipper in the front between
the time he left his rooming house at 1026 North Beckley,
around 12:55 p.m., November 22, 1963, until shortly after
he shot Dallas Police Officer J. D. TIPPIT at approximately 1:17 p.m., November 22, 1963. (The PENNINGTONs
described the jacket as definitely medium brown with
dark brown vertical stripes.)

        The movements of LEE HARVEY OSWALD from the time
of the shooting of President KENNEDY at approximately
12:34 p.m., November 22, 1963, until his arrest at the
Texas Theater at about 2:00 p.m., November 22, 1963, have
been accounted for as follows:

        (1) President KENNEDY was shot at approximately
12:34 p.m. in downtown Dallas.

        (2) OSWALD boarded a bus in downtown Dallas
near his place of employment, but left same shortly
thereafter, about 12:40 p.m., due to traffic congestion.

        (3) OSWALD boarded a taxicab at the Greyhound
Bus Station in downtown Dallas at about 12:45 p.m.

        (4) OSWALD got out of the taxicab on North
Beckley and walked north toward his rooming house at 1026
North Beckley, Oak Cliff section of Dallas, at about
12:55 p.m.

DL 100-10461
RJB:jtf
2

        (5) OSWALD entered the rooming house about
1:00 p.m. and left shortly thereafter.

        (6) OSWALD is accused of shooting officer
J. D. TIPPIT at 1:17 p.m.

        (7) OSWALD was arrested by local Dallas Police
inside the Texas Theatre at 2:00 p.m.

It is noted that the PENNINGTONs advised they are not sure of the time they were in the laundromat, but after they returned to their residence a few blocks from the laundromat, they shortly thereafter received a telephone call from their daughter in Phoenix, Arizona, advising them of the assassination of President KENNEDY, which was unknown to them at that time. The PENNINGTONs believe they were in the laundromat sometime between 12:00 noon and 1:00 p.m., Friday, November 22, 1963.

It is further recalled that the PENNINGTONs stated that the individual they saw and that they believe was OSWALD drove up to the laundromat, and then left, after making a telephone call, walking south on North Clinton Street. Extensive investigation regarding OSWALD has not revealed that he owned a motor vehicle or even knew how to drive a car.

The distance between the Tidy Lady Launderette, 1227 Davis Street, and the Texas Theatre is a little over one mile.

Mr. and Mrs. JOHN WESLEY PENNINGTON are an elderly couple.

"At this stage, we are supposed to be closing doors, not opening them."
(July 1964 response to staff counsel Wesley Liebeler's request that a conspiracy lead (Silvia Odio) be pursued, quoted in Epstein, "Inquest")

him, or others close to him. According to Edward Epstein's respected account of the Warren Commission investigation, *Inquest,* when Liebeler tried to explain the important unsolved allegations of Odio's testimony to General Counsel J. Lee Rankin, Rankin angrily told him that, "At this stage, we are supposed to be closing doors, not opening them."[18]

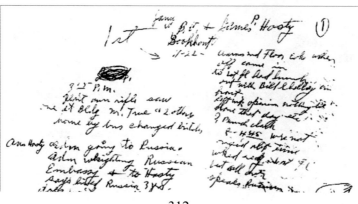

**Transcription of Captain Fritz Notes From
Oswald Interrogations**
Friday, November 22-24, 1963
*Note: Prepared by Review Board staff to assist the
reader, but not an official transcription*

(1)

1st 11-22
B.O. + James P. Hosty
Jame W Bookout

3:15 p.m.
Didn't own rifle saw
one at Bldg M. True + 2 others
home by bus changed britches

Ans Hosty adm going to Russia
adm wrighting Russian
Embassy + to Hosty
says lived Russia 3 yrs.
Does write over then now
school in Ft W. - to Marines
says got usual medals
claims no political belief
belongs Fair Pl
Hdqts NY off N.O.
says supports Castro Rev.

claims 2nd floor Coke when
off came in
to 1st floor had lunch
out with Bill Shelley in
front
lft wk opinion nothing be
done that day etc.
? punch clock
8-4:45 wre not
rigid abt time
wked reg 1st Fl
but all over
speaks Russian

?Why live O.H. Lee
says landlady did that

Terminate interview
with line up
4:15

4 man left to right as #2

(2)

Time of filing 11:26 pm Johnson Pres 22nd   Precinct 2
F154
Received evidence 1st then filed

313

2nd Interview 23rd
Present 10:35-11:34
T.J. Kelly Robt Nash
Grant ??
B.O + myself
Boyd + Hall

Says 11-22-63 rode bus
got trans same out of pocket
says 1 p.o. box denied bringing
 package to wk. Denied telling Frazier
purpose of going to Irving - denied
curtain rods - got off bus after seeing
jam got cab etc .85 fare told you wrong before
at apt. Changed shirts + tr. Put in dirty clothes - long sleeve red sh
            + gray tr.

14

The Chicanery of Joseph Ball

"As with Watergate, numerous lawyers were involved with the Warren Commission; in neither case did these lawyers act as lawyers. Rather, they participated in a cover-up and acted as accessories in serious crimes."

—Howard Roffman, *Presumed Guilty*

"If it is not an act of God, it is a conspiracy."

—Jim Marrs

"I will tell you something else I forgot, but it illustrates what a theater show this Warren Commission was. Chauncey Holt relates that two of his CIA superiors were Joseph Ball and Frank Belcher. They were business partners in California. Joseph Ball was a big shot lawyer who served on the Warren Commission . . . At some point Chauncey Holt was told by his parents that FBI agents had come to their home looking for Chauncey. That worried Chauncey, so he called Frank Belcher . . . Belcher reported back to Chauncey "not to worry," but just to make sure, they moved him and some other people to a CIA safe house in Acapulco. Out of reach of the Warren Commission. It was a splendor holiday mansion that Ball and Belcher owned there."

—JFK Researcher Wim Dankbaar (*Chauncey Holt: Self Portrait of a Scoundrel*)

Joseph Ball spanned most of the 20th century as one of the top lawyers in the country. He cut his teeth in the oil and gas industry in the 1920s and was a member of the firm Ball, Hunt and Hart from Long Beach and Santa Ana, California. He also taught criminal law and procedure at the University of Southern California. At one point in his life he was offered, but turned down, a seat on the California Supreme Court. Over the years, some of his clients included John D. Ehrlichman of Watergate fame, automaker John DeLorean, and Saudi financier Adnan Khashoggi. He died 21 September 2000.[1]

As Assistant Counsel, Joseph Ball was one of the most prolific

Warren Commission lawyers, leading and taking more than 100 depositions, most of them in Dallas, Texas.[2] For all of his qualifications, distinctions and immaculate reputation, it seems Mr. Ball was seduced by the dark side—the cabal that assassinated John F. Kennedy 22 November 1963. It is time to put Joseph Ball's Warren Commission activities in the proper perspective, as they lay bare by the record.

Sixth Floor Cartridges—The "Empty Shell" Game, Part I

Joseph Ball took the testimony of Deputy Sheriff Luke Mooney, who first found the shell casings on the sixth floor of the TSBD, which supposedly came from Oswald's Mannlicher-Carcano.[3] In *Bloody Treason: The Assassination of John F. Kennedy*, Noel Twyman[4] established how Ball orchestrated the scenario where two empty shells and one live round, which had been found by Mooney, and documented by the FBI, was sanitized to officially become three empty shells, presumably left behind by Oswald in the sniper's nest, and which later would become part of the Warren Commission record.[5]

From Mooney's testimony:

> Mr. BALL. Is that the empty shells you found?
> Mr. MOONEY. Yes, sir.
> Mr. BALL. Are they shown there?
> Mr. MOONEY. Yes, sir.
> Mr. BALL. Now, will you take this and encircle the shells?
> Mr. MOONEY. All right.
> Mr. BALL. Put a fairly good sized circle around each shell. That is the way they were when you saw them, is that right?
> Mr. MOONEY. Yes, sir. I assume that this possibly could have been the first shot.
> Mr. BALL. You cannot speculate about that?
> Mr. MOONEY. You cannot speculate about that.
> Mr. BALL. Those were empty shells?
> Mr. MOONEY. Yes, sir.
> Mr. BALL. They were turned over to Captain Fritz?
> Mr. MOONEY. Yes, sir; he was the first officer that picked them up, as far as I know, because I stood there and watched him go over and pick them up and look at them. As far as I could tell, I couldn't even tell what caliber they were, because I didn't get down that close to them. They were brass cartridges, brass shells.
> Mr. BALL. Is this the position of the cartridges as shown on 510, as you saw them?
> Mr. MOONEY. Yes, sir. That is just about the way they were laying, to the best of my knowledge. I do know there was—one was further away, and these other two were relatively close together—on this particular area. But these cartridges—this one and this one looks like they are further apart than they actually was.
> Mr. BALL. Which ones?
> Mr. MOONEY. This one and this one.

Mr. BALL. Now, two cartridges were close together, is that right?

Mr. MOONEY. The one cartridge here, by the wall facing, is right. And this one and this one, they were further away from this one.

Mr. BALL. Well——

Mr. MOONEY. But as to being positive of the exact distance——

Mr. BALL. You think that the cartridges are in the same position as when you saw them in this picture 510?

Mr. MOONEY. As far as my knowledge, they are; pretty close to right.

Mr. BALL. Well, we will label these cartridges, the empty shells as "A", "B", and "C."

From *Bloody Treason*:

"The answer was clear (a) the evidence of three empty cartridge cases was fabricated, and (b) deputy sheriff Luke Mooney was led into testifying that there were three empty cartridges when there were in fact only two. I wondered how an honorable man such as Joseph Ball could have gotten himself involved in such a transparent scheme."[6]

From Commission Exhibit 2003:

Q6 6.5 millimeter Mannlicher-Carcano cartridge case from building
Q7 6.5 millimeter Mannlicher-Carcano cartridge case from building
Q8 6.5 millimeter Mannlicher-Carcano cartridge from rifle

"One more important note in Joseph Ball's questioning of deputy sheriff Mooney, he focused on Exhibit 10-14 (CE510). Why did he choose Exhibit 10-14 instead of Exhibit 10-15 (CE512), both of which are in the Commission report? The answer could be that Joseph Ball knew that Exhibit 10-14 was authentic, and he could not understand Exhibit 10-15, so he avoided attracting attention to it."[7]

Dougherty's story of "one noise" from this location comports with the discoveries of Shaw discussed in *Cover-Up* and expounded in Twyman's *Bloody Treason* that only two, not three, spent shells were found in the assassin's lair on the 6th floor, the third being an intact cartridge which can be seen upon careful study of one of the official photographs published as a Warren Report Exhibit, and altered reported evidentiary inventories reported by those authors.

From the article, "Have We Ignored the Key Witness to the Depository Shot or Shots?" by Frank A. Cellura, March 2000

As far as calling Ball an "honorable man," the rest of this chapter will show how generous Twyman appears to have been in his assessment of Ball.

Joseph Ball's manipulation of Mooney's testimony was only the beginning of his involvement with the empty shell game. As we move on, the stakes will move higher, and the shell game will rear its ugly head later, when we cover African-American witnesses Harold Norman, Junior Jarman and Bonnie Ray Williams.

Commission Exhibit 361—"Parking" Area for TSBD Employees

CE361 was prepared in the exhibit section of the FBI by Inspector Leo Gauthier, Eugene Paul Airy, exhibit specialist, with the assistance of Charles D. Musser, illustrator, with particular reference to showing the TSBD, and the immediate area with relation to the parking lot the employees used.[8] The exhibit was presented upside down, south side up, with north pointing downward, "instead of the top, as usually the case."[9] It was originally introduced by Arlen Specter during the testimony of James Richard Worrell.[10] The exhibit did not show Main and Commerce streets or the Dal-Tex Building.

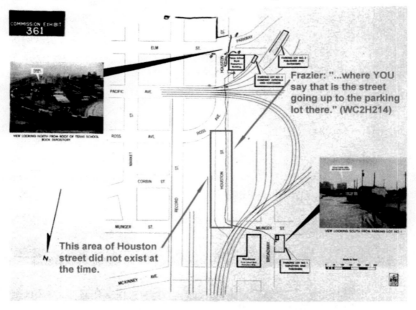

COMMISSION EXHIBIT 361

It is clear, when one compares this map to contemporary maps of the period, that it has been misrepresented by the FBI. There is not a single witness, of the few who were shown this map, who was not surprised by the oddity of its orientation and landmarks that were out of place and/or nonexistent.[11] Furthermore, the Commission published maps of downtown Dallas that are totally illegible, when compared to regular road maps found in any gas station in Texas at the time.[12]

This is CE371:

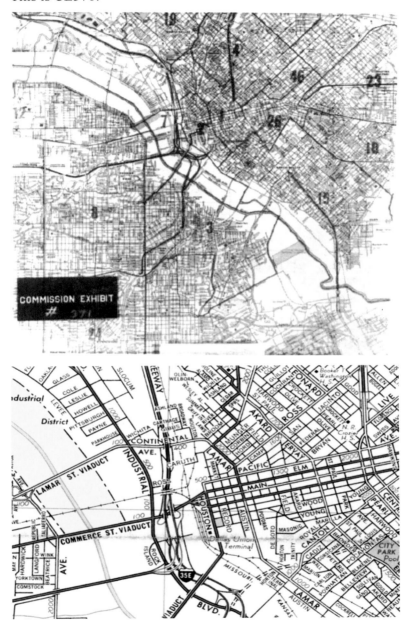

1962 Dallas Road Map

Aerial photographs of Dealey Plaza and photograph from CD496, p. 51, confirm that Houston Street ended right after the TSBD and

Dal-Tex Building, and actually curved into Ross Avenue. Houston Street re-emerged well beyond the railroad yards north of the TSBD, where today it heads northbound and crosses Continental Avenue. (Google Maps)

38. VIEW FROM ROOF OF TEXAS SCHOOL BOOK DEPOSITORY LOOKING NORTH TOWARD PARKING LOT NO. 1. (ARROW)

Apparently, and judging from the following exchange, Buell Wesley Frazier tried to blow the whistle on this deception by advising Ball, when talking about "Houston" Street in CE361: ". . . that is where *you* say that is the street going up to the parking lot there."[13] After this remark, Ball did not care to elaborate as to the problems with the map, and immediately changed the line of questioning to Frazier's car:

Mr. BALL. We have here a map which has been marked as Commission's Exhibit No. 361.
Mr. FRAZIER. I see.
Mr. BALL. And north is to the bottom of the map.
Mr. FRAZIER. Yes.
Mr. BALL. Instead of the top, as usually the case.
Mr. FRAZIER. Right.
Mr. BALL. It has two pictures over here, one to the left and one to the right of the map.
Mr. FRAZIER. Right.
Mr. BALL. Let's take a look at the picture to the right of the map. Do you recognize that area?
Mr. FRAZIER. Yes, sir; I do.
Mr. BALL. What is it?
Mr. FRAZIER. I see that is right there where you say that is the street going up to the parking lot there.
Mr. BALL. Do you recognize this car?

When interviewed recently by the Sixth Floor Museum on 13 July 2013, Frazier stated the following about Joseph Ball: "I ran into one of the sharpest attorneys I have ever seen in my life, Mr. Ball. He was good—but I could not accept what he was trying to feed me."

Frazier describes the extremely difficult terrain around his "parking lot": ". . . it has more trenches, and it gets muddy and slimy and you can get bogged down."

there are not any cars, it is usually a long train that moves up pretty soon but I usually move up in this direction here, especially when it is dry. When it is wet I walk on this because it is harder. But when it is raining, I usually walk around here, because in this area right here, <u>when you get up closer to the railroad tracks it has more trenches, and it gets muddy and slimy and you can get bogged down.</u>

So, when it is bad weather, I usually walk on this side. But I say nine times out of ten I come up right down here.

Mr. BALL. Let's look at the map. Here is the parking lot here, is that the parking lot where you usually park?

Mr. FRAZIER. Yes, sir: it is.

Mr. BALL. This is parking lot No. 1.

Mr. FRAZIER. That is parking lot No. 1, isn't it?

Mr. BALL. Right.

Mr. FRAZIER. Right.

These images and testimony combined, allows us to visualize the deception committed by Ball in his deposition of Frazier, where the actual terrain and obstacles, make it impossible to reconcile CE361 as accurate and truthful.

Thanks to Joseph Ball, this is the terrain and distance the Commission established that Oswald and Frazier traversed that rainy morning of 22 November 1963, with Oswald walking ahead and hauling a 7.5-pound, broken-down rifle cupped under his arm pit. And of course, his trusty dime—10¢—to reassemble the rifle, with its five individual screws, each torqued exactly to the correct number of foot-pounds, (lest the Carcano become misaligned), all of this in no more than six minutes.[14]

Linnie Mae Randle and Lee Oswald's "Package"

This is not the first time Joseph Ball's actions have been questioned by Warren Commission critics. Howard Roffman wrote how Ball tried to mislead Linnie Mae Randle about the "long and bulky package."[15]

From *Presumed Guilty*:

"When Oswald held the package, he apparently tried to lead her into providing a false description for the record; she corrected him:

Mr. Ball: And where was his hand gripping the (middle) of the package?

Mrs. Randle: No, sir; the (top) with just a little bit sticking up. You know just like you grab something like that.

Mr. Ball: And he was grabbing it with his right hand at the top of the package and the package almost touched the ground?

Mrs. Randle: Yes, sir.

Mr. BALL. Was he carrying any package?
Mrs. RANDLE. Yes; he was.
Mr. BALL. What was he carrying?
Mrs. RANDLE. He was carrying a package in a sort of a heavy brown bag, heavier than a grocery bag it looked to me. It was about, if I might measure, about this long, I suppose, and he carried it in his right hand, had the top sort of folded down and had a grip like this, and the bottom, he carried it this way, you know, and it almost touched the ground as he carried it.
Mr. BALL. Let me see. He carried it in his right hand, did he?
Mrs. RANDLE. That is right.
Mr. BALL. And where was his hand gripping the middle of the package?
Mrs. RANDLE. No, sir; the top with just a little bit sticking up. You know just like you grab something like that.
Mr. BALL. And he was grabbing it with his right hand at the top of the package and the package almost touched the ground?
Mrs. RANDLE. Yes, sir.
Mr. BALL. He walked over to your house, did he?
Mrs. RANDLE. Well, I saw him as he started crossing the street. Where he come from then I couldn't say.
Mr. BALL. You don't know where he went from that?
Mrs. RANDLE. Where he went?
Mr. BALL. Did you see him go to the car?
Mrs. RANDLE. Yes.
Mr. BALL. What did he do?
Mrs. RANDLE. He opened the right back door and I just saw that he was laying the package down so I closed the door. I didn't recognize him as he walked across my carport and I at that moment I wondered who was fixing to come to my back door so I opened the door slightly and saw that it—I assumed he was getting in the car but he didn't, so he come back and stood on the driveway.
Mr. BALL. He put the package in the car.

248

Mr. Ball led Linnie Mae throughout most of her testimony. Certainly, he would have failed any of his students who would have exhibited this type of behavior in class, and as the opposing counsel in a court of law, he would have objected to no end. As a judge, he would have sustained the objections. Ball kept molding her testimony to fit most of the characteristics of a rifle wrapped in packing material, except for the most important feature: the length. When Linnie Mae started to chop it down to only two feet, he had to regroup:[16]

> Mr. Ball. This package is about the span of my hand, say 8 inches, is that right? He would have about this much to grip?
> Mrs. Randle. What I remember seeing is about this long, sir, as I told you it was folded down so it could have been this long.
> Mr. Ball. I see. You figure about 2 feet long, is that right?
> Mrs. Randle. A little bit more.
> Mr. Ball. A little more than 2 feet.

There were more problems with the paper wrapping. He decided to switch to another exhibit, trying desperately to elongate the package.[17]

> Mr. Ball. What about length?
> Mrs. Randle. You mean the entire bag?
> Mr. Ball. Yes.
> Mrs. Randle. There again you have the problem of all this down here. It was folded down, of course, if you would take it from the bottom —
> Mr. Ball. Fold it to about the size that you think it might be.
> Mrs. Randle. This is the bottom here, right. This is the bottom, this part down here.

Her testimony hints at being rehearsed, where she is still trying to help him set the script.[18]

> Mrs. Randle. About this.
> Mr. Ball Is that about right? That is 28½ inches.
> Mrs. Randle. I measured 27 last time.
> Mr. Ball. You measured 27 once before?
> Mrs. Randle. Yes, sir.
> Mr. Ball. How was Lee dressed that morning?

With that in mind, when Linnie Mae blurted this out, it appears that Ball wanted no part of any insinuation that he could be involved in this scenario, and finally settled for 27" but not without fighting for an extra 1.5" and of course, changing the subject to Lee's attire that morning.

Railroad Yard Blues: Lee Bowers

Lee Bowers was manning the railroad control tower on 22 November 1963 at 12:30 PM. He was immediately singled out at as a witness who should know what happened at the picket fence. Joseph Ball made sure, for the record, that Lee Bower's so very important testimony got mangled, and cut him off when he was about to go into detail about what transpired there from his vantage point. J. Gary Shaw wrote about this in *Cover Up* (1976) and filled in the blanks of what Bowers should have said for the record. Shaw continued:

> In an interview with researcher-author Mark Lane, Bowers revealed what he was about to say in his testimony: ". . . there was some unusual occurrence—a flash of light, or *smoke* or something which caused me to feel like something out of the ordinary had occurred there."[19]

Mr. BALL. When you said there was a commotion, what do you mean by that? What did it look like to you when you were looking at the commotion?

Mr. BOWERS. I just am unable to describe rather than it was something out of the ordinary, a sort of milling around, but something occurred in this particular spot which was out of the ordinary, which attracted my eye for some reason, which I could not identify.

Mr. BALL. You couldn't describe it?

Mr. BOWERS. Nothing that I could pinpoint as having happened that——

Mr. BALL. Afterwards did a good many people come up there on this high ground at the tower?

For the time being, Joseph Ball was successful in suppressing Bower's first-hand witness account of what occurred behind that picket fence and the parking lot before and after the shots.

Despite Ball's attention to irrelevancies, the amount of detail provided by Bowers left him very little wiggle room and prompted him to finish Bower's testimony as soon as possible.

Fortunately, he left the door open for investigators to scrutinize his actions, and question why he did not allow Bowers to finish his thought. As seen above, he proceeded to cut him off in mid-sentence. With Mark Lane's interview of Bowers, we can complete the picture and illustrate how biased and premeditated Ball's actions were. Two years later, Bowers perished in a one-car accident.

Lee Bowers, Jr.
August 9, 1966

Lee Bowers, Jr., a railroad towerman for the Union Terminal Company, was in the 14-foot railroad control tower behind the Grassy Knoll on the morning of the assassination. During the morning, he witnessed several unusual events. On three occasions, he saw three unauthorized cars enter the parking area behind the Picket Fence, drive around the area, then leave. Even though this area had supposedly been secured by police, the three vehicles entered unhampered and "checked out" the area. On one occasion Bowers saw what appeared to be a man talking on a radio.

Bowers gave evidence that he observed a blue and white 1959 Oldsmobile station wagon with out-of-state license tags and a "Goldwater for '64" sticker drive through, followed by a black 1957 Ford—whose driver appeared to use a radio microphone—which in turn was followed by a white 1961 Chevrolet Impala with out-of-state tags (and another Goldwater sticker). The last car left approximately 12:20, ten minutes before the shooting.

But Bowers saw more than just strange vehicles in the area. According to the Warren Commission, "...Bowers saw two 'strangers' standing near the wooden fence prior to and at the time of the shooting. One of these men was middle-aged and fairly heavy-set. The other was in his mid-twenties and wearing a plaid shirt or jacket; this fits the description of the man carrying the rifle case seen by Miss Mercer." This last statement referred to what was witnessed earlier by Julia Mercer who saw a man carrying a rifle case up the Grassy Knoll from a pickup truck that stopped in the street prior to the assassination.

Bowers, when testifying before the Warren Commission, began to describe (and later did describe to Mark Lane) what he saw happen behind the Picket Fence, but was cut short by Warren Commission attorney Joseph Ball. What Bowers attempted to get on record was: "There was some unusual occurrence—a flash of light or smoke or something which caused me to feel like something out of the ordinary had occurred there."

Bowers died at the age of 41 in a single-car accident near Midlothian, Texas. The medical examiner said that when Bowers died, he was in some kind of a "strange shock." It should be noted that at this time the intelligence services world-wide had access to drugs that produced various mental conditions ranging from a catatonic state to grogginess to death.

Cause of death: Single car "accident" under suspicious circumstances.

TSBD Entrance: Joseph Ball's Masterpiece—How the Deception of Doorway Man Took Place

The doorway of the TSBD was a huge problem for the Commission. (To this day it remains an extremely volatile and controversial subject.) As soon as Ike Altgens's photograph circled the globe, many were questioning the figure in the doorway, who had an uncanny resemblance to Oswald. They asked, if Oswald was in the doorway, then how could he have been shooting at JFK from the sixth floor? It was up to Ball to dispel these rumors and rearrange history for the Warren Commission.

"Divide and conquer" is a common technique used in many fields to break down complex issues and problems. Its origins can be traced back to *The Art of War* by the Chinese military strategist Sun Tzu. The fingerprints of this methodology are all over the issue of the witnesses who were in the TSBD doorway on 22 November 1963. By analyzing Weigman 658 and Warren Commission testimony, it can be established that at least 10 people were standing on the entrance stairs that led to the doorway of 411 Elm Street.

The following table reveals how Joseph Ball methodically divided and conquered these witnesses to arrive at the official version of Billy Lovelady as Doorway Man. From the evidence, it appears that Ball might have been designated to make it work for the Commission, and the reason his actions deserve to be singled out. Older employees Reese, Sanders, Stanton, and Williams were ignored and never called to testify. They were very superficially interviewed by the FBI in CE1381. Seventeen-year-old, African-American Roy Lewis was also thrown into this mix and completely ignored. The next five witnesses who were brought in for the record were fully pliable, except Joe Molina, who was never called to testify. As seen in Chapter 5, Joe was the only one who initiated contact with the Commission because of his treatment right after the assassination.

	Arce	Frazier	Shelley	Lovelady	Molina	Reese	Sanders	Lewis	Stanton	Williams
Identified Doorman as Lovelady	X	X		X?						
Identified Frazier in Doorway	X	XX	X							
Identified Shelley in Doorway	X	X	X	X					X	
Identified Molina in Doorway					X					
CE1381 Asked if had seen LHO	NO	NO	NO	NO	NO	NO	NO	NO	NO	NO*

Warren Commission testimony & CE1381   CE1381 Only-------->

Billy Lovelady

It is impossible to assess Lovelady's role without considering his court-martial from the USAF for the theft and attempted sale of guns in 1961 at Andrews AFB. With the TSBD company historically being a very strict employer, his mere employment and presence at TSBD suggests a very special relationship with O.V. Campbell and James "Jack" Charles Cason, owners of the company.[20] Lovelady told Ball he was "standing on the top level" and, when shown CE369, he drew an arrow to the figure represented by what is commonly known as Black Hole Man.[21] This study by Richard Hooke and Ralph Cinque explains Ball's interaction with Lovelady.

Commission No. 4578

SIGN OF THE BLACK ARROW

First arrow already marked beforehand by Buell Wesley Frazier

Lovelady indicated to Ball where he was before he drew the arrow; that's why Ball told him to put the arrow in the black (a black arrow in the black is no arrow at all) And then, subconciously, we are willing to excuse the fact there is only one arrow because we are thinking, 'well, it's OK, they were pointing to the same place anyway'; which of course, in reality(we realize 50 years later), they were not.

Ralph.

What I see is this:
1) a mark on **Black Hole Man's** right forearm (his right)
2) discoloration in the central area under his arms like the rest of the arrow was colored over with a slightly lighter shade of black.
3) after Ball saw Lovelady was pointing in the wrong place he told him to **mark it in the dark**, why? So Ball could color it over later.

Ball just told Lovelady to mark his arrow in the dark, and then Ball acknowledges there is an arrow in the dark but tells Lovelady it's the arrow in the white that is pointing toward him.

"Please note the semantics trick: at this point the court reporter's notation would read like the arrow in the dark was pointing where the arrow in the white was; which, in reality, was not the case at all.

Let me ask you this: why would someone ask you to mark an arrow, with a black pen, in the black?
Obviously Ball was not happy where Lovelady was pointing, so he told him to mark it in the black so it could be colored over afterward (they left the tiny part on the forearm) and then BALL is telling Lovelady he is somewhere, and somebody, else: Doorman by the post

Ralph. I knew these attorneys were some sneaky sons of bitches but, now I've heard everything!!! Ralph Cinque and Richard Hooke 3/9/2012

Mr. BALL - I have got a picture here, Commission Exhibit 369. Are you on that picture?
Mr. LOVELADY - Yes, sir.
Mr. BALL - Take a pen or pencil and mark an arrow where you are.
Mr. LOVELADY - Where I thought the shots are?
Mr. BALL - No; you in the picture.
Mr. LOVELADY - Oh, here (indicating).
Mr. BALL - Draw an arrow down to that; do it in the dark. You got an arrow in the dark and one in the white pointing toward you. Where were you when the picture was taken?
Mr. LOVELADY - Right there at the entrance of the building standing on the top step, would be here (indicating).
Mr. BALL - You were standing on which step?
Mr. LOVELADY - It would be your top level.
Mr. BALL - The top step you were standing there?
Mr. LOVELADY - Right.

In now predictable fashion, Ball interrupted Lovelady when he was about to elaborate as to who was with him on the steps.[22]

> Mr. BALL. Who was with you?
> Mr. LOVELADY. Bill Shelley and Sarah Stanton, and right behind me——
> Mr. BALL. What was that last name?
> Mr. LOVELADY. Stanton.
> Mr. BALL. What is the first name?
> Mr. LOVELADY. Bill Shelley.
> Mr. BALL. And Stanton's first name?
> Mr. LOVELADY. Miss Sarah Stanton.
> Mr. BALL. Did you stay on the steps?
> Mr. LOVELADY. Yes.

This image shows how Lovelady could have named Wesley Frazier, Otis Williams, Joe Molina, Pauline Sanders, Roy Lewis, and Maggie Reese, had Joseph Ball not cut him off.

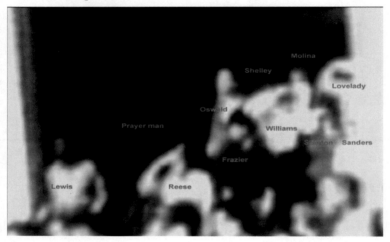

Danny Arce, 19-Years-Old

What appears to be the most obviously coached and perverted testimony of all.[23] In the words of Harold Weisberg, ". . . it is Arce's testimony that provides a key to solving the mystery of this conspiracy."[24] Arce was caught in Altgens6 talking on a radio device.

Arce's affidavit was taken on 22 November 1963 by the DPD within a few hours of the assassination.[25] The information contained in this document contradicts his Warren Commission testimony taken by Joseph Ball. A couple of items require further examination:

• Without any hesitation, he placed himself at Elm and Houston, which happens to match the position of the individual talking on a radio device in the image. While being deposed by Ball, he was

Man positioned in front of the
Dal-Tex Building at the time of
the assassination

Danny Arce

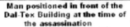

Arce was caught in Altgens6 talking on a radio device.

•   literally all over the place, and Ball's frustration was evident as he failed to convincingly set Arce's exact position during the shooting.[26]

•   In his affidavit, he saw Oswald at 11:50 AM on the fifth floor. During Ball's deposition of Arce, he made absolutely no mention of this.

> saw named Lee Oswald. He was on the first floor of the building when I saw him at
> 8:00 am. He is the same man I saw the police bring into the Homicide Bureau about
> 2:00 pm. I also saw him on the 5th floor as we were leaving for lunch at 11:50 am.
>
> *Danny Garcia Arce*

And of course, we must address the "feeble individual."[27] Arce was a very busy man in the 40 minutes before the motorcade arrived. He allegedly helped an older man in a brown suit and cowboy hat to the men's room on the first floor, towards the back of the building. Nobody ever corroborated Arce's Good Samaritan ways.

The Warren Commission report insinuated he spotted the man from the sixth floor when he happened to look out the window, then bolted down the elevator and helped the man because he felt pity for him.[28] Thereafter, he went back upstairs to participate in the famous elevator race.

The Warren Commission report set this at about 40 minutes before the assassination, which would have been 11:50 AM.[29]

> in the building on the morning of November 22.[18] Only one employee
> saw a stranger whom he described as a <u>feeble individual</u> who had
> to be helped up the front steps of the building. He went to a public
> restroom and left the building 5 minutes later, about 40 minutes
> before the assassination.[79]

Here is what Ohio researcher James DeLuzia wrote about Danny
Arce's actions that day:

> The fact that the Warren Commission was disingenuous in this account
> of a "feeble individual" who was seen by "only one employee" does not mean
> that the employee, Danny Arce, was completely truthful in his deposition
> before Joseph Ball. Had the Commission applied the same scrutiny to Arce's
> testimony that it did to Mr. Rowland's, it might have noted that Arce first
> claimed to have eaten his lunch <u>before</u> he went outside (VI,365), then claimed
> that he ate it <u>after</u> helping the stranger into the building (VI,367); Arce
> first claimed to have ridden the elevator* with Bonnie Ray Williams from
> the sixth floor to the first at lunch-time (VI,364), then claimed that
> Williams "stayed upstairs with Hank"(VI,365); Arce's account of his move-
> ments on the grassy knoll and railroad yard at the time shots were fired
> (VI,365-6) is abstruse, if not suspicious. Item 071 *"The Feeble Individual"* DeLuzia

Danny Arce: "Yes, that's Billy Lovelady," Arce said three times
in a matter of seconds.[30] Arce was about to finish his deposition
when Joseph Ball, as a matter of fact, and in belated manner, asked
him to identify Doorway Man in CE369. Of course, after all the
inconsistencies and omissions, perhaps Ball had to make sure Arce
identified Lovelady as Doorway Man, not once, but three times, as if
each time would enhance his credibility.

Charles Givens, 37-Years-Old

African-American Givens was not deposed by Joseph Ball. However,
his forced participation in the cover-up needs to be included here, due
to the timeline the Warren Commission tried to establish for Oswald
around noon on 22 November 1963.[31] The following is an excerpt
from his official Warren Commission testimony, taken by David
Belin without any witnesses present, except for a court reporter.[32]

Mr. BELIN. When did you see Lee Harvey Oswald next?
Mr. GIVENS. Next?
Mr. BELIN. Yes.
Mr. GIVENS. Well, it was about a quarter till 12, we were on our way down-
stairs, and we passed him, and he was standing at the gate on the fifth floor.
I came downstairs, and I discovered I left my cigarettes in my jacket pocket
upstairs, and I took the elevator back upstairs to get my jacket with my cig-
arettes in it. When I got back upstairs, he was on the sixth floor in that
vicinity, coming from that way.
Mr. BELIN. Coming from what way?
Mr. GIVENS. Toward the window up front where the shots were fired from.
Mr. BELIN. Just a second, where did you go? Where were you when you
saw him on the sixth floor?
Mr. GIVENS. I had went and got my jacket and was on my way back to the
elevator.
Mr. BELIN. All right, just a second. I am going to get a plan of the sixth
floor, if I have one, and try and have you point that out to me.
Mr. GIVENS. Yes, sir.

AFFIDAVIT IN ANY FACT

THE STATE OF TEXAS
COUNTY OF DALLAS

BEFORE ME, _____ Mary Rattan _____

a Notary Public in and for said County, State of Texas, on this day personally appeared _____

Charles Douglas Givens c/m/37, 2511 Carpenter, RI2 4670

Who, after being by me duly sworn, on oath deposes and says: I work for the Texas School Book Depository, 411 Elm Street. I worked up on the 6th floor today until about 11:30 am. Then I went downstairs and into the bathroom. At twelve o'clock I took my lunch period. I went to the parking lot at Record and Elm street. I have a friend who works at the parking lot. We walked up to Main and Record when the President passed by. We then walked back to the parking lot after the President had passed by. We had just got back to the lot when we heard the shooting. I think I heard three shots. I did not see anyone in the building that was not supposed to be there this morning.

Charles Douglas Givens

Sylvia Meagher did a comprehensive and chronological breakdown of Charles Givens's many stories about his 22 November experience, and how it kept morphing from one account to the next.[33]

Meagher even wrote that Givens, with his police record and narcotics conviction, could have been on the take for his story. The first impression is usually the correct one, so here is his statement of 22 November 1963. No mention of Oswald, or the trip back to the sixth floor to fetch his cigarettes.

April 8, 1964
Charles Givens gives sworn testimony to the Warren Commission in a deposition taken by lawyer David Belin, with no one else present except the court reporter. Now, for the *first time*, Givens tells the story (later embodied in the Warren Report) about the cigarettes forgotten on the sixth floor and the encounter with Oswald (6H 345-356, WR 143). Belin should have been fully aware that Givens had told a completely different story to the FBI and the police on the day of the assassination, and subsequently to the Secret Service and the FBI, since Belin had co-authored the report which discussed Givens' accounts of his movements in considerable detail. But Belin did not

From the article "The Curious Testimony of Mr. Givens," The Texas Observer, 13 August 1971, by Sylvia Meagher

GIVENS said all employees enter the back door of the building when JACK DOUGHERTY, the foreman opens the door at about 7 A.M. On the morning of November 22, 1963, GIVENS observed LEE reading a newspaper in the domino room where the employees eat lunch about 11:50 A.M.

From CD5, p. 329, 22 November 1963, FBI Statement File DL 89-43 Griffin and Odum

Bill Shelley, 37-Years-Old

Bill Shelley had already sworn an affidavit the day of the assassination at the DPD and Joseph Ball knew it. *"I have been working close*

with this man since he has been there," [Emphasis added] said Shelley on 22 November 1963, about Oswald, perhaps hinting that he knew more about him than established.

He also said how he had *not seen* Oswald on the sixth floor at noon.[34] Ball did not depose Shelley until 7 April 1964 in Dallas. Shelley was a tough nut to crack for Ball. He left no angle for him to pursue and filled his testimony with irrelevancies like chicken bones and clipboards.

He did not ask him if Lovelady was Doorway Man. When he tried twice to steer him towards Vicky Adams, Shelley expressed his lack of knowledge about her whereabouts.[35]

AFFIDAVIT IN ANY FACT

THE STATE OF TEXAS
COUNTY OF DALLAS

BEFORE ME, _____ Patsy Collins _____ .

a Notary Public in and for said County, State of Texas, on this day personally appeared _____
William H. Shelley, w/m/37 of 126 S. Tatum, FE-7-1969. Bus 411 Elm, RI-7-3521

Who, after being by me duly sworn, on oath deposes and says: Approximately October 10th or 12th, 1963
a man by the name of Lee Oswald w/m/21, came to work uher I do. I was put in
charge of him by Mr. Truly to show him what to do. I have been working close
with this man since he has been there. This man stayed by himself most of the
time, and would go for a walk at noon time. Lee would bring his lunch and usually
eat with us in the lounge and read the paper. He would usually read about politics.
Today I arrived for work about 8 am and went about my usual duties. Lee was
already filling some orders just outside my office. I saw him periodically all
morning with the exception of when we were on the sixth floor. At noon I
started eating my lunch in my office and I went outside to see the President.
W.S. After the President accident, I started checking around and I'd missed Lee.
I ask Mr. Truly about him and He told me he had not seen him. I didn't see Lee
until the Police brought him in to the Police Homicide Bureau.XXXXXXXXXXXXXXXX

William H. Shelley

There are, however, some very important aspects about his deposition.

He established Oswald on the first floor at 11:50 AM. This time seemed to be a very important nexus between Danny Arce, Charles Givens and Bill Shelley.

All three had Oswald in their vicinity at the same time on different floors of the building. As mentioned above, the Warren Commission accepted Givens's testimony, where he said he saw Oswald on the fifth floor at 11:45 AM, then went down to the first floor, returned for his cigarettes, seeing him again, only now on the sixth floor and close to the southeast window. This was even included in the report itself.[36]

Mr. BALL. On November 22, 1963, the day the President was shot, when is the last time you saw Oswald?

Mr. SHELLEY. It was 10 or 15 minutes before 12.

Mr. BALL. Where?

Mr. SHELLEY. On the first floor over near the telephone.

Mr. BALL. Did you ever see him again?

Mr. SHELLEY. At the police station when they brought him in.

Mr. BALL. Did you see him in the building at anytime after 12?

Mr. SHELLEY. No.

Ironically, in the pre-civil rights era in 1963 Dallas, *the story of an African-American man with a police record, Charles Givens, would prevail over the account of a white man who happened to be a foreman and supervisor in the TSBD company!*

Buell Wesley Frazier, 19-Years-Old

As covered earlier, Ball allowed Frazier to establish two different positions in the doorway. First, he was one step down from the top, standing by the rail, consistent with Weigman footage, and his handwritten statement and affidavit of 22 November. Second, when trying to accommodate Lovelady as Doorway Man, Frazier changed his position to "I was back up in this more or less black area here."[37] The physical aspects of the top landing, which only measured about three feet, made it totally impossible to accommodate Frazier in that position because it was already populated by other employees of the TSBD, as seen in the Weigman slide shown above.[38]

Ball did not care to correct this ambiguity, perhaps because he was intent on establishing Lovelady as Doorway Man. As stated earlier, and as recently as July 2013, Frazier said this about Ball: ". . . but I could not accept what he was trying to feed me." Thus, Frazier, perhaps reluctantly, became the lone witness to identify Lovelady as Doorway Man.

Mr. BALL. When you stood out on the front looking at the parade, where was Shelley standing and where was Lovelady standing with reference to you?

Mr. FRAZIER. Well, see, I was standing, like I say, one step down from the top, and Mr. Shelley was standing, you know, back from the top step and over toward the side of the wall there. See, he was standing right over there, and then Billy was a couple of steps down from me over toward more the wall also.

Upon further scrutiny, we note that Frazier had, at one time or another, given six different stories about his and Lovelady's positions in the doorway. (see Chapter 10)

Joe Molina, 38-Years-Old

Joseph Ball's grand finale with Molina was to prevent him from testifying about super communist spy infiltrator William Lowery, who just two months earlier had made national headlines by testifying about communist organizations in Texas.[39] Molina has never revealed what he wanted to say that day.

Of the nine other individuals named here, not one was asked about the presence of Joe Molina. Molina, on the other hand, identified Pauline Sanders and Otis Williams, his boss, as being with him—then Ball changed the subject and asked him about Roy Truly.[40]

He was not asked about Lovelady, Frazier, or Shelley. For the obvious reasons, he did not mention Oswald standing right next to him, to his right, as seen in Altgens6.

Mr. MOLINA. I know there's a fella that I talk with that belongs to the or had worked with the FBI that knows my position in this thing.

Mr. BALL. I never heard anybody accuse you of any wrongdoing in connection with this matter.

Mr. MOLINA. In fact, Bill Lowery worked with the FBI.

Mr. BALL. You don't have to worry about that; no one is accusing you of anything.

Mr. MOLINA. Except the local people here.

Mr. BALL. Do you want to sign it or do you want to waive your signature; how do you feel about it? It's your option; you can do either way.

Mr. MOLINA. Well, I would like to.

Mr. BALL. See it and sign it?
Mr. MOLINA. See it and sign it.
Mr. BALL. She will notify you then. She will tell you when to come in.
Mr. MOLINA. Thanks very much.

Tom Dillard and the Smell of Gun Powder

Dallas Morning News chief photographer Tom Dillard was particularly experienced in the use of firearms and expressed this during his deposition. Unfortunately for Ball, he volunteered more than Ball could allow for the record, and following the pattern he had clearly established earlier, he moved to limit how much of this information Dillard was to reveal.[41] Note how Ball attempted to steer Dillard to place the smell of gun powder further up Elm street, in front of the TSBD. In this letter, Harold Weisberg questioned Ball's motives for obfuscating his testimony and requires no further analysis.[42]

> Dillard said he is "a gun nut" and had "a great number of high-powered rifles ... so I know a bit about guns." He said, with respect to the origin of othe shots, "We were getting a sort of reverberation which made it difficult to pinpoint the actual direction", and "I very definitely smelled gun powder when the car moved up at the corner."
>
> Could he have smelled gunpowder from a sixth floor shot, if he
> 2
> really did smell gunpowder? With a "brisk north wind"? Ball drops this line of questioning right there.

Mr. BALL. You have had experience with rifles?
Mr. DILLARD. Yes. I have shot a great deal, so I am familiar with the noise that they made in that area. We were getting a sort of reverberation which made it difficult to pinpoint the actual direction but my feeling was that it was coming into my face and, in that I was facing north toward the School Depository—I might add that I very definitely smelled gun powder when the car moved up at the corner.
Mr. BALL. You did?
Mr. DILLARD. I very definitely smelled it.
Mr. BALL. By that you mean when you moved up to the corner of Elm and Houston?
Mr. DILLARD. Yes; now, there developed a very brisk north wind.
Mr. BALL. That was in front of the Texas School Book Depository?
Mr. DILLARD. Yes, it's rather close—the corner is rather close. I mentioned it, I believe, that it was rather surprising to me.
Mr. BALL. Who did you mention it to?
Mr. DILLARD. Bob, I'm sure.
Mr. BALL. Bob Jackson?
Mr. DILLARD. Yeah, Bob and I were talking about it.
Mr. BALL. You developed your pictures, didn't you?
Mr. DILLARD. I don't remember.
Mr. BALL. Or did you turn them over?
Mr. DILLARD. I printed them.

African-American Witnesses Norman, Williams and Jarman— The "Empty Shell" Game, Part II

COMMISSION EXHIBIT 488

COMMISSION EXHIBIT 482

The presence of African-American witnesses Bonnie Ray Williams, Harold Norman and James Jarman, who were photographed at the fifth floor windows by Tom Dillard right after the shots, has been examined at length by researchers and investigators.[43] They were brought to D.C. on 24 March 1964, and were interviewed by Joseph Ball in the presence of John McCloy, Allen Dulles, Gerald Ford, and Earl Warren himself.[44] This should give the reader an idea of the importance of the testimony of these three gentlemen—and the degree of intimidation they must have been subjected to. Roy Truly accompanied the three to D.C. for his first deposition as well.[45] All three of them had been thoroughly prepared and coached four days earlier—Friday, 20 March 1964—in Dallas, when they did photo shoots, rehearsals, and re-creations with Joseph Ball on the fifth floor of the TSBD for the Commission.[46]

Of the three, Norman was the only one who said he heard a rifle bolt being operated in-between shots, and the shells falling, after being ejected, onto the wooden floor right above the three men. On 26 November 1963, Norman was interviewed by the FBI and made no mention about hearing shells and rifle action bolts. Alas, by 4 December, he was brought in to swear an affidavit where he now stated he heard the above-mentioned sounds.[47] This document was used later to buttress his Secret Service interview of 7 December 1963.

Patricia Lambert wrote about Secret Service Report (SS491) in *The Continuing Inquiry* 22 October 1977, Vol 2, No 3 :[48]

Norman's allegation that he heard the shells hit the floor and the bolt action of the rifle surfaced in toto in SS491. Twelve days after the assassination and eight days after his interview by the FBI, Norman's startling disclosure made its belated appearance. Norman's sworn affidavit to the Secret Service states:

I knew that the shots had come from directly above me, and I could hear the expended cartridges fall to the floor. I could also hear the bolt action of the rifle. I also saw some dust fall from the ceiling of the fifth floor and I felt sure that whoever had fired the shots was directly above me.

Missing entirely from this new version is the description of Norman putting his head out the window and looking up toward the roof, a gesture which was witnessed by at least four people. Norman permanently eliminated this event from this testimony at this point. Also, the particles of dirt, which he told the FBI fell outside the building and prevented him from seeing anything when he looked up, are changed in this version to "some dust." This dust fell "from the ceiling" inside the building and the intended implication appears to be that it was dislodged by the shells hitting the floor of the sniper's nest.

This then is Norman's new story. Not only are the sounds of the gunman added for the first time, but one part of his earlier statement to the FBI is excised and another part altered to accommodate the new information. This new story transformed Norman from an inconsequential witness to one of major importance who provided firsthand evidence linking the shots that were fired at 12:30 to the hulls that were found on the sixth floor 40 minutes later. This important information became the focus of his interview three months later before the Warren Commission.

COMMISSION EXHIBIT 489

Jarman and Williams both "corroborated" that Norman *said he heard these sounds* but they did not hear anything themselves.[49] Once again, an accomplished professor of law and veteran attorney such as Joseph Ball surely would have known both Jarman's and Williams's statements about Norman telling them about shells hitting the wooden floor above them would have been pure hearsay, and would have been objected to by any competent opposing counsel. So why did he pursue this line of questioning and allow it to stand for the record?

Below is a sample of Bonnie Ray Williams's testimony: (WC3H175)

Mr. BALL. Norman said he could hear it?
Mr. WILLIAMS. He said he could hear it. He was directly under the window that Oswald shot from.
Mr. BALL. He was directly under. He told you as he got up from the window that he could hear the shells ejected from the gun?
Mr. WILLIAMS. Yes; he did.

Ball *leads Williams hearsay*, and in the process allows Williams to declare Oswald the shooter! Law students should use this as an example of what *not* to do when taking depositions and testimonies, unless of course, you have an ulterior motive.

The onus of proof here obviously lies with Harold Norman. How could he specifically hear the shell casings hitting the floor, but—he nor the others—not hear the footsteps of a person *running on the wooden floor* right above him,[50] and which had empty spaces where flooring was supposedly in the process of being laid? Ball tried to sucker him into this and Norman refused to go along:[51]

> Mr. Ball. How many shots did you hear?
> Mr. Norman. Three.
> Mr. Ball. Do you remember whether or not you said anything to the men then as to whether or not you heard anything from above you?
> Mr. Norman. Only I think I remember saying that I thought I could hear the shell hulls and the ejection of the rifle. I didn't tell I think I hear anybody moving, you know.
> Mr. Ball. But you thought, do you remember you told the men then that you thought you heard the ejection of the rifle?
> Mr. Norman. Yes, sir.
> Mr. Ball. And shells on the floor?
> Mr. Norman. Yes, sir.
> Mr. Ball. Falling?
> Mr. Norman. Yes.

As pointed out above, the Warren Commission conducted a re-creation, placing Norman on the fifth floor and working a rifle bolt right above him and letting empty shells hit the floor. Obviously, the Warren Commissioners were not convinced with Norman's testimony, and they later made three different trips to Dallas to re-enact the shell game and find out for themselves if it was possible.[52]

> had up there."[56] The experiment with the shells and rifle was repeated for members of the Commission on May 9, 1964, on June 7, 1964, and again on September 6, 1964. All seven of the Commissioners clearly heard the shells drop to the floor.

This shows how desperate they appear to have been to establish three shots, three shell casings and one patsy in a sling. Regrettably, and with Joseph Ball leading the way, three blue-collar African-Americans got caught in this intricate web of deception, having to go along with a very vital part of the Warren Commission's railroad of Oswald.

We close the shell game with this from Shirley Martin:[53]

> All of the Negro boys involved–Givens, Williams, Norman, Jarman, Piper, etc.–were scared to death. I am intrigued by the following:
>
> > McCloy: You testified you had not seen Oswald except this one occasion in the morning. Did you hear any of your friends or coworkers say whether they had seen Oswald on that morning?

```
      Norman: Not until after...
      McCloy: After the assassination?
      Norman: Yes, sir; that is the only time.
            (Belin breaks in)
      Belin: Offtherecord.
      Discussionofftbreord.
```

It all seems obvious to me that Lee went into the domino room for his
lunch where Norman probably saw him, after having spoken to Givens
while Givens was enroute down from 6th at 11:30--Lee having been on
5th at this point. After getting his lunch Lee wandered out onto
the first floor near the telephone where his confrontation with
Jarman took place. Meanwhile Shelley saw Lee at this point and
gave testimony in this regard. The Commission however dismissed this
and accepted instead Givens rather questionably-orientated testimony.)

The Strange Case of Jack Dougherty

Jack Dougherty was a U.S. Army veteran who had received a
medical discharge after World War II. Dougherty had quite an amount
of seniority as he began working for the TSBD company in 1952 as a
shipping clerk.[54] At the age of 40, he was unmarried and living with
his parents. "His father indicated his son had considerable difficulty
coordinating his mental facilities with his speech."[55] Even FBI
Special Agent William O. Johnson found it necessary to document
his own impression of Dougherty, confirming what his father said
during his FBI interview of 18 December 1963.[56] The only thing they
did not write was that he was retarded, perhaps even autistic. Could
this have been some kind of cover? It would be wise to allow Harold
Weisberg's previous work in this area speak for itself. Joseph Ball
initiated Dougherty's deposition in this fashion:

> Mr. BALL. Now, did you ever have any difficulty with your speech?
> Mr. DOUGHERTY. No.
> Mr. BALL. You never had any?
> Mr. DOUGHERTY. No.
> Mr. BALL. Did you ever have any difficulty in the Army with any medical
> treatment or anything of that sort?
> Mr. DOUGHERTY. No.
> Mr. BALL. None at all?
> Mr. DOUGHERTY. No.

The truthful answers to the four questions posed here are the
complete opposite! Yes.

Weisberg was quite disturbed by Joseph Ball's "abusive" treatment
of Jack Dougherty.[57]

```
                                          ing
        Unhappy with his results in the questionin of Daugherty and
    undoubtedly completely aware of Dougherty's emotional problem, Ball
                                    usive
        then treated him in an abmmm fashion that I cannot precall being used
```

upon any of the other witnesses:

"Mr. Ball. Is that the truth?

Mr. Dougherty. That's right." (p.378)

Mr. BALL. When you talked to the FBI men, I've got a statement here dated the 19th of December 1963, a statement from Special Agent William O. Johnson, and he reports that you told him that you saw Lee Harvey Oswald at approximately 8 a.m. when he, Oswald, arrived.

Mr. DOUGHERTY. That's right.

Mr. BALL. That you saw Oswald again at approximately 11 a.m. on the sixth floor?

Mr. DOUGHERTY. That's right.

Mr. BALL. But you didn't see him again after that, is that your testimony?

Mr. DOUGHERTY. Yes.

Mr. BALL. Is that the truth?

Mr. DOUGHERTY. That's right.

From Weisberg, (At the TSBD: Statement of Witnesses—Jack Edwin Dougherty)

In the light of this, we face the question "How dependable a witness was Jack Dougherty?" The Commission leaves us only one way of answering this question, the Commission regarded him as a dependable witness. They used his testimony in the report. Dougherty is, not because he was, but because the Commission has chosen to make him so, an important witness.

And how anxious was Ball to establish Dougherty seeing Oswald with a package that morning? Consider these two exchanges in his deposition.[58]

Mr. BALL. Did he come in with anybody?

Mr. DOUGHERTY. No.

Mr. BALL. He was alone?

Mr. DOUGHERTY. Yes; he was alone.

Mr. BALL. Do you recall him having anything in his hand?

Mr. DOUGHERTY. Well, I didn't see anything, if he did.

Mr. BALL. Did you pay enough attention to him, you think, that you would remember whether he did or didn't?

Mr. DOUGHERTY. Well, I believe I can—yes, sir—I'll put it this way; I didn't see anything in his hands at the time.

Mr. BALL. In other words, your memory is definite on that, is it?

Mr. DOUGHERTY. Yes, sir.

Mr. BALL. In other words, you would say positively he had nothing in his hands?

Mr. DOUGHERTY. I would say that—yes, sir,

Mr. BALL. Or, are you guessing?

Mr. DOUGHERTY. I don't think so.

Mr. BALL. You saw him come in the door?

Mr. DOUGHERTY. Yes.

Mr. BALL. The back door on the first floor?

Mr. DOUGHERTY. It was in the back door.

Four pages later, Ball reverted to the imaginary package. (WC6H381)

Mr. BALL. Did you ever see Lee Oswald carry any sort of large package?
Mr. DOUGHERTY. Well, I didn't, but some of the fellows said they did.
Mr. BALL. Who said that?
Mr. DOUGHERTY. Well, Bill Shelley, he told me that he thought he saw him carrying a fairly good-sized package.
Mr. BALL. When did Shelley tell you that?
Mr. DOUGHERTY. Well, it was—the day after it happened.
Mr. BALL. Are you sure you were on the fifth floor when you heard the shots?
Mr. DOUGHERTY. Yes, I'm positive.

From: Weisberg, (At the TSBD: Statement of Witnesses—Jack Edwin Dougherty)

In using Dougherty, the Commission was in the unfortunate position of honest people not knowing how to successfully be dishonest people. They felt for some strange reason that they had to show Oswald entering the building. Countless witnesses established that Oswald was in the building. If it wasnecessary to get him to the building, Frazier did that. But Jack Dougherty was the only person who saw him as he entered the building.

This immediately raised the question, did Dougherty see Oswald carrying a package? Unfortunately for the Commission, he didn't.

Even Shirley Martin chimed in on the Jack Dougherty issue:[59]

On top of this is the fascinating testimony of Daugherty. This was so confusing that I can't believe it wasn't deliberate. If a man is REALLY this dumb can he hold a job year after year? We should know more about Daugherty? What were his politics? I have the inference that he was an insane fan of the right-wing. Was he interested in guns, rifles? Did he belong to any organizations?

From Weisberg: (At the TSBD: Statement of Witnesses—Jack Edwin Dougherty)

Although Dougherty has already testified, and testified very clearly on the point of when and where he ate lunch, Ball, in an effort to trip up his own witness, whose testimony by this point he certainly wasn't happy with, and knowing full well of the speech problem the witness had, asked him whether he heard the shot before or after lunch and elicits the reply that it was before lunch (p.381)

So having proved beyond doubt that the only package Oswald had on leaving for and arriving in the area of o his place of employment could not possibly have contained the rifle, theCommission then proves that Oswald could not possibly have carried the package into the building.

Because the testimony of these three witnesses, Frazier, Randle, and Dougherty, is the only testimony the Commission has on whether or not Oswald had a package of any kind and whether or not he took it into

the building, the Commission is left in the position where it had to
ignore or misrepresent(and it chose the latter course) its only testimony.

Hence, the Commission's conclusions in the Report are in contradiction to the only sworn evidence the Commission took and can be classified only as pure fiction.

The Eisenberg Memorandum

On 12 March 1964, Assistant Counsel Melvin A. Eisenberg wrote an
ultra-secret memorandum to J. Lee Rankin that was not declassified
until 1998 by the ARRB.[60] In this memo, Eisenberg expressed his
suspicions about Dougherty, and the need to investigate him further.
The memo pointed out the various discrepancies and omissions in
Dougherty's different interviews, statements and testimonies.[61]

I am suspicious of Dougherty for several reasons.

(1) He has no alibi. Of the six employees on the floor laying
crew, Givens claims to have been with a friend at a parking lot
several blocks away when the assassination took place; Williams
and Jarman were together on the fifth floor with another employee
named Norman; Lovelady was standing outside the TSBD (and was photographed); and Arce claims to have been standing outside the TSBD.
Dougherty was inside the TSBD and all alone.

(2) His story is very thin.

(a) It does not make sense that Dougherty, one of a six-
man floor laying crew, should begin working before the other five
members returned from lunch.

(b) It is questionable that Dougherty would have had to go
to the fifth floor to get "stock" in connection with the floor-laying
project.

(3) If Dougherty is "mentally retarded," it may explain some of
the inconsistencies in his story. On the other hand, the "mental
retardation" may be an emotional problem, which would itself be
grounds for suspicion. In this connection, I find disturbing
Truly's comment that Dougherty "has been especially confused since
the assassination."

MAE

In the final analysis, the Eisenberg memorandum exposes sensitive areas which few have looked at before and leaves us tantalized by the notion that it might have come from people inside who were working for the Warren Commission, who realized the injustices that were being perpetrated. Its contents would explain why it was deep-sixed into oblivion, not to see the light of day until 29 May 1998.

Unlike Joseph Ball, it would seem that at least there was one other Warren Commission assistant counsel without an agenda, who was actually convinced that Oswald did not shoot anyone on 22 November 1963 and tried to do something about it. Melvin Eisenberg seemed to object to the whitewash his partners were trying to push.[62] (see below)

> Mr. Eisenberg, who appears to be the principal member of the staff interested in the exact locations of where the shots were fired, indicated that the staff of the President's Commission were all in agreement concerning the locations that had now been established based on the viewing of the Zapruder film. However, he stated that when comparing the Zapruder film with the film taken by Nix, there were certain objects which could not be reconciled, particularly at the point where it was believed the third shot was fired. Mr. Eisenberg pointed out that it was not a matter of questioning the measurements taken by either the Bureau or the Secret Service of the models that had been made, but rather to try and resolve the exact circumstances under which the Nix film was taken so that there would be no possibility of allegations being made at a later date that the facts concerning the shooting were different than the President's Commission arrives at as being the correct situation.

The Rosen Memorandum

Were there mid-to-high-level FBI employees in-the-know who were concerned about Joseph Ball's conduct? You bet! On 9 March 1964, and in response to a memo written on 3 March 1964, by W. V. Cleveland to Courtney Evans,[63] Alex Rosen, assistant director in charge of the General Investigative Division,[64] wrote a memorandum to Alan Belmont, assistant to the director, reporting on the possibility of the FBI investigating Ball under Executive Order 10450, which pertains to security concerns of federal employees.[65]

They were concerned, and with good reason, that there might have been a connection between fellow Californians Earl Warren and Joseph Ball. This investigation never took place because the Warren Commission did not request it.

JOSEPH ANTHONY BALL
President's Commission on the
Assassination of President Kennedy
SECURITY OF GOVERNMENT EMPLOYEES

Mr. Belmont   **3/9/64**

A. Rosen

Memorandum from Cleveland to Evans dated 3/3/64 recommended a letter be delivered to Mr. J. Lee Rankin at the President's Commission, advising Mr. Rankin the Bureau did not contemplate an investigation of Ball under Executive Order 10450 (Federal Employees Security Program) in the absence of a request from the President's Commission.

Mr. Rankin was advised that the Bureau knew nothing concerning any association of Mr. B'l with the Chief Justice and that if the President's Commission desired the Bureau to conduct the investigation we would be more than glad to proceed immediately. He was told that the only reason we did not go ahead with this investigation was because we felt the President's Commission should be aware that the Civil Service Commission had requested this type of investigation concerning one of its employees and that because of the type of inquiry being handled by

Mr. Rankin stated he did not quite follow the situation wherein the Bureau was not conducting this investigation, inasmuch as it was his understanding that in those instances where there was an allegation of a subversive nature, such investigations were handled by the FBI. Mr. Rankin said there was a question in his mind as to whether or not we did not desire to conduct this investigation because we felt there might be a connection between Mr. Ball and Chief Justice Warren. (Joseph Ball has been a resident of California since he completed his education at the University of Southern California Law School in 1927.)

Was Alex Rosen of the FBI leaving a paper trail pointing at Joseph Ball as the master of deceit for the Warren Commission, much in the same manner that J. Edgar Hoover left one pointing at "George Bush of the CIA" in his memorandum of 29 November 1963?[66] There is the distinct possibility. Coincidentally, Alex Rosen happens to be one of three FBI individuals copied in the Hoover memorandum, so that in itself shows his importance in the hierarchy of the FBI. The following passage refers to ". . . and the additional information furnished to him (Rankin) orally." How close was Joseph Ball to being processed for misconduct? We will never know, as the memo concludes: "ACTION: None—for information."

Memo to Mr. Belmont from A. Rosen
Re: Joseph Anthony Ball

the President's Commission we felt they should be the ones to decide whether they did or did not desire the investigation.

Mr. Rankin then commented that he sincerely appreciated the Bureau calling this matter to his attention by letter and the additional information furnished to him orally. He advised that he would present this matter to the seven-man Commission in order that they could make a decision as to whether they did or did not desire the Bureau to proceed with a loyalty-type investigation.

ACTION: None - for information.

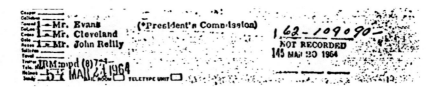

The FBI vs Warren Commission Attorneys: The Origin of the Single-Bullet Theory

There appear to have been serious conflicts between the FBI and the Warren Commission attorneys, as evidenced by this portion of an eight-page memorandum written three years later by Al Rosen to Cartha DeLoach on 8 July 1966, and Joseph Ball seems to have been right in the middle of it all.[67]

> Although Epstein did not make any direct derogatory remarks against the Bureau, he did quote several Commission staff members who were primarily dissatisfied with communications with the Bureau. He quoted Joseph A. Ball, Assistant Counsel, who said that on his first trip to Dallas he called the FBI Field Office for assistance in a problem. Ball was told the request must come from FBI Headquarters, Washington. Thereafter, Ball had to telephone Mr. Howard P. Willens, Assistant Counsel, who prepared a formal request which was forwarded to the Bureau. Ball said three days later he was notified that this request had been approved, but by this time Ball had resolved his problem. Ball was quoted as saying the FBI was "exasperatingly bureaucratic." Epstein said that other lawyers on the Commission staff were less satisfied with FBI cooperation. Mr. Melvin Eisenberg, Assistant Counsel, said that although relations gradually improved, FBI Agents were resentful of "amateurs" doing what they considered to be their job. Joseph Ball was again quoted as saying that FBI Agents cooperated only on "express orders" from "Hoover." J. Lee Rankin, General Counsel, said, however, that although there were some "communication problems" between the staff and the FBI there was a liaison officer with the Bureau on whom he could call at "any time of the day or night" to expedite important problems.

That Epstein implied endorsement of that purpose—of the sacrifice of justice and truth to the dirty imperatives of politics—is scarcely possible. Why *Inquest*, in that case? But Epstein *has* been excessively delicate and equivocating in confronting the moral issues which attend the Warren Report in his public statements as well as in *Inquest*.

Sylvia Meagher book review: "Four Books on the Warren Report: The Summer of Discontent"

On 27 January 1964, Leo Gauthier and Special Agent Lyndal Shaneyfelt of the FBI met with Warren Commission staff members Joseph Ball, David Belin, Melvin Eisenberg and Norman Redlich.[68]

The Secret Service was represented by Inspector Thomas Kelley, and John W. Howlett.[69] This meeting lasted eight and a half hours and its purpose was to discuss the Zapruder and Nix films and how they were going to frame the three shots to coincide with the film evidence. This is exactly the time when the "single-bullet theory" was concocted. This passage mentions "one staff member" as the originator of this "wild" concept.

Despite Kelly rejecting this "ridiculous" notion as a "spur of the moment" thing, the truth of the matter is that this is the exact scenario that eventually prevailed and became part of the official record. It appears the FBI did not want to get involved in any "ridiculously wild" interpretations or scenarios that Ball and company might have been attempting to advance.

Furthermore, the Secret Service is on record here as outright rejecting the single-bullet theory as ridiculous.

Is it any wonder the FBI never really took center stage in developing the single-bullet theory? Of course not, they left that up to Warren Commission Assistant Counsel Arlen Specter.

> One staff member, according to Inspector Kelley, quietly spoke about the "outside" possibility of shot one going through the President with sufficient velocity remaining to penetrate Connally's body, wrist and leg. Inspector Kelley mentioned this to me confidentially. He was of the opinion that this was a personal remark made on the spur of the moment. Shot two under those ridiculous facts would have gone completely "wild" according to Kelley.

Conclusion

In the end, the sad conclusion of this research indicates that Warren Commission Assistant Counsel Joseph Ball was most actively involved in the suppression of vital testimony, leading, suborning, rehearsing and coaching witnesses, aiding and abetting perjury, using falsified exhibits to obtain false testimony, encouraging hearsay testimony and allowing it to stand for the record.

We now know there were people in the FBI who were concerned about his behavior and tried to do something about it, to no avail. In fact, he did most of his dirty work after the Rosen memorandum. In the meantime, we are left with no doubt that he was fully committed to doing everything in his power to make Lee Oswald posthumously appear guilty.

Unfortunately, and shamefully for him, his Warren Commission activities will tarnish his reputation forever.

The Joseph Ball Scorecard (partial list)

Cunningham WC2H251-252	Martin WC6H289
McWatters WC2H262	Mitchell WC6H175
Frazier WC2H210	Molina WC6H368
Linnie WC2H	Murphy WC6H256
Whaley WC2H253	Pinkston WC6H334
Boone WC3H291	Piper WC6H382
Callaway WC3H351	Erlene Roberts WC6H434
Davis WC3H342	Rowland WC6H177
Jarman WC3H198	Shelley WC6H327
Markham WC3H305	Skelton WC6H236
McDonald WC3H295	Underwood WC6H167
Mooney WC3H281	Ables WC7H239
Norman WC3H186	Caster WC7H386
Williams WC3H161	Clark WC7H235
Arce WC6H363	Guinyard WC7H395
Bledsoe WC6H400	Hicks WC7H286 insists he not sign (twice)
Bowers WC6H284	Leavelle WC7H260
Brown WC6H231	Lujan WC7H243
Burns WC6H397	Perry WC7H232
Crawford WC6H171	Piper WC7H388
Dougherty WC6H373	Potts WC7H195
Foster WC6H248	Rose WC7H227
Hine WC6H393	Shelley WC7H390 (2nd)
White WC6H253	Shields WC7H393
Kaiser WC6H341	Stovall WC7H186
Lovelady WC6H336	Truly WC7H380 (2nd)

ENDNOTES

1. longbeachbar.org/single-post/2017/03/16/Joseph-A-Ball
2. JFK Assassination Debate, Mark Lane vs Joseph Ball, 4 December 1964 (2:04 YouTube video) He also wrote Chapter 4 of the Warren Commission report, which happens to be the most important chapter that railroads Oswald. "I never talked to an FBI agent about my investigations" (3:38)
3. WC3H281
4. Twyman, Noel, *Bloody Treason*, pp. 91-97
5. CE 510 & CE 512

6. Twyman, Noel, *Bloody Treason*, p. 94

7. Ibid. 97

8. WC2H195

9. WC2H214

10. WC2H190 (see in appendix)

11. WC2H195 Brennan, Baker, Frazier, Worrell

12. See CE371 and WC16H968. Weisberg also wrote about the illegibility of the maps.

13. WC2H214

14. WC2H251-252

15. Roffman, Howard, *Presumed Guilty*

16. WC2H249

17. CE142

18. WC2H250

19. Shaw, J. Gary, *Cover-Up*, p.11, also references back to *Rush to Judgment* by Mark Lane, p. 32

20. Laura Kittrell unpublished manuscript, p. 68, The Armstrong Collection. Also, FBI 3-25-64 DL100-10461 Switzer and Petrakis.

21. CE369

22. WH6H338 Lovelady

23. WC6H363-367 Arce

24. Weisberg Item 71, The Feeble Individual, The Weisberg Collection. Hood College, Frederick, MD, USA

25. Arce DPD affidavit 22 November 1963

26. WH6H366 Arce

27. Warren Commission report, p. 234, "feeble individual"

28. Weisberg Item 71, "feeble individual"

29. Warren Commission report, p. 234, "feeble individual"

30. WC6H367 Arce

31. WC6H345 Givens

32. Meagher, Sylvia, "The Curious Testimony of Mr. Givens," *The Texas Observer*, 13 August 1971, pp. 11-12, The Weisberg Collection. Hood College, Frederick, MD, USA

33. Ibid

34. WC24 CE2003 No.60, signed Shelley affidavit 22 November 1963, by Patsy Collins

35. WC6H330-331 Shelley

36. Warren Commission report, p. 143

37. WC2H233 and 242

38. Rivera, Larry, "Why Buell Wesley Frazier was removed from Altgens6," 19 February 2013

39. WC6H373 Molina cut off about Lowery

40. WC6H371 Molina cut off about who was with him

41. WC6H165 Dillard

42. Tom C. Dillard deposition, 1 April 1964, 6H162-7 (Item No. 3), The Weisberg Collection. Hood College, Frederick, MD, USA

43. *The Continuing Inquiry*, Vol. V, No. 7, 21 February 1981, p. 3

44. WC3H140

45. HSCA Norman interview by Day, also WC3H140

46. CE482, CE490

47. CE493

48. SS491 (CD87 pp. 775-797)

49. WC3H161 and WCH198 (Jarman and Williams)

50. *The Continuing Inquiry*, Vol. V, No. 7., 21 February 1981, p. 3

51. WC3H191: How could Norman have heard spent shells and rifle bolt action over the report and reverberation of the shots themselves?

52. Warren Commission report p. 71

53. Martin letter, 25 January 1967, (Item No. 3) The Weisberg Collection. Hood College, Frederick, MD, USA

54. WC6H374-375 Dougherty

55. WC19H622

56. WC19H620

57. Weisberg, Harold, "At the TSBD: Statement of Witnesses—Jack Edwin Dougherty," The Weisberg Collection. Hood College, Frederick, MD, USA

58. WC6H377 and 381

59. Shirley Martin letter to Weisberg 25 January 1967, The Weisberg Collection. Hood College, Frederick, MD, USA

60. 12 March 1964, Eisenberg memorandum to F. Lee Rankin, released by ARRB 29 May 1998, (from the Armstrong Collection, box 16, notebook 3, tab 31)

61. WC19H620-622: Did Eisenberg inadvertently stumble upon some kind of intelligence operation to which he had not been made privy to?

62. FBI Memo, Alex Rosen to Alan Belmont, 29 January 1964

63. Cleveland to Evans, 3 March 1964: This memo is unavailable. We only know about it because it is mentioned in the Rosen memo. Apparently, this information filtered through unaltered.

64. Harold Weisberg letter 18 September 1989, with FBI memorandum regarding David Lifton. (Item 05) The Weisberg Collection. Hood College, Frederick, MD, USA

65. archives.gov/federal-register/codification/executive-order/10450

66. Hoover memo, 29 November 1963

67. Rosen to DeLoach memo, 8 July 1966, p. 7. Joseph Ball later claimed Epstein made this up but never sued. See *Law Quarterly Review*, 1 January 1967, p. 44

68. FBI Inspector Leo Gauthier memo to Nicholas Callahan, Assistant Director dated 28 January 1964. Callahan—considered an "old Hoover hand" by the mid-1970s, was later fired by FBI Director Clarence Kelly in July 1976.

69. See Warren Commission Hierarchy in appendix, including Thomas Kelley's role as a liaison between the Secret Service, the legal staff of the Warren Commission, and the FBI.

APPENDIX

James Richard Worrell WC2H197 (CE361)

Mr. SPECTER. Mr. Worrell, before we leave this Exhibit 361, are you able to testify as to the accuracy of the scale drawing here which represents the part of it that you have testified about, specifically the presence of the Texas School Book Depository Building on the northwest corner of Elm and Houston. Is that the accurate location of that building?

Mr. WORRELL. Yes, sir.

Mr. SPECTER. And is it an accurate reproduction of the intersection of Elm and Houston leading into the parkway on Elm Street?

Mr. WORRELL. As far as this?

Mr. SPECTER. Yes.

Mr. WORRELL. Yes.

Mr. SPECTER. As far as all the parts you have testified about Elm and Houston. Is it accurate that Pacific is one block in the northerly direction away from Elm Street?

Mr. WORRELL. Yes, sir.

Mr. SPECTER. And Ross is another block, generally, in a northerly direction away from Pacific?

Mr. WORRELL. No, Ross is over here. This is Record Street.

Mr. SPECTER. Well, first there is Elm, then there is Pacific, and then there is Ross. Is that much accurate as the map shows it to be, is that the way the streets are laid out?

Mr. WORRELL. I think so.

Mr. SPECTER. How about the general width of Houston Street in relation to the general width of the Texas School Depository Building, is that about right?

Mr. WORRELL. I don't know, sir.

Mr. SPECTER. All right, that is fine.

197

This exchange proves the deception of CE361, where Specter is trying to establish the accuracy of exhibit, and in the process confusing Worrell as to where each street is actually located. Out-of-towners trying to confuse locals. Perhaps Specter was trying to single out the FBI for CE361 (p. 195).

(Author's note: Drew Pearson circulated a rumor that in Dallas, Joseph Ball insisted on the FBI providing him with a car. One other FBI cable mentions Ball requested that the FBI locate witnesses for the Commission, to which the FBI replied negative.)

Since the FBI denied the issue of the automobile, it could not be included in this research, however the Epstein information detailed above seems to dovetail with this "rumor."

FBI WASH DC

MAY 1 1964

FBI-DALLAS

555 PH CST URGENT 5-14-64 FLL

TO DIRECTOR (105-82555) ATTENTION: INSPECTOR JAMES R. MALLEY

FROM DALLAS (100-10461) 3P

LEE HARVEY OSWALD, ALSO KNOWN AS INTERNAL SECURITY - RUSSIA - CUBA.

RE TELEPHONE CALL FROM INSPECTOR MALLEY THIS DATE, REFERRING TO CALL FROM DREW PEARSON, WHICH REPORTED THAT HE HAD A TIP THAT JOSEPH BALL OF THE WARREN COMMISSION HAD COME TO THE DALLAS OFFICE OF THE FBI AND ASKED FOR THE LOAN OF A CAR TO INTERVIEW PEOPLE. IT WAS ALSO INDICATED THAT THE DALLAS OFFICE DELAYED FOR APPROXIMATELY TWENTYFOUR HOURS AND THEN FLATLY TOLD BALL HE COULD NOT HAVE THE CAR.

THE DALLAS OFFICE HAS AT NO TIME RECEIVED A REQUEST FROM JOSEPH BALL OR ANY OTHER MEMBER OF THE PRESIDENT'S COMMISSION FOR THE USE OF AN AUTOMOBILE.

From a different cablegram

PAGE TWO

JOSEPH BALL. MR. SANDERS STATED THE PRESIDENT'S COMMISSION MEMBERS HAD THE ADDRESS AND TELEPHONE NUMBERS OF CERTAIN WITNESSES THEY DESIRED TO INTERVIEW AND THAT THEY WOULD LIKE THE FBI TO LOCATE SUCH INDIVIDUALS FOR PURPOSES OF HAVING THEM APPEAR AT THE UNITED STATES ATTORNEY'S OFFICE FOR THE NECESSARY INTERVIEWS WITH PRESIDENT'S COMMISSION MEMBERS.

IMMEDIATELY AFTER THE RECEIPT OF THE TELEPHONE CALL FROM MR. SANDERS, CONTACT WAS HAD WITH INSPECTOR MALLEY, WHO STATED THAT MR. SANDERS SHOULD BE ADVISED THAT SINCE THIS WAS A PRESIDENT'S COMMISSION MATTER, THAT THE FBI SHOULD NOT GET INVOLVED WITH LOCATING WITNESSES TO APPEAR AND TESTIFY BEFORE THE COMMISSION REPRESENTATIVES, BUT THAT SHOULD IT DEVELOP THAT DIFFICULTY WAS HAD IN LOCATING A PARTICULAR WITNESS, THAT A REQUEST TO ASSIST IN THE LOCATION OF A WITNESS WHOULD BE CONSIDERED.

Warren Commission Hierarchy

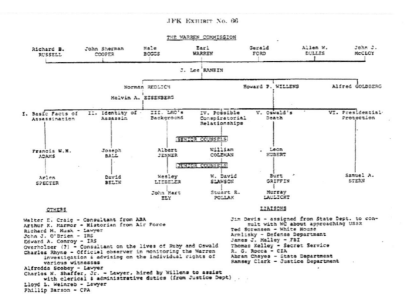

JFK Exhibit No. 66

THE WARREN COMMISSION

Richard B. RUSSELL	John Sherman COOPER	Hale BOGGS	Earl WARREN	Gerald FORD	Allen W. DULLES	John J. McCLOY

J. Lee RANKIN

Norman REDLICH   Howard P. WILLENS   Alfred GOLDBERG

Melvin A. EISENBERG

I. Basic Facts of Assassination	II. Identity of Assassin	III. LHO's Background	IV. Possible Conspiratorial Relationships	V. Oswald's Death	VI. Presidential Protection

SENIOR COUNSELS

| Francis W.H. ADAMS | Joseph BALL | Albert JENNER | William COLEMAN | Leon HUBERT | |

JUNIOR COUNSELS

| Arlen SPECTER | David BELIN | Wesley LIEBELER | W. David SLAWSON | Burt GRIFFIN | Samuel A. STERN |
| | | John Hart ELY | Stuart R. POLLAK | Murray LAULICHT | |

OTHERS

Walter E. Craig - Consultant from ABA
Arthur K. Marmor - Historian from Air Force
Richard M. Mosk - Lawyer
John J. O'Brien - IRS
Edward A. Conroy - IRS
Overholser (?) - Consultant on the lives of Ruby and Oswald
Charles Rhyne - Official observer in monitoring the Warren
    investigation & advising on the individual rights of
    various witnesses
Alfredda Scobey - Lawyer
Charles N. Shaffer, Jr. - Lawyer, hired by Willens to assist
    with clerical & administrative duties (from Justice Dept)
Lloyd L. Weinreb - Lawyer
Phillip Barson - CPA

LIAISONS

Jim Davis - assigned from State Dept. to con-
    sult with WC about approaching USSR
Ted Sorensen - White House
Armlinsky - Defense Department
James J. Malley - FBI
Thomas Kelley - Secret Service
R. G. Rocca - CIA
Abram Chayes - State Department
Ramsey Clark - Justice Department

From HSCA Vol 11 pg 315

It is interesting to note that although
Joseph Ball had deposed Roy Truly and
had attended the deposition of Marrion
Baker --- and therefore knew all about
the alleged stopping of the car --- he
never confronted B.J.Martin with the
allegation. (Dealey Plaza Echo 11/2005 pg 48)

15

Whalen's Blunder

The news media came of age on 22 November 1963, in ways we could have never imagined. Information and news dissemination attained unprecedented heights, as the evolving media transmitted the events almost simultaneously as they occurred.

That efficiency could have been counterproductive to information control, as spontaneous accounts of eyewitnesses and newsmen seemed to provide the most accurate accounts of what was going on. Mary Woodward, Roger Craig, Malcolm Kilduff, Seth Kantor, Jean Hill, and others gave us immediate impressions that when analyzed, gave a true portrait of what was really happening that day. Primitive communications required newsmen and news networks to improvise with what was available at the time.

NBC dedicated the rest of the weekend to continuous coverage of JFK's assassination, and during this coverage their complicity in suppression of the truth was evident as early as 51 minutes into the assassination!

The following are images from actual footage of NBC's assassination coverage immediately after it happened. At 2:21 PM CT, Bill Ryan, still trying to grasp what was happening, was suddenly patched into

2:21 pm, E.T.

WPAB-TV in Fort Worth, as the nation was still reeling from the news of the president's assassination.

The disturbing actions of Tom Whalen cried out for further investigation and suggest the Dallas media was actively suppressing the truth right from the beginning.

Bill Ryan (from NBC New York): Now for late details, we go to newsman Tom Whalen at WBAP-TV Fort Worth.

Whalen: This is Tom Whalen in Fort Worth, the scene of the presidential shooting, WBAP-TV newsman James Darnell on the scene of the presidential shooting, where president Kennedy and Governor Connally were shot, has an eyewitness interview with a Mrs. Jean Hill—here is the interview (phone interview from Dallas is patched into WBAP studios in Fort Worth):

Darnell: What is your name ma'am?

Hill: Jean Hill.

Darnell: From Dallas?

Hill: That's right.

Darnell: Did you see the shooting, Miss?

Hill: Yes sir.

Darnell Can you describe what happened?

Hill: Yes sir.

Darnell: Can you do that now?

Hill: Ah, they were driving along, ah, and we were the only people in this area, on our side and the shots came from directly across the street, just as the president's car directly came even with us, . . . we took one look at him and he was sitting there, and he and Jackie were looking at a dog that was in the middle of the seat and at that time two shots rang out just as he looked up, this is the president who looked up, and two shots rang out, these two shots rang out and he grabbed his chest, looked like he was in pain and he fell over in his seat, and Jackie fell over on him and said "My God he's been shot." After that, more shots rang out and the car sped away.

Darnell: What kind of car was it?

Hill: What kind of car was it? The president's car!

Darnell: I mean, where did the shots come from?

Hill: The shots came from the hill. (Whalen's immediate reaction to this statement!)

Darnell: From the hill?

Hill: It was just east of the underpass, we were on the south side.

Whalen again motions to silence Jean Hill (second time).

Whalen gives the "cut" sign to his producer—get this woman off the air NOW!

Whalen's glares at his producer or whoever was in charge of Hill's phone call.

Darnell: Ah ha . . .

Hill: Off the south side of the street.

Darnell: Did you look up there where the shots came from ma'am?

Hill: Yes sir.

Darnell: Did you see anyone?

Hill: Ah, I thought I saw this man running, but, I looked at the president, you know, for a while, and I thought I saw a man running, so I started running up there, too.

Darnell: Ah huh, now what is your name?

Hill: Jean Hill.

Whalen's reaction after they finally got rid of Jean Hill.

The assassination was not even an hour old and Whalen and/or NBC/WBAP seemed to be actively trying to suppress any mention of shots from the hill (hence, from the front). Why? Was this just an innocent effort by NBC to wait for all of the facts to come out before committing to any particular version or interpretation of the events of the day? Was there something more sinister going on?

(Author's Note: Even though this video is now on YouTube, the author obtained it in 1988 when the A&E Network broadcast the program: "JFK: As it Happened," to commemorate the 25th observance of the assassination. Three full VHS tapes were recorded and transferred years later to DVDs for a total of about eight-hours running time.)

16

The Backyard Photos

Of course, we would be remiss if we failed to conduct overlay studies of the famous backyard photographs, which convicted Oswald in the public eye. This chapter will establish the same hypothesis as those early researchers who concluded these had been artificially produced and set out to confirm or refute their results using the computer overlay techniques extensively outlined in Chapter 8. In that chapter, we introduced the concept of the probe image, which is our control or unknown, versus our gallery image, which we superimposed onto our probe. The Luce empire published this one three months after the assassination, on 21 February 1964:

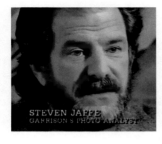

There is a mountain of research already done related to these photographs. In the 1992 video, *The Garrrison Tapes*, produced and directed by John Barbour, photographic expert Steven Jaffe (26:25) concisely demonstrated how these had been fabricated by superimposing transparencies of the two photos, paying particular attention to the head and body:

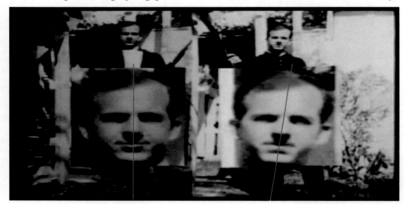

"Whoever framed Oswald, evidently used only one picture of his face, and planted it onto someone else's body, then to give the face on the right a different look, it seems they airbrushed some facial features and tilted the head slightly, and in doing so, they tilted the shadow under his nose. That it was one face is easily demonstrated. If you take the face on the right, and superimpose it over the face on the left, the features line up, but when you slide the face back, you see that it had to be tilted."

360

"The second and more obvious proof is with the position of the bodies. The body on the right seems to be closer to the camera—if so, the head should be larger—however, you see when you slide it over the face on the left, the faces are the same size. This means the bodies should be the same height—they are not."

—Steve Jaffe, *The Garrison Tapes*

Jack White

Jack White also did brilliant and extensive work on the backyard photos, and his research is covered in his famous 1990 video *FAKE— The composite photographs fabricated to frame Lee Harvey Oswald for the murders of President Kennedy and Officer Tippit*. (White starts at 18:19 of video)

When he flipped CE133-A, he showed how ridiculous the figure looked and questioned its ability to remain upright and balanced. Other observations are shown below:

He also explained the belated arrival of the third photograph, which did not surface until 1976, which had been in the hands of Roscoe White's widow, Geneva. "It had been suppressed for 15 years," according to Jack.

The video points out the simple, relevant fact: "Furthermore, an intensive search of Oswald's possessions failed to turn up either the dark shirt or the dark pants seen in the photographs."

Robert and Patricia Hester, who worked at a Dallas photo lab that weekend, told Jim Marrs they saw the backyard photos in the hands of the FBI *the night of the assassination,* which Marrs pointed out was the day before they were officially discovered by the DPD. "They (the Hesters), were processing film and photographs for the FBI and Secret Service," reported Marrs:

"I first interviewed Robert Hester in the late 1970s. He told me he saw the backyard photos in the hands of the FBI the night of the assassination; he was quite insistent on this fact. Of course, that is the day before the photos officially were discovered. In later years, his wife Pat confirmed this story, and told me and other Texas researchers that the FBI even had a color transparency of one of the photos, as well as a picture of Oswald's backyard, but with no one in the picture! They were very certain about all of this."

Michael Griffith wrote an exhaustive article in 1996 in the *Dealey Plaza Echo* which discussed the many anomalies with the photograph. The article validated and confirmed Jack's work such as the edit lines across the chin, the bulging neck, the non-movement of features between the three photographs, and the shadows which show that the same photo of Oswald was used in all three photos.

So, what in the world is there to debate? Is this evidence not enough to sway the reader that these photos were fabricated and were the linchpin that clinched Oswald's guilt, on the cover of *Life* magazine, no less?

Even More Proof

The overlay results of this next battery of tests should help decide as to the authenticity of the backyard photographs.

These are actual overlays of known photographs of Oswald onto one of the backyard photos, CE133A, the one on at top left, which will be our probe. Our gallery images are the same ones used in Chapter 8, the NOPD and DPD mug shots.

Recall that in Chapter 8 the importance of lining up the eyes and scaling the gallery image by establishing the interpupillary distance when rendering overlays onto unknown images was stressed. The same concept obviously applies here. This overlay sequence combines the DPD *and* NOPD photographs over the backyard photo shown above.

6 panel collage of two layers showing increasing levels of opacity. Layer 1: Probe image which is backyard man Layer 2: Gallery image which is the NOPD mug shot.

This technique yields startling results. In these overlays, the outline in red belongs to the backyard figure.

Whereas the eyes, nose, mouth and left ear line up perfectly when the probe and gallery images are overlaid onto each other, the right side of the backyard subject protrudes in absurd fashion. This includes the right side of the neck, right ear and all the right side of the head on up to the crown.

Why the extra space around the head?

Consider the following photographs found later to have been in possession of the DPD, which Dr. Jim Fetzer discusses in his paper "Farid's Folly: A Flawed Study of the Famed "Oswald" Backyard Photos":

91-001 /427

"What is this photo about? I used to work for Steck-Vaughn Publishers in Austin, Texas. We would cut out an area and place dark red cellophane in that spot. Then we could slip a different photo in the cutout area. The cutout is created to place a different photo in the space. Why did the Dallas police have such a cutout in their possession? They said they were just testing to see if a cutout was possible. Of course, the answer is "yes."

"A negative of a cutout, found in the possession of the Dallas police. White would be black in a photo made from this negative. In 1963, the cutout section would have been created with red cellophane cut to create the 'white' area on the negative. It would film as black and the photo of "Oswald could be quickly dropped into place."

Why Blender is So Important

As discussed in previous chapters, with Blender we can set our models up in 3D space and simulate the position of the sun at any time of day. How does a Blender model behave when subjected to a single light source from above, in this case the sun? Here is our Blender layout in front and right orthographic views:

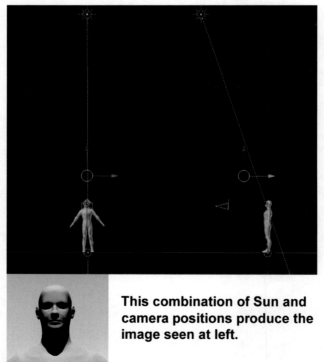

This combination of Sun and camera positions produce the image seen at left.

Above we show the shadow of the nose, which is symmetrical, points directly at 6 o'clock, as with the first of the backyard photos, CE133A.

This is what we see when we overlay the Oswald head onto our model. The eyes and nose shadows are symmetrical and consistent with this type of light source and clearly indicates that the sun or other light source is directly above, which we have replicated in our Blender model:

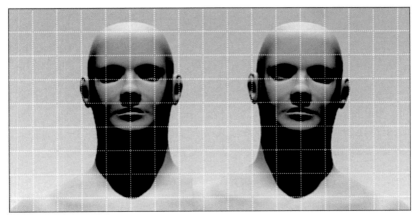

In this collage, the head is tilted 5-6° and the shadow under the nose becomes slightly distorted towards the right and becomes noticeably asymmetrical:

An interesting and unintended result of this experiment is the vast amount of shadow cast below the model's chin, covering all the neck and upper chest down to the upper sternum. This occurs in both the straight and the tilted model. This effect, however, is not seen in the backyard figure. This suggests the possibility that Oswald's face might have been pasted above the chin line in the following manner:

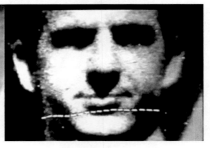

Many researchers, especially Jack White, have proposed that the chin and body actually belonged to Roscoe White, and have pointed out an edit line below "Backyard Man's" lower lip.

The following image shows that Oswald's chin was tapered with a very particular and unique cleft:

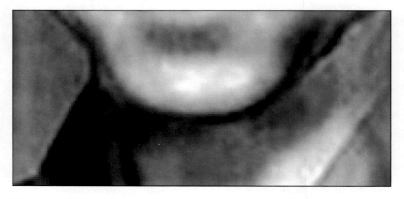

This next image is an actual 50% overlay of White's chin onto the chin of Backyard Man. They seem to line up perfectly.

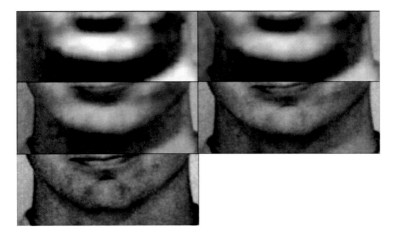

Jack also discovered that a bulging anomaly above the individual's right wrist, possibly from a prior fracture which never healed properly, seemed to match Roscoe White's wrist as well.

Mock Trial Testimony: The Roscoe White Overlays

(Author's note: The following is my presentation, which was supposed to have been given on 18 November 2017, in Houston, Texas, at the People v. Lee Oswald mock trial held at the University of Houston School of Law. For reasons beyond my control, I was excluded from the witness list six days before the trial.)

"The famous backyard images of Oswald holding two weapons and two left wing publications, were used to paint him as a violent malcontent capable of assassinating the president of the U.S. Life magazine did their very best to disseminate and propagate one of these images, by prominently publishing it on the cover of its 21 February 1964 issue."

"These are the images, which we now enter as exhibits, using the same names that were established by the Warren Commission: Commission Exhibits from left to right, CE133A, CE133B, and CE133C. The first two were shown to Oswald the evening of 23 November 1963."

"Curiously, CE133C did not surface until the 1970s, among the possessions of former Marine and DPD Officer Roscoe White. At that time, the HSCA took possession of it, and returned it later to the White family."

"On the evening 23 November 1963, Oswald was interrogated by Captain Will Fritz, FBI agent James Bookhout, and Secret Service Inspector Agent Thomas Kelley, about these images:"

at 2515 West 5th Street, Irving, Texas. When the photographs were presented to Oswald, he sneered at them saying that they were fake photographs; that he had been photographed a number of times the day before by the police and apparently after they photographed him they superimposed on the photographs a rifle and put a gun in his pocket. He got into a long argument with Captain Fritz about his knowledge of photography and asked Fritz a number of times whether the smaller photograph was made from the larger or whether the larger photograph was made from the smaller. He said at the proper time he would show that the photographs were fakes. Fritz told him that the smaller photograph was taken from his effects at the garage. Oswald became arrogant and refused to answer any further questions concerning the photographs and would not identify the photographs as being a photograph of himself. Captain Fritz displayed great patience and tenacity in attempting to secure from Oswald the location of what apparently is the backyard of an address at which

Oswald formerly lived, but it was apparent that Oswald, though slightly shaken by the evidence, had no intention of furnishing any information.

The interview was terminated at about 7:10 P.M.

mffpdf_29106: Interviews with Lee Harvey Oswald on November 23, 1963

From the very notes of Inspector Kelley, here is what Oswald said the evening of 23 November 1963: "He said at the proper time he would show that the photographs were fakes."

(Author's note: Thanks to Amy Joyce for bringing attention to the below).

• *The figure in CE133A is not wearing a ring on either ring finger. CE133B is wearing a ring on his right ring finger.*

• *The figure in CE133C is wearing a ring on his left ring finger. This figure is also wearing a watch on his left wrist.*

- *When we go back to CE133B, we note the figure is not wearing a watch, while in CE133A the wrist is blocked by the hand holding the rifle.*

Color-coded horizontal photogrammetry suggests the same face was inserted into all three photographs, with simple airbrushing used to slightly alter the mouth, head and hair:

Photogrammetric comparison

LR

When these three are superimposed, this is the result—all features line up perfectly: (left).

Side-By-Side Chin Comparison

When we isolate and do a side-by-side study of the chins, this is the result:

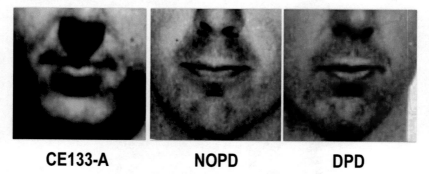

CE133-A   **NOPD**   **DPD**

Vertical Photogrammetry

As detailed in Chapter 8, setting interpupillary distance allows the alignment and scaling of all other features. This can be accomplished by overlaying a grid onto our test images. This exercise will validate the accuracy of our overlays. As noted at right, the result is perfect geometry in the areas of mouth, eyes, nose, and left ear.

372

When we project the grid in the vertical plane, however, it becomes obvious that the right side of the face, including the ear, does not fit the photogrammetric parameters defined by our grid. Empirically speaking, our gallery image covers 5.5 squares from ear-to-ear, where our probe image covers 6.5 squares, at least a 15% difference in the horizontal plane.

Furthermore, the junction between the neck and distal jawbone differ significantly between left and right, which indicates space had to be filled in to finish the composite:

To summarize these observations, the inconsistent rings, the wrist watch, the chins, and the bulging right side of the head and neck, need to be pointed out, when known photos of Oswald are superimposed onto CE133A.

Enter Roscoe White

In 1990, Ricky Don White, the son of Roscoe, shocked the JFK assassination community by claiming that his father had played an active and crucial role in the events of the weekend of 22 November 1963.

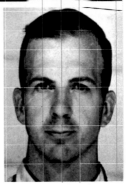

Perhaps in his naivete, and as a result of what can be considered harassment and intimidation, Ricky allowed the FBI access to his father's diary and cablegrams—which, by the way, have disappeared—contained a trove of information, some of it cryptic, which described his father's activities that weekend. Consequently, up until now, no one had bothered to conduct forensic overlay studies to determine if his father had anything to do with the backyard photos.

It would not have been necessary to wait until the computer age to do overlay studies—simple plastic transparencies scaled to the correct dimensions, like Ray Marcus did with the man in the doorway in Chapter 8, would have allowed investigators to replicate this procedure, but in analog fashion, if you will. Roscoe had a stout physique, with a broad chest, thick neck, square chin and wide face and head. This photograph of Roscoe at a beach with some friends vividly illustrates this point:

The fact that CE133C was found among the possessions of Roscoe White raises all kinds of questions about his possible involvement in the production of these composites.

The very first observation happens to be that both "Roscoe at the beach" and Backyard Man are standing with their weight on the right hip.

As an aside, before we continue with what we would have covered in our testimony, an intriguing paper found at the Harold Weisberg JFK repository, which does not cite its author or its sources, posits the following information about Roscoe:

1. "Roscoe White grew up in the Red River Valley and married Rickey's mother Geneva before joining the Marines. He was a crack shot with rifle and pistol, an accomplished photographer with a penchant for altering or obliterating the faces of his subjects, and he probably had access to microdot technology. "Rock" also had the uncanny ability to change his appearance so drastically that even family members had trouble recognizing him in photographs."

2. Roscoe and Oswald trained in the Marines together and knew each other for years. They also worked together at JCS, which the Reverend Jack Shaw asserted was involved as a base of operations on 22 November 1963, as detailed in Chapter 2 of this book. "He is also known to have had an affair with a woman named Hazel who worked at Jagger-Chiles-Stovall, a Dallas company that worked on top-secret defense contracts and where Lee Harvey Oswald was hired upon his return from the Soviet Union."

"A confidential source has stated that Roscoe was a contract operative during this period and knew then that there was a plan to eliminate President Kennedy, who was seen as a threat to national security. This source also confirmed that Oswald's employment at [JCS] and Roscoe's involvement with Hazel gave both men access to the company's micro-dot technology, which may explain the FBI's persistent interest in Roscoe's personal effects and agents' remarks about microdots overheard during their searches of Geneva's house in Paris."

3. Roscoe was trained in photography, having been hired in that capacity by the DPD, on 7 October 1963, only weeks before the assassination. Roscoe took pride in his photographic skills and was in the habit of altering the faces of people in photographs. "His relatives thought it curious that he went to the trouble of erasing the faces of all the people in his pictures. They wondered where he had learned to do that, but naturally he never offered any explanation." "After eight months, Roscoe was finally classified a mechanic and remained

in the [584th Marine Air Control (MAC) Motor Pool] and continued sending home doctored photographs he had taken and developed himself."

4. "Roscoe continued to take advantage of his position with the police department to engineer (or sabotage) the crime scene investigations and may have supplied doctored photographs of Oswald."

5. Roscoe participated in the search at the Paine residence. "Due to his being assigned to Crime Scene Search, Roscoe took part in searches of Oswald's room in Oak Cliff and the house in Irving where Marina stayed with the children. It was this involvement that enabled Roscoe to take the photographs that he kept in the blue suitcase. Naturally, it also provided him an excellent opportunity to remove, plant, or alter evidence."

6. Roscoe and J.D. Tippit were neighbors and lived across the street from each other. "Although Tippit and Roscoe had been neighbors and friends, and their families had been close, Roscoe did not attend the fallen officer's funeral."

7. 24 November 1963, was Ricky's third birthday, and the family gathered together in their home waiting for Roscoe to come home for his party. Like Americans everywhere, they watched Jack Ruby shoot Oswald in the basement of the Police Courts Building amid a throng of reporters, and they were stunned. Moments later, Roscoe stormed into the house, screaming for them to hurry and get into the car. In a matter of moments, the White family was on the road, racing north toward Paris. Roscoe left his wife and kids with family there and disappeared for several days. Ricky had his birthday party the next day, without his dad.

8. Evidence suggests that Rock may have spent the missing days in a "safe house" in Central Texas, a place seen after by a colleague. He finally returned to Paris for his family, and they spent what Ricky remembers as a normal Christmas there.

9. "When Oswald was murdered, Roscoe suspected that the conspirators had decided to eliminate everyone who could implicate them, and he went to ground. After laying low in the safe house for several days, he received assurances, and reappeared. But he took steps to ensure that Geneva was not seen as a threat by having her submit to shock therapy."

"It is unlikely that Roscoe was murdered because he had threatened to disclose the Kennedy conspiracy. What is likely, and perhaps even more unsettling, is that after 1963 he continued in his role as a contract assassin, and the number of murders he committed may never be known. He was killed simply because he wanted out. This is supported by John Doe, who told Ricky that "nobody leaves the Company alive," "or words to that effect. Roscoe White's code name was 'MANDARIN.'"

(Author's note: Anything in quotations above comes from the original document.)

Indeed, Roscoe was a chameleon, as suggested above and seen in this collage:

Going back to our mock trial testimony, here is a very possible scenario, based, once again, on computer imaging technology. These overlays, which were supposed to have been shown at the mock trial on 18 November 2017, confirm an anatomical match to Backyard Man.

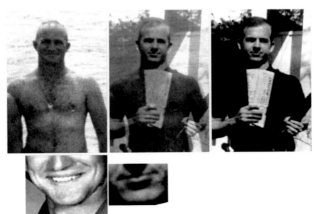

Zooming in, a detailed positive match is obtained, as the chin, neck, trapezoids, shoulders, arms, and torso fall into perfect alignment.

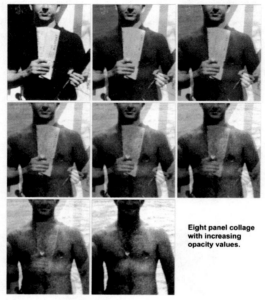

Eight panel collage with increasing opacity values.

And finally, it is also important to see how Oswald's torso fares when trying to overlay it onto CE133A. In this case, using a cutout of CE133A and color-coded probe and gallery image for easy visualization. Using the chins as a frame of reference, the following results are obtained:

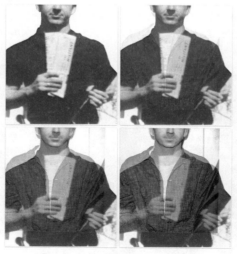

Four panel collage LHO at DPD over CE133C

Final Thoughts

A careful evaluation of the evidence requires one to consider what technology was available at the time. Despite the "ghost image" found at the DPD, it is doubtful that the entire body was superimposed onto a cutout matrix. The shadows of the body seem to be cast in the correct direction and flow naturally. It is the nose shadow which is at odds with the rest of the composition. The body also appear to be seamless, with no evidence of retouching. The question that remains is why would the DPD leave the "ghost" image behind? The information provided in the "lost" paper on Roscoe White certainly narrows it down to a much simpler technique, one which Roscoe refused to share with his family. This would be simple matte insertion of only the face, the same technique used to produce the autopsy photographs of the back of JFK's head.

"That's when two photographic elements come together visually and there's an overlap."

Roscoe had at his disposal probably the two best image processing labs available at the DPD and at JCS. The reader can refer to *The Last Investigation* by Gaeton Fonzi, p. 218, for a description of this process.

PART IV
DEALEY PLAZA IN DALLAS

17

Crossfire in Dealey Plaza Reexamined: The Shot from the Front

Over the years, many researchers have known and accepted that the JFK limousine was caught in a crossfire with multiple shooters from different locations in Dealey Plaza. One of the shot trajectories that has always been a focus of investigation has been the frontal shot, due the presence of a bullet hole in the windshield of the limousine, which was witnessed at Parkland Hospital by motorcycle patrolmen Sergeant Stavis Ellis, James Chaney and Harry Freeman,[1] and the fact that the doctors who attended President Kennedy that day immediately discovered that he had been hit from the front, right below the Adam's apple.

Doctor Malcolm Perry performed a tracheotomy by slightly enlarging that wound of entry by creating two small incisions, one of which was a very small vertical incision large enough to insert the tubing which would have assisted in providing oxygen to the moribund president.

Author and reporter Jimmy Breslin described this in the 14 December 1963 issue of *The Saturday Evening Post*:

> There was a mediastinal wound in connection with the bullet hole in the throat. This means air and blood were being packed together in the chest. Perry called for a scalpel. He was going to start a tracheotomy, which is opening the throat and inserting a tube into the windpipe. The incision had to be made below the small bullet wound.

Dr. Perry spoke about a gunshot wound to the president's throat in a 3:16 PM press conference that was broadcast live from Parkland Hospital:

Reporter: "Which way was the bullet coming on the neck wound? At him?"

Dr. Perry: "It appeared to be coming at him."

Reporter: "Doctor, describe the entrance wound. You think from the front in the throat?"

Dr. Perry: "The wound appeared to be an entrance wound in the front of the throat; yes, that is correct."[2]

After the press conference, the story began to change. The anatomically precise expression "throat wound" turned into the less specific "neck wound" after the Bethesda autopsy. In turn, the Warren Commission subtly began to alter the historical record by referring to the "neck wound" to give the impression that the president had experienced a shot from behind. But the medical staff at Parkland was in complete agreement that the wound was frontal. Speaking for the Parkland medical team, Charles Crenshaw, M.D., witnessed "a small opening about the diameter of a pencil at the midline of his throat to be an entry bullet hole. There was no doubt in my mind about the wound. I had seen dozens of them in the emergency room."[3]

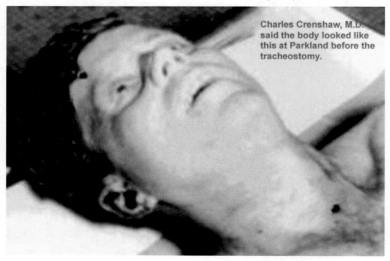

Charles Crenshaw, M.D. said the body looked like this at Parkland before the tracheostomy.

The Windshield

Robert Cutler, an architect and early researcher, who dubbed himself an "assassinologist," prepared meticulous and very accurate drawings of Dealey Plaza which are still relevant today because they predate the subtle changes that have been made to the landscape there. In late 1992, Charles Putensen published an article in *The Third Decade* titled "More about the Neck wound," which tried to deal with the frontal shot and its resultant throat wound. In response to this article, Cutler submitted the following drawing and comments on his take of where this shot came from and its trajectory:

The following was submitted by Robert Cutler in response to the Putensen article:

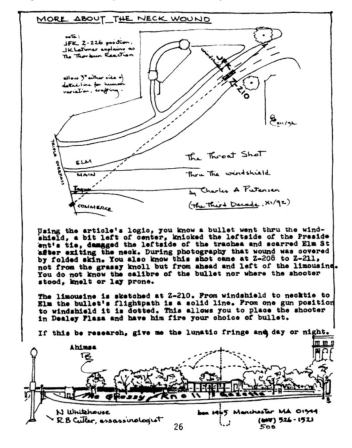

Clearly, Cutler understood the impossibility of the throat wound having originated anywhere to the right of JFK, hence the grassy knoll, the sidewalk, or anywhere on the north side of Elm Street. Cutler's logic is defined by the position of the limousine when the Zapruder film shows that JFK has obviously been hit between frames 208 and 211, and the orientation of the limo at that precise moment. This shot had to have gone through the windshield, and Cutler mentions it above.

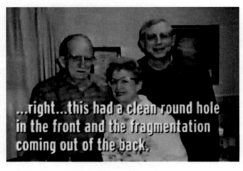

...right...this had a clean round hole in the front and the fragmentation coming out of the back.

Later on, the late Doug Weldon researched and provided the JFK assassination research community with the definitive study which answered all the questions surrounding the windshield of the JFK limousine and the possible source of the frontal shot which perforated the windshield. In *Murder in Dealey Plaza*, Weldon described an elaborate shell game in which multiple windshields appear to have been used by the Secret Service in an attempt to reenact the hole in the windshield.

Moreover, Weldon discovered that the Secret Service attempted to document the existence of a second windshield which contained a crack instead of a through-and-through bullet hole, with the inference being that it would have been caused by a fragment of concrete or possibly the shot that missed and presumably hit bystander James Tague. In his research in 1993, Weldon interviewed an ex-Ford Motor Company employee who witnessed events there the following Monday, 25 November 1963, related to the SX100 Lincoln Continental convertible limousine in which President Kennedy was assassinated. This witness spoke about the total reconstruction of the limousine's interiors and the removal and replacement of the windshield using the old one as a template which was subsequently destroyed. Even though Weldon knew the identity of this person, the information was withheld, at his request, until his demise in 2001. Nigel Turner, in *The Men Who Killed Kennedy*, identified George Whitaker, Sr., as the Ford Motor Company employee mentioned in Weldon's work. Douglas Horne, in his book, *Inside the Assassination Records Review Board: The U.S. Government's Final Attempt to Reconcile the Conflicting Medical Evidence in the Assassination of JFK—Volume V* (p. 1447) also identified Whitaker as the employee who witnessed the condition of the windshield and verified that the hole had been caused by a shot from the front, with fragmentation and beveling present on the inside. Shards of this fragmentation, called stippling, were known to have struck the president in the face and neck. These were later removed, and its effects covered with wax during the process of embalming and preparation of the body for burial.[4]

The accounts of both Weldon and Whitaker can be seen in *The Men Who Killed Kennedy*, episode No. 7. In *Murder in Dealey Plaza* (p. 154), the Weldon study concludes:

The windshield shot offered a perfect trajectory for a sniper firing from the top of the south side of the underpass, because of the unique downward slope of Elm Street, it is only a slight downward trajectory as a vehicle approached the overpass on Elm Street after the turn from Houston Street. Also, the angle of Elm Street, as one turns from Houston Street points the vehicle almost directly at the area of the south underpass. It is, for all practical purposes, not even a moving target, since for a couple of seconds the vehicle is virtually approaching the area head on.

Note that this conclusion exactly follows Cutler's earlier location of an overpass shooter near the south knoll right above Commerce Street.

Roy Schaeffer provided this UPI article published by the *Dayton Daily News* on 14 December 1963, which clearly refers to work being done in Detroit on the limousine after the assassination:

Kennedy Death Car Undergoing Refitting

Dayton
Daily News
12/14/63

DETROIT, Dec. 13 — (UPI)— The car in which President Kennedy was assassinated is being refitted with bulletproof glass and armor plate for use by President Johnson.

The work on the famous "bubbletop" presidential Continental is being done at a Ford Motor Co. experimental garage in suburban Dearborn. But Ford officials and the secret service declined to comment.

HOWEVER, sources said the limousine in which Mr. Kennedy was killed and Texas Gov. John Connally was wounded in Dallas Nov. 22 was brought to Dearborn under a cloak of secrecy Saturday night.

It was learned that the following work is being done:

ONE—A new windshield has been installed, lending credence to reports the old one was damaged in the shooting.

TWO—Springs and shock absorbers have been strengthened so the car can carry an additional 1,600 pounds of bullet proof armor plate.

THREE—The brakes also have been stiffened and the exhaust system reworked to accommodate the heavier load.

FOUR—New trim and carpeting have been installed in the back seat where Mr. Kennedy was riding when he was shot.

"A new windshield has been installed, lending credence to reports the old one was damaged in the shooting." (in red above)

Anthony DeFiore discovered the reaction of Roy Kellerman in Zapruder frame 306 to what appears to be stippling, where he can be seen touching his left cheek in reaction to the shot that came through the windshield.[5] DeFiore also verified with Vince Palamara, an authority on the Secret Service, that the Secret Service did not use earpieces at the time, therefore, the actions of Kellerman cannot be attributed to the use of this device.[6] Furthermore, studying the radio transcripts, DeFiore established that Kellerman was not speaking on the radio at this point either.[7]

The Hole in the Windshield Seen in Altgens6

As described in *Murder in Dealey Plaza* and *Assassination Science*, Roy Schaeffer is credited with finding the hole in the windshield in Altgens6, depicted as a hole in the center of a nebulae, slightly to the right and above the rear-view mirror.

In 1994, Schaeffer produced a DVD called *Photographic Interpretation of President Kennedy's Assassination*, in which he studied possible locations from which a frontal shot would have caused the damage described by Weldon and Fetzer. Schaeffer proposed that the frontal shot indeed originated from the south side of Dealey Plaza, specifically the south side of Commerce Street, but possibly not from as high a location as the overpass would have provided, and as suggested by Weldon.

He proposed a lower and flattened out trajectory to this shot and the possibility that it might have come from the sidewalk area of the tunnel under the overpass. Furthermore, Schaeffer discovered an electrical utility junction box which conveniently could have been used to stash away any weapon that could have been used after the deed. More on this will follow.

The Vertical Angle

Anthony DeFiore's study, "Z225," agrees with Doug Weldon's conclusion that the frontal shot originated from the corner of the overpass at the south side of Dealey Plaza. Even though the lateral angle seems to verify a shot from this general area, the vertical angle, plus the down slope of Elm Street, seem to create a problem for this hypothesis. The following images show the limousine as it made its way from the intersection of Houston and Elm Streets down Elm. By plotting a simple line between the area of the hole in the windshield and the president's throat, the vertical angle changes drastically:

In this Towner slide, the trajectory is downward from the front to back.

As the limousine advances down Elm Street, this angle begins to level off as seen in the Croft photograph below:

At this point we must begin to account for the down slope of Elm Street.

This is an image taken from Daryl Weatherly's land plot survey published in 1994, mapping the down slope of Elm Street, and which also shows matching marks for Zapruder frames 61, 171, 232 and 285.

These empirical results confirm the degree of down slope of Elm Street.

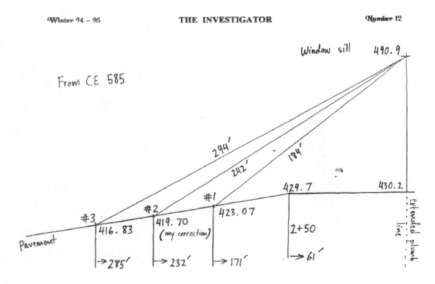

This image at Z230 from DeFiore's study, shows a very slight downward angle between the hole in the windshield and JFK's throat.

And this image is the same line plotted at Zapruder frame 246, well after the frontal shot, which is estimated to have occurred between Z208 and Z211, while the limo was hidden behind the Stemmons Freeway sign.

Many witnesses, among them TSBD manager Roy Truly, witnessed the limo almost jumping onto the curb while making the turn onto Elm Street. Truly was standing right at the curb where this happened.[8] Secret Service Agent—and driver of the limousine—William Greer, made that turn wide from Houston onto Elm Street, forcing him to make a correction which would have brought the limo into perfect alignment for this shot. This image, using the Queen Mary, and taken during the FBI reenactment of the shooting, shows the orientation of the limousine after it negotiated the turn onto Elm Street:

On the weekend of 22 November 2014, Professor Jim Fetzer, Gary King, and the author visited this spot to verify Roy's findings. The area in question is this one:

As seen in this image, the first "cubby hole" provides an excellent position for a sniper with a silenced weapon where the cement railing and column meet to form the perfect rifle support stand. Here is the view from that position which offers a perfect flat and low trajectory with the vehicle being practically a stationary target for various seconds as described in the paragraph cited from *Murder in Dealey Plaza* above. This photograph was taken while standing. The actual posture of a sniper from this position would possibly have been slightly lower as he would have used the cement railing for support and the vertical column for cover. Professor James Norwood has noted that this angle is also in a perfect crossfire position for a shot coming from the second floor of the Dal-Tex Building in the background.

This next image reveals that the sidewalks on both the north and south ends of the overpass connect all the way to the other side as one enters Dealey Plaza from the west. This means that access to the area would have been easily controlled by the deployment of either a DPD officer who was aware of what was about to happen, or a DPD impostor.

As far as cars being able to interfere with a shot from this area is concerned, this blowup from the Cancellare photograph shows there was ample clearance for this shot. Furthermore, James Tague testified that his intention originally had not been to see the parade, rather he was forced to do so because the cars in front of him on Commerce had come to a stop.[9] This suggests that the cars seen in this photograph, which are at a standstill, would have provided even more cover for our proposed shooting position.

James Tague at right standing next to abutment and his car.

And finally, as suggested by Schaeffer, the most astonishing and peculiar feature enjoyed by a sniper at this position is that he would have been able to easily stash away his weapon in this utility box and just walk away and mingle with the crowd. He would not even have gotten dirty by making his escape via the underground drainage system that exists under Dealey Plaza.

JFK researcher Ray Hale happened to come upon the box while it was open, and supplied these extraordinary images showing the inner dimensions of the box:

(Author's note: Special contributions to this chapter were made by Roy Schaeffer and Professor James Norwood.)

ENDNOTES

1. Fred Newcomb tapes, 1971, transcribed by Larry Rivera, 2014
2. Horne, Douglas, *Inside the Assassination Records Review Board: The U.S. Government's Final Attempt to Reconcile the Conflicting Medical Evidence in the Assassination of JFK—Volume 2*, p. 646; see also Mary Ferrell Foundation website (maryferrell.org). The audio and video recordings of Dr. Perry's press conference were lost. However, a stenographer's transcript of the conference surfaced in the Lyndon B. Johnson Presidential Library decades later.
3. Crenshaw, M.D., Charles A. with Hansen and Shaw, *JFK—Conspiracy of Silence*, (1992), p. 4.
4. ARRB, Thomas Evan Robinson, 26 May 1992 interview
5. Anthony DeFiore, "Z225" Part 2, pp. 142, 161
6. Ibid. "Z225" Part 2, p.142
7. Ibid. 161
8. WC3H220
9. WC7H553

> Mr. TRULY. That is right.
>
> And the President's car following close behind came along at an average speed of 10 or 15 miles an hour. It wasn't that much, because they were getting ready to turn. And the driver of the Presidential car swung out too far to the right, and he came almost within an inch of running into this little abutment here, between Elm and the Parkway. And he slowed down perceptibly and pulled back to the left to get over into the middle lane of the parkway. Not being familiar with the street, he came too far out this way when he made his turn.
>
> Mr. BELIN. He came too far to the north before he made his curve, and as he curved—as he made his left turn from Houston onto the street leading to the expressway, he almost hit this north curb?
>
> Mr. TRULY. That is right. Just before he got to it, he had to almost stop, to pull over to the left.
>
> If he had maintained his speed, he would probably have hit this little section here.

220

18

Zeroing in on JFK's
Fatal Head Shot

*The occipitoparietal, which is a part of the back of the head, had
a huge flap. The damage a rifle bullet does **as it comes out of a
person's body** is unbelievable.*

—Dr. Malcolm Perry, *The Saturday Evening Post*
14 December 1963

Dr. David Mantik, M.D., Ph.D., has published the definitive
study which locates the so-called "Harper Fragment" in the
rear of JFK's skull, the occipitoparietal area. These two images,
from Dr. Mantik's book, *John F. Kennedy's Head Wounds: A Final
Synthesis—and a New Analysis of the Harper Fragment*, illustrate
the exact location where a massive blowout in the back of the head
was observed by more than 20 witnesses at Parkland Hospital and
Bethesda Hospital, among them seven trained doctors who were used
to dealing with gunshot wounds on a daily basis.[1]

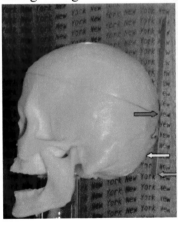 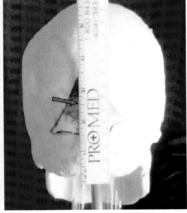

Two Working Hypotheses

In order to ascertain how the Harper Fragment and its corresponding
defect was produced, it is necessary to establish two distinct
hypotheses, which should in turn allow us to study and possibly

determine the origin of the shot that caused it. The two hypotheses covered in this chapter are:

1. The shot over JFK's right eye and brow ridge, near the hairline, which appears to line up with the location of the exit wound established by Dr. Mantik.

2. Its upward trajectory, based on the position and forward tilt of the president, and the position of the limousine on the down slope of Elm Street.

Over the years, researchers have hypothesized that the dramatic and shocking source of the head shot that instantaneously killed JFK came from either the picket fence atop the grassy knoll, or further down the way, where a raised sewer opening and grill cover abuts with the triple overpass cement railing and the picket fence itself.

Malcolm Kilduff, when announcing the death of President Kennedy, pointed above his right eyebrow and issued this stunning statement: "Uh, Dr. Burkley told me that it's, it's a simple matter, Tom, of, uh, of a bullet, right through the head."[2]

By using as a base Dr. Mantik's groundbreaking work, in conjunction with simple geometrical and computer imaging analysis, this chapter will attempt to establish the origin and trajectory of the shot which produced the fatal wound which took the life of our 35th president.

The second working hypothesis mentioned above follows the research of Tom Wilson and Jack Brazil, who independently of each other, in the early 1990s, established that the head shot which took JFK's skull off could have originated from the storm drain on the north curb of Elm Street.[3]

This hypothesis, however, is nothing new. In 1967, Jim Garrison sent investigators to Dealey Plaza, and following leads that he had received from Lillian Castellano, his men explored the intricate underground system of storm drains and sewers that led to the nearby Trinity River. In the mid-1960s Castellano obtained and disseminated among first-generation researchers, the actual plans and blueprints that showed this intricate system that was beneath Dealey Plaza.[4]

Penn Jones (above right) used to give journalists who were brave enough to enter the storm drain via the manhole cover on the sidewalk, live demonstrations, by standing in the middle of Elm Street where the President was struck at Z313, and showing them what a clear shot a concealed sniper would have enjoyed from that position.[5]

Garrison's Photograph

This very important photograph snapped by Jim Garrison's investigators was taken for the purpose of showing that an assassin inside the storm drain would have had ample clearance to execute a virtually point-blank shot, especially if the conspirators, including Secret Service driver Bill Greer, were in on the plot and had planned to bring the limousine, in coordinated fashion, to stop right in the middle of Elm Street.

The third photograph was described as taken from the inside of a sewer opening facing the north side of Elm Street, showing people in a convertible visible from the chest up.

Garrison said a small truck was parked "for an unusually long period" directly over a manhole leading into this sewer opening on the day of the assassination.

Garrison said last week one of the shots fired at Kennedy came from one of these sewer openings.

The Evening Star 12/15/67

(Author's note: The position of the car shown above is exactly abreast of the storm drain and is not representative of JFK limousine position at Z313.)

Moreover, Garrison was completely convinced that this is where the shot that did most of the damage came from,[6] adding that:

. . . *a small truck was parked "for an unusually long period" directly over a manhole leading into this sewer opening on the day of the assassination.*

In the late 1960s, Beverly Brunson pointed out Roy Kellerman's Warren Commission testimony at Volume 2, p. 66, which unequivocally stated that he felt that shots came into the vehicle in an upward trajectory, "an upshot into the vehicle," were Kellerman's exact words. Brunson observed how, in predictable fashion, and showing a pattern that he had already established, Arlen Specter tried to muddy the waters as soon as this sensitive piece of information was being discussed and put into the record. Specter clearly did not want to elaborate, and Brunson's comments bear this out. Brunson's research is reproduced in the next chapter in its original state.

All of which is to say, that the Commission, especially Arlen Specter, was well aware of the possibility that the fatal shot could have had an upward trajectory, seriously jeopardizing the rear shot conclusion that was eventually adopted and seared into the historical record.

The Observations of John Judge

Legendary JFK researcher, activist, and Coalition On Political Assassinations—COPA—co-founder John Judge was completely convinced of a shot coming from the storm drain. In this 2001 email, he expressed why he believed this to be the case:

"I [missed the earlier part of this exchange but] have always believed the fatal shot came from the storm sewer on Elm Street to the right front of the motorcade.

This was not from speculation or photo angling. The letter from Ed T, whoever that is, hits the nail on the head. I used to crawl down in the sewer with Penn Jones in '60s and it is quite different today. For one thing, the bottom has been filled in (note the flattening of the pipe opening at the bottom) and the opening that used to come up to my armpits now only reaches my waist.

Oliver Stone repaved the street for his film and considerably reduced the size of the opening onto the street. It was more than ample and wide for the head shot. And Penn Jones, Jim Garrison and other critics placed the shot there from reports by witnesses and the physical evidence. It was Mark Lane in the late '60s who tried to move everyone up to the grassy knoll.

1. Ear-witnesses heard a completely different sound from the last shot fired, one saying it echoed as if in a sewer.

2. Connally and others in the motorcade smelled gunpowder during the events. Smoke rose upwards from the fence area atop the grassy knoll and would not have reached them. However, the passing of the first car in the motorcade would suck air and smoke out of the sewer hole and along the route of the motorcade.

3. A shot from the grassy knoll would have reached JFK's head at a downward angle, exiting from the base of his skull, and driving him down into the seat as it sent him backwards. A close examination of his reaction in both Zapruder and Nix films shows that he rises up from the seat as he is thrown back at over 100 mph. The fatal shot blew out the upper right portion of his skull. Both are consistent with a shot from below.

4. Brain matter and skull fragments explode upwards and travel back and to the left with great velocity at the moment of impact. Jackie later revealed that she picked up a portion of skull on the left rear of the car behind her seat, before being pushed back in by Clint Hill. A portion of skull was found near the curb on the south side of Elm, nearly 30 feet behind the position of the car at the point of the fatal shot and across the street.

5. Officer Billy Hargis was riding his motorcycle to the left rear of JFK's limousine and witnessed the head shot. He was quoted in the Warren Commission testimony saying that he was hit so hard with a skull fragment through his leather jacket that he thought he had been hit by a bullet. He looked down to see he was covered with blood, stopped and got off his motorcycle, and said "Am I hit?" He later parked the motorcycle over the opening of the sewer and ran up the grassy knoll with other witnesses. Quoted in *The Dallas Morning News* on the 30th observance of the assassination, Hargis recalled the event and said the brain and blood matter arced up and came down on him. Again, all this is more consistent with a shot from below and to the front.

6. The storm sewer is a good hidden location, one that a military sniper would choose. Penn Jones crawled through the pipes and discovered that going west along Elm leads to the vertical pipe that opens behind the grassy knoll fence near the overpass, and going across Elm and to the east leads to a grate in the basement of the Dallas jail. He yelled out when he got there, but no one responded." [7]

The Harper Fragment

The Harper Fragment was found by Billy Harper on 23 November 1963 at approximately 5:30 PM beyond the south infield of Dealey Plaza, well in front of JFK's limousine position.[8]

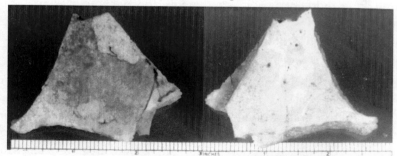

Harper Fragment From CD1269: Outer (left) and Inner (right)

Fortunately, it was immediately photographed at the behest of Billy's uncle Jack, who was an M.D. in his own right.[9] That is the only reason that today we know what it actually looked like. Later on, the FBI also photographed *and* **X-rayed** this piece of skull bone.[10] It ultimately fell into the hands of Admiral George Burkley and subsequently disappeared.[11] It was, in effect, a very large piece of skull measuring 2.73" x 2.13", the images of which, over the years, Dr. Mantik has thoroughly studied to determine its exact anatomical source.[12] Here are some 3D renderings of the Harper Fragment using the 3D program Blender:

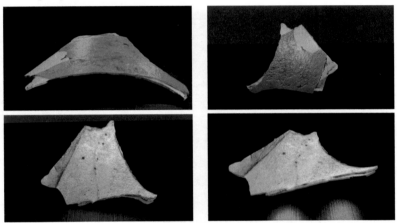

In September 1969, Harper pinpointed for Howard Roffman the location where he found it and marked the spot in this diagram:

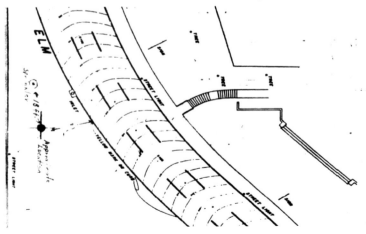

It would seem inconceivable that such a large piece of skull could have remained undetected for close to 30 hours after the fatal head shot which killed JFK. Several of the Murray photographs show "agents"—within minutes of the assassination—combing the infield beyond the south side of Elm Street in Dealey Plaza looking for, locating, and pocketing crucial evidence which was never inventoried and entered as evidence.[13]

Dr. Mantik clearly remains skeptical about how, when and where the Harper Fragment might have landed where it was found:

Section 7. Conclusions

1. If Harper's "spot" had been just 25 feet left (i.e., south) of the limousine at Z-313 and if HF had been ejected at Z-313 (e.g., from a frontal shot), then an occipital site of origin for HF would be credible. This has been the traditional view of WC critics—even though Harper's discovery site is inconsistent with this. I agree that if HF had landed at Harper's site then the ensuing argument for a frontal shot seems desperate. However, much uncertainty attaches to this scenario. In particular, the Harper fragment was probably moved after it landed. Moreover, it is no longer certain *when* HF was ejected, much less what JFK's head position was at that critical moment. This uncertainty derives from critically placed witnesses (who describe a headshot well after Z-313), from the WC data in Marler's review, from the *Newsweek* illustration, and from the early Secret Service photographs. In fact, HF may have been ejected farther down Elm Street (well beyond Z-313), much closer to Harper's discovery site. If HF was parietal, though, then Harper's discovery site becomes a bit more likely (than an occipital origin would be). *Based on the discovery site alone* though, we cannot know when HF was ejected, or exactly where it landed. In my opinion, Harper's discovery site is not very useful.

Sargent Stavis Ellis

Sergeant Stavis Ellis

The stunning revelations of Dallas Police Sergeant Stavis Ellis, who was interviewed via telephone on 21 April 1971, by Gil Toft on behalf of Fred Newcomb for his book *Murder from Within: Lyndon Johnson's Plot Against President Kennedy*, offer a tantalizing possibility of the provenance of the Harper Fragment: [14]

(Author's note: Toft used the pseudonym "John Whitney.")

Whitney: Did you see any of the wounds on him at all?
Ellis: No I didn't, I didn't get that close, I know that down on the street a piece of his skull blew out of the car and blew over on the grass, and a kid picked it up, a Secret Service man took it away from him and threw it in the back of the car. (pause) We, our people, right there at the motor knew how bad he was hurt, I knew he was hit, I didn't know how bad he was hit until my man Chaney came up there and said he - no chance, he ain't got no chance but let's go - he said his head was just - well I didn't really know for sure until we got to the hospital, there wasn't any chance for him, after talking to how often they come in. (last part unintelligible)
Whitney: That piece of bone that the Secret Service man took from that young boy you say in the grass - when he came to the hospital he threw it in the car there.
Ellis: No, he put it in the car back at the - right there as it happened as I remember.
Whitney: As it happened at the street there on Elm?
Ellis: Yes sir.
Whitney: The President's limousine stopped for a while, right at that point?
Ellis: Well no it didn't stop, it almost stopped.

The interviewer was so taken aback by the revelation of the skull fragment, that he later came back to that subject towards the end of the interview, and asked for a clarification:

Whitney: So much stuff coming into my head, I can hardly hold it all together. Ah, I'm trying to think, you saw the SS, Secret Service man put the piece of skull in the car was that as you said at the hospital he did that you said? (52:35)
Ellis: He put it in there, I think, I believe he put it, threw it back in there, right.....(pause) right there where it happened there I remember, cause the kid that gave it to him it was on the grass on the side of the street there that - where it happened..
Whitney: He picked it up right there on Elm St.
Ellis: The kid picked it up, had it and gave it to the Secret Service man took it away from him.
Whitney: You remember seeing that, you say over on Elm Street.
Ellis: I beg your pardon?
Whitney: You say you remember seeing that over on the by the Depository, when the Secret Service man took the skull...
Ellis: No I didn't see him put it in there at all.
Whitney: You didn't,
Ellis: No I just..
Whitney: What made you feel - how'd it get in there?
Ellis: One of my men saw him do it - motorcycle officer...
Whitney: You don't remember who that was.
Ellis: It was either Chaney or Jackson, one of the two.

Clearly, this event is not seen in the extant Zapruder film, however, that is subject for another day. What is important to note here is that this fragment did not remain in Dealey Plaza and was removed immediately from the scene by an unidentified Secret Service agent, who tossed it into the limousine. Outside of speculation, it is not inconceivable that this was actually the Harper Fragment which later, well after the fact, could have been re-positioned down Elm Street, southwest of the location of the head shot at Z313, where it was found the next day by Billy Harper. The purpose of this, of course, would have been to create "evidence" that would have supported a shot from behind, hence, the southeast window of the sixth floor of the TSBD.

In 2000, Dr. Mantik created this diagram for Jim Fetzer's *Murder in Dealey Plaza*, where he roughly set the anatomical location of the Harper Fragment: [15]

405

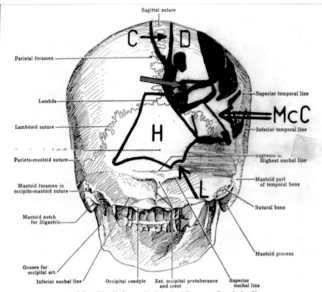

485   Skull from behind—Norma Occipitalis

The Opinion of Dr. Robert Grossman

Dr. Robert Grossman, a neurosurgeon who attended to JFK at Parkland Hospital that day drew this diagram about his recollections. When shown the HSCA Ida Dox drawing, (above) which showed the back of the head intact, he unequivocally remarked: "That's completely incorrect."[16]

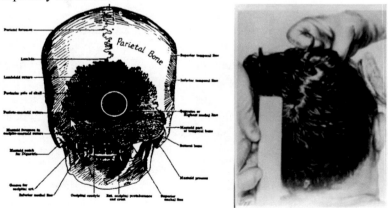

As stated in the introduction of this chapter, Dr. Mantik has updated and reiterated his expert analysis by introducing actual skull images with an overlay (shown earlier above), which represents the Harper

Fragment, to show the reader where it came from. The actual anatomical and technical reasoning for Dr. Mantik's conclusion is beyond the scope of this chapter, therefore, the reader is referred to that source. Dr. Mantik's image has been enhanced to more clearly show the exact position of the Harper Fragment:

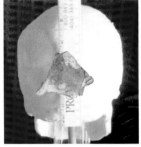

In January 2015, irrefutable proof was discovered revealing the magnitude of the blowout of the back of the head when we obtained a very clear copy of Zapruder frame 343, which showed the hole enhanced by the position of Jackie's white glove, providing the perfect background that enabled us to unequivocally identify the defect.

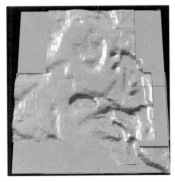

When this image is rendered in 3D by Blender, the blowout's dimensions and shape are shown in shocking detail (left).

This rendering of Jackie reacting to the blowout in the back of the head of JFK at Z343 shows the capabilities of Blender in "solid mode." The extrusion of figures in images and the ability to

407

render 2D images in 3D is one of the most important functions of the program.

JFK's Forward Tilt

In Dealey Plaza, the very first impression which strikes the visitor is undoubtedly the dimensions of the site and the way angles come into play. For example, the gentle "S" curvature of Elm Street, along with its down slope are very important considerations when trying to discern the possible direction of shots which were fired upon the JFK limousine. It is therefore of utmost importance that we consider not only the downward angle of the JFK limousine, but more importantly, the forward tilt of the president's head—one crucial millisecond before the head shot(s)—seen at Zapruder frame 313. This is not a new concept. Joseph Riley, Ph.D., addressed this in 1993, stressing its importance in the vertical plane.[17] In the same manner, Riley wrote about the importance of the lateral plane, which would have been affected by the rotation of JFK's head.

Indeed, Dr. Mantik also discusses the forward tilt at Z313 in his book and puzzles over how the Harper Fragment could have landed where it was found based on this position.[18] Another interesting point raised by Dr. Mantik is the wind, clearly seen by observing the overcoats of Mary Moorman and Jean Hill, blowing in a brisk easterly direction, away from the limo, and how this could have affected the flight of the Harper Fragment.[19] Dr. Mantik also raises the possibility of the re-positioning of the Harper Fragment,[20] bolstered many years later by the rediscovery of the Sergeant Ellis tapes, cited above. (Author's note: At the time of publication of his book, Dr. Mantik was not aware of the Stavis Ellis tape.)

The following illustration—video enhanced—shows the exact position of JFK's head prior to the head shot which shows the spray of matter.

A video enhanced display—the exact moment between frames Z312 and Z313, perhaps one thousand-millionth of a second (nanosecond)—showing the exact position before head shot.

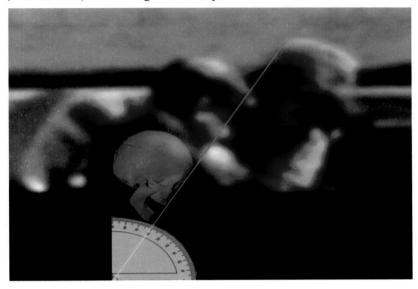

Costella Z312—JFK's forward tilt measures out to approximately 60° (this of course, relative to the Zapruder film. These frames from the Z film show absolutely no Elm Street down slope.)

For reasons unknown and never revealed to this day, strange, out-of-the-ordinary, yellow stripes had been painted on the south curb of Elm Street *the day before*, where this paint had not yet completely dried by the time the motorcade drove down Elm Street. These visual signs clearly would have offered perfect markers to guide the stoppage of the JFK limo.[21]

Kill zones depicted by yellow paint on curb offered visual signals for coordination of shots.

This next image from the Couch film shows the storm drain and the lateral angle it would have provided a sniper positioned inside the structure:

409

This amazing image actually shows the position JFK would have been relative to the storm drain, in the center lane of Elm Street, when he received the head shot at Z313, practically a head-on shot.

This drawing is from Architect/Researcher Robert Cutler's diagram of Dealey Plaza, showing overhead relative positions of the storm drain, the limousine and the yellow markers. Two very important details to consider here are: 1) The location of limousine at Z313 exactly at the yellow marker at Mary Moorman's feet, and 2) The trajectory lines up with Charles and Joey Brehm, where an object of some kind is known to have landed right at their feet.[22] As stated above, Stavis Ellis confirmed a piece of skull landed on the infield grass of the south side of Elm, which was snatched by a Secret Service agent from a boy who had picked it up.

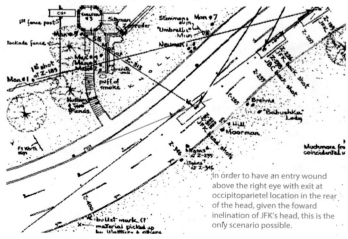

In order to have an entry wound above the right eye with exit at occipitoparietel location in the rear of the head, given the foward inclination of JFK's head, this is the only scenario possible.

410

Professor Jim Fetzer points out the storm drain with manhole cover as it looked on 22 November 2014. Notice the down slope of Elm and how several layers of asphalt have narrowed the gap. Cover has been welded shut. (photo credit Larry Rivera)

View from area of storm drain while standing.

View at street level from storm drain as car approaches in center lane.

Blender rendering at Z313, with a camera positioned inside the storm drain.

Hargis And Martin Sprayed with Debris

The next image, courtesy of Tyler Newcomb, whose father Fred co-wrote *Murder from Within*, shows an approximate pattern of debris from JFK's head and how it actually affected all four of the motorcycle escorts, more so on the left, where Bobby Hargis was hit with such force that he thought he himself had been hit by gunfire.

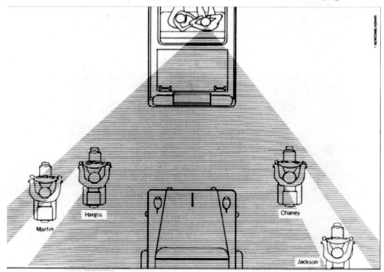

Fig. 3-8 Positions of motorcycle escort officers and limousine at the time of the fatal shot. Shaded area depicts debris forced out by shot fired directly ahead of the President.

Dino Brugioni's Observations

Douglas Horne interviewed National Photographic Interpretation Center's (NPIC) Dino Brugioni in 2015 about his recollections the weekend of the assassination when the Zapruder film was delivered to the NPIC by the Secret Service. Here is a transcript of what Brugioni told Horne and Peter Janney in different interviews:[23]

Dino Brugioni: The one that I remember was that there was a chunk of body, the head in . . . above his head and . . . then there was . . . like a little mist or cloud around it. (35:12)

Douglas Horne: The most startling thing I learned about the missing briefing boards made from the true original film is that Dino Brugioni, in the film that he studied on November 23rd, saw a very different head explosion than we see today in the film in the National Archives. Dino Brugioni as he explained to Peter Janney in a personal interview in April of 2011—Dino Brugioni saw a much larger head explosion that went three or four feet into the air (35:48) above President Kennedy's head. He described the head explosion that we see today in frame 313 of the extant film as being too low in the image, his head explosion was very high into the air, and when Dino found out that the present version of the Zapruder film only has one frame showing the head explosion, frame 313, he was astounded.

Brugioni: What I saw was more than that.

Peter Janney: This is frame 313, so you saw more pink mist, going up, straight up?

Brugioni: I remember the splatter was high, you know, say, three or four feet from his head.

Janney: Ah, huh, up in the air?

Brugioni: Yeah, uh huh.

Janney: This is the only frame on the whole Zapruder film that you get to see . . .

Brugioni: No, there is more than that.

Janney: So, you're saying there was more than one frame, for sure. How many more frames do you think there would be?

Brugioni: I don't know. But all I know is that we were shocked . . . when we saw it.

413

Janney: Right, right.

Brugioni: Have you been down to the archives yet for the Zapruder film? They claim that's the true one?

Janney: That's the true one, right. The one with the frames that we just looked at. No—you're shaking your head. It's not the true one, is it? Is that what you mean?

Brugioni: I'd say the one that I saw, his head was way high on, up in his head.

Janney: Yeah, the debris . . .

Brugioni: And I can't imagine that there would only be one frame, what I saw was more than what, what you have there.

Clearly, the action of the debris field seen by Brugioni was more vertical than horizontal, which would suggest a shot from a lower level, going in an upward direction, exactly as described by Kellerman.

Frangible Bullets—James Jenkins

Many researchers have assumed that frangible or exploding bullets were used in the assassination. James Jenkins was present during the entire autopsy, even remaining in the room while he tried to take a break to have a sandwich.[24]

```
"Were you there all of the time?"
"I was there all of the time. The only time I was away from
the table was probably five or ten minutes when I was told to
get a sandwich. But I did not leave the room."
```

Here is what Jenkins saw that night:

```
May 24, 1991

     Jenkins discussed exploding bullets. Prussic acid explodes
on contact. If used in exploding bullets, there would be
fragments throughout the brain if there was an explosive bullet.
"But the brain that I saw was virtually intact, and there were
no fragments. The flap in the Zapruder film is much bigger than
in the pics and at the autopsy."     James Curtis Jenkins Confidential 05/24/91
```

This key observation by someone who was present throughout the autopsy suggests a bullet or bullets that traversed the entire skull, leaving no fragments behind.

It is extremely important to point out that the position of the Harper Fragment is off-center, meaning that it lays somewhat slightly left of center, of the posterior view of the skull. This would suggest a shot coming in from right to left as the limousine moved west on Elm

Street. Here is a bisected version of the posterior view shown earlier:

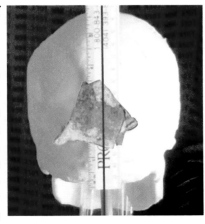

The Shot Above the Right Eye

Since the HSCA interview of mortician Tom Robinson by Andrew Purdy in 1977, there have been documented references to a hole above the right eye of JFK. Douglas Horne summarized these references in his historic five-part video series *Altered History: Exposing Deceit and Deception in the JFK Assassination Medical Evidence.*

From: "Altered History Exposing Deceit and Deception in the JFK Assassination Medical Evidence"

Multiple Lines of Evidence indicate that this damage above JFK's right eye was the result of surgical tampering prior to the autopsy:

- In 1988, **Dr. Paul Peters** of Parkland Hospital described this damage in a documentary televised by PBS as **"an incision"** and confirmed that it was **not present** when JFK was treated at Parkland Hospital.
- Two witnesses---**Joe O'Donnell and Dennis David**---profess to have seen autopsy photos *not in the official collection today* that depicted a small bullet entry wound at this exact site. (The removal of these photos from the official autopsy collection indicates intent---*namely, the elimination of any forensic evidence supporting frontal shots.*)
- Mortician Tom Robinson first described seeing a small hole in JFK's cranium, at this approximate site, to the HSCA staff in 1977.
- Dr. Boswell, one of the two Navy pathologists, first attempted to describe this V-shaped damage as a "laceration" during his testimony to the ARRB; later during his deposition he described it as **"an incised wound"---i.e, an incision**---an obvious Freudian slip.

As noted above, Dennis David and Joe O'Donnell were actual witnesses to seeing photographs of JFK before the autopsy. Dennis David was shown these photographs by Navy Photographer Lt. Commander William Pitzer, which showed what appeared to be a clean entrance wound at this location.

Joe O'Donnell was even more specific, estimating its size to have been 3/8". This ARRB call report by Horne, dated 28 February 1997, is an extremely important document:

CALL REPORT: PUBLIC

Document's Author: Douglas Home/ARRB   **Date Created:** 02/28/97

The Players
Who called whom?   Jeremy Gunn called Joe O'Donnell of Witnesses/Consultants, Douglas Home called Joe O'Donnell of Witnesses/Consultants, Dave Montague called Joe O'Donnell of Witnesses/Consultants, David Marwell called Joe O'Donnell of Witnesses/Consultants

Description of the Call
Date: 02/28/97
Subject: ARRB Interviewed Joe O'Donnell (Revised 3/03/97)

-First Viewing: He said Knudsen showed him about 12 each B & W glossy prints, about 5" X 7" in size, which were post mortem images of the President. He said the images were quite clear and that he assumed they were first generation prints. He said some images were close-ups of the head, some were close-ups of the shoulders, and that some were views of the entire body. He said that in some images the President was lying on his back, and in some images he was lying on his stomach. He said he remembers a photograph of a gaping wound in the back of the head which was big enough to put a fist through, in which the image clearly showed a total absence of hair and bone, and a cavity which was the result of a lot of interior matter missing from inside the cranium. He said that another image showed a small round hole above the President's right eye, which he interpreted as an entry wound made by the same bullet which exited from the large wound in the back of the head.

-Second Viewing: At a subsequent private viewing, he said Knudsen showed him approximately 6 to 8 (and no more than 10) additional glossy B & W prints of post mortem photographs of President Kennedy, in which the small round hole above the right eye was no longer visible, and in which the back of the head now looked completely intact. He said that the appearance of the hair in the "intact back of the head" photograph(s) was wet, clean, and freshly combed. His interpretation of the differences in the photographs of the President's head was to attribute the differences to the restorative work of the embalmers.

-On the first occasion, he was shown approximately 12 ea 5" X 7" B & W photos. The views included the President lying on his stomach, and closeups of the back of the head. He said that the back-of-the-head photograph(s) showed a hole in the back of the head, about 2" above the hairline, about the size of a grapefruit; the hole clearly penetrated the skull and was very deep. Another one of the photographs showed a hole in the forehead above the right eye which was a round wound about 3/8" in diameter which he interpreted as a gunshot wound.

Not only did O'Donnell estimate the size of the wound, he even associated it as being the shot that caused the blowout in the back of the head, which we have shown to be clearly visible in frame 343 of the Zapruder film.

This modified version of the "Stare of Death" photograph—seen in Chapter 18—shows what Charles Crenshaw, M.D., saw when JFK was

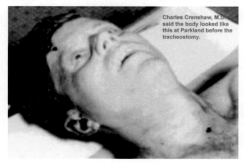

Charles Crenshaw, M.D., said the body looked like this at Parkland before the tracheostomy.

wheeled into the emergency room, right before an emergency tracheostomy was performed by Dr. Malcolm Perry. Note the clean entry wounds above the right eyebrow near the hairline and right below the Adam's apple:

As noted by Horne above, the entrance wound was later obliterated and made to look like a "V-shaped incised wound," according to Dr. Thornton Boswell, who was one of the Navy pathologists who performed the autopsy the night of 22 November.

Quentin Schwinn

Dr. Mantik presents the observations of Quentin Schwinn and offers some of his background:

"Quentin Schwinn, an imaging specialist who, while a student at the Rochester Institute of Technology (several years after the sunset of the HSCA), saw an apparent authentic autopsy photo with a frontal entry wound in the right high forehead, near the hairline."[25]

In 2010, Horne was contacted by Mr. Schwinn, subsequently maintaining a three-year interview relationship with Schwinn, where he thoroughly verified his credibility, background and credentials.[26] As far as Horne is concerned, Schwinn is "The Real Deal" and qualifies him as a "reliable witness."[27] In late 1982 or early 1983, as part of the recruitment process for a job, Schwinn was shown a positive color transparency of JFK right before autopsy, which Schwinn vividly recalled as being completely different from what is in the public domain today, which shows a grotesque jagged anomaly in the area of the throat and what appear to be V-shaped cuts above and around the right temple area, and above the right eye.

Horne has established that this image is not part of the official collection of autopsy photographs and X-rays. Absent this image, Horne and Schwinn decided to try to re-create the image by recruiting medical illustrators to draw what Schwinn had seen.[28]

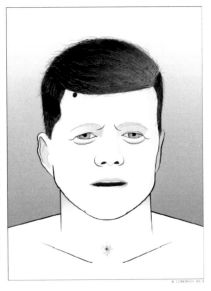

After some trial and error, and the evaluation of several certified medical illustrators, Schwinn's re-creation of what he was shown in 1982/83, is shown above right. This is almost an exact match to what David and O'Donnell described seeing.

So, when we put all of this data together in a comprehensive collage, using Dr. Mantik's images as a frame of reference to try to trace the trajectory of the head shot which produced the Harper Fragment, this is the result:

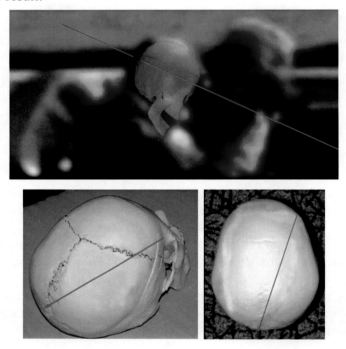

These modified images from Mantik's book trace the movement of the hypothetical shot that produced the Harper Fragment.

The very first observation that may be interpreted from this collage is that the wound of entry above the right brow ridge, lines up perfectly with its corresponding wound of exit at the occipitoparietal location from which the Harper Fragment was blasted out. This happens to also be the area to which Malcolm Kilduff pointed to at the press conference at Parkland Hospital within minutes after JFK was pronounced dead. The forward tilt of JFK's head, *plus the down slope of Elm Street*, strongly suggest that this shot came from below, as Kellerman described in his Warren Commission testimony, "an upshot into the vehicle." Garrison's and Jones's earlier work confirmed an assassin placed inside the storm drain would have had the clearance to execute this shot, and the yellow stripes painted on the curb would have offered the perfect visual cue for Greer to stop the vehicle to line JFK up for the coup de grâce.

This is what the storm drain looked like in 1963.

The Downward Trajectory

The alternative hypothesis is a shot tracking from above in a downward trajectory towards the limousine. This simple overlay traces a shot from the direction of the corner of the picket fence and triple overpass cement railing:

The exit vector does not even come close to the position of the Harper Fragment and the wound of exit seen in Zapruder frame 343 shown above.

It is extremely important to consider the downward trajectory of any shot that might have originated from any position along the picket fence atop the grassy knoll. Any forensic re-enactment, clearly would have to take these angles into account. The position of JFK's head at Z312 and Z313 creates a problem for the proposed trajectories from these positions.

Conclusion

Summarizing the findings presented here we begin with Dino Brugioni's observation of the vertical debris he saw in the original Zapruder film the weekend of the assassination of President Kennedy, "I remember the splatter was high, you know, say, three or four feet from his head," and Roy Kellerman's long forgotten Warren Commission testimony about "an upshot into the vehicle." In addition to this, we must consider the extremely important forward tilt orientation of the president's head at the moment of impact seen in Zapruder frame 312, coupled with the down slope of Elm Street. Dr. Mantik's exact placement of the Harper Fragment and the identification of a wound of entry above the right eye and brow ridge, which lines up perfectly with the exit wound in the occipitoparietal area, offer tangible evidence that in all likelihood, the shot that created the Harper Fragment and killed JFK on 22 November 1963 came from the storm drain on the north curb of Elm Street, just as Jim Garrison had proposed in 1967.

ENDNOTES

1. Fetzer, Jim, *Murder in Dealey Plaza* (2000), p. 197
2. NBC News file footage, transcribed by Gary Mack, *COVERUPS!*, No. 22, May 1985
3. *The Men Who Killed Kennedy*, Part 6 (5:00)
4. Lillian Castellano letter, 24 July 1968
5. *Texas Monthly Magazine*, November 1983, p. 152, "Still on the case"
6. Garrison's thesis was confirmed by Vincent Salandria in email to author dated 29 June 2016, "I know that Jim Garrison was convinced of the shot from the storm drain. He told me so. Your article convinces me that you are right about it."
7. "Sewer Shot in JFK Assassination," ratical.org/ratville/JFK/JohnJudge/sewerShot.html
8. FBI report, James Anderton, 25 November 1963
9. Ibid. Jack Harper, M.D., photographed Harper Fragment and studied it at the Pathology Department at Methodist Hospital (see CD1269)
10. Item 06, Hoover to Burkley letter, 29 November 1963. Howard Roffman files at Weisberg repository at Hood College. Needless to say, these X-rays have never surfaced. (see appendix)
11. CD1269, Burkley made the Harper Fragment disappear
12. Fetzer, Jim, *Murder in Dealey Plaza* (2000), p. 175
13. Shaw and Harris, *Cover-Up: The Governmental Conspiracy to Conceal the Facts About the Public Execution of John Kennedy* (1976), pp. 72-74

14. These tapes were transcribed in 2014 by the author.
15. Fetzer, Jim, *Murder in Dealey Plaza*, p. 227
16. Ibid. 201
17. *The Third Decade*, Vol. 9, No. 3, March 1993, p. 7
18. Mantik, David, M.D., Ph.D, *John F. Kennedy's Head Wounds: A Final Synthesis—and a New Analysis of the Harper Fragment*, pp. 65-66
19. Ibid. 65
20. Ibid. 66
21. Fetzer, Jim, *Murder in Dealey Plaza* (2000), insert p. 11 Jack White. Jack used these markers to prove Zapruder film alteration by using them as a measuring device to determine the impossible sizes of Ike Altgens and Toni Foster.
22. see Roberdeau map
23. "The Zapruder Film Mystery," Douglas Horne, Dino Brugioni, Peter Janney (video removed by YouTube February 2018)
24. jfk.hood.edu/Collection/Weisberg%20Subject%20Index%20Files/Weisberg-Subject-Adds%201-23-09/Jenkins%20James%20Curtis%20Confidential%20Part%202
25. Mantik, pp. 115-117
26. Horne, Douglas, *Altered History Exposing Deceit and Deception in the JFK Assassination Medical Evidence*, Part 2 (28:15) youtube.com/watch?v=5m8lSUB6K5o
27. Ibid.
28. Ibid.

APPENDIX

Figure 36. The three headshot scenario.

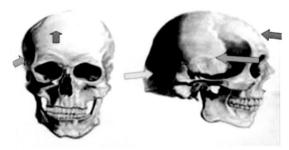

Figure 36. Schematic illustration of the three headshots. Entry sites are only approximate. Each color defines a different shot.

If HF really did initially alight at Harper's discovery site, then how did it escape from the back of the skull (especially at Z-313) and fly so far forward? That answer, of course, depends not only on where the shot occurred, but also on how far forward JFK's head was tilted. At Z-313 (Figure 27), JFK's head was indeed tilted far forward, but it still seems unlikely that an occipital fragment would go so far forward. Judging from the bystanders (see Mary Moorman's coat[26]) the wind was blowing briskly toward the rear of the limousine and would have strongly resisted the bone's forward flight.

Another bone fragment was found in Dealey Plaza that day; it was picked up—and then put back down again:

> As we [Jack Faulkner, deputy sheriff, and A. D. McCurley] were crossing Elm Street, McCurley picked up a white piece of bone near the north curb.[77] He asked me, "Do you suppose that could be part of his skull?" I said, "There's no blood on it," and he put it down. Later, we got to thinking, and somebody said your skull doesn't necessarily have to be touching something that's bloody. We went back and looked for it later but never found it. To this day, I believe it was a piece of Kennedy's skull.[78]

Likewise, someone might have picked up the Harper fragment and then later dropped it, perhaps even some distance from its original site, leaving it for Harper to discover later. Possible reasons for dropping it are easy to understand: (1) a reluctance to get involved, (2) a distaste for the macabre, or (3) simple embarrassment. It should also be emphasized that 29 hours had passed before Harper arrived—and this very plaza was the focus of world-wide attention for that entire weekend: Is it credible therefore that no one else spotted this bone until Harper saw it?[79] I strongly suspect that we cannot now know where this bone initially landed—that information is forever lost to history. After all, Harper could only tell us where he found it, but that may well be useless information.

Headshot #2. (Red in Figure 36). A frontal (forehead) shot most likely produced the particle trail now seen in the X-rays. (Even if the debris is attributed to a posterior shot, this trail must still count as a separate shot; it is far too high to derive from a posterior EOP shot.) This bullet entered high on the right forehead, near the hairline (where the incision is seen in the autopsy photographs—an incision that was *not* seen at Parkland). The metallic trail on the AP X-ray goes nearly straight back; therefore this shot should *not* be called "tangential," as some writers have mistakenly done.[197]

For a shot from anywhere on the triple overpass, the observed particle trail is really only possible when JFK's head is nearly erect, i.e., it cannot occur with the forward head orientation seen in Z-312 (or in Z-313).[198] If JFK's head had been rotated far enough to the left, then this particle trail might derive from a South Knoll shot, although not too close to Z-312. On the other hand, since the moment of this shot is not precisely known, so also is JFK's head orientation unknown at this moment. That leaves open the possibility that this shot might have come from elsewhere, e.g., the north side of the overpass (e.g., the storm drain there). However—and this is critical—this shot cannot explain the large hole at JFK's right rear (the one that so many witnesses recalled)—after all, *the particle trail is far superior to that large defect.*

Robert McClelland, MD, who believes the (single frontal) headshot came from the Grassy Knoll, said the president had been struck "...around the hairline near the middle of his forehead."[199] Like many others, though, McClelland has conflated the forehead shot (#2) with the temple shot (#3); the Grassy Knoll shot was #3, not #2. The forehead shot (#2) produced the metallic trail on the X-rays, but *not* the occipital blowout. Another possible example of this confusion shows Dennis David pointing to his right lateral eyebrow and Malcolm Kilduff pointing (vaguely) toward his right forehead.[200] However, at least one other Parkland witness, Charles Crenshaw, MD, has recalled (on video) a bullet entry in the high right forehead, near the hairline.[201]

About a week after the assassination, Robert Knudsen (a White House photographer) showed JFK photographs to Joe O'Donnell; one showed a hole in the right forehead, above the right eye. This was round and about 3/8" in diameter; O'Donnell interpreted this as a gunshot wound.[202]

In the final inning of this essay (which was written during the baseball playoffs), an astounding witness (for this right forehead shot) emerged. After he heard my interview on Black Op Radio (October 8, 2014),[206] he telephoned and e-mailed me. See Appendix L for details and for his sketch of the entry site (in the high right forehead). He had seen an apparent JFK autopsy photograph (not present in the Archives). His entry site matches the metallic trail on the X-rays very closely indeed, and also matches the recollections of Crenshaw, O'Donnell, David and Robinson. McClelland's recollection is only modestly different, and Custer may even be in the ballpark.

> Jerrol Custer, the radiology technologist recalls an entry wound above the mid-right eyebrow.[203]

And Dennis David (also at the autopsy) made this statement:

> But there was a small hole that looked like an entry wound. It was about the size of the tip of my finger. Maybe a little over a quarter of an inch [6 mm], 5/16 of an inch in diameter. It was located right in this area here (LAW: indicates a point at the hairline above the pupil of the right eye).[204]

Tom Robinson, the embalmer (while before the HSCA) also recalled a small wound in the right forehead, near the hairline:[205]

Purdy: Did you notice anything else unusual about the body…?

Robinson: Probably, a little mark at the temples in the hairline. As I recall, it was so small, it could be hidden by the hair. It didn't have to be covered with make-up. I thought it probably [was] a piece of bone or a piece of the bullet that caused it.

Purdy: In other words, there was a little wound.

Robinson: Yes.

Purdy: Approximately where, which side of the forehead or part of the head was it on?

Robinson: I believe it was on the right side.

Purdy: On his right side?

Robinson: That's an anatomical right, yes.

Purdy: You say it was in the forehead region up near the hairline?

Robinson: Yes.

Purdy: Would you say it was closer to the top of the hair?

Robinson: Somewhere around the temples.

Purdy: Approximately what size?

Robinson: Very small, a quarter of an inch [6 mm].

Purdy: Quarter of an inch is all the damage. Had it been closed up by the doctors?

Robinson: No, he didn't have to close it. If anything I just would have probably put a little wax on it.

7/24/68

Dear Harold —

I apologize for the delay but I have to work fulltime now and find it hard to devote as much time as I would like to the case.

Thank you for the plans — I had them in the batch of small films sent to me by West which I had given to Steve Jaffe and asked him to have larger copies made but which he never had done — so, I used your larger copies and had copies made for me, Ray, Maggie and Fred Newcomb. I also send you a copy of another plan showing the outline of the pergolas etc. What I intend to do if I ever get the time and the money is to have ① the survey plat map ② the plan showing the outline of pergolas ③ the plan showing the sewers and ④ the plan showing the buildings that were razed — all reduced to the same size and photographed on transparent overlays so that they can all be laid one on top of another. It will probably be expensive and I may never do it but I have hopes.

We have just heard that the permanent injunction

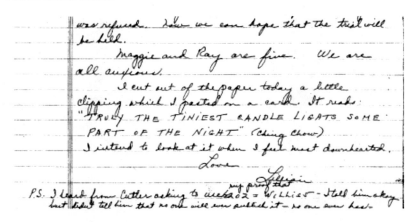

was refused. Now we can hope that the trial will be held.

Maggie and Ray are fine. We are all anxious.

I cut out of the paper today a little clipping which I pasted on a card. It reads:

"TRULY THE TINIEST CANDLE LIGHTS SOME PART OF THE NIGHT" (Ching Chow)

I intend to look at it when I feel most downhearted.

Love

Lillian

P.S. I heard from Cutter asking to check $2 = Willies - I tell him okay but didn't tell him that no one will ever pull it - no one even has-

Photoshop Color adjusted images of the Harper Fragment:

In this transcript, Douglas Horne talks about Quentin Schwinn in his video *Altered History: Exposing Deceit and Deception in the JFK Assassination Medical Evidence*, Part 2 (28:15):

I was contacted in the year 2010 by a person named Quentin Schwinn. He's a contractor with a high-level security clearance who works at one of the 8 NASA centers. He was once a student of photography at the Rochester Institute of Technology. He has a vivid recollection of being approached during what was clearly a job interview in late 1982 or early 1983 while he was a student at RIT, he was approached by one of his professors, a Professor David Hazy, and by an unknown stranger from out of town. The stranger had a brief case, stranger pulled out two photographs, one was a satellite image of airplanes parked on a runway, obviously taken from a great distance, and they asked Mr. Schwinn all kinds of photogrammetric questions about how would you determine the size of this airplane, the length of the wings, the length of the shadows, and apparently he satisfied them with his answers and he indicated to them that he had a good knowledge of photogrammetry, photography and photographic analysis. They then showed him one color positive transparency, a postmortem image of JFK after death. And I spent three years off and on, interviewing Mr. Schwinn on the phone, assessing his credibility I even had him contact RIT and had them send me a sealed transcript of his matriculation there. I received the sealed transcript, I verified that he was in school there when he said he was, he did receive the two degrees in photography that he said he did, and my considered judgment after interviewing him for 3 years, is that Quentin Schwinn is a reliable witness, and that he was shown a postmortem image of President Kennedy, which is not in the official collection today, by two individuals as part of a recruitment pitch - by the way, he was subsequently offered two federal jobs in photography and declined both of them, but this event happened, and ah, so this is what I encouraged him to do: this image is the result of Quentin Schwinn going to a qualified medical illustrator describing for him what he recalled seeing in the image, and getting the medical illustrator to draw a picture, and I believe this is the third of fourth attempt, of the effort, I mean Quentin Schwinn is a perfectionist and he had, in fact more than one artist work on the project and he finally settled on the best artist, and then he, I think this is the 3rd attempt made by the second artist. This is important for two reasons. One is the apparent entrance wound above the right eye, the second reason the condition of the throat wound which we will talk about later in this presentation.

So, this is the wound that apparently Dennis David and Joe O'Donnell recall seeing in photographs—the week after the autopsy. I forwarded this image to Dennis David, with a minimum of description, and asked him if it was similar in any way to the photographs he was shown by Lt. Commander Pitzer, and he said the entrance wound above the right eye is exactly what he recalls, the condition of the throat wound is different, which we'll talk about later in this presentation, which is significant, but he said that the small entrance wound above the right eye, he said the small entrance wound above the right eye, is 100% consistent with the photographs shown to him by Lt. Commander Pitzer a week after JFK's death. Joe O'Donnell is now deceased so could not contact him, but I think this gives the viewer a good impression of an entry wound of a shot from the front which was later removed from President Kennedy's skull by illicit clandestine postmortem surgery before the autopsy began."

425

OFFICE OF THE DIRECTOR

UNITED STATES DEPARTMENT OF JUSTICE

FEDERAL BUREAU OF INVESTIGATION

WASHINGTON 25, D.C.

November 29, 1963

BY LIAISON

Rear Admiral George G. Burkley
Physician to the President
The White House
Washington, D. C. 20501

Dear Admiral Burkley:

　　　　　This letter confirms the information furnished to you telephonically by Special Agent Roy H. Jevons of the FBI Laboratory on November 27, 1963, concerning the piece of bone reportedly found by a student near the place where the President was shot.

　　　　　In accordance with your request, this piece of bone was X-rayed and examined microscopically to determine the presence of bullet metal but none was found. A small amount of blood appearing on the surface of the bone was determined to be of human origin. There was not a sufficient amount of blood present for grouping purposes.

　　　　　This specimen was delivered to you on the afternoon of November 27, 1963, by special courier.

Sincerely yours,

J. Edgar Hoover

234

3

PART V
QUEEN HECATE AND THE JFK HORSEMEN

19

The Forgotten Research of Beverly Brunson

"Passion is the Ultimate expression of the Intellect"

—Beverly Brunson

Beverly Brunson, from Baxter Springs, Kansas, was an author and poet. She was born 7 November 1928 and died 21 February 2000.[1] She graduated from the University of Missouri in 1950 Phi Beta Kappa. Her father, Leroy Brunson, who worked in the 1940s for Root Manufacturing,[2] served one year in the Kansas House of Representatives, and also served as mayor of Baxter Springs for 10 years, from 1954-64. Beverly lived in New York for a while,[3] she never married, and lived a more or less secluded life with her parents and her longtime companion Mary Gibson.[4] This chapter will offer a perspective on Beverly's research and studies pertaining to the JFK assassination, which only spanned a couple of years from 1966-1968.

According to her second cousin Glenna Shanks Vernon, most of Beverly's records and writings perished in an accident while they were being transported and moved from one location to another. The transport truck became submerged in one of the many creeks of the area of Baxter Springs during a storm. Only her original desk remains in the possession of her extended family.[5]

Ms. Brunson's obsession with the JFK case centered on a few of the more important and controversial issues, which she felt had not been resolved, and is summarized in this quote from a 1968 letter to Harold Weisberg:

You will, I trust, forgive me for sending you so much and at my own

The JFK Horsemen

will. This case has come apart. I eat and sleep it. And I think the time is crucial. I have acquired a number of gray hairs, my first, these last two months, but I am not ashamed of them.

—Beverly Brunson, 28 March 1968

In 1966 Beverly established her first contacts with Harold Weisberg. They never met, however, they maintained a casual relationship for a couple of years, where she sent many unsolicited letters and manuscripts detailing her theories while she pored over the 26 volumes of the Warren Commission and other printed media available at the time. She was an extremely well-versed and informed writer who meticulously sourced her work with precision for others to follow and verify. Weisberg never discouraged Brunson from sending her research, however, with everything that he had on his plate, he admitted that he could not properly address and analyze her work, opting instead to place her investigations in a university archive. In prophetic fashion, Weisberg wrote the following in 1968:

Generally speaking, even I can find no immediate use for it, I'll welcome anything you might care to send. I may then be able to make it available to others (like the occasional newspapermen who has an interest), have it in case there is an investigation, and will have it in my files for the day when, as I've been told, my files will wind up in a university archive. I've asked that this be broadened to include the files of all working on the case.

Thanks to Weisberg's foresight, we can revisit Ms. Brunson's impressive work and appreciate the significance of her insights, industry and perceptiveness. Perhaps the reason Weisberg did not take much of her research seriously might have been because he did not believe in photographic alteration, and Beverly was emphatic that most of the photographic record was tainted. Time and modern technology has confirmed that Ms. Brunson may have been right in many of her theories. Beverly had superior analytic skills which she used to break down and analyze many of the inconsistencies that she found in the 26 volumes of the Warren Commission.

This chapter will take a look at her work with Altgens6 and its controversies, including diversionary tactics she believed to be embedded in the photograph, and also analyze her work with the Zapruder film using the few Zapruder frames that the Warren Commission published as exhibits, and those filtered by *Life* magazine, and Altgens6 versus Zapruder frame 255. In between, we will delve into other areas of Brunson's investigations, such as the DPD and the motorcycle escort officers, the phantom ambulance and the third victim of the shooting, and her findings on the Moorman

430

photograph. These are but a handful of the areas of investigation that Brunson was involved in. Bear in mind that all of her analysis and research was done in the late 1960s.

These passages from a couple of her letters to Weisberg suggest her lifelong partner Mary Gibson aided in her research:

Miss Brunson sounds stiff at this late date. Mary and I are working hard. We think it best to do it right. It is going to take some more time. It is all there. -I wish I could talk to you. Feel the need very much. The next time you are this way, perhaps we could come to meet you and talk an hour or so. Perhaps you might have a layover at the Kansas City or Wichita airport some time.

(Item 04)

4-1-68

Dear Mr. Weisberg:

A picture of me? Lawsamercy. Ok, I'll see if I can get Mary to take one of me on her new color polaroid. And I will obtain one of her too. Somehow though I can't see a picture of me in anybody's files. Except for comic relief.

(Item 06)

She minced no words when expressing who she believed was responsible for the assassination, from the president, all the way down to individuals in the DPD who she suspected were closely affiliated with right wing organizations. Brunson was convinced the original plan of the conspirators was to set up Oswald as part of a "Red" conspiracy which would bring about an outright response and provoke a retaliatory invasion of Cuba.

For example, the Julia Ann Mercer incident she suspected, was planned to "draw attention to the knoll."[6]

The Goldwater stickers on two vehicles that cruised the west parking lot of the TSBD behind the knoll were indications that whoever was behind the assassination wanted to make sure the Republican right wing could have also been suspected, and would have provided a special personal name brand, or "pathological stamp" belonging to whoever was behind it.[7] Brunson came just short of naming LBJ as the mastermind of it all. She concluded that all of this attention was dropped in favor of a lone nut scenario, much to the detriment and objection of the DPD.[8]

Film/Photograph Alteration

Years before the release of most of the films of the assassination, and well before it was later confirmed by modern technology, Brunson was already suspecting that these had been altered, edited, and in many cases suppressed. Moreover, she considered the control over photographic evidence to be of the utmost importance in the success of the assassination and subsequent cover-up:

> You have proved that the powers that be were desperately afraid of photographic evidence. I merely submit that it could be what I am interested in that they wanted to suppress. Especially since they suppressed the fourth rider also. The fact that Featherstone descended so fast on Mrs. Moorman (and didn't Jean Hill say that Featherstone turned out to be a cop?) might indicate that the assassins had planned on the possibility that they might be photographed and were prepared to grab the film? In which case they would also have taken pains to concoct an assassination that would reveal the minimun on film. They would have known in advance that many cameras would be in evidence. I think they were counting on a trick assassination to escape the camera. Which it did. Almost.
>
> Beverly Brunson
> Box 296
> Baxter Springs, Kansas 66713

(Item 37 pg 3)

Firecrackers, Silent Shots and Other Diversions

More than 50 witnesses claimed they heard and saw firecrackers and streamers explode during the assassination.[9] The documentation is extensive, and it is beyond the scope of this chapter to go into the details of each and every case. Secret Service men who were in the follow-up car, witnesses who lined the parade route in the area of Elm and Houston Streets, etc., are all included in this documentation. The smell of gunpowder and abundant smoke permeated the area despite higher than normal winds around noon time on that fateful day.

Brunson wrote extensively about this and was convinced that the use of diversionary tactics such as firecrackers and streamers was fundamental to the success of the operation and pointed out the misconception most people had regarding "smoking" rifles, an

432

impossibility given the characteristics of modern rifles, which emit very little smoke, if any at all.[10]

For instance, in Altgens6, on the hood of LBJ's car, right below the left windshield wiper, she noted a foreign object not part of the car she called a "streamer." This object could have carried some kind of firecracker or exploding device that would have provided a diversion to attract attention while other snipers or closer shooters (such as one possibly placed in the storm drain of the north curb of Elm Street) zeroed in on the kill. Obviously, those who threw the streamer did not intend for it to land on the hood of the vice president's car. This is how Beverly described it:

2. The other possible firecracker streamer may be lying on the (Item 28 pg 3) hood of the Vice-President's car. It is a long whitish object in the position of, roughly, the windshield wiper, but it is too large and glowing to be the wiper and does not correspond to the wiper on the other side of the hood. This would explain why Yarborough said he smelled gunpowder on the car all the way to the hospital and nothing else will explain it. And it explains why (Vol 18) Agent Warren Taylor reported that after the first shot he thought he saw a firecracker or streamer fly past the tail of the Vice-President's car. This was Shot One, and may have come from the Dal-Tex building.

And as noted by Brunson above, the presence of streamers and firecrackers was confirmed by Secret Service Agent Warren Taylor in this report:

Our automobile had just turned a corner (the names of the streets are unknown to me) when I heard a bang which sounded to me like a possible firecracker--the sound coming from my right rear. Out of the corner of my eye and off slightly to the right rear of our car, I noticed what now seems to me might have been a short piece of streamer flying in the air close to the ground, but due to the confusion of the moment, I thought that it was a firecracker going off. **SSA Warren Taylor Vol 18 page 782**

Secret Service Agent Roy Kellerman, who was riding shotgun in JFK's limousine described what he heard as they turned onto Elm Street:

Mr. KELLERMAN. This noise which I attribute as a firecracker, when this occurred and I am in the process of determining where it comes because I am sure it came off my right rear somewhere; the voice broke in right then.   WC2H75

Was A Streamer Thrown From The Second Or Third Floor Of The TSBD?

Brunson pointed out the strange, open mouthed reaction of this gentleman, whose attention seemed to have been drawn to something above street level, which was happening in the direction of the second or third floor of the TSBD.

He seemed to have been pointing this out to the woman in the dark business suit right in front of him and Altgens6 happened to catch her in the process of turning leftward to see what he was so freaked out about. Is it possible that someone threw one of the "streamers" from a window of the second or third floor? This would have been the perfect place to throw from to avoid detection, as opposed to throwing from the open and crowded street:

I want to draw your attention to one more thing: in the Altgens photograph there is a man standing on the curb in the far right top end of the picture who is obviously looking up into the air openmouthed, and seems in fact to be pointing out something to a woman standing in front of him with her back to the camera. This man is *not* looking up at the sixth floor. He is looking into the air over the Vice President's car - about the level of the second or third floor, no higher. He has either seen something happen in the air over the VP car; or in a lower window of the TSBD. And it is startling enough to cause his mouth to drop open and to cause him to lift his right arm and call the woman's attention to it. Also one of the women in the Dal-Tex window just to the right of the projecting arm or object, is looking into the air at about the same position. What have they seen happen in the air? Additionally, a woman on the second floor of the TSBD said the second floor windows shook. I suggest that this could very well mean that a large "torpedo" exploded in the air in front of those windows.   **(Item 37 pg 2)**

Silenced Shots

Why use firecrackers and streamers, one might ask? These, according to Brunson, would have been used to divert attention away from what really did the damage that day: silenced weapons. By carefully studying Zapruder film still frames, Brunson determined that shots could be detected in Zapruder frames Z227 and Z234, where Kennedy and Connally were reacting independently of each other to being struck by different bullets. When she combined this information with Weisberg's discovery that there had been a shot prior to frame 210, perhaps as early as Z189, she was able to ascertain that silenced weapons were the only means of achieving this.

Different reactions by Kennedy and Connally at Z227 and Z234

The only problem with ear witnesses, she wrote, was that most of them heard one shot followed by a long interruption. In between, she detected reactions from Kennedy and Connally that were out of sync with those reported gunshots:

In other words we are faced with the astounding evidence that the shot that hit President Kennedy in Frame 227 and the shot that hit Governor Conally in Frame 234, two shots, were not heard by the overwhelming majority of witnesses, including even those who heard more than three shots. They say over and over again, there was a long pause after the first shot.   **(Item 25 pg 3)**

This is nothing short of amazing to me. I do not dispute that other shots were fired, nor that other shots were heard by a few people. But I simply cannot ignore the fact that two shots occurred on the film which occurred precisely in that long pause that most people noted after the first shot. It seems irrefutable to me that a silencer was used in the assassination.   **(Item 25 pg 4)**

Some witnesses were definite that they did <u>not</u> hear rifle sounds. They thought they heard firecrackers, torpedoes, dumballs, backfires and blow outs. Other s were certain they heard rifle shots. One man who heard rifle shots even remarked that the shot didn't hang in the air long enough to be a rifle though. These discrepancies might be explained by assuming that the sound of exploding firecrackers (or shots) was immediately followed by the sound of a silencer. Some witnesses heard the one, some heard both the primary and the secondary sounds. Governor Conally, for instance heard <u>one</u> shot from a <u>rifle</u> before he was hit, when he should have heard <u>two</u> shots.   **(Item 25 pg 4)**

Another thing: there was too much attention drawn to rifles in this case and much of it before the assassination. Especially the events at the Sports Drome Rifle Range. There, there was absolutely no attempt to incriminate Oswald as a <u>lone</u> gunman with a Mannlicher Carcano. Instead, attention was drawn to <u>men</u>, one of whom resembled Oswald, with rifles - sporterized rifles, rifles passed over the fence, etc. Rifles, rifles,rifles. But if the attempt had been primarily to incriminate Oswald his name could have been left on the register at the range as Mrs. Davis makes clear in her testimony. If the plan was primarily to draw attention to <u>rifles</u>, it succeeded.   **(Item 25 pg 5)**

Where was the man with the silencer? What would have been the advantage of a silencer when shots were loudly going off on the knoll and up toward the corner of Elm and Houston? (I didn't mean to suggest in my last letter that a man in the Dal-Tex building couldn't have hit Kennedy. Of course he could have. But an assassin firing from the

TSBD bldg. and one in the Dal Tex building should have fired as the
motorcade turned the corner. The President was a much better target
for them then than she was for <u>three</u> men down by the Stemmons sign.
Anyone who has seen the FBI re-enactment photos through the scope;

and who has fired a rifle will tell you that they would have fired
then. They could have got him. The fact that they didn't get him
then when they could have got him makes me doubt that rifles were
seriously involved in those buildings.)   **(Item 25 pg 4)**

These excellent passages by Brunson require no further analysis as
they more than adequately establish her argument.

Bill Turner in an article on The Minutemen in the January <u>Ramparts</u>
quotes a Minuteman manual on silencers: -"the advantages of a gun
which makes no sound when fired are obvious." Yes, indeed. And right-
wing activists (including the CIA) love and <u>use</u> these gimmicks. We
have no right to assume that the latest and <u>best</u> could not have been
used on the man they hated most. The use of a silencer on the
President is far less fantastic than cyanide in the airconditioning
system of the United Nations. And much easier to get away with.
It only took about 8 seconds. You could do it at the dinner table.
                                                          (Item 25 pg 4)

(see William Turner article in *Ramparts*, "The Minutemen: The
Spirit of 66," p. 6)

What is quite obvious here is that Brunson believed that the only
rifle that was actually fired that day is the one which would incriminate
Oswald: the Mannlicher Carcano that was found on the sixth floor of
the TSBD, and that concerted efforts were made to draw attention to
rifles to make sure that any other weapon used would be excluded
from suspicion.

It would be painfully ironic if we have spent three years searching
for rifles while a murderous pistoleer sat under our very noses. I
don't insist that it is so, of course; I am interested in the truth,
not my own theories. But I become more and more convinced that the
assassins pulled a fast one on us. And that we can discover it, and
pull the ground out from under them. For, in spite of the fact that
they have got away with it for three years, I don't think they are
very smart. There are two sets of elephant tracks in this case; one
real and one false. The false conspiracy and the real conspiracy.
And the false conspiracy, which was amazingly bold, is also amazingly
obvious. They created the false Oswald prior to the assassination
and since you discovered him, I believe they have not slept well. The
false Oswald was a mistake. Maybe they made another big mistake,
thinking they could kill the President with a gimmick and get away
with it.

Beverly Brunson
Beverly Brunson
Box 296
Baxter Springs, Kansas 66713
(Item 25 pg 5)   1-3-67

One more thing, at the risk of boring you further: if you
were going to kill the President of the United States and
had planned this long and this hard to kill him and had
spent all that time setting Oswald up for the fall, you
could not <u>afford to fail</u>. You would have to be sure beyond
the shadow of a doubt that you would get him. With the
Kennedys you would never have a second chance. And suppose
you killed Jacqueline Kennedy and left Jack Kennedy alive -
which could so easily have happened with snipers as far away

as the knoll and the TSD building; even if you hit him, you
could have left him alive and her dead. Where would you
have hidden then? And the only way to be sure you would get
him would be to have an executioner near enough not only not
to miss but to blow his head off. **(Item 27 pg 3)**

Without specifically pointing it out, this passage foreshadows the
now generally accepted opinion of many researchers, that the fatal
shot that struck JFK at Z313 came from the storm drain of the north
curb of Elm Street. Brunson continues:

This would explain the Commission's stubbornness. They simply
could not see how he could have received a right-left, upward
missile. So they turned it downward by a gross distortion of
his position. As for the patrolman on the left getting matter
on his helmet and windshield, he was riding into it, and the
wind could have been blowing it. Or he might have lied. If
the shots were originally supposed to be thought from the knoll.
Several people told stories they got stuck with and had to
repeat before the commission, even though they no longer fit
the case.
And Zapruder 313 plainly shows an explosion, upward and forward,
with the explosion over Mrs. Kennedy's face which was above
and ahead of the President's head. **(Item 27 pg 4)**

As noted in the previous chapter, Brunson did even more brilliant
research on a possible upward trajectory which she found in Secret
Service Agent Roy Kellerman's Warren Commission testimony:

AGENT ROY KELLERMAN: "..it was now known to be an upshot into the
vehicle..."
1-24-68

Dear Mr. Weisberg:

I am pleased to be able to report that I have discovered that I
do not stand utterly alone in my theory of the mechanics of the
assassination; it seems that the Secret Service -or at least the
Kellerman faction -held the theory that there were bullets fired
into the car on an upward trajectory as late as March 9, 1964, when
Kellerman testified.

KELLERMAN: Well, I have tried to study that, sir. The angle
of the back as an example which is -what degree I
don't recall, hoping that -of course, it was now known
to be an upshot into the vehicle... (Italics mine)
Vol. 2, page 66

Spector jumped in and asked a question having nothing to do with
Kellerman's statement and trying to confuse the issue. The rest of
the statement reads like gibberish, deliberate stenographic jumble,
I'm sure.

Kellerman as you know tried hard to get into the record that the
entry to the man's head was below exit. He was graphic and insistent
about it. **(Item 13 pg 1)**

On page 93, Vol 2, Kellerman quotes Colonel Finck as saying of the
back wound, "There are no lanes for an outlet of this entry in this
man's shoulder." Notice that Kellerman does not go on and add that
the wound was at a 45 degree downward angle. (This was the FBI line,
a rough guess at the TSBD 6th floor window angle, I think. It is
in fact possible that Dr. Finck might have said it was a 45 degree
upward angle. A 45 degree downward angle is impossible from any building
in Dealey Plaza; but a 45 degree upward angle would about fit the
head wounds, and possibly also the back wound.) Kellerman plainly
did not think any of the wounds to the President were at a downward
angle. He is just as plainly of the opinion that the wounds were at

437

angle. He is just as plainly at the opposite
an upward angle. Specter asked if Dr. Finck had any other conversation
with him at the time. Kellerman said no but Dr. Humes did.

> KELLERMAN: Well, from Dr. Humes, who was the other gentlemen out
> there, from the entry of the skull, from this hole
> here.

> SPECTER: You are now referring to the hole which you describe
> being below the missing part of the skull?

> KELLERMAN: Yes, sir. It was confirmed that the entry of the
> shell here went right through the top and removed that
> piece of the skull.

> SPECTER: ...So you are saying that it confirmed that the hole
> that was below the piece of skull that was removed,
> was the point of entry of the one bullet which then
> passed up through the head and took off the skull?

> KELLERMAN: Right, sir. That is correct.

Vol 2, page 95 **(Item 13 pg 2)**

Again, as covered in the last chapter, the upward trajectory theory would be confirmed many years later when Tom Wilson and Jack Brazil demonstrated the likelihood of this bullet trajectory in the landmark TV series, *The Men Who Killed Kenney*, Episode No. 6, by Nigel Turner.

youtube.com/watch?v=_0D3pWBwqzU (4:50)

The view is consistent with the trajectory described by Kellerman and the direction of a piece of skull which landed at the feet of Joey Brehm, as Stavis Ellis highlighted in the 1971 Newcomb phone interview.

In her reasoning, Brunson was convinced that the fatal shot that took JFK's head off came from a silenced weapon with a short and upward trajectory, not from a rifle. The only thing that Brunson was not able to deduce was the exact location of the silenced weapon:

(Item 25 pg 5)

"Please understand that the important thing is not where I think the silencer may have been located, but that the evidence that a

438

silencer was located somewhere is, in my opinion, almost proven. If you re-read the evidence—what the witnesses said, especially those in the president's car and in the follow up car, keeping in view that a silencer may have been used, you will have a revelation. There could have been two silencers of course. There were many more seen shots (on the street) smoke in the trees, scaring the sidewalk, hitting the turf, hitting the manhole—than there were heard shots."

And here is what Weisberg answered regarding the silenced shot theory of Brunson on 7 January 1966:

> Your theory onbthe silenoerrs is intriguing. I'd never thought of it. It is also logical. On the rifles, ditto. Since the whole campaign to make it seem that the pictures and Xrays of the autopsy can validate the report among the things I have been emphasizing is that they cannot show the KIND of weapons used.

Sadly, Weisberg never pursued or developed Brunson's theories and filed them away where they remained dormant until now.

Altgens6

Which logically brings us to Brunson's analysis and extensive study of Altgens6. Her early work with Altgens6 shows she was highly suspicious of what the government was trying to push on the American public. She noted many anomalies in the photograph and discovered there were three versions of Altgens6 in circulation, the so-called "Parallax" version, the AP version which was published by Weisberg in *Whitewash II*, and the version published by *The Saturday Evening Post* on 14 December 1963.

Bobby Hargis
Anomalies

This comparison above between two different versions of the photograph illustrates what Brunson was on to and is one of the reasons why she insisted it had been doctored. The blob over Officer Bobby Hargis's left shoulder and the right edge of the bumper at the end of the front grill are quite evident. A different version of the photograph shows a white anomaly which she called a "brilliant glare," covering part of the dark blob. Also, notice the "streamer" on the hood of LBJ's car mentioned earlier in this chapter.

3-13-68

Dear Mr. Weisberg:

Here is what I see in the Altgens. I think the white objects were streamers, some of which carried firecrackers.

Beverly Brunson
Box 296
Baxter Springs, Kansas 66713

(Item 28)

Mr. Weisberg:

8-2-67

I sent you on 7-31 material evidence that two versions of the Altgens photograph exist, one with a brilliant glare near the right hand grip of the cyclist off the lefttrunk of the limosine and one without the glare and instead a neat black blob, circular and appearing to be something on the cycle.

I send you today the left side of the Altgens photograph, in two versions, one from the Post and one from the Parallax Torch is passed, which show distinct differences in the arm line of the cyclist off the right trunk of the limosine. (Item 39)

If you should get to look over the originals mentioned in the carbons you sent me, and if you still think there is something wrong, then I would like to talk to you about it. Also, it goes without saying that if something is wrong with the Altgens, just in these places, then we know where to look for other faked evidence. I doubt very much if any clean pictures still exist anywhere, after all this time. But it could. I have always felt a cunning but essentially careless and crude type of mind involved in this whitewash, and black out. There has been an arrogance approaching carelessness in the whole case starting probably from the day it was first planned. An utter contempt for the American people. An ad man's attitude. You can sell them anything, no matter how crude.

Item 38 pg 3

3

is the grillwork on the Johnson limosine as you can see by studying it and comparing it to the grillwork on the Kennedy car. The left hand may be in the shadows below the gearshift on the handgrip. The right hand should appear just behind that black blob, which is peculiar to the Hargis cycle. It does not appear on any other cycle. Either Hargis had a black or dark circular object way off to the right of his headlights or a black blob of paint has been placed on the photograph there. I ca not find a photograph of Hargis in which I can determine whether he was wearing black gloves or whether he did actually have an anomolous round black object attached to his cycle which the others did not have. (Item 37 pg 3)

I am unlucky enough to have a very clear light copy of the Dec. 14,1963 Post. I also have a copy of the issue which contains a much darker print. Nothing can be made from the latter. From the light clear copy much can be made. But in both copies there appears the circular smear in the front of Hargis' windshield, about the size of a thumbprint. The interesting thing about this is that when magnified this smear discloses several scratches and pinholes that cannot have been on the windshield since if magnified to life size the scratches would be an inch thick and the pinholes the size of bullet holes. These defacing marks definitely appear to be on the negative. I wish you would look at this. (Item 37 pg 3)

440

Anyway, it's like having hold of a hot grenade. I almost wish you would prove me utterly and totally wrong so that I could write poetry again. However, I am convinced enough to feel compelled to bring this to the attention of those qualified to judge it. I trust you will believe in my good faith and advise me, if you have time, how to proceed with good sense.

Sincerely,

Beverly Brunson
Box 296
Baxter Springs, Kansas 66713

(Item 38 pg 3)

Oswald in the Doorway?

Weisberg was the first Warren Commission critic to write extensively on Altgens6 and the so-called "man in the doorway." In *Whitewash*

II (1966), he documented nine points of similarity between the shirt worn by Doorway Man and the shirt worn by Oswald during the day and night of 22 November 1963.[13]

Furthermore, and as noted throughout this book, Weisberg pointed out the dissimilarity between the shirts worn by Oswald and coworker Billy Lovelady, who was identified by the Commission as the man in the doorway. He extensively studied the actual shirt at the National Archives in Washington, D.C., and concluded that neither the vertical striped shirt worn by Lovelady during his FBI photo shoot on 29 February 1964, nor the checkered plaid shirt worn by a man shown in the Martin film outside the TSBD on 22 November 1963, could possibly have been the shirt worn by Doorway Man.

Contemporary computer enhanced techniques by JFK author, researcher and anthropologist Richard Hooke, have recently identified at least 50 points of similarity between Doorway Man and Oswald, including head and facial features such as eyes, hair, chin, head, ear, and nose, as well as many of the original elements discovered by Weisberg pertaining to the shirt of Doorway Man. And, of course, Beverly concurred with Weisberg that it really was Oswald standing right there on the top step of the doorway of the front entrance of the TSBD. "The Lovelady Caper" she refers to below is the name of Chapter 16 of Weisberg's book *Whitewash II*, in which he detailed the shenanigans that the government went through to turn Oswald into Lovelady, the figure in the doorway. Below, in these original excerpts, Brunson eloquently and decisively offers the results of her investigation on "the man in the doorway."

"I do think it is Oswald in the doorway."

—Beverly Brunson

Before going on to the false Oswald I would like to offer a thought on the Lovelady caper. I do think it is Oswald in the doorway. Certainly any reasonable person ought to go on the possibility that it could be him. But what about Lovelady? Why would Lovelady say it is himself? FBI armtwisting is one answer, of course. But Lovelady must have been very stubborn in one respect: he absolutely refused to pose in a shirt that could be mistaken for the one worn by "him" in the picture. He must have been shown the picture, have identified himself and then gone and got a shirt. If he had forgotten what he wore that day, he would look among his shirts for one that resembled the picture he had looked at and identified. If he wasn't sure then he would have picked one resembling it, going on the theory that that was probably it. He would have picked a darker long sleeved shirt. Instead he picked a short

2.

sleeved shirt that couldn't possibly be the right one. This discloses a great deal of craftiness on his part, at the least. On the one hand he admits it is a picture of him. On the other hand he poses in a shirt that proves beyond a shadow of a doubt that it isn't him - if that was the shirt he wore that day. What can explain this? Lovelady obviously wanted an out. He had to say that it was he in the picture because that is what the FBI wanted. Yet he left himself an opening. He proved to

everyone that it w sn't he. This can xxdyx mean two things: one, either
he knows perfectly well that it is Oswald and fears it may be proved sometime; or he knows it is himself and that the person was up to something;
as I have suggested there is an object in front of the person's chin and
shoulder. Whatever that is out in the air is in front of the person,
since it cuts off the chin and shoulder. And there is a third possibility,
of course. It is Oswald and one of the other men who are obviously up to
some shenanigans in front of Oswald is Lovelady. In any case it would seem
obvious that Lovelady has some guilty knowledge, the most innocent being
that he swore it was himself when he knew it was Oswald. That is the minimum
that can be inferred from his refusal to put on a shirt that would condemn
him to being the person in the doorway. He did not want to prove that it
was himself in the doorway. He wanted for some reason to prove that it was
not. Which he did by putting on a shortsleeved, striped shirt. At any rate,
something was going on in that doorway and Lovelady knew it.

(Item 37 pg 1-2)

In my opinion if it was Oswald in the doorway, then the men in the doorway -
Shelley, Lovelady, Frazier must have some guilty knowledge, the minimum
being that they have lied and condemned a man. And who is the colored man
in the niche in front of Oswald? Oswald's left arm is out in the air over
his shoulder (if it is not in the air then it is cozily on his shoulder) -
surely he must have known if Oswald was standing there with his arm so sweetly
on his neck? However the arm is out in the air. And it is moving. **(Item 37 pg 2)**

This last explanation by Brunson about the proximity between Doorway Man and Black Profile Man, however, was flawed because she was interpreting the doorway image in two dimensions, not three, as revealed in Weigman slide 658 from the NBC film taken by Dave Weigman. As seen here, the figure of Doorway Man is nowhere near Black Profile Man, who, by the way, has been identified as 17-year-old employee Roy E. Lewis.

At the time of her interpretation in the late '60s, Brunson obviously did not have access to the Weigman film, which was not released until the 1970s:

NBC is also the owner of several important pieces of photographic evidence. A TV film taken by NBC photographer David Weigman was suppressed by NBC and not made available to researchers. It shows the grassy knoll in the background just a fraction of a minute after the shots. Some of the assassination participants can be seen on the knoll. *Taking of America 1,2,3* Richard Sprague 1976 pg 53

As noted in the beginning of this section, Brunson postulated that the white marks over Doorway Man's left shoulder were streamers that were being thrown from the entrance of the TSBD doorway that were actually well in front of the doorway figures, and the strange position of the arms and hands of those seen in the doorway were the result of the action of throwing these objects into the air as the motorcade made its way down Elm Street.

This is a concept that has never been discussed in JFK research circles. The purpose of the streamers has already been covered in this chapter. Finally, her conclusion about Shelley, Frazier and Lovelady "having some guilty knowledge" regarding Oswald in the doorway is something that is still being debated to this day.

Buell Wesley Frazier, the only surviving witness of the group, has never spoken publicly about this. However, his erasure from Altgens6 and the seizure of an Enfield rifle with ammunition at his sister's house, raises serious questions about his role as an alternate patsy.[14]

The Station Wagon Ambulance, Blood on the Ground and the Third Shooting Victim

Some researchers have always suspected that there were more victims of the crossfire in Dealey Plaza that day. Brunson figured that given the fusillade of gunfire aimed at the limousine, any collateral damage was a distinct possibility. (James Tague is a great example of this collateral damage.)

She discovered several passages in the radio transcripts, which when combined with the reports of blood on the ground and the documented experiences of other witnesses that day, suggest that this may have indeed been the case.

Here are a few examples of what she meant:

> The ambulance running loose on the way to Parkland was carrying a third victim of the shooting on Elm Street. This is made clear when Sgt. Burkhart, in front of Parkland, asks the dispatcher (time about 12:38), "What's this emergency on this ambulance?" The dispatcher answers, "We had a shooting in the downtown area." The FBI transcript adds "involving the President". This makes it explicit that there was an ambulance running for Parkland carrying someone shot at the assassination scene. This ambulance is #601. It later shows up at Parkland. **(Item 08 pg 1)**

It has been documented that there was a strange 1959 Oldsmobile station wagon with out-of- state license plates behind the picket fence

and sporting a "Gold-water for 64" bumper sticker in the rear window.[15]

In those days, most ambulances were converted station wagons, which had been adapted by installing sirens, and what were known as "lolli-pops," double-sided, flat, round flashers on the roof, which identified the vehicle.

This is the same type of vehicle in which Aubrey Rike transported the epileptic around 12:20 PM that day.

youtube.com/watch?v=YjhCbt5X4hA

Brunson surmised that the station wagon parked behind the fence could have been a getaway vehicle *which was equipped to also double as an ambulance, in case it was necessary.* In the event of a casualty, this vehicle would become a phantom "ambulance" and drive one "Mr. X" to Parkland Hospital. In retrospect, having this type of vehicle available seems to have been a brilliant strategy designed to deal with unforeseen circumstances. According to Brunson, those circumstances dictated that it would be pressed into service as an "ambulance."

```
Most ambulances are station wagons. An ambulance-station wagon
would make a good getaway car. A station wagon without a red light
on top, but with a siren and sidelights could quickly become an
ambulance.  It would seem reasonable, in view of the peculiar
testimony on the station wagon behind the fences, and the ambulance
described running loose on the way to Parkland in the radio log
of Ch. 1 about 12:34, that the assassins had placed such a station
wagon at the top of the knoll, as a getaway car, or ambulance,
in case it was needed.  The dispatcher did tell Sgt. Burkhart at
Parkland that the ambulance expected was one which had to to with
the shooting downtown involving the President.      (Item 01 pg 1)
```

From FBI Tape:

```
12:37 p.m.
     ..........
          20 ( Sgt. Samuel Burkhart ) : " I'm on Hines in front of Parkland.  What
          is this emergency on this ambulance ?"
          Dispatcher ( Hulse and Jackson) : " 20 (Sgt. Burkhart), there's been a shoot-
          ing in the downtown area involving the President."
          20 (Sgt. S.Burkhart) : "10-4."
```

With this passage shown above, which is contained in the radio logs of 22 November, Brunson was able to infer that something very strange was going on that day regarding an ambulance that nobody wanted to be involved with. She determined that this ambulance was "running loose on the way to Parkland" and it "was carrying a third victim of the shooting on Elm Street."

The ambulance that Sergeant Samuel Burkhart was referring to above, was ambulance "601." Moreover, Brunson makes it quite clear that this ambulance "may have been difficult to recognize," based on the radio exchanges with Patrolman D.L. Pate:

```
That this "ambulance" may have been somewhat difficult to recog-
nize as such is indicated by the question of D.L. Pate, a patrol-
man sent to watch for the ambulance.  "Was APB supposed to be
following it?"  It appears that Pate may have arrived in time to
see an accident squad car traveling behind a station wagon which
he could not definitely determine was an ambulance.  The dispatcher
informs Pate he does not know if APB was following.  However,
Patrolman Hawkins, APB, calls in shortly to ask the dispatcher:
"Numerous people asking questions, can you give us some information?"
"Was he shot or what?"  And the dispatcher answers: "Wounded the
President."  In the Sawyer version of Ch. 2, Hawkins is told to
call Operator One from Parkland.  Operator One would be a telephone
extension in the dispatcher's office.  This is not carried in #705
of #1775.  It appears the dispatcher has information for Hawkins
```

2.
which he doesn't want to put on the air.
Hawkins testified that he was working an "accident" at the time of
the assassination. It was on Industrial somewhere. He is vague
about the time. It seems he was working this "accident" from the
time of the assassination until he left to go the scene of the
Tippit shooting. The radio logs however tell us he was at Parkland,
shortly before one o'clock. This indicates that he was the APB
following the "ambulance" which Pate inquired about. (Hawkins later
shows up as an arresting officer of Oswald in the Texas Theatre. His
name appears in Jack Ruby's notebook.)

(Item 1 pg 1-2)

In November 1985, renown editor and publisher of *The Third Decade*, Jerry Rose, wrote a piece titled "Dallas Police: Manufacture of Confusion," in which he, too, questioned the DPD radio logs which referred to a "mystery ambulance":

The <u>mystery ambulance.</u> Further diversionary communications---or possibly encoded messages to assassination conspirators---are suggested by the inexplicable radio references to an "ambulance" containing the stricken President. There was no ambulance as such in the Presidential motorcade; yet the dispatcher directed patrol units to cut traffic for "the ambulance" on its way to Parkland after a shooting involving the President.[9] At least two patrol squads were asked---and answered negatively---if they had seen the "ambulance" pass their location.[10] Faced with a lost "ambulance," the dispatcher signalled ambulance 602 for its location. The response: "We're at the Trade Mart" and a moment later: "enroute to Parkland."[11] Any possible reason for an (apparently) empty ambulance going from the Trade Mart to Parkland escapes my understanding.[12] Wouldn't it have been far more reasonable for the dispatcher to do what he apparently never did: to dispatch ambulances to <u>Elm and Houston</u>? This would be especially an indicated action in the light of the dispatcher's early misinformation that "six or seven more" people may been shot at the scene.[13] Did he assume that all these folks were crowded into "the ambulance" going to Parkland?
   Strangest of all, perhaps, the dispatcher was apparently ignorant not only of the motorcade vehicles but of Dallas geography. One patrol unit was directed to cut traffic at Inwood and Stemmons for "the ambulance going to Parkland."[14] In fact Inwood is <u>beyond</u> the exit off the Stemmons Freeway for Parkland when one proceeds there from downtown Dallas. It seems that either the dispatcher did not know Inwood's location; or he somehow visualized the motorcade as proceeding downtown as it headed for Parkland. Neither of these seeming alternatives is remotely credible, however, since a dispatcher must maintain above all a clear sense of just who and what are where at every given moment. The whole "ambulance" set of messages makes no sense if they are regarded as genuine instructions for police movements. The meaning of these messages awaits, I suspect, the results of a de-coding operation which is informed by a strong suspicion of a police-coordinated assassination operation.

9. 23H841.
10. 23H842.
11. 23H842.
12. A glimmer of light on the role of the Trade Mart-to-Parkland ambulance after the assassination may be shed by an item in the police radio log, again as it appears only in Bonner's version thereof. After the presidential party left Love Field, the dispatcher contacted Captain J.N. Souter, in charge of traffic arrangements for the motorcade's arrival at the Trade Mart. Souter was informed that ambulance 601 had completed its assignment at Love Field and would report to "your location." There is nothing irregular about this, as it might be assumed that ambulances were assigned to "stand by" both at the air field and at the end of the motorcade route; and one ambulance could conceivably have been assigned to standby at both locations, which are not really so far apart. The strange element is the dispatcher's statement to Souter that a "transfer ambulance" would also be stationed at this location. Was ambulance 602 the "transfer" ambulance; and (shades of "Best Evidence") who or what or to where was anyone supposed to be transferred on November 22?
13. 23H915.

446

Going back to our discussion, the radio logs suggest that Patrolman D.L. Pate was totally oblivious as to what was going on with the phantom ambulance and who was in it. Another DPD patrolman was about to throw a monkey wrench into the whole operation.

Enter DPD Patrolman Willie Price

Unknowingly, Patrolman Willie Price might have given it all away. Price was driving a three-wheeler that day and was stationed at the Trade Mart. The Brunson narrative continues:

```
While looking for the ambulance going to Parkland, the dispatcher
calls 601 ambulance.  It announces it is at the "market".  ᴀxᴢᴀᴡ
An "Unknown" comes in and says, "We are at Parkland!.  Later #601
announces it is at Parkland and "standing by." At some point the person
carried away from the assassination scene in the ambulance-station
wagon may have been transferred to 601 ambulance.  Or there may
have been two men in 601 ambulance, one using the ambulance number 601
and one using the number #35.  In which case "601" ambulance would
have been the station wagon itself, and there would have been no
transfer.

It appears, however, that the "car" carrying the third victim of
the shooting at the triple underpass stopped somewhere briefly.
For one thing, the dispatcher lost it.  For a second, there is a
most peculiar call on Ch. 2 at 12:40.  A three wheeler with the
number #295, J. Price, comes on the air in answer apparently to
a query from Batchelor about the President's condition.  Price
says "Believe the President's head was practically blown off." The
dispatcher ignores him for a call or two, then calls and is told
by Price to "disregard what I said.  It's not for me to say."
On Sawyer Ex. A Ch. 2, when Price is asked "Where did you get your
information?", Price replies "I was at the car." This mysterious
and astounding message is dropped from the subsequent versions of
the log #705 and #1775.  No wonder.  For it is impossible for
                                                          (Item 01 pg 2)
```

```
Price to have been at the President's car at any time from 12:30
when he was shot to 12:40 when he had already been at some car and
found out, second hand it appears, that the President's head had
been blown off.  Price was a three wheeler assigned to the Trade
Mart with the notation "After".  This would mean that Price was
a member of the Trade Mart pool that was to appear at the Trade
Mart after fulfilling some previous assignment along the motor-
cade route, after the motorcade has passed his point.  It goes
without saying that a three wheeler was not at the President's
car at the time the shots were fired and he was hit in the head.
Nor could Price had been at Parkland by the time the President
arrived and was taken into the hospital since he was neither part
of the motorcade itself; nor did any of the Trade Mart crew join
the motorcade as it passed at high speed on the way to the hospital,
most especially not in time to lead it there and be there in time
to see the President's head, which was immediately covered by
Hill's coat.  In addition Price's doubtful language "Believe the
President's head was practically blown off", "Disregard what I
say, it's not for me to say", seems to mean that Price was at
some other car by 12:40 where he was told the President's head
was blown off, and told on good authority.     (Item 01 pg 3)
```

The timeframe in which Price makes his transmissions is crucial. A scant 10 minutes after the assassination, a time when nobody knows much about what is happening, and he has an encounter that defies all logic, which is at variance with what stands as the official story. Perhaps somebody in that station wagon/ambulance told him the president's head had been blown off, and as Brunson writes, "and told on good authority." Of course, it's conceivable that Price arrived at Parkland in time to see the president removed from the limousine.

447

When Mary Ferrell investigated this possibility, this is what she commented in her chronologies for 22 November 1963 on Willie Price:

> A151 **Officer William Price** (21:392; 23:915) Radio #295 [Probably was <u>not</u> a witness - See N422 back]
> a. Radios over Channel 2 at 12:40 p.m. that President's head was practically blown off. (Curry tape - 21:392; FBI tape - 23:915)
> b. Price said, "I was at the car." Might have meant at Parkland Hospital.
>
> [- A151   DPD Officer **William Price** was assigned to Harwood & McKinney and then to Motor
>
> Pool at Trade Mart (20:489)]   (From: Mary Ferrell Chronologies - November 22, 1963, Book 1 Narrative 411 and 422 back)

Motor Pool (Trade Mart Command Post):

Sgt. R. L. Striegel-130	J. O. Fenley-274 (After)	J.W. Williams-162
Sgt. W. C. Campbell-280 (After)	R. K. Higgins-282 (After)	ED. Waffco - 159
L. H. Marshall-139	E. Jones-293 (After)	J.H. Taylor - 157
W.J. May-241	W. Price-295 (After)	W.R. Featherstn - 154
W.R. Featherston-154 (After)	O. L. Purnell-277 (After)	
J. H. Taylor-157 (After)	C. F. Fields-275 (After)	
E. D. Mafford-159 (After)	C. W. Watt-265 (After)	
J. W. W. Williams-162 (After)		WC20H489

Did Price anticipate the motorcade speeding toward Parkland when he heard Chief Jesse Curry and Sheriff Bill Decker's broadcasts, then drove his three-wheeler in time to see the stricken president there? If so, then why, as Brunson notes, was his remark so "doubtful" where he stated, "*Believe* [Emphasis added] the President's head was practically blown off," when he should have said, "The President's head was practically blown off."

Here is the log to which Brunson is referring to above (see CE1974 pp. 169, 170, and CD1420):

Batchelor	12:40PM	2-531	Where did it happen? At Field and Main?
Batchelor		531-2	No, sir, the tripple under pass between the triple under pass and Stemmons. Possibly six or seven more people may have been shot.
W. Price		295-531	Believe the Presidents head was practly blown off.
Homicide	12:40PM	303-531	What hospital did the President go to?
Homicide		531-303	Parkland Hospital. Where are you?
Homicide		303-531	300 is enroute.
Homicide		531-303	Is 300 in route to the store Elm and Houston?
Homicide		303-531	300 enroute to the Hospital.
W. Price		295-531	Disregard what I said.
W. Price		531-295	Do you know the extent of the injury?
W. Price		295-531	It's not for me to say, I can't say, disregard that remark,
W. Price		531-295	Where did you get your information.
W. Price		295-531	I was at the car.

W. Price=295
Dispatcher=531

Vol 21 pg 392

Clearly, the radio transmissions by Willie Price need to be re-examined and explained. How did he know about the severity of the president's condition when he was nowhere near Dealey Plaza!? He obviously realized his bonehead mistake when he blurted, *"Disregard what I said," "It's not for me to say, I can't say, disregard that remark,"* and later, *"I was at the car"* when the dispatcher asked him where he got his information. Was he *really* at the car?

The same goes for D.L. Pate. As an innocent police "bystander" who was just trying to do his job, who documented the fact that there was a mysterious ambulance "on the loose" which should not have been where it was. Both Price and Pate show how difficult it was to cross all the "t"s and dot all the "i"s in an operation of this magnitude. If, as Brunson concluded, there had been a third victim riding in an unmarked ambulance to Parkland Hospital, then there had to have been evidence of this in Dealey Plaza and at the hospital itself. She found plenty of information indicating this was indeed the case.

Blood on the Ground

When Jean Hill went running up the country steps that lead to the north side monument, she spoke about seeing "red stuff" on the ground in her Warren Commission testimony (WC6H212/214). Brunson expands and comments on this:

(Item 12)

BLOOD ON THE GROUND
(AND A BIG RUNAROUND?)

1-6-68

Brunson
Box 296
Baxter Springs,
Kansas 66713

Jean Hill testified that as she crossed the street and went up the hill by the steps she thought she saw blood on the ground. It turned out to be Koolaid. An FBI interview says a red snow cone. Mrs. Hill was about 30 years old, a substitute school teacher and the mother of two children. There is no chance that she would mistake blood for Koolaid. Besides Koolaid will not retain its red color if spilled on either the grass or the walk. A red snow cone will retain its color only if it is not melted and ice is not mistaken **byxhhnkx** for blood except in metaphor. There is, however, every chance that she was bullied and confused into saying she was wrong.

In July 1995, Alan Houston published a short article in *The Fourth Decade* titled "The Vanishing pool of blood." The article narrates the story of *Dallas Morning News* photographer Jim Hood and how he was alerted to the presence of a pool of blood at the top of the steps by two witnesses who had been in Dealey Plaza that day, *Dallas Morning News* employee Jerry Coley and his friend Charlie Mulkey. Hood actually dipped his finger in the pool of blood and tasted it to confirm what it was.[16] By the time Hood reached the spot with Coley and Mulkey, the blood had already started to coagulate. Hood was then able to take several photographs which were confiscated by the FBI a week later, never to be seen again. This excerpt reports on what happened to the negatives:

> A little over a week later, the atmosphere in Dallas had begun to settle down, so Jerry Coley returned to work. The following day, two men, who identified themselves as FBI agents, showed up and said they wanted to talk to him and Jim Hood, the photographer. Jerry and Jim began to tell their story, but one of the agents cut them off, and asked about the photograph that they had. Coley was startled, because he had not yet mentioned the pool of blood or the photograph, but he produced the picture and handed it to one of the agents. The agents then requested to see the camera, negatives, and any prints that they had in their possession. Coley left and returned with the items, which he handed to the agents. After placing the photos and the negatives in an envelope, one of the agents stated "All right gentlemen, that's the end of the interview, the end of the story, and the end of the blood." Coley asked him what he meant, and the agent told him "For your benefit, it never happened. You didn't see it. Someone just fell and got hurt and it's ridiculous to carry this thing any further." The agent warned Coley that if he continued, he was going to cause himself a lot of problems, and told Coley just to forget the entire incident.   **TFD July 1995 pg 22**

The information was later confirmed by Texas U.S. Marshall Clint Peoples. "When asked if he knew about the pool of blood and if it was involved in the assassination, he simply replied, 'It most definitely was involved.'" He declined to elaborate."[17]

Bertha Lozano and the Mysterious "Mr. X"

Nurse Bertha Lozano was sitting at the triage desk at 12:30 PM on 22 November 1963, when all hell broke loose in Parkland Hospital. "I remember noticing a patient in a dark suit coat with his face and head covered with a suit coat roll past me . . ." and "Blood technicians came to ask me who 'Mr. X' was who did not have an ER number.

Hematology also came with the same problem and was told the same thing."[18]

Here is Ms. Brunson's analysis:

The mysterious "Mr. X" whom nurse Bertha Lozano refers to must have been this third shooting victim. There was no mystery about Kennedy or Connally at that time and they both had room numbers. Miss Lozano says that blood technicians and hematologists were coming to her to find out who "Mr. X" was who had no room number. We know from Nurse Henchcliffe that she went to get blood from the bank for Kennedy and at that time was told their patient was the President. It is impossible that the blood technicians did not know for whom they were supplying blood. What they did not know was who "Mr. X" was. -The third bloody stretcher could not have been Fuller's since two nurses state that Fuller had been just prepared for suturing when the President was declared dead. This was one o'clock and Fuller had not yet been treated. Tomlinson saw the third bloody stretcher just after one o'clock.

Item 08

There is ample circumstantial evidence in Brunson's studies for her to conclude that there was a third victim involved in the Elm Street ambush at the top of the country steps leading up to the monument on the north side of Dealey Plaza, and that this unidentified victim arrived at Parkland Hospital where he

Service Agent, Policeman Killed

DALLAS (AP) — A Secret Service agent and a Dallas policeman were shot and killed today some distance from the area where President Kennedy was assassinated.

No other information was immediately available.

was treated without any records being kept. Nurse Lozano confirmed the person was wearing a suit, so it could not have been a uniformed DPD officer. Furthermore, early dispatches out of Dallas reported a Secret Service agent had been killed during the ambush, and Walter Cronkite initially reported that Secret Service agents "fanned out into the crowd, looking for the assassin."[19]

The DPD radio logs contained in Vol. 21, p. 392, shown earlier, and noted by Jerry Rose in the passage reproduced above, certainly mention more victims to the shooting: "Possibly six or seven more people may have been shot."

If the victim on the knoll was indeed a Secret Service man who was transported in the station wagon/ambulance out of Dealey Plaza and on to Parkland Hospital, the implications are just unimaginable. It would introduce the notion that casualties were anticipated, and the conspirators were ready to deal with them as contingencies. It opens a Pandora's box on Secret Service complicity where the notion of not leaving the killed and/or wounded behind takes on new significance.

Also, any Secret Service agent taking gunfire head-on obviously did not know what was about to occur and was treated as expendable. Moreover, the mere fact that all Secret Service agents would have known about this casualty speaks volumes about the hermetic bonding of their "brotherhood," not to mention their families.

This radio log tells a story in itself. Another DPD patrolman, J.W. Brooks, call No. 174, had been in the thick of the events of the day. He had been at the TSBD and at Parkland Hospital. While dispatcher Henslee and Sergeant R.E. Duggar were carrying on a conversation regarding the possibility of other victims of the shooting, Brooks interrupted and innocently stated, "One of the Secret Service men on the field—Elm and Houston—said that it came over his teletype that one of the Secret Service men had been killed."

Re: ASSASSINATION OF PRESIDENT
JOHN FITZGERALD KENNEDY,
NOVEMBER 22, 1963, DALLAS, TEXAS

Caller	Conversation
Dispatcher (HENSLEE)	That's the latest I had on it, 18. (Sergeant R. E. DUGGER).
Dispatcher (HENSLEE)	18 (Sergeant R. E. DUGGER), there were some more injured but I don't know who they were or how severe.
18 (Sergeant R. E. DUGGER)	I didn't read you. You know anything about an injured Secret Service Agent?
Dispatcher (HENSLEE)	No, I do not. There were some more injured but I don't know who they were.
174 (Patrolman J. W. BROOKS)	One of the Secret Service men on the field -- Elm and Houston; said that it came over his teletype that one of the Secret Service men had been killed.
Dispatcher (HENSLEE)	Well, 10-4. I don't have that information.
18 (Sergeant R. E. DUGGER)	I believe this is going to be incorrect. He's not at Parkland. Can you have someone canvass the major hospitals please?
	(Garbled)
139 (Patrolman L. H. MARSHALL)	I have a man out here that doesn't know anything about that.
Dispatcher (HENSLEE)	10-4.

- 210 -

The experiences of Hood, Coley and Mulkey, of whom Brunson was unaware of at the time she wrote her paper, "Blood on the Ground (and a big runaround?)," coupled with her discovery of the cryptic radio logs and Willie Price and D.L. Pate's ill-timed transmissions, certainly establish that her conclusions were well-founded, and point at the distinct possibility that there indeed might have been more victims to the shooting on Elm Street than previously reported and accepted by researchers.

The transmission by J.W. Brooks follows the same pattern of Price and Pate, who as men just trying to do their jobs, found themselves right in the middle of the most important historical event of the 20th century.

Who Exactly Died on the Knoll?

A very enigmatic figure who predicted the JFK assassination was a Cuban exile by the name of Homer Echevarria. A rabid anti-Castro militant, he arrived in Chicago in 1960 and was working as a bus driver at the time of the assassination.

He allegedly had very close ties to another anti-Castro exile by the name of Paulino Sierra Martinez. A quote that has been cited by many assassination authors and researchers was attributed to Echevarria in Secret Service Document C-2-34;030, dated 3 December 1963, where on the day before the assassination a very reliable informant heard him state: "we now have plenty of money—our new backers are Jews—as soon as 'we' (or 'they') take care of Kennedy . . . " [20]

A Homer Echevarria has been identified by Chauncey Holt as being very much involved in the operation behind the picket fence on 22 November 1963.[21] Holt writes that he provided Echevarria with fake Secret Service credentials[22] and "parked a "souped up" Oldsmobile station wagon containing several handguns and an extra set of identification papers . . . "[23] Holt continues: "Echevarria was carrying forged Secret Service credentials and was dressed to fit his role . . ."[24]

According to A.J. Weberman, "In 1995, the CIA released 16 heavily deleted pages from Homer Echevarria's CIA file all generated in 1965. A Top Secret document, SSS-53-265, on Homer Echevarria, was filed in the Top Secret safe in SR/OSR/BIO. NARA 1994.04.26.09:23:43:250005"

jfkassassination.net/weberman/10-75.htm

(Author's note: The "Homer Echevarria" with whom Weberman corresponded claims his identity might have been compromised and used for nefarious purposes.)

It is common knowledge that there were men with fake Secret Service identifications behind the picket fence. One of these was encountered by DPD Policeman Joe Smith[25] several moments after the limousines sped off to Parkland Hospital.

If "Echevarria" was playing the part of a Secret Service agent, is it possible that another yet unidentified bogus Secret Service agent might have been felled by gunfire as postulated by Brunson that day?

Another very distinct possibility could be an angle investigated by JFK researcher Richard Hooke, who informed this author that a Secret Service agent by the name of Chuck Robertson disappeared after 22 November 1963, and his family continued to receive his paycheck indefinitely, mailed directly to his home.[26]

The Motorcycle Escort

According to Brunson, the security-stripping of JFK's limousine took place in two stages: The removal of the bubble top, and the last-minute modification of the escort assignments that day. Over the years, the responsibility of the removal of the bubble top has been a hot potato.

Kellerman blamed Lawson, Lawson blamed Kellerman, and eventually the blame had been placed on the shoulders of JFK aide Kenny O'Donnell: [27]

```
                              B. Brunson
                              Box 296           1-26-68
                              Baxter Springs,Kansas 66713
    BUBBLETOP

    Kellerman states in his testimony that Lawson called him in Fort
    Worth about 10:00 on the morning of the 22nd to ask specifically
    whether the bubbletop could come off.

    Lawson states that Kellerman called him.  Lawson does admit that
    he gave the final word to take off the bubbletop (which was on the
    car that morning).  Lawson's lie, if it was that, was then not to
    hide the fact, which he could not, that he ordered the bubbletop
    off; but to conceal the fact that there was anxiety in Dallas as
    to whether they would be able to get the bubbletop off, that a
    special call was made to get permission to remove the bubbletop.
```

Secret Service guru and specialist Vince Palamara revealed in his book, *Survivor's Guilt: The Secret Service and the Failure to Protect President Kennedy*, that the order ultimately came from Secret Service Agent Sam Kinney.[28] Palamara obtained his information directly from Sam Kinney.[29]

Kinney was captured in this photo at Parkland, belatedly re-installing the bubble top with the help of Officer James Chaney. Could this have been out of remorse?[30]

Originally, Marrion Baker, Clyde Haygood, H.B. McClain and Jimmy Courson, were supposed to flank the limousine during the motorcade:

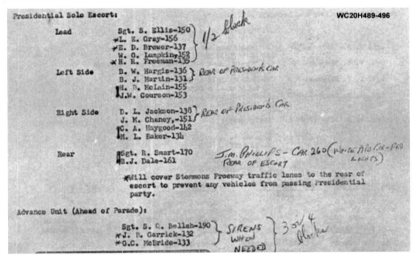

This assignment chart submitted the day before by Captain Will Lawrence, clearly shows where these men were supposed to have ridden.

At the Eleventh Hour, only five to 10 minutes before the motorcade, and while they were still at Love Field, the Secret Service removed these four outriders, and assigned them well back of the motorcade. Brunson wrote:

Switch now to Marion Baker's testimony. You will find a blockbuster buried in it. Baker states that he and his partner (and as you will see two other officers) were scheduled to ride beside the President's car. It was not until about 5 to 10 minutes before the motorcade departed from Love Field that Baker received orders from his sargeant to fall back behind the press cars: putting these four officers way to hell and gone out of the way when the shots were fired. (Item 13 pg 6)

Douglas Jackson, the Knoll Rider

Perhaps Brunson's most significant research, however, centered on Motorcycle Patrolmen Douglas Lavelle Jackson and James Chaney, the two outriders to JFK's immediate right. There is not a single more intriguing story than that of Douglas Jackson, who Beverly baptized as "the knoll rider." When she realized that Jackson was apparently being protected and hidden away, she began to dig deeper as to the actions of this "motor jockey."

By studying the few images that were available, as well as all relevant testimony and FBI interviews, she inferred that Jackson rode up the embankment of the grassy knoll to confront shooters behind the picket fence. She noted how the newspapers were replete with stories about the actions of the immediate outriders dropping their motorcycles and racing up the knoll with their guns drawn. Here are a couple of examples:

Brunson wrote several very important studies about the events right after the head shot which killed JFK, and what the motorcycle patrolmen did in the immediate aftermath.

Jackson's unusual "disappearance" and unavailability further fueled her suspicions that members of the DPD were very much involved in the logistics of the assassination and its subsequent cover-up.[31]

(Roberts saw one jump the curb, right himself and go on up.)
At any rate I am glad Mr. Sprague agrees that D.L. Jackson is
an important missing witness.

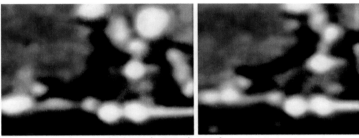

Jackson jumps the curb

These two frames from the Orville Nix film show Jackson looking to his right before jumping the curb of Elm Street, as Secret Service Agent John Ready rushes past him on foot.

Richard Sprague, however, tried to dispel and discourage Brunson's analysis by inventing and speculating careless scenarios whereby the witnesses cited by Brunson had to have been mistaken, indicating perhaps his desire to reformulate what these witnesses had seen and reported. If anything, it exposed the superficiality of Sprague's own research because Brunson thoroughly backed her work with actual testimony and many published sources.[32]

Now much of the above, proven by photos, conflicts directly with the statements
of witnesses you quote; namely Altgens, Zapruder, Hargis, Mrs. Newman, Simmons,
Winborn, Johnson, Holland and Bowers. Why would all of these witnesses lie
about a cop riding up the knoll? They didn't lie. They thought they saw it or
something like it. In Holland and Hargis' case, imagination about what they
should have done or what they would like to have done, took over their memories.
Holland certainly did not want to remember standing rooted to one spot for over
two minutes. Hargis being a cop, looks even sillier leaning against a lamp post
for nearly a minute during the crucial two or three minutes after the shots. He
looks much better remembering running up the slope and looking behind the wall.

The problem with Sprague's flawed analysis has to do with the alteration of many of the photographs and film that he cites in his explanations to Brunson. Sprague and Weisberg were much too trusting of the photographic record, and why they ran into many unexplained conundrums and dead ends. Brunson, on the other hand, was wide open to alteration, and time and technology apparently are proving her right.

The conspirators could not have possibly known if Oswald was going to remain out-of-sight during the assassination. The best they could do to manipulate Oswald was to keep him at the top of the stairway of the entrance of the TSBD. After the assassination, his supposed presence on the second-floor lunchroom placed him inside the building.

According to Brunson, the evidence is clear that a cross-section of different elements who wanted JFK dead were present in Dealey Plaza and the grassy knoll. Rogue CIA operatives, elements of the Mafia, Cuban exiles, and other mercenaries offered a kaleidoscope of possible suspects who could be moved into a frame if Oswald happened to be caught on film or other irrefutable media.

```
As for the rest of the plot, you will make this look like a leftwing
assassination. The layer underneath that will look like a rightwing
assassination, just in case the top one falls of its own sheer
imppobability (which in fact it did). (Remember you like insurance.)
And you will certainly use other people to do the dirty work for you:
Cuban refugees, rightwing, gangsterdom, the paramilitary, a dissident
wing of the CIA. In fact this second level of the plot which Garrison
is getting at -probably the people who pulled off all the hocus pocus
with rifles, firecrackers, milling around, etc. -the guerilla operation
may have been calculated to substitute for the failure of the Oswald-
Hidell-FPCC as fall guys.                           (Item 35 pg 2)
```

Once Oswald was moved into at least partial culpability, the DPD spent that Friday night trying to find confederates, and this is obviously the case as we have already discussed what happened to Joe Molina and Buell Wesley Frazier the night of the 22nd.

We saw how Molina was paid a visit by the top brass of the DPD and Assistant District Attorney Bill Alexander at 1:30 AM, where his house was searched for evidence linking him to Oswald, while Frazier was pressured by Captain Fritz late Friday night to sign a confession—which he refused—that he was involved in the plot.[33]

These two events are indicative of the fluidity of the situation, and proves how the plotters were actually improvising as they went. The transformation of the final lone nut story did not finally evolve until Saturday the 23rd, when Henry Wade spoke for the record that this was the man who had planned and executed the assassination all on his own. Brunson's analysis appears to have been spot on.

Zapruder Film Anomalies and Alterations

Clear versions of the Zapruder film were not released and made available until the 1990s. The very first still images were released by *Life* magazine in their 29 November 1963 issue, where only 31 frames were published in black and white.

Some selected frames were later published in Vol. 18 of the Warren Commission hearings and exhibits. The very first public showing was made by Jim Garrison, after he had subpoenaed the film from Time Life for the 1969 Clay Shaw trial. Garrison had bootleg copies distributed throughout the country. From those, second and third generation copies were made available to researchers and other people interested in the case. The anomalies discovered by Brunson were based on these early images and speak volumes of her analytic abilities. We will now discuss some of these.

There are many who have noticed the strange behavior of the limousine tail lights in the Nix film, which are indicative of Secret Service Agent Greer pulling the limo to a stop. As we see here, Brunson noted that only the left tail light was on and wondered why this could have been:

> In the *Life* Magazine Oct 1964 Women Report issue – on one of the big "Z" color frames – has one of the limousine's taillights been shot out? My young friend discovered this too – he says the brakes have been suddenly applied & yet only one of the taillights is working ? It looks like it. I don't know the magazine here – but it's the frame in which Mrs Kennedy is on top of the Trunk, I think ? They could have replaced that tail light before Kellerman saw the car.

Transcription of above:

"In the Life magazine Oct 1964 Warren Report issue—on one of the big "Z" color frames—has one of the limousine's taillights been shot out? My young friend discovered this too—he says the brakes have been suddenly applied & yet only one of the taillights is working. It looks like it. I don't have the magazine here—but it's the frame in which Mrs. Kennedy is on top of the trunk, I think? They could have replaced that tail light before Kellerman saw the car."

Right brake light on in Muchmore film, off in Zapruder

Zapruder Frame 240 and Jackie's Navy Blue Lapel/Collar

Brunson believed there was bleeding and extension of "blue paint" over Jackie's right shoulder. When we blow up the area in question, however, we realize that shadows are consistent with the time of day which bring about what seems to be a merging of the collar and shoulder pad.

This blow up reveals more detail:

In this particular case, Brunson seems to have erred in her analysis. When we take a closer look at frame 240 and compare the faces of the three occupants of the limousine, we can't help but notice that JFK looks like a faceless caricature where his face has been painted over, and his features have been removed. The faces of Jackie and Governor Connally seem to be intact as their features are clearly visible. JFK's facial features, on the other hand, which are facing the bright noon sun, are indistinguishable.

A comparison of Frame 240 with Frames 254, 258 and 260.

Zapruder Frame 255: Comparison of Altgens6 with Frame Z255

Photographs taken of the same event but from different perspectives or angles of vision should show the same figures according to the difference in perspectives. We saw this phenomenon earlier when we compared Weigman frame 658 to Altgens6, where we placed Roy Lewis in his relative position to Doorway Man. Even though at least 30 seconds had already elapsed, the figures in the doorway had remained relatively stationary when Weigman passed by the TSBD in camera car No. 2 that day. Staring researchers right in the face has been the fact that from a photographic point of view, Altgens6 and Zapruder frame 255 should also show the same event, but from different perspectives due to the position of the photographers.

This passage by Brunson explains her findings regarding these Zapruder film anomalies:

with the SEP Dec. 14, 63 one? As best I can see, it definitely was. And two, where exactly is the motorcycle officer (yes, I still have my yellow eye on him) located in that photograph, in regard to the right side of the limosine? I place him where he appears to be, beside the limosine, about five feet to the left of it, at a position about even with or slightly ahead of the President. Why then isn't he in or around Z frame 255? I suspect he may be the reason for all that blue paint scattered all over the frames as published in the Nov. 66 Life, especially frame 240 and afterward. Some of those spots seem to appear in the black and whites in Vol. 18, but not all of them, as if someone got busy with the blue paint brush, just before Life went to press –notably, the series of blobs around Mrs. Kennedy's neck in Life 240. I maintain that anyone cut to blue in or out something in these frames would have been painting in the vicinity of the limosine.

Handwritten above:

Same goes for the blue discoloration you noted on 207—the bottom half. 210 is all spotty as published and it indicates to me they were working on the left hand side of the missing frames & made such a mess they had to eliminate them altogether. You know who was in the left hand corner of 210: my man (Chaney not Jackson)

(Author's note: Weisberg obviously had no answer to this because he did not believe the Zapruder film had been altered.)

It may seem at first glance that Ms. Brunson's analysis and comparison of Altgens6 with Z255 would seem somewhat farfetched. However, when we follow her research, we find that there are definite anomalies that perhaps might have been overlooked by others in the past. If we place Officer James Chaney in the proper position in this overhead view by Fred Newcomb, author of *Murder from Within*, (courtesy of his son, Tyler Newcomb) we find he is more abreast with the limousine—indeed, in Altgens6 he is shown looking to his immediate left and seems to be almost in line with JFK on the horizontal plane. He can be no more than four feet away from JFK, and almost seems close enough to touch the president.

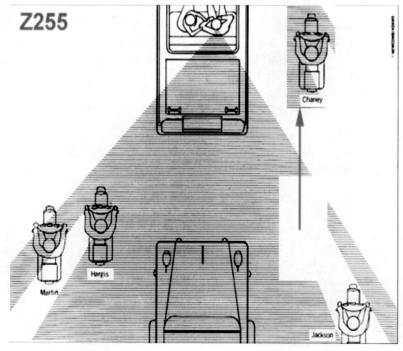

It is for this reason that Brunson determined that Chaney might have been painted out of the Zapruder film in its most crucial frames, namely around Z240 and beyond. This would make Beverly Brunson one of the very first researchers—if not the first—to conclude that the Zapruder film itself might have been extensively altered, which is amazing when we consider that up until then, she had never seen the actual movie, only a limited collection of individual frames.

In her research, Brunson referred to Willis slide No. 5, (above) which corresponds to Z202, as she traced the movements of Chaney, arriving at the assumption that he advanced from a position slightly in front of the Queen Mary, in between both limousines, to his position next to JFK as seen in Altgens6. Z172-207 shown below confirm that he remained off of the rear right fender until he disappeared behind the Stemmons Freeway sign:

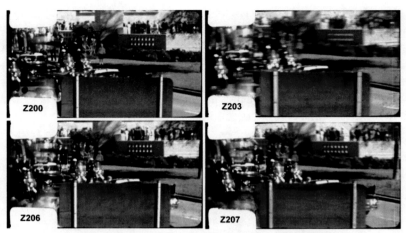

Movements of James Chaney from Z172-Z207

Chaney's movements were the result of either him accelerating his motor, the limo itself slowing down, or a combination of both. After Z313, he came to a complete stop along with Douglas Jackson, who was right next to him as shown in the Nix film, and by his own admission in an interview with Fred Newcomb in 1971:

Chaney: . . . I don't believe that it actually stopped, it could have, but I don't know—I know that the second car did 'cause I recall the officers . . . and Officer *Hargis jumped off the motor and run in front of me.* [Emphasis added][34]

Whitney: Right, right, that's another thing . . .

Chaney: I don't recall myself stopping—I must have or come almost to a stop. Hargis did, he got off of his motorcycle over on the left-hand side and run between those two cars . . . *and run in front of me, so apparently I did too. I don't recall stopping, but I must have.* [Emphasis added][35]

This excerpt of a letter by Brunson to Weisberg dated 14 February 1968 explains her findings regarding James Chaney:

I wrote you some time ago that I thought this officer was painted off the side of the limosine in the vicinity of Z255, which corresponds to Altgens' picture. Z193 shows the inside rider is inside the same traffic lane as the President's car and moving steadily up. Willis #5 shows him still moving up. At that rate he would be where he appears in Altgens right next to the car and far enough up on it to have to look back or square to the left to see the President. Thereafter he falls back. Thus in Z255 he ought to be pictured up against the trunk of the limosine.

Zapruder couldn't have shot over him since he didn't shoot over the arm and head of the waving man who disappears in Z243. This officer would appear in any picture above the waving man. And he

can't be too far in the rear for Zapruder to have caught him in
the picture since he has had to turn his head to look back at
the President. He is next to the car and up on it. Yet he does
not appear in Z255 at all, and I think possibly this is a paint job.
This would explain all the blue paint. And it would explain the
sudden cessation of reflections on the body of the limosine after
the waving man disappears. Up until then this officer had reflected
brightly on the trunk of the limosine. Other reflections show too.
Suddenly no more reflections.

Beverly Brunson
Box 296
Baxter Springs, Kansas
66713

"*And he can't be too far in the rear for Zapruder to have caught him in the picture **since he has had to turn his head to look back at the President. He is next to the car and up on it**.* [Emphasis added]

"*Yet he does not appear in Z255 at all, and I think possibly this is a paint job. This would explain all the blue paint. And it would explain the sudden cessation of reflections on the body of the limousine after the waving man disappears.*

"*Up until then this officer had reflected brightly on the trunk of the limousine. Other reflections show too. Suddenly no more reflections.*"

Z255

These collages offer a summary of Beverly's astute observations and what she was on to. Z193 below shows the limousine before it becomes blocked by the Stemmons Freeway sign and illustrates Brunson's point about the reflections of Chaney and his motorcycle projected onto the impeccably waxed and shiny side of the JFK limo. The reflections should have remained visible after the limo emerged from the sign, and the apparent presence of a different tone of ink along the side of the car further stirred her suspicions of alteration.

Chaney and his motorcycle brightly reflected on the side of the SS100X

After the limousine emerges from behind the Stemmons Freeway sign, the side of the limousine becomes dull and lacks the shiny, polished surface seen in earlier frames.

Photoshop magic: The figure of Chaney at Z206 inserted into Z255

Norwegian researcher Sverre Avnskog independently corroborated Brunson's findings in 2011, as shown in this illustration. Avnskog did not mention, however, the absence of reflections on the side of the limousine. (Author's note: Avnskog inserted the Hargis figure into the frame.) toward-the-light.net/Kennedy.html

Closeup of Z255 showing side of limo without any reflections.

Blender model of frame Z255 clearly shows reflections on side of limousine

It does not take a photographic expert to realize that Altgens6 and Z255 should display the same event from different perspectives and angles of vision, yet, they do not. This demonstrates that either one or the other, and most probably both, have been subjected to alteration. The most remarkable difference in Zapruder frames noticed by Brunson must be the absence of any reflections on the side of the limousine after it emerges from behind the Stemmons Freeway sign. Also, note that after Z255, as the limousine passes Zapruder's position, the bottom of the film from above the door line on down vanishes and appears to have been cut out of the frames, as if by design.

Why Erase James Chaney from the Zapruder Film?

The obvious question that needs to be answered is why erase Officer Chaney from the Zapruder frames after the JFK limo emerges from behind the Stemmons Freeway sign. On 4 May 1964, the FBI and the Secret Service reenacted the assassination for the Warren Commission. Once again, we look at the forgotten research of Beverly Brunson, but before doing so, it must be pointed out that the automobiles used in the reenactment were not the SS100X Lincoln Continental where JFK was seated, who was in a position that elevated him above all the other occupants of the limousine.[36]

COMMISSION EXHIBIT 875—Continued

(Author's note: The original document that follows had to be enhanced electronically due to its partial illegibility. The transcript is accurate. Warren Commission images are provided to allow the reader to follow her reasoning.)

Brunson:

I also wanted to point out to you something about "The reconstruction photos." You will notice that those taken on Houston Street show a rider on the right rear trunk. Suddenly on Elm Street, this rider falls so far behind he does not appear in the picture at all at the crucial time. I think there is a very simple reason for this: they couldn't lay the crosshairs on the Kennedy stand-in without getting such a rider in the picture from the sixth-floor window.

And this would mean that from almost any point to the right rear below the sixth floor, they couldn't lay the crosshairs on the Kennedy stand-in without laying them on this man. Kennedy was protected from the right rear by this rider and anyone behind him, on the right rear.[37]

The shot would go for right rear wound to Connally. Connally would be covered by this man. And it goes for the Dal-Tex Building, too, which was to the right rear when the car is in the assassination position.

Also, to anyone in the TSBD or the Dal-Tex Building, Kennedy's head would simply be one among many. There was the escort and the 10 men in the follow-up car, some of them standing up or sitting on the top of the car. They had to pick out that one head. Thus, the reconstruction photos are entirely deceptive.[38]

That isn't the way it was that day. There were many heads, Kennedy may have been almost entirely protected by the cycle escort, and the standing men or high-sitting men in the follow-up car. But the reconstruction photos lay him out there empty of protection. And especially is the scene denuded of this right trunk rider, who offered him the most protection from the right rear. He is deliberately dropped from the pictures taken on Elm Street. [39]

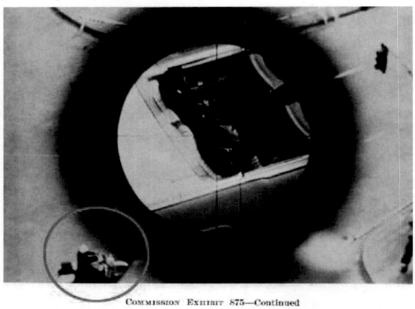

COMMISSION EXHIBIT 875—Continued

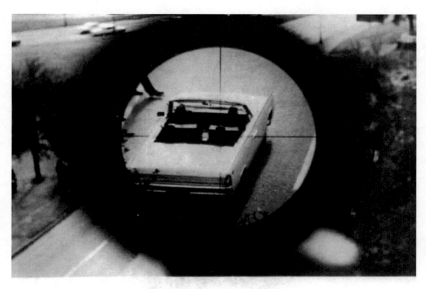

COMMISSION EXHIBIT 875—Continued

Reenactment position of limousine for the "magic bullet" shot.
(Z289-290)

This reenactment photograph was taken by the DPD the Wednesday after the assassination. Notice how distant and separated from the car Chaney's stand-in motorcycle rider is. According to John Costella and Jack White, this photograph is the smoking gun that proves the Zapruder film has been altered. (*The Great Zapruder Film Hoax: Deceit and Deception in the Death of JFK*, pp. 89, 124-125)

Master of deceit Arlen Specter supervises Secret Service reenactment sans motorcycle escort.

These images from the Elsie Dorman film capture Chaney and Jackson abreast of the JFK limousine while on Houston, right before making the turn on to Elm Street with Chaney riding inside the traffic line, within only a couple of feet of JFK.

To illustrate the deception orchestrated in the reenactment pointed out by Brunson, notice the position of the motorcycle outside the traffic line and well-removed from the stand-in automobile. This is not even close to the position of Chaney seen in Z193 shown below:

James Chaney rides inside the traffic line almost abreast with the right rear fender of limousine

Chaney had this to say the night of the assassination in an interview broadcast by ABC[40]:

Lord: I understand you were riding next to the president's car when the assassination took place.

Chaney: I was riding on the right rear fender.

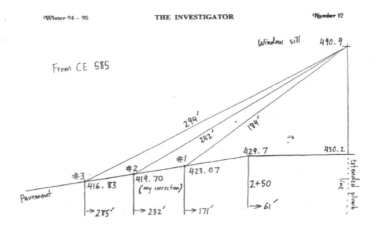

This image from Daryll Weatherly's study, introduced in chapter 17, published in the journal *The Investigator* in 1994-95, allows the reader to appreciate the pronounced downward slope of Elm Street going away from the TSBD.

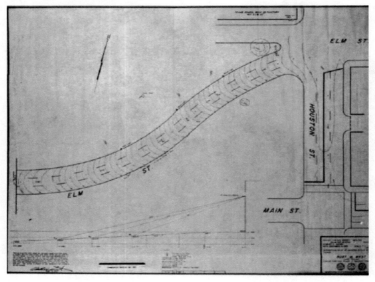

Another factor to consider must be the fact that the alleged sniper's nest position was confirmed to be at a lateral angle of 9° 21'.[41] Both the down slope and the lateral angle suggests that any motorcycle riding to the right rear of the limousine would have essentially blocked the view of any shooter from the southeast window of the sixth floor of that building.

Commission Exhibit CE898 shows the limousine is not following the correct path according to traffic lines which mark the lanes on Elm Street. Other images in this exhibit seem to be missing traffic lines altogether.

What this implies is that they were very conscious of the unusual angles and down slope which existed in the "kill zone," which brought the motorcycle escort on the right rear dangerously close to being in the line-of-fire of a sniper perched in the southeast corner of the sixth floor. Notice the reenactment image below which shows stand-in limo in the correct position, which is angled in the opposite direction from that shown above in CE898. Also, notice how the photograph was taken at a horizontal angle that seemed to minimize the down slope of Elm Street which made it appear virtually flat.

The Mary Moorman Photograph

And how close was Chaney to being in the line of fire of a hypothetical shot from the sixth floor of the TSBD? Check out the Moorman photograph: by definition, it can also be postulated that the Moorman photograph must be tilted, presumably to hide the down slope of Elm Street. How else can one explain the leveled horizontal plane the limousine and the motorcycle riders exhibit in the image? In fact, the limousine *appears to be going uphill!*

When we rearrange the Moorman photograph, we come up with this: Chaney's position becomes much higher when we match the down slope shown in Weatherly's study.

This photograph was taken by the author in October 1991. It approximates the Moorman position, but the point in presenting it here is to show the true down slope of Elm Street and how the retaining wall is supposed to be tilted to the left. This tilt is absent in the Moorman photograph but is restored when we tilt the image as shown above.

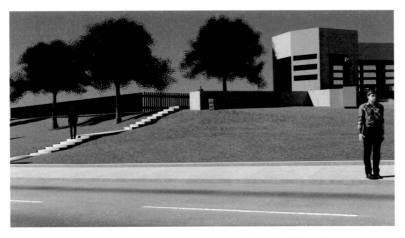

Blender also confirms the down slope of Elm Street

The following study by Roy Schaeffer proves the Moorman photo has been tilted to hide and reduce the down slope of Elm Street. While re-enacting the Moorman photograph, Roy snapped this photograph with his 35mm camera, while he had his friend Mel Snyder pose on the steps that lead to the north monument. He happened to capture a police cruiser driving by at the time, which greatly enhanced the image, by providing a comparison basis which allows us to analyze both photographs side-by-side.

The differences in the horizontal planes are obvious:

Years later, French researcher Marcel Dehaeseleer, while researching the correct orientation of Moorman's Polaroid camera, inadvertently confirmed that Mary held her camera in a perfectly horizontal plane, which would have preserved the downward slope of Elm street and prevented the absence of tilt seen in the image today.

Mary Moorman's camera is perfectly horizontal, not tilted in any way.

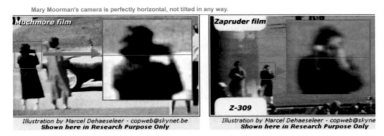

Muchmore film

Zapruder film

Z-309

Illustration by Marcel Dehaeseleer - copweb@skynet.be
Shown here in Research Purpose Only

Illustration by Marcel Dehaeseleer - copweb@skyne
Shown here in Research Purpose Only

This excellent analysis published by Dr. John Nichols in 1968 proved the major problems the Commission confronted with the lateral angles required to make the "magic bullet theory" feasible.

To that we must now add the problem of Officer James Chaney and his position in the police escort of the motorcade that day.

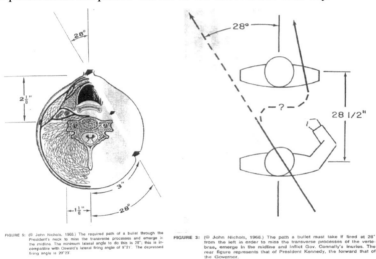

FIGURE 5: (© John Nichols, 1968.) The required path of a bullet through the President's neck to miss the transverse processes and emerge in the midline. The minimum lateral angle to do this is 28°; this is incompatible with Oswald's lateral firing angle of 9°21'. The depressed firing angle is 20°23'.

FIGURE 3: (© John Nichols, 1968.) The path a bullet must take if fired at 28° from the left in order to miss the transverse processes of the vertebrae, emerge in the midline and inflict Gov. Connally's injuries. The rear figure represents that of President Kennedy, the forward that of the Governor.

(Author's note: Recently, Oswald Innocence Campaign senior member Ralph Cinque has proposed that perhaps Mary did not really take her picture, after all. He points at the fact that Jim Featherstone immediately confiscated her camera and photograph, where she did not know what she had captured. Also, the fact that she waited until the president had passed her to snap her picture, when she had him slowly making his way down Elm Street and could have had him centered and facing her, as well as B.J. Martin, who was the original reason for Mary and Jean Hill to seek that position to begin with.)

"The doctoring here is obvious and grotesque."

—Beverly Brunson

479

But Brunson had even more to say about the Moorman photograph, and she suspected it had been "hastily and grotesquely doctored." This letter to Harold Weisberg dated 12 March 1968, sums up her opinions on Moorman alteration.

We have never before in public print been allowed to see this picture of "Jackson". As you can readily see he has only one arm and a neck like a giraffe. The doctoring here is obvious and grotesque. It ought to stand up in court. The blur at his stomach and chest, which at first glance would appear to be Mr. Newman's little boy, cannot be, I think, since the little boy, I believe, was standing on the other side of Newman. Nor could that be Newman's xxxx shadow as the shadows were falling northeast.

An interesting point is that I think it possible that they may have, in their haste that afternoon, painted out the wrong arm. The one arm cuts off from the trunk rather than the shoulder, and instead of a shoulder, we have a big gap which makes the man's neck grotesquely long, as it was not, of course. No one's is this long. There was an effort in the Nix frame published in color in the Post (SEP), the issue that mentioned you, to make it appear that this man was looking toward the knoll. As you can see he was not.

Profile and chin strap comparison

This Moorman also seems to show a wound to the top of the President's head, which I have not seen in poorer prints. It appears that a bullet has exited from the top of the head and caused a flap of skin to fly forward and upward. This wound does not appear to be the same wound which is visible on the side of the head in Zapruder after 313. It also looks as if there may be a small portion of skull exposed on the left top of the head, but the quality of the picture is so poor, it is not possible to make a decision on the matter.

480

It is of course very easy to ruin a Polaroid, just smear it before
it is dry. Or fail to paint it and let it fade. But this one
definitely appears to have been smeared. Hargis has a number of
arms as a result. The one thing possible to determine from his
picture is that his left hand is not on the left handlegrip but
up toward the center of the machine. I believe the right hand
is at the approximate position of the black blob and the flash
of light in various versions of the Altgens; but it is not possible
to say so flatly from this Moorman.

Are they opening your mail?

Brunson's painstaking research clearly offered concepts that, even
though radical at the time, seem to have been confirmed by the release
of new documents and technological advances in computer imaging
techniques and analysis.

In most cases, she was probably spot-on with her research, to the
point where she suspected her correspondence with Weisberg was
being subjected to inspection by forces unknown. If that was the case,
then those who had her under surveillance were certainly aware of
where her research was taking her.

Perhaps this is what prompted a very strange and mysterious
incident in Joplin, Missouri, possibly designed to dissuade her from
pursuing her investigations.

The Joplin Incident

On 5 September1967, Beverly made the short eight-mile drive to neighboring Joplin Missouri, to meet up with a young woman, presumably to exchange JFK research information and perhaps track down a lead. She carried in her purse pages upon pages of her research and correspondence with Weisberg. (One of the letters she had with her was correspondence with Richard Sprague regarding the motorcycle escort.) This person was a slim, short-haired young woman Beverly had never met. After a couple of drinks, Brunson found herself a few hours later being pulled out of her car by five "irate" cops who told her they had been chasing her for the past hour-and-a-half, where she had been driving on the wrong side of the road, with headlights turned off, speeding and running red lights, and causing a minor accident. She had been cut in her leg and had a nasty knot in the middle of her forehead. The last thing she remembered was that the woman had been driving Brunson's car before she blacked out. The woman turned out to be a friend of one of the arresting officers and the policemen examined the JFK documents and correspondence that she had in her purse with amusement, while commenting what a nut she was. She was never charged with anything because the doctor who treated her advised the police she was not drunk. (Source: Brunson letter 13 September 1967) Weisberg was convinced Beverly had been drugged and was lucky to be alive.

(Authors note: After carefully thinking this through, it is obvious to me that the "Joplin Incident" was a clear warning and a "shot across the bow" aimed at Weisberg, to lay off of this facet of the investigation—Douglas Jackson and James Chaney. In one of his letters, he clearly tells Beverly that he thought if something like this were to happen, it would have been to him. He realized not only that his mail was being compromised, but that these "powers" could take him out anytime they chose to.)

This letter, dated 26 September 1967, which had to be enhanced to make it legible, vividly describes "The Joplin Incident":

Dear Mr. Weisberg:

Thanks for your letter and interest. It looked like I was behind the wheel. Blood on the floor there and a crack in the windshield above the steering wheel. The steering wheel was badly twisted back toward the dash, but I had no bruises in chest or soreness from that. There was a [unintelligible] *tear in the carpeting on the passenger side.*

There were no witnesses. The police said they heard the crash.

By chance I knew the ambulance driver. He had been monitoring the police radio. He told his sister-in-law that there were calls out on my car at least 30 minutes before the crash and that there was an early report of a young man or boy running from the scene. He later [unintelligible] on this but did not deny it. (If true it could be the young woman: short hair, blue jeans, tall.)

I have found out the following that happened during my black-out period. The car was seen parked behind a saloon downtown. The young woman went in, made a phone call, came back out, talked to police, who she said warned her out of a yellow zone. The car was next in Webb City, Missouri, 8 miles away parked on a side street. The Webb City police came up to the car and asked what was going on and specifically what was wrong with me as I was sprawled across the seat. She told them I was sick. (I assume unconscious since she had to answer for me.) She admits to all this. And she says that then she drove us back to Joplin and turned the car over to me. Minutes later, by her timetable, the crash occurred about 6 blocks from her house. I having stirred up 5 police cars!

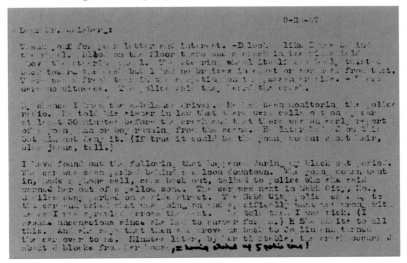

This I remember: earlier in the evening she had lent her car to two young men and a girl to take to the drive-in movie in Webb City. They left about 8 o'clock. I did not know them. (Her explanation of the phone call and the trip to Webb City was that she was trying to check upon her car. She was parked on the side street to wait for these people to show up. They did not so she came back to Joplin. 10

is a little early to start out looking for your car if you have lent it to someone to go to a drive-in movie in another city. So maybe the Webb City incident is an indication that I was given a fixed drink and taken over there [unintelligible] *circumstance peculiar enough to arouse the attention of the Webb City police. But a fixed drink would not explain* [unintelligible] *ride behind the wheel a short time later)*

The police are telling the insurance people that I was drunk and running. I was not charged with either. My lawyer got this across and when the case got into the hands of the city prosecutor he was very nice and to recommend a fine of $50. I could plead Not Guilty. So now all I got stuck with is the reputation and in trouble with the insurance company. I've only drank hard liquor twice this year, once too many. I don't go out. I've never had a blackout [unintelligible] *where I have been and what I have done. There are several other very* [unintelligible] *little things—but I would* [unintelligible] *to tell them* [unintelligible] *I can't see what significance they could have. Suffice it to say that the whole thing . . ."*

These are just speculations, except for the first and
second paragraphs. That's a phony. And I don't like it.
Turner has my rundown and wrote me a gingerly wrought
letter about the Parallax Altgens. He said he couldn't
see what significance it could have and that the flash
of light was too close to the ground to be a muzzle flash.
I hadn't said it was a muzzle flash. And it isn't close to
the ground. I had Turner's letter on me when I had that
accident fixed on me in Joplin on Sept. 5, 1967. Since
then I have not been in touch with him and don't plan to
be. I trust he is an honest front shotter but he must
have a plant on him, if he is.

                                    Beverly Brunson
                                    Box 296
                                    Baxter Springs, Kansas 66713

The above passage shows how Brunson suspected William Turner,
or someone in his auspices, of orchestrating the Joplin incident.

From this letter and others that she wrote to Harold Weisberg, she
clearly suspected Turner of working for the other side and who was
planting false information in the research community. (Weisberg Item
09) She also thought that Turner was burying information she was
making available to him.

Julia Mercer. I am not saying that she is a plant on
Garrison. But there is a possibility of it. If she
witnessed what she said she witnessed then the event was
staged. If she didn't witness it, then she was pre-designed
to come forward with it. Now that she has turned up again,
the effect has been, it seems, to confirm Garrison in his
view that there was a shot from the knoll, or the front.
I don't doubt it could have been Ruby driving the truck.
But if it happened, it was still staged and meant to be
noticed. You don't block traffic to take your weapon up
to position. -I think we ought to keep in mind that
Mercer, Bowers, Holland evidence was all turned over by
the DSO: they could have put their affadavits in a hot
Xerox. Instead they obligingly turn it all over to the
Commission and thereby the public. There are many indications that Dallas was not happy when the front shot
and the rifle conspiracy from knoll and building were
squelched in favor of the lone assassin line. Walker
wasn't happy either. These people had gone to a lot of
work to create the impression of a red rifle conspiracy. Now they were stuck with it and weren't a bit
happy.   **(Item 09 pg 5)**

                                    3-21-68

Mr. Weisberg:

Another one-subject letter. You will recall that David
Welsh, in the famous Nov. 1966 Ramparts, expresses his
surprise that Bill Turner on a "whirlwind" trip to Dallas
could turn up five witnesses who not only knew Tippit, but
saw him racing around at 1 o'clock. In retrospect, I am
very surprised too. This is false information. Turner
supposedly got it on a tip from David Lifton, who is, I
believe the tunnel man, a theory in my opinion just a
hop, skip, and jump from those of Mr. Geo. Thomson, and

with the same charm. It contains a grain of truth, that
tunnel, since it implies an upshot; but it makes nonsense
of the truth and is utterly misleading.

Turner's "witnesses" also have charm. It turns out that
the direction in which they saw Tippit go was the same
as that of Jack Ruby's apartment. Obviously news most
welcome to outside conspiracy theorists.

You might be interested to know that I have determined to my own
satisfaction that I was not driving my car when that wreck happened
and I got into so much trouble and bad publicity. When I received
my car back, about a month ago, there had been $1000. damage to the
right front repaired, but the inside had not been touched. The dash
board on the passenger side is bent out of shape, the metal part
beneath the padded part almost half an inch on the passenger side,
and the carpeting is torn loose deep in the passenger's feet compartment,
right where there is a large belt, just the size of the scar I bear on
my left instep. Since it was a right side accident, and since I
had on a soft shoe that absorbed the first bleed, I must have moved
my feet to the driver's side to try to get out. There was blood all
over the driver's side floor, but none at all on my right shoe or
right shoe sole; and long drip marks on the left shoe, very plain to
see. Thus neither of my feet were ever in the blood on the driver's
side floor. One foot hung off there and bled. The crack in the
windshield was a spreading from a preexistent defect. One thing
disturbs me mightily - I had a bad bruise on the left side that
nothing fits but the seat belt on the passenger side which was opened,
put in so that the belt buckles on the left side. This exactly fits
my bruise. And I never use seat belts. I am convinced that I must
have been strapped in there.

I now think that you were right the first time, I must have had a
fixed drink. (An Oklahoma State police veteran who has heard the
whole story says there is no doubt in his mind that this is what
must have happened. He said the motive would be sex.)However, I
knew that I was not molested; not robbed, so the motive eludes me.

Also, since I knew to my satisfaction that there was a passenger, it
is a virtual certainty that it was me and that the early report heard
by the ambulance driver of someone running must have been correct and
that the driver left the car immediately and ran. Thus the behavior
of the police is mystifying. They said that they were in pursuit of
the car, rounding a corner when it crashed in the middleof the block.
They were therefore upon it immediately, and must have known that I
was not driving - which I told them repeatedly though I could not say
who was. They risked a suit for false arrest and one for libel (which
they would and will get if I ever get hold of a shred of proof) just in
order to arrest and publicly slander me when they must have known for
a certainty that I was not even driving. The fact that the first one
on the scene and the one that insisted on the arrest was the friend
of the young woman driving at my last memory makes the whole thing
still somewhat sinister. They could not have known, were they innocent
of any prior knowledge, that I would not remember and be able to prove
that I was not driving. As a matter of fact the city prosecuter was
very nervous about the whole matter and the newspaper dropped the
story from all subsequent editions, since I was not charged with what
I was accused of, no doubt... that is running from the police and being
drunk.

At this point, it begins to look to me as if the motive may have been
exactly what was accomplished. I was fed a fixed drink in order to
be taken for a wild ride. The motive should scarcely have been blackmail
since I would have been given it in a stationary place and pictures made
or something. Attention was drawn to the car throughout the evening
so that the police were looking for it. It was reported "coming into
town" on a certain street, the police found it nicely waiting at a
closed service station on Main Street, it ran when they appeared and
the crash occurred. It looks as if the car was waiting for the cops -
one of them - her friend - to find it, so this wild run and pursuit could
occur and give someone a chance to do some damage to my reputation.

The ambulance driver, interestingly enough said that my clothes were
unbuttoned and unzipped; yet I knew that I was not molested, nor in
any sex siutaion voluntarily, so I think that it is possible that was
arranged too. I was simply to be found in the condition most damaging

to a woman of my age and occupation. It has even occurred to me that
the report of the "young man" running might have been a fake and originally
intended to serve the purpose of damaging me but been dropped when it
turned out I was not drunk and could express myself. I knew one or two
young men better than I want to - they keep hanging around - and it is
conceivable that someone wanted to pin me to some kind of carouse with
an unknown youth - which would be very damaging. Since both of these
young men are queer, there is nothing there, needless to say; but someone
might think they could make it look like it.

At any rate, it is still a dense mysterious event; and to me still
sinister and alarming.

Beverly Brunson
Box 546   (296)
Baxter Springs, Kansas, 66713

It appears by the studies provided here that Beverly Brunson was well ahead of her contemporaries in the scrutiny, examination and interpretation of the evidence pertaining to the JFK assassination. Consequently, many of her discoveries that are now being re-examined are being confirmed to have been correct.

Brunson's research and interest in the JFK assassination mysteriously and dramatically came to an end after the Joplin incident. She was obviously touching on aspects of the case that were considered taboo and apparently moved much too close for comfort to those who are still covering up what happened to JFK.

Technology and the passage of time has shown that JFK Queen Hecate's work needs to be placed with the best researchers of her generation. May she rest in peace.

(photo credit Glenna Shanks Vernon)

487

Thank you for saying there is nothing wrong with my prose. It's
a matter of stamina. I am not too modest: I know I swing a
formidable phrase but I am apt to strike out at the end of about
three of them. Prose is a long art - the long meticulous art of
the truly civilized. Poets are not too civilized. We like to
leap suddenly out of the dark. Or, to put it another way, poetry
is still an incantation to produce the god. Poets (and witchdoctors
and other magical operators) are impatient souls; and, like Milton,
when they attempt the art of prose, they are apt to keep that old
bullroarer going, in the sly hope that, if their reasoning won't
prevail against the opposition, Queen Hecate will come and throw
a bright bolt in their eyes.

Sincerely,

Beverly Brunson
Box 296
Baxter Springs, Kansas 66713

Item 4 pg 3

July 25, 1967

Dear Mr. Weisberg:

Please forgive this letter following so fast on the last one. As you
know I do not expect an answer unless you think one appropriate. I
have read Photographic Whitewash. (Thank you for your kind mention of
me.) As with all your books, each chapter is a revelation and carries
to the reader that sense of shock that is at once pleasant and un-
pleasant: it is sickening to learn that the whitewash has been so
blatant and wide; but it is exciting and redeeming to know that the
truth is going to be known. You may remember I once believed that
Nothing Would Ever Be Done. I now think, thanks largely to your work,
the whole story will one day be told. And I have hope that it will
be in our lifetime. A second factor contributes to my optimism. I
experienced a cold fury when CBS pushed its four hours of propaganda.
I stared at Cronkite and Severeid and swore that I would never
give up. Therefore, in spite of the fact that I know you do not agree
with my reconstruction of the mechanics of the assassination, I have
continued to send you material, one, because you requested it, and two,
because I am still convinced that I am turning up a fresh perspective.
If, for instance, the photos and X rays are ever viewed by an impartial
body and it does turn out that they by and large resemble the Commission's
case; if for instance, the Garrison case for snipers on the knoll should
fail to be established, I will still have provided a coherent and
thorough explanation of what could have happened. I think it is what
must have happened, simply because I am a reasonable person (Phi Beta
Kappa, Mo., 1950) and my reason leads me to the same answer from every
direction in which I approach the mechanics of the assassination.

2

Is it necessary to point out that assassins may have theatrical
talent? That assassins would not park a truck part way up on
a curb and then remove what looks like a gun case from it and
walk about with it? That the end of a gun case cannot become
entangled in the grass, and that even if it did, a good jerk
would release it? That assassins desiring to place a rifle on
this grassy knoll would have driven in the back way on the parking lot and no one the wiser? That assassins are not likely
to make their cars suspicious by covering them up with mud
putting big Goldwater stickers on them and talking on micro-
phones? That assassins are too busy shooting and getting
away to throw anything into the bushes? And what would they
throw anyway? That modern rifles smoke very little and on
a windy day are not like to smoke 8 feet in the air? A firecracker is far more likely to smke at that height if it is
thrown there. Diversionary tactics? Many thought they heard
firecrackers, many experienced gunmen in that motorcade.

THE ALTGENS'PICTURE   3-13-68

There exist at least three different version of this picture
taken at the time President Kennedy was assassinated in Dallas,
Texas, on Nov. 22, 1963. One version appeared in the Saturday
Evening Post, Dec. 14, 1963; a second version is that published

```
by Harold Weisberg in  Whitewash II, with assurances from AP
that it was made from the original untouched 35 mm negative;
a third version is that published in Esquire, May, 1967, the
National Enquirer, May 7, 1967, and by Parallax Press in a
paperback version of The Torch Is Passed in July, 1967.  I
shall refer to these versions as the Post Altgens, the Whitewash
Altgens, and the Parallax Altgens.
```

(Author's note: All Brunson JFK research material cited in this article resides at jfk.hood.edu/Collection/Weisberg%20Subject%20 Index%20Files/B%20Disk/Brunson%20Beverly. Some documents that were illegible were computer-enhanced and transcribed by the author.)

ENDNOTES

1. findagrave.com/cgi-bin/fg.cgi?page=gr&GRid=29088330
2. *Baxter Springs Citizen* obituary 23 April 1983, Leroy Brunson, courtesy Baxter Springs Historical Society, Ms. Earlene Spaulding
3. Glenna Shanks Vernon email, 6 February 2014
4. Earlene Spaulding email, 12 February 2014, companion Mary Gibson
5. Glenna Shanks Vernon email and telephone conversation, 6 February 2014
6. Item 9, p. 5
7. Item 27, p. 2
8. Item 9, p. 5
9. Jones, Milton, *The Third Decade*, "Skulduggery in Dallas," January 1993 (makes reference to: WC4H160, 4H352, 18H723, 2H73, 7H447, 7H473, 18H750-762, 2H150, 7H474 and 18H778)
10. Item 27, p. 5
11. CD897, pp. 36-37
12. Ibid.
13. Weisberg, Harold, *Whitewash II* (1966), pp. 192-193
14. Rivera, Larry, "Who was in the TSBD Doorway?" 11 February 2015
15. Also seen by S.M. Holland (*The Saturday Evening Post* 2 December 1967)
16. *The Fourth Decade*, July 1995, p. 22
17. Ibid. 23
18. WC21H213
19. CBS, 22 November 1963 transmission
20. Secret Service, 26-29 November 1963, File: CO-2-3;030 Special Agents Edward Z. Tucker and Joseph E. Noonan
21. Holt, Chauncey, *Self-Portrait of a Scoundrel* (2013), edited by Wim Dankbaar, pp. 161-162
22. Ibid. 161
23. Ibid. 170
24. Ibid. 173
25. "After the shooting, Dallas Police officer Joe M. Smith encountered another suspicious man in the lot behind the picket fence [on the grassy knoll]. Smith told the Warren Commission that when he drew his pistol and approached the

man, the man 'showed [Smith] that he was a Secret Service agent.' (Warren Commission Vol. VII, p. 535; see interview of Joseph M. Smith, 8 February 1978, House Select Committee on Assassinations [JFK Document 005886]) I looked into all the cars and checked around the bushes. Of course, I wasn't alone. There was some deputy sheriff with me, and I believe one Secret Service man when I got there. I got to make this statement, too. I felt awfully silly, but after the shot and this woman, I pulled my pistol from my holster, and I thought, this is silly, I don't know who I am looking for, and I put it back. Just as I did, he showed me that he was a Secret Service agent." (Warren Commission Hearings, Vol. VII, p. 531)

26. Conversations and emails with Richard Hooke
27. *The Fourth Decade*, September 1994, p. 27
28. Palamara, Vince, *Survivor's Guilt: The Secret Service and the Failure to Protect President Kennedy* (2013), p. 10
29. Ibid.
30. Kinney footnote: Later in life, Sam Kinney had even more nefarious revelations in store. As an aside, on 20 November 2013, Professor Jim Fetzer interviewed Gary Leuchs, a neighbor of Kinney of many years. According to Leuchs, the former Secret Service agent revealed that he was responsible for finding CE399, the famous magic bullet, which was found on a stretcher at Parkland Hospital. Leuchs informed Fetzer that Kinney told him he recovered the bullet from the limousine and placed in on the stretcher himself. Furthermore, Kinney insisted that this information not be disclosed until his demise. (http://radiofetzer.blogspot.com/2013/11/gary-leuchs.html)
31. see Brunson items 10, 11, 16A, 16B, 36, 37
32. By using FBI reports, Warren Commission testimony, magazine and newspaper accounts/
33. Rivera, Larry, "Who was in the TSBD Doorway?" 11 February 2015
34. 1971 telephone interview by Gil Toft, commissioned by Fred Newcomb, transcribed by Larry Rivera
35. Ibid.
36. Newcomb and Adams, *Murder from Within* (1974), pp. 46-47
37. Brunson item 16A, computer-enhanced for legibility
38. Ibid.
39. Ibid.
40. youtube.com/watch?v=x0gcAQNunbM
41. Dr. John Nichols, 1968

APPENDIX

8/10/68

Mr. Weisberg:

Thanks for your letter. I haven't sent you much because I haven't
worked much on the case specifically. Since the new assassinations
I have devoted a good amount of time to trying to get a realistic grasp
on the national picture. I think I've got it. Although really it is
now child's play to figure it out. The symbols are big and broad.
The politicians, the press, even the citizen on the street, or a number
of them, seem to know the score exactly, if you read between the lines.

As a result of this analysis I have been making, for my own satisfaction,
I have come to the conclusion that there is nothing we can do. As you
said, they have the power. I, at least, can no longer go on the assumption
that the truth is the turtle in a race and will ultimately win. That is
an assumption we might reasonably have made in the old democracy. But it
is now a new ball game. And we have no bat, no ball. In such a situation,
the truth seems a little beside the point and hope pernicious.

I also have come to estimate my own role in this as amusing: here I was
on the outside flailing away about the great discoveries I had made. It
is no wonder all the "critics" -or I mean those except you with whom I
have been in contact -fought me so ferociously or made a pariah of me.
What I thought I had discovered was known to them all the time. They
were playing various games. Perhaps some of those games were to protect
the Kennedys. It may have been the only thing they felt they could do.
But it did not work. -I also do not think for a moment that Garrison
can have been in ignorance of what happened in Dallas for four long years.
He would have been among the first to know, in his position. So there
is no use for me to do the work. There is, in short, no longer any place
for a citizen investigation or an armchair detective.

My regard for you and my trust in you is undiminished. -If you think
that there is still hope and room to work I want to know it. But I can't
see where it could come from. I am not equipped to play the power game.
And what citizen is? When giants fight.

Mary feels the same way, though she is not responsible for this decision
of mine to merely watch events. She concurs, however.

Yes, Bobby made the wrong choice. And as the existentialists say, he
made it for all of us. The establishment made it for all of us. It
ected according to its nature and did not go to the people with the truth.
Then when it saw not only all honor but all power slipping away, it
let Bobby go out and fight. All by himself.

Do not think I am too bitter. I am resilient. But I feel that I have
been just a citizen trying to do my duty. When my voice got around, I
should have been let in on the secret that what I was coming with was
no secret. I am particularly bitter about Mrs. Meagher whom I believed
in. And Richard Sprague -I suspect he was in the Kennedy faction.

Beverly Brunson
Box 296
Baxter Springs, Kansas 66713

I have written you a number of letters, but mailed few. They were
mainly dry runs. Even this one I had to rewrite. It is hard for me
to say exactly what I want to say.

Item 01

491

20

The JFK Horsemen

In the wake of the JFK assassination, J. Edgar Hoover and his FBI embarked on a vicious campaign of persecution and intimidation against the DPD.[1] One of the casualties of this abuse was Chief of Police Jesse Curry himself, when Hoover intervened directly to make sure the FBI took over the investigation, despite the protests of Chief Curry.[2] Curry was eventually forced into retirement and later published his own account of the investigation, where he raised issues that he felt were never resolved.[3] Immediately after the assassination, Chief Curry held press conferences informing that the FBI had prior knowledge about Oswald in Dallas, and that they had been monitoring his activities.[4] Hoover was so outraged that he forced the DPD and Curry to retract these statements.[5] This "show of force" by the FBI intimidated the DPD into obeying every directive, and set forth an environment of fear and submission that trickled all the way down to the policemen and motorcycle escort, known as "motor jockeys" amongst themselves, who witnessed the assassination up close and personal. They also referred to their Harley Davidson's as their "motors."

Despite being the closest law enforcement officers and witnesses to the assassination, these four men became *personae non grata* to the FBI, the Warren Commission, the Secret Service, and the DPD. This chapter will examine the photographic record versus the documentary record, and the historical, and perhaps reluctant roles, each of them played in the assassination and its aftermath.

The Fred Newcomb and Perry Adams Tapes

In 1971, Fred Newcomb and Perry Adams commissioned Gil Toft to speak to and interview the motorcycle escort. A very small portion of the transcripts of the tape recordings was used for the book *Murder from Within: Lyndon Johnson's Plot Against President Kennedy* (1974). At a time when even seasoned local investigators such as Penn Jones were having extreme difficulties talking to any of the members of the DPD, who in any way had information regarding the events of 22 November 1963, it was truly remarkable that Toft, using the pseudonym John Whitney, was able to engage them in any type of conversation.

Whitney soon discovered that none of the motor jockeys he spoke to had seen the Zapruder film, and immediately had Newcomb send bootleg copies of the film to these officers.

Once they were in possession of the film, Whitney could point out discrepancies and obtain their reactions.

In the case of Douglas Jackson, he welcomed the opportunity to obtain a copy of the film for the benefit of his children and grandchildren. Jackson figured it wouldn't matter 50 years into the future. The Newcomb and Adams tapes seemed to resolve the following issues:

Issues that are resolved by the Newcomb tapes

- The hole in the windshield
- The limo stop
- Movements of Hargis, Jackson, Chaney, Martin, Freeman and Ellis.
- Besides Clint Hill, the actions of Secret Service Agents in the follow up car
- Second Secret Service Agent in the limousine.
- Piece of skull that was picked up by a young boy on the infield of the South curb of Elm Street.
- The knoll rider

As seen in Chapter 19, security assignments for JFK's motorcade in Dallas on 22 November 1963, were arranged by Captain Perdue W. Lawrence, as noted in a 21 November 1963 memo written by Lawrence to Chief Curry dated the day before.[6]

Motorcycle Patrolman Douglas Lavelle Jackson had escorted JFK on a previous visit to Dallas in 1961. He was hoping he would be selected to escort him again. Jackson appreciated how JFK made the extra effort to acknowledge the police escort and shake hands with them.[7]

As noted in the previous chapter, JFK's SS-100-X Ford Lincoln Continental limousine was flanked by four DPD motorcycle officers. These patrolmen had been given instructions to keep spectators at bay and to ride right off the rear bumpers of JFK's limousine for the motorcade that day.[8]

Mr. MARTIN. They instructed us that they didn't want anyone riding past the President's car and that we were to ride to the rear, to the rear of his car, about the rear bumper.   (WC6H293)

A review of the Warren Commission volumes reveals that of the 18 motorcycle officers only B. J. Martin, Bobby W. Hargis, E. D. Brewer, Clyde A. Haygood, and M. L. Baker were interviewed by the Commission.

Of the four "motor jockeys" that were escorting JFK on 22 November 1963, only Bobby Hargis and Billy J. Martin testified, so very briefly, before the Warren Commission for a total 7.5 pages of testimony between the two.[9]

Marrion Baker, who was not in the immediate vicinity of the limousine, was the only motorcycle patrolman interviewed by the FBI. The others were ignored by the FBI, the Secret Service and the DPD.[10] In 1975, FBI Inspector James R. Malley, acting as a spokesperson for the FBI, tried to explain why:

Malley said that, generally, only those persons the FBI knew had information, or who were brought to our attention as having information, were interviewed. Regarding the motorcycle officers, he speculated that they never came to our attention as being persons who could furnish pertinent information. He feels that if they had pertinent information, they should have come forward.   (mffpdf-62474 pg 171)

Malley, was actually brought out of retirement that year to help the FBI document this abomination.[11]

This is exactly the role adopted by retired CIA operative George Joannides, of the CIA's JM/WAVE—the codename for a major secret U.S. covert operations and intelligence gathering station in operation from 1961 until 1968—station in Miami in 1978 as liaison between the CIA and the HSCA.[12]

It will soon become evident why none of the officers came forward to tell their stories. Malley also questioned the motorcycle escort' supposed inability to be good witnesses simply because they were riding their bikes. It is absurd and downright disrespectful that Malley would try to infer that "numerous people who were in the immediate vicinity on foot"[13] "would have a better view," and therefore would be better suited as witnesses, than the four escort that were within a few feet of the limousine during the entirety of the assassination, men who were trained to be prepared for emergencies and other contingencies.

> It is noted from the Warren Commission testimony of the five motorcycle officers above that they were pretty much preoccupied at the time of the shooting with maintaining balance on their motorcycles at the slow speed of the motorcade and looking ahead to avoid hitting anything. The Dallas Office interviewed numerous people who were in the immediate vicinity on foot and had a better view of the area.

Consider this letter to Quin Shea of the National Archives, from Harold Weisberg, regarding his JFK assassination records appeals dated 16 June 1979, on Dallas Policemen Jim Chaney, D.L. Jackson; "no law enforcement purpose."[14]

> Previously I have appealed withholdings relating to Motorcycle Policeman Jim Chaney, who was one of the four closest to the President. In amplifying this I add Douglas Lavelle Jackson, also one of these four. Both are among the approximately dozen and a half Dallas motorcycle policemen ostensibly never interviewed by the FBI in its greatest investigation ever, no doubt because policemen might be better than average observers and had the responsibility of being alert to any untoward events.
>
> Clearly, therefore, 15 years after the event the FBI has nothing to hide.
>
> That Jackson saw the second shot he heard strike Governor Connally is not in accord with the Commission's conclusion that the first shot hit both Kennedy and Connally. (Serial,7344, 62-109060, attached.) That the third shot hit the President above the right
>
> ear and his head exploded out to the left (page 2) also is not what the Commission concluded.
>
> That he had an excellent opportunity to examine Governor Connally as he assisted him from the limousine at the hospital apparently also tended to disqualify him as a witness for the FBI. (Page 2) Ditto for the President because he only helped put the President on the stretcher. (Page 2) And that he guarded the emergency room door and assisted in transporting the President's body to Love field also meant to the FBI that he had no information of any value at all. (Page 2)
>
> The indices reflect that it was not by accident that the FBI did not interview any of the 18 motorcycle police escorts. (Page 2)
>
> In providing explanations of these omissions, and I'm inclined to agree there was a need, this memo repeats still again that there was no law-enforcement purpose. (Page 2, penult. graf.)
>
> Inspector Malley was questioned because he had been sent to Dallas immediately. He helped explain away the FBI's failure to interview any of these 18 policemen:
>
> "Mr. Malley said that, generally, only those persons the FBI knew had information, or who were brought to our attention as having information, were interviewed." Now about these trained and experience police, there is a Malley/Orwell explanation:"... he speculated that they never came to our attention as being persons who could furnish pertinent information. He feels that if they had pertinent information, they should have come forward."

Bobby Hargis

Most researchers are familiar with the story of how Bobby Hargis was hit with brain and skull matter with such force that he thought he himself had been shot.[15]

How important did the Commission consider Hargis's experience that day? They dedicated a total of 3.5 pages to his testimony. We must begin by tracing Hargis's movements after the shots.

Hargis testified that he "ran to the light post" and then ran up to the "little wall," obviously reacting like everyone else to what was going on at the top of the knoll.[16]

Mr. STERN. And did you run up the incline on your side of Elm Street?
Mr. HARGIS. Yes, sir; I ran to the light post, and I ran up to this kind of a little wall, brick wall up there to see if I could get a better look on the bridge, and, of course, I was looking all around that place by that time. I knew it couldn't have come from the county courthouse because that place was swarming with deputy sheriffs over there.   (Vol 6 page 295)

These images from the Mark Bell film show Hargis standing at the lamp post, but they fail to show him running up to the little wall of the pergola where Abraham Zapruder had been filming.

Notice how Zapruder and his secretary Marilyn Sitzman have already abandoned their position. This will prove to be extremely important later on in this chapter.

After standing there for a few seconds, looking north toward the monument arches atop the grassy knoll, he is shown turning around and crossing the street to get back on his bike.

The Bell film, however, does not show Hargis's dash to the "little wall" as stated in his testimony and corroborated by several witnesses, among them S.M. Holland. This is how Jesse Curry described Hargis's experience and movements that day:[17]

> President John F. Kennedy had been shot and the motorcycle officers on each side of the rear of the Presidential car knew that he was hurt and hurt badly. No one knew any more forcefully than motorcycle Officer Bobby Hargis. He had been following close, just behind the left rear fender of the limousine. A red sheet of blood and brain tissue exploded backward from Kennedy's head into the face of Officer Hargis. The trajectory must have appeared to Hargis to have come from just ahead and to the right of the motorcade. He parked his motorcycle and started running in that direction. (From Jesse Curry's Personal JFK Assassination File page 30)

Curry's description of Hargis's movements cannot be verified with the Bell footage either. Of the four escort, Hargis was the only motorcycle officer who remained in Dealey Plaza.

"He ran across the street, then looked over to the railroad overpass," leaving his bike right in the middle of the left lane of Elm Street. Hargis described what he did next in his Warren Commission testimony (WC6H296):

> Mr. HARGIS. Then I got back on my motorcycle, which was still running, and rode underneath the first underpass to look on the opposite side in order to see if I could see anyone running away from the scene, and since I didn't see anyone coming from that direction I rode under the second underpass, which is Stemmons Expressway and went up around to see if I could see anyone coming from across Stemmons and back that way, and I couldn't see anything that was of a suspicious nature, so, I came back to the Texas School Book Depository. At that time it seemed like the activity was centered around the Texas School Book Depository, so, that is when I heard someone say, one of the sergeants or lieutenants, I don't know, "Don't let anyone out of the Texas School Book Depository," and so, I went to a gap that had not been filled, which was at the southwest corner.
> Mr. STERN. And you remained there until you were relieved? (WC6H296)
> Mr. HARGIS. Yes.

In the 2 December 1967 issue of *The Saturday Evening Post*, Josiah Thompson erroneously identified Hargis as the policeman who ran parallel to the picket fence, circled above right, atop the grassy knoll.[18]

These two Wilma Bond images confirm:

a.) That Hargis momentarily parked his "motor" right on Elm Street, and

b.) He re-mounted and drove under the triple overpass as stated in his Warren Commission testimony above.

As first pointed out by Beverly Brunson,[19] the Bond image at left shows Hargis in the process of re-mounting his motorcycle. The image at right shows the motorcycle is no longer there, confirming Hargis's testimony and the Bell images above.

The motorcycle patrolman at the top of the hill (circled red) is officer Clyde A. Haygood, who was part of the third tier of motorcycle escort and was just turning from Main onto Houston when the shooting began.[20]

Clyde Haygood looks in the direction of the picket fence, then dismounts and runs up to where the stockade fence meets the corner of the triple overpass where a steam pipe is located.

This is a different view of Hargis, as shown in the Weigman film, as he remounts his motorcycle in the left lane of Elm Street after crossing the street from his position next to the lamppost. At right, smoke drifts from the embankment of the grassy knoll.

The real exciting one [photograph] *is atop the grassy knoll where the curved concrete rail of the underpass joins the stockade fence. It is behind the fence near the sharp angle in it, under the steam pipe. I have exciting pix of that. It is also consistent with all front right trajectories, and what a perfect pill box, 6 ft deep, 3 ft square, hidden from everyone!*

—Harold Weisberg, February 1968 note to Robert Cutler

While Hargis was trying to expand on blood, skull, and brain matter in his Warren Commission testimony, Counsel Samuel Stern was trying to shift him away from that very sensitive line of questioning. Stern repeatedly cut him off, then desperately tried to establish the "sounds of shots." Hargis did not acknowledge "sounds," only that he "knew they were shots" *because of the chaos he was seeing.* This testimony also confirms that Hargis was not concerned with the TSBD at the time, because people were not reacting as if shots had been fired from there. The great majority of witnesses were attracted to the area of the railroad yard, grassy knoll and picket fence areas.

could have been coming from the railroad overpass, because I thought since I had got splattered, with blood—I was just a little back and left of—just a little bit back and left of Mrs. Kennedy, but I didn't know. I had a feeling that it might have been from the Texas Book Depository, and these two places was the primary place that could have been shot from.

Mr. STERN. You were clear that the sounds were sounds of shots?

Mr. HARGIS. Yes, sir; I knew they were shots.

Mr. STERN. All right, what did you do then? You say you parked your motorcycle?

Mr. HARGIS. Yes, uh-huh——

Mr. STERN. Where?

Mr. HARGIS. It was to the left-hand side of the street from—south side of Elm Street.

Mr. STERN. And then what did you do?

Mr. HARGIS. I ran across the street looking over towards the railroad overpass and I remembered seeing people scattering and running and then I looked——

Mr. STERN. People on the overpass?

Mr. HARGIS. Yes; people that were there to see the President I guess. They were taking pictures and things. It was kind of a confused crowd. I don't know whether they were trying to hide or see what was happening or what—and then I looked over to the Texas School Book Depository Building, and no one that was standing at the base of the building was—seemed to be looking up at the building or anything like they knew where the shots were coming from, so——

Mr. STERN. How about the people on the incline on the north side of Elm Street? Do you recall their behavior? (WC6H295)

499

In his later years, Hargis said he suffered recurring nightmares about the assassination, where he said he saw a shiny weapon sticking out of a window of the TSBD and tried to alert the Secret Service men who were oblivious to his pleas, and to his dismay, was never able to prevent assassination and save JFK.[21]

Mike Robinson's "End of Innocence"

The story of Mike Robinson, as told to Larry Howard at the Assassination Information Center (AIC) back in 1993, deserves our attention at this time, because the information available has mostly checked out.[22] Mike walked into the old AIC in Dallas and stunned Howard and his editor, Robert Johnson, with an experience he had been withholding since 22 November 1963.[23]

Mike had been good friends with Kirk Martin, the son of Captain Frank M. Martin, who was head of the Juvenile Division of the DPD at the time of the assassination. With permission from school and his parents, Mike had been invited to see the parade accompanied by his buddy Kirk.

Afterward, they were supposed to go to The Majestic Theater on 1925 Elm Street. They were in the theater ready to go in, with their popcorn and all, when they found out about the shooting. Mike and Kirk raced back to Captain Martin's office and spent most of the afternoon and early evening at the DPD at City Hall.

Mr. Robinson's story is so dramatic, it needs to be reproduced here as it was originally published, so the reader can appreciate the impact of the shooting on the motorcycle escort, who by process of elimination can be none other than Bobby Hargis.[24]

The estimated time of this encounter was about 3:00-4:00 PM, 22 November 1963.

stepped out to see what all the commotion was about and noticed a motorcycle policeman walk toward me from down the hall. As he got close I realized he was covered in dried blood. His face was weathered, his eyes were glazed—he was vacant looking. The left side of his neck was coarse and sunburned and splattered with Kennedy's blood. His shirt and his helmet had what looked like chunks of brain matter and hair. I noticed tears started swelling in his eyes then fall down his face. He put his hands over his eyes. I had never seen a grown man cry, much less a policeman. His sorrow quickly turned to a rage. He started pounding on the wall with his fists and then beating his head against the wall with his helmet. It was sad. I remember thinking how proud he probably was in his spit shined boots, his neatly pressed blue uniform, and his shiny white helmet. It looked like he was going to open the door to Homicide where the suspect was and I thought maybe he might have been going after him; he seemed so hopeless and unhinged. I thought he felt guilty that he wasn't able to have protected the President and stopped what had happened. Several people tried to calm him down which angered him more; he wanted no part of it. He wrestled for a moment with those trying to restrain him and finally gave in. He was escorted down the hall toward the elevators and into the crowd.

I looked down on the tile floor near where the scuffle took place and saw something I'll never forget. It was shiny gray and about the size of my thumbnail. It looked like skin and bone with hair on it. I looked closely. "Kirk, that's a piece of the President's head." At that moment the total shock of what had happened reached its impact level. Listening to the story unfold on the scanner, knowing what happened down the street, seeing the suspect hustled by—it all seemed unreal, but when I saw the blood, heard his crying, felt his sorrow, and then almost touching a piece of the President's skull, it became horribly real—President Kennedy was dead.

The President of the United States had been killed a few blocks away and I saw his blood and bits of his brain freshly splattered all over a policeman who was proudly escorting him. I tried to push what I had just seen out of my mind by thinking about the cheers, the applause and Kennedy smiling as his car was rushed by people who loved him, but I couldn't. How could this have happen? How? It was the end of innocence.

Hargis Saw the Limousine Stop

On 26 June 1995, Hargis was interviewed:

Hargis: This is . . . not to be shown publicly, but that guy slowed down—maybe his orders was to slow down whether the rest of the guys . . .

Interviewer: Mr. Greer, the driver of the presidential limousine . . .

Hargis: *Yeah, the presidential limousine—slowed down, almost to a stop.* [Emphasis added]

Hargis: I don't think if he had slowed down, that Oswald would've had another shot.[25]

James Chaney

James Chaney was never called before the Warren Commission and was not interviewed by the FBI until 1975. As noted by Beverly Brunson, the Commission references to Chaney are indirect, one from Marrion Baker (WC3H366) and the other from Bobby Hargis (WC6H294). Chaney was the only DPD motorcycle escort interviewed by the media—ABC—the evening of the assassination.[26] Here is the transcript of that interview:

Lord: I understand you were riding next to the president's car when the assassination took place.

Chaney: I was riding on the right rear fender.

Lord: What happened?

Chaney: We proceeded west on Elm Street at approximately 15-20 miles an hour . . . I heard the first shot, I thought it was motorcycle backfiring, and I looked back over to my left and also President Kennedy looked back over his left shoulder.

Then when the second shot came, I looked back just in time to see the president struck in the face by the second bullet.

He slumped* forward in Mrs. Kennedy's lap and it occurred to me that we were being fired upon. I went ahead of the president's car—to inform Chief Curry that the president had been hit—he instructed us over there to take him to Parkland Hospital and he had Parkland Hospital stand by—I went up ahead to notify the officers that were leading the escort that he had been hit and we had to move him out.

Lord: You did not see the person who fired the shot?

Chaney: No sir, it was back over my right shoulder.

Lord: What preventive measures had been taken to preclude such an incident?

Chaney: I don't know what [unintelligible] . . . that part of town.

Studio: This patrolman was so close to the president following the three shots, his uniform was splattered with blood.

(*Author's note: John Hankey has noted the extensive use of the term "slumped" to describe JFK's reactions to gunshots. The term was widely used in all media that weekend to describe JFK's reaction, including FBI interviews, Warren Commission exhibits, and well beyond, and even persists in grade school history books to this day.[27])

As Chaney's interview is analyzed, two statements deserve additional scrutiny:

1. ". . . also President Kennedy looked back over his left shoulder."

The Zapruder film simply *does not* show JFK doing this. What comes to mind is how Paul Mandel in LIFE Magazine tried to justify JFK's throat wound when he supposedly turned to his right "exposing himself to the sniper's nest"—causing a wound of entry.[28] Regarding Chaney turning to *his* left, he is not in enough frames of the Zapruder film to determine this.

2. "We proceeded west on Elm Street at approximately 15-20 miles an hour."

In 1979, Dallas Sheriff James C. Bowles wrote, however:

At 12:29, the microphone again stuck open and remained open for more than five minutes. At that time, the motorcade was nearing Main and Houston Streets. In the next period of some two minutes, the motorcade would almost stop while turning right onto Houston, ease its way north to Elm Street, then turn left onto Elm, westward toward the triple underpass. During this segment, the motorcade speed was reduced to less than 4 mph, and one or two stops were required as well as a considerable amount of "walking-speed" travel.[29]

Sergeant Stavis Ellis confirmed Chaney had been "sprayed" by blood and noted so when they arrived at Parkland Hospital.[30] Chaney himself confirmed he was splattered with blood in a 1971 phone interview arranged by Fred Newcomb mentioned at the beginning of this chapter:

Chaney: Well, on this film that I've got everything, looks like it's powdered in white, real white.

Whitney: Right, right, right, but you know you just see it at that one split second, you don't see anything flying anywhere . . .

Chaney: No.

Whitney: . . . which is kind of strange.

Chaney: Yeah . . . all over with as soon as it hit—it did splatter everything.

Marrion Baker stated before the Commission that "the car stopped completely, pulled to the left and stopped." The only reason they brought in Baker was because of his famous encounter on the second floor of the TSBD with Oswald.[31] The Commission had no other choice than to depose Officer Baker. He climbed all the way up to the roof looking for the sniper. This exchange illustrates why the Warren Commission wanted no part of the DPD motorcycle cops.

Mr. BELIN. Did you talk to any of the other officers who were in or about the President's vehicle at the time of the shooting?

Mr. BAKER. Yes, sir; I talked to several of them and all of them had kind of had the same story, you know. It had to come from above and behind.

Mr. BELIN. When did you talk to these officers, like Officer Martin?

Mr. BAKER. That was—I didn't talk to him until we got back to the city hall, which we got off, we were supposed to get off at 3 o'clock that day, we got off around 4 the same time, they called us all in together.

Mr. BELIN. What other officers did you talk to and what did they say that you remember?

Mr. BAKER. I talked to Jim Chaney, and he made the statement that the two shots hit Kennedy first and then the other one hit the Governor.

Mr. BELIN. Where was he?

Mr. BAKER. He was on the right rear of the car or to the side, and then at that time the chief of police, he didn't know anything about this, and he moved

up and told him, and then that was during the time that the Secret Service men were trying to get in the car, and at the time, after the shooting, from the time the first shot rang out, the car stopped completely, pulled to the left and stopped.   WC3H266

The limo stop will be further discussed below.

Regarding the sound of gunfire in Dealey Plaza, this is what the FBI determined Chaney heard that day:

Chaney stated that as the President's car passed the Texas School Book Depository (TSBD), he was four to six feet from the President's right shoulder. He heard three evenly spaced noises coming seconds apart, which at first he thought to be a motorcycle backfire. Upon hearing the second noise, he was sure it was not a motorcycle backfire. When he heard the third noise he saw the President's head "explode" and realized the noises were gunshots. He said that the shots did not come from his immediate vicinity and he is positive all the shots came from behind him.   (mffpdf-62474 pg 169)

None of the witnesses in Dealey Plaza described "three evenly spaced noises."

Most of them described one report followed by two more in quick succession, which is exactly what Chief Curry described in his 1969 book, *Retired Dallas Police Chief, Jesse Curry Reveals His Personal JFK Assassination File*:

504

For a brief moment I almost started to relax. I made the left turn (west) and proceeded at a speed of approximately 8-10 mph toward the triple underpass. I did see a few unauthorized people on the overpass and wondered how they had gotten up there. About half-way between Houston and the triple underpass I heard a sharp crack. Someone in the car said, 'Is that a firecracker?' Two other sharp reports came almost directly after the first. All of the reports were fired fairly close together, but perhaps there was a longer pause between the first and second reports than between the second and the third.[32]

Chaney told news reporters the next day the first shot missed, and it was duly reported by the *Houston Chronicle* the next day.[33] There are many references to bullet marks on the pavement and the south curb of Elm Street.[34]

Here is what Chaney told Marrion Baker:[35] (also see 3H266)

Though efforts of researchers to speak with Chaney prior to his death were shunted aside by the Dallas Police Department, Officer Marrion Baker, who also rode escort that day, stated that Chaney told him that two shots struck Kennedy, and a separate shot struck Connally. These three shots, along with the "miss" that struck bystander James Tague, would account for at least four shots—proving a single gunman could not have performed the feat. It would have been a conspiracy.

Chaney was finally interviewed 12 years later by the FBI on 8 September 1975, by unknown special agents, their names redacted from the report.[36]

He was not quoted directly. The entire report is nothing more than "he said, he stated, he advised," etc. This is what the FBI retroactively decided Chaney's actions had been:[37]

CHANEY said he immediately rode up to the car occupied by Chief CURRY and someone in the car asked how bad it was in the President's car and CHANEY told them "bad." Someone in the car then gave orders for CHANEY to lead them immediately to Parkland Hospital. CHANEY said he cleared other motorcycles from in front of Chief CURRY's car and he led the way to Parkland Hospital. Upon arrival at Parkland Hospital, CHANEY ran inside the hospital and ordered a stretcher to be brought outside, not knowing that two stretchers would be needed, one for Governor JOHN B. CONNALLY. CHANEY said that he then participated in other activities at Parkland Hospital in carrying out his duties as an officer.   (mffpdf-62475 pg 171)

This FBI report states that Chaney "immediately rode up to the car occupied by Chief Curry." The Nix film however, shows Chaney and Jackson *both* pulling up to a complete stop.

Did Chaney "immediately" ride up to the car occupied by Chief Curry, as stated in this FBI report?

The photographic record indicates otherwise and will be scrutinized as we proceed with our analysis.

Interviewed on ___9/8/75___ at __Dallas, Texas__ ____ File # _Dallas 89-43_

by SAs ▓▓▓▓▓▓▓▓▓▓▓▓▓▓▓ and ▓▓▓▓▓ Date dictated ___9/12/75___
▓▓▓▓▓▓▓▓/CTB/dah

This document contains neither recommendations nor conclusions of the FBI. It is the property of the FBI and is loaned to your agency; it and its contents are not to be distributed outside your agency. *6 - 1 ... - 7369*
ENCLOSURE:

Document redaction of agents[38]

Even though the FBI attempted to hide the identities of the special agents that made up this report, Harold Weisberg was able to cleverly identify one of them as Charles T. Brown:[39]

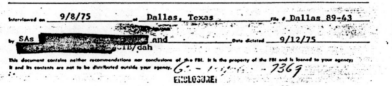

With this kind of situation the withholding of the name of the reporting SA, appealed 10 months ago, when I said I believe the agent was Charles T Brown, serves an interest other than in protecting his non-existing privacy, his name having been disclosed early, in the records made available through the Commission. An obvious purpose is obfuscation. Another may be to cover up or impede searching. In any even, subsequently the processors slipped up. They failed to withhold his name in a second copy of the same record. One is 89-43-9614, the other is 62-109060-7257.

Interviewed on ___9/8/75___ at __Dallas, Texas__ ____ File # _Dallas 89-43_

by SAs _CHARLES T. BROWN, JR._ and _____ Date dictated ___9/12/75___
DAVID H. ISRAELSON/CTB/dah

This document contains neither recommendations nor conclusions of the FBI. It is the property of the FBI and is loaned to your agency; it and its contents are not to be distributed outside your agency.

In 1999, (see appendix) the ARRB finally released these documents in their pristine state, which identified *both FBI agents* involved in the interviews: Charles T. Brown Jr. and David H. Israelson.

Charles T. Brown Jr.

Chaney's and Jackson's Reactions

Where did Chaney and Jackson look when shots were fired in Dealey Plaza? These images from the Muchmore and Nix films show them reacting toward the area of the picket fence/grassy knoll. The FBI report shown above states Chaney thought shots were fired from "behind." The photographic evidence shows otherwise:

In James Chaney's 1971 phone interview commissioned by Fred Newcomb, Chaney surprised the interviewer (John Whitney) by expressing that he did not think that Kennedy and Connally could have been hit by the same bullet:

> Chaney: Well now...I noticed that part...'cause it always, you know, been ah, how many shots were fired and all that, and I, uh, seems strange that uh, maybe Connally was hit with the same bullet that first hit Kennedy....Connally in the arm, shoulders, whatever it was I don't remember ....just uh, one bullet couldn't account for all that.

Toward the end of the same interview, Chaney revealed that he also owned a rifle similar to the one found on the sixth floor of the TSBD and had actually been involved with other people re-enacting the three-shot sequence attributable to a lone gunman. Furthermore, Chaney felt quite comfortable that the feat could be achieved, even while shooting at a moving target.

> Chaney: I don't remember what it was, but I've taken this rifle, and uh, had someone else time - I don't remember what the time was, but actually squeezed off 3 well aimed shots well within those, that time period.
> Whitney: U-huh.
> Chaney: Of course this rifle I have doesn't have a scope on it and it does take a little time to align the scope back on the target, but the direction he was going, it was no effort at all, because he was almost going straight away, he didn't have to pan or turn you know, or track or anything, and, it's very, very easy - 5 seconds is a long time, whatever time it was, I remember we kept trying it - see here, you don't actually,

> don't have any time period running for the first shot,
> because the first shot is in the barrel and time starts after
> the first shot is fired, so I believe all he had to do was work
> off two more shots in the 5 or 6 seconds what it was, it really
> - it's easy to do.

Chaney died on 18 April 1976 at the very young age of 54, per this death notice: [40]

> NEWS BRIEF: Dallas Police officer James Chaney, 54, suffered a fatal heart attack on April 24 of this year. Chaney, the motorcycle escort riding to President Kennedy's right rear on November 22, 1963, told reporters at Parkland Hospital that he had seen the President "struck in the face" by one of the bullets. He was never called as a witness before the Warren Commission.

James Chaney can be considered one of the many mysterious witness deaths surrounding the JFK assassination.[41]

Billy J. Martin

Jean Hill's *JFK: The Last Dissenting Witness*, tells about her short romance with Billy J. Martin,[42] which was the reason she found herself at that particular location in Dealey Plaza that day, accompanied by her friend Mary Moorman. Hill was helping Moorman process her Polaroid pictures as they were handed to her after being taken by Mary.

Here is B.J. Martin's description of the events he witnessed that day:

"I couldn't hear the shots over the noise of my cycle, but I could see what was happening," J. B. explained. "When that

Hill: JFK, The Last Dissenting Witness page 55

56   JFK: THE LAST DISSENTING WITNESS

head shot hit Kennedy, I was sure it was coming from the right front because of the direction the blood flew. It looked to me like at least two people were firing from a forward position, and I thought there might be as many as six in all. The first thing I thought was, 'Oh, shit, they're going to pick all of us off like ducks in a gallery.' So I started circling, figuring a moving target would be harder to hit."

"That's what you were doing when I ran right past you," Jean said. "I saw a puff of smoke and a figure with a gun behind the wooden fence at the top of the grassy knoll, and I started running that way. You almost ran over me."

Hargis (left) Martin (right)   Martin at Zapruder Frame 166

Inexplicably, Martin's Warren Commission testimony mentions nothing about his true actions, instead, he stated he looked back to his right, toward the TSBD, while riding his motorcycle, to look in the direction of the shots he supposedly "heard."

Warren Commission Counsel Joseph Ball leads him to testify "he turned his body" while riding his motorcycle.

Mr. MARTIN. Yes, sir; I looked back to my right.
Mr. BALL. After which shot?
Mr. MARTIN. After the first shot.
Mr. BALL. You looked to your right?
Mr. MARTIN. I looked back to my right.
Mr. BALL. What did you look at?
Mr. MARTIN. At the building on the right there.
Mr. BALL. Is that the Texas School Book Depository Building?
Mr. MARTIN. Yes; it is.
Mr. BALL. Did you see anything?
Mr. MARTIN. No, sir.
Mr. BALL. As you turned to the right, did you turn your motorcycle also, or did you turn your body?
Mr. MARTIN. I believe I just turned my body. I don't believe I ever turned my motor. I believe I kept my motor headed down Elm Street—west on Elm.

WC6H291

Trial of Clay Shaw Transcript (pp. 48-50)

Q. Now Officer Martin, as the motorcade was proceeding on Elm Street, did you have occasion to see or hear anything unusual?

A. Yes sir, after we turned onto Elm Street I heard what I thought was a shot and then I heard, *I looked back to my right* and two more or what I thought to be two more shots or what I thought to be two more shots I heard.

Q. Officer, do you know where these shots were coming from?

A. No, sir, I do not.

Q. Were you able to hear the third shot distinctly?

A. Yes, sir.

Q. Were you able to see the effects of the third shot?

A. No, sir, I did not.

Q. What were you doing at the time of the third shot, if you recall?

A. *All during the shots I was looking to my left and right*, trying to find out where the shots were coming from.

Q. Now, Officer Martin, shortly after hearing the third shot did you notice the presidential limousine's speed?

A. Yes, sir, it was after the third shot it had almost come to a stop, it was going very slow.

Q. Officer Martin, what did you do after hearing the third shot in relation to the presidential limousine?

A. We had instructions before going on the escort not to leave the limousine and to stay with it regardless of what happened. When they left, I kept up my position as best I could and we proceeded on down Elm Street and out Stemmons Expressway there to Parkland Hospital on Harry Hines.

Did B.J. Martin turn his head or body toward the right, facing the TSBD, during the shooting as recorded in his Warren Commission and Shaw trial testimony above? Upon close examination, he mentions it three times in his Warren Commission deposition. If he did turn over his shoulder to his right, or "turn his body," it is not shown in the extant Zapruder film. Martin and Hargis are clearly visible for approximately eight seconds between Z136 to Z275.

In his testimony at the Shaw Trial, he mentioned turning both "left and right, trying to find out where the shots were coming from." According to the FBI and the Warren Commission, two out of three "evenly spaced shots" had already been fired between these two Zapruder points of reference.

Z255/Altgens6 composite showing B.J. Martin.

There is not a single frame, however, that shows Martin turning back to his right. In fact, as he motors along, he remains facing forward towards the west, then turns toward JFK until he disappears from view, around Z276.

He seems oblivious to gunfire as he maneuvers his motorcycle down Elm Street, next to Bobby Hargis, who does not seem to react to shots either.

Simply put, Martin's Warren Commission *and* Shaw Trial testimony *are not* supported by the Zapruder film record. Martin's angle in Altgens6, shows a possible reason why he was sprayed on his *left side* with blood and debris.

> Mr. BALL. And were there any other spots of any other material on the helmet there besides blood?
> Mr. MARTIN. Yes, sir; there was other matter that looked like pieces of flesh.
> Mr. BALL. What about your uniform?
> Mr. MARTIN. There was blood and matter on my left shoulder of my uniform.
> Mr. BALL. You pointed to a place in front of your shoulder, about the clavicle region?
>
> Mr. MARTIN. Yes, sir.
> Mr. BALL. Is that about where it was?
> Mr. MARTIN. Yes.
> Mr. BALL. On the front of your uniform and not on the side?
> Mr. MARTIN. No, sir.
> Mr. BALL. That would be left, was it?
> Mr. MARTIN. Yes; on the left side.
> Mr. BALL. And just below the level of the shoulder?
> Mr. MARTIN. Yes, sir.
> Mr. BALL. And what spots were there?
> Mr. MARTIN. They were blood spots and other matter.   (WC6H292)

Trial of Clay Shaw Transcript (p. 54)

Q: Did you have occasion to examine your police helmet?

A: Yes, sir.

Q: Did you notice anything unusual about either of these?

A: Yes, sir, there was on my helmet, there was red splotches on it and to the left side of my uniform there was other matter, grey matter, and I don't know what the matter was but as an officer I would say it was ...

The Court: If you didn't get it examined, officer, that is as far as you can go.

Returning to Jean Hill's account, we get an idea of the incredible pressure the motorcycle cops were under from the FBI:[43]

Jean had never realized until then just how worried J. B. really was.

"The Feds are tearing our whole department to pieces," he said. "They're slipping around and talking to guys' partners behind their backs, telling them a lot of lies about incriminating stuff their partners supposedly said about them."

"What kind of stuff?" Jean asked.

"You know, stuff like 'He's told us all about you and that kickback you took or that woman you're sleeping with.' Or anything else that might be incriminating in any way. Then, when they get something on some guy who might be able to cast some doubt on that 'Oswald-acted-alone' bullshit, they start leaning on him. I know of cases where they've told cops to alter their locations at the time of the assassination or deny something they might've heard over the radio. And they tell 'em, 'If you don't cooperate, we'll take your badge.'

From Jean Hill's, *JFK: The Last Dissenting Witness* (p. 85)

"It's a kind of divide-and-conquer situation, and they've been especially rough on all the guys who were on motorcade duty that day. To tell you the truth, McGuire and I both expect

to be kicked off the force just about any time now. So do a lot of other people. It's got everybody so damned on edge, they can't stand it. I've seen a half-dozen fistfights break out between guys I thought were best friends just in the past couple of weeks. One guy even tried to shoot his partner right there in the basement where Ruby killed Oswald."

B.J. Martin continued on to Parkland Hospital to work traffic around the emergency entrance.[44] He left that same afternoon on a hunting trip to Colorado and did not return until eight-and-a-half days later.[45] Or did he? In his testimony, however, he stated he saw Bobby Hargis the following day, Saturday 23 November.[46]

> Mr. BALL. And did you ever see his helmet or his uniform or the windshield of his motorcycle?
>
> Mr. MARTIN. No, sir—I never recall seeing him again until the next day.

> They also asked me if I was surprised when the motorcade turned from Main Street onto Houston Street. My only reply was "No". They said they wanted me to come to New Orleans to testify but I told them I would not come unless a subpoena made it mandatory that I appear.

In August 1968 and January 1969, Jim Garrison sent Messrs Bethel, Alford and Oser to Dallas to interview Chaney, Hargis and Martin. Not surprisingly, they avoided Garrison's men, and it was only by subpoenaing Martin that they were able to make him comply and testify at the Shaw Trial in New Orleans.[47] There is no mention of

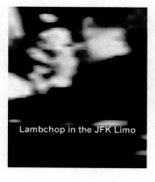

Lambchop in the JFK Limo

Douglas L. Jackson in their efforts.

Jean Hill's Credibility

Jean Hill's credibility as a witness to the assassination, and the details she provided, were immediately attacked by the FBI, Secret Service and the Warren Commission. They tried to portray her as someone with a vivid imagination who had embellished the facts and attacked and ridiculed her. Her references to a stuffed "little dog" and to witnessing as many as six shots had to be suppressed. Later, Arlen Specter tried to dodge her during her Warren Commission testimony and framed it to fit what the Commission wanted.[48]

This very rare photograph from the Bell film, published in *The Saturday Evening Post*, 2 December 1967, shows Jean Hill in her red raincoat, charging up the grassy slope of the knoll, as she chased a shooter she saw running away from the crime scene. The famous "Babushka Lady" is right behind her. When she reached the top of the steps, however, she was intercepted by a couple of "Secret Service" agents who confiscated her Polaroid pictures and then led her to the fourth floor of the County Records Building.[49] Once there, she was introduced to two other "agents" who had a perfect view of the "kill zone," and who proceeded to dictate what she was going to say thereafter: she would adhere to the story of three shell casings and three shots as the official version.[50]

This arm-twisting had very little effect on Hill, as we saw in Chapter 15, because at 2:21 PM ET, she was being interviewed by James Darnell, where reporter Tom Whalen tried to suppress her comments as to where the shots came from, just 51 minutes after the shooting.

Darnell: I mean, where did the shots come from?

Hill: The shots came from the hill. (Whalen's immediate reaction to this statement!)

Due to her relationship with B.J. Martin, Jean Hill's impressions during and after the assassination were extremely important.

It is the only inside information which gives an accurate portrayal of what the motorcycle policemen were going through in the aftermath of the JFK assassination.

The extreme measures that were taken to disregard Jean Hill are perhaps an indication that she was telling the truth, therefore she deserves a great deal of credibility.

Douglas L. Jackson

Up until 1974, nothing had ever actually been published about Douglas Lavelle Jackson, the fourth motorcycle to JFK's immediate right.[51]

The City of Dallas JFK Collection has not a single document that references Jackson, and Jackson was not interviewed by anyone on 22 November 1963.

No FBI, no Secret Service, no DPD, no district attorney. On one of the most tragic days in the history of the U.S., he did however, record his experiences, and he "prepared a detailed written account for his personal retention."[52]

Why would Jackson find it necessary to record what happened that day? Why did Beverly Brunson consider him a crucial witness to the assassination?

Jackson (left) Chaney (right)

This image shows Jackson keeping pace with the Queen Mary on Main Street with Chaney ahead of him. People are spilling into the street, directly in front of him.

516

As covered in the James Chaney section above, in 1975, almost 12 years after the fact, the FBI decided it might be time to interview the four law enforcement officers that were closest to JFK during the ambush in Dealey Plaza.

The FBI interviewed Douglas Jackson in Mesquite (Dallas) on 15 September 1975.[53]

> Reference is made to B. H. Cooke to Mr. Gallagher memorandum of 9/12/75, concerning Dallas, Texas, Police Department motorcycle officers who escorted the Presidential car in Dallas on 11/22/63, not being interviewed by the FBI regarding the assassination. It was recommended that motorcycle officer D. L. Jackson be interviewed in view of his pertinent location in the motorcade, in view of the fact he had never been interviewed, and in view of the fact he had retained notes regarding his observations during the assassination. (mffpdf-62475 pg 97)
>
> By teletype of 9/15/75, (attached) the Dallas Office advised that Jackson was interviewed on that date. He stated he heard three distinct shots which he feels came from the vicinity of the Texas School Book Depository. On the night of 11/22/63, he prepared a detailed written account of the incident for his personal retention and still has it. He advised he was never interviewed by the FBI or the Warren Commission.

His statement appears to follow the same pattern as Chaney's above, with Jackson "stating" the shots came from behind him, meaning the TSBD.

As seen in the various photographs leading up to Dealey Plaza, besides James Chaney, nobody had a better view of JFK's assassination than D.L. Jackson. Although he was right off of the Queen Mary, Altgens6 does not show Jackson, as he seems to be blocked by Secret Service Agents Paul Landis and John Ready.

Again, we encounter an FBI report taken 12 years after the fact, with the names of the FBI agents who wrote the report erased from the document.[54]

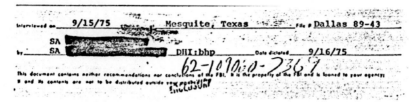

As noted earlier, Harold Weisberg was livid about this and resolved to find out who were the agents and why they had to be redacted from the report, 12 years later.[55] When we follow Weisberg's cogitation, we find the HSCA had the original, non-redacted documents in their possession and failed to make them public.

The National Archives continued to withhold these until the ARRB released them in 1999. As revealed in the Chaney interview earlier in this article, we find FBI agents Stephen G. Rand and David H. Israelson identified as the men who were deleted from this document, where Israelson now became the common denominator in both the Chaney and Jackson interviews.

Interviewed on __9/15/75__ at __Mesquite, Texas__ File # __Dallas 89-43__

    SA STEPHEN G. RAND
by __SA DAVID H. ISRAELSON DHI:bhp__ Date dictated __9/16/75__

This document contains neither recommendations nor conclusions of the FBI. It is the property of the FBI and is loaned to your agency; it and its contents are not to be distributed outside your agency.

This telex tells about Jackson hearing a loud report *as he was turning* from Houston onto Elm Street, much too early for any shots to have been fired from the southeast window of the sixth floor.

ON SEPTEMBER 15, 1975, OFFICER DOUGLAS LAVELLE JACKSON,
PATROLMAN, DALLAS POLICE DEPARTMENT, DALLAS, TEXAS, INTERVIEWED
AT DALLAS. JACKSON ADVISED HE WAS ASSIGNED NOVEMBER 22, 1963,
AS MOTORCYCLE OFFICER IN PRESIDENT KENNEDY'S MOTORCADE, AND
WAS RIDING TWELVE TO FIFTEEN FEET TO THE RIGHT REAR OF THE
PRESIDENTIAL CAR ALONG WITH OFFICER JAMES CHANEY, DALLAS PD.
AT APPROXIMATELY 12:30PM, JACKSON WAS TURNING CORNER FROM
HOUSTON STREET ONTO ELM STREET FOLLOWING THE PRESIDENTIAL CAR
WHEN HE HEARD A LOUD REPORT, WHICH HE THOUGHT TO BE A MOTORCYCLE
BACKFIRE. HE LOOKED TOWARD THE PRESIDENTIAL CAR AND ABOUT
THE SAME TIME HEARD A SECOND LOUD REPORT, WHICH HE THEN RECOG-
NIZED AS GUNFIRE. HE OBSERVED GOVERNOR OF TEXAS JOHN CONNALLY

Furthermore, none of the four escort reacted to any gunshots, as we see in Willis slide No. 5, which roughly corresponds to Z202.

Willis slide No. 5 (Z202).

The JFK Limo is well down Elm Street and at least one and possibly two shots fired with no visible reaction from the four escort.

According to Harold Weisberg, this portion of a telex dated 15 September 1975, tells a totally different story which does not coincide with the official version.

```
AND OBSERVED BYSTANDERS FALLING TO THE GROUND.  AS HE TURNED
TO LOOK AT THE PRESIDENTIAL CAR, HE HEARD A THIRD SHOT AND
OBSERVED PRESIDENT KENNEDY STRUCK ABOVE THE RIGHT EAR AND
THE TOP OF HIS HEAD EXPLODED TO THE LEFT OF THE PRESIDENTIAL
CAR.  JACKSON AGAIN LOOKED BACK TOWARD THE INTERSECTION OF
HOUSTON AND ELM; HOWEVER, HE DID NOT LOOK UP AT THE WINDOWS
OF THE BUILDINGS.  THE PRESIDENTIAL CAR STARTED SPEEDING
UP AT THIS POINT AND OFFICERS JACKSON AND CHANEY LEFT WITH
THE CAR.  WHILE CHANEY CLEARED THE WAY FOR THE PRESIDENTIAL
CAR, JACKSON STAYED IN THE SAME POSITION, TWELVE TO FIFTEEN FEET
TO THE REAR OF THE VEHICLE, FOR THE TRIP TO PARKLAND HOSPITAL.
```

FBI 62-109060 7344 (JFK HQ File, Section 181)

And this is how Rand and Israelson reported it 12 years later.[56]

```
        JACKSON advised he had recognized three distinct
noises at the time President KENNEDY was shot and could identify
two as definitely being gunfire.  He further stated he is posi-
tive the shot that struck President KENNEDY in the head was
fired from his right rear, the vicinity of the Texas School
Book Building.
```

Another interesting fact about Jackson—if the FBI was so interested in his personal written account of 22 November 1963—why did Rand and Israelson not elaborate as to its contents during his interview in 1975? His manuscript eventually found its way into the hands of a handful of researchers and was used extensively in Dallas Sheriff James C. Bowles's book, *The Kennedy Assassination Tapes: A Rebuttal to the Acoustical Evidence Theory.*[57]

(According to Doug Jackson, Jr., it seems to have been transcribed by DPD clerks or secretaries.) Bowles redacted parts of the manuscript but published most of it verbatim.[58]

Douglas Jackson's Personal Account

In 1981, Dallas County District Attorney Henry Wade obtained Douglas Jackson's personal manuscript and had it transcribed and typed up for Harold Weisberg, as Weisberg at the time needed Jackson's manuscript for litigation against the government. Jackson's account was quite a revelation for those familiar with the actions of the motorcycle officers.

Jackson described how difficult it was to control the curbside crowds as they approached downtown, and how he kept hitting people in the stomach with his handlebars because they were focused on JFK and not paying attention (see bus picture above). Of particular interest was his use of the term "motor jockey," mentioned earlier, to refer to other motorcycle policemen in the motorcade.

He described how slow the motorcade was traveling after the turn from Houston to Elm Street. "Drove only a short way traveling very slowly."[59] This is also supported by Newcomb and Adams, who quoted Jackson as saying, "The car just all but stopped . . . just a moment"[60] He heard what he thought was motorcycle backfire. He saw Connally hit as he was turning to face him, with a "shocked expression" in his face.[61]

Jackson was quoted by Newcomb and Adams:[62] "Mr. Connally was looking back toward me. And about that time then the second shot went off. That's the point when I knew that somebody was shooting at them because that was the time he [Connally] got hit—because he jerked. I was looking directly at him . . . he was looking . . . kind of back toward me and . . . he just kind of flinched."[63]

Jackson saw the president hit "above the right ear," then saw the top of his head "fly away" from him. He said shots were fired from "behind," but did not see exactly where because he did not look up.[64]

This portion of his manuscript confirms the actions of Secret Service Agent Clint Hill, who jumped on the limo to protect Jacqueline

Kennedy, but also mentions the actions of "Secret Service men" that are not seen in the extant Zapruder or Nix films:[65]

```
back that way but I never did look up. Looking back to the
front again I saw the Secret Service Agent lying down across
the car over Mr. and Mrs. Kennedy the Presidential limosine was
beginning to pick up speed and Secret service men were running
past the presidental car drawing there guns as they ran. I
```

Secret Service Men Fanning Out Into The Crowd

"After that shooting incident, of course pandemonium broke out. The Secret Service men—well trained in their job—immediately began fanning out into the crowd, looking for the assassin."

—Walter Cronkite, 22 November 1963, 1:21 PM ET

James Altgens confirmed this in his Warren Commission testimony:

```
                              There was utter confusion at the time
I crossed the street.  The Secret Service men, uniformed policemen with drawn
guns that went racing up this little incline and I thought——    WC7H519
```

Warren Commission counsel Wesley Leibeler did not all allow Altgens to finish his thought. Gayle Newman, who was within 10 feet of the president at the time, was never brought before the Warren Commission to testify. The iconic images showing Gayle and her husband Bill, lying face down covering their children as bullets flew overhead is forever burned into the history of what happened that day. She was interviewed the Sunday following the assassination—24 November 1963—and this passage offers a hint as to why she was never called to testify, where the possible insertion of the word "probably" sticks out like a sore thumb:

```
CD5 (CE1431) Gayle Newman 11/24/63
         She stated that after the President was shot officers and
probably Secret Service men started running toward the arcade near
the point where the photographer was taking his pictures.
```

As cited above, Douglas Jackson, noted in his manuscript that he witnessed "Secret Service men running past the presidental (sic) car, drawing there (sic) guns as they ran."

When speaking to John Whitney (Gil Toft) in in 1971, Jackson was much more specific about the actions of the agents in the follow up car:

Jackson: There was four people that come out of that follow up car,(22:06) and <u>run out to</u> <u>either side of that Presidential limousine with rifles of some type</u>. (22:11)
Whitney: How many would you say - there were about?
Jackson: I'd say 2 or 3 on each side.
Whitney: They came up from the follow car, Kennedy's follow up car?
Jackson: Right.
Whitney: When did they do that? (22:21)
Jackson: <u>Ah, about, between that second and third shot, I believe, on both sides of the car.</u>
Whitney: <u>They ran on both sides of the car.</u>
Jackson: <u>Right.</u>
Whitney: It was what, two of them you said.
Jackson: I believe there was 3 of them on one side (22:39), on that right side I believe there was 3 of them.
Whitney: That is what you are saying.
Jackson: Right
Whitney: There were 3 of them.
Jackson: I believe I saw two of them on the other side. I wouldn't swear to that.
Whitney: And, ah, but neither of the two or the 3 are the ones that climbed in the car.
Jackson: No, that, that Hill, he just ran apparently, to me evidently he had just run up there and jumped on the back of that car.

Jackson also puzzled over why certain events were not seen in the Zapruder film:

Jackson: Now Life magazine printed that picture on, I would argue the fact that, that uh, he missed it, you know, ah, he stepped at that car and they started accelerating about that time and he missed that step.
Whitney: Right, right. I really think that's what happened also.
Jackson: But uh, I would argue that he missed that step, but I didn't see it. <u>Ah, Life magazine</u> <u>printed that picture, of that film, but it's been cut up.</u>(23:35) <u>It's been edited, part of it's been</u> <u>cut out</u>, but it does show Mrs. Kennedy get up, leaning over of the back of that car. (23:42) And ah, some of 'em said Mrs. Kennedy was leaving that car, trying to get away from him, I don't think so, I think that she was just reaching back there to help that Secret Service man on there, 'cause she knew he was coming. (23:54)

Clearly, Douglas Jackson believed the Zapruder film had been edited: ". . . but it's been cut up, it's been edited, part of it's been cut out," he told Whitney as noted above.

After shots were fired, he lagged behind and actually stopped along with Chaney, who both "put their feet down . . . to decide what to do next."[66] In 1981, Gary Mack interviewed Jackson and wrote this paragraph for the assassination journal *The Continuing Inquiry,* published by Penn Jones, where he wrote that Chaney supposedly motored ahead to supposedly talk to Chief Curry "through the right front window" while Jackson supposedly led the way on to Parkland Hospital, dodging spectators on Stemmons Freeway, who were not aware of what had just happened. We will analyze these alleged actions shortly.

Since my last letter I've had the pleasure of talking with another witness who can partially corroborate the timing of Curry's first broadcast. Doug Jackson was one of two motorcycle officers at the right rear bumper of the President's car. He and the late Jim Chaney came to a dead stop on Elm Street, "put their feet down" and looked around the Plaza for anyone suspicious and trying to decide what to do next. They then sped off to catch Curry and when they did, Chaney talked with him through the right front window while Jackson remained at the rear of Kennedy's car. Curry often stated he didn't know if anyone had been hit until a motorcycle officer drove up and told him. When I asked Jackson how long this took, he replied "30 seconds...maybe a little more or less." I then asked if it could have been as long as 45 seconds and he agreed it was quite possible. This was an area of his activities which he had never considered important and which no one had ever inquired.(TCI VI #4 11/81)

As they arrived at Parkland Hospital's emergency room, he helped remove Kennedy from the limousine:

"I could see the top of his head was gone, his left eye was bulged out of socket."[67]

And this is how FBI agents Stephen Rand and David Israelson molded his interview regarding JFK's head wound. Despite this being an interview of Douglas Jackson, these two FBI agents steered the observation of a head wound to an unnamed "Secret Service Agent," who observed "a massive wound on the President's *left forehead*," [Emphasis added] with the inference obviously being that this was the result of a shot from the right rear of the president. Can there be anything more deceptive than this passage? This would explain why the names of Rand and Israelson had to be removed from this document.

Parkland Hospital. After arriving at Parkland Hospital, he walked over to the Presidential car with a Secret Service Agent. Mrs. KENNEDY would not let them place President KENNEDY on a stretcher. He helped remove Texas Governor CONNALLY from the vehicle and placed him on a stretcher, and at this time, the Secret Service Agent convinced Mrs. KENNEDY to let them take the President into the hospital. As the President was being removed from the vehicle, the Secret Service Agent observed a massive wound on the President's left forehead and used his coat to cover the President's head as he was being transported into the hospital. President KENNEDY was taken directly to the Emergency Room and a Secret Service Agent assigned JACKSON to guard the Emergency Room door and not let anyone into the room except doctors and nurses. JACKSON remained in that position until President KENNEDY was pronounced dead and was then asked by a Secret Service Agent to assist in escorting the body back to Love Field. JACKSON provided a motorcycle escort for this trip to Love Field at that time. FBI 62-109060 JFK HQ File Sec181 pg 174

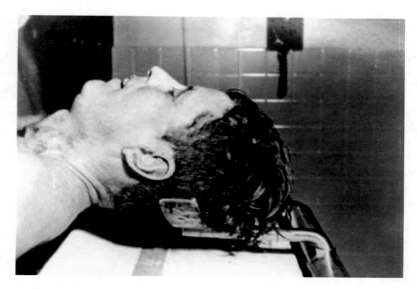

This JFK autopsy photo fails to show a "massive" wound to left forehead. In fact, it shows no wound at all. Neither does it show the left eye "bulged out of socket."

Moments later, while on a cigarette break, he noticed blood running all the way from top to bottom on his left side but assumed this had occurred as he helped remove the president from the limousine. "I noticed I had blood on my hands looked and *I had blood on my left sleeve, down the left side of my riding breeches and on the outside of my left boot.*"[68]

Jackson, who did not know the president was already dead, turned away a justice of the peace, whom he could not identify, who showed up at the emergency room. The hospital administrator advised him the justice of the peace "owned" the body and it could not be moved until he showed up.[69]

Jackson then ran into Mrs. Cabell, who advised Mayor Earle Cabell was in the emergency room with Kennedy! As he entered the emergency room, Cabell recruited him to use the radio on his motorcycle to summon a justice of the peace to Parkland Hospital as soon as possible.[70]

According to his account, and upon Secret Service request, he was the one who arranged with the DPD dispatcher for motorcycle patrolmen to escort the body and lead the way to Love Field for the trip back to Washington.[71]

Jackson leads hearse to Love Field [72] (from Executive Action)

Of course, Cabell's insistence in securing a justice of the peace merits scrutiny. JFK was still being attended to and everything medically possible was being performed. Estimating the first justice of the peace to have been turned away by Officer Jackson around 1:00 PM, his account reveals the apparent desperation the conspirators showed to get the body airborne and out of Dallas.

The newest revelations contained in documents released by the ARRB identify Cabell as a CIA asset. (see appendix)

Brunson's Investigation—The Motor Jockey Hero

In 1967 and 1968, after months of investigation and careful evaluation of the pertinent testimony and FBI interviews, Brunson determined that one of the motorcycle jockeys, who was part of the immediate escort, ran his bike *up the grassy knoll* chasing what was presumably one of the shooters.

The Warren Commission report went as far as trying to dispel the ugly "speculation" about the "knoll rider," with the outright and blatant lie: "There are no witnesses who have ever stated this and there is no evidence to support this claim."[73] For some unknown reason, and even though it was duly reported in the newspapers that weekend, Brunson discovered that the actions of this escort were ignored and never pursued by researchers and investigators. In a letter written in 1967, she lamented: "In fact, so far as I know nobody but me has ever been interested in him."[74] In her paper titled, "The President's Motorcycle Escort: Activities Immediately after the Shots Were Fired," Ms. Brunson cited four crucial witnesses who observed the "knoll rider": George Davis, James Simmons, Luke Winborn, and

525

Clemen Johnson, who never testified before the Warren Commission, and were only interviewed by the FBI:[75]

Mr. DAVIS stated his attention was directed to the motorcycle escort and the car in which President KENNEDY was riding, and he saw very little, if any, other activity in the area at that time. (Vol 22 page 837 CE1424)

SIMMONS said he recalled that a motorcycle policeman drove up the grassy slope toward the Texas School Book Depository Building, jumped off his motorcycle and then ran up the hill toward the Memorial Arches. SIMMONS said he thought he saw exhaust fumes of smoke near the embankment in front of the Texas School Book Depository Building. SIMMONS then ran toward the Texas School Book Depository Building with a policeman. He stopped at a fence near the Memorial Arches and could not find anyone. (Vol 22 pg 833 CE1416)

Mr. WINBORN stated that very shortly thereafter the motorcycle escort dispersed and one motorcycle was abandoned by the police officer riding it on the grassy slope on the north side of Elm Street and this officer rushed up the steps leading to the pavillion and was lost from sight. The vehicle carrying the President immediately left the area at a high rate of speed. Mr. WINBORN then moved away from the east edge of the viaduct, where he could get a clear view of the area to the shed of the Texas School Book Depository Building (TSBD). He remained at this spot and observed the approach to the railroad tracks for a few minutes, but failed to see anyone moving toward the railroad tracks. (Vol 22, pg 833 CE1417)

JOHNSON stated his attention was attracted to the motorcycle escort and the automobile carrying President KENNEDY as this section of the motorcade came into his view. He stated he first realized something was wrong when the motorcycles began moving from their regular course and at or just before this he heard sounds that could have been shots. Mr. JOHNSON stated at that time he did not know that it was shots and he could not say how many shots he heard. His attention remained on the vehicle carrying President KENNEDY and he observed this car until it sped away. Mr. JOHNSON stated that white smoke was observed near the pavillion, but he felt that this smoke came from a motorcycle abandoned near the spot by a Dallas policeman. (Vol 22, pg 836 CE1422)

And here is Ms. Brunson's analysis:

These statements from Simmons, Winborn and Johnson are unmistakable; the rider on the slope was a member of the escort immediately at the rear of the limousine. It could not have been Martin, Hargis, or Chaney. Therefore, the officer must be Mr. Jackson, who was not called to testify to the Commission about what he saw when he rode up the slope, or why, indeed he rode up there. It is also strange that this ride is not pictured in any of the films, taken from the south side of the street. That it happened and that it involved one of the escort at the right rear of the president's limousine is clear from the testimony of two witnesses who saw it from widely different angles, S.M. Holland, on the overpass and Lee Bowers, on the north terminal railroad tower. S.M. Holland saw Hargis drop off his cycle on the south side of the street and an officer of the same escort ride up the knoll.[76]

> Now, do you want to know about the two policemen that were riding in that motorcade and one of them throwed the motorcycle down right in the middle of the street and run up towards that location with his gun in his hand.
>
> Mr. STERN. Toward——
>
> Mr. HOLLAND. The location that——
>
> Mr. STERN. Where you saw the puff of smoke?
>
> Mr. HOLLAND. Where I saw the puff of smoke. And another one tried to ride up the hill on his motorcycle and got about halfway up there and he run up the rest of the way on foot.
>
> Mr. STERN. Go ahead. This is at the time of the——
>
> Mr. HOLLAND. At the time of the——
>
> Mr. STERN. That the shots were fired?
>
> Mr. HOLLAND. The shots was fired.
>
> Mr. STERN. Two motorcycle policemen who were in the motorcade?
>
> Mr. HOLLAND. In the motorcade, and one of them throwed his motorcycle down right in the middle of the street and ran up the incline with his pistol in his hand, and the other motorcycle policeman jumped over the curb with his motorcycle and tried to ride up the hill on his motorcycle, and he tipped over with him up there, and he ran up there the rest of the way with his—— (Vol 6 page 247)

Note above how S.M. Holland had to practically force Counsel Samuel Stern to allow this part of his testimony, to which Stern reluctantly acquiesced. Furthermore, Holland was just about to say, "with his pistol (or gun) drawn," when Stern abruptly cut him off:

Mr. Stern: Did you see anything further involving those two?[77]

Samuel Stern had had enough of S.M. Holland.

In 1966, Mark Lane interviewed S.M. Holland for his documentary film *Rush to Judgment*. Not only was Mr. Holland still adamant about what he witnessed regarding the two motorcycle officers and their actions that day, but Lane allowed him to finish what he was about to say in his Warren Commission testimony when Stern rudely cut him off:

Holland: "And a policeman throwed (sic) his motorcycle down in the middle of the street and run up the embankment with his pistol drawn. He was running toward that particular spot, and also another motorcycle policeman right behind him, tried to ride up the embankment on his motorcycle and it turned over about halfway up there—embankment—and he got out, got off of his motorcycle and left it laying there and run on over to the fence with *his* [Emphasis added] gun in his hand."

And the FBI, in totally dishonest and deceptive fashion, "documented" S.M. Holland's observations thusly, mentioning only one motorcycle officer:

(Oswald 201 File, Vol 3, Folder 9A, Part 1 page 59) FBI Report Dated 11/24/63 SA Kennedy & Griffin

> When the first shot was fired, HOLLAND stated that a motorcycle officer behind the car stopped his motor, left it in the street, drew his gun, <u>and began running back toward the intersection of Elm and Houston Street.</u>

Lee Bowers confirmed what S.M. Holland saw, but as noted by Brunson, from a different angle atop the railroad tower behind the picket fence and pergola structure. Bowers confirmed a very important detail: that the motor jockey was only there momentarily and he *"abandoned his motorcycle for a moment **and then got on it and proceeded** . . ."* [Emphasis added]

> Mr. BOWERS. At the time of the shooting there seemed to be some commotion, and immediately following there was a motorcycle policeman who shot nearly all of the way to the top of the incline.
> Mr. BALL. On his motorcycle?
> Mr. BOWERS. Yes.
> Mr. BALL. Did he come by way of Elm Street?
> Mr. BOWERS. He was part of the motorcade and had left it for some reason, which I did not know.
> Mr. BALL. He came up——
> Mr. BOWERS. He came almost to the top and I believe abandoned his motorcycle for a moment and then got on it and proceeded, I don't know.
>
> Mr. BALL. How did he get up?
> Mr. BOWERS. He just shot up over the curb and up.
> Mr. BALL. He didn't come then by way of Elm, which dead ends there?
> Mr. BOWERS. No; he left the motorcade and came up the incline on the motorcycle.   (Vol 6 pg 288)

Even Abraham Zapruder testified about "motorcycle cops" . . . "running right behind me."[78] The timeline of Zapruder's presence on his pedestal is crucial in determining when the motorcycle patrolmen climbed up the embankment. The Bell images shown earlier in this chapter show Zapruder is no longer at that position, therefore, he cannot be referring to Hargis, who is seen standing at the light pole, then crossing the street to get back on his motor.

> Mr. LIEBELER. As you were standing on this abutment facing Elm street, you say the police ran over behind the concrete structure behind you and down the railroad track behind that, is that right?
> Mr. ZAPRUDER. After the shots?
>
> Mr. LIEBELER. Yes.
> Mr. ZAPRUDER. Yes—after the shots—yes, some of them were motorcycle cops—I guess they left their motorcycles running and they were running right behind me, of course, in the line of the shooting. I guess they thought it came from right behind me.   (Vol 7 page 572)

Ed Hoffman

Ed Hoffman was a true American hero. Hoffman, a deaf-mute, took up a position off Stemmons Freeway that permitted him to see what happened behind the picket fence during the assassination.[79]

He tried to communicate what he witnessed, specifically a shooter, handing his rifle to a confederate dressed as a railroad worker, who in turn disassembled it and placed it in a leather tool bag. This man disappeared between the railroad cars. The shooter nonchalantly turned and walked east, parallel to the fence, when Hoffman witnessed an unidentified policeman who stopped him and witnessed as he pulled out some type of identification.[80]

Apparently satisfied with what he saw, this unidentified policeman turned around and disappeared back under the tree line. Hoffman then witnessed the JFK limo as it sped right below him on Stemmons Freeway and saw the nature of JFK's wounds. He was so disturbed by what he saw, that he got back in his car and drove around Dealey Plaza to the rear of the TSBD to try to find this individual. Jim Marrs interviewed Hoffman in the 1980s and corroborated different elements of his account. Marrs wrote: ". . . his story may be the best version of what happened behind the picket fence to date."[81] Was this policeman Douglas Jackson? Hoffman spent the rest of his life trying to get the DPD, FBI, and later the Warren Commission and HSCA to heed his experience that fateful day.

In 2008, his story was finally told by Casey J. Quinlan and Brian K. Edwards in the book, *Beyond the Fence Line: The Eyewitness Account of Ed Hoffman and the Murder of President John F. Kennedy.*

Haygood stops and parks his bike at the north curb of Elm Street (Bell film)

In trying to eliminate possible candidates for the motor jockey who drove up the grassy knoll, Brunson made sure she studied all the available documentation. She was soon able to discard Clyde Haygood as the possible "knoll rider."

Motorcycle Patrolman Clyde Haygood confirmed in his Warren Commission testimony that he did not ride up the embankment because the curb was too high for him to clear.[82]

> way, and I immediately tried to jump the north curb there in the 400 block, which was too high for me to get over.
>
> Mr. BELIN. You mean with your motorcycle?
>
> Mr. HAYGOOD. Yes.
>
> Mr. BELIN. All right.
>
> Mr. HAYGOOD. And I left my motor on the street and ran to the railroad yard.
>
> Mr. BELIN. Now when you ran to the railroad yard, would that be north or south of Elm?
>
> Mr. HAYGOOD. The railroad yard would be located at the—it consist of going over Elm Street and back north of Elm Street. **(Vol 6 page 298)**

Earlier in this chapter, it was mentioned that Brunson had identified Haygood as the motor jockey that Josiah Thompson erroneously identified as Bobby Hargis running parallel to the picket fence, and who is seen in the Wilma Bond image No. 6. But why would Haygood even mention jumping the curb if not to emulate what another motor jockey had already done?

Brunson ends her manuscript in the following manner:

Thus, of the four men at the immediate rear of the car who were in a position to have observed events in the immediate aftermath of the shooting and who could have taken action, the only one who appears to have taken direct and purposeful action is the one completely missing from the Commission's evidence. We cannot even be sure of the man's name! Yet he is the officer pictured directly to the right of the president in the famous Altgens photograph and looking right at him: in short this is the witness closest to the president of any except those in the limousine. And he is completely missing from the official case. Why?[83]

Another letter by Brunson dated 17 March 1967, reveals how convinced she was of her identification of Doug Jackson and the identity of the fourth motor jockey: [84]

> I insist that the kind of confusion that appears in the various stories put out by Hargis, Martin, & Chaney — and the "burial" of the unsung Jackson is significant. Why was that wild ride ignored and the man who made it never identified (until now?)?

Why keep Jackson so much in the dark since, in fact, as I have discovered, Jackson was the great unsung hero of that day. He was in fact the officer whom Lee Bowers, Jr., saw riding up the steps on the knoll, wrecking his cycle, etc. Several people on the overpass (Walter Luke Winborn, for one, and Holland, for another) were fascinated by the behavior of the motorcycle escort. And in film you can see spectators turning away from the sight of the century, Mrs. Kennedy on top of the limousine trunk, to watch something transpiring on the knoll near the steps. (Nix, Muchmore). The papers that day were full of the event of this cyclist riding up the knoll. Who was it?[85]

From Executive Action

Jerry Coley

The reader will recall last chapter where we discussed Jerry Coley, the witness who revealed what he knew about the pool of blood at the assassination site. During this same interview, Coley spoke about the motorcycles he encountered there:

". . . but I went ahead and started down that esplanade, made a left, started down towards, besides the picket fence corner there, and at the top of those steps that go down the grassy knoll. And it was there that I saw people laying all over in the median grass between there, *a couple of motorcycles up on—laying on the side of the hill*, [Emphasis added] people and police running up towards the picket fence to the right of me."

Which appears to have been the result of what the *Oklahoma City Times* reported in their final edition of 22 November 1963 (left).

OKLAHOMA CITY TIMES

Circulation 313,289 *A.M.-P.M. Daily Average, October 1963*

VOL. LXXIV, NO. 240   42 PAGES—50¢ N BROADWAY, OKLAHOMA CITY, FRIDAY, NOVEMBER 22, 1963   FINAL HOME   FIVE CENTS

3 Shots—

'It Was

Horrible'

By Allan Cromley
(Washington Bureau)

Wall Hurdled

The first tip-off of tragedy was when several spectators jumped over a stone wall and started running toward what apparently was the scene of the shooting.

A motorcycle patrolman rode pell-mell up a railroad embankment, apparently in pursuit of the assassin.

When we compare these Muchmore and Nix images, we see Emmett Hudson and his two unidentified companions *standing* on the steps leading up to the west side of the north monument of Dealey Plaza.[86] The Muchmore slide above corresponds roughly to Z338, which is more than one full second after the head shot, and Hudson has not even moved. Next thing we see, Hudson and his two companions (Nix frame below) are cowering as they try to get away from something or someone who is coming their way. They were not looking at the

JFK limousine and the spectacular action that was going on there. If they were fearful of gunshots "above and behind them,"[87] then why were they running in the direction of the obvious source of danger? Hudson's Warren Commission testimony is a morass of ambiguity and contradictions as he claimed he was already on the ground when "the third shot" rang out,[88] but this same image shows him running and dodging up the stairs after all shooting had ceased.

The third man in the white shirt actually ran full speed all the way to the top and disappeared into the shadows. (see Nix enlargement below)

> Mr. LIEBELER. Did you see that shot hit anything—the third shot?
> Mr. HUDSON. No, sir. I'll tell you—this young fellow that was sitting there with me—standing there with me at the present time, he says, "Lay down, Mister, somebody is shooting the President." He says, "Lay down, lay down," and he kept on repeating, "Lay down," so he was already laying down one way on the sidewalk, so I just laid down over on the ground and resting my arm on the ground and when that third shot rung out and when I was close to the ground—you could tell the shot was coming from above and kind of behind.
> Mr. LIEBELER. How could you tell that?
> Mr. HUDSON. Well, just the sound of it.   **(WC7H561)**

As we follow Brunson's observation, it is noted that the Nix image (below left) captures other witnesses astonished with what is happening at the embankment, as they totally ignore Jacqueline Kennedy being pushed back into the limo by Clint Hill. At right, Hudson and his unidentified companion turn their backs to Jackie on the trunk of the limo, as they bolt back up the steps, *in the direction of shots fired above and behind.*

In her letter of 17 March 1967, Brunson continued:

The report never identified the man but managed to give the impression that it was Hargis or Haygood. Hargis testified that he left his cycle in the street. Haygood said he left his at the curb. Martin and Chaney rode on with the motorcade to Parkland Hospital. That leaves the unmentioned and, apparently unmentionable, Jackson, who rode right rear. He bolted, or raced, up that hill just as Jacqueline Kennedy came over the right trunk of the limousine. Jackson was in the in-crowd that day. Apparently he was one of the two officers (Hargis, the other) who took Johnson to Love Field. Escorted, that is. Jackson #138, is also the officer who called at 1:44 P.M. on the 22nd of Nov. 1963, for a JP-Code 3 (emergency lights and signals) to Parkland Hospital. (In an effort to keep the body in Texas?)[89]

As stated earlier in this chapter the Nix and Muchmore films confirm that Chaney and Jackson stopped their motorcycles on Elm Street and put their feet on the ground. Brunson's extraordinary research indicates a high probability that Chaney went on to Parkland and Jackson was the motor jockey who immediately skipped both curbs leading to the embankment and drove up the grassy knoll adjacent to the steps, dropped his motorcycle, and drew his gun, in reaction to shots fired from that area. Jackson was a very experienced motorcyclist and this maneuver would have come easy to him.[90]

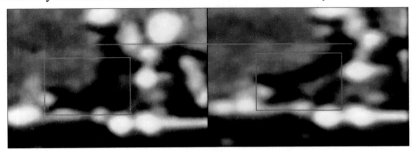

Willis slide No. 5 and Altgens6 show that Jackson had lagged slightly behind Chaney as they made the turn onto Elm street, and he seemed to slow down as he passed the TSBD. The angle Jackson found himself in would have been perfect to see what was happening at the knoll and picket fence. That is why he stopped along with Chaney on Elm Street. The Bell film is not uniform in its sequence. Since the Bell film captured the immediate aftermath of the area of the grassy knoll and Elm Street right after the assassination, it must be assumed that the actions of the "knoll rider" and Bobby Hargis's dash to the "little wall" of the pergola were removed, and the film was tampered with. This is not farfetched, given the fact that both the Nix and Zapruder films have been proven to have been altered to hide Secret Service complicity in the stopping of the limo.[91]

This is Doug Jackson looking down as he gets ready to jump the first curb.

James Chaney looking toward the knoll.

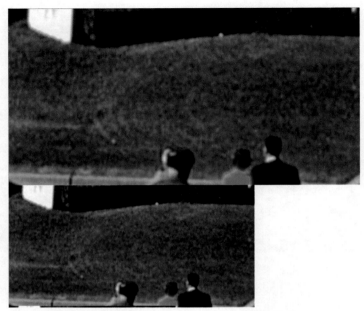

**This frame from the Bell film shows what appear
to be tire marks running up the embankment.**

Which brings us back to Jackson's "detailed written account" of 22 November 1963. If Beverly Brunson's research and analysis is correct, Douglas Lavelle Jackson was without a doubt, "the great unsung hero of the day!" [92]

He was the only officer who reacted quickly and decisively as the president was being driven through a hail of bullets. The question that begs to be answered is why did he leave out his drive up the embankment of the grassy knoll and his confrontation with the shooters?

Did Jackson run into other DPD officers who were known to him? Why was Jackson the only escort who committed his recollections to paper, only to have them stashed away with no intention of making them public? Finally, why did he disappear and make himself unavailable until his supposed FBI interview of 1975? Beverly Brunson summed it up best:

Let's see if Jackson can. Let's see if Jackson, or any other motorcycle officer, will admit to having ridden this position that day. I think Dallas made a serious mistake in burying this man in the evidence and pretending he didn't exist. They might have produced him to tell the official story or something as harmless as the stories of Martin and Hargis. Perhaps they could not produce him because they could not. At any rate he must be heard from.[93]

Photographer Bob Jackson was recently interviewed by the Sixth Floor Museum. Recall that Jackson took the photograph of Lovelady standing on the third step of the TSBD in the 1971 doorway re-enactment discussed earlier. Here, Jackson—in less than 20 seconds—describes the actions of the knoll rider in astonishing detail, confirming what S.M. Holland told Mark Lane!

youtube.com/watch?v=KTNXGT4leas

"A motorcycle cop rode his motorcycle up the grassy knoll - and just let it keep running - he jumped off, the motorcycle went on 'till it fell over"

These Blender images show Lee Bowers's view from the control tower:

537

Blood, Brain Matter and Debris

Interestingly enough, there is abundant documentary evidence that shows that all four patrolmen were sprayed with blood and debris from the headshot seen in Z313.

To recap, there is Bobby Hargis's Warren Commission testimony, B.J. Martin's Warren Commission and Clay Shaw trial testimonies, Douglas Jackson's personal manuscript of 22 November 1963 and Jim Chaney's ABC interview the evening of 22 November 1963, where ABC News mentioned that Chaney had been splattered: *"This patrolman was so close to the president following the three shots, his uniform was splattered with blood."* Stavis Ellis confirmed he saw Chaney splattered with blood at Parkland immediately after the assassination.[94] In 1971 Hargis, however, was unsure if any of his partners had been sprayed with blood and matter:[95]

Whitney: Were the rest of you guys around the car also covered or were you the only one.

Hargis: No, I believe I was the only one. I was the only one close enough.

This schematic drawing is from Newcomb's and Adams's *Murder from Within: Lyndon Johnson's Plot Against President Kennedy*, (1974), p. 61, showing the motorcycle escort:

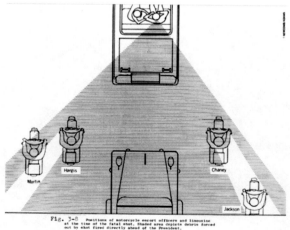

Fig. 3-8 Positions of motorcycle escort officers and limousine at the time of the fatal shot. Shaded area depicts debris forced out by shot fired directly ahead of the President.

Caption under image reads:

"Positions of motorcycle escort officers and limousine at the time of the fatal head shot. Shaded area depicts the zone where debris was forced out by a shot fired directly ahead of the president." (courtesy of Tyler Newcomb, Fred's son)

Who Removed JFK from the Limousine?

In this 1971 interview, also recorded by Fred Newcomb, Jackson downplayed the amount of blood on him, claiming it happened when he helped move Kennedy onto a stretcher at Parkland. As discussed earlier, Jackson noticed blood all over his left side from head-to-toe and wrote about it in his manuscript.

> Whitney: Were you hit by any spray, by the way?
> Jackson: No. U-uh.
> Whitney: You weren't hit at all.
> Jackson: No everything that, everything that hit him - that's how come they know the shots came from my right rear is because uh, all of the - I guess his brains and what have you that came off the top of his head went toward Hargis and BJ Martin who was on the left side of that car.
> Whitney: U huh.
> Jackson: And uh, the force of the bullet caused it to go that way. I didn't get anything on me till I got to Parkland Hospital. When I got out there, of course, I got some blood on me trying to get him out of the car, but that's the only blood I got on me.

These are very odd places to have blood on as a result of supposedly only helping JFK out of the limo, but perfect areas for having been sprayed according to Newcomb's diagram shown above. Chaney would not have shielded him entirely.

Officer Jimmy Courson also said he helped remove JFK from the limousine at Parkland Hospital, so Jackson allegedly was not the only motorcycle patrolman claiming to do this.[96]

But did Jackson and Courson actually help remove JFK from the limo? Not according to Chief of Secret Service James J. Rowley:[97]

> Special Agent Lawson entered the hospital and obtained two stretchers on wheels. Special Agents Hill, Roberts, Greer, Kellerman and Lawson assisted in removing the President and Governor Connally from the car.

Rowley was pretty specific about who helped remove the president from his death car. Moreover, Dave Powers, Winston Lawson, Clint Hill, Roy Kellerman and Sam Kinney all wrote in their reports and/or Warren Commission testimonies that it was they who helped remove both Connally and Kennedy from the car.

Upon our arrival there at approximately 12:34 p.m., I rushed into the emergency entrance, met persons coming with two stretchers and helped rush them outside. Governor Connally was being removed from the car when the stretchers arrived and he was placed on the first one. Mr. Powers, myself and one or two others placed President Kennedy on a stretcher and we ran pushing the stretcher into the emergency area which hospital personnel directed us to. I remained out-

Lawson CE771 Vol. 17.

We proceeded at a high rate of speed to Parkland Hospital. Upon arriving at the emergency entrance, I raced over to where President Kennedy lay and Special Agent Hill and I, along with Special Agent Kellerman, placed him on a stretcher. The three of us and Special Agent Greer pushed him into the emergency area. I stayed with Mrs. Kennedy the entire time at the hospital.

Dave Powers WC7H473

When we arrived at Parkland Memorial Hospital, Dallas, I jumped off th Presidential automobile, removed my suit coat and covered the President's head and upper chest with it. I assisted in lifting the President from the rear seat of the automobile onto a wheel type stretcher and accompanied the President and Mrs. Kennedy into the Emergency Room. Governor Connally had been placed in an Emergency Room across the hall.

Clint Hill CE1024, p. 742.

Then Mr. Hill removed his coat and laid it over the President's face and shoulder. He and I among two other people—I don't know—we lifted up the President and put him on a stretcher and followed him right into the emergency room. **WC2H79**

Roy Kellerman.

n arrival I jumped from my car and ran to the right rear of the President's , where I assisted in removing Gov. Connally and the President.

Kinney CE1024, p. 731.

There is absolutely no mention here by any of the Secret Service agents or Dave Powers, who was riding in the middle seat of the Queen Mary, about any Dallas policemen of any kind assisting in the removal of the president and Mr. Connally.

Additionally, the motorcycle police officers were ordered to secure the perimeter and not allow spectators and other members of the public access to Parkland's emergency entrance and other adjacent areas, and James Chaney did help Secret Service Agent Kinney replace the bubble top onto the limo.

There does not seem to have been any involvement on the part of any Dallas policemen with any of the limousine's occupants.

What Happened After the Shots

While Jackson appears to have been rambling up the knoll confronting at least one shooter, and Hargis was stopping his motor in the middle of the left lane of Elm Street, Chaney separated and rode ahead with B.J. Martin as they tried to catch up to the Secret Service and JFK limos.

Subsequently, it was Chaney and Sergeant Stavis Ellis who were the actual leaders of the convoy that sped to Parkland on Stemmons Freeway. Their route being Stemmons to Industrial, and then on to Hines Boulevard, which took them right in front of the hospital. [98]

The McIntire image shows Chaney and Martin still under the viaduct of the triple underpass while Chief Curry has allowed the presidential limousine to pass him as they approach the exit ramp to I-35E (Stemmons Freeway).

The three "motor jockeys" who first made the turn on to Elm Street at Z19 (inset), as seen in the foreground, are part of Sergeant Stavis Ellis's group, identified by Todd Vaughan as Gray, Lumpkin and Ellis. [99] They seem to have been waiting just past the triple underpass as seen in these frames from the Mark Bell film. More significantly, by the looks on their faces, they seem to be unaware of what has just happened. Officer E.D. Brewer, who was also part of this group, testified he never heard any gunshots at all. Brewer had dismounted and was on the shoulder of Stemmons Freeway at the end of the ramp awaiting the motorcade to assist in directing traffic. [100]

From the Bell film

Thayer Waldo, a reporter from the *Fort Worth Star-Telegram*, and very reputable witness to most of the events of the weekend of the assassination, documented what happened to the lead motorcycles. The only problem here is that it is impossible to determine which two patrolmen pulled in to the Trade Mart.[101]

> 2) The motorcycle officers riding to the <u>left</u> and just behind Mr. Kennedy's open convertible have testified that they were spattered with blood and particles of flesh at the moment of impact of the second shot. Those riding on the right side of the car were apparently unaware that anything had happened, <u>since when the speeding motorcade reached the Trade Mart, these two officers turned into the parking lot, as per schedule, and only swerved back into the street when they observed the cars continuing on toward Parkland.</u>

The Curry-Chaney Encounter

It has been well established that Chief Curry found out about the casualties of the assassination when Chaney raced up "immediately" and informed the occupants of the lead car.[102] We will now examine the official record versus the photographic, radio and other complementary information. For example, this passage is from a letter from Gary Mack to Professor Norman Ramsey of Harvard University:[103]

> Curry, on the other hand, told the Warren Commission he didn't use his radio until after confering with Officer Jim Chaney. Chaney's was one of two motorcycles at the immediate right rear of the JFK limousine; in the Orville Nix film he can be seen coming to a stop as the fatal shot was fired. From the Jack Daniel film, an extension of the Zapruder film "clock" shot from west of the Underpass looking up into the Plaza, we know that as late as 15 seconds after the last shot Chaney was still stopped on Elm.
> (TCI VI #2 9/22/81)

The radio evidence clearly indicates Curry called the dispatcher *at 12:30 PM and said*:

"Go to the Hospital, Parkland Hospital. Have them stand by. Get a man on top of that Triple Underpass and see what happened up there."[104] From the Bell Film:

Certainly, these are not the actions of someone who claimed he was not aware of what was going on, and needed a motorcycle patrolman, who had stopped on Elm Street, to tell him what was happening. The evidence is clear that Curry's call to the dispatcher probably occurred while he was stopped under the Triple underpass, as seen in these images.

From the Jack Daniel Film.

These images confirm Curry did not speed ahead to lead the motorcade. The photographic evidence indicates he stepped on the brakes, slowed down, and pulled over to the left, allowing JFK's limo to come abreast of his vehicle.

The Daniel video confirms Chief Curry then sped along with the limousines and did not wait for Chaney. So why did Curry find it necessary to misstate his actions?

Someone in the Presidential car said, *"Let's get out of here."* A solo motorcycle officer pulled up behind my car and I asked, *"What has happened in the Presidential car--has someone been hit?"* He answered, *"Yes,"* and I told him to head for Parkland Hospital which is the nearest hospital from that location. I immediately went on the air as the motorcycles formed an escort for our vehicles which were rapidly gaining speed. The radio transcript was as follows: (Curry page 30)

Daniel was standing with his three sons (two of whom are seen in the foreground of the film) about 200 feet west of the underpass on the north side of Elm Street. The film sequence begins as the president's limousine emerges from the railroad underpass en route to the Stemmons Freeway and Parkland Hospital. To the left and behind Kennedy's car is the car of Police Chief Jesse Curry (the motorcade's lead car). Directly behind JFK's

car is a Secret Service car, followed by LBJ's car and his Secret Service backup car. One motorcyclist, who has been identified by Texas researcher Gary Mack and by Bob Groden as Policeman B.J. Martin, is visible.

Origin of the Jack Daniel Film

This review of the Daniel film by David Lifton is still valid today, and its importance cannot be overstated. The positions of the vehicles, as they exit the triple overpass, fail to support the official record.[105]

A small side mystery emerges from the order of the cars, according to the film. Secret Service Agent Will Greer, the driver of the president's limousine, told the Warren Commission specifically that he followed Chief Curry's car to Parkland Hospital. Greer testified that he didn't know the way. As the Zapruder film shows, Curry's car was the lead car until the triple underpass. Curry apparently slowed down and pulled over to the left side of Elm Street just after the final head shot, and the Daniel film clearly shows Curry's car behind Greer when they emerge on the other side of the tunnel. According to Sigalos, "The President's car was first, no question about it. The followup Secret Service car is next and Curry's car was the third car." Others who have seen the film, including Bob Groden, verify this description. How did Greer know where to go?

New York critic David Lifton has pointed out this discrepancy. "The popular conception has always been that Chief Curry led the president's car to the hospital," said Lifton. "This conception is proved wrong, at least at the point of the Stemmons ramp by the Daniel film."

Lifton points out that Curry's testimony on this matter is vague and that he only says the motorcade went to the hospital under "siren escort." "He doesn't say whether he led them or tailed them," says Lifton. "But three Secret Service officials [Greer, Forrest Sorrels, and Winston Lawson] all give testimony that is specific and completely contradicted by the Daniel film." (Sorrels, Secret Service Chief of Dallas, and Lawson, the advance agent from Washington, were both riding in Chief Curry's car.)

Lifton points out, for example, that Greer told the commission "I never passed it [Curry's car] . . . I was led to the hospital by the police car who was preceding me." Lawson was asked by the commission if Greer actually passed Curry's car at any time. Lawson replied, "No sir, they never did. We stayed ahead of them."

The explanation to this is either that these highly-trained agents panicked in this emergency and totally forgot what did happen or that somebody is lying. What could the reasons be? Another mystery. (Clandestine America Vol 3 No 1 1979 page 12)

"Once on Stemmons Freeway, Clint Hill looked at Jackson and gave him the 'thumbs down' sign."[106]

The above passage from Jesse Curry's book is particularly puzzling, because Stavis confirmed it was he and Chaney who led the JFK limousine on to Parkland Hospital. In 2013, this author established contact with Douglas L. Jackson Jr., and this is what he had to say in several emails.

Email No. 1:

However, my impression from the Nix film (as you pointed out, Dad and Chaney came to an almost complete stop and therefore lagged behind the presidential limo for several seconds) would be that Dad can't be ahead of the limo by this point and is likely the shadowy officer directly under the Triple Overpass on the left background in this picture. His Harley would have had a very difficult time getting him to the position of these three officers from that far behind the limo in the short distance covered between the grassy knoll and the entrance to I-35E North which is where these three bikes are located. From Dad's notes, I would presume these three jockeys are three of the four who rode with Sgt. Ellis one block ahead of the limo. Also, from his notes, it's clear he stayed close to the car en route to Parkland, rather than out in front of it like this picture. Here's what he said:

". . . I said to Jim Chaney, 'Let's go with them,' and we sped away. He pulled past the president's car and up toward Chief Curry's car . . ."

". . . As we were traveling north on Stemmons Freeway, agent Hill raised up, looked over toward me and shook his head from side to side and held up his hand thumb down . . ."[107]

Email No. 2:

In the [McIntyre] photo you sent, isn't the white car to the right of the limo Chief Curry's car, being passed by the accelerating limo? I would assume Chaney is the officer on the right background of this shot, whose lights can be seen in the shadows just about to emerge from under the triple overpass.[108]

It must be pointed out that Douglas Jackson was the only motor jockey who was asked to write an account of what he experienced that day. As far as the official record is concerned, Chaney, Martin and

Hargis did not. There must be a reason for this. The Newcomb tapes appear to redefine what happened on Elm Street and the subsequent trip to Parkland Hospital. These tapes will be now be thoroughly analyzed.

What Happened During the Limousine Stop

Remarkably enough, the 1971 interviews of the motorcycle patrolmen conducted by Fred Newcomb for *Murder from Within*, reveal significant details about the amount of time, and what actually occurred when the motorcade stopped on Elm Street. In these excerpts transcribed from the actual interviews, the four policemen in the immediate vicinity of the JFK limousine claimed that it stopped, or almost stopped, after the "first" shot.

> Hargis: Well uh, what struck me strange was when he fell over, he fell over to his left she was sitting on the left, and that secret service man almost stopped that car.
> Whitney: A huh. Right.
> Hargis: After the first shot he almost stopped the car, then and after the second shot, well he fell over on Jackie, and uh, she didn't want anything - she didn't want to touch her (him). She was trying to get out of that car. She wasn't concerned with getting that Secret Service agent in there, he was just blocking her way from getting out.

> Whitney: Do you remember how long it stopped when it was on Elm Street.
> Hargis: Oh - you mean after that first shot?
> Whitney: Right.
> Hargis: Only about uh, oh 3-4 seconds. Maybe about 5-6. That's all.
> Whitney: You say it stopped for about 5 or 6 seconds.
> Hargis: Yeah, but you won't find that in the Warren Commission Report.
> Whitney: Don't they claim that it stopped?
> Hargis: Huh?
> Whitney: Don't they claim that it stopped?
> Hargis: Ah no I don't think it didn't - you've seen a rolling stop have you? It's going less than one mile an hour?
> Whitney: Right, right.
> Hargis: Well that's what he was doing he wasn't completely stopped or dead still.

Whitney: You do - OK. Is that you in that
picture or is that Chaney?
Jackson: That's Jim Chaney
Whitney: That was Jim Chaney in that
picture
Jackson: U huh
Whitney: OK...What you think of the film?
Jackson: I liked it. The only thing is I
thought that caravan stopped and it didn't.

Douglas Jackson's impression of the
Zapruder film in phone interview dated
1971 by Fred Newcomb for his book
"Murder From Within."

Whitney: Do you remember by what shot the limousine
stopped?
Martin: No sir, I don't
Whitney: You remember how long it stopped?
Martin: It was just for a moment.

Whitney: 'Cause we see a lot of things in there. In fact we
see one thing which is very disturbing, that the car doesn't
even stop in that film, doesn't even slow down.
Martin: Doesn't slow down at all?
Whitney: No, somebody's monkeying around with, some
things...
Martin: I would've sworn that, that it was, uh, the time that
he, uh, tried to get up, that the car stopped....
Whitney: You say who was trying to get up.
Martin: ..the agent - after the shooting? That when he came
up to, and jumped up to the back of the car - at that instant is
when it stopped, and I believe he lost his balance. Then they
started again, and of course was throwing him off and that's
when she turned around and - I thought was trying to help
him get up on the, help him up on the back of the limousine.

Chaney: I don't know whether the lead car stopped or not but I know that
uh, I mean uh, Kennedy's car, the one behind them,..apparently did
because it was officers that run from the left hand side, in front of me -
Whitney: U huh.
Chaney: I know I stopped.
Whitney: Right
Chaney: Whenever I seen what happened there, then, I know Hargis, the
motorcycle escort on the other side run across the front.
Whitney: Yeah, Bobby, I just spoke to him just a few minutes ago. Yeah,
you know I think at least between 60 and 75 people that day who claimed
the car stopped. But even if it didn't stop...
Chaney: Whether the lead car did or not - I don't believe that it did....it

> slowed down enough that this agent, whats his name Clint Hill?.
> Whitney: Right, right.
> Chaney: ...slowed down enough that he did get on that car, now whether
> or not he was on there or not you know - several different times during
> the procession there, he would run up and jump on this little step and
> ride there for a couple of seconds and jump off, and - that all depends on
> how fast it was going along and where we were at - so whether, I don't
> believe that it actually stopped, it could have, but I don't know - I know
> that the second car did 'cause I recall the officers....and Officer Hargis
> jumped off the motor and run in front of me.
> Whitney: Right, right, that's another thing -
> Chaney: I don't recall myself stopping - I must have or come almost to a
> stop. Hargis did, he got off of his motorcycle over on the left hand side
> and run between those two cars...and run in front of me, so apparently I
> did too. I don't recall stopping, but I'm not sure.

The same series of interviews done by Newcomb, this one with Chaney, offers further proof that the limousines stopped on Elm Street for quite some time.

Chaney spoke about how Bobby Hargis, after dismounting from his motorcycle and parking it on the left lane of Elm Street, ran in front of him and in between the two limousines on his way up the grassy knoll and right up to the pedestal where Abraham Zapruder had been standing. (WC6H295)

For Bobby Hargis to have had enough time to park his motor *and run between the two limousines **and** in front of Chaney*, means that both limousines stopped for a substantial amount of time, perhaps for as long as five or six seconds, as stated by Hargis above. The only problem with this is that none of the films that exist today show the true actions of Hargis. The Bell film tracks Hargis as he stands by the lamppost on the north curb, then shows him turning around and crossing Elm Street to get back on his motorcycle, after which he rode underneath both triple overpasses and doubled back to help search the railroad yard. The absence of Hargis's initial movements across Elm Street and in between the limos after he dismounted his motorcycle, would indicate that the Bell film was hacked and edited just like the rest of the JFK photographic and film record.

James Simmons was standing on the railroad overpass over Elm Street along with S.M. Holland. Simmons was a car inspector employed by Union Terminal Company. He had been working for the company for 11 years.[109]

At the 1969 Clay Shaw trial, Simmons, who was never called before the Warren Commission, testified as follows:

Oser: What did the limousine do then?

Simmons: It paused and then accelerated real fast *after the motorcycle got out of the way.* [Emphasis added]

This exchange had never been properly analyzed by researchers except for Penn Jones, Jr., who summed it up in this manner:

⁵⁴ So that is   **FORGIVE MY GRIEF III**
why the Secret Service driver did not burn-off in that especially powerful Presidential automobile! The damn police had him trapped!
    Many of us have been puzzling over this point. We knew the shooting went on for almost six seconds. (Try holding your breath, or see how far you can run in six seconds.) Why did the car stop instead of plunging out of that spot?
    Now we know. The police had the President literally trapped, while he was being shot to pieces from several directions.

The same recently transcribed interviews by Fred Newcomb with the motorcycle patrolmen contains the following exchange with Officer Harry Freeman:

Whitney: What position did you have at that point, when they were coming down Elm Street toward the triple underpass? (9:33)

Freeman: *I was right to the left front, I was out, oh a few feet out the left front.* (9:41) [Emphasis added]

Whitney: The lead car—Curry's car?

Freeman: *No, at that time I was between Curry's car and the limousine.* (9:55) [Emphasis added]

Whitney: And you were at that position when the shooting took place?

Freeman: Right.

If Penn Jones, Jr.'s suspicions are correct, there is a high probability that Patrolman Harry Freeman, who admitted he was riding in front of the JFK limousine, and right behind Chief Curry's lead car while the motorcade drove down Elm Street, *might have been the one individual who brought the entire motorcade to a halt, by stopping his motorcycle in between Chief Curry's lead car and the SS100-X, driven by Secret Service Agent Bill Greer*! In retrospect, this would have been a brilliant way to innocently bring the limousine to a halt, and is possibly the reason the beginning of the Zapruder film has been removed—to hide the fact that Freeman was riding right between Curry's lead car and the JFK limousine:

Who were the policemen who had the opportunity to do such a deed? There were a total of eight motorcycle cops in front of the President. Three motorcycles abreast were three or four blocks ahead, and a second line of five motorcycles abreast were one half block ahead of the motorcade. Some of these officers had orders to stop at the underpass and hold the traffic while the President proceeded to Stemmons Expressway to the luncheon site at the International Trade Mart.

Names of the motorcycle officers (and apparently their numbers) are given in Vol. XX, page 489. The three out front were Sgt. S. C. Bellah—190, J. B. Garrick—132, and G. C. McBride—133. The five only half a block ahead of the President were: L. E. Gray—156, E. D. Brewer—137, W. G. Lumpkin—152, and H. R. Freeman—135.

Five of the eight officers were instructed to fall to the rear at the underpass and cover the motorcade from the rear on to the Trade Mart. The burden for the trapping of the President falls, most likely, on one of these five officers.

We have only talked to three policemen, but we always get the same answer: "We have been instructed not to talk about it at all." Simmons said he believed it was the motorcycle cop at the left front of the automobile who got in the way, and who made it appear he was trying to find out what the shooting was all about.

Whoever the man is, we hope he has been punished by conscience that will drive him out of his brain. **FMG III pg 55**

Underlined in red above: *"Simmons said he believed it was the motorcycle cop at the left front [Emphasis added] of the automobile who got in the way and who made it appear he was trying to find out what the shooting was all about."*

550

The only man riding in that position, by his own admission, was Motorcycle Officer Harry R. Freeman. But wait, the story does not end here. Sergeant Ellis revealed what was reported to him by the motorcycle officers under his command, and why the limousine stopped for as long as five-six seconds. This information would contravene every version of what actually happened on Elm Street that day. A huge chunk of Kennedy's skull was blown to the left and onto the inner grass beyond the south curb of Elm Street. Since the motorcade was at a standstill, an unidentified boy picked up the piece of skull and a Secret Service agent snatched it from him and threw it into the back seat of the limo. As farfetched as it may seem, Sergeant Stavis Ellis was quite certain this happened as shown in this exchange.

The interviewer was so surprised and taken aback by the revelation of the kid and the piece of skull bone, that he came back to the subject toward the end of the interview, assuming of course, that this had occurred at the hospital:

Whitney: So much stuff coming into my head, I can hardly hold it all together. Ah, I'm trying to think, you saw the SS, Secret Service man put the piece of skull in the car was that as you said at the hospital he did that you said?
Ellis: He put it in there, I think, I believe he put it, threw it back in there, right..... (pause) right there where it happened there I remember, cause the kid that gave it to him it was on the grass on the side of the street there that - where it happened..
Whitney: He picked it up right there on Elm St.
Ellis: The kid picked it up, had it and gave it to the Secret Service man took it away from him.
Whitney: You remember seeing that, you say over on Elm Street.
Ellis: I beg your pardon?
Whitney: You say you remember seeing that over on the by the Depository, when the Secret Service man took the skull...
Ellis: No I didn't see him put it in there at all.
Whitney: You didn't,
Ellis: No I just...
Whitney: What made you feel - how'd it get in there?
Ellis: One of my men saw him do it - motorcycle officer...
Whitney: You don't remember who that was.
Ellis: It was either Chaney or Jackson, one of the two.

Whitney: Did you see any of the wounds on him at all?
Ellis: No I didn't, I didn't get that close, I know that down on the street a piece of his skull blew out of the car and blew over on the grass, and a kid picked it up, a Secret Service man took it away from him and threw it in the back of the car. (pause) We, our people, right there at the motor knew how bad he was hurt, I knew he was hit, I didn't know how bad he was hit until my man Chaney came up there and said he - no chance, he ain't got no chance but let's go - he said his head was just - well I didn't really know for sure until we got to the hospital, there wasn't any chance for him, after talking to how often they come in. (last part unintelligible)

> Whitney: That piece of bone that the Secret Service man took from that young boy you say in the grass - when he came to the hospital he threw it in the car there.
> Ellis: No, he put it in the car back at the - right there as it happened as I remember.
> Whitney: As it happened at the street there on Elm?
> Ellis: Yes sir.
> Whitney: The President's limousine stopped for a while, right at that point?
> Ellis: Well no it didn't stop, it almost stopped. If you've ever ridden a motor, you know if you go so slow, your motor will want to lean to one side, you have to put your foot down and balance it, but we were going so slow, that's what was happening we were having to kick our foot down, a very slow pace, this was, after the first shot was fired, we were - we cut the speed, the Secret Service cut the speed, on the convoy.
> Whitney: You know for how long?
> Ellis: Well, it was just momentarily, it never did stop, it almost stopped, it got so slow, we were just barely moving - and then they hollered Go Go Go! Lets go. Get him to the hospital as quick as you can.

The Hole(s) in the Windshield

In 1971 Sergeant Stavis Ellis and patrolman Harry Freeman told John Whitney that when JFK's limousine arrived at Parkland Hospital there was a visible bullet hole clean through the glass. The hole was of such a caliber that one could pass a regular-sized pencil right through it.

> Ellis: Yes sir I sure did, it was a mass blood in the back seat, and a piece of the skull bone, and there was a hole in the left front windshield..ah (17:30)
>
> Whitney: You sure it was a hole? 'cause we were just thinking it was a crack...
> Ellis: It was a hole, you could put a pencil through it (18:04) I showed it to Officer Chaney out there at the hospital, and the angle on it was like if something came over high on the right rear side came down right in front of the driver and out the glass into the street about 5 or 6 inches to the right of the left post of the windshield, it would have been right, just over and to the front of the steering wheel and out at that angle. The trajectory of the hole and the building and the place where it hit the street would have been just exactly right. I showed it to Chaney at the hospital, you could take a regular standard writing pencil, wood pencil, and stick it through there, about that size, and said that's where that first one went, he says, some Secret Service agent that's no bullet hole that' a fragment. It wasn't a damn fragment - it's a hole. The bullet hit the street down there, the FBI come out there and cut a plug of that concrete curb out for the investigation, where the bullet hit.

> Whitney: You remember seeing the windshield exploding things like that? (16:55)
> Freeman: You mean the front of the car?
> Whitney: Right.
> Freeman: No I didn't see the blood, I don't remember it had a hole in it until we got to the hospital.
> Whitney: You saw the hole at the hospital?
> Freeman: Yes.
> Whitney: You say we, who else saw it?
> Freeman: Who else was out there?

Whitney: Yeah, who saw the hole.
Freeman: Oh gosh, I don't know.
Whitney: Ellis?
Freeman: Yeah. Should have.
Whitney: It really was a hole and not a crack. (17:24)
Freeman: It was a hole on the left side, to the left of the driver.
Whitney: How close were you when you looked at it?
Freeman: At that time? Oh heck right beside it.
Whitney: You did touch it or anything.
Freeman: No Nah-ah.
Whitney: You were quite sure it was a hole.
Freeman: Oh yes! Bullet hole, you could tell it was a bullet hole.

The significance of the interviews conducted by Fred Newcomb of these policemen back in 1971 are only now being understood. The information gleaned from these recordings has confirmed what researchers had long suspected, and why the investigative bodies involved wanted no part of their testimony.

Conclusions

It is clear that the Warren Commission, the FBI, the Secret Service and DPD did not want these basic facts to come out from the four policemen closest to JFK at the time of shooting:

1. There were two limousine stop events, the first one on Elm Street not seen in the extant Zapruder and Nix films, but reported by at least 60 different witnesses, including Marrion Baker. The Fred Newcomb interviews, conducted in 1971, reveal disturbing aspects about the magnitude of the cover-up orchestrated by the Warren Commission, the Secret Service and the FBI. As first noted by Penn Jones in 1971, the reason the motorcade came to a stop on Elm Street might have been because a motorcycle officer feigned problems with his motor, bringing JFK's limousine to a complete stop right in the kill zone. This was witnessed by James Simmons. The motorcade stopped long enough for Bobby Hargis to pass in between the two limousines and in front of Chaney on his way to the pedestal where Zapruder had been filming, and long enough for a Secret Service agent to snatch a piece of skull from a young boy who had picked it up from the grass on the infield beyond the south curb of Elm Street. The second limo stop occurred under the Stemmons Freeway, on the entrance ramp leading up to it. This afforded enough time for a second Secret Service agent to enter the limousine.

What is left of the Nix film confirms that Chaney and Jackson did pull up to a complete stop before Chaney advanced ahead along with Sergeant Ellis, to lead the stricken JFK to Parkland Hospital. Jackson lagged behind when he drove his motor up the knoll and later joined Chaney and Martin at Parkland Hospital. Bobby Hargis was interviewed in 1971 and 1995 and admitted the limousine slowed down "almost to a stop." Chaney, Jackson, Martin, and Ellis also confirmed this.

Other film and images show that Chief Curry also slowed down and waited under the triple underpass for the limos to reach his position. Courson, who was posted behind JFK's car along with J.B. McClain, caught up to the limousine on the entrance ramp to Stemmons and had enough time to peer into it as it was still stopped at that position for at least 30 seconds. Meanwhile, the lead motorcycle escort had to literally stop and wait for the motorcade beyond the triple underpass, (see Bell film) and the peculiar separation of the three lead patrolmen to the motorcade is proof positive the motorcade stopped behind them as well.

2. As first proposed by Newcomb and Adams in 1974, *all four* of the patrolmen were sprayed with blood and matter from the head shot seen at Z313. The pattern of debris clearly indicates this fatal shot to JFK's head came from his right front, possibly the corner where the picket fence meets the cement railing of the overpass, but more than likely from the storm drain on the north curb, as described in Chapter 18.

3. If Beverly Brunson's research is correct, one of the deep and dark secrets the DPD has been keeping all of these years may be the fact that Douglas Jackson drove up the grassy knoll and confronted shooters behind the picket fence, only to be turned away when he was possibly shown bogus identification. Furthermore, we can now add the Bell film to the catalog of film evidence that has been edited and altered.

There are obvious gaps in the film which indicate that it was torn asunder to perhaps hide the actions of Bobby Hargis and Doug Jackson, both of whom dismounted from their motorcycles and headed up the embankment of the grassy knoll. Mark Bell's film was so complete, that he panned all the way around to show Main and Commerce Streets, which were behind him at the time. It is highly probable that he never stopped filming during those crucial two minutes after the head shot. As a matter of fact, the current version of the Bell film available is not as sharp as the crystal-clear image published by *The*

Saturday Evening Post issue of 2 December 1967. Also, notice the cropping of the individual frames. A complete, frame-by-frame and thorough study of the Mark Bell film is definitely in order.

Brunson cited no less than six different witnesses in her work who saw the "knoll rider" in action. She went as far as calling him an "unsung hero." Hargis went up to the area of Zapruder's position at the pergola (monument arches) and Jackson, emulating Evel Knievel, probably popped a wheelie to clear the curbs, and drove his bike almost to the top of the hill, dismounted and disappeared under the tree line, only to emerge within seconds to get back on his motor and go on to Parkland Hospital. According to S.M. Holland and Bob Jackson, he lost control and actually flipped his bike over halfway up the knoll. These were precisely the actions that Brunson cited—witnesses she described as being "fascinated by the behavior of the motorcycle escort." A possible scenario could have been that Jackson, having been met with bogus Secret Service agents, was turned back and told to "stay with the president, this area has been secured." Moreover, the movements of Emmett Hudson and the two men with him who were standing on the steps, and the direction in which they were looking, seem like people who were startled and surprised to see a motorcycle jumping the curb and driving up the hill.

They were getting out of the way of the oncoming bike—not reacting to gunshots "above and behind" them. Had they been avoiding gunfire, they would have *moved away* from the picket fence, not toward it as they are shown in the Nix film. Haygood, unable to follow in the footsteps of Jackson, calmly parked his bike on the north curb, and scoured the area of the railroad yard, as he moved parallel to the picket fence, moving west, all the way to the triple overpass, where he was finally photographed standing atop the cement railing. It is highly unlikely that Jackson helped carry JFK out of the limousine where he claimed he was spattered with blood from head to toe. According to Sergeant Stavis Ellis, Jackson did not lead the emergency convoy to the hospital—Ellis and Chaney led the way.

4. As first pointed out by David Lifton, and upon close analysis of the Daniel film, which was not made public until 1979 (thanks to Daniel's sons), the famous encounter between Chaney and Curry never occurred at the leading point of the motorcade as generally accepted. As noted by the photographic record presented here, Chaney and Jackson stopped together after the head shot at Z313, and *"put their feet on the ground,"* which delayed their progress on Elm Street. They did not leave Dealey Plaza *together* as documented in an FBI telex. While the limousines and Chief Curry were approaching the entrance ramp to Stemmons Freeway, (exit to I-35E North) Chaney was still under the triple underpass.

Martin presumably did his evasive maneuvers on Elm Street and later followed on to Parkland right behind Chaney. Meanwhile, Curry pulled left and allowed JFK's limo to catch up to him. Decker was plainly seen in Altgens7 looking back toward Kennedy. Certainly Curry, Secret Service Agent Winston Lawson, Sheriff Bill Decker and Secret Service SAIC Forrest Sorrels could see the distress going on and Secret Service agents on the running boards of the Queen Mary with their weapons drawn. And how could they have missed Hargis dismounting and running in between the limousines, Jackson riding up the embankment, a second agent jumping into the limousine, and a kid picking up the piece of skull and handing it to one their agents? The official version of "Secret Service Agent" Hill communicating the severity of the situation with his "thumbs down" signal was obviously contrived and invented.

5. At least one of the four officers, Billy J. Martin, admitted he could not hear the report of shots over the din of both his *and* his partner Bobby Hargis's motorcycle, the sirens, and the background noise of the crowd. Note how close together they were in the Zapruder film and other images presented in this chapter. What he did react to, is what he could *see*. Furthermore, the Zapruder film does not show Hargis and Martin turning over their shoulders to look in the direction of the TSBD, and neither does it show them flinching or visibly reacting to the sounds of gunfire. James Bowles wrote about background noise: "Background noises are clearly present with Chief Curry's transmissions in the downtown area, and he was in an enclosed sedan, not an open motorcycle."[110]

6. More than likely all four of them knew exactly the true direction of the shots. Surely Hargis and Martin who were both sprayed with a "sheet" of blood, skull, and brain matter. Martin was an avid hunter and he thought for sure they were caught in a multi-sniper ambush and kept circling his bike to present a more difficult target for the shooters.

This probably delayed him enough where Chaney was able to ride ahead of him. Hargis pulled his bike over, parked it in the middle of the left lane of Elm Street, ran with his gun drawn in between the limousines and in front of Chaney, and then climbed the embankment to see what was going on in the railroad yard, where so many people thought shots had been fired from. Then, he stood by the lamppost for a few seconds, got back on his bike, and went under the triple overpass and doubled back into the railroad yard.[111]

He could not tell who was storming the grassy knoll versus who may have been trying to get away. Chaney and Jackson both looked in the direction of the grassy knoll in reaction to gunfire. Jackson seems to have been the famous "knoll rider," so-christened by Beverly Brunson in the 1960s. Jackson told the FBI 12 years later that he witnessed JFK hit above the right ear and the top of his head "explode" to the left of the limousine. Chaney, who originally reported the first shot missed, told fellow officers that two shots hit JFK and one shot hit Connally. So much for the single-bullet theory. He also said in his interview the night of 22 November that he saw the president shot in the face. After his interview the next day with the *Houston Chronicle,* he clammed up and was never heard from again until 12 years later, when the FBI supposedly interviewed him, one year before his death at 54.

7. The 1975 FBI interviews of the remaining motorcycle officers, if they ever happened, were a complete and total sham and cover-up. This study has revealed for the first time the names of all the agents involved in the belated interviews of Chaney and Jackson. FBI agents Charles T. Brown, Stephen G. Rand and David H. Israelson "mopped up" 12 years after the fact, but in doing so, opened up areas that cannot be reconciled with the photographic and documentary evidence presented here. While in motion on their bikes, none of the motor jockeys looked over their shoulders towards the TSBD in reaction to any shots. Hargis noted in his Warren Commission testimony how he did not even pay any attention to the TSBD because he noted there was no reaction there at all.

There were no "evenly spaced noises or reports," and the Zapruder and Nix films, Willis slide No. 5, and Altgens6 fail to show any reaction as well. Beverly Brunson's theory of the silenced weapons appears to be more likely than ever before. Chaney did not "immediately" race up to meet with Curry; in fact, it is doubtful the encounter even took place. Douglas L. Jackson wrote his own personal account, and FBI agents Stephen G. Rand and David H. Israelson were totally negligent in not asking Jackson to produce this document when they interviewed him 12 years later in Dallas.

With the information presented here, it is not hard to imagine why this was so. Moreover, FBI agents Rand and Israelson mangled his interview by inserting supposed observations by an unnamed "Secret Service agent" regarding JFK's head wounds, which turned out to be incontrovertibly and completely false.

But *who were* Stephen G. Rand and David H. Israelson? A thorough search of maryferrell.org yields only three documents containing:

A. The two non-redacted 1975 FBI interviews of Chaney and Jackson cited above, which were held back by the HSCA in the late '70s in their so-called "Administrative Folder;

B. Another 1975 document where Israelson was asked to respond to a request by *Dallas Morning News* reporter Earl Goltz pertaining to bullet marks that lined up to the west window of the sixth floor of the TSBD, and which had been reported and studied by a Dallas citizen by the name of Eugene Aldredge.[112]

There is nothing on Rand and Israelson in the Harold Weisberg Archive Digital Collection, the City of Dallas JFK Collection, the Penn Jones *The Continuing Inquiry* Collection, and the John Armstrong Collection of JFK documents. Were these perhaps "Men in Black" phantoms who were recruited to obfuscate extremely sensitive aspects of the FBI cover-up of the JFK assassination? Were they actually real people?

8. The "Committee" (Warren Commission) was actively involved in coaching the motor jockey's version of events, as evidenced by J.B. McClain's quote in James C. Bowle's, *The Kennedy Assassination Tapes*:[113]

"Now, the Committee staff report says that I was from 80 to 90 feet west of Houston, west bound on Elm Street when the president was hit with the last shot. That's completely wrong! I never left Houston Street until after the chief said for us to go to the hospital and for someone to check the overpass.

The agent didn't get onto the back of the limousine until some seconds after the last shot. I saw that happen while I was still on Houston Street, so while I only heard one shot, I could not have been on Elm Street until after the shots had been fired. *Had the Committee staff told me what they had in mind, it would have made a difference in my testimony. They were at least deceitful if not outright dishonest with me.*" [Emphasis added]

There is also compelling evidence that the four patrolmen were told to avoid the issue of blood sprayed from JFK as much as possible.

Many years later, Chief Curry would take the stance that indeed shots had been fired from JFK's front right because Hargis and Martin had been sprayed by a "sheet" of blood and brain matter. In an interview of Curry in his later years he stated the following:[114]

"There's the possibility that one shot could have come from in front of us. We were never—we've never been able to prove that. But just in my mind and by the . . . direction of the . . . blood and brain from the president from one of the shots it would just seem that . . . it would have to be fired from the front rather than behind. I can't say that I would, could swear that I believe there was one man and one man alone, I think that there's a possibility there could have been another man." youtube.com/watch?v=Qcd_3tBtRu4&f

In the meantime, and no doubt intimidated by the FBI, these officers became fully insulated from the public, where even Jim Garrison's prosecutors had one heck of a time finding them and were only able to serve a subpoena to B.J. Martin after much resistance.

Again, Martin's Warren Commission testimony and his testimony at the Shaw trial under oath does not comport with the photographic and film record. The same can be said about Hargis and his immediate movements after he dismounted his motorcycle. Any attempt by anyone outside of Dallas to contact these men was immediately reported in writing to their superiors, which further isolated them. Under extreme pressure by the FBI, the four motorcycle horsemen appear to have been forced to comply and gallop away with the government's big lie.

Cancellare photograph showing Patrolman Haygood atop the railing of the triple overpass.

ENDNOTES

1. Livingstone, Harrison, *Killing Kennedy: And the Hoax of the Century* (1995), pp. 21-22
2. Ibid. 22 (under the pretext of being a civil rights violation case)
3. Curry, Jesse, *Retired Dallas police chief, Jesse Curry reveals his personal*

JFK assassination file (1969). Curry raises many questions based on the photographic and physical evidence.

4. North, Mark, *Act of Treason: The Role of J. Edgar Hoover in the Assassination of President Kennedy* (1991), p. 393

5. Ibid. 417, reference back to CBS documentary *4 Days in November*

6. WC20H489-496

7. Jackson, Douglas Lavelle, unpublished manuscript, *I saw the President Assassinated,* 22 November 1963, The Weisberg Collection. Hood College, Frederick, MD, USA

8. WC6H293

9. WC6H289 Martin, WCH293 Hargis

10. Chaney 06-00, The Weisberg Collection. Hood College, Frederick, MD, USA

11. FBI 62-109060 JFK HQ File Section 180

12. Morley, Jeff, *Miami New Times*, "Miami Revelation 19," p. 13

13. FBI 62-109060 JFK HQ File Section 180

14. Item 67, The Weisberg Collection. Hood College, Frederick, MD, USA

15. Marrs, Jim, *Crossfire: The Plot That Killed Kennedy* (1989), p. 15

16. WC6H295

17. Curry, Jesse, *Retired Dallas police chief, Jesse Curry reveals his personal JFK assassination file* (1969), p. 30

18. *The Saturday Evening Post*, 2 December 1967, Beverly Brunson, *"The President's Motorcycle Escort: Activities Immediately after the Shots Were Fired,"* p. 1

19. Ibid. 5

20. Ibid. 8

21. Turner, Nigel, *The Men Who Killed Kennedy*, "The Cover-Up" episode (12:14)

22. Except for his reference to the movie he allegedly went to watch that day with Kirk, *The sons of Kady Elder* with John Wayne, which was not released until 1965.

23. *Dateline Dallas*, "Eyewitness to History," Mike Robinson, 22 November 1993, p. 36

24. Jackson, Chaney and Martin were at Parkland until late that afternoon. Jackson then led the way to Love Field. Hargis remained in Dealey Plaza.

25. youtube.com/watch?v=hrX8lsb2WTk

26. youtube.com/watch?v=x0gcAQNunbM

27. Hankey, John, *JFK II* at youtube.com/watch?v=we3vEvOhKR0

28. Mandel, Paul, *Life*, 6 December 1963, "End to Nagging Rumors: The six critical seconds," p. 52F

29. Bowles, James, *The Kennedy Assassination Tapes*, Chapter 4, p. 32, jfk-online.com/bowles.html

30. 1971 taped interview of Stavis Ellis by Fred Newcomb

31. FBI 62-109060 JFK HQ File, Section 181mffpdf-62475, p. 98, B.H. Cooke to Gallagher 22 September 1975

32. Curry, Jesse, *Retired Dallas police chief, Jesse Curry reveals his personal JFK assassination file* (1969), p. 30, also see Kellerman Testimony WC2H76

("double bang")

33. Marrs, Jim, *Crossfire: The Plot That Killed Kennedy* (1989), p. 14, Shaw, J. Gary, *Cover-Up*, p. 123

34. Ibid., *Cover-Up*, p. 124

35. Author's note: unable to locate reference to image which obviously exists

36. FBI 62-109060 JFK HQ File, Section 181 mffpdf-62475, p. 169

37. Ibid. 171

38. Ibid. 169

39. Chaney 06-00, p. 3, The Weisberg Collection. Hood College, Frederick, MD, USA

40. *The Continuing Inquiry* Vol 1, No. 1, first edition, 22 August 1976, editor Penn Jones

41. assassinationresearch.com/v1n2/deaths.html

42. Using the pseudonym J.B. Marshall, see *Inside the ARRB* by Douglas Horne, p. 1433

43. Jean Hill, *Eyewitness to History*, p. 85

44. WC6H291

45. Jean Hill, *Eyewitness to History*, p. 41

46. WC6H291

47. Dallas City Docs 2490-001 and 3644-001 and 002

48. WC6H207

49. Jean Hill speech 1991

50. Ibid.

51. Newcomb and Adams, *Murder from Within* (1974)

52. Douglas manuscript, 22 November 1963, The Weisberg Collection. Hood College, Frederick, MD, USA

53. FBI 62-109060 JFK HQ File, Section 181 mffpdf-62475, p. 97

54. Ibid. 172

55. See Weisberg item No. 67, The Weisberg Collection. Hood College, Frederick, MD, USA

56. FBI 62-109060 JFK HQ File, Section 181 mffpdf-62475 p. 174.

57. Bowles, James: *The Kennedy Assassination Tapes* jfk-online.com/bowles. html

58. Ibid.

59. Jackson, Douglas, *I Saw The President Assassinated 11/22/63* (unpublished manuscript), p. 3

60. Newcomb and Adams, *Murder from Within* (1974), interview with Doug Jackson, p. 62

61. Jackson, Douglas, *I Saw The President Assassinated 11/22/63* (unpublished manuscript), p. 3

62. Newcomb and Adams, *Murder from Within*, (1974), interview with Doug Jackson, p. 53

63. Ibid.

64. Jackson, Douglas, *I Saw The President Assassinated 11/22/63* (unpublished manuscript), p. 3

65. Ibid.

66. Mack, Gary, *The Continuing Inquiry* Vol. VI, No. 4, November 1981 letter

to Professor Norman Ramsey
67. Jackson, Douglas, *I Saw The President Assassinated 11/22/63* (unpublished manuscript), p. 4
68. Ibid. 4
69. Ibid. 5
70. Ibid.
71. Ibid. 5-6
72. *Executive Action*, identified by Doug Jackson, Jr. in an email
73. Warren Commission, p. 640
74. Brunson letter to Weisberg, 17 March 1967, p. 3, The Weisberg Collection. Hood College, Frederick, MD, USA
75. Warren Commission, Vol. 22, pp. 833, 836, 837
76. Brunson, Beverly, *"The President's Motorcycle Escort: Activities Immediately after the Shots Were Fired,"* p. 9, The Weisberg Collection. Hood College, Frederick, MD, USA
77. WC6H247
78. Meagher, Sylvia, *Accessories After the Fact: The Warren Commission, the Authorities & the Report on the JFK Assassination*, (1966), p. 16, also see WC7H572 and *Op. Cit.*, p. 4
79. Marrs, Jim, *Crossfire: The Plot That Killed Kennedy* (1989), pp. 81-85
80. Quinlan and Edwards, *Beyond the Fence Line: The Eyewitness Account of Ed Hoffman and the Murder of President John F. Kennedy*, (2008)
81. *Op. Cit.*, p. 85
82. WC6H298
83. Brunson, Beverly, *"The President's Motorcycle Escort: Activities Immediately after the Shots Were Fired,"* p. 11, The Weisberg Collection. Hood College, Frederick, MD, USA (Note: Brunson erroneously identified Jackson for Chaney. Chaney was ahead of Jackson, who is blocked and not seen in Altgens6.)
84. Brunson letter to Weisberg, 17 March 1967, p. 1
85. Ibid. 3
86. Mark Bridger, *Emmett Hudson and the Two Anonymous Bystanders, Dealey Plaza Echo*, Vol. 14, No. 3, pp. 35-50, November 2010 (Note: In 2010, Casey Quinlan identified them as Earl Schaeffer and Jerry Williamson. This has not been corroborated or attributed.)
87. WC7H561
88. Ibid.
89. Ibid.
90. Several emails certainly give the impression of this. Doug Jackson, Jr., 19-20 August 2013
91. Horne, Douglas, *Inside the ARRB Vol IV* pp. 1185-1365, Jim Fetzer, *Murder in Dealey Plaza*, pp. 311-360
92. Brunson letter to Weisberg, 17 March 1967, p. 3, The Weisberg Collection. Hood College, Frederick, MD, USA
93. Brunson letter to Weisberg, 1 April 1968, (Item 06)
94. Newcomb and Adams, *Murder from Within* (1974), interview with Doug Jackson, p. 59

95. Fred Newcomb phone interview, 1971

96. "At Parkland, Courson helped the First Lady get out of the car, and assisted others to get the president out of the vehicle, his son said." dallasnews.com/obituary-headlines/20140214-jimmy-courson-retired-dallas-motorcycle-officer-dies-at-81.ece (Courson obituary)

97. WH 18 CE1026, p. 2

98. 1971 Stavis Ellis interview by Fred Newcomb

99. *Presidential Motorcade Schematic Listing* (1993), p. 9-Vaughan's interviews with Ellis and Lumpkin

100. WC6H303

101. Thayer Waldo letter to Maggie Field - University of the Americas D.F. Mexico 5 April 1967, The Weisberg Collection. Hood College, Frederick, MD, USA

102. WC12H28 Testimony of Jesse Curry

103. Gary Mack, *The Continuing Inquiry* Vol. VI, No. 2, 22 September 1981, letter to Professor Norman Ramsey

104. CE1974, p. 163

105. *Clandestine America*, Vol. 3, No. 1, March-April/May-June 1979, p. 12

106. Curry, Jesse, *Retired Dallas police chief, Jesse Curry reveals his personal JFK assassination file* (1969), p. 30

107. *Clandestine America*, Vol. 3, No. 1, March-April/May-June 1979, p. 12

108. Jackson, Douglas, *I Saw The President Assassinated 11/22/63* (unpublished manuscript), p. 3

109. Jackson, Jr., Doug, email, 17 September 2013

110. Lane, Mark, *Rush to Judgment* film (1966), James Simmons interview

111. James Norwood email, 3 April 2014 (Norwood transcribed interview of Courson shown in the 50th observance program "Capturing Oswald" shown on "The Military Channel.")

112. Bowles, James, *The Kennedy Assassination Tapes*, Chapter 2, p. 19 (jfk-online.com/bowles.html)

113. WC6H296

114. FBI 62-109060 JFK HQ File, Section 184, p. 2

115. Bowles, James, *The Kennedy Assassination Tapes*, Chapter 6, p. 62

116. youtube.com/watch?v=Qcd_3tBtRu4&f

APPENDIX

This is how the Warren Report attempted to dispel the "knoll rider":

Speculation.—Immediately after the shooting a motorcycle policeman was seen racing up the grassy embankment to the right of the shooting scene pursuing a couple seeking to flee from the overpass.

Commission finding.—There are no witnesses who have ever stated this and there is no evidence to support the claim. A motorcycle policeman, Clyde A. Haygood, dismounted in the street and ran up the incline. He stated that he saw no one running from the railroad yards adjacent to the overpass. Subsequently, at 12:37 p.m., Haygood reported that the shots had come from the Texas School Book Depository Building.⁴ **(WC Report Page 640)**

The Hartford Times *dated 22 November 1963: "Dallas motorcycle officers escorting the President quickly leaped from their bikes and raced to the grassy hill."*

Presidential Motorcade Schematic Listing (1993) by Todd Vaughan

B. LEAD MOTORCYCLES

1. DPD Leon E. (L.E.) Grey
   (DPD Call #156)
   (DPD Equipment #351)
2. DPD E.D."Buddy" Brewer
   (DPD Call #137)
   (DPD Equipment #348)
3. DPD Harold B. (H.B.) Freeman
   (DPD Call #135)
   (DPD Equipment #345)
4. DPD W.G. Lumpkin
   (DPD Call #152)
   (DPD Equipment #343)
5. DPD Sgt. Stavis Ellis
   (DPD Call #150)
   (DPD Equipment # ?)
   (NPOA)

vehicles: Harley-Davidson two-wheel motorcycles
aka: lead police vehicles (CE 767)
     motorcycles (CE 768)
     lead motorcycle squad (N&A)
relevant photos/film: DCA film, Altgens 1-2,
     Bothun 1, Croft 1, Bond 1, Weaver 1, Moorman 4 (missing),
     Bell film sequence, McIntyre 1.
occupant sources: Lawrence Exhibit 2, 6H303-308 Brewer, authors
     interviews with Stavis Ellis and W.G. Lumpkin.
notes: At Main and Houston Brewer and Freeman join the 3 Advance
     Motorcycles to assist in Stemmons Freeway traffic control,
     leaving Ellis, Grey and Lumpkin leading the motorcade through
     Dealey Plaza (Lawrence Exhibit 2). None of the three leave the
     motorcade as is claimed to be seen in the Zapruder film, as
     all three can be seen beyond the underpass in the Bell film
     and in the McIntyre photograph. Ellis, Grey, and Lumpkin
     escort the motorcade to Parkland (author's interviews with
     Ellis and Lumpkin, Bowles Manuscript). After the shots and
     traffic control on Stemmons, Brewer reports to Dealey Plaza by
     driving back the wrong way on Elm Street. Freeman goes on to
     Parkland (Lifton). However, officer TA Hutson testified that
     he thought Freeman was at the entrance of the Depository
     shortly after the shooting (7H28). Brewer is later inside the
     TSBD on the 6th floor. Moorman #4, missing, shows Lumpkin and
     the sixth-floor corner window of the Depository (Mack).

C. PRESIDENTIAL MOTORCYCLES

1. DPD William Joseph (Billy Joe, B.J.) Martin
   (DPD Call #131)
   (DPD Equipment #344)
2. DPD Robert Weldon (Bobby, B.W.) Hargis
   (DPD Call #136)
   (DPD Equipment #347)
3. DPD James M. (J.M.) Chaney
   (DPD Call #151)
   (DPD Equipment #337)
4. DPD Douglas L. (D.L.) Jackson
   (DPD Call #138)
   (DPD Equipment #356)

vehicles: Harley-Davidson two-wheel motorcycles
aka: motorcycles (CE 768)
relevant photos/film: many.
occupant sources: Lawrence Exhibit 2, 6H289-293 Martin, 6H294-296
   Hargis, Steve Barber interview of Robert Hargis, Bowles
   Manuscript.
notes: Chaney and Jackson stop for a few seconds in Dealey Plaza
   after shooting. Chaney then moves ahead and informs Chief
   Curry that The President has been hit. Jackson follows him
   and the two escort the motorcade to Parkland Hospital (WFAA
   Tapes, Bowles Manuscript). Hargis "parks" his motorcycle in
   the middle of Elm after the shots and runs over to the north
   (cont.) Elm sidewalk near the fallen Newman family. He
   returns to his motorcycle and rides under the Triple
   Underpass to check the other side. He then returns to Dealey
   Plaza, specifically outside the TSBD (6H295-296). Hargis
   does not run up the grassy knoll as is often claimed. Officer
   Martin escorts the motorcade to Parkland Hospital (Paschall
   film sequence, Bell film sequence, Daniels film sequence 1,
   6H291-292, Bowles Manuscript).

3. LEAD CAR

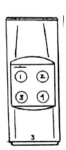

1. DPD Chief Jesse E.(J.E.) Curry
   (DPD Call #1)
2. SA Winston George "Win" Lawson (SSR)
3. DC Sheriff James Eric (J.E.) "Bill" Decker
   (DPD Call Dallas #1)
4. SAIC Forrest V. Sorrels

vehicle: white Ford Mercury 4-door sedan
   Lisc. TX #N or M U 8631 - provided by DPD
aka:
relevant photos/film: DCA film, Croft 1, Altgens 1-3,
   Martin film sequence, Hughes film sequence, Weaver 1, Altgens
1-7.
occupant sources: CE 768, CE 771, 4H170 Curry, 17H628 Lawson.
notes: SA Lawson has portable DCN SS radio tuned to "Charlie"
   frequency, however, according to Curry it "wasn't working
   too well" at the time of the assassination, and thus there
   was "no radio contact" between the Lead Car and the
   Presidential Limousine (Curry 2).

4. PRESIDENTIAL LIMOUSINE
   (SS WHCA code-SS-100-X)

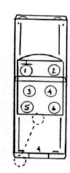

1. SA William R. "Bill" Greer
2. ASAIC Roy H. Kellerman (SSR)
   (SS WHCA code-Digest)
3. Mrs. Nellie B. "Nell" Connally
4. Governor John B. Connally
5. Mrs. Jacqueline B. "Jackie' Kennedy
   (SS WHCA code-Lace)
6. President John Fitzgerald "Jack" Kennedy
   (SS WHCA code-Lancer)

vehicle: midnight blue 4 door 1961 Lincoln
        Continental Convertible (modified)
        Lisc. DC #GG 300 (3/31/64) - provided by SS
aka: President's Car, SS-100-X (CE 767 & 768)
relevant photos/film: many.
occupant sources: CE 767, CE 768, 2H68-70 & 18H724-727, 728-729
        Kellerman, 2H115 & 18H723 Greer, 4H130-131 Connally.
notes: "#7" in right-front windshield. Limousine has mounted SS
        radio tuned to "Charlie" frequency. All SS agents armed with
        .38 revolvers. SA Hill moves back and forth from the SS car
        to the limousine, finally staying there following the
        shooting until arrival at Parkland. Presidential Limousine
        comes abreast of and passes the Lead car on west side of
        Triple Underpass. Limousine armor plated for President
        Johnson by Hess & Eisenhart of Cincinnati and is presently on
        display at Henry Ford Museum, Dearborn, Michigan.

5. PRESIDENTIAL SECRET SERVICE FOLLOW-UP CAR
   (SS WHCA code-Halfback)

1. SA Samuel A. "Sam" Kinney
2. ASAIC Emory P. Roberts (SSR)
   (SS WHCA code-Dusty)
3. P. Kenneth "Ken" O'Donnell-Special Assistant to
   President (SS WHCA code-Wand)
4. David F. Powers-Assistant to President
   *-private color movie (last sequence 12:25)
5. SA George W. Hickey Jr.
6. SA Glen A. Bennet
7. SA Clinton L. "Clint" Hill
   (SS WHCA code-Dazzle)
8. SA William "Tim" McIntyre
9. SA John D. "Jack" Ready
10. SA Paul E. Landis
    (SS WHCA code-Debut)

vehicle: black 4 door 1956 Cadillac
        Touring 4-door convertible
        Lisc. DC #GG 301 - provided by SS
aka: SS Follow-Up Car SS-679-X (CE 767 & 768)
        Secret Service Follow-Up Car (N&A)
        Queen Mary (Youngblood p.109)
relevant photos/film: many.
occupant sources: CE 767, CE 768. 2H68-70 Kellerman, 2H134-136 &
        18H809 Hill, 7H472-474 Powers, 7H446-447 O'Donnell, 18H 730-
        765 (SS agent reports).

HEARSE MOTORCADE FROM PARKLAND MEMORIAL HOSPITAL TO DALLAS LOVE FIELD

1. LEAD CAR

1. DPD Officer
2. SA Winston George "Win" Lawson
3.
4.

vehicle:
aka:
relevant photos/film:
occupant sources: 18H744 Hill
notes:

A. LEAD MOTORCYCLES

1. DPD Leon E. (L.E.) Grey
   (DPD Call #156)
   (DPD Equipment #351)
2. DPD Douglas L. (D.L.) Jackson
   (DPD Call #138)
   (DPD Equipment #356)

vehicle: Harley-Davidson two-wheel motorcycles
aka:
relevant photos/film:
occupant sources: Bowles Manuscript p. 122
notes:

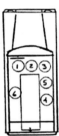

2. O'NEAL MORTUARY COMPANY HEARSE

1. SA Andrew E. Berger
2. SA Stewart G. Stout, Jr.
3. ASAIC Roy H. Kellerman
4. SA Clinton L. Hill
   (SS WHCA code-Dazzle)
5. Mrs. Jacqueline B. Kennedy
   (SS WHCA code-Lace)
6. Rear Admiral George G. Burkley, MD, US Navy,
   Presidential Physician (SS WHCA code-Market)
7. President John Fitzgerald Kennedy (deceased) [in casket]

vehicle: white 1964 Cadillac Hearse

Source of non-redacted interviews of Jackson and Chaney: maryferrell.org.

Title: ADMIN FOLDER-I8: HSCA ADMINISTRATIVE FOLDER, JFK MOTORCYCLE OFFICERS INTERVIEWS
Author: n/a
Pages: 66
Agency: FBI
RIF#: 124-10370-10000
Subjects: HSCA ADMINISTRATIVE FOLDER, JFK MOTORCYCLE OFFICERS INTERVIEWS
Source: AARC

```
                                                    Date : 02/02/99
                                                    Page : 1

                    JFK ASSASSINATION SYSTEM
                      IDENTIFICATION FORM
------------------------------------------------------------------
                        AGENCY INFORMATION

                 AGENCY : FBI
          RECORD NUMBER : 124-10370-10000
          RECORDS SERIES : HQ
     AGENCY FILE NUMBER : 62-117290-ADMIN FOLDER-I8
------------------------------------------------------------------
                        DOCUMENT INFORMATION

             ORIGINATOR : FBI
                   FROM : DL
                     TO : HQ
                  TITLE :
                   DATE : 10/07/75
                  PAGES : 61
               SUBJECTS : HSCA ADMINISTRATIVE FOLDER, JFK MOTORCYCLE OFFICERS
                          INTERVIEWS

          DOCUMENT TYPE : PAPER, TEXTUAL DOCUMENT
         CLASSIFICATION : UNCLASSIFIED
           RESTRICTIONS : OPEN IN FULL
         CURRENT STATUS : OPEN
   DATE OF LAST REVIEW : 02/02/99
       OPENING CRITERIA :
               COMMENTS : INC FOLDER, A/T, MEMO, TTY, FAX, NOTES, S/S, INTERVIEWS
```

B.J. Martin's Shaw Trial Testimony:

Q   Now, Officer Martin, as the motorcade was proceeding on Elm Street did you have occasion to see or hear anything unusual?

A   Yes, sir, after we turned onto Elm Street I heard what I thought was a shot and then I heard, I looked back to my right and two more shots or what I thought to be two more shots I heard.

Q   Officer, do you know where these shots were coming from?

A   No, sir, I do not.

Q   Were you able to hear the third shot distinctly?

A   Yes, sir.

Q   Were you able to see the effects of the third shot?

A   No, sir, I did not.

Q   What were you doing at the time of the third shot, if you recall?

A   All during the shots I was looking to my left
    and right trying to find out where the
    shots were coming from.

Q   Now, Officer Martin, shortly after hearing the
    third shot did you notice the Presidential
    limousine's speed?

A   Yes, sir, it was after the third shot it had
    almost come to a stop, it was going very
    slow.

Q   Officer Martin, what did you do after hearing
    the third shot in relation to the
    Presidential limousine?

A   We had instructions before going on the
    escort not to leave the limousine and to
    stay with it regardless of what happened.
    When they left I kept up my position as
    best I could and we proceeded on down
    Elm Street and out Stemmons Expressway
    there to Parkland Hospital on Harry Hines.

Q   Did you have occasion to examine your police
     helmet?

A   Yes, sir.

Q   Did you notice anything unusual about either
     of these?

A   Yes, sir, there was on my helmet, there was
     red splotches on it and to the left side
     of my uniform there was other matter, grey
     matter and I don't know what the matter
     was but as an officer I would say it was --

THE COURT:

     If you didn't get it examined, officer,
          that is as far as you can go.

From: Harrison Livingstone, *Killing Kennedy and the Hoax of the Century*, p. 152:

Governor John Connally said: "... then, after the third shot, the next thing that occurred, I was conscious the Secret Service man, of course, the chauffeur, had, ah, had pulled out of line ..."[94]
Officer Billy Martin said the car stopped "just for a moment."[95] Martin was on the motorcycle next to Hargis. Officer Douglas L. Jackson said "that car just all but stopped ... just a moment ..."[96] Officer Marrion L. Baker said that the other police told him the limousine stopped completely.[97] Joe H. Rich, a Texas highway patrolman driving Vice President Lyndon Johnson's follow-up car, said that "the motorcade came to a stop momentarily."[98] Robert Baskin, one of the reporters in the motorcade, said "the motorcade ground to a halt."[99] UPI's book *Four Days* said in a caption to a photograph made from a film: "The driver slams on the brakes ..."[100] *at 10 mph.*

I cannot pretend to understand this or to be able to evaluate
what significance it has. I do know it strikes me as quite unusual.
Martin was in the outermost of the 2 left-hand motorcycles. If the
tiny segment of the Zapruder film between the sprokket holes can be
pxmpaxpixhxm properly read, at the moment of impact, Hargis was ahead
of Martin at that point and Martin is not visible. From the other fi
it is clear there can be little distance between them. But how could
all this be on his left side unless he was turned to his right? It
was the right side of the President's head that was so badly injured,
and the President was not turned noticeably to the left, nor was his
head cocked in that fashion

It is interesting to note that although
Joseph Ball had deposed Roy Truly and
had attended the deposition of Marrion
Baker --- and therefore knew all about
the alleged stopping of the car --- he
never confronted B.J.Martin with the
allegation. (Dealey Plaza Echo 11/2005 pg 48)

FBI Worksheet regarding motorcycle officers who were interviewed
or deposed regarding the incidents of 22 November 1963, from
ADMIN FOLDER-I8: HSCA ADMINISTRATIVE FOLDER, JFK
MOTORCYCLE OFFICERS INTERVIEWS:

Name	DL	HO	DC
James M Chaney	No	No	No
D. L. Jackson	No		No
B.J. Martin	No	No	Yes
Bobby Hargis	No	No	Yes
S. Q. Bellah	No		No
J. B. Garrick	No		No
G. C. McBride	No		No
Stavis Ellis	No		No
L. E. Gray	No		No
C. D. Brown	No		Yes
W. G. Lumpkin	No		No
H. R. Freeman	No		No
Roll Smart	No		No
B. J. Dale	No		No
H. B. McLain	No		No
J. W. Courson	No		No
Clyde A. Haygood	No		Yes
M. L. Baker	Yes		Yes

Mr. BELIN. Say this again, Officer Baker. When you say some were on the left-hand side?

Mr. BAKER. Yes, I believe Officer B. J. Martin——

Mr. BELIN. Is he a motorcycle policeman?

Mr. BAKER. Yes, sir; he is.

Mr. BELIN. On a one- or two-wheeler or three-wheeler?

Mr. BAKER. He is a solo motorcycle, two-wheeler.

Mr. BELIN. Where was he riding at this time?

Mr. BAKER. He was on the left front.

Mr. BELIN. Of what?

Mr. BAKER. There were five motorcycle officers in front. There were four, two on each right side behind.

Mr. BELIN. When you say in front and behind of what vehicle?

Mr. BAKER. We are referring to the President's car.

Mr. BELIN. All right. He was on the front and to the left of the President's car.

Mr. BAKER. Yes, sir; that is right.

Mr. BELIN. What did he say to you about blood or something?

Mr. BAKER. Like I say, we were talking about where the shot came from, and he said the first shot he couldn't figure it out where it came from. He turned his head backward, reflex, you know, and then he turned back and the second shot came off, and then the third shot is when the blood and everything hit his helmet and his windshield .

Mr. BELIN. Did it hit the inside or the outside of his windshield, did he say?

Mr. BAKER. It hit all this inside. Now, as far as the inside or outside of the windshield. I don't know about that. But it was all on the right-hand side of his helmet.

Mr. BELIN. Of his helmet?

Mr. BAKER. On his uniform also.

Mr. BELIN. On his uniform.

Mr. BAKER. That is right.

Mr. BELIN. And he was riding to the left of the President and you say ahead of the President?

Mr. BAKER. On the left-hand side.

Mr. DULLES. But a little ahead of him?

Mr. BAKER. Yes, sir. They were immediately in front of the car.

Mr. DULLES. Any other conversations—pardon me, does that answer your question?

The New York Times, 23 November 1966, Peter Kihss:

In another Dallas interview, S. M. Holland, a railroad signal supervisor who had been a commission witness, insisted "there definitely was a shot fired from behind that fence" — a point ahead of President Kennedy's car. Oswald was allegedly behind the President.

"Four or five of us saw it, the smoke," Mr. Holland was quoted as saying by The Associated Press. "One of my employes even saw the muzzle flash. The way the Warren Commission published my testimony, it was kind of watered down some. It made it seem that I wasn't really sure whether I'd heard a shot from the fence."

Mr. Holland said he was certain at least four shots were fired, and perhaps five. He said those from Oswald's alleged position in the Texas School Book Depository Building had been "quite a bit louder than the one from the fence," so he "could tell they were from different rifles."

UNITED STATES GOVERNMENT

Memorandum

TO : SAC, DALLAS (89-43) DATE: 11/27/63

FROM : INSPECTOR JAMES R. MALLEY

SUBJECT: ASSASSINATION OF PRESIDENT KENNEDY, 11/22/63
AFO

Section Chief HANDLEY telephonically advised
that the Director desired District Attorney HENRY WADE and
Chief of Police CURRY to again be contacted and requested to
refrain from making press releases concerning events taking
place in Dallas. HANDLEY stated that newspapers throughout
the country were quoting both Chief CURRY and the District
Attorney WADE, and that it was imperative that they refrain from
making comments concerning the Dallas situaton which would interfere with successful prosecution of the case, as well as investigation being conducted.

Chief of Police CURRY was located at 12:50 PM and
this matter was discussed by me with Chief CURRY. The Chief
advised that he was not making any press releases of any kind
and that he had specifically requested individuals in the
Department to refrain from comments to the press, but that
he was having difficulty in controling this phase of the
Police Department's activities. He assured me that he
personally would try to make every effort to see that no comments
were made and that he had not personally made any comments since
this matter had been discussed with him on Sunday, Nov. 24th.

HENRY WADE, District Attorney, was located at his
home at 1:15 PM, and this matter was discussed with him in
detail. WADE stated that he had made no statements to the
press of any kind since I discussed this situation with him
on Sunday evening; that he understood he was being quoted in
various newspapers, the latest being the "Houston Post" and he
wanted to assure me that he had made no comments of any kind
concerning the activities of the Police Department or the FBI,
but did tell a representative of the "Houston Post" that he
knew nothing concerning the FBI's activities in the Dallas
situation. He stated his Assistant BILL ALEXANDER was talking
to representatives of the press this morning and when he saw
this, he called ALEXANDER away from the reporters and told him
to refrain from making any comments; that the District Attorney's

89-43-4136

SEARCHED
SERIALIZED

NOV 27 1963
FBI - DALLAS

2 - Dallas
JRM:mfr
(2)

DL #89-43

office had a case to prosecute and he wanted no further
information given out. He advised he was leaving for Houston,
Texas very shortly and that he would be in Houston until
Friday, and that he was not furnishing his whereabouts to
anyone, so there would certainly be no comments from him in
the meantime.

I've just skimmed Bowles' version of the Douglas Jackson. At the key part I think
it is different. I'll enclose a copy of the copy I have. I should explain that but please
keep my source secret. He did not ask for this but I also do not want him getting letters
to answer. When I learned that the FBI had refused to accept Jackson's mémoire I asked
Henry Wade to ask him to lend it to me. Henry got it and had his secretary retype it,
making no changes or corections. If you find any differences please let me know pronto
because Bowles was a source for Posner, who praises him and his impartiality.

archives.gov/files/research/jfk/releases/104-10215-10213.pdf

104-10215-10213

MATERIAL REVIEWED AT CIA HEADQUARTERS BY

HOUSE SELECT COMMITTEE ON ASSASSINATIONS STAFF MEMBERS

FILE TITLE/NUMBER/VOLUME: _CABELL, EARLE_
3 of 121104 (FICHE)

INCLUSIVE DATES: _____

CUSTODIAL UNIT/LOCATION: _____

ROOM: _____

DELETIONS, IF ANY: _____

DATE RECEIVED	DATE RETURNED	REVIEWED BY (PRINT NAME)	SIGNATURE OF REVIEWING OFFICIA
			NOT REVIEWED BY HSCA

NO DOCUMENTS MAY BE COPIED OR REMOVED FROM THIS FILE

SIP

SECRECY AGREEMENT

1. I acknowledge the fact that because of the confidential relationship between myself and the U. S. Government, I will be the recipient of information which, in itself, or by the implications to be drawn therefrom, will be such that its unlawful disclosure or loose handling may adversely affect the interests and security of the United States. I realize that the methods of collecting and of using this information, as well as the identity of persons involved, are as secret as the substantive information itself and, therefore, must be treated by me with an equal degree of secrecy.

2. I shall always recognize that the U. S. Government has the sole interest in all information which I or my organization may possess, compile or acquire pursuant to the understanding. No advantage or gain will be sought by me as a result of the added significance or value such information may have, due to the Government's interest in it.

3. I solemnly pledge my word that I will never divulge, publish, nor reveal either by word, conduct, or by any other means such information or knowledge, as indicated above, unless specifically authorized to do so, by the U. S. Government.

4. Nothing in this understanding is to be taken as imposing any restriction upon the normal business practices of myself or my organization: i.e., information normally possessed by us or gathered in the regular course of business will continue to be utilized in accordance with our normal practices.

Signature: _____

Representative of U. S. Government

17 Oct 1956
Date

Signature: _____

(Earle Cabil)

Organization

17 Oct 1956
Date

Index

189, 202, 209, 210, 214–216,
221–223, 226, 228–232, 236,
237, 242, 249, 265–267, 274,
276, 279, 280, 288, 290, 292,
294, 298, 299, 302, 303, 315,
316, 322, 326, 329, 330, 332,
338, 339, 344–350, 353, 370,
384, 400, 402, 418, 420, 430,
437, 441, 449, 459, 468, 489,
490, 492, 494, 497, 499,
502–504, 510–512, 514, 521,
525–527, 529, 530, 533, 538,
539, 549, 553, 558–560, 563

Weigman, Dave 62, 70, 84, 90, 97,
100, 221, 223, 225, 228, 232,
235, 243, 246, 247, 326, 333,
443, 461, 499

Weisberg, Harold ix, 13, 32, 38, 40,
41, 55, 56, 61, 69, 70, 82,
83, 87, 108–110, 112–114,
150, 151, 153, 154, 165, 177,
195–197, 209, 214, 240, 242,
272, 274, 291–293, 302, 303,
329, 335, 340–342, 349, 350,
375, 420, 421, 429–431, 435,
439, 441, 442, 457, 462, 464,
480–482, 485, 489, 495, 499,
506, 518–520, 559–564

Whalen, Tom, interviewer on NBC
355

Whaley, William 274–295, 298–302,
303, 305, 348

White, Jack, backyard photo analysis
361

White, Roscoe 32, 362, 368, 369,

370, 373–375, 377, 379
overlays 369
Williams, Bonnie Ray 336
Williams, Otis 36, 68, 70, 73, 75, 76,
109, 115, 202, 211, 216, 232,
249, 250, 318, 326, 328, 334,
336, 338, 348, 350

Willis, Phillip 7, 14, 26, 49, 90, 92,
97–100, 254, 463, 519, 535,
558
slide No. 8 90, 92, 98, 254

Wilma Bond images 497
Windshield, JFK limousine 384,
388, 552
Wirephoto 9, 10
Woman and Child 63–65, 68
Woodward, Mary 42, 44, 45, 354

Y

Yarborough, Senator Ralph 44
Youngblood, Rufus 44

Z

Zapruder film 42, 43, 46, 47, 88,
243, 385, 405, 409, 413, 414,
416, 420, 421, 430, 434, 458,
461, 462, 463, 471, 493, 503,
511, 512, 522, 550, 557
anomalies 458